me(anura)

(Nouvelle Zélande)

Messiaen

Messiaen

Peter Hill and Nigel Simeone

Yale University Press
New Haven and London

For information about this and other Yale University Press publications please contact:
U.S. Office: sales.press@yale.edu   www.yalebooks.com
Europe Office: sales@yaleup.co.uk   www.yalebooks.co.uk

Set in Minion 10.5/13 pt by J&L Composition, Filey, North Yorkshire
Printed in China through World Print

Library of Congress Control Number 2005930976

ISBN 978–0–300–10907–8

A catalogue record for this book is available from the British Library

10 9 8 7 6 5 4 3

Contents

Acknowledgements

This book would have been impossible without the overwhelming generosity of Olivier Messiaen's widow, Yvonne Loriod-Messiaen. Initially, we wrote to her requesting information about photographs and other materials which she might have in her possession. Her reaction was an immediate invitation to Paris in order to discuss our plans. During this visit she showed us Messiaen's pocket diaries, letters and photographs, and offered us the use of the archives which she had been putting in order since the composer's death in 1992. This extraordinary opportunity set us the challenge of writing the first detailed biographical study of Messiaen, one that is based to a very large extent on unpublished material. The vast photographic collection in Mme Loriod-Messiaen's possession also made it imperative that such a book should be generously illustrated. Throughout our research, Mme Loriod-Messiaen has given us every possible assistance, without at any time seeking to guide or influence our work and our conclusions. She has given freely of her time in answering our many questions about material, about people and about events, invariably providing us with answers which went far beyond the specific question. We owe her an immeasurable debt of gratitude.

We are also greatly indebted to many friends and colleagues who have answered queries, put material in their private collections at our disposal, provided specific support and encouragement, or helped in other ways. These include Felix Aprahamian, Caroline Atherton, George Benjamin, Pierre Boulez, Stephen Broad, Christopher Dingle, Robert Fallon, Raymonde Guéritte, Robert G. Heittman, Roy Howat, Marie-Louise Jaquet-Langlais, Père Jean-Rodolphe Kars, John Kline, O.W. Neighbour, Caroline Potter, Alex Ross, Claude Samuel, Matthew Schellhorn, Manuela Schwartz, Richard Langham Smith, Jacques Tchamkerten, Dame Gillian Weir and Philip Weller. Roger Nichols, in particular, has been invaluable not only for his assistance with translations, but also for his extremely detailed advice and guidance, and for some welcome corrections. We are also grateful to the publishers, Yale University Press, and in particular to Malcolm Gerratt and Robert Baldock, for their enthusiastic support throughout the project, and to Stephen Kent for producing such an elegant design. In the final stages Michael Wood gave the text the most rigorous scrutiny, for which we tender heartfelt thanks.

Special thanks are due to Catherine Massip and her colleagues at the Département de la Musique at the Bibliothèque Nationale de France for their unfailing helpfulness and courtesy. Other libraries and archives to which we are grateful for allowing us to reproduce materials in their collections include: the Société des Auteurs et Compositeurs Dramatiques (Florence Roth); the Musée des Beaux-Arts in Troyes (Chantal Rouquet); in Portugal, the Serviço de Música, Fondação Calouste Gulbenkian (Mariana Portas); and in New York, the Pierpont Morgan Library (J. Rigbie Turner).

We are grateful to the University of Wales, Bangor, and the University of Sheffield, both of which granted periods of study leave, and to colleagues in their music departments who supported and encouraged our research in numerous ways.

The Arts and Humanities Research Board provided generous funding for our research on this book, making it possible to spend extended periods in Paris for work in the Messiaen Archives and the Bibliothèque Nationale de France, to visit important Messiaen sites in France and elsewhere, and to commission translations.

Finally, with a substantial undertaking of this kind, we have both made considerable demands on our wives Charlotte and Jasmine, our families and friends. Without their support, patience and love the book would never have been written.

Peter Hill and Nigel Simeone
Sheffield
2005

List of Illustrations

Unless otherwise stated, photographs and documents are reproduced from originals in the collections of Yvonne Loriod-Messiaen and the authors.

Introduction

Of the leading composers of the twentieth century Messiaen is without doubt one of those about whom most remains to be discovered. More than a decade after his death, our knowledge of him is still largely conditioned by what he said about himself. Throughout his life Messiaen was apparently remarkably open about his music, which he discussed publicly, in lectures, press interviews, and in his teaching. The drive to explain himself led him while only in his mid-thirties to publish *Technique de mon langage musical*, and for the last forty years of his life he worked at a monumental seven-volume treatise that encompassed the whole of his composing world. Three of the best-known books on Messiaen – by Goléa, Samuel and Rössler – are based largely or wholly on interviews with the composer, while two further studies – by Halbreich and Périer – were written under his watchful supervision. Not unnaturally, independent studies of Messiaen have tended to draw heavily on his published recollections.

In fact Messiaen's publications conceal as much as they reveal. Read carefully, his accounts of the music are more descriptive than explanatory, telling us what is in the music but seldom why it is there, or what complexities went into its making. We know little of how individual works were conceived or how they evolved, and almost nothing of Messiaen's working practices, let alone of the creative decisions that he took during the course of composing.

Indeed, Messiaen became fanatically secretive about any work in progress, and was similarly reticent about his private life, of which he divulged little, apart from a few details of his childhood. His wife, Yvonne Loriod-Messiaen, only discovered the existence of his final composition – the *Concert à quatre* – when she found it among his papers after his death, despite the fact that he had been working on the piece for much of the previous year. For six years, during the 1970s, she was even kept ignorant of *Saint François d'Assise*, the existence of which was known to only one other person, the Director of the Paris Opéra. In the surviving correspondence there is just a single instance where Messiaen discussed the progress of a composition – when driven to offer excuses for failing to deliver *La Transfiguration de Notre-Seigneur Jésus-Christ* on time.

Otherwise, his current work was always kept rigorously private, and anyone enquiring about it would be met with a polite snub.

Against such a background, this life of Messiaen is the first to explore the world that he was at pains to keep hidden. A great deal of it would not have been possible without the access granted to the unpublished papers sorted and catalogued by Mme Loriod-Messiaen since the composer's death in 1992. These include remarkable musical sketches, correspondence, lectures and lecture notes, rough jottings, and a complete set of diaries, which Messiaen kept from 1939 onwards; before this date the archive's most valuable source is a marvellous collection of early photographs, many published here for the first time.

Details of Messiaen's ancestry, childhood and student days at the Paris Conservatoire in the 1920s have come from a variety of sources, including correspondence with family and friends, and the recollections of surviving relatives. A particularly precious document is a letter from Jean de Gibon, which recalls the days when he taught Messiaen the piano (and introduced him to Debussy's *Pelléas et Mélisande*) during the time when Messiaen's father, a schoolteacher, was transferred to Nantes after the end of World War I. The Messiaen family at the time was marked by tragedy. An aunt and two of Messiaen's uncles perished as a result of the conflict, and his mother, Cécile, died young in 1927. Family tradition holds that Messiaen's parents' marriage was unhappy, although a moving letter from his father, written after Cécile's death, suggests otherwise.

Messiaen's unique musical language formed strikingly early. The power and originality of his music already impressed his teachers and fellow-students at the Conservatoire, and by the time he was appointed organist of the church of the Trinité in central Paris (in 1931) his supporters included some of the leading figures of the French musical establishment.

Our image of Messiaen in the 1930s is conditioned by the high-minded seriousness of his output, which is almost entirely on religious themes, and equally by photographs of him at the organ of the Trinité, an earnest bespectacled figure, alone in the church's vast and rather gloomy interior. The portrait that emerges here may therefore come as a surprise. Messiaen's lively correspondence shows him to have been gregarious, with a wide circle of friends, and not without a sense of fun. The letters also show him establishing a network of contacts, as he set about determinedly building a career with characteristic thoroughness and tenacity. In early press interviews Messiaen appears confident and astute, sure of his powers and of his opinions, a young man in a hurry to succeed, and not afraid on occasions even to criticize celebrated contemporaries, such as Ravel or Stravinsky.

Early in his professional life, Messiaen recognized the need to ensure the best possible performances of his music. Composition and performance were inseparable. Sketches of later works for piano or organ show that even early drafts carry precise details of fingering and pedalling. Messiaen never forgot what he owed to performers. Musicians who visited his home to rehearse would receive a letter in advance with instructions on how to find the apartment, at the same time gravely thanking them for having learned his music. As far as possible Messiaen made a point of attending rehearsals and performances of his music. No doubt this was partly to ensure high standards, but equally he never lost the excitement of hearing his music well played, and he was generous in his comments, whether made publicly or confided to his diary.

The two song-cycles of the 1930s are among Messiaen's most personal works, and reflect his domestic happiness. His wife, Claire Delbos, was an ideal partner: devout and musically gifted – a composer and violinist. Messiaen became a regular visitor to the Delbos rural home, a small château at Neussargues, in the hills of the Cantal. In 1936 the couple constructed a modest retreat at Petichet, in the mountains south of Grenoble, and it was here that Messiaen continued his well-established practice of devoting holidays in the country to intensive work on composition. Both Messiaen and his wife enjoyed taking photographs, and these provide an intimate portrayal of their life together, and of their son, Pascal, who was born in 1937.

The record of their relationship continues in the letters Messiaen and Claire exchanged during the years of separation, which began with the outbreak of World War II. By the end of 1939 Messiaen was serving with the French army. His attempts to get transferred to more congenial war work seemed likely to succeed, but were overtaken by the rapid German advance in May 1940, during which he was one of the many thousands of French servicemen to be captured. Letters to Claire continued from the prisoner-of-war camp near Görlitz, and provide a context for the *Quatuor pour la fin du Temps*, Messiaen's transcendent response to the first-hand experience of suffering and despair.

Messiaen was repatriated early in 1941, and after working briefly for a cultural organization in Vichy, took up a post as a harmony teacher at the Paris Conservatoire. The hazards of wartime concert life in Paris are recorded in his correspondence with Denise Tual concerning the première of *Visions de l'Amen*, the first commission to come Messiaen's way after his return from captivity.

Despite the difficulties, privations and dangers of life under the German occupation, the next few years were a ferment of creativity, graphically reflected in the pages of Messiaen's diaries; at times these are so congested as to be all but illegible. As well as recording appointments, addresses and telephone numbers, the diaries present a mosaic of Messiaen's daily life. There are notes for lectures or articles, lists of works taught in his class at the Conservatoire, domestic details ('order coal, get the boiler repaired'), lists of books and music to pack, and arrangements for cover at the Trinité when he was away. Improvisations were carefully planned, with the required duration noted and an outline of tempi and dynamics. Most importantly, Messiaen used the diaries to jot down ideas for compositions. Among the revelations of the war years are notes for a symphony (later to become *Turangalîla*), made as early as 1944. In the event, that project had to be postponed. First, Messiaen was side-tracked by a commission to write short piano pieces for the radio that were to grow into his longest work to date – the *Vingt Regards sur l'Enfant-Jésus*. Then, in 1945, he composed the song-cycle *Harawi*, subtitled 'Song of Love and Death', Messiaen's anguished tribute to Claire, whose mind had begun the deterioration that would cause her to pass the last six years of life in a nursing home. She died in 1959.

In the wake of the publication of *Technique de mon langage musical* (in 1944), Messiaen suddenly found himself a figure of controversy, subject to a campaign of vilification in sections of the press. 'Le Cas Messiaen', as the affair is known, rumbled on for some years, during which he resumed work on the symphony, his first overseas commission (from Serge Koussevitzky, musical director of the Boston Symphony Orchestra). The *Turangalîla-Symphonie* was to be a watershed in Messiaen's development: the climax to a decade of exceptional magnificence but also a forerunner of the rhythmic experiments to come in the late 1940s and early 1950s. While the composers of the avant garde were suspicious of *Turangalîla*, the radicalism of Messiaen's ideas in works like the *Quatre Études de rythme* could not be ignored. He became an iconic figure, and his class a kind of finishing school which attracted brilliant young composers from all over the world.

Almost no sketches survive of Messiaen's early music. Either he discarded them, or (more probably) they perished as a result of the damp in his Paris home that also destroyed his pedal piano. However, by the early 1950s a new source for Messiaen's music becomes available. It was while at the height of his influence in progressive circles that Messiaen made the extraordinary decision to dedicate himself to a huge series of compositions based on birdsong. He began a rigorous study of birds, noting their songs in specially dedicated manuscript notebooks – his *cahiers*; over the next forty years he filled nearly 200 of these, carefully preserving them as a treasure-trove for composition. A priceless feature of the *cahiers* is that each entry is meticulously dated. Moreover, since Messiaen used the *cahiers* as musical sketchbooks as well as an ornithological record, it becomes possible to trace the evolution of musical ideas with considerable precision.

The *cahiers* also tell us much about Messiaen as a person. They are wonderfully vivid documents, the margins filled with extensive descriptions of scenery, and even sketch drawings (for example of flamingos in flight in the Camargue). And they have their lighter moments, as Messiaen's obsession with timbre led him to record everything that flies – including geese, turkeys, parrots and insects – to say nothing of frogs, gurgling water, or the sound of the wind humming in the trees.

By the early 1960s, the *cahiers* are supplemented by extensive musical sketches; their survival is due to the more orderly conditions at the rue Marcadet where Messiaen moved after his marriage to Yvonne Loriod in 1961. As a result, the emphasis changes in the second half of the book as we piece together the genesis of Messiaen's later compositions. At the same time we decided to refer less to press comment on Messiaen's music, which, though a fascinating record of his early career, became less significant once his reputation was established. The one startling exception to this came in 1961 with the reports on *Chronochromie*, which are of outstanding interest since the early performances of this work provoked storms of protest, even driving Messiaen to a rare public defence of his music.

Ironically, the controversy came at precisely the moment when the French establishment was beginning to view Messiaen as a national asset. The city of Paris commissioned a piece to celebrate the centenary of Debussy, and for the government he composed a work to commemorate the dead of two world wars: *Et exspecto resurrectionem mortuorum* received its first public performance with due ceremony at Chartres Cathedral in the presence of General de Gaulle. A return to writing on the grandest scale came with *La Transfiguration de Notre-Seigneur Jésus-Christ* (1965–9), a work of whose composition we have a detailed record thanks to the protracted correspondence with the commissioning body, the Gulbenkian Foundation in Lisbon.

Messiaen's difficulties with *La Transfiguration* were a portent of much greater trials attending the composition of his only opera, *Saint François d'Assise*, on which he worked for twelve years. Messiaen approached the project with the utmost circumspection. He delayed almost five years before accepting the commission, during which he carried out meticulous research in Assisi and the Pacific island of New Caledonia, trips recorded vividly in the *cahiers* and diaries. Although the bulk of the music was composed rapidly in short score, the orchestration became agonizingly protracted, and the result was a serious crisis of confidence.

During the 1980s the nature of Messiaen's diaries changed somewhat, with more space available for him to record observations. This arose partly because Messiaen initiated a parallel diary to keep track of his correspondence, but also because of the gap in his life left by his retirement from the Conservatoire, which took place in 1978, at the end of the term before his seventieth birthday. He was hardly less busy, however, since the demand for his music meant that in some years he spent almost half his time travelling to rehearsals and concerts. Messiaen revelled in acclaim, and recorded in his diary audience reaction using a system of exclamation marks – fourteen being the record. Important though the accounts of these concerts are, we have decided to limit them, preferring to concentrate on the fascinating story unfolding behind the scenes. The difficulties experienced with *Saint François d'Assise* continued, and throughout the

1980s Messiaen was engaged in a painful struggle to regain his inspiration. Thankfully, the story has a happy outcome, with his determination crowned by a final orchestral masterpiece, *Éclairs sur l'Au-delà*.

Throughout the book we have tried to show something of the world as Messiaen experienced it. Sustained by his faith, and by marriages to two remarkable women, his music aimed for the heights. At the same time, the foundation of his achievement was a passion for order. Nothing was so trivial that it was not worth checking and rechecking, until at last a line could be drawn – 'relu et *bien*'. By contrast, the *cahiers* reveal a different side of his character: the virtuosity of mind and hand needed to capture birdsong shows Messiaen at his most spontaneous, creating with an improviser's flair and speed of thought. The most revealing documents are those intended for his use alone, the *cahiers*, sketches and diaries. They show the lengths Messiaen went to in organizing the strands of his career – as composer, organist, concert performer and teacher – so that not a minute was wasted. His was a life dedicated, to a heroic degree, to work. Above all, it is in these private documents that one finds side by side the balancing forces – the sense of the sublime allied with a craftsman's love of detail – which sustained and renewed his immensely long creative life.

Childhood and the Conservatoire
1908–1929

The Register of Births at Avignon records that Olivier Eugène Prosper Charles Messiaen was born on 10 December 1908 at 11 o'clock in the evening, and his parents' address is given as 20 boulevard Sixte Isnard.[1] His father Pierre Messiaen had been appointed as an English teacher at the Lycée Frédéric Mistral in the city, and thus it was in Avignon that Cécile Messiaen (*née* Sauvage) gave birth to her first son. The birth was registered on 12 December and the entry is signed by both parents. Olivier was baptized at Saint-Didier in Avignon, on Christmas Day 1908 – an event now commemorated by a plaque in the church.[2]

1 Messiaen's grandfather, Charles, by his uncle, Léon.

2 The church at La Chaise, near Fuligny (photo: Peter Hill).

Pierre Messiaen (13 March 1883–26 May 1957) was born at the other end of France – close to the Belgian frontier, in the hamlet of Le Blaton near Wervicq in Flanders – one of Charles and Marie Messiaen's seven children (three brothers: Pierre, Léon and Paul; and four sisters: Marthe, Madeleine, Marie and Agnès). After schooling by the Jesuits, Pierre became a student at the Catholic University of Lille in 1900. That same year, the Messiaen family moved from Flanders to the village of Fuligny, in the Aube, east of Troyes. Charles and his wife Marie were taken on as tenant farmers by the de Tilly family who were looking for devout Catholics to work their land.

3 Léon Messiaen: *L'Énergie fauchée* (Musée des Beaux-Arts, Troyes).

Among the Messiaen children, one of the most artistically gifted was Léon, born in 1885, a graduate of the École Nationale des Beaux-Arts; he was at the start of a promising career as a sculptor when killed in action in 1918. The Messiaen family tomb, in the churchyard of La Chaise near Fuligny, is surmounted by a striking sculpture after Léon Messiaen entitled *L'Énergie fauchée* ('Energy spent'). This was based on the original plaster sculpture commissioned to mark the centenary of the battle of La Rothière (1814). It was subsequently exhibited at the 1919 Salon des artistes français in Paris and was given by Léon's mother Marie to the Musée des Beaux-Arts at Troyes in 1920.[3] The tomb reveals some of the history of the Messiaen family. Charles died aged 63 on 26 May 1904. His wife Marie (*née* de Myttenaere) was to outlive several of her children: born in 1853, she died in 1932. Pierre's sister Marie died in a hospital at Merxplas (Belgium), on 26 August 1918 after years of insanity, 'in her forty-second year'; and Paul, the third brother, died in January 1919, 'in his forty-first year', as a result of wounds sustained in the Great War. With the deaths of three siblings (Léon, Marie and Paul) in the space of less than a year, 1918–19 was a melancholy time in the family's history – though the Great War made such tragedies a grim commonplace. Marthe was born in 1880 and died in 1938, and the youngest sister was Agnès: born in 1894, she died as recently as 1977. The longest-lived of the seven children was Madeleine, who was born in 1890, married Paul Guéritte in 1912 and lived until 1987.[4] It was Marthe and Agnès – both spinsters – with whom the young Messiaen often stayed in Fuligny during his holidays. Messiaen's own recollections of the house, and some of his visits, were evoked for Claude Samuel:

4 *L'Énergie fauchée*: reworking of the sculpture by Léon Messiaen on the Messiaen family tomb at La Chaise, near Fuligny (photo: Peter Hill).

My memories [of nature] go back to the age of fourteen or fifteen, chiefly to a period when I went and stayed in the Aube with aunts who owned a rather odd farm, with sculptures by one of my uncles [Léon], a flower-bed, an orchard, some cows and hens. [. . .] To 'restore' my health, my brave aunts would send me out to tend a little herd of cows; it was really a very small herd (there were only two or three cows) but even so I looked after them very badly, and one day they managed to escape and wrought havoc in a field of beetroot which they munched through in a few hours. I was told off by everyone in the village. The Aube countryside is very beautiful and very simple: the plain, its big fields surrounded by trees, magnificent dawns and sunsets, and a great many birds. It was there that I first began noting down birdsong.[5]

So, while the adventure with the cows is almost worthy of Huckleberry Finn, Fuligny was also a place of formative experiences for Messiaen. Agnès seems to have been particularly close to Pierre Messiaen's family, and it was to her that

Messiaen's mother Cécile sent a heartfelt letter of condolence on 28 November 1918, following the death of Léon:

> My dear Agnès
>
> It gave me such grief to hear from you of the death of our poor Léon, and I cannot get used to the idea – we were worried for him as he hasn't written anything since the start of September. His was a wonderful mind and a big heart. [...] Give my best to your poor mother, for whose recovery I prayed for when she was ill, and for whom I will pray now, that she will have the courage to bear this new tragedy. Tell her that I will always keep reverently the memory of her poor Léon. I have asked for a Mass to be said here which we will attend. [...] The children are well. They are at the Lycée, and Zivier [i.e. Olivier] has learnt the catechism. They join me in sending our warmest love, and both say that neither of them will forget their Uncle Léon.
>
> Cécile Messiaen[6]

Clearly Cécile felt able to write on very personal terms to her sister-in-law, but how had she come to marry into the Messiaen family? As a student Pierre developed a passion for poetry (especially English poets) and in 1905, after qualifying as a teacher, he became an editorial assistant for the literary journal *La Revue forézienne*, based in Saint-Étienne. It was at just this time that Cécile Sauvage was beginning her literary career. She was born on 20 July 1883 at La-Roche-sur-Yon in the Vendée, the daughter of Marie (*née* Jolivet) and Prosper Sauvage, a teacher who was appointed the following year to a post at Digne-les-Bains in Haute-Provence, where Cécile grew up. She was one of three talented children: her sister Germaine – referred to by Messiaen, using her married name, as 'Tante Tatin' – went on to a career as a physics and chemistry teacher at Romans, and her brother André became a surgeon in Grenoble. With the encouragement of the great Provençal writer Frédéric Mistral (who addressed her as his 'chère petite Aréthuse'),[7] Cécile submitted her poem 'Les Trois Muses' for publication. The *Revue forézienne* decided to publish it, and in November 1905 she went, with her brother André, to see Fournier-Lefort, the director, and his young editor Pierre Messiaen. After this first meeting, Cécile returned to Digne: her father was going blind and needed her to accompany him to the Lycée and to help with correcting pupils' work.

Neither family was particularly enthusiastic about the marriage of Pierre and Cécile: in the Sauvage household there was concern that their eldest daughter was marrying a young man who was about to do his military service;[8] Pierre's family was worried that Cécile was too delicate. These reservations were evidently overcome, since the couple were married in the church at Sieyes (the part of Digne in which the Sauvages lived) on 9 September 1907, and they moved

5 Pierre Messiaen, left, on military service.

into Cécile's family home. In 1908 Pierre was appointed to the Lycée Frédéric Mistral in Avignon, and the couple moved there. Cécile became pregnant and began her most famous collection of poems, *L'Âme en bourgeon* ('The Soul in Bud'), while carrying her child. The poems were published in 1910 by Mercure de France, as part of her collection *Tandis que la terre tourne*.

The extraordinary poems written to Messiaen during and just after his time in the womb were things he always considered immensely precious. Though the 1910 first edition of *L'Âme en bourgeon* contains no dedication to Messiaen, it is clear that Cécile wrote them for him: she said as much in a letter from 1917, presumably written to Pierre at the front: 'With [Olivier], I leafed through *L'Âme en bourgeon*. It's for you, I said to him, with its bees and grasshoppers. Mummy, he said, you're a poet just like Shakespeare. Like him, you have suns, planets, ants, frightening skeletons.

6 Sauvage family group, with Cécile on the left, her sister Germaine and brother André, and her maternal grandparents.

7 The house at Digne-les-Bains, Provence, where Cécile Sauvage lived from 1888 until her marriage to Pierre Messiaen (photo: Peter Hill).

8 Cécile in c.1905.

9 Pierre Messiaen, photograph inscribed to Cécile Sauvage, 1906.

10 Cécile with the baby Olivier, early 1909.

I prefer things which are frightening.'[9] In the posthumous 1929 edition of Sauvage's poems, *L'Âme en bourgeon* has a dedication, 'pour Olivier Messiaen'.

Messiaen spoke often about the inspiration of his mother and of her work; this is unsurprising, but his comments about her poetry are much warmer than those of an affectionate and loyal son. Reading Sauvage's poems, it is not hard to see why he admired them so much. Not only are there the prophetic qualities in *L'Âme en bourgeon* about Messiaen's future interests (music, the Orient, and birdsong), but her work as a whole is impressive and original. Shortly after her death, tributes were paid by a number of other writers, and an article by Léon Daudet declared that she was 'the leading woman poet – by some distance – of our time'.[10] Her poems deal frequently with music and with nature, and she brought unique insights, honesty and lyric eloquence to the subject of maternity.

In 1909 Pierre was appointed to a school at Ambert in the Auvergne and the family lived there until 1913.[11] Messiaen's younger brother Alain was born on 30 August 1912, and the same year Cécile finished another collection of poems, *Le Vallon*, which often evokes the Auvergne landscape.[12] Mercure de France issued *Le Vallon* in 1913 and it was to be the only other volume of Cécile Sauvage's poetry to be published during her lifetime. The birth of Alain apparently took its toll on her health, which was to remain precarious for the remaining years of her life.[13]

11 Olivier and Alain Messiaen in 1914.

12 2 cours Berriat in Grenoble, where Messiaen lived during World War I (photo: Peter Hill).

Pierre joined the French army on the outbreak of war, and Cécile moved with her two boys to Grenoble, where they were to spend the war years. It was a time recalled affectionately by Messiaen in a speech he gave in 1984:

> It was the First World War (1914–18). During the five years of wartime, my father and all the men in my family were at the front. So it was that I lived in Grenoble, at 2 cours Berriat, in the flat belonging to my uncle, the surgeon, Dr André Sauvage, with just my grandmother and my mother. Here I spent the formative years of my life, those when the personality forms: I was five when I arrived in Grenoble and ten when I left. [. . .] But I have never forgotten Grenoble with its marvellous mountain landscape, and every year, during the three months of the summer, I come to one of the loveliest places in the region [Petichet], simply to compose music. [. . .] It was in Grenoble that I realized I was a musician. I was seven-and-a-half and had just been bought, from Deshairs [Grenoble's largest music shop], Gluck's *Orphée*, and with my present under my arm, I went into the park.[14]

This account intriguingly leaves out Cécile's father, who was also living there. He was completely blind by then; Messiaen later likened him to Arkel in Debussy's *Pelléas*, and recalled evenings in the Grenoble flat: 'Alain and I played games with him, to frighten us. In the evening we would go into the room where he was, in darkness which didn't worry him at all, and we would say "Grandad, scare us!", which he did. Wasn't that an atmosphere quite close to Maeterlinck's in the old castle of Allemonde!'[15] Messiaen continued his story of the revelation he had when reading the vocal score of Gluck's *Orphée* in conversations with Claude Samuel:

13 Place Victor-Hugo in Grenoble (photo: Peter Hill).

14 The jardin de ville in Grenoble (photo: Peter Hill).

I went to sit on a stone bench in the large Jardin de Ville, the old garden of the Hôtel de Lesdisguières, near the church of Saint-André, the Palais de Justice and the Hôtel de Ville. [. . .] I looked at the theme in F major from Orpheus's great aria in the first act, which is probably the most beautiful passage Gluck ever wrote, when I noticed that I was 'hearing' it. So I could already hear a score, and I had only been learning music for a few months.[16]

However, Messiaen's boyhood enthusiasm for opera was not explored just by quietly reading scores on park benches in Grenoble, but by sitting at his uncle's piano (which Messiaen was teaching himself to play) and giving performances in which he would also sing the principal roles in his piping treble voice. The works he specifically mentioned as childhood gifts included Mozart's *Don Giovanni* and *Die Zauberflöte*, Gluck's *Alceste* (as well as *Orphée*), Berlioz's *La Damnation de Faust*, and Wagner's *Die Walküre* and *Siegfried*.[17] This was a lifelong passion and he was even to return to private singing of opera in his seventies: with Yvonne Loriod at the piano, Messiaen sang parts of *Saint François d'Assise* on tape so that singers would have an idea how he wanted the music to go.[18] In the early Grenoble years, Messiaen was also given some modern piano music, and the repertoire suggests his progress as a self-taught pianist was impressive: Debussy's *Estampes* and Ravel's *Gaspard de la nuit* made a lasting impact.[19] It was in Grenoble, too, that he composed his first piece, *La Dame de Shalott*, inspired by Tennyson's poem and described half a century later by the composer as 'obviously a very childish piece, but not entirely silly, and not completely devoid of sense. I still think of it with a certain tenderness.'[20]

Messiaen's love of literature developed quickly during the war years. He was aware from an early age that his mother was a poet and writer, but as well as her influence, there was also the discovery of drama, particularly Shakespeare, where his early favourites were *Macbeth* ('because of the witches, and Banquo's ghost'[21]), Puck and Ariel in *The Tempest* and 'the greatness of the mad King Lear berating the storm and the lightning'.[22] Perhaps the most intriguing aspect of his enthusiasm was his interest in the stage directions, especially 'the famous instruction in the historical plays: "alarums, skirmishes, the enemy enters the city"'.[23] But by then – as he related many times – he was putting on regular Shakespeare performances for his brother Alain, acting all the parts himself. Since he also experimented with lighting effects and placed model characters on the stage of his toy theatre, a fascination with the details of stagecraft becomes less surprising. However, his lifelong enthusiasm for Shakespeare, Keats and others makes Messiaen's reluctance to learn English all the more baffling, especially given his father's impressive series of published translations.[24]

Pierre was serving as a soldier, away from home, throughout the war, so it was not the future translator of Shakespeare, Milton, Blake and Whitman who introduced his son to Shakespeare's plays.[25] While the young Messiaen had plenty of encouragement from his mother to explore great poetry and drama, it was his Uncle André (Cécile's brother) who gave him 'an edition of Shakespeare's works which I loved very much, a romantic edition with woodcuts depicting all the characters in all possible attitudes – that made a deep impression on me as a child'.[26]

Messiaen was already developing an understanding of the Catholic faith which was to underpin his adult life. Though he often spoke of his parents being non-believers, it is clear that they were happy to support their son's religious beliefs. As we have seen, Cécile reported to Aunt Agnès that he had learned his catechism by the time he was ten years old. Two years earlier, she had observed that 'Childhood is completely wonderful because its whole being is filled with belief',[27] suggesting that she was greatly touched by Olivier's religious disposition.

Following demobilization in 1918, Pierre was appointed to teach at the Lycée Clemenceau in Nantes, and it was there that the family lived in 1918–19, at 1 place des Enfants Nantais,[28] a square dominated by the handsome church of Saint-Donatien. As the precocious Olivier was already playing the piano and had even tried his hand at composition, his parents recognized the need to find him some specialist music teaching. According to his Nantes schoolfriend Maurice Poté,[29] Messiaen's music teachers there included Mlle Véron,[30] Gontran Arcouët[31] and Jean (sometimes Jehan) de Gibon.[32] It was de Gibon (1873–1952) who was to make a lasting impact on the young Messiaen, with the inspired act of kindness for which he is now best remembered: a gift to the ten-year-old Olivier of the vocal score of Debussy's *Pelléas et Mélisande*. This was a moment of awakening for Messiaen which he was to recall many times in later life, never with more affection than in the obituary notice he wrote for de Gibon:

15 Place des Enfants-Nantais, Nantes, where the Messiaen family lived in 1919 (photo: Peter Hill).

He was a good, honest, generous man, full of tact, with the deepest sensibility, a man such as you are unlikely to find any more. And what a musician – ardent and enthusiastic! His passionate discussions about music are still ringing in my ears!

After a long career as professor of harmony at the Conservatoire in Nantes, he suffered the tragedy of losing his wife, whom he loved above everything, and retired to his home town of Redon. He lived there in his world of memories, speaking often of his friend the pianist Gontran Arcouët and of his former pupils: Louis Martin, conductor; Maurice Bagot, conductor; Maurice Poté, organist; Gilette Justice, pianist; and the author of this article. Each day, a Panama hat on his head (and clogs on his feet when it was raining), he went to put flowers on his wife's grave. Then, returning to his small room in the Grande Cour, he wrote music criticism for *L'Écho du Pays de Redon*.

He left us numerous works for piano, two pianos and organ. Particularly notable is *Cimetière breton* for piano, dedicated to Gontran Arcouët, written in 1919, where the bell effects using superimposed fifths, the imaginative harmonies, the use of the whole-tone scale and modes from plainchant must have sounded strangely 'modern' at the time.

I must also mention a beautiful *Pastorale* for organ, dedicated to me, which has a similar harmonic daring (we even find ninths with an added sixth) to which should be added the finesse of the timbres and a sweet and unspoilt melodic freshness which bear witness to the touching sincerity of the composer. I have often played this *Pastorale* on my organ at the Trinité and will play it again regularly, along with his other works, in memory of my old master.

To finish, a marvellous story that I have often told my students at the Conservatoire de Paris: it is the story of a young boy aged nine and a half who from the age of eight had an unstoppable passion for music, played the piano and composed with typical awkwardness. He came to Nantes in 1918, with his family, and there met his first harmony teacher who took a liking to him from the first instant and refused any payment for the lessons he gave. After six months, pupil and teacher needed to separate because the little boy went to Paris with his family. What did the teacher give to the child as a souvenir of these beautiful lessons? A classic work, a harmony treatise? No: he gave him a score which at the time was the height of daring (rather like serial music, or *musique concrète*, or a sonata by Pierre Boulez nowadays). He gave him *Pelléas et Mélisande* by Debussy! This present served to confirm the young pupil's vocation, and point him in the direction he wanted. The pupil was me; the master was Jean de Gibon.[33]

Pelléas was perhaps given to Messiaen as a birthday or Christmas present in December 1919. In a draft New Year letter (undated, but almost certainly from late December 1919) he wrote to his grandmother, aunt and uncle Sauvage, describing a remarkable haul of gifts, with *Pelléas* at the head of the list:

I miss very much the nice visits to Romans and Grenoble, and I hope to see you again as soon as possible. I have had a superb Christmas. *Pelléas et Mélisande* by Debussy, and the same play with just the text by Maeterlinck, then *Monna Vanna* by the same author. Then I was given some characters of all sorts for my little theatre: halberdiers made of lead, some *santons* [Provençal statuettes], and above all some Breton and Spanish characters

16 Rue Rambuteau, Paris, home of the Messiaen family in the 1920s (photo: Peter Hill).

17 Messiaen with friends at Romans in 1919.

from the Middle Ages. Everything I could have wished for. [. . .] I won't list all of Alain's presents as he will do that in his own letter. I just want to tell you about one thing: a pistol which makes the devil's own racket. He also got a book of plays by Calderón which he is copying out in large letters and illuminating, which uses up all my crayons. Despite the holidays at the Conservatoire, I still have harmony lessons over Christmas, then a harmony competition to prepare for. As that will be a lot of work, you will forgive me for writing just a few pages. Happy New Year once again!
Your Olivier who loves you,
    Olivarnus.[34]

In an interview he gave in 1931, Messiaen mentioned two other musicians with Nantes connections who encouraged him to continue his studies in Paris: Lucy Vuillemin and Robert Lortat.[35] Both had successful careers (and both were living in the capital): the pianist Robert Lortat was a friend and interpreter of Fauré (and the dedicatee of Fauré's Twelfth Nocturne), while Lucy Vuillemin was a distinguished singer, and wife of the Nantes-born composer Louis Vuillemin.[36]

The Messiaen family's move to Paris was a result of Pierre's appointment (in July 1919) to teach at the Lycée Charlemagne, in the Saint-Gervais quarter of the 4e arrondissement; initially the family lived on the quai de Bourbon, on the Île Saint-Louis.[37] Subsequently they moved to 67 rue Rambuteau, at the corner of the rue Quincampoix, in the Beaubourg district on the edge of the Marais. The date Messiaen himself gave for his arrival at the Paris Conservatoire was 1919,[38] and it is likely that the eleven-year-old attended classes, at least as an 'auditeur', for a year before his official enrolment. Moreover, the New Year letter quoted above indicated that he was studying for the Conservatoire harmony exams during the 1919 Christmas holidays. However, his first appearance in a formal register of students seems to be in October 1920.[39] Messiaen was clearly proud of the many prizes he won over the next decade, and he kept all the certificates:[40]

1922	Deuxième médaille de piano
	Deuxième accessit d'harmonie
1923	Première médaille de piano
1924	Second prix d'harmonie
	Second prix d'accompagnement au piano

1925	Premier prix d'accompagnement au piano.
1926	Premier prix de fugue
1928	Premier accessit d'orgue
	Deuxième accesit de composition
	Cours d'histoire de la musique Second prix
1929	Premier prix d'orgue
	Second prix de composition
	Cours d'histoire de la musique Premier prix
1930	Premier prix de composition

In 1929 Messiaen was also presented with the coveted *Diplôme d'études musicales supérieures*, an award from the governing body of the Conservatoire in recognition of consistently high achievement by a student.[41]

18 The piano class of Georges Falkenberg at the Paris Conservatoire in 1919. Messiaen is in the middle row, second from the right.

Messiaen's earliest teachers at the Conservatoire included Georges Falkenberg[42] for the preparatory piano class (the test piece in 1922 – the year of his earliest Conservatoire award, a 'deuxième médaille' – was one of Mendelssohn's Preludes and Fugues op.35[43]). His harmony teacher was Jean Gallon, and photographs of his class show Messiaen wearing spectacles, something he was to do for the rest of his life. Throughout his time at the Conservatoire, Messiaen also took private lessons with Jean Gallon's younger brother Noël.[44] It was an overworked Jean Gallon who suggested that the eleven-year-old Messiaen should go to his brother for extra teaching, and he was to continue seeing Noël Gallon regularly for the next decade. In November 1991, at one of his last public appearances, Messiaen spoke at a concert 'dédié à la mémoire de Noël Gallon':

19 The harmony class of
Jean Gallon at the Paris
Conservatoire in 1924.
Messiaen is at the far right.

I went to Noël Gallon's, at 1 rue Gaillard, once a week for about ten years. [...] Noël Gallon was a marvellous teacher. I was aware of his prodigious technique and I put my complete confidence in him. He was extremely kind. When I showed him an unsuccessful harmony exercise, he put it patiently on the table and wrote the whole exercise for me again. When I played him a Chopin étude on the piano, awkwardly and with inadequate technique, he would sit at the piano and play me the same Chopin étude, then without any hesitation, and to encourage me to work harder on piano technique, he would play six or seven more Chopin études. But the area where his teaching was indispensable was counterpoint. [...] I learned all my counterpoint, from A to Z, with Noël Gallon. [...] He taught me from when I was eleven years of age until I was twenty-one. He was always courteous, kind and affectionate. He had known me as a laughing child, as a worried and tortured adolescent, and as a young man smitten with the avant-garde. In every case, he knew how to adapt to my age and my tastes, and he treated me like his own son. He even listened with patience to my earliest attempts at composition: a song for voice and piano on the *Ballade des pendus* by François Villon; a piece which was meant to be revolutionary and just sounded clumsy, *La Tristesse d'un grand ciel blanc*; and finally I played him (when I was twenty) my Opus One, the *Préludes* for piano.

One last recollection. He invited me to dinner with my brother Alain. [...] After dinner, Madame Gallon (his mother), Madame Noël Gallon (his wife), Noël Gallon himself, my brother Alain and I declaimed an entire act of *Hamlet* together. It must have been very funny, but I was playing the role of Hamlet and was taking myself extremely seriously. Noël Gallon was nice enough not to laugh, and to join in this over-long bit of whimsy with his usual kindness.[45]

For piano accompaniment – which also involved other keyboard skills such as score-reading and improvisation – Messiaen was taught by César Abel Estyle (pipped at the post for the *premier prix* for piano accompaniment in 1902 by his classmate André Caplet), and for fugue by Georges Caussade, who had previously taught three of Les Six (Auric, Milhaud and Tailleferre), as well as Noël Gallon. Music history classes particularly excited Messiaen since Maurice Emmanuel – a pupil of Delibes and friend of Debussy – helped to ignite his interest in ancient modes and non-Western music. Emmanuel's *Sonatine IV: sur des modes hindous* was composed in

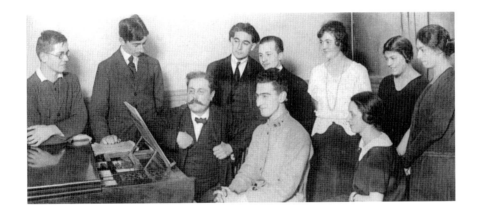

20 The piano accompaniment class of César Abel Estyle at the Paris Conservatoire in 1924. Messiaen is standing at the far left.

21 The composition class of Paul Dukas at the Paris Conservatoire, 1929–30. Left to right, near the piano: Pierre Maillard-Verger, Elsa Barraine, Yvonne Desportes, Tony Aubin, Pierre Revel, Georges Favre, Paul Dukas, René Duclos, Georges Hugon, Maurice Duruflé. Seated at right: Claude Arrieu, Olivier Messiaen.

1920 and published in 1923 (the same year as Albert Roussel's opera-ballet *Padmâvatî* which also took its inspiration from the East). Messiaen was to become an enthusiastic advocate for Emmanuel's music, especially the folk-song arrangements, *Trente Chansons bourguignonnes* (1913). In the late 1920s, Messiaen also attended the percussion classes of the redoubtable Joseph Baggers, whose pioneering *Méthode de timbales et instruments à percussion* had been published in 1906 with enthusiastic endorsements from Debussy, Fauré, d'Indy and Massenet.

The Conservatoire records show that Messiaen's composition teacher for the academic year 1926–7 was Charles-Marie Widor.[46] Though Messiaen seldom mentioned his lessons with Widor, master and pupil evidently got on, since a few years later, when Messiaen applied for the post of *titulaire* at the Trinité, he used Widor as one of his referees. But in autumn 1927, Messiaen joined the composition class of Widor's newly appointed successor, Paul Dukas. Widor's class had evidently become something of a production-line for the Prix de Rome, and Dukas wrote a witty letter to his friend Guy-Ropartz in November 1927 about the need to restore geniune creativity (rather than competition-winning formulae) to the centre of the composition curriculum: 'If there is ambition, it's been along the lines of M. Citroën rather than *père* Franck! I shall very gently try to deindustrialize music.'[47]

As Messiaen was to assert on many occasions, Dukas was an inspiring teacher, and the expert encouragement of the composer of *Ariane et Barbe-bleue* and *La Péri* was indispensable. Dukas's surviving output as a composer had more or less ground to a halt in 1911 with the ballet *La Péri*. Despite some tantalizing later projects (a ballet in 1930; a work for the Boston Symphony Orchestra in 1932), only a piano piece in memory of his friend Debussy and a song for *Le Tombeau de Ronsard* saw the light of day during his lifetime (both in musical supplements for *La Revue musicale*). For over twenty years, until his death in 1935, this great musician's ruthless self-criticism prevented him either from finishing any major works or allowing them to survive. This extreme case of 'composer's block' makes Dukas's generosity of spirit towards his pupils all the more remarkable.

Only weeks before starting his studies with Dukas, Messiaen's world fell apart. Though Cécile Sauvage had been in failing health for several years, her death from tuberculosis on 26 August 1927 had a profound effect on her sons. Olivier was with Cécile during her final illness, and the day before her death he summoned his father and brother back to Paris from a short holiday they were taking. One of the few family papers to survive from these years is the moving letter which Pierre Messiaen ('Pio') sent to his teenage sons on 6 September, just over a week after Cécile had died.

Mes chers petits,

I arrived this morning very tired. The house is so sad and empty. Your dear mummy is no longer here, nor her beautiful eyes, nor her smile and her wonderful voice which I can imagine saying: hello – be wise, sensible, distinguished. Make your grandmother and your uncle André happy, through your love for her and through affection for me. Go to pray at her grave, listen to what she says to you from above, for her thoughts are around all three of us. [. . .] Write down your memories of your mummy and we can make a beautiful book about her, and we will publish everything that we can of her works. [. . .] I will write to you again tomorrow and on the days which follow. Write to me too. Be good and brave children, full of courage and tenderness for your poor, poor papa.

   Goodbye, my dear Olivier, my dear Alain. In my thoughts, there are still four of us.

   Pio[48]

Messiaen's musical remembrance to his mother is found in the *Trois Mélodies*. The second of these, 'Le Sourire', was of great personal significance to the young Messiaen, his only setting of a text by his mother. In an interview in 1931 Messiaen recalled:

I wrote three songs in which I framed a poem by my mother with two poems of my own.
So you are a poet?
Oh no! She was that.
And [. . .] you aren't thinking of setting more of her work?
No! I wouldn't dare. It would be dabbling in matters that are far too precious.[49]

Short and gentle, Messiaen's music is an expression of the most intimate sadness, using the second poem in Sauvage's 1913 collection, *Primevère*:

A certain word murmured
By you is a kiss
Intimate and prolonged
Like a kiss on the soul.
My mouth wants to smile
And my smile trembles.[50]

This touching memorial is enclosed by settings of poems by the composer. The words of 'Pourquoi?' express grief as the poet wearies of the beauties of nature. In the final song, 'La Fiancée perdue', Messiaen portrays his mother as a bride in radiant apparel: the eager phrases of the voice are accompanied by a brilliant toccata on the piano, before a long coda in which the music sinks to rest with a serene prayer for Christ's blessing. Near the end of his life, Messiaen confided to George Benjamin that he believed his mother had continued to watch over him as a 'guardian angel'.[51]

Everywhere there are signs of a personal musical language beginning to form. In 'Pourquoi?', for example, the harmonies of the reiterated cadence – gliding between F sharp major (the tonic) and A minor – hint at a central feature of Messiaen's language, the octatonic mode of alternating semitones and tones favoured by (among others) Rimsky-Korsakov, Ravel and Stravinsky. (In Messiaen's terminology this is the second of his 'modes of limited transposition', so called because the pattern of intervals ensures that only two transpositions up a semitone are possible before arriving back at the original collection of pitches.) Also characteristic of Messiaen's early work is the music's intense emotional charge, which causes it to break through the slightly stilted conventions of the poem with an impassioned upsurge, before dying away to the icy frisson of the final 'Pourquoi?'

Messiaen joined not only Dukas's class in autumn 1927, but also that of his other great 'maître', Marcel Dupré, whose preparatory organ course he attended on Jean Gallon's advice, initially as a way of developing his improvisation skills. Forty years later, in a letter dated 27 December 1967, Dupré recalled his first encounter with Messiaen: 'In my preparatory course for the organ class, you played to me, by heart and impeccably, the Fantasia in C minor by Bach. You had been playing the organ for . . . eight days!'[52] In another account, Dupré gave more details, including some interesting comments on the nature of Messiaen's relationship with his father at the time:

> He joined my class in October 1927. When he came out to Meudon for the first time (he was nineteen), he sat stupefied in front of my organ keyboards. He had never seen an organ console before. After an hour of explanations and demonstrations, I gave him the Bach C minor Fantasia to learn. He came back a week later and played it to me by heart, perfectly; an astonishing feat! In class he didn't fidget, but seemed to me to be rather distracted. I confided this to his father, an English teacher at the Lycée Charlemagne, who replied: 'I've had hundreds of children pass through my hands, but Olivier is the only one I've completely failed to understand. All I can say is that, at table, he interrupts every conversation to talk about you.'[53]

The May exams for the organ class in 1928 included a composition to be based on a given theme. In *Technique de mon langage musical* Messiaen listed a

22 Fuligny (photo: Peter Hill).

set of *Variations écossaises* for the instrument, and the records in the Archives Nationales show that one of the themes set that year was the well-known Scottish folksong 'Comin' through the rye'.[54] Mind-boggling as the prospect may seem to us now, this is almost certainly the melody on which Messiaen's variations, now lost, were based. That summer he stayed with his aunts in Fuligny and composed the orchestral work which he later called *Le Banquet eucharistique*, and the organ work derived from part of it, *Le Banquet céleste* (both discussed below).

Dupré also recalled the organ exams a year later, in 1929, when Messiaen was given special dispensation to perform Widor (the finale of the Second Symphony) in place of a work by Franck.[55] After the exams at the Conservatoire in May–June 1929, which produced a bumper crop of awards (two first prizes, one second prize, and the *Diplôme*), Messiaen again spent the summer with his aunts at Fuligny. From this isolated village in the undulating landscape north of Bar-sur-Aube, he wrote on 17 August to Jean Langlais (a fellow-pupil in Dupré's organ class) about his holiday, which he was using to compose: the *Préludes* for piano, and perhaps some work on the *Diptyque* for organ and *Trois Mélodies*.[56] Using the summer months for intensive composition was to become a lifelong habit. Whether in Fuligny, Neussargues or Petichet, the summer was always Messiaen's most productive time for creative work; in some years it was his only time, given his heavy teaching commitments at the Conservatoire and, in later years, numerous concerts and foreign tours.

Elsa Barraine, another friend from the Conservatoire, gave an interview in 1968 in which she recalled Messiaen as a fellow-student. They first met in Jean Gallon's harmony class:

Messiaen must have been 14 or 15 – he was still in short trousers and had an open-necked shirt. After that we moved up through classes in parallel, that's to say he was normally one year ahead of me, but in Dukas's class we found ourselves together and it was there that I saw a lot of him and in a more regular way. [. . .] There's a great contrast between the Messiaen we know nowadays, who is open, radiant and fulfilled, and the young Messiaen who was extremely reserved, extremely timid and inward-looking. His face reflected feelings of submissiveness and humility. For example, many of our fellow-students enjoyed free discussions with our teacher Paul Dukas and were vociferous in class. Messiaen, as I remember, never spoke, just brought his music and played it on the piano. We could tell what power and technique he already had, what passion and originality of language was making itself felt. But you couldn't discern any of that from him personally, he was so self-effacing right from his beginnings as a composer. [. . .] I didn't dare try to be familiar with him or crack jokes, as I did with some of the others. When I heard him play his piano *Préludes*, which he brought one by one as they were written, and all his music from those years [. . .] it was all so impressive and extraordinary coming from such a young man, you felt already such a humane, musical personality, that it commanded respect and placed him on a level too far above us for us to be able to treat him as a crony. [. . .] He never came empty-handed, he always had a large briefcase, stuffed full of scores, and he always had something to show our teacher.[57]

The Trinité and marriage
1930–1934

On 22 January 1930 an event advertised as an 'Exercice des élèves' by the chorus and orchestra of the Conservatoire included the one and only performance of an orchestral work billed as *Le Banquet céleste*. This was the piece usually described by Messiaen as *Le Banquet eucharistique*. The *Guide du concert* gave the whole programme: D'Indy's *Camp de Wallenstein*, Messiaen's *Le Banquet céleste*, Saint-Saëns's *Havanaise* and Beethoven's Ninth Symphony, all conducted by the Conservatoire's director, Henri Rabaud.[1] Composed at Fuligny in 1928, Messiaen always considered his orchestral *Banquet* to be something of a failure, but during the same summer vacation in 1928 he had salvaged the best of it for the organ piece *Le Banquet céleste*: 'When I was in Paul Dukas's class, I composed a work first for orchestra, and then for organ in a second version, at least of a passage which I had taken from the work. [. . .] I was only nineteen years old when I composed *Le Banquet eucharistique*, it was a very long work, neither very well scored nor very well constructed.'[2] 'I found it bombastic, in other words, not good.'[3] Whatever the shortcomings of the piece, this was valuable experience for Messiaen: it was the first time any of his orchestral music had been performed.

It was in the summer of 1930 that Messiaen's formal years of study came to an end and he embarked on the perilous career of composer. The *Préludes* for piano was the work which Messiaen always considered his true opus one,[4] but his early works present a more complex picture than such a tidy starting point suggests. Among the pieces written during his time at the Conservatoire, several are lost or remain to be rediscovered,[5] but Messiaen's enthusiasms for orchestral and piano music, as well as works for voice and organ, can clearly be seen in the compositions that have survived; even the writing of his own sung texts is something which goes back to his student years. Perhaps more important than any of this, though, is the emergence of a thoroughly original voice even before his studies were over. In the early 1930s, it was the works written in the last couple of years in Dukas's class which were to form the basis of his reputation as a new voice in French music.

« LES AMIS DE L'ORGUE »
— 1929-1930 —

TROISIÈME   CONCERT

SECRÉTARIAT GÉNÉRAL
6, Place du Pré-t Mithouard
PARIS - VII°

AUDITION
de
M. Olivier MESSIAEN
sur le Grand Orgue de
L'ÉGLISE DE LA TRINITÉ
avec le Concours de Mlle LINA FALK, Cantatrice

10 FÉVRIER 1930   20 HEURES 45

Ce Programme est vendu 3 francs au profit de la Caisse de Secours des Organistes Pauvres ou Malades.

23 Programme for Messiaen's first public recital in Paris, at the Trinité on 20 February 1930, including the première of the *Diptyque*.

Dukas had encouraged René Dommange, the Managing Director of Durand et Cie, to sign up his brilliant protégé, and by the time Messiaen won a *premier prix* for composition in June 1930, three of his pieces had been taken by Durand: the *Préludes* for piano, the *Diptyque* for organ (dedicated to Messiaen's two 'maîtres', Dupré and Dukas) and the *Trois Mélodies*. The young composer wasted no time in arranging performances of these pieces – a task made easier with the backing of a publisher whose catalogue included the masterpieces of Debussy, Ravel and, of course, Dukas. The *Diptyque* has the distinction of being Messiaen's first work to appear in print, in May 1930, quickly followed by the *Préludes* in June, and the *Trois Mélodies* in October.

Messiaen gave the première of his *Diptyque* in a concert for Les Amis de l'Orgue on 20 February 1930, at the Trinité. Since autumn 1929 he had been the regular deputy for the Trinité's ailing *titulaire* Charles Quef, and this event appears to have been his public concert début in Paris. The autobiographical note mentions that he 'gave two organ recitals last summer at Tencin (Isère)'. These concerts, in a small town just to the north-east of Grenoble, were apparently Messiaen's first public organ recitals anywhere, given on 15 and 22 September 1929.[6]

The *Diptyque*, described in the programme as 'unpublished' but 'in preparation from Durand', is explained in a short note by Messiaen with a mixture of musical and theological commentary that was to become characteristic: 'The composer is at present a composition pupil of Paul Dukas. The first part of this work expresses the anguish and useless torment of life. It is a prelude in C minor containing four statements of the same theme, separated by short developments. The second part takes up the theme of the first and transforms it. An Adagio in C major, based on a single serene ascending phrase, it expresses the peace and charity of Christian paradise.' The concert also included music by Bach (the Fantasia and Fugue in C minor – which had so impressed Dupré after Messiaen's eight days' work on it two years earlier – and the Choral Prelude *Schmücke Dich, o liebe Seele*) and pieces by two of Messiaen's fellow-students in Dupré's class: Henriette Roget's *Complainte*, and two *Préludes* by Jean Langlais, 'Un Ange en prière' and 'Adoration des bergers'. The programme ended with two extemporizations by Messiaen: 'Improvisation sur un thème donné': *Prélude, Fugue, Toccata*, and *Sortie improvisée*. Langlais gave the *Diptyque* its second performance for Les Amis de l'Orgue at Saint-Antoine-des-Quinze-Vingts on 27 December 1930.

On 28 January 1930, a few weeks before the official première, Messiaen gave a private performance of the *Préludes* in Durand's salon at 4 place de la Madeleine (Dukas was also present on this occasion[7]). The first public performance of six of the *Préludes* ('Chant d'extase dans un paysage triste', 'Le

Nombre léger', 'Instants défunts', 'Les Sons impalpables du rêve', 'Cloches d'angoisse et larmes d'adieu' and 'Un Reflet dans le vent') was given by Henriette Roget at a Société Nationale concert in the Salle Érard on 1 March 1930.[8] The *Préludes* are dedicated 'à Mademoiselle Henriette Roget' and fifty-five years later she reminisced about the première:

It is always dreadful to speak about oneself, but I want to recall a date which has been one of the most significant of my entire career: 1 March 1930 (it seems like only yesterday!). It was on that evening that I gave the first performance of one of the works written when Messiaen was about twenty: the *Préludes* for piano, which he had the kind idea of dedicating to me, as if I was his best friend. Already very conscious of the parallels between sounds and colours, Olivier Messiaen asked me not to wear white or pink. He wanted sky blue or pale green, the colour of water, of leaves, of the sky. These *Préludes* caused a sensation among a group of enthusiasts; there are in these pieces more than a promise of a very individual musical palette, a modal style of writing inspired by Hindu scales, experimentation with rhythms and a unity of conception. Consequently it was only a few years later that Messiaen became famous. A hundred years from now, if my name hasn't been forgotten entirely by musicologists, it will undoubtedly be because it appears on the score of the *Préludes*.[9]

Composed (and first performed) while he was still studying with Dukas, the *Préludes* were among the first pieces by Messiaen to attract critical attention. Georges Dandelot reviewed the first performance:[10]

There is no doubt that we are here in the presence of a musician, and a gifted musician too. That is rare enough to deserve a mention, and we predict a fine career for the composer of these *Préludes*. But I do not know why these pieces which should, by definition, be short, have such elongated proportions. All this does is to tire the listener without any benefit to the music. The second prelude is the most charming and the most successful of the six performed.[11] All the others would gain from greater conciseness. But that doesn't matter as there is real quality here, and that's the essential thing: beautiful sonorities, light and lively rhythms, interesting counterpoint, much delicacy, and unexpected endings. [. . .] Mademoiselle Henriette Roget, as refined a pianist as she is a sensitive musician, contributed greatly to the success of these pieces.[12]

No doubt Dandelot would have found more to his liking the two *Préludes* unaccountably omitted by Henriette Roget – 'La Colombe' and 'Plainte calme' – both of which are true miniatures. The former is the opening piece of the set and is very characteristic of Messiaen's early language. The harmony hovers between Messiaen's 'second mode' – which gives the tritone intervals (F to B) on which the melody is poised and the harmonies of the fluttering descant – and a solid underlying tonality (E major) which articulates the two halves of the structure. The texture is transparent, with a typically exquisite effect at the closing cadence where a reminiscence of the melody is given a slightly acid colouring by a parallel line two octaves minus a semitone higher. The refinement of mood is true of the *Préludes* as a whole, with one notable exception, 'Cloches d'angoisse et larmes d'adieu', whose Apocalyptic vision makes it the piece most prophetic of later Messiaen. The stillness that Messiaen achieves in its immense coda – the 'farewell' of the title – is a hallmark of all his great slow movements, and the final page is superbly imagined: silence creeps in and the music distils into fragments.

The Prix de Rome for music was awarded annually by the Académie des Beaux-Arts from 1803 until 1968, though several outstanding French composers never entered at all (especially those, such as Fauré, Chabrier and Duparc, who did not attend the Conservatoire), while others were unsuccessful despite repeated attempts. Notable among the failures were Saint-Saëns (in 1852, and again in 1864), Dukas for four years running (1886–9), Ravel on no fewer than five occasions (1900–3 and 1905), and Messiaen in 1930 and 1931. Two pieces are known to have been written by Messiaen for the 1930 competition, in which he failed to reach the final round: a four-voice fugue on a subject by Georges Hüe in 2/2 time,[13] and *Sainte-Bohème (extrait des Odes funambulesques)*, a setting for chorus and orchestra of a text by Théodore de Banville. The words for this may have had a special appeal for Messiaen: 'Nous sommes frères des oiseaux' ('We are brothers of the birds') and, later, 'des lys de diamant, des couleurs d'or et de miel' ('lilies of diamond, colours of gold and of honey').[14]

Messiaen may have failed to win, but in a long article on the 1930 Prix de Rome for *Le Courrier musical*, the composer and critic Gustave Samazeuilh considered his emerging importance. Samazeuilh, a good friend of Dukas and Ravel, clearly felt that the judges might have got it wrong again:

While the winners are savouring their success [. . .] I cannot help thinking about two of the best recruits from the class of Monsieur Dukas: Georges Hugon and Olivier Messiaen, winners of the composition prize [at the Conservatoire] and composers, respectively, of a Trio and String Quartet, and some *Préludes* for piano, and organ pieces. In them are to be found the most reassuring portents for the future and both seem to have been granted the rare and precious gift of a truly musical nature. They have the right not to be passed over in silence, since they have succeeded in another competition held behind closed doors [the Conservatoire's own prize for composition] which requires, I must tell you, preparation no less serious than that for the Prix de Rome.[15]

Though the competition was conducted under strict rules, the candidates did not have an entirely joyless time while competing in the preliminary rounds of the competition at Fontainebleau. Some informal snapshots show Messiaen, Henriette Roget, Tony Aubin (the eventual winner that year), Yvonne Desportes and others enacting some student *tableaux vivants* which border on slapstick, including a mock religious ceremony and the death of Jeanne d'Arc. Though Messiaen had no luck in the Prix de Rome – which had traditionally favoured aspiring opera composers – he did win a *premier prix* in composition at the Conservatoire in 1930, and the booklet listing the prize-winners for the 1929–30 academic year shows that Messiaen also picked up several additional scholarships as a result of his success.[16]

24 Fontainebleau, 1930. Messiaen is on the left, Henriette Roget in the centre.

25 Fontainebleau, 1930, enacting Jeanne d'Arc. Messiaen is kneeling with his head on the block.

Following his 1930 attempt at the Prix de Rome, Messiaen again spent the summer holidays with his aunts at Fuligny, and here completed his first acknowledged orchestral work, the astonishingly assured 'méditation symphonique', *Les Offrandes oubliées*, a work in which the influence of Honegger and Roussel (in the central section) is heard side by side with a highly original musical voice in the slower passages. Messiaen wrote to Charles Tournemire on 30 August 1930 to announce that he had 'just finished the music for a symphonic poem'.[17]

Les Offrandes oubliées was first performed six months later, on 19 February 1931, by one of the most distinguished advocates of modern music in Paris at

THÉATRE DES CHAMPS-ÉLYSÉES
15, avenue Montaigne

CONCERTS

WALTHER STRARAM

SAISON 1931

Le Jeudi soir

CINQUIÈME CONCERT

JEUDI 19 FÉVRIER, à 9 heures

PROGRAMME

C.-M. WEBER . . . . . . Jubel-Ouverture.
E. CHABRIER . . . . Suite Pastorale.
O. MESSIAEN . . . . Les Offrandes Oubliées 1re audition.
L. VAN BEETHOVEN Symphonie n° 5 en ut mineur.

Prix des Places : de **2** francs à **40** francs

Le Concert commencera strictement à l'heure indiquée.

LOCATION :
THÉATRE DES CHAMPS-ÉLYSÉES, 15, avenue Montaigne.
Maison DURAND, 4, place de la Madeleine.
ABONNEMENT :
THÉATRE DES CHAMPS-ÉLYSÉES.

6e Concert : le Jeudi 26 Février 1931

26 Handbill for the first performance of *Les Offrandes oubliées* at the Concerts Straram on 19 February 1931.

the time. Walther Straram was born in London in 1876, as Walter Marrast (of which Straram is an anagram), and after posts as *chef de chant* at the Opéra and Opéra-Comique, he established a series of concerts with his own orchestra. Straram's emphasis on contemporary music was a much-needed corrective to the famously conservative repertoire of the Orchestre de la Société des Concerts du Conservatoire. In 1927 Straram conducted the French première of Berg's Chamber Concerto, and the following year gave the first performance of Ravel's *Bolero*. The musicians in Straram's orchestra included several of the best in Paris (Marcel Moyse was the principal flute); it was the only Parisian orchestra Toscanini was happy to conduct, and Stravinsky recorded *Le Sacre du printemps* with it in 1929. In 1931 Stravinsky conducted the orchestra again in the first recording of the *Symphony of Psalms*. The sessions were at the Théâtre des Champs-Élysées on 17–18 February 1931;[18] since Messiaen's première was the next day, it is not surprising that the rest of the programme was of more traditional repertoire.

Les Offrandes oubliées received a great deal of attention in the press, much of it enthusiastic. A sour note was struck by Louis Schneider in *Le Petit Parisien* (24 February), who dismissed it as 'an academic exercise [. . .] without personality'.

André George, an insightful critic best remembered as the author of the first serious study of Honegger's music (1926), was enthusiastic:

I want to draw your attention above all to the arrival on the scene of the twenty-two-year-old musician Olivier Messiaen, whose *Les Offrandes oubliées* has just been introduced by the Orchestre Straram. His work is testimony to an artistic temperament in which the spirit of his mother's poetry is rediscovered, and where I find again the magnificent gifts which I first glimpsed when the composer was just ten years old.[19] The composer of *Les Offrandes oubliées* – entirely mystical in character – has no fear of the human, nor of that which goes beyond the human. But though he follows his heart, he realizes that he must express himself in clear structures. [. . .] The rhythmic variety in the first section and the beautiful handling of the orchestra in the second are enough to place this composer among those who make their mark from the outset.[20]

Guy Chastel, in *Les Amitiés* (March 1931), was equally impressed, and quoted a charming remark by Messiaen – one which suggests that the composer was delighted with the performance:

A phrase which dares to sustain itself for more than three notes, and music which is emotional and knows how to move people: in our day and age that is a rare and novel pleasure. [. . .] The subject-matter of this work is not one which the moderns would usually choose for musical themes: the *Offrandes oubliées* are the Cross and the Host; Olivier Messiaen's symphonic meditation brings us closer to them. [. . .] We know that the son of Cécile Sauvage has the most refined sensibilities. But we greatly admire the way in which this young man of twenty-two, who has already gathered several first prizes at the Conservatoire, allies this sensibility with a power which reveals rare qualities, even if it has not yet reached its fullest expression. [. . .] And what a modest young man! He said to a friend in the wings of the Théâtre des Champs-Élysées just as the musicians of the Straram Orchestra had finished his *Offrandes*: 'It is so much more beautiful than I thought. These musicians play it like champions.'

The early months of 1931 saw the premières of two more Messiaen works. On 14 February, a few days before the Straram concert, the *Trois Mélodies* were given at the Société Nationale by the experienced soprano Louise Matha accompanied by the composer. Six weeks later, on 25 March, Messiaen's *La Mort du Nombre* for soprano, tenor, violin and piano was performed for the first time. It has an interesting place in Messiaen's output and is the closest he came – outside the constraints of the Prix de Rome – to writing an operatic *scena*; it may be no coincidence that it was started in Fuligny just after his first attempt at that competition. This concert was one of the few times when Messiaen worked with Nadia Boulanger, as she was a committee member of the Société Musicale Indépendante (SMI) which put on the concert.

Boulanger and Messiaen never had an easy relationship. In the 1930s they were colleagues at the École Normale de Musique, and later both taught at the Conservatoire, but Boulanger was unconvinced by Messiaen's music and was not afraid to say so. After Messiaen's appointment as *titulaire* of the Trinité in September 1931, she had ample opportunity to hear his work as this was her local parish church; it was also where the Requiem Masses took place for her sister Lili (1918), for her mother Raïssa (1935) and, finally, for Nadia herself (1979). Boulanger worked tirelessly on behalf of the SMI until its eventual collapse in 1935. Messiaen's letters to her reveal a young composer fretting over arrangements for the première of *La Mort du Nombre*.[21] His first letter to Boulanger, dated 1 February 1931, outlined the difficulties of fixing the artists for the performance – initially planned for the end of February – in the absence of precise details about the date and time. Messiaen wrote again the next day (2 February) giving complete information about the intended performers, and the 'personnages' (cast-list: 'First Soul – soprano' and 'Second Soul – tenor') – perhaps a suggestion that he viewed the piece as a quasi-dramatic one. On 12 February Messiaen was preoccupied with arrangements for the premières of *Les Offrandes oubliées* and the *Trois Mélodies*, but he took time to write to

Boulanger, reporting that he was still having problems finding the singers and the violinist needed for the SMI concert, though the première had now been put back to 25 March.

This care over choosing performers was to become characteristic of Messiaen's preparation for concerts, and while it may at first seem like undue fussiness, the strategy certainly paid off: the premières of Messiaen's works in the 1930s were often praised in the musical press for the exceptionally high standard of execution, and this was to remain the case, with very few exceptions, throughout his professional career. On 23 February he informed Boulanger that he was correcting the proofs of *La Mort du Nombre* and that the work should be in print by the time of the concert; this was unduly optimistic, but it was published – in an edition of 500 copies – in May 1931, a few weeks after the first performance.[22] The concert took place as planned, at the École Normale on 25 March, but at the last minute (after the programme was printed) the soprano Georgette Mathieu was indisposed, and her place was taken by Mlle Guiberteau. Like the first and third of the *Trois Mélodies*, the poems were by Messiaen himself, something mentioned by Simone Plé in her perceptive review.

Plé commented on the work's apparent stylistic disunity, and complained about harmonic progressions which at times seemed closer to Massenet than to Messiaen: 'In the second section he uses chromatic progressions which really come too near to grand opera, or the post-romantic symphonic poem.' In particular, she was bothered by the musical language of the closing pages: 'We encounter virtuoso passages in double notes à la Chopin, arpeggios in simplistic harmonies – all a long way from the promise of the opening. Messiaen will no doubt realize, having completely acquired the critical sense which is so indispensable to an artist, that his work suffers from a lack of aesthetic unity. [...] If we stress this point, it is because Messiaen's individuality inspires such confidence.'[23] Simone Plé was probably right to detect a stylistic divergence between the closing pages and the rest of *La Mort du Nombre*, but this richly expressive cantata for two 'souls' deserves to be better known: the lyrical ardour of the concluding bars may owe a large debt to Wagner's *Tristan*, but the musical language is still very much Messiaen's own.

For the first round of the 1931 Prix de Rome competition, Messiaen composed *La Jeunesse des vieux*, a short choral setting of a poem by Catulle Mendès (1841–1909), poet, librettist, and one of the leading French Wagnerites of the nineteenth century.[24] This time, Messiaen was admitted to the final round. The cantata libretto was by Paul Arosa, a poet and playwright (whose works included some *grand guignol* melodramas).[25] Messiaen and the other finalists worked on their settings of *L'Ensorceleuse* ('The Enchantress') behind closed doors at Fontainebleau during June 1931, and their cantatas were first performed at the Institut on 4 July. The review by Paul Bertrand in *Le Ménestrel*[26] tells us about the jury, which included, among others, Widor, Alfred Bruneau (composer of a string of successful operas in the 1890s such as *Le Rêve*, *L'Attaque du moulin* and *Messidor*), Gabriel Pierné (distinguished both as a composer and conductor, and a friend of Ravel), Henri Rabaud (Director of the Conservatoire and composer of the enormously popular *Mârouf*) and Philippe Gaubert (principal conductor of the Paris Opéra, and also a composer).

The winner was Jacques Dupont (or Jacque-Dupont as he styled himself), with Yvonne Desportes[27] as runner-up. Of the remaining finalists, only Henriette Roget was awarded a prize (she went on to win the Prix de Rome in 1932). Messiaen's unplaced setting of *L'Ensorceleuse* was scored for soprano, tenor, bass and piano (or orchestra) and was performed – for the one and only time – at the 4 July competition by the soprano Georgette Mathieu, the tenor Louis Arnoult, and the bass Louis Guénot, with Messiaen at the piano. Bertrand, in *Le Ménestrel,* predicted a successful future for the young composer:

> If he is some way from writing the best cantata, M. Messiaen has nonetheless demonstrated an incomparable musical talent. [. . .] Messiaen has an intense inner life, and he was clearly uneasy grappling with the conflict of the fates and the clash of human emotions. This is why his cantata gave an impression of slightly chaotic imbalance, not entirely free of monotony. Even so, remember his name. It is doubtful whether he will succeed in dramatic music, but I will be surprised if he does not reach the heights in abstract music.

Samazeuilh continued to champion Messiaen in *Le Courrier musical,* as he had the previous year, and he was clearly scandalized by the jury's failure to award Messiaen a prize for *L'Ensorceleuse*:

> It is impossible for me to accept the singular severity of the judges at the Institut in refusing to give any prize to Olivier Messiaen, a pupil of Paul Dukas and the most musically gifted of all the competitors: the only one, in my view, who brought a sense of poetic construction to his composition, which he demonstrated particularly well in his duo, with exquisite inflections which would have enchanted Emmanuel Chabrier. He has an inventive gift of rare quality. [. . .] That has not done him any good here, and it is possible that Messiaen is unfamiliar with the tricks of the trade which are needed to manufacture these cantatas. [. . .] But Messiaen remains what he was before the 1931 Concours de Rome: one of the greatest hopes of his generation. [28]

Messiaen's own view of *L'Ensorceleuse* was characteristically modest. In a letter to Langlais on 3 August 1931 he wrote: 'My cantata was good as music, but inferior as theatre. So the judgment was very fair.'[29]

Following Charles Quef's death in the summer of 1931, Messiaen applied to be his successor as *titulaire* at the Trinité. Messiaen had been the regular deputy for two years, even though he had been playing the organ only for a couple of years. It was Marcel Dupré who first recommended his star pupil: 'Messiaen had just won his first prize for organ when I met Charles Quef on the train to Meudon. [. . .] "I am very ill with diabetes and won't live for much longer. Is there one of your students who could deputize for me and eventually become my successor?" I sent him Messiaen, and the two immediately became friends. Quef died eighteen months later.'[30] Quef (born in 1873) succeeded Alexandre Guilmant at the Trinité in 1898 and was his pupil, as well as studying with Widor and Vierne. Though his music was in the Guilmant tradition, Quef was involved in at least one controversial venture: in 1908 he composed the music for the Charles Pathé film *La Vie de Jésus* which earned the condemnation of Pope Pius X for its cinematic depiction of Christ.[31]

27 Messiaen on the steps of the Trinité, early 1930s.

Messiaen's campaign to become Quef's permanent successor was supported by several distinguished musicians, including Dupré, Emmanuel, Marchal, Tournemire and Widor.[32] On 7 July 1931 Messiaen wrote to the parish priest, Curé Hemmer, to apply for the job:

> For the last two years I have been the only deputy for Monsieur Quef. I started to substitute for him in 1929. I know the organ of the Trinité and the regular parishioners. My greatest wish is to be Monsieur Quef's successor as organist of the *grand orgue* at the Trinité. [. . .] My organ teacher was Marcel Dupré. He told me that I should have a good chance of obtaining this position, given my qualifications and my deputizing, and he has strongly encouraged me to apply. Moreover, I enclose a letter from Widor recommending me to you. Widor was my composition teacher for one year. He also encouraged me and fully supports my application.

Widor's letter recommended 'young Messiaen who is worthy in every respect of the post for which he is applying, besides being chosen by Quef as his deputy for the last two years. M. Messiaen brings honour to the tradition of Catholic organists – our French tradition.' Tournemire wrote to Curé Hemmer on 15 July: 'The musical value and the future of this Christian organist are of the highest order: a transcendant improviser, an astonishing performer, and a *biblical* composer. [. . .] With Messiaen, all is prayer.' The composer and historian Maurice Emmanuel provided an eloquent testimonial, describing Messiaen as 'one of the most brilliant graduates of the Conservatoire', and also captured something of his former pupil's character: 'Messiaen is a modest man who does not show off his gifts to others. But we place on him our highest hopes. His considerable academic success has been confirmed by compositions which are very remarkable and very daring musically speaking, almost all of them inspired by deep religious feelings. This young artist is a complete believer; and, in an environment where faith plays little part, he has commanded admiration and respect through the dignity of his lifestyle and the genuinely Christian warmth of his personality.'

Despite this support, Messiaen's candidature was not without problems. He spent much of the summer in Fuligny, and was alarmed when he heard that Langlais might also apply for the post, but his old friend reassured him straight away. Messiaen was greatly touched, and wrote on 3 August 1931: 'Your quiet rage about my lack of self-confidence cheered me greatly, and I see just how faithful a friend I have in you. [. . .] For the Trinité, I wait, and I want it, though without much hope. The future seems very black. Is this because of my capricious and perverse nature? After all, the flowers are in bloom and the sun is shining.'[33]

Curé Hemmer had concerns of his own. The most serious of these was that the young composer might upset the parishioners with too much dissonant music. Messiaen replied:

When I was deputizing at the Trinité, I know that I sometimes exhibited tendencies which were too modern, and I regret that now. I was only twenty years old when I deputized for the first time; I am now twenty-two-and-a-half, and at this time of life one evolves very quickly. My current view is that music should always search for the new, but in works for chamber ensembles or orchestra, where the imagination can run free. For the organ, especially the organ in church, what matters above all is the liturgy. The environment and the instrument are not well suited to modern music and it is important not to disturb the piety of the faithful by using chords which are too anarchic.

Messiaen was being diplomatic; so was Dupré when he wrote to Curé Hemmer assuring him that 'Messiaen – who has a technique and artistic self-control of the highest order – will easily be capable of repressing some of his youthful ardour.' André Marchal, the organist of Saint-Germain-des-Prés, also supported Messiaen, and his letter reveals that he even advised some of his own pupils to stand aside:

Even though this young man was never my pupil, I have often had the opportunity, at the Conservatoire and elsewhere, to admire the real artistic worth of his very individual talent as an organist and improviser, as well as the high standing of his character. Moreover, he had the complete confidence of his predecessor as deputy for a long time. All these reasons have led me to advise those of my pupils who could have applied for the post to renounce any applications, and it is in their name that I write in support of a young artist who seems to me to be worthy in every way of the honour of becoming *titulaire* for one of the most famous instruments in Paris.

Messiaen was offered the job, and on 14 September he wrote to Curé Hemmer, undertaking to 'perform my duties with wisdom and classical restraint'. Three days later he wrote to Langlais, expressing delight at the appointment, but also revealing a lack of confidence about his compositions:

I have been named organist of the Trinité. I'm writing to you with the good news as soon as possible. I will always remember your extreme kindness during this affair. [...] At the organ, everything goes by so quickly that the conception does not have time to become fixed. But in composition what a difference there is between sublime heights on the one hand, and lamentable platitudes on the other. The more I work at music, the more I become aware of my uselessness when faced with this unattainable ideal.[34]

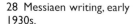
28 Messiaen writing, early 1930s.

The appointment of such a young *titulaire* was newsworthy. Under the headline 'Organist of the Trinité at 22' an article appeared in *L'Intransigeant* on 18 October 1931:

A very young man answered the door. I thought this must be the new organist's son. The young man asked me in and invited me to sit down. He then did the same. I was going to ask him if he would like to comment on the appointment, since his father seemed not to be at home. The young man stretched out his hands on the table in front of him: they are very pale, very supple, extraordinarily lively, and I wondered if he too was an artist who might succeed his father one day. Did Messiaen sense this? An ironic look passed across his face and a childlike expression lurked behind his glasses. [. . .] Olivier Messiaen is enjoying himself, and I am in front of a master who is just twenty-two years old. 'I am replacing M. Charles Quef, the previous organist of the Trinité. I'm a pupil of Marcel Dupré and I would very much like you to mention him, a perfect artist, an astonishing virtuoso. I owe him everything. One detail may interest you: Alexandre Guilmant, who was, as you know, organist at the Trinité, was also Marcel Dupré's teacher. In the old days Dupré used to listen to this great musician with such respect. And he did me the honour of coming to hear me play last Sunday.' You must, of course, have been studying the organ for a long time? 'I knew nothing about the instrument until three years ago.'

The longest of the interviews Messiaen gave at the time of his appointment was to José Bruyr, though it was not published until two years later, in 1933.[35] Bruyr (1889–1980) was a critic, writer on music, and occasional librettist. His intelligent questioning produced the most revealing of Messiaen's published conversations from his early years, with some valuable observations on musical trends of the time. And while comments about Messiaen's mother and his teachers were often repeated in later interviews, some remarks on his earliest works appear for perhaps the only time. Bruyr was an observant writer and his opening describes the Messiaen family home at 67 rue Rambuteau:

Something hangs over the centre of a round, extending table; there is a cabinet in which books and missals are lined up on shelves and an upright piano with a long organ bench; on the wall, some devotional images. If I am mistaken about some of the details of this interior, the atmosphere is certainly right. The house is in the heart of the Marais – the road bustles with activity, with the smell of vegetables and of petrol fumes – Daudet might have made this the home of a benevolent ecclesiastic, a gentle, somewhat dotty recluse. But no! for he would have sensed that this presbytery dining-room was filled with a feminine presence. [Georges] Bernanos described Cécile Sauvage as one of those poets who watch over the threshold of our homes. Above all, she watches over the threshold of this room where her son shakes me by the hand.

Messiaen described his childhood to Bruyr as one in which the 'spiritual climate was that of poetry itself. My mother was not a musician and no longer a believer; but poetry allowed her to explore the mysteries of faith in the same way as music. It often seems to me now that it is my mother, after her death, who guides my hand or my spirit.' Bruyr asked Messiaen why he had never posed the question 'Whom should I imitate to be original?' Messiaen's reply included some reflections on his earliest works: 'It was while I was still a pupil of Dukas that I wrote my *Préludes*. They don't form a suite in the usual sense of the word, but are essentially a collection of successive states of the soul and of personal feelings. Besides, I think that with my *Diptyque* for organ, I was able, straight away, to expand the horizons of my art: I wanted, for the first time, to contrast terrestrial life with eternal life.' And what of the state of music in 1931? Messiaen was unambiguous in his views about composing techniques which destabilized tonality, and his quest for other ways forward:

I think that today the most important thing is not to destroy tonality but to enrich it. In this regard we have terribly neglected Gregorian chant: a source which is still living. By returning to it, this is how a musician of the age – of our age (I'm thinking of Malipiero) – has been able to create such a special mood in his work, just as other composers in other countries have been able to base music on folk songs. However, I think it's above all in the mystic sense that this source can give life to our art.

A question about the current vogue for neoclassicism provoked a vigorous response, including Messiaen's reaction to Ravel's brand-new Piano Concerto, and to Stravinsky:

It is possible to be a humorist and a great musician at the same time. Ravel is like that. I think it's inconceivable that Ravel could really have taken the Largo of his new concerto seriously, this Largo which turns a phrase reminiscent of Fauré on a bad day into Massenet.[36] A return to classicism? Always that same old refrain? But *Le Tombeau de Couperin* returned there already, and it's a masterpiece, a true masterpiece on the same level as *Daphnis et Chloé*. The best model for French music today seems to me to be Albert Roussel – the Suite in F and some of the symphonies – and early Stravinsky. I say early because I still hear nothing in his later music. And though, to my shame, I haven't yet heard the *Symphony of Psalms*,[37] *Apollo* still strikes me as like a piece by Lully with the wrong bass notes.

Bruyr then turned to the religious aspects of Messiaen's music: 'Olivier Messiaen seems to want to claim a kingdom for which there is little competition: that of the mystical composer. Is music a pleasure or a prayer? It is one or the other, but perhaps each is the same as the other. [...] Needless to say, Messiaen's music has nothing of the "mystical striptease" of which Huysmans accused Gounod. It is orthodox: Catholic, Apostolic and Roman.' As the interview drew to a close, Messiaen spoke about the importance of his faith to his work as a creative artist:

Since my second work, *Diptyque*, I have wanted to contrast the earthly life and the life beyond. I wrote a *Banquet eucharistique* which I have now disowned, but which I heard performed by the student orchestra at the Conservatoire conducted by Rabaud. This 'Banquet' was inspired entirely, as is *Les Offrandes oubliées*, by the mystery of the Eucharist. In *La Mort du Nombre*, I wanted to create a dialogue between two souls who, at the end, discover themselves in a supernatural love: the words being thus silenced, I confided their voices to a violin. Finally, in *Le Tombeau resplendissant*, I wanted to write a kind of Beatitude for those who discover in their faith something more than the illusions of a distant youth. [...] To discover the same ideals, we must return to Charles Tournemire, whose *L'Orgue mystique*, washed clean of any sentimentality, relies also on the art of Gregorian chant. Unfortunately there are lots of ways of relying on it, not all of them good! Some simply take the themes in order to construct fantasy variations; others write in semibreves and minims to make the motifs for chorale preludes. The mania for disturbing beautiful things knows no ends. I have heard Schoenberg inflate a wonderful Bach chorale beyond endurance with an immense Wagnerian orchestra. No! The only admissible way is that which Falla has used with Spanish popular song: to rediscover the depths of the soul – the mystical soul – and faith.

In November 1931 the full score and orchestral parts of *Les Offrandes oubliées* were published by Durand, and the work's second performance was given on 6 December by the usually unadventurous Société des Concerts du Conservatoire, conducted by Philippe Gaubert; Maurice Emmanuel supplied the programme note. For a young composer to appear in this most traditional of concert series was a considerable achievement, and Louis Aubert, in *Le Journal* (16 December), noted that Gaubert 'had the happy idea of opening the doors of the Société des Concerts to *Les Offrandes oubliées*', while *Le Monde musical* (31 December) commented on the work's 'genuine expressive power, which the orchestra underlined with subtlety under the invigorating direction of its conductor'.

During 1932 Messiaen composed several short works: *Apparition de l'Église éternelle* for organ (his first piece for the instrument since taking up his post at the Trinité), *Hymne au Saint-Sacrement* for orchestra, the *Fantaisie burlesque* for piano (written quite early in the year, and published by Durand in July), and the *Thème et variations* for violin and piano which was just about finished in time for its first performance on 22 November. In May, he started work on *L'Ascension*, completing a short score in July, though it was not orchestrated until the following year.

Curiously, only one of these works was known to be performed during 1932, the *Thème et variations*, though Messiaen probably played *Apparition de l'Église éternelle* at the Trinité soon after its composition. But this was a momentous year in Messiaen's private life. In an undated letter ('Avril 32' has been added later in pencil) Messiaen wrote to tell Langlais that he was engaged to be married:

29 Claire Delbos, aged 5, with her sister Marie-Rose, c.1911.

I particularly wanted to send a note to you, as one of my closest friends, to let you know some important news which will explain why I am so snowed under with a combination of hectic musical activities and those connected with the above news. I am engaged and I am to be married on 22 June to Mademoiselle Louise Delbos, a violinist and the daughter of Victor Delbos, the eminent professor at the Sorbonne. You'll receive an invitation in a few days, with all the details. I hope you will give me the great pleasure of seeing you at the ceremony, if you are free. It will be a very grand occasion – following my mother-in-law's wishes and not mine, as I hate display in something so intimate and spiritual. No point in saying more. All the best to your wife and yourself. I end with a magnificent line from the English poet Keats: 'A thing of beauty is a joy for ever.'[38]

On 6 June Messiaen wrote to another old friend from the Conservatoire, Claude Arrieu – who won a *premier prix* for Composition in Dukas's class that summer – inviting her to be Maid of Honour.[39]

Claire Delbos was born in Paris on 2 November 1906, and though she was usually known after her marriage as Claire (or occasionally as Claire-Louise), she was baptized Louise Justine Delbos, and the programme for a recital she gave at the Schola Cantorum on 5 February 1932, a few months before her wedding, gives her name (as Messiaen does in his letter to Langlais) as 'Louise Delbos, violiniste'. Her father, Victor Delbos (1862–1916), had been a distinguished philosophy professor at the Sorbonne and she was brought up in a comfortably-off academic family; an early photograph of Claire shows her with her elder sister Marie-Rose in about 1911. She went on to study the violin, chamber music and composition at the Schola Cantorum; in June 1925 the Chamber Music class gathered in the garden of the Schola for a group photograph with the austere figure of the director, Vincent d'Indy, seated at the centre; the eighteen-year-old Delbos can be seen standing immediately behind him. Her teachers included Nestor Lejeune and Guy de Lioncourt (respectively, on the progressive and traditional wings of the Schola's teaching staff), and in 1928 she was awarded a diploma for completing Lejeune's course for 'violon du deuxième degré' (with a mark of 'très bien'); this enabled her to enter the class for the 'Cours supérieur de violon' in the academic year 1928–9. How and when she first met Messiaen remains a mystery, and he kept their courtship and engagement a secret until shortly before the invitations to the wedding were sent out.

Messiaen and Claire were married on 22 June at the church of Saint-Louis-en-l'Île,[40] and the guests included Arrieu and Langlais. The only known photograph of the wedding shows Claire arm in arm with her husband, both looking rather serious, the bride in a fine wedding dress and the groom in formal black. By 27 June Messiaen was writing thank-you letters; he was particularly enthusiastic about Arrieu's wedding present, ending his note to her with the line from Keats which he always enjoyed quoting: 'I send you a thousand thanks. First of all for being Maid of Honour, then for the flowers, and above all for the magnificent crystal decanter. It is elegant, slender, and the sun plays on it beautifully. It makes me think of a light, fragrant wine, transparent and clear. In the face of such a success, I would like to quote a phrase of Keats which I love: "A thing of beauty is a joy for ever".'

30 Claire, right, with her sister Marie-Rose and her mother, 1918.

31 Schola Cantorum chamber music class, 16 June 1925. Claire Delbos is in the centre, behind d'Indy.

32 Handbill for a recital given by Louise Delbos in February 1932, a few months before her marriage to Messiaen and before she adopted the name Claire.

33 The wedding of Messiaen and Claire Delbos, 22 June 1932.

34 Claire and Messiaen in the country.

On 5 September he wrote to Arrieu again, from Lévigny (the village next door to Fuligny) where he was taking a short break: 'I am taking only three weeks holiday in the countryside and have had to endure the stifling heat of Paris. I have not had time to compose, and that distresses me.' Much of the summer had to be spent moving house from the Beaubourg to 77 rue des Plantes, in the 14th arrondissement at the southern end of the city. This was to be the Messiaens' home for the next five years.

Back in Paris after his short holiday in the Aube, Messiaen wrote again to Claude Arrieu (on 10 October 1932), urging her to visit the conductor Walther Straram ('you can usually find him at home, 78 avenue Kléber, around 11 in the morning') and to support his own ambitions at the Société Nationale: 'If you can, please be at the general assembly of the Société Nationale this year. I am standing for membership of the committee. If that is something you would like, then come and vote for me.' The Société Nationale de Musique – founded in 1871 by Franck, Fauré, Duparc, Saint-Saëns and Massenet, among others – was long established as the leading forum for new French chamber music, piano music and songs. Messiaen had already appeared several times on the programmes of the Société Nationale (notably the premières of the *Préludes* and the *Trois Mélodies*), but election to its committee was an important further step in establishing himself with this institution. Messiaen was successful in the election, and his duties soon required all his formidable keyboard skills; in an undated letter to Arrieu, he wrote: 'Your work has been taken up straight away by the Nationale. Bravo! I've had to sight-read something like one to two hundred manuscripts!'

A much smaller society, the Cercle Musical de Paris, put on a joint programme of music by Messiaen and Arrieu on 22 November 1932. It was just five days before the concert that Messiaen finalized his contribution, adding the newly written *Thème et variations* for violin and piano, composed for his wife (and dedicated to her: in the first edition 'Mi' appears in musical notation, as a semibreve E – 'Mi' in French). One could hardly imagine a more flattering wedding gift. The theme, passionate but withdrawn, is allowed gently to uncurl (Variation 1) before being put through its paces in a trio of bravura variations, from which the violin emerges high on the E string, the theme transformed into a triumphant march. The passion and vigour of the music suggests a side of Claire's temperament not apparent from photographs of her, while the virtuosity of the writing for violin testifies to her talent. Surprisingly, perhaps, the piano part that Messiaen devised for himself is, if anything, even more challenging; this is particularly true of the second variation where the pianist must play streams of chords quickly and lightly, and negotiate a tricky double canon, the right hand a quaver behind the violin and the left hand a quaver behind the right. Messiaen sent Arrieu a *pneumatique* announcing the work's completion on 17

November: 'I have decided to perform the *Thème et variations*, which I have just finished. [. . .] I will play it with my wife and will place it straight after [Arrieu's] *Clowneries*. I hope you don't see any problems with that. [. . .] Would you like to come to Dukas's house on Saturday to get used to turning the pages for me in the mélodies and in the *Thème et variations*? It's very difficult to turn as I'm playing from a manuscript and I would very much like you to do it.'

The programme also included six of Messiaen's *Préludes* played by Mlle Hennebains, the *Trois Mélodies* sung by Mme Hérault-Harlé (who ran the Cercle Musical de Paris) with the composer at the piano, and an 'Improvisation sur un thème donné' by Messiaen. The *Thème et variations* was added too late for inclusion in the listing in the *Guide du concert*, but two days before the concert Messiaen wrote to Langlais: 'As an additional item [. . .] my wife and I will give the first performance of my *Thème et variations* for violin and piano. It would be very nice of you to come along and make lots of noise so that this work – one of my best – gets an encore. Unless you would prefer to whistle, which would make just as much noise.'[41]

The early months of 1933 were dominated by three premières, and started with a second performance, when Messiaen and Claire gave the *Thème et variations* at the Société Nationale on 14 January. One of Messiaen's least-performed (and oddest) works, the *Fantaisie burlesque* for piano, had been published by Durand the previous year and this was given in a concert of the SMI at the École Normale on 8 February 1933, by one of the outstanding French pianists of the day, Robert Casadesus – a friend of Ravel, who greatly admired his playing. In a much later programme note, Messiaen wrote about the piece with an ironic detachment which he found sadly lacking in the music itself, and revealed something of how he was seen by his friends and contemporaries in 1932:

> The title is surprising. There exists very little truly comic music, and my music is not at all humorous. In 1932, my old classmates from Paul Dukas's composition class found me too serious, too contemplative: they thought I didn't know how to laugh. I wanted to prove them wrong . . . and failed to do so. In this unduly traditional ABA piece, the first and third parts are meant to be comic (without succeeding). The middle section is the best: there are many things there which foreshadow the colours of chords and the rhythms in my later works.[42]

The contemporary press judged the first performance more generously. In *Le Ménestrel* (17 February) Marcel Belvianes wrote that 'this Fantaisie has a clownish motif [. . .] which appears at the start and comes back at the end. At the centre of the piece, a much more tender motif unfolds. M. Olivier Messiaen certainly has a sense of colour and lacks nothing in ideas, nor in amusing techniques to give them form. His success was all the greater since he had the excellent pianist Robert Casadesus as his interpreter.'

Le Tombeau resplendissant was composed at Fuligny in 1931, a few months after the first performance of *Les Offrandes oubliées* and, though far more typical of its composer than a piece like the *Fantaisie burlesque*, it was to remain unpublished until 1997. Messiaen seldom mentioned it (though it is listed in his 1944 worklist[43]). According to Harry Halbreich, 'Messiaen does not want it to be performed, nor for it to be discussed'.[44] The reasons for this are hard to determine, unless Messiaen felt it to be a poor relation to *Les Offrandes oubliées*, which it resembles, particularly in terms of structure. But the work was never withdrawn and it was always available from the hire library at Durand. It was first performed by one of the most celebrated conductors of the day, Pierre Monteux, with the Orchestre Symphonique de Paris. *Le Monde musical* (28 February) printed a very positive review by Tristan Klingsor, who is best remembered as the poet of Ravel's *Shéhérazade*:

> It is the 'tombeau' of the composer's youth. [. . .] I am very grateful to Olivier Messiaen for yielding nothing to the false impassiveness of a certain school, and to placing some value on the impulses of the innermost being, its heartbreaks and its joys. For this new work is captivating. There is quite audacious modernism in the writing; the dissonant style troubles our ears and our hearts; but a long, melancholy phrase draws us into repose and serenity.

For a young composer to have two orchestral works given their premières by leading Parisian ensembles within a few weeks of each other was unusual, but this is just what happened in the early months of 1933, when six weeks after *Le Tombeau resplendissant*, the *Hymne au Saint-Sacrement* was first performed on 23 March. As with *Les Offrandes oubliées* two years earlier, the work was conducted by Walther Straram in his enterprising series at the Théâtre des Champs-Élysées. It was to be one of the last works introduced by this pioneering musician: he died in Paris on 24 November 1933. The musical press turned out in force for the performance of the *Hymne au Saint-Sacrement*, and Paul Le Flem in *Comœdia* (27 March) wrote that it

> evokes a mysticism where ecstasy and fervour are combined. The presence of Jesus in the Eucharist is glorified in it, the battle of mankind against sin is commented upon harshly, and the spiritual union of Jesus and the communicant is affirmed. Religious fervour, serenity and human violence are portrayed through musical means which are bold to the point of fierceness. [. . .]

This memorable score is by a musician who has something to say, knows how to say it, and whose intentions are clearly expressed.

In *Le Petit Journal* (27 March), Paul Dambly noted a paradox which was to be echoed by later critics: 'All this, which is full of beautiful things, is the work of a remarkable artist. But it seems to have virtually no connection with the title, and it would undoubtedly have gained from being presented without a commentary, which only emphasized the disparity between the subject matter and the music itself.'

Messiaen continued to give concerts of his own music and that of his old Conservatoire friends. Early in 1933 he sent plans to Claude Arrieu for another joint programme, at the Concerts Servais on 1 April. As well as his own and Arrieu's works, he wanted to include music by two other Dukas pupils: Elsa Barraine, and Jean Cartan (who had died in 1932 at the age of twenty-five). Messiaen thought it best to discuss the programme at Arrieu's home as he was 'afraid of tiring my wife if we meet at mine' – perhaps a reference to one of the doomed pregnancies which cast a tragic blight over the first few years of the Messiaens' marriage: Claire was to suffer several of these distressing miscarriages before the birth of Pascal in 1937.

In his letters to his classmates from the Conservatoire, there are virtually no references to Messiaen's faith, but one sent to Arrieu on 16 May 1933 is an intriguing exception and shows him trying a little gentle evangelization:

> I am sending you an excellent translation of the Gospels without too many annotations. Firstly read the Gospel according to Saint John, particularly chapters 14, 15, 16, 17 and the very end of chapter 13. Above all, read chapter 17, which is the most beautiful passage in all scripture, and the least wordy. It has a sublime and unaffected tone, with such direct words, enriched by a new feeling, being spoken by one who was not a mortal man. Forgive me if this bores you. You must think me a terrible zealot.

Messiaen's reputation as an organist was growing, despite the fact that by 1933 only one of his organ works (the *Diptyque*) had been published. The *Bulletin trimestrielle des Amis de l'Orgue* noted that a recital on 1 April by Marcel Lanquetuit, organist of Saint-Godard in Rouen, had ended with an improvised organ symphony on themes by four composers: Pierre de Bréville, Alexandre Cellier, Duruflé and Messiaen.[45]

The young composer was also starting to make the acquaintance of the more influential figures in Parisian musical life. One of these, who was to become an enthusiastic champion of Messiaen's music, was Roger Désormière (1898–1963). Désormière studied composition with Charles

Koechlin, and had his first big success as a conductor in 1924–5 with the Ballets suédois (including the notorious première of Satie's *Relâche*).[46] 'Déso' was credited by the composer as one of his 'most devoted interpreters' in the Introduction to *Technique de mon langage musical*.[47] For three years running (1936–8) he conducted the annual orchestral concerts of La Jeune France and later he gave the première of the *Trois petites Liturgies de la Présence Divine* and the first European performance of the *Turangalîla-Symphonie*. However, this relationship had an unpromising start. Messiaen had a meeting with him on 20 June 1933 to discuss a concert of music by the 'Four' (Messiaen, Arrieu, Barraine and Cartan), but it was a dismal failure. He sent an emotional account to Arrieu in which his frustration and disappointment are all too apparent; so, too, is his ability to take a longer view and not to rush into an unsatisfactory arrangement:

> I've just left Désormière. Lamentable! He knows about us, values our work etc., but won't do a thing without 50,000 francs! He is very kind, but at a price! He told me to write to M. Marie, administrator of the OSP [Orchestre Symphonique de Paris]. In the event of his conducting the OSP, it's a relatively short evening – so just 20,000 francs! We could try knocking on Mme de Polignac's door, but that would be a matter of luck. I think all we can do is to abandon the idea.
>
> Don't blame me for this: it isn't my fault and I spoke to him with all possible vigour. But money is the sinews of war. . . [a quotation from Cicero]. Well-known amateurs have money thrown at them and Les Six have profited from society connections which we've never had, and from special circumstances which no longer exist: Cubist painting, Picasso, Chirico, Dadaism, etc.
>
> Here is my view, which I hope is a wise one: it would mean nothing to be played alongside mediocrity and to compose pot-boilers ['demi-œuvres']. Since we are four genuine talents, let's keep looking, collect our thoughts and write our masterpieces. Then it will be the sheer beauty of our ideas which gets us noticed; and if it doesn't, at least we'll have had the satisfaction of doing something important.
>
> That's it. I have seen Barraine who will, I think, be of the same opinion. My friendship with you is so important. If the opportunity arises again I ask no more than to be able to take matters in hand. You know in what esteem I hold my three fine comrades. But it would be vanity and folly to spend so much money on a kind of glory which would be dubious and transitory.

Messiaen spent the summer of 1933 in the Cantal, at the country house of the Delbos family, the Château de Saint-Benoît, at Neussargues, where he worked

35 The Château de Saint-Benoît at Neussargues.

36 View of Neussargues taken from the Château de Saint-Benoît. On the right is the church built in the 1920s by the Delbos family.

37 Claire and Olivier in the garden at Neussargues, 1933.

on the orchestration of *L'Ascension* and composed the Mass for eight sopranos and four violins,[48] a work which appears never to have been performed and which has yet to be rediscovered. Claire and Messiaen seem to have been at their most relaxed during this stay. One photograph presents an idyllic image of the young couple in the garden, with Claire playing the violin to her husband. This was a picture of unclouded happiness which Messiaen treasured for the rest of his life.

By the academic year 1932–3, Messiaen had almost certainly started teaching at the École Normale de Musique.[49] Confirmation of this is not a simple matter, as the École Normale no longer has any records of Messiaen's employment.[50] However, there are references to his work there in letters to Arrieu, and in at least one little-known publication from 1933. His 'Solfège' first appeared in the supplement to *Le Monde musical* for 30 September 1933 and is described at the head of the music as 'Solfège donné au Diplôme d'Enseignement de l'École Normale de Musique'. Scored for an unspecified melody instrument and piano, it was presumably composed as a test piece for the exams that summer; the supplement is a facsimile of Messiaen's autograph, and its later version as no.14 of *Vingt Leçons de solfège moderne* differs from the original in at least two respects: in this publication (issued by Lemoine in 1935) the melody is transposed down an octave, notated in the bass clef, and a metronome marking (crotchet = 100) has been added. The Lemoine collection of *Vingt leçons* includes five by Messiaen and it is likely that most, if not all, of these had their origins as examination pieces.

Messiaen's compulsory military service started in Autumn 1933.[51] With the rise of Hitler in Germany, and with the manifestations – in Paris – of General La Rocque's proto-fascist *Croix de Feu* party in February 1934, the prospect of fighting was not that remote. But in a letter probably written early in January 1934, Messiaen wrote to Arrieu about the rather unusual direction his own activities as a soldier had taken: 'At the moment I am doing a rather gentler kind of military service. I am giving harmony lessons to the officers and soldiers and write on average two assignments for them every day. (It's just as well that I work fast, half an hour for a melody or a bass!)'

In March Messiaen's relations with Nadia Boulanger, already strained, took a turn for the worse. Boulanger had invited Joseph Bonnet, the organist of Saint-Eustache, to play for her sister Lili's memorial service at the Trinité, but Bonnet failed to turn up, and as Messiaen was on hand he agreed to play. Boulanger disapproved of his improvisations and obviously made her feelings known; in a letter written soon afterwards, Messiaen attempted to explain what he had been doing:

I am completely distraught that things did not happen according to your wishes. You asked me if I could play the first of Bach's Advent chorales at the

38 Messiaen on military service, c.1933.

39 A sight-reading piece written by Messiaen for the exams at the École Normale de Musique, published as a magazine supplement in October 1934.

beginning of the service. I did that. I was given no other instructions whatsoever. Seeing that Monsieur Bonnet had not arrived and not knowing the keys of the pieces with the small organ,[52] or the time that you had set aside for me between these pieces, I thought that the wisest course was to improvise from start to finish. There you are! I am not to blame!

Messiaen's military service continued through the summer of 1934. During this time he composed examination pieces for the École Normale, including sight-reading tests (as he reported to Arrieu on 23 July). At least one of these sight-reading pieces was published: twenty bars long and marked 'Lent, expressif', the *Morceau de Lecture à vue pour les Examens de piano de l'École Normale de Musique: Déchiffrage I* appeared as the musical supplement in *Le Monde musical* for 31 October 1934. It is in 6/8 time, with a key signature of four sharps, ending on a long C sharp major dominant seventh chord, and is a delightful footnote to Messiaen's piano works from the early 1930s.

A month later, on 21 August, Messiaen wrote again to Arrieu, and mentioned an unspecified 'incident' which seems to have resulted in his being confined to barracks:

> I've recently had a lot of bother at the barracks and a ridiculous incident has prevented me from going out for the last fifteen days (Sundays excepted!). I'm calmer about it now and should be free in forty-five days. I am really sorry not to have been able to help you with *Noé* [Arrieu's opera]. But what can be done when one is locked up? If you still need me I am at your disposal, always assuming there is no further military catastrophe!

During the summer, Messiaen and Claire were able to spend some time on the Côte d'Azur and in Monte-Carlo. It was probably on this holiday that Messiaen put the finishing touches to the organ version of *L'Ascension*, but there was time for relaxation too, as can be seen from a photograph which Messiaen took of Claire in Monaco's botanical gardens, standing in front of the giant cacti. These plants fascinated Claire, and photographs taken a year later show her tending an impressive collection of her own cacti. Another photograph, taken on the same trip, shows the couple sitting on a stone wall, gazing lovingly at each other, with the bay near Beaulieu-sur-Mer behind them.

40 Messiaen and Claire at Beaulieu-sur-Mer in 1934.

La Jeune France
1935–1939

A new production of Dukas's *Ariane et Barbe-bleue* opened at the Paris Opéra in January 1935, conducted by Philippe Gaubert. Messiaen was very eager to see the *Ariane*, but was prevented by illness from attending the first night. He went as soon as he could, and wrote an eloquent fan-letter to his old *maître*:

> Yesterday evening I put on my smartest clothes and rushed off to the Théâtre National [de l'Opéra] to see this work, at last, in all its splendour. I thought the performance was superb. The orchestra played with such magnificence, such incredible radiance! The sets are very beautiful. [. . .] The high-point was the Second Act. I couldn't stop myself from weeping like a baby, from the appearance of the light[1] until the end, and my neighbours must have wondered what was the matter with me! [. . .] The music of this act is of incomparable beauty. Its subject is eternal. For some it will be the tragic conflict of darkness and light, for others Prometheus bringing divine fire. As for me, I couldn't help thinking of the words of Saint John: 'The light shines in the darkness and the darkness could not overpower it.'[2] And to this sublime subject you have given music which is marvellously noble, pure, serene, of incomparably high ideals, of adorable compassion, and of musical substance which is intensely vibrant harmonically and which develops in a way that nobody has matched since. Over a period of at least three-quarters of an hour,[3] the music rises from the blackest darkness in the orchestra to the most intense light [. . .] with not a single moment when the emotion or the grandeur of thought weakens. Forgive me, dear Maître, for this dithyrambic fan-letter! To speak to you about it like this seems foolish. In the presence of true beauty it is best to remain silent. But I was so overwhelmed last night that I felt I had to tell you.[4]

The start of 1935 was also dominated by the first performances of an important new work, *L'Ascension*. According to the dates in the published orchestral score, this was started in Paris in May 1932 and finished at Neussargues in July the same year. Nothing further was done until May 1933 when Messiaen began the orchestration, which was completed in Monaco that July. The first performance of the original orchestral version did not take place for a further eighteen months: it was given in the Salle Rameau, Paris, on 9 February 1935 at the Concerts Siohan, conducted by Robert Siohan.[5] *Le Monde musical* (28 February 1935) published an unsigned commentary by Messiaen including reproductions of music examples in his own hand. At the time of the première Messiaen was very positive about the originality of *L'Ascension*:[6] after giving performance details and providing the movement titles and subtitles, he went on to assess the work's stylistic innovations. Using language which is a clear pre-echo of the theoretical ideas laid out in the preface to *La Nativité du Seigneur*, published the following year, Messiaen explained the technical principles used, including an early reference to the 'modes of limited transposition', the scales evolved by Messiaen as a highly individual resource for both melodic and harmonic material.

The first movement of *L'Ascension* is a majestic brass chorale. The solo trumpet sings and rises up on a mode of limited transposition, supported by spacious dominant chords.

The construction of the second movement is descended from plainchant graduals and hymns. Through the medium of solo woodwinds, the theme, a kind of vocalise, develops melodically, accompanied by appoggiatura-fragments and pedal-fragments based on the second mode of limited transposition. After the cor anglais, the oboe and the clarinet, the wind ensemble sings 'Alleluia' under a luminous haze of trills and harmonies in the strings.

A joyful 3/8, vigorous and sunlit, constitutes the third movement. Again the appoggiatura-fragments can be heard clearly. After a long crescendo, the theme appears on the whole orchestra, fortissimo, in an augmentation, and gives way to a sort of Dance before the Ark.

The fourth movement leads us into the mysteries of the Divine plan. The second movement is the most important part of the work from the point of view of its innovations in technique, form and musical language. But the fourth movement is its emotional peak. It grows from a serene phrase, ecstatic and palpable, given to the strings which rise up and float ever higher, finally arriving on a simple seventh chord which seems to have no end.

The first performance was the subject of a thoughtful review by Maurice Imbert in *Le Courrier musical* (1 March 1935). He appeared to share Messiaen's own view that the emotional peak was to be found in the last movement: 'Played by strings alone, without double-basses, the musical imagination takes flight here and rises up on the agile wings of inner prayer. Here the music is noble, beautiful and pure, more so than anywhere else in the work.' Imbert then produces an architectural analogy for the structure of the work which he says 'resembles the art of the master-craftsmen who dreamed up Gothic cathedrals, with their forests of majestic pillars continuing into audacious vaults; their stained glass with linear designs or primitive-looking people, dyed in transparent colours through which the rays of the sun flicker'.

The issue of *Le Monde musical* with Messiaen's introduction to the work also included a review of the first performance. It was written by Daniel-Lesur, a very old friend who had known Messiaen since they shared childhood classes at the Conservatoire. He was particularly enthusiastic about the third movement: 'The "Alléluia sur la trompette" is a supra-terrestrial hymn of triumph, blazingly announced by trumpets and horns. Abundantly energetic rhythms express the joys of mystical order. It is, in our view, the most eloquent of the four movements, thanks to the magnificent development of its memorable opening phrase and the powerful conclusion.' Clearly this enthusiasm was shared by other musicians, as the orchestral version of *L'Ascension* was regularly performed before the score was published in 1948. For example, in autumn 1943 – hardly the most propitious time for new music in Paris – the work was broadcast *twice* in the space of fifteen days: on 10 October conducted by Siohan at the Concerts Pasdeloup, and on 25 October conducted by Gustave Cloez at Radio-Paris (the radio station run by the occupying Nazis).

By the time of the première of the orchestral version, the alternative for organ had already been published (in November 1934) and played in public (29 January 1935). This transcription had the newly composed 'Transports de joie d'une âme devant la gloire du Christ qui est la sienne', written during 1934, as a replacement for the original third movement, 'Alléluia sur la trompette, Alléluia sur la cymbale'. Messiaen considered this colourful and decidedly Dukas-like orchestral scherzo unsuitable for the organ, and substituted a new and dazzlingly idiomatic toccata: the first of several such organ pieces he was to write.

The Trinité organ was undergoing restoration in 1934–5, so the première of the organ version was given by Messiaen (29 January 1935) on the Cavaillé-Coll at Saint-Antoine-des-Quinze-Vingts, near the Gare de Lyon. The recital was reviewed in *Le Ménestrel* (3 February 1935) by a critic identified only as 'M.P.': 'M. Messiaen gave us the first performance of his *L'Ascension*, a poem in four movements, written in a very refined style with colours which often seem more orchestral than organistic, and of a mystical tendency. This serenity expresses itself sometimes through quite turbulent music which is adjacent to passages of great poetry, of real beauty.' Félix Raugel in *Le Monde musical* (28 February 1935), after claiming (wrongly) that the organ version had been conceived first, went on to describe Messiaen's achievement in terms which must surely have delighted the composer: 'Messiaen has planned this symphonic paraphrase on the Gospels in a way which recalls the broad and luminous work of the master glassmakers in our cathedrals. An ardently religious soul expresses itself in these passionate pieces with a tumultuous daring, but also at times with a delicate sweetness.'

Messiaen played *L'Ascension* on his own instrument at the Trinité on 28 May 1935, as part of a recital he shared with Marcel Dupré to inaugurate the newly restored organ, to which seven new stops had been added while the instrument was out of action.[7] As well as *L'Ascension*, the concert included two movements from Dupré's *Le Chemin de la Croix* played by Messiaen, and *Le Banquet céleste* played by Dupré.

Messiaen's *Vocalise-étude* was published by Alphonse Leduc in March 1935, as no.151 of the 'Répertoire moderne de Vocalises-études publiées sous la direction de A.L. Hettich, Professeur au Conservatoire National de Paris'. Started

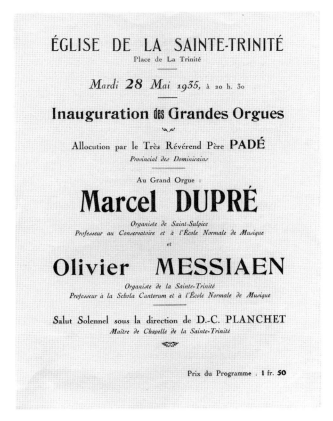

41 Programme for the recital on 28 May 1935 at which Messiaen and Marcel Dupré inaugurated the restored and expanded organ at the Trinité. Messiaen played his own *L'Ascension* and two movements from Dupré's *Le Chemin de la Croix*.

many years earlier, this series already included vocalises by the likes of Fauré, Milhaud, Nielsen, Poulenc, Ravel, Szymanowski and Tailleferre. In its modest way, the *Vocalise* represents an important stylistic step forward for Messiaen. He was soon to embark on two large song-cycles, and in this short piece he used – for the first time – the elaborate, ecstatic vocal melismas that were to be such an important feature of the *Poèmes pour Mi* and, to a lesser extent, the *Chants de terre et de ciel*. It is likely that the work was used at the 1935 *concours* at the Conservatoire, but Messiaen soon included it in recitals with his other songs, always calling it by the simpler title – without didactic overtones – of *Vocalise*. He performed it with the soprano Henriette Quéru-Bedel in a concert organized by Le Triptyque on 18 May 1936,[8] and at another Triptyque event a couple of weeks later, on 5 June 1936,[9] with Madeleine Chardon.

Messiaen spent the summer of 1935 in Grenoble. He wrote to Claude Arrieu on 12 September about the work he had been doing: 'I have been able to compose a little and I think I have made progress from a rhythmic point of view (though perhaps I am fooling myself!). I've seen the most stunning mountain landscape here. The Dauphiné is really one of the greatest things in France!' Since the 'little' composing activity referred to here included Messiaen's most ambitious work to date, *La Nativité du Seigneur*, he was being unduly modest. There was another, smaller work too: a few months after Messiaen had sent his panegyric about *Ariane et Barbe-bleue* (quoted above), his teacher Paul Dukas died, on 17 May 1935. During his summer vacation, Messiaen received a letter from Henry Prunières, editor of *La Revue musicale*, asking about Dukas pupils who might contribute to a 'Tombeau'. His undated reply listed several classmates, including Arrieu and Barraine ('perhaps the most fervent of all the master's disciples'), and he readily agreed to write a piece himself. He ended with a heartfelt tribute:

> At the moment I am in Grenoble where I am spending my holidays – that's to say, my time for real work. [...] You can definitely count on me. You have had a noble and touching idea which will be dear to the hearts of all who admired the master. The task will be a heavy one for all of us: what heights and what depths must be reached in order to offer a tribute to his memory which is worthy of him! He was a great mind, as well as a great musician.[10]

Le Tombeau de Paul Dukas was published as the musical supplement to *La Revue musicale* in May–June 1936; it included Messiaen's striking memorial, entitled simply 'Pièce', along with works by eight other composers. Messiaen wrote his contribution for the *Tombeau* before returning to Paris for the start of the new academic year in October. Many years later, he described the musical language of his tribute to Dukas: 'My piece is quite simple: it uses mode 3 in its first transposition, whose orange, white and gold light perpetually falls onto a long dominant seventh. It is static, solemn and stark, like a huge block of stone.'[11] The piece was first performed at the École Normale on 25 April 1936, in a concert which included all nine contributions to *Le Tombeau de Paul Dukas*.[12] The pianist was another Dukas pupil, Joaquín Nin-Culmell.[13] A few months later Messiaen played his own piece, as well as those by Rodrigo and Falla, at a concert in Lyon on 11 January 1937.

The group La Spirale was founded in 1935 under the leadership of the composer Georges Migot[14] and with the active support of Nestor Lejeune, who had recently been appointed Director of the Schola Cantorum following the inflammatory political infighting there at the end of 1934. One of Lejeune's most vigorous supporters (in what his opponents considered a kind of *coup d'état*) was Jules Le Febvre, who sat on the committee of La Spirale. So too did the distinguished Breton composer and critic Paul Le Flem, his erstwhile pupil André Jolivet, Édouard Sciortino, Daniel-Lesur, Claire Delbos and Messiaen. Almost all of them had close connections with the Schola.

The first encounter between Messiaen and Jolivet had taken place in 1934. Messiaen read Jolivet's String Quartet for the Société Nationale and wrote a short note to its composer: 'Monsieur, you write the music I would like to write. Can we meet?'[15] Hilda Jolivet left a somewhat jaundiced account of their earliest meeting, at Messiaen's apartment in the rue des Plantes, when the Jolivets and the Messiaens spent an evening together. 'We had heard about the white wedding of these two ethereal beings, so I was astonished when my hostess started to confide in me about her difficulties with pregnancy, and her regret at not having children. The conversation between our two husbands must have been more enthralling, because it went on and on.'[16] More helpfully, Hilda Jolivet also recorded that her husband introduced Messiaen and others (like Daniel-Lesur) to recent music from abroad, especially the Second Viennese School and Bartók.[17]

La Spirale gave its inaugural concert on 12 December 1935 at the Schola Cantorum.[18] The enterprising programme included the première of Jolivet's *Mana*, a work hugely admired by Messiaen, who later wrote the preface to the published edition.[19] Messiaen played his own *L'Ascension* and three organ pieces by Claire Delbos. The group's aims were printed on the front of the programme:

> The committee of La Spirale intends to participate in the promotion of contemporary music, through concerts of French works, and through organizing exchange concerts with composers from other countries. It wishes to serve music and in order to do so, it will give fewer world premières; instead, it will give repeat performances of significant works.

SALLE DE LA SCHOLA CANTORUM
269, Rue Saint-Jacques, 269

Jeudi 30 Janvier 1936
à 21 heures précises

CONCERT DE MUSIQUE MODERNE
donné par

Claire DELBOS
Violoniste

avec le concours de

Marcelle GERAR
Cantatrice

et d'

Olivier MESSIAEN
Pianiste

PLACES : 15 et 10 francs

Autobus : AB · AR bis · H · H bis · S · W · AA · AX · BB · U.
Tramways : 8 · 16 · 43 · 51.

42 Programme for a concert at the Schola Cantorum on 30 January 1936 given by Delbos, Messiaen and Marcelle Gérar.

The press response was enthusiastic and so, evidently, was the audience: according to Jean Douël (*Guide musicale*, December 1935), 'several encores demonstrated the interest which an enthusiastic public took in these performances'. Douël does not specify which works received repeat performances, but the habit of giving encores, even on unlikely occasions, was nothing new in Paris.[20] The group's manifesto mentioned no particular stylistic standpoint, though the programming in this and its subsequent concerts signalled a clear aversion to neoclassicism – the one contemporary style left unexplored in the Spirale concerts.

The Schola Cantorum was the venue for another 'Concert de musique moderne' (unconnected with La Spirale), on 30 January 1936. This was given by Delbos, Messiaen, and the distinguished soprano Marcelle Gérar (one of Ravel's favourite singers, who made one of the first recordings of his *Shéhérazade*, in 1929). The programme opened with the Violin Sonata by Germaine Tailleferre, whose music was to appear a few months later in the first concert of La Jeune France. Gérar sang Messiaen's *Trois Mélodies*, Arrieu's *Quatre Mélodies* and *Clowneries*; later in the programme she sang Delbos's *Primevère* – a cycle of short songs on poems from Cécile Sauvage's collection of the same name – and three songs by Elsa Barraine. The other instrumental items were Messiaen's *Thème et variations*, the finale of Jolivet's Violin Sonata, and Bartók's Second Violin Sonata. This was a tough programme, which suggests that at the time Claire's capabilities as a violinist were considerable. It was also one of the comparatively few occasions when Messiaen and Claire appeared together as performers in public. Daniel-Lesur reviewed the concert in *Tablettes de la Schola Cantorum* (February 1936), a rare chance to read an account of Claire's playing, albeit one written by a friend and close colleague of the Messiaens:

Claire Delbos took on the toughest part of this back-breaking programme. After giving a spirited account of the spicy and polytonal sonata by Germaine Tailleferre, then a generously expressive version of the nobly developed *Thème et variations* by Olivier Messiaen, Claire Delbos demonstrated the highest qualities of energy and fire – one could call it Gypsy fervour – in the powerfully streamlined finale of the Jolivet [Sonata], and in the Second Sonata by Béla Bartók, where the rhythmic vigour was never allowed to slacken for a moment. The last movement of this Sonata, in particular, was given with all the sense of fantasy and the folkish ferocity which it requires. Marcelle Gérar sang with intelligence, the innate interpretative gift that best characterizes her [...] the fresh *Primevère* by Claire Delbos, written in a very personal style, and finally three little masterpieces by

Olivier Messiaen: 'Pourquoi', 'Le Sourire' and 'La Fiancée perdue'. These three songs contain some unforgettable music.

Four weeks later the musical press was out in force for Messiaen's next important concert, one of the turning-points in his career. *La Nativité du Seigneur* was composed in summer 1935 and individual movements were probably played by Messiaen at the Trinité that autumn.[21] The first complete performance was a special concert by Les Amis de l'Orgue at the Trinité on 27 February 1936, where the nine movements were shared between three players: Daniel-Lesur played nos.1–3, Jean Langlais nos.4–6, and Jean-Jacques Grunenwald nos.7–9. It was an enormous challenge – even for such gifted organists – to get to grips with this new work, but according to Daniel-Lesur, Messiaen had tried, rather charmingly, to reassure his three friends that the music 'wasn't as difficult as all that'.[22] Why did Messiaen not perform *La Nativité* himself on this occasion? Almost certainly it was because he wanted his friends and colleagues to take up his newest and most ambitious work, and to perform it in their own churches and elsewhere.

Messiaen was feeling buoyant about *La Nativité* when he wrote to Claude Arrieu inviting her to the first performance: 'As this is my most substantial work – and represents for me the result of several years' reflection – I will be so pleased if you can come to hear it. I am counting on your being there, and on your friendship. Thank you! We can see each other on the evening of the concert for a chat.' At this première, a small slip of paper (printed for the composer) was distributed to the audience, outlining Messiaen's musical and theological leanings:

> The emotion, the sincerity of the musical work: to be at the service of the dogmas of Catholic theology.
>
> To be expressed by melodic and harmonic means: the progressive growth of intervals, the chord on the dominant, pedal notes, embellishments and extended appoggiaturas.
>
> Still more by rhythmic means: rhythms immediately preceded or followed by their augmentation and sometimes increased by a short note-value (half the added value).
>
> And above all by modes of limited transposition: chromatic modes, used harmonically, the strange colour of which derives from the limited number of their possible transpositions (2, 3, 4 and 6 according to the mode).
>
> Theological subject matter? The best, since it contains all subjects. And this abundance of technical means allows the heart to overflow freely.

That final phrase encapsulates Messiaen's aesthetic position very clearly: the technical procedures and innovations in his compositions were there to expand the emotional range and to enhance the expressive power of his music, to liberate the imagination – 'to allow the heart to overflow freely'.

Such was the extent of the press coverage of *La Nativité* that Messiaen prepared a four-page leaflet containing extracts from reviews, several of them by composers.[23] Georges Auric (in *Marianne*) admitted an interesting paradox: he was reluctant to accept some of Messiaen's ideas, but had a genuine enthusiasm for the music: 'It seems to me that on many issues we would be poles apart. [. . .] So it is a great delight for me to write that some of these pieces are among the most beautiful and the most moving which I have encountered in a long time.' Henri Sauguet was clearly bowled over:

> In this work, comprising nine mystical meditations for organ on the Nativity of Our Lord Jesus Christ, Olivier Messiaen has achieved a perfect and brilliant mastery of his art, at the same time as expressing a mystical sensibility of an incomparable nobility and quality. We would like to go into detail about each of these nine pieces, to describe their beauty. They are written in an extremely personal language, using a musical vocabulary which Olivier Messiaen has created himself, using particular modes which he calls 'modes of limited transposition'. In *La Nativité du Seigneur*, Olivier Messiaen has reached the highest level of religious expression which music can achieve.[24]

Messiaen's later view of *La Nativité* made it clear just how important a work this was in his musical development: 'With the use of Hindu rhythms in *La Nativité* I produced the proof, at least I believe I did, that it was possible to write music for the organ other than in a post-Franckist aesthetic.' He added that the work was partly an indirect homage to his composition teacher Dukas, 'perhaps to his remarkable open-mindedness'.[25] As early as 25 May 1936, five pieces from *La Nativité* ('Les Bergers', 'La Vierge et l'Enfant', 'Le Verbe', 'Les Anges' and 'Les Mages') were heard again at the Trinité, played on this occasion by Messiaen's gifted assistant organist and fellow Dupré pupil, Line Zilgien. Her all-Messiaen recital – possibly the first ever given by a performer other than the composer – also included *Le Banquet céleste*, the *Diptyque*, 'Transports de joie' from *L'Ascension*, and *Apparition de l'Église éternelle*.

The third La Spirale concert, given on 5 March 1936, revealed the international flavour of the group's programming policy. Devoted entirely to music by American composers, it included songs by John Alden Carpenter and Charles Ives, sung by an American baritone (Victor Prahl) accompanied by Messiaen. They performed a group of four songs by Carpenter ('Slumber Song', 'Serenade', 'Youngman, Chieftain' and 'Dark Hills') and five by Ives: the first known performances anywhere of 'The Innate', 'Requiem', 'Paracelsus', 'Resolution' and 'Majority'. Exactly three weeks later, on 26 March 1936, La Spirale mounted its fourth concert. This was an all-French programme including the String Quartet by Jean Cartan, two pieces by Elsa Barraine played by Messiaen, and five of Maurice Emmanuel's *Chansons bourguignonnes* sung by Mme Bourgeois Félix, with Messiaen at the piano. Messiaen's admiration for Emmanuel – and for the *Chansons bourguignonnes* in particular – is well known (largely through his 1946 article in *Revue musicale*[26]), but this concert provided a rare opportunity for him to put this enthusiasm into practice. In his later article, Messiaen wrote admiringly of the modal flavour of the settings, the poetic feeling, 'drenched in sunlight', of some harmonizations, the ability to create a mood (citing the *Dies irae* tune 'in the style of a danse macabre' in 'J'ai vu le loup'), and, in 'Adieu, Bergère', a 'great melodic and modal sweetness, in which the chords, without thirds, are close relatives of those of Ravel, or of Debussy's *Images*, and which prolong the caresses and the melancholy'. The 'veritable pearl' of the collection, according to Messiaen, was no.13, 'La Mal Mariée'.

Messiaen, Jolivet and Daniel-Lesur all served on the committee of La Spirale, but it was a fourth composer, the self-taught Yves Baudrier, who first had the idea of bringing together a group of composers with diverse musical styles but shared ideals, as La Jeune France:

> [Baudrier] never forgot the day when [. . .] he first heard Olivier Messiaen's *Les Offrandes oubliées* at the Société des Concerts du Conservatoire. It was at that moment, he said, 'that he became conscious of a spiritual movement which was going to carry along a number of young artists in France'. He immediately arranged a meeting with Messiaen, and the union was quickly sealed between the two musicians. To complete the group, Messiaen suggested two of his friends, who only knew each other slightly: Daniel-Lesur and André Jolivet. [. . .] Jolivet was the *enfant terrible* of the Société Nationale; his music scandalized its regulars. But it found a champion in the person of one of the committee members, none other than Olivier Messiaen. Subsequently they met at each others' homes; there they plotted various ideas and schemes, mainly at Yves Baudrier's house. He lived in a small ground-floor flat, cluttered with books, scores and records, all muddled up with his pots and pans in an indescribable mess.[27]

The first Jeune France concert took place on 3 June 1936.[28] It was well publicized in advance, notably on the front cover of the *Guide du concert* (15 and 22 May 1936), next to a photograph of the occasion's celebrity soloist, the pianist Ricardo Viñes – a legendary figure by the mid-1930s: he had been a close friend of Debussy, Ravel, Satie and Falla, was the dedicatee of Ravel's *Oiseaux tristes*, Debussy's *Poissons d'or* and Falla's *Noches en los jardines de España*, gave first performances of numerous major works (including Debussy's *Pour le piano* and Ravel's *Miroirs* and *Gaspard de la nuit*), and was Poulenc's piano teacher. In short, Viñes was a remarkable catch. Apparently the event only took place 'after much difficulty',[29] mostly the need to find the necessary money (much of which came from Baudrier – a fact which makes his later penury all the sadder). However, the musical forces lined up for the occasion were impressive: not only Viñes, but also the conductor Roger Désormière and the Orchestre Symphonique de Paris, as well as Maurice and Ginette Martenot showing off the latest version of the ondes Martenot. It was a conscious tribute from 'Les Quatre' to 'Les Six' to include Tailleferre's *Ballade*, in which Viñes was the soloist.

Among the most influential early supporters of La Jeune France was the critic André Cœuroy,[30] and his papers include letters from Messiaen and Jolivet about the group's activities. In an undated letter written shortly before the inaugural concert, Messiaen wrote to Cœuroy for an article which the critic was preparing, enclosing his *curriculum vitae*, and a copy of the small manifesto (circulated at the première of *La Nativité*). Messiaen also sent the spoken commentary he was going to read out at the concert to introduce his two works, *Les Offrandes oubliées* and the *Hymne au Saint-Sacrement*:

'The body lives through the spirit. Why deny the unknown power of the spiritual body to see the spirit itself through the body?' Thus wrote Saint Augustine. And it seems that true beauty is that which comes closest to this simple vision. Every artist thus needs to try, according to the words of [Paul] Valéry: 'to enlarge our conceptions to the extent where they become inconceivable'. This state of the spirit maintains a proper humility and contempt for the work itself: these are the necessary conditions in any quest for the new. How is this ideal to be realized? Do we not possess the gift of tears? And a sense of the divine which can allow us to be drawn into the gift of grace which the Father sends to the Son? And what of the best of these new expressive ways, lying dormant and unexploited, in the music of those who have gone before us? All that can elevate us towards higher things.

Emotional sincerity, put at the service of the dogmas of the Catholic faith expressed through a new musical language – or at the very least an attempt to achieve this. Such is the programme of Olivier Messiaen which he puts into practice in the *Hymne au Saint-Sacrement*, in *Les Offrandes oubliées*.

These two meditations are based on 'modes of limited transposition': chromatic modes, used harmonically, whose strange colours derive from the limited number of possible transpositions.

The *Hymne au Saint-Sacrement* is dedicated to the real presence of Jesus in the Eucharist. It attempts to depict the marvellous gifts of communion: the growth of love and grace, the force against evil, and the promise of eternal life. *Les Offrandes oubliées* differs from the *Hymne* through its expressive freedom which is more marked in its rhythm, and in the rhythm of its breathing. In three short sections, the work evokes Sin – which is oblivion, the Cross, and the Eucharist – which are the divine offerings.[31]

Cœuroy in fact wrote two articles about La Jeune France at the time. The first appeared in *Gringoire* – a right-wing Catholic newspaper – on 29 May 1936. Messiaen immediately wrote to thank him: 'All of the "Four" have now received and read your article in *Gringoire*. It is beautifully presented and absolutely accurate. A thousand thanks. [. . .] You understand, effortlessly and charmingly, how to bring out the important and striking characteristics. This is extremely perceptive and persuasive: here is real living criticism!'[32]

The manifesto of La Jeune France was distributed at the first concert, and most of it was quoted in Cœuroy's second article, published in *Beaux-Arts* on 5 June 1936. This first appeared in English a few months later, in the programme book for the Boston Symphony Orchestra concert on 16 October 1936 (discussed below) which included the American première of *Les Offrandes oubliées*:

As the conditions of life become more and more hard, mechanical and impersonal, music must always bring to those who love it, its spiritual violence and its courageous reactions. *La Jeune France*, reaffirming the title once used by Berlioz, pursues the road upon which the master once took his obdurate course. This is a group of four young French composers who are friends: Olivier Messiaen, Daniel-Lesur, Yves Baudrier and André Jolivet. *La Jeune France* proposes the dissemination of works [that are] youthful, free, [and] as far removed from revolutionary formulas as from academic formulas.

The tendencies of this group will be diverse; their only unqualified agreement is in a common desire to be satisfied with nothing less than sincerity, generosity and artistic good faith. Their aim is to create and to promote a living music.

At each concert *La Jeune France*, assembling an unbiased jury, will arrange performances, as far as its means allow, of one or several works characteristic of some interesting trend within the bounds of their aspirations.

They also hope to encourage the performance of recent French scores which have been allowed to languish through the indifference or the penury of official powers, and to continue in this century the music of the great composers of the past who have made French music one of the pure jewels of civilization.

Cœuroy's *Beaux-Arts* article went on to describe a meeting with the group, and reported on its inaugural concert, which he heard over the radio. The portrait of Messiaen is an affectionate one, and includes an enthusiastic reference to Line Zilgien's recital the previous week:

> The one among them who could be considered the most other-worldly, with his baggy trousers and his halo-like hat, is Olivier Messiaen (who is the son of the poetess Cécile Sauvage). But in fact he is not at all other-worldly. The other evening at the Trinité, during an organ recital of his works (where the young organist Line Zilgien revealed an exceptional technique, a depth of feeling and an intelligence which put her in the front rank of today's virtuosos), I thought I had found him out: I read, in the programme, that 'Les Anges', one of the pieces from *La Nativité du Seigneur*, was 'a sort of heavenly dance', 'an exultation of disembodied spirits'; in short, either drugged to the eyeballs or indescribably boring. Well, *never* have I heard an organ piece which had such a vibrant sense of jubilation or such powerful poetry, where there was, at the same time, such taste, such delicacy and such colour.
>
> I don't have space to explain how Messiaen obtained this colour, and the role played in his music by 'augmentations of rhythms' and the 'modes of limited transpositions'. But if I make allusion to them, it is to underline the novelty of the group's spiritual position, which embraces research into their art. They are human and want to be musicians above everything else; but the musicians in them are inspired by their pursuit of the human.
>
> This was demonstrated in the concert which they gave the other day with the collaboration of dear Ricardo Viñes and the dynamic Roger Désormière. Away from Paris, I was only able to hear the concert on the radio, and the broadcast from the Eiffel Tower was not one of the best from a technical point of view. [...] The *Hymne au Saint-Sacrement* and *Les Offrandes oubliées* by Messiaen demonstrate that a sense of the divine has no need of theatrical gestures or Jansenist rigour in order to express itself. [...] La Jeune France is not an isolated or gratuitous enterprise. It celebrates the profundity of youth. The year 1936 will be one to remember in the history of music.

A sense of national identity is self-evident in the title La Jeune France, and by evoking Berlioz, the group placed itself firmly in an explicitly French tradition – and perhaps, too, an explicitly Romantic lineage. The political instability in Europe (and particularly in France at the time) was perhaps another reason for the choice of name, but if the group's motivation was to some extent nationalistic, the music of its composers was seldom so, except in terms of a characteristically French sensibility and, in Messiaen's case at least, French spirituality. Their first concert was given under the distinguished patronage of several eminent French writers and thinkers of the day, including no fewer than four members of the Académie Française: Georges Duhamel, François Mauriac, Marcel Prévost and Paul Valéry. According to Jean Roy, 'the manifesto and the concert generated a unanimous wave of fellow feeling'.[33] In *Marianne*, Georges Auric emphasized 'the spontaneity of these musicians, whose names will be remembered in the future'; in *Le Jour*, Henri Sauguet praised 'their sureness of touch, their skill, their technical suppleness and their resourceful orchestration'; and in *Comœdia*, Paul Le Flem was a fellow-member of the La Spirale committee with Messiaen, Jolivet and Daniel-Lesur, so hardly an impartial observer. He greeted the birth of a group which 'must now hold a dominant position in musical life'.[34] Florent Schmitt, writing in *Le Temps*, commented wryly on the presence of Tailleferre's name in the programme, and the bewildering stylistic diversity of the concert. His remarks were quoted in the Boston Symphony programme (16 October 1936): 'The first contest of the *Jeune France* of 1936 mustered [...] everything from the most academic traditionalism to the most dishevelled revolt, a grouping of works as unlike [one another] as such a promiscuity, necessarily arbitrary, could be expected to produce.'

Tailleferre's appearance in the concert and Auric's review in *Marianne* were not the only instances of encouragement for 'Les Quatre' – and especially for Messiaen – from the erstwhile members of Les Six. In *Je suis compositeur*, published in 1951, Honegger declared: 'I have much admiration and fellow-feeling for Olivier Messiaen. He certainly stands at the head of his generation. [...] I love his sweeping melodies, even though some have denounced their sensuality. But I much prefer melody – voluptuous or not – to no melody at all. I am impressed by the grand conceptions which Messiaen strives for.'[35] In his postwar conversations with Claude Rostand, Poulenc admitted that 'Messiaen and I do not genuflect in the same way, but what matters is that we both try to share our faith with the public';[36] and he thought highly of Messiaen's organ music, if not his poetry:

> I admire it deeply, since Messiaen has put the best of himself into it. *La Nativité* and *Les Corps glorieux* contain passages of genius. If I bristle (above all from a literary point of view) when Messiaen invents a pseudo-hindu language mixed with outdated symbolism, [...] it gives me pleasure to salute, in his organ music, the very great musician that he undoubtedly is.[37]

In an article by Milhaud dating from early 1938 (but not published until 1998), Messiaen was singled out as 'one of the most striking personalities of young French music: his harmonic language that is so free, his tender heart, his profound mysticism, and his ardent faith are all at the service of his great talent'.[38] Messiaen was also acquainted with the sixth (and least-known) member of Les Six, Louis Durey, and he visited him on several occasions during the Occupation.[39]

After an intensely busy few months, Messiaen and Claire spent the summer of 1936 in their new house set in the spectacular Alpine surroundings of Petichet (Isère), where Messiaen was to do most of his composing for the rest of his life, and close to which he now lies buried. Presumably it was the isolation of Petichet which not only fulfilled Messiaen's needs as a composer but which also enabled the young married couple to buy the land, and to pay for the construction of their very modest country retreat. The Messiaen house looks down to the Lac de Laffrey and beyond to the looming hogsback of the Grand Serre; not far above the house is the main road, the Route Napoléon, which runs past a chain of four lakes before carving a spectacular route through the mountains between La Mure and Gap.

43 The house at Petichet in 2003 (photo: Peter Hill).

44 Le Grand Serre (photo: Peter Hill).

The first fruit of Messiaen's composing at Petichet was to be one of his most rapturous works of the 1930s, the *Poèmes pour Mi*, written as an extended love song to Claire. A photograph shows the two of them together in their new house, poring over a manuscript which is likely to be either the *Poèmes pour Mi* or the work Claire was composing at the same time, her setting for voice and piano of poems from Cécile Sauvage's *L'Âme en bourgeon*.

In the *Poèmes pour Mi* the bond linking man and woman in marriage serves as a symbol of the union between Christ and his Church. The fifth song, 'L'Épouse', reads: 'Go where the Spirit leads you, / Nothing can separate that which God has joined [...] / The wife is the extension of the husband [...] / As the Church is the extension of Christ.' Messiaen's texts are filled not only with evocations of Claire but also with images reflecting the setting at Petichet:

45 Delbos and Messiaen at Petichet during summer 1936, their first holiday there.

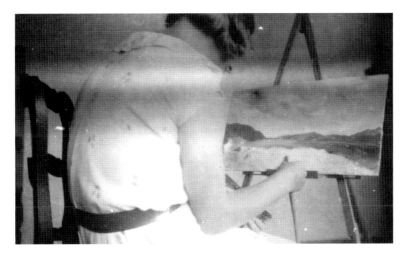

46 Claire painting.

The sky,
And the water that follows the variations of the clouds,
And the earth, and the mountains ever waiting,
And light which transforms.[40]

The lake like a big blue jewel,
The road full of sorrows and hollows,
My feet that falter in the dust,
The lake like a big blue jewel.
There she is, green and blue like the landscape!

47 Claire's painting of the Grand Lac de Laffrey.

48 The Grand Lac de Laffrey (photo: Peter Hill).

Between the corn and the sun I see her face:
She smiles, her hand over her eyes,
The lake like a big blue jewel.[41]

Disturb the lonely old mountain of sorrow,
That the sun may get to work on the bitter waters of my heart![42]

In terms of Messiaen's international reputation, the afternoon of Friday, 16 October 1936 was a significant one. In Symphony Hall, Boston, Serge Koussevitzky conducted Messiaen's music for the first time in the USA when the Boston Symphony Orchestra gave the first American performance of *Les Offrandes oubliées*. The programme notes by John N. Burk included a very thorough account of Messiaen's career to date, as well as a description (in a long footnote) of the modes of limited transposition by no less an authority on scales and modes than Nicolas Slonimsky. On 20 October, four days after the Boston concert, the French organist Noëlie Pierront[43] introduced Messiaen's music to London audiences for the first time: at St John's, Red Lion Square, she performed *Le Banquet céleste* in a recital for the Organ Music Society; three weeks later, on 12 November, André Marchal played *Apparition de l'Église éternelle* at the same church.

The new year began with a concert at the Salle Béal in Lyon on 11 January 1937, billed as the second concert of the 'Société Liszt'. Messiaen was joined by the soprano Suzanne Dupont-Royer for the vocal items. The programme began with memorial pieces: *La Plainte au loin du faune*, which Dukas had written in memory of Debussy, then the pieces by Falla, Rodrigo and Messiaen from the Dukas *Tombeau*. These were followed by Delbos's song-cycle *Primevère* and two of Milhaud's *Saudades do Brazil*. The second half was all Messiaen: three *Préludes*, the *Trois Mélodies*, the *Vocalise*, and finally the *Fantaisie burlesque*, a work which the composer seldom played in public.

On 28 January 1937 La Spirale brought together several of Paris's leading organist-composers for a concert of contemporary organ music in which Messiaen gave the first performance of the *Prélude, Aria et Final* by Jules Le Febvre as well as three pieces from *La Nativité*. A year after its first performance, the Trinité was once again the venue for the 'seconde audition intégrale à Paris' of *La Nativité du Seigneur*, on 23 February. As with the première, Messiaen did not play the work; this time he entrusted it to André Fleury, the *titulaire* of Saint-Augustin and a player he much admired. In an undated letter to Felix Aprahamian from the end of 1937, Messiaen described Fleury as 'one of the finest organ virtuosos in France!'[44]

Always mindful of the historical tradition associated with his post as a church musician, Messiaen was a member of the committee established to celebrate the centenary of Alexandre Guilmant, the most illustrious of his predecessors at the Trinité. On 12 March he was one of eight players who gave a special concert of Guilmant's works at the Trinité. The others were his teacher Marcel Dupré (Saint-Sulpice), Ludovic Panel (Sacré-Cœur), Édouard Mignan (Madeleine), Joseph Bonnet (Saint-Eustache), Alexandre Cellier (Temple de l'Étoile), Georges Jacob (organist of the Société des Concerts du Conservatoire) and Abel Decaux (honorary organist at the Sacré-Cœur).

Messiaen was a regular performer at the Société Nationale during the 1930s. He appeared on 6 March 1937, at the École Normale, playing three songs by Claire Delbos with the singer Eliette Schenneberg, and two of his own *Poèmes pour Mi* with Mme Bourdette-Vial (replacing Renée Mahé at the last moment):

this was the first performance anywhere of 'Paysage' and 'Action de grâces'.[45] The first complete performance of the *Poèmes pour Mi* took place a few weeks later at La Spirale. That concert, at the Schola Cantorum on 28 April 1937, was perhaps the most historically significant in La Spirale's brief history. It included three works for solo piano – Ravel's *Valses nobles et sentimentales*, six of Milhaud's *Saudades do Brazil,* and Samazeuilh's Suite in G – all played by Messiaen – and the premières of two song-cycles: *L'Âme en bourgeon* by Claire Delbos (on poems by Cécile Sauvage), and the *Poèmes pour Mi*, sung by the distinguished Wagnerian soprano Marcelle Bunlet, with Messiaen at the piano. It seems to have been largely up to Messiaen to find an audience for the concert, as intimated in a letter to Claude Arrieu:

> I have just sent you 100 programmes and tickets for my concert at La Spirale on 28 April. I am relying heavily on your propaganda to fill the hall. Thank you. It is so kind of you to go to such trouble for me. You will notice that I have put an announcement for the *Jeune France* concert at the bottom of each programme. Your name is there, of course. I spoke to my three accomplices about putting *Mascarades* into the *Jeune France* concert and it's done: this charming and spicy fantasy will end the concert!

Arrieu's *Mascarades* was indeed on the programme of the second Jeune France concert, and this letter provides evidence of the quaintly informal selection process of the 'unbiased jury' described in the original manifesto.

As well as annual orchestral concerts, La Jeune France was also involved in smaller events. The group generated a lot of interest, and other concert-giving organizations started to invite them to perform. On 16 March 1937 La Jeune France appeared at one of the regular Tuesday concerts promoted by *La Revue musicale*. An unsigned review made some perceptive comments on the nature of the group:

> One is struck by the diversity of styles which exists among the musicians of La Jeune France. Nothing – or almost nothing – seems to unite these composers, but they have a clearly manifested willingness to express themselves in a very personal language whose boldness is uneven. [. . .] Our Jeune France composers share an aversion to music which is complacently harmonized, to Impressionist prettiness and also – one of their most distinctive features and one which does them the greatest credit – to the artistic materialism of the generation which preceded them.[46]

Like the 1936 concert, the group's second orchestral concert, on 4 June 1937, was trailed on the front cover of the *Guide du concert* (14 and 21 May 1937), this time next to a photograph of Désormière. A most unexpected source for a review of this event is the *New York Times* (20 June 1937), which published a long article entitled 'Young French Composers' by the pianist Elen Foster, a specialist in contemporary repertoire who lived and worked in Paris. The concert included an important Messiaen première: the first performance anywhere of the orchestral version of 'Action de grâces', first of the *Poèmes pour Mi*. This review is particularly noteworthy for its well-informed comments on Messiaen, one of the earliest serious assessments of him in English:

> Olivier Messiaen's 'Action de grâces,' sung by the exceptionally gifted Marcelle Bunlet, received a veritable ovation. Messiaen, already in complete possession of a style intensely personal and original in character, has achieved in this work what seems a veritable masterpiece. The song is one of a cycle entitled *Poèmes pour Mi*, originally conceived for voice and piano. The orchestral version serves to enhance the qualities inherent in the original score. Most effective is the use of the voice in unaccompanied phrases, thus alternating its discourse with that of the orchestra – a device of great dramatic intensity.
>
> Messiaen's style, with its rhythmic canons, harmonic modes and absence of fixed measure, contrives to transport the hearer into something which sounds like a new musical dimension. Nowhere else in French contemporary music has this reviewer encountered such a coupling of intense power with perfect repose. [. . .] Messiaen's *Offrandes oubliées*, given its first hearing last year, was repeated. Again Messiaen's extraordinary magic transports and sustains the attention in a progression of sound at once static yet evolving; and the final chord opens up a new vista still unexplored. [. . .] Widely differing in their personal endowments, the four musicians of 'Jeune France' have one characteristic in common: their instinctive search for a vocabulary which, expressing something more than cerebral theories and formulas, will give voice to human nature in its entirety.

Michel-Léon Hirsch in *Le Ménestrel* (11 June 1937) drew a parallel between Messiaen and one of the most original French visual artists of an earlier generation in his review of 'Action de grâces': 'The orchestral writing is at once rich and strange, of a knowing naivety: that of a musical Douanier Rousseau.'

On 15 June, a few days after the Jeune France concert, the pianist Bernadette Alexandre-Georges gave the first complete performance of Messiaen's *Préludes*, at the École Normale. This was the first time all eight were played in public; Henriette Roget's Société Nationale concert in 1930 had included only six of them, and Messiaen's performances of them in the 1930s were confined to selections.

The motet *O sacrum convivium* was composed in Paris, probably in early 1937, apparently as a commission from an enterprising clergyman, Abbé Brun.[47] It was published by Durand in June 1937. The scoring of the work – unusually flexible for Messiaen – is given on the first page as 'four-part mixed choir or four soloists (with organ accompaniment *ad libitum*)'. In later life, Messiaen came to a less equivocal view: in the worklist he compiled for *Musique et couleur* (1986), the forces are given as 'chœur mixte a cappella', the way it is almost always performed today. However, it is interesting to examine what little evidence there is for early performances. A copy of the first printing was annotated by Messiaen for use at his own church.[48] It has detailed organ registrations (headed 'Trinité') written in pencil – including a 16-foot Bourdon on the Récit – as well as an instruction to play the bass line of the organ part on the pedals. The work may well have been performed at the Trinité in its year of composition, probably with organ accompaniment; but the first known performance was early the following year, in a concert by Les Amis de l'Orgue, at the Trinité on 17 February 1938, in which Jehan Alain and Messiaen played their own compositions (including the premières of Alain's *Le Jardin suspendu* and his famous *Litanies*) and Jean-Jacques Grunenwald played works by an indisposed Daniel-Lesur. The recital ended with the customary 'Salut' to the Blessed Sacrament, when three works – by Messiaen (*O sacrum convivium*), Daniel-Lesur (*Ave Maria*) and Jehan Alain (*Tantum ergo*) – were performed by the singers Mme Bourdette-Vial and Lucile Darlay, with organ accompaniment. This indicates another variation in the scoring – for solo soprano(s) with organ – one that for a time evidently appealed to Messiaen, since in *Technique de mon langage musical* the scoring is given as 'four mixed voices a cappella, or soprano and organ'.[49]

O sacrum convivium enjoyed enormous success during Messiaen's lifetime. After a slow start (the first printing of 1,000 copies was not exhausted until the mid-1950s), it was reprinted eighteen times between January 1954 and December 1991, amounting to a total of over 138,000 copies. Yet it had no successors: Messiaen's only small-scale liturgical setting was destined to remain a one-off. Almost three decades later, he wrote a letter, dated 11 May 1964, to Abbé Pézeril, at the parish of Saint-Jacques-du-Haut-Pas (Paris 5ᵉ), which provides a possible explanation for his reluctance to compose any other simple liturgical pieces:

> I understand completely your desire to renew the liturgy and your horror of recent hymns – which I share! Unfortunately, I believe my music to be much too complex to be of use to you: it can only be played on the piano, on the organ, and above all by an orchestra, and is intended only for an initiated élite. I think it would be unsingable by a congregation and also by young

children. [. . .] Besides, no hymns, however successful they are, can match
the beauty of the most humble plainchant Alleluia! Why is so little plainchant sung, and even that without observing the rhythmic laws and the
neumes?[50]

The summer of 1937 was a blissful time in Messiaen's life: his son Pascal was
born on Bastille Day (14 July) 1937, to be immortalized the following year as
'Le Bébé-Pilule' in the *Chants de terre et de ciel*. Before Pascal's birth, Claire had
suffered several miscarriages, so the arrival of their son was a moment of
tremendous joy, mingled with relief, for both parents. Pascal Emmanuel
Messiaen was baptized on 22 September.

During the final months of what must have been an anxious pregnancy,
Messiaen made one of his rare forays into purely occasional music, for the
1937 Paris Exposition. The *Exposition Internationale des Arts et des Techniques
appliqués à la Vie Moderne* ran in Paris from the end of May 1937 throughout
the summer and into the autumn. But while the city was *en fête*, it was also in a
state of political chaos: Léon Blum's Popular Front government, elected in 1936,
was already doomed, and a series of short-term fixes failed to restore international confidence until the spring of 1938, when Édouard Daladier returned
to power. However, this instability did nothing to stifle the response of the arts
to the scientific and technological emphasis of the Exposition. In the visual arts,
the special exhibits included Dufy's *La Fée électricité* and Picasso's *Guernica*. Of
the new buildings erected, two examples remain today: the Palais de Chaillot
and the Palais de Tokyo (now the Musée d'Art Moderne de la Ville de Paris);
and among the temporary buildings, immense figures in a monumental
'heroic' style, brandishing hammer and sickle, glared balefully from the roof
of the Russian pavilion at the giant eagle which perched on the top of Albert
Speer's German pavilion. From a musical point of view, the most innovative
feature was the series of *Fêtes de la lumière*: spectacular sound, water and light
shows along the banks of the Seine accompanied by newly commissioned
music.

Messiaen's contribution was the *Fête des belles eaux*, given its première on
Sunday, 25 July at 10 p.m. Just as electricity had been an inspiration to
Dufy's huge painting, so an electronic instrument was Messiaen's stimulus:
his commission was scored for a sextet of ondes Martenot, the electronic
instrument invented by Maurice Martenot that caused a sensation when it
was first heard at the Paris Opéra in 1928. *Fête des belles eaux* has sometimes
been written off as little more than a *pièce d'occasion* (this tended to be
Messiaen's own later view), but it contains some music of real beauty and,
indeed, a passage of startling familiarity, one that was to be reused, pretty well
note-for-note, as the cello and piano movement, 'Louange à l'Éternité de
Jésus', in the *Quatuor pour la fin du Temps*. This music occurs twice in the

49 La Jeune France: André Jolivet, Daniel-Lesur, Messiaen and Yves Baudrier, May 1937 (photo: Lipnitzki-Viollet).

Fête des belles eaux, the first time scored for four ondes, and the second time in a version elaborated with delicate electronic rills by the other two instruments, at the point marked 'The water (at its greatest height)' in Messiaen's manuscript score.[51]

Though Messiaen is more associated with this most French of instruments than any other composer, this was his first work for the ondes Martenot. Other composers had already written for earlier versions of the instrument, including the four ondes called for by Canteloube in his opera *Vercingétorix* in 1933, and Honegger's *Sémiramis* (two ondes) in 1934, as well as Jolivet's *Danse incanta-toire* which also employed two ondes – and which had featured on the inaugural programme of La Jeune France in June 1936. The use of half a dozen of them

– in the newly developed 1937 version – was Messiaen's own choice. *Fête des belles eaux* was performed at three of the *Fêtes de la lumière*, on 25 July, 12 September and 3 October.

Another innovative feature was that all the new pieces for the *Fêtes de la lumière* were pre-recorded and relayed using 78 rpm discs. In the case of the *Fête des belles eaux* this recording was made under the direction of Ginette Martenot. The *Fêtes de la lumière* involved the illumination of the Palais de Chaillot, the Trocadéro gardens, the Eiffel Tower and many of the pavilions along the banks of the river, a spectacular fireworks display on the Eiffel Tower, and breathtaking effects using the Seine itself to produce immense jets of water; it was these aquatic marvels which were the particular focus of the extravaganza for which Messiaen provided the music. Only one fragment – the passage for four ondes later reused for the *Quatuor* – was published, and then only in a little-known musical supplement to a Belgian periodical: the 'Cahier de musique inédite' issued with the first number of the Brussels-based *Revue internationale de musique*.[52]

In the programme book for a 1974 concert by L'Itinéraire at which the Sextuor Jeanne Loriod performed the work, Messiaen recalled how he composed *Fête des belles eaux*. It is interesting to note that he described it as an

50 Maurice Martenot, inventor of the ondes Martenot (photo: Harlingue-Viollet).

'improvisation'. Written at great speed (and thus not, in Messiaen's mind, a true 'composition'), it was also the closest he ever came to the constraints of composing for film or television, since both the timings and the title were imposed on Messiaen. The 'one worthwhile passage', depicting water as a symbol of divine grace and eternity, was the music he reworked in the *Quatuor pour la fin du Temps*.

> At the time of the great Paris Exposition of 1937, a number of commissions were given to young composers for the fêtes of water and of light which took place at night on our river Seine. [. . .] The only real interest of this very old improvisation lies in the fact that it uses a sextet of ondes Martenot. [. . .] Musically speaking, there is in this hurried and foolhardy work, one worthwhile passage, which I liked (and have always liked) because it symbolizes for me an escape from the dimension of 'time', a humble approach to true Eternity. But that is just a very personal opinion, and even if it is justified, one short passage is not much to justify the effect of a whole score.[53]

In the same programme book, Maurice Martenot set out the historical perspective, and spoke warmly of Messiaen's piece and the impression it made at the time:

> When the architects Beaudouin and Lods conceived a spectacular symphony of water, of music and of light for the 1937 Exposition, they wanted music to be the driving force. Seven composers wrote scores which were intended to give life, in a way that was as carefully synchronized as possible, to the sprays of fountains, the spiralling rockets, the streams of water . . . While all made use of the expressive flexibility of the ondes, only Messiaen limited himself to a sextet of them, seeking in this paring-down the closest possible relationship between music, water and light. He succeeded to such an extent that each sequence of the work evokes the scene perfectly, as much through the choice of timbres as through the dynamic fluidity of the music, creating an extraordinary delight for the ear and the eye.[54]

Messiaen was back at the Société Nationale for its concert on 22 January 1938, in the Salle Chopin. With Marcelle Bunlet, he gave complete performances of the two song-cycles which had formed the core of their concert for La Spirale in April the previous year: Delbos's *L'Âme en bourgeon* and the *Poèmes pour Mi*. He gave the *Poèmes pour Mi* again with Bunlet a few months later, in the voice and piano version, at the third of the annual orchestral concerts of La Jeune France, which took place at the École Normale de Musique on 12 May. There are signs of economies being made, since this hall was generally used for cham-

51 Messiaen in May 1937 (photo: Lipnitzki-Viollet).

52 Claire at the piano, November 1937 (photo: Lipnitzki-Viollet).

ber music, and the large symphony orchestra of the first two concerts was replaced by a chamber orchestra, though it was again conducted by Désormière. A review by Paul Bertrand appeared in *Le Ménestrel*, and made some thoughtful comments on the *Poèmes pour Mi*:

> This work reveals a composer whose dominant quality is the sincerity with which he expresses an intense inner life. In this cycle of nine songs glorifying the Sacrament of Marriage, on words by the composer himself, he writes with great stylistic freedom: no bar lines, a modal language oscillating between plainchant and Hindu music, irregular rhythms following the natural patterns of the words, and vocal writing where psalmody alternates with an expressive vocalise.

Twelve days later, on 24 May 1938, La Jeune France made another appearance at the Tuesday concerts of *La Revue musicale*. An unsigned report in *La Revue musicale* (September–November 1938) discussed two contrasting interpretations of the *Poèmes pour Mi* given less than a fortnight apart, on 12 and 24 May 1938 – an unusual luxury for a thirty-year-old composer, especially with such a demanding work. It is particularly interesting to read the description of Bunlet's highly dramatic vocal style:

Mlle Flore Wend gave, a little later, an intimate and inward-looking per-formance of the *Poèmes pour lui* [*Mi*] by Messiaen. A few days after hearing these sung with appropriately dramatic expression by Marcelle Bunlet, it was curious to hear them again, transposed into an altogether different ambi-ence, and sung with a diametrically opposed sensibility. It is very possible, indeed probable, that Marcelle Bunlet was closer to the author's wishes, and that her violent accents and melodramatic contrasts were carefully planned to correspond with the composer's intentions. It would be presumptuous to declare a preference for a work of art interpreted in a way that differs from that which the composer wanted. In order not to fall into that trap, I shall keep my personal feelings to myself. On the other hand, I believe I can report something which helps, perhaps, to explain why the work has received such widespread praise: these songs are sufficiently substantial and complex, and exude such a true poetic sensibility, that it is possible to express them in two completely different ways.

Bunlet was especially noted for her Wagner performances. She was born in 1900 (in the Vendée) and made her début at the Paris Opéra in 1925. Three years later, she sang Brünnhilde there (in *Götterdämmerung*), and in 1931 she appeared at Bayreuth for the first time. Significantly, one of her most celebrated roles at the Paris Opéra was Ariane in Dukas's *Ariane et Barbe-bleue* which she sang in alter-nation with Germaine Lubin (the production which Messiaen had attended in January 1935). By the time Messiaen came to know her, she was very well estab-lished as an international opera singer and recitalist, and she continued to sing with Messiaen even after her retirement from the stage. Their only known recording together was made at a concert in Vichy in 1954; though Bunlet's voice is clearly starting to age, its power is unmistakable, and Messiaen's piano playing (both in Debussy's *Cinq Poèmes de Baudelaire* and his own *Harawi*) has the kind of calm, relaxed authority that comes from years of familiarity with a musical partner: it is clear that they were a formidable duo. After Bunlet's retirement, she taught in Strasbourg for a number of years. She died in 1991.[55]

In March 1938 works by all of La Jeune France were featured for the first time in a concert outside France: the Société Philharmonique de Bruxelles devoted a programme to the group's works (along with music by Saint-Saëns and Roussel) in one of the Concerts Symphoniques Populaires, at the Palais des Beaux-Arts on 18 March 1938, conducted by Hans Ebbeke.[56] This was a time when Messiaen's name was appearing with increasing frequency in concert programmes abroad, and as a result he started to travel overseas. In June 1938 he visited London for the first time, to play two movements from *La Nativité du Seigneur* at the ISCM Festival (on the organ of the Concert Hall at Broadcast-ing House on 22 June), and to perform the whole of the cycle at St Alban the

Martyr, Holborn (on 25 June). It was thanks largely to Felix Aprahamian, Honorary Secretary of the Organ Music Society, that Messiaen's music had already been introduced to London audiences by Noëlie Pierront, André Marchal and André Fleury. Aprahamian also made the arrangements for Messiaen's London visit, sending him the specifications of the two organs he was to play, and ensuring that the trip went smoothly. On 13 June Messiaen wrote to Aprahamian with a frank admission about his lack of English, and characteristically diligent plans for rehearsals: 'I will arrive in London on Tuesday 21 [June] at 6 a.m. and will stay until the afternoon of Sunday 26. Would you like to come and find me at the station? As I don't speak a word of English it will be impossible for me to sort myself out. [. . .] As for my working hours, I will be at the organ all day on the 21st and 22nd, so as to rehearse as much as possible.'[57]

La Nativité was greeted with dumbfounded incomprehension in more tradi-tional quarters. Archibald Farmer, writing in the *Musical Times*, seemed to believe that any enthusiasm for Messiaen was a passing craze: 'As a composer he is enjoying at the moment a vogue, owing to the support of some whose approach to music is rather more sensational than intellectual. Whether this will endure I very much doubt.'[58] The verdict of London critics in general was largely negative, a striking contrast with the French reception of Messiaen during the 1930s. Even so, Messiaen enjoyed his first trip across the English Channel, and he was to return many times after World War II; eventually the British critical tide, thanks to writers like Felix Aprahamian, David Drew and Colin Mason, turned decisively in his favour.

The first year for which any Messiaen diary is known to survive is 1939. The earliest significant event recorded in it was on 23 January: the third concert in the 1938–9 season of the contemporary music society Triton, at the École Normale, when Bunlet and Messiaen gave the first performance of a work billed as *Prismes: Six poèmes d'Olivier Messiaen, pour soprano et piano*. Within a mat-ter of weeks (in time for the work's publication in April 1939) Messiaen was to change this to *Chants de terre et de ciel*; the individual songs are listed with the same titles and subtitles as the published edition, with the tiny exception of 'Minuit pile et face', described as 'pour la peur' (in the programme) rather than 'pour la mort' (in the score).

Very possibly, Messiaen's first title was intended to describe the way the spir-itual dimension of marriage – now extended to parenthood – is viewed from different perspectives. 'Bail avec Mi', which opens the cycle, is a love song very much in the vein of the *Poèmes pour Mi*. In 'Antienne du Silence' Claire is replaced as the object of contemplation by an angel, inspiring one of Messiaen's most inscrutable creations to date, with the voice floating amid a texture of rig-orously independent lines. The central pair of songs, dedicated to 'mon petit

Pascal', come firmly down to earth with a celebration of childhood and its bois-terous and playful moods. After this idyll comes a tormented scena ('Minuit pile et face') complete with a macabre fugal dance, a nightmare dispelled by a meditation on the untroubled innocence of the sleeping child. Finally, Pascal's name is the cue for a paean of praise to Easter, and the new life symbolized by Christ's resurrection.

Michel-Léon Hirsch in *Le Ménestrel* (3 February 1939, p.28) wrote a warmly appreciative review of the cycle, but he also alluded to the 'isolated protests' which it aroused. Messiaen responded to the controversy with 'Autour d'une parution', an article in the April issue of *Le Monde musical*, in which he provided a robust defence of his new work:

> My *Chants de terre et de ciel* (for soprano and piano) has just been pub-lished by Durand. As this is a very individual work (more than just its title!) which has been, is, and will be vigorously discussed and attacked, I want to provide some commentary on it. As the author of both the poems and the music, I can plead neither for nor against, but to set out honestly my intentions.
>
> First of all, I wanted to compose a religious, Catholic work. I wrote recently in *Art sacré*: 'If there is such a thing as essentially religious art, then it is equally essentially diverse. Why? Because it expresses ideas about a sin-gle being, who is God, but a being who is ever-present and who can be found in everything, above everything, and below everything.' Every subject can be a religious one on condition that it is viewed through the eye of one who believes. Why should 'Bail avec Mi' (for my wife) be any less religious than

53 Messiaen and Pascal in 1938.

54 Messiaen with Pascal at the rue des Plantes, 1938.

55 Messiaen reading in a deckchair, Petichet, 1938.

56 Claire tending her cacti, 1938.

57 Messiaen at the piano, Petichet, 1938 or 1939.

'Antienne du Silence' (for the day of the Guardian Angels)? Why should the same spirit of faith not run through 'Arc-en-ciel d'innocence' (for my little Pascal) and 'Résurrection' (for Easter Day)?

The third song, 'Danse du Bébé-Pilule' (for my little Pascal) has caused more surprise than the others. It has been said to resemble – as has the whole cycle – a nursery rhyme ['enfantine']. Written for my son, it seeks to express the exuberant and unbounded enchantment of childhood: 'The fascination of stairs, surprises behind doors; all the light birds fly from your hands. Light birds, pebbles, refrains, creamy light. As blue fish, as blue moons, the halos of earth and water. One lung alone in one reed.' I really cannot understand what connection there is between these words and those of nursery rhymes.

The heart of the work is really the fifth song: 'Minuit pile et face' (for death). If you realize that I wanted to depict – in a setting of nocturnal bells – the remorse, the prayers, the anguish and the agony, followed by the heavenly calm of the dead, then you must also admit that the end of the poem can have a poignant effect (and not a childish or comic one).

It is clear that Messiaen felt the need to defend his work, and his intentions in writing it, but his concluding paragraph is the most arresting. As a response to criticism, it is a robust assertion of his musical integrity:

Now I turn to the matter of musical language. No – it isn't crazy! For many years I have studied harmony, fugue and composition so that I can lay claim to knowing my craft. And if there is more vigour in this work than in previous ones, my favourite 'modes of limited transposition' are still there, and also my juxtaposed harmonies, my pedal-groups, my cluster-chords. Still in place as well are my customary rhythms, based on added note values, on augmentation, on the absence of measured bars, offering a very simple but completely unconventional use of note values and duration. Besides, I am not alone in this. My models were first Debussy, then plainchant and the work of the great Hindu rhythmician Çarngadeva. Certain pages of Schoenberg and Jolivet, certain French and Russian traditional melodies have moved me as well. Add to that the fact that I love Massenet, because his music is tonal and well harmonized, and you have some idea of my style. As for those who moan about my so-called dissonances, I say to them quite simply that I am not dissonant: they should wash their ears out![59]

The aristocratic supporters of La Jeune France had formed themselves during 1938 into 'Les Amis de la Jeune France' and private concerts became a feature of the group's activities.[60] In one of these, on 24 February 1939, at the home of M. et Mme Edme Sommier (57 quai d'Orsay), the programme ended with a comparatively rare performance of *La Mort du Nombre,* given by the singers Madeleine Dubuis and Georges Cathelat, the violinist André Proffit and Messiaen at the piano. The same week, Messiaen visited Milhaud with Yvonne de Casa Fuerte to discuss plans for the forthcoming concert given by La Sérénade in which Messiaen appeared as both organist and composer. This took place on 14 March, in the Trinité, and the programme included Satie's *Messe des pauvres,* the first performance of Delbos's *Paraphrase* for organ, six movements from *La Nativité,* Sauguet's *Petite Messe pastorale,* Poulenc's *Litanies à la Vierge Noire* (sung by the Chorale Yvonne Gouverné), and, to finish, de Grigny's *Dialogue sur les Grands Jeux.* In the handsome programme book issued for this event, Messiaen is specifically named as the player for each of the solo organ items, including the Satie – a surprising choice for him, though of all Satie's works this is perhaps the only one which might have had any appeal for Messiaen. As no other organist is listed, it is probable that Messiaen also played for the Poulenc *Litanies.*

Billed as a 'Concert spirituel', this event was a new departure for the resolutely secular La Sérénade. Stan Golestan in *Le Figaro* (24 March) expressed a mixture of amazement and pleasure:

Who would have thought it? The worldly and daring La Sérénade showing penitence among the shadows of the columns in the Trinité. The Marquise de Casa Fuerte welcomed her customary audience from the Salle Gaveau, but to the sounds of the *Messe des pauvres* by Erik Satie, a *Paraphrase* by Claire Delbos, and the *Petite Messe pastorale* by Henri Sauguet. The rose window at the centre of the programme was Messiaen's *La Nativité du Seigneur.*

In sum, highly attractive, simple in style but nobly conceived, with the Chorale Yvonne Gouverné enhancing a beautiful liturgical ambience.

La Sérénade was a distinguished society which boasted Auric, Désormière, Markevich, Milhaud, Nabokoff, Poulenc and Sauguet among its active committee members, and a group of founders which constituted a veritable constellation of Parisian musical patrons: the Princesse Edmond de Polignac, the Vicomtesse de Noailles, Marie-Blanche de Polignac, Coco Chanel, Edward James and Comte Étienne de Beaumont. Of these *mécènes* it was Étienne de Beaumont who was to take a particular interest in Messiaen during the 1940s, and who was to promote performances of his music in the dark years of the Occupation.

Marcelle Bunlet was now firmly established as Messiaen's singer of choice. On 23 May 1939 there was a gathering at Bunlet's house (4 villa Malakoff, near the Trocadéro) for 'Une heure de musique contemporaine'. The programme shows that Messiaen and Bunlet performed three songs from the *Poèmes pour Mi*, five from Delbos's *L'Âme en bourgeon* and the whole of the *Chants de terre et de ciel*. Just over a week later, on 1 June, Messiaen was back

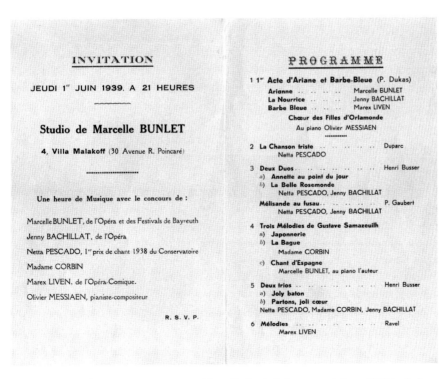

58 Programme for a private concert at Marcelle Bunlet's home on 1 June 1939, including Act I of Dukas's *Ariane et Barbe-bleue* with Messiaen at the piano.

59 Messiaen and Pascal at Petichet, 1938.

60 Claire leaning against a mantelpiece.

at the villa Malakoff for another of Bunlet's private concerts – one that would have been a special occasion for him. Described in the programme as 'pianiste-compositeur', Messiaen accompanied Bunlet and several other singers in works by Duparc, Busser, Gaubert, Samazeuilh and Ravel, and he served as the piano-cum-orchestra for the complete first act of Dukas's opera *Ariane et Barbe-bleue* which opened the evening.

On 20 March Messiaen noted in his diary that he had written an article, 'Autour d'une œuvre d'orgue', which appeared in the April issue of the magazine *L'Art sacré*.[61] This is considerably more wide-ranging than its title might suggest, with discussion of the religious nature of the *Poèmes pour Mi* and the *Chants de terre et de ciel*, as well as orchestral works and, finally, organ pieces, especially *La Nativité*, whose musical language Messiaen described as one which caused some consternation, but which 'really seeks to delight more than to shock'. On 14 April he was visited by the Benedictine composer and theologian Dom Clément Jacob (1906–77), and two days later he played *La Nativité* for Jacob at the Trinité, when the poet René de Obaldia was also present.

During spring 1939 Messiaen was busy compiling the harmony exercises which he was going to include in a collection to be published by Leduc. On 19 May he went to visit his old harmony teacher Noël Gallon to show him these exercises, written for his classes at the École Normale and the Schola Cantorum over the past few years, in the styles of various composers from Monteverdi to Messiaen. One had been published a couple of years earlier: the supplement of *Le Monde musical* for 27 February 1937 included a

61 The villa du Danube, in the 19th arrondissement, to which the Messiaens moved in 1938 (photo: Peter Hill).

62 Interior of the house at the villa du Danube.

'Chant à harmoniser', a 36-bar melody marked 'Très lent, expressif' with a time signature of 6/8 and a key signature of six sharps. A note at the foot of the music announced that 'L'harmonisation de l'auteur paraîtra dans le prochain numéro'. So it did: in the 31 March issue, *Le Monde musical* published Messiaen's 'solution' to the harmonization of his extended melody, a four-part realization in open score written in soprano, alto, tenor and bass clefs. The subsequent publication of this realization in the *Vingt Leçons d'harmonie*, issued by Leduc in May 1940, is identical to the version in *Le Monde musical* apart from the final chord (a bar longer in the earlier printing). In the Leduc collection it appears as no.15: 'Chant donné (style mi-Franck, mi-Debussy)'.

The fourth – and last – of the annual Jeune France concerts was on 20 June 1939, in a new venue: Rolf de Maré's Archives Internationales de la Danse at 6 rue Vital, Paris 16ᵉ. The programme included Bunlet and Messiaen in Jolivet's *Romantiques* as well as the *Chants de terre et de ciel*. Just over a week later, on Wednesday, 28 June, Messiaen left for his summer holidays in Petichet. He was due to travel to Venice in September for a performance of the *Chants de terre et de ciel* with Bunlet at the Teatro La Fenice (as part of the ISCM Festival), but this was abandoned with the outbreak of war: a poignant note in Messiaen's diary stated that the concert was 'postponed'. As usual, the summer was Messiaen's most productive time for composition, and at Petichet on 25 August he finished *Les Corps glorieux*, recalling later that it was 'the last work I composed as a civilian. It was just being finished when I was called up.'[62]

Messiaen was in Petichet when France declared war on Germany on 3 September 1939. He was apparently the only man in the village to be called up

63 Claire with Pascal in 1939.

64 Claire, Pascal and Messiaen in 1939.

for the army (others were sent to work in the nearby coal mine at La Mure) and he returned to Paris to take up his posting.[63] During August, Claire and Pascal had left for her family's château at Neussargues to be with her mother and sister; they were to remain there for the next two years. During his time in the army and as a prisoner of war, Messiaen kept no diary, but it is possible to reconstruct some of his activities during this painful period in his life. Letters from friends always gave him the greatest pleasure, and on 2 November he wrote to Jean Langlais, recording the sender as 'Soldat Messiaen Olivier, 620ᵉ R.I. Pionniers, 2ᵉ Bataillon, 5ᵉ Compagnie – secteur postale 42':

I was infinitely touched by your letter. The slightest expression of affection goes straight to my heart at the moment, and there is no better time than when the letters arrive. I am certain that civilian life – while maybe less painful than the military – means that you have to endure some quite disagreeable changes in time of war. [...] As for me, my grazed and blackened hands, manhandling a pickaxe, the flies, the unbelievably heavy weights (ranging from tree trunks to lithographic stones) – these all prevent me from getting very close to music. I try nevertheless to read a few orchestral scores (packed in my bag on top of my survival kit) when I have a free moment, so as not to lose touch. Besides, I left a work unfinished when I was mobilized. I receive a letter from my wife almost every day, which is a consolation beyond words for me. But I can't watch my little boy growing up! ... A terrible sorrow! Pray for peace, and also for your old pal.[64]

The 'unfinished work' is a reference to *Les Corps glorieux*. But composition was not really a priority for Messiaen. As he admitted to Langlais, Claire's regular letters to the front – with news of her and young Pascal – were his greatest source of joy. One such letter survives, a long and extraordinarily moving document which gives an evocative description of Claire's life with the two-year-old Pascal at Neussargues. It is dated Friday 24 November, continued on Saturday 25 November:

A letter which does not have a happy beginning! Wanting, my darling, to protect my nice inner warmth against the outer cold that descends after dinner, I slid into bed with a nice hot water bottle at my feet. What a cheerful Mie she was, getting ready to write to her old man! I open the Bible [. . .] and, carried away by my reading, grab hold of the ink bottle. Splat! all over the sheet, the flowery apron, my sweet little pale blue sweater and the top of my skirt! No more keeping warm for me! It was a three-quarters naked Mi who rushed into the kitchen to heat up some water and soak all her fancy nightclothes in a basin of saving suds. It was only 'Aunt Rose's' sheet which was left to its fate (a good rinsing with bleach at the next wash, and there won't be a mark left), and the poor Bible in which Psalm 45 (not the one you showed me, numbered here as 46) will bear the memory of Mi's outburst of trust in the strength of Yahweh's protection.

So much for that! Then . . . a dull thud in the nearby corridor where Pascal sleeps. A call: 'Mummy! Big Teddy has fallen out!' Poor Mummy, who had slid back with such relief into her warm bed. Will I ever get back to reading my Psalm? With Pascal tucked back in and the pale caramel figure of Big Teddy snuggled up against his master's blond head (as for minute Tiny Teddy, continually manhandled and dragged hither and yon, he too went missing for a moment), I go back to bed. An excellent lesson in trusting to the protective power of the Almighty, this psalm, my Zouvier,[65] is even more consoling and fortifying because it takes account of all possible outcomes of events – the thought that directs it is an unbelievable and infinite goodness.

Pascal is overexcited by the ink incident and goes on chattering; the little voice pipes up: 'Darling Daddy . . . Pascal's Mummy . . . Kiss for Daddy . . . letterbox . . . goat . . . Daddy there (the photo).' Talking about the photo over the small bed: I've put Pascal's bed up against the wall opposite the one where it used to be. It's better like that, but I've deliberately left Daddy's photo and Jesus on the Cross where they were so that, when the young gentleman is letting off steam in the corridor, he can, in passing, give an affectionate glance at the two people he loves ('Take that always, as you go past' – do you remember, my darling, those little furtive, discreet kisses your Mie used to give her old man as she went past?).

Sometimes it's a caress, sometimes a big kiss. It's very touching to see the dear little boy: Jesus is placed rather high up, so Pascal has to stretch slightly to reach Him, but Daddy is below Him, a bit lower down. Pascal's fat little bottom moves to the right, his little legs bend, taking him down a few centimetres: and his little mouth is just level with Daddy's heart. Meanwhile his 'active life' continues as ever: either pushing his parrot-on-wheels or else curling up in a ball on the floor, with his legs stretched out over his head, shouting with glee. Then silence descends on the corridor. It's a respite for Mummy, who extends her 'mixed joy' to the Light of her Life, and who is no doubt on the edge of sleep, unless he is on guard duty this evening – something which is very distressing and makes the heart of your Mie beat a little faster with fear of the unchanging stillness in the cold of the night – but which gives her beloved artist a chance to read his orchestral scores. Good night, my dearest love. Have you still got a fairly comfortable mattress and bed? Let me know every now and then all about your surroundings. I remain your Mie, full of love and hope.

Saturday
My vanity promised you yesterday a copy of various passages from *The Book of Wisdom* [in fact, Proverbs 31] which relate to a Mie-type character. Here they are: 'the heart of her husband doth safely trust in her . . . She seeketh wool, and flax, and worketh willingly with her hands . . . She considereth a field and buyeth it: with the fruit of her hands she buyeth a vineyard (Petichet, rue du Danube) . . . Her candle goeth not out by night . . . She hath set her hand (or her mind) to important matters and her fingers hold the distaff (composition; my Zouvier's sweater) . . . She maketh herself coverings of tapestry (Mie's dear little bonnets) . . . Her husband is known in the gates of the city (the works of Zouvier are becoming ever more powerful and filled with life) . . . She looketh well to the ways of her household, and eateth not the bread of idleness . . . Her sons arise up, and call her blessed; her husband also, and he praiseth her.'

Oh the vanity of Mie! But no! Simply a few hours of satisfaction, spent calling to mind these various points of contact with that ideal of strength and of completeness of life which she would so greatly have wished to realize within herself, and which her moral and physical weakness has prevented from rising beyond the level of wishful thinking. The eighth level of the spiritual heights.

1 p.m.: Heavens! I had only just lain down for my siesta when there was Adèle already on the doorstep. Pascal was stirring and my letter wasn't finished. And I have to post another one too, to the Banque de France. Help like that is more disruptive than anything else. It destroyed the peace of

mind in which I'd gone to bed, deeply touched by a loving gesture from our little son. I'd been thinking of Peace and I suddenly said to Pascal: 'Just wait, my darling, when the war's over the bells in Jesus's House will ring really loudly', and thinking about that hour of deliverance made me sob even as I spoke (I'm still weeping as I write this). Pascal was distraught at my emotion and hurled himself on me: 'Mummy, little Mummy. Come, come, Mummy, come here.' And his little arms were held out to give a passionate embrace to his poor Mummy. I repeated what I'd said, with the same mixture of distress and hope, and my little boy embraced me in desperation. Five minutes earlier he had been behaving appallingly at table.

Talking of our dear boy, Oli, I should like to suggest something to you. The poor little fellow is so keen on having a toy truck 'Like Bob's'. I hardly ever mention it, but you alluded to it in your first letter 'for him' and also his two other toys and the big car from 'Tante Rose' have whetted his appetite. Are you absolutely determined to keep this big surprise for the day when Peace comes? Will Pascal be able to tell the difference between your arrival on leave and the end of the war? Won't he be disappointed (despite his real and absolute happiness at seeing his Daddy) if behind Daddy there is not a 'Like Bob's'?[66] In any case he's so tall and strong now that for him to get any wear out of it he would already have to have the largest size, to fit a 4- or 5-year-old. Could you see your way to *bringing the moment forward* and agreeing to this large expense (nearly 200 francs, I think – 150 anyway, because of the size ...)? On the off chance I got hold of some toy catalogues from La Samaritaine and Le Bazar, which are the shops that offer the best deal. Please feel free to say what you think. If you prefer to wait until the clouds of war

65 Pascal in his pedal car.

have lifted, tell me. Otherwise I'll order it and hide it until you arrive on leave. I would much prefer – if we had the choice – that you take this leave at the very end of December – or the end of January, if possible. My darling, I must write my letter to the bank. I leave you – all Adèle's fault – rather abruptly but not without telling you again that you are my little all-beloved, my reason for living and my glory. Olivier, my pet, I love you so much. May nothing make you suffer, be happy and confident – and brave in the face of days without a letter from me. Keep your spirits up as best you can. To that end, I slip my hand into yours, having first kissed it tenderly. I am your little Mie x Pascal x[67]

Messiaen's war
1940–1944

Early in 1940, 'soldat pionnier d'infanterie O.M.' wrote to the journal *L'Orgue* about his experiences as a soldier:

> After digging holes or sawing up trees, carrying heavy loads or pushing trucks, it's hard to think about music, to return to it as to a comforting elder sister. However, every night, during the hours which are meant to be for sleeping, I resolved to read a few pages of the pocket scores which are arranged with loving care at the bottom of my kit-bag. Whenever I have been able to find a light, I have kept my resolution, and I have read them closely, in a corner, analysing forms, harmonies and timbres in symphonies by Beethoven, *Ma Mère l'Oye* by Ravel, *Les Noces* by Stravinsky, and *Horace victorieux* by Honegger. Another musical joy was meeting the composer and conductor Maurice Jaubert, at present a captain in the sappers, with whom I was able to chat about things other than the din of the shells or the time of the early morning parade.
>
> Finally, I was allowed – and even asked – to play the organ on 11 November, on Christmas Day and on 1 January. The same privilege has been granted to me on some Sundays. Here, I have found abandoned instruments, riddled with ciphers. However, among all of them, two at least were very good. One, a Cavaillé-Coll, is equipped with lovely 8-foot foundation stops and powerful reeds. I played a few pieces on it by heart (the memory is a tenacious thing!): the sixth Trio Sonata by Bach, the Toccata and Fugue in D minor by the same, two Noëls by Daquin and Widor's Toccata. The other organ was modern, with lots of gentle mixtures. I treated myself to numerous improvisations, in an avant-garde style, with one solo for the 16-foot Bourdon and the Tierce on a harmonic scheme which would have frightened Schoenberg himself! Here's a curious thing: unlike the pious Parisian ladies, the soldiers were not shocked by these surprising sonorities!

66 Messiaen and other soldiers enjoying a moment of relaxation, Metz, 1940.

While out on marches, trudging over bridges covered with sacks, or during the hours on watch when the only company is an enormous red moon and my feet feel as if they're burning with cold in the deep snow, I often find myself singing certain melodies, certain favourite rhythms, and going over in my head the most important parts of my latest organ work, interrupted by the war ... Whether it was a presentiment or a painful irony, I don't know – but it deals with the Resurrection of the bodies. Will I ever be able to complete it? I'll wait, because you have to know how to wait, especially as a soldier, and so 'I hitch my wagon to a star' (as the Mexican proverb says), to the only star which is really useful at the moment: Christian hope.[1]

Messiaen's letter to *L'Orgue* has several touching details: his mention of meeting Maurice Jaubert (*mort pour la France* a few months later in the fighting of June 1940), the solace he drew from reading his treasured pocket scores, the receptiveness of his fellow-soldiers to his most daring improvisations, and a rather despairing reference to *Les Corps glorieux*. He was certainly not suited to the tough manual work which was required in the Pioneers, and he applied for a transfer to work as a nurse. But he wanted above all to find some kind of war work which would involve music, and wrote to Claude Arrieu on 31 January 1940 to ask for her help:

Since you are in Rennes, you must have occasion to see Tony Aubin. I have already written to him (he has not replied). Here's why: you know that many musicians (including several of our old friends at the Conservatoire) are with radio stations working in music, being considered indispensable and mobilized *in situ*. [. . .] In a radio station I could take on any of the duties which they might give me: producer, broadcaster, announcer, chorus master, organist, pianist. The thing which would best suit me, because I have a special aptitude for it, would be to work as a piano accompanist for soloists, singers, etc. I am not a bad pianist, know a lot of music and can *sight-read anything with ease*. It is necessary to send a request for an *immediate recall* for me to the Colonel Commandant of the 620th regiment of the Pioneer Infantry, postal sector 42. The head of the radio station needs to do that. If I were to be in Rennes with you and Aubin, my wife and little Pascal could live there, which would make me happy![2]

Nothing came of the request to Tony Aubin, nor of Arrieu's follow-up. However, while Messiaen was putting a brave face on things, Claire was working hard on his behalf and kept in touch with her husband's most loyal supporters in Paris, including Marcel Dupré, who wrote to her on 29 January 1940:

67 Claire composing.

I have waited a little while to reply to your kind letter, because I had hoped to see you and your father-in-law at the same time. I was delighted to see him when he came to St-Sulpice yesterday morning. I asked him to sit close to me, and on the beautiful organ I played for him *Apparition de l'Église éternelle*. He gave us a touching and sumptuous present: his splendid translation of Shakespeare.[3]

I hope to see [Emmanuel] Bondeville on Thursday about the Radio. In any event, I will find out whether we have any serious hope or not. There are two other possibilities which I learned of yesterday. As you realize, I have a passionate desire, just as you do, to succeed on behalf of my dear and inspired kid![4]

It is a measure of Dupré's commitment to Messiaen's cause that he persuaded a musically inclined officer in the French army to take a personal interest in the case. On 4 April Commandant [Major] Parisot wrote to Messiaen – then stationed near Verdun – from his office at 93 boulevard Montparnasse:

Maître Marcel Dupré has brought your current situation to my attention and he has stressed the necessity of placing you in a posting which will enable you to continue dedicating yourself to your art. Personally, I share this opinion entirely, for I am a fervent admirer of Maître Marcel Dupré.

I assure you of my complete support and will do everything possible for you. You understand that my actions are unofficial and that the examination of your military situation which I propose to undertake cannot have a formal character. I ask you to send me a sort of military curriculum vitae, a description of your present activities, and to indicate what your wishes are. Please send me as well the names of your superior officers.[5]

Historical events soon made any question of a new posting an irrelevance: in May the German army entered France and established overwhelming military superiority. Verdun fell on 15 June and Messiaen was among the many thousands of French servicemen taken prisoner and placed in makeshift camps. He was taken to a huge field in Toul (just west of Nancy), where he soon met other musicians, notably the clarinettist Henri Akoka and the cellist Étienne Pasquier. This encounter was to produce an immediate burst of creativity from Messiaen, recalled over half a century later by Pasquier:

> While we were waiting to be transferred, the Germans had assembled us in the open air, near Nancy. One of our friends was a clarinettist who had been allowed to keep his instrument. His name was Henri Akoka. [. . .] Messiaen composed a solo clarinet piece for Akoka which was to become the third movement of the *Quatuor pour la fin du Temps*. It was in this field that Akoka sight-read the piece for the first time. I served as his music stand, that is I held the music for him. He groused from time to time, because the composer made him do difficult things: 'I'm never going to get it,' he said. 'But you will, you will. You'll see,' Messiaen replied.[6]

This field was also where Messiaen first met Guy Bernard-Delapierre, an event of immense significance to both men, though they could not have known this at the time. Bernard-Delapierre's most important article on Messiaen, 'Souvenirs sur Olivier Messiaen', appeared in 1945 (just after the première of the *Trois petites Liturgies*), in the lavish Lausanne-based art periodical *Formes et couleurs*. The author's name is given as 'Guy Bernard'. The article includes an evocative account of their first meeting, under grim circumstances:

> The first time I saw Olivier Messiaen, he appeared to me like a character from legend amid the most horrendously real of realities. It was in June 1940, that time of catastrophe, that fate brought us together, in one of those improvised camps in Lorraine into which the Nazi army all too easily scooped up thousands of exhausted, betrayed soldiers as though into a net. [. . .] It was in these tragic surroundings that I got to know Messiaen. In his pale, thoughtful face, his gaze was as utterly calm as the sky above. I was struck by the kind of tender deference with which his faithful comrades treated him. They included Étienne Pasquier, the cellist of the Pasquier Trio, [Henri] Akoka, a cultivated young man who played the clarinet, and a music-hall singer whose name I've forgotten. When some of the more resourceful of us managed finally, by some miracle, to get hold of some food,

I can still see these comrades of Messiaen bringing him a spoonful of soup or a quarter of a litre of water – treasures beyond price, which he accepted with the unemotional gentleness of some Hindu anchorite. Despite his hunger, despite his thirst, he seemed far away, he appeared to be thinking of something else: of something very pure and brilliant, something which moved very slowly in the distance, something which unceasingly absorbed his gaze, full of life and love. [. . .] There was a story that he had retreated dragging a pram that contained a cargo of miniature scores – his musical library and his most precious possession. He spent his time reading them and lent me some of them including, I remember, Stravinsky's *Les Noces*. It was this tiny score that got my brain working again and restored my hope. [. . .]

Messiaen and I would wander through this strange village [i.e. the camp] discussing all sorts of topics – music, religion, philosophy. Things of the mind were resuming their rightful place. It was then that Messiaen confided to me his views on the music of the future, the form of the works he wanted to create, the inspiration that he felt to be his. [. . .] In general, he said, the means of expression in Western music make too little use of certain rich possibilities. Our music is too impoverished in the areas of modes and rhythms. So in my music I use new modes and new rhythms. All that leads to modal polyphony (by superimposing modes) and rhythmic counterpoint (by superimposing rhythms), which bring a definite enrichment to the expressive and architectural possibilities of music. Nor do I hesitate to take my inspiration from the forms of plainsong and of Hindu ragas.

Messiaen also confirmed that he found his inspiration in Christian faith. 'Religious matters', he has written, 'include everything: they are God and his entire creation.' I underline these last words because it is precisely Messiaen's love for nature, both for what is most obvious in it and for what is most hidden, that gives listeners to his music that hallucinatory impression of making contact with the heart, with the essence of things. In his music, objects become as transparent as in Cubist painting. But in this manner of transcending reality, the wind of the spirit never dries out this love that goes to the centre of things so that it becomes a dangerous abstraction. Also, this Christian mysticism often expresses itself, side by side with purely contemplative melodies, in an utterly pagan violence, an abandonment to sensuality such as we no longer find except among 'primitive' peoples still living at one with nature. With Messiaen, the senses are never in opposition to the spirit. They engage immediately and directly with the physical joys and sufferings of creation. With Messiaen, music has suddenly regained the religious, cosmic sense that it had lost for so long in Europe, with all that the word 'religious' contains of magic in its original sense – the sometimes terrifying element of magic that is found today only in atomic science or in a study of the stars. Messiaen indeed, even if he fills any number of note-books with the astonishing rhythmic and melodic virtuosity of birdsong (which he often uses in his music), is also a passionate reader of the latest textbooks on physics and astronomy, the sites of the 'marvellous' in our times.

All that formed part of Messiaen's conversation in the prison camp. Rainbows, stained glass, perfumes, the dances of planets and atoms – he spoke of all that, suggesting to me an unknown music full of rhythms and new colours of sound. He would also read me poems by Reverdy and talk about Eluard – they were his favourite poets. [. . .] Those were the topics of conversation following our strange meeting. Finally, one day while I was asleep he left with the comrades of his unit to follow a different path from mine. When I woke up, his place was empty. But on my chest I found a small piece of paper with his Paris address. This meeting was to haunt my dreams for years before I was at last able to hear his music.

In July 1940 Messiaen was transported to Silesia, and on 19 August he wrote to Claire (at Neussargues) on German PoW stationery:

Ma Mie chérie,
For the last month I have been a prisoner in Germany and I am sending you my first letter today; you should receive a second one in August. Reply to me at the following address: Messiaen, Olivier, prisoner no.35333, Stalag VIIIA, Germany. Are you in Paris? How is Pascal? How are you? I am well. I have a kit-bag, my miniature scores and some underwear. Could you send me a parcel containing: a razor, a shaving brush, razor blades, shaving soap, shoelaces, a kit-bag, a sweater (a large one!), a pair of socks, a handkerchief, chocolate, sugar, cake, gingerbread, altogether weighing 5 kilos (ask at the Post Office)? Embrace for me my father, Alain, Mario Meunier and Alfred Cortot. Give my news to Abbé Hemmer, to Mme Hunger and to Marcel Dupré, so that I can go back to my posts as organist, and as a professor of harmony at the Paris Conservatoire. Every day, I pray for Pascal and for you, and ask for all of us to be granted patience, a gift of the Holy Spirit. I long for my home, my music, and above all for your sweet presence, and I embrace you with all my heart. I hope this note arrives quite quickly so as to calm your worries! Stroke my little Pascal's fair hair, and a huge kiss for my Mie whom I love.[7]

The reference in this letter to a post 'as a professor of harmony at the Paris Conservatoire' is intriguing: it suggests that Messiaen may already have been approached about applying for the job before the outbreak of war, and certainly before he was taken captive. Interesting, too, is the mention of Cortot – his erst-while employer at the École Normale – among those to be greeted, and it is certainly possible that Cortot had put in a good word on Messiaen's behalf. However, at the time of writing his letter, it is most unlikely that Messiaen knew of the pianist's involvement (starting in June–July 1940) in forming the artistic policy of the Vichy regime. It is probable that he was aware of Cortot's more honourable conduct during the 'phoney' war (September 1939–June 1940) when he cancelled his engagements in order to be at the service of the French government's cultural administration, particularly to coordinate all artistic activity likely to be a source of entertainment or comfort to the troops.[8]

During Messiaen's time as a prisoner, Claire was able to send him recent photographs of Pascal and herself; some have survived, each stamped 'Stalag VIIIA 49 geprüft' on the reverse. The camp was situated near the town of Görlitz (or Zgorzelec: the town is now German at one end and Polish at the other), just over 130 miles (210 km) south-east of Berlin and about 70 miles (110 km) due east of Dresden. One description was published in London soon after the end of the war:

> The former huts of the Hitler Jugend had a new identity. By early 1940 they had been surrounded by wire, overlooked by sentry-boxes and signposted *Stammlager* VIIIA. Polish prisoners, the first arrivals, numbered fifteen thousand by June [1940] and were being employed in building huts until absorbed in factories. A Franco-Belgian influx in June and July of that year overcrowded the camp still further, thousands being accommodated in tents under primitive conditions. When it is realized that some eight thousand Belgians and forty thousand French reached a camp of thirty barracks, each capable of holding five hundred under crowded conditions, the immediate effects are apparent. [. . .][9]

Messiaen's time as a PoW in Görlitz was to produce one of his most remarkable works, the *Quatuor pour la fin du Temps*. Two movements (the two 'Louanges') had earlier incarnations: that for cello is a reworking of part of the *Fête des belles eaux* (1937, see pp.73–6 above), and the concluding violin 'louange' existed in a primitive form as the second part of the *Diptyque* for organ (1930); another movement ('Abîme des oiseaux') was the one that had been composed for the clarinettist Henri Akoka during the time in the makeshift camp at Toul. The 'Intermède' was the first movement to be written after transportation to Görlitz, probably in August or September 1940, when it was rehearsed by Akoka, Pasquier and the violinist Jean Le Boulaire in the camp's washrooms. Once it was agreed by the authorities that a piano would be found for Messiaen, he got down in earnest to composing the rest of the *Quatuor*, beginning with the first movement, using manuscript paper (printed in Germany) provided by one of the guards, Hauptmann Karl-Erich Brüll.[10]

Thus, the startling fact is that four of the eight movements already existed in some form before Messiaen had the idea of writing the *Quatuor*. His point of departure was the 'unpretentious little trio'. This became the fourth movement (the 'Intermède'), oddly out of place in its Apocalyptic surroundings, but musically important as the source of a number of motifs used in the four newly composed movements, as well as the theme of the sixth movement, 'Danse de la fureur, pour les sept trompettes'.

The instruments available to Messiaen made a problematic ensemble in terms of blend and balance. The answer was to explore them in different combinations. There is one unaccompanied solo (the clarinet's 'Abîme des oiseaux'), solos with piano accompaniment for cello and for violin ('Louange à l'Éternité de Jésus' and 'Louange à l'Immortalité de Jésus'), and a trio (the 'Intermède'). The second movement ('Vocalise, pour l'Ange qui annonce la fin du Temps') is in effect another trio, its long central section scored for strings with piano, although all four instruments contribute to the explosive gestures at either end of the movement. Similarly, the opening 'Liturgie de cristal', although involving the whole ensemble, is really a solo for clarinet with piano, against which the strings play remote descants, the cello in artificial harmonics, the violin in brittle *spiccato* tremolos. The first time the ensemble plays on equal terms is the sixth movement; even so, the way this is done is strikingly odd, with the instruments in unison throughout. Thus it is only in the climactic seventh movement ('Fouillis d'arcs-en-ciel, pour l'Ange qui annonce la fin du Temps') that the sonority of the ensemble as a whole is fully unleashed. The odd-one-out in Messiaen's scheme is the piano, which has no solo, presumably on account of the imperfect working order of the instrument provided.

In the second movement the piano accompaniment to the cantilena for violin and cello consists of cascades of 'blue-orange' chords, the first time Messiaen identified specific colours in one of his scores. It is possible, indeed, that Messiaen's perception of music as colour was heightened in the *Quatuor* not only by the work's subject matter (from Revelation) but by his wonder at seeing displays of the Northern Lights, which at first he took to be hallucinations brought on by hunger and by the intense cold that gripped Europe during the winter of 1940–1.[11]

The piano is again the backbone of the 'Liturgie de cristal', its part formed out of cycles of harmonies and rhythms (with values of 29 and 17 respectively) against more regular cycles on the cello. Since the process would take some two hours to return to its starting point, Messiaen offers merely a glimpse of the whole, a symbol of infinity or, as the Preface puts it, 'the harmonious silence of Heaven'. The birds whose songs appear on clarinet and violin are named, if rather vaguely ('a blackbird or a nightingale'), another first in a Messiaen score. The whole movement is of exceptional importance for Messiaen's future, a tiny seed that would germinate into the complexities of *Chronochromie* two decades later. By contrast, the two 'Louange' movements are both from Messiaen's past. Why Messiaen should have turned to earlier music for the emotional core of the *Quatuor* is unknown; we may guess that he must have wished to give new life to these marvellous inspirations by rescuing them from their rather ordinary surroundings (in the *Fête des belles eaux* and *Diptyque*). The fascination lies in the way the music gains through Messiaen's transcriptions. Since the piano lacks the sostenuto of the ondes Martenot or the organ, Messiaen makes virtue of necessity by giving its accompaniments rhythmic significance – in the pulsing chords under the cello solo, or the double-dotted 'shudder' that marks each crotchet beat in 'Louange à l'Immortalité de Jésus'. Similarly, melodies which are effortlessly legato on ondes or organ, when transferred to strings become charged with perilous difficulty – memorably so in the high pianissimo harmonic that ends the cello movement, and the climactic high C sharp of the violin solo, sustained fortissimo in Messiaen's impossibly slow tempo ('Extrêmement lent').

Messiaen later recalled his time at Görlitz in conversation with Antoine Goléa:

When I first arrived at the camp [. . .] I was stripped of my clothes, like all the prisoners. But naked as I was, I clung fiercely to a little kit-bag containing all my treasures, that is to say, a little library of miniature scores which served as my consolation when I suffered, as did the Germans themselves, from hunger and cold. This very eclectic little library went from Bach's *Brandenburg Concertos* to Berg's *Lyric Suite* [other works included Debussy's *Prélude à l'après-midi d'un faune*, Honegger's *Horace victorieux*, Ravel's *Ma Mère l'Oye*, and Stravinsky's *Petrushka* and *Les Noces*]. The Germans considered me to be completely harmless [. . .] and since they still loved music, not only did they allow me to keep my scores but an officer gave me pencils, erasers and some music paper.

In the Stalag with me were a violinist, a clarinettist and the cellist Étienne Pasquier. I wrote an unpretentious little trio for them which they played to me in the washrooms, because the clarinettist had kept his instrument and someone had given the cellist a cello with three strings. Emboldened by this first experiment, called 'Intermède', I gradually added the seven movements which surround it, and it is thus that my *Quatuor pour la fin du Temps* has a total of eight sections.

[The first performance] was preceded by a speech which I made on the Apocalypse [Revelation] of Saint John, in front of the priests among the prisoners, who approved of what I had to say. An upright piano was brought into the camp, very out of tune, the keys of which seemed to stick at random. [. . .] On this piano I played my *Quatuor pour la fin du Temps*, in front of an audience of five thousand people – the most diverse mixture of all classes in society – farmworkers, labourers, intellectuals, career soldiers, doctors and priests. Never have I been listened to with such attention and such understanding.[12]

This stirring account needs to be treated with circumspection. While some details are confirmed by other sources, two were corrected by the cellist Étienne Pasquier, interviewed by Hannelore Lauerwald shortly before his death:

Messiaen had helped to establish the camp theatre [in Hut 27B]. He also had a corner in the hut that was used as a church and where he could compose. He then came across a violinist who had a violin. For my part, I was able to buy a cello from an instrument maker in Görlitz after we'd organized a collection among our fellow-prisoners. I was allowed to go into the town to buy it escorted by one of the guards. Soon after that, Messiaen wrote a trio for us [the 'Intermède'].

[The first performance of the *Quatuor* took place] in the hut that we used as the theatre. It consisted of an auditorium, a stage and a room where the props were stored. Once Messiaen had finished the *Quatuor*, we rehearsed there at six o'clock every evening after work. The rehearsals lasted till lights out at ten. A piano had been provided for Messiaen, but its keys used to stick. We rehearsed for months. An officer always sat at the back and listened. [. . .] Expectations among the prisoners ran high. Everyone wanted to come and hear us, including the camp commanders. They sat in the front row. All the seats were taken, about four hundred in all, and people listened raptly, even those who may have been listening to chamber music for the first time, their thoughts turning inward. It was extraordinary. The performance took place on Wednesday, 15 January 1941, at six in the evening. It was bitterly cold outside the hut, and there was snow on the ground and on the rooftops. Our clothing was bizarre in the extreme. The four of us who were performing – Messiaen included – wore old Czech uniforms covered in patches, with clogs on our feet. They were warmer, and good for walking in the snow, but they also hurt your feet. Messiaen was known as a natty dresser[13] – and now here he was in this shabby get-up! But the performance was a great success, and we often repeated it.

Messiaen repeatedly made the claim [that there were only three strings on my cello], but in point of fact I played on four strings. [. . .] In telling this story, he presumably wanted to highlight the inadequacies surrounding the first performance.[14]

While the circumstances of this performance make Messiaen's mythologizing of the event entirely understandable, Pasquier's points about the cello and the size of the audience are persuasive. Inevitably, there is little contemporary documentation of this famous occasion. However, a copy of the small handwritten programme sheet for the performance, preserved in Messiaen's archives, gives the movement titles in blue pencil on the verso. Two of these differ from those which Messiaen established soon afterwards. The sixth movement is given as 'Fanfare' (changed to 'Danse de la fureur'), while the eighth movement appears as 'Seconde louange à l'Éternité de Jésus' (changed to 'Louange à l'Immortalité de Jésus'). The programme also has inscriptions to Messiaen from his three fellow performers. Pasquier wrote: 'The camp at Görlitz . . . Hut 27B, our theatre. Outside, night, snow, misfortune. Here, a miracle – the *Quatuor pour la fin du Temps* transports us into a marvellous Paradise, and takes us away from this terrible place. Unending thanks to our dear Olivier Messiaen, poet of eternal purity.'[15]

The first issue of the French-language camp newspaper *Lumignon: Bimensuel du Stalag VIIIA* , dated 1 April 1941, included a review of the performance with the headline 'Première au Camp'. This article, signed with the initials V.M., is of particular interest for its description of the audience reaction, and for its recognition that something out of the ordinary had taken place:

It was our good fortune to have witnessed in this camp the first performance of a masterpiece. And what's strange is that in a prison barracks we felt just the same tumultuous and partisan atmosphere of some premières, latent as much with passionate acclaim as with angry denunciation. And while there was fervent enthusiasm along some rows, it was impossible not to sense the irritation on others. Reminiscences of the time speak to us of such a storm when one evening in 1911 [*recte* 1913] at the Théâtre des Champs-Élysées, *Le Sacre du printemps* was first performed. It's often a mark of a work's greatness that it has provoked conflict on the occasion of its birth.

With the first words of introduction spoken by the composer, we already sensed that his music was full of daring. It delighted me to recognize in Messiaen, normally so unassuming and almost invisible, a singular mastery. [. . .] There are certain works which are like a bridge thrown towards the absolute, an attempt to go beyond time. [. . .] It is a real pleasure to report that the applause itself did not burst out immediately. The last note was followed by a moment of silence which established the sovereign mastery of the work.

Because the composer's quest has been undertaken with all the humility and patience of his faith, I believe that the *Quatuor pour la fin du Temps* is truly filled with the idea of God. Between movements you reflect on what has been heard: this music honours everyone. This is its true grandeur, which draws us to it. [. . .] When the concert was over, all the work's admirers rushed up to Messiaen. We were among those to witness this delightful moment, where only deference and friendship surrounded a rather anxious young master.

Another witness to the event published his recollections in the newspaper *Nice-Matin* on 15 January 2001. Charles Jourdanet recalled the day of the concert, providing yet another estimate of the size of audience gathered to hear the work. He paints a vivid portrait of cultural life in the camp (including the publication of *Lumignon* and the performances in Hut 27), and of Messiaen himself, a fellow-inmate in Hut 19A:

> It was Wednesday, 15 January 1941. [. . .] On that memorable day for the one hundred and fifty or so in the audience who were privileged to hear not only a first performance but also a world première, the routine had been much the same as usual. At 6 a.m., distribution of rations. From 8 a.m. until 12 noon, each prisoner worked on the task assigned to him. At midday, cauliflower soup for everybody. From 1 p.m. until 4 p.m., various jobs. At 5 p.m., more rations, with each prisoner given a small piece of black bread, with a little soft white cheese. [. . .] Finally, at 6 p.m. the concert was held in Hut 27, where a 'theatre' had been set up for a few months.
>
> This Stalag, like many others in Germany, was no holiday camp. [. . .] But these were not concentration camps either. Protected by the Geneva Convention and visited by the International Red Cross, the prisoners of war were often able to benefit from better living conditions, particularly in the areas of sport and culture. In Stalag VIIIA, at Görlitz (Silesia), the 'KG' (Prisoners of War) had access to, among other things, a library, and a 'university' where various languages could be studied, a sports ground (mainly for football), a theatre from the second half of 1940 and a monthly newspaper (from April 1941).
>
> The theatre was set up by a man called Mouchet, succeeded, after his release, by Oriou, a poet and Jack-of-all-trades. The camp authorities allowed them to transform Hut 27 into a real theatre. Shows were given weekly. Sometimes there were additional filmshows or even concerts during the week. Performances started at 6 p.m. so that they would be over before the curfew, fixed at 9 p.m. Admission cost 20 pfennigs. Faced with daily demands by the prisoner-organizers about practical problems, Oberfeldwebel Pluscher and Lagermeister Vogl always attempted to find a solution quickly. So it was that the theatre was gradually fitted out with some scenery, some musical instruments, fabric for costumes, wigs, and so on. For his part, Olivier Messiaen was able to obtain what he needed to compose his *Quatuor pour la fin du Temps*.
>
> Over the years, the theatre at Stalag VIIIA presented the widest possible range of shows: plays by Labiche and Courteline, operettas composed and

staged by the prisoners, some music-hall, and even a 'corps de ballet' with the prisoners in drag. There were song recitals, recitations, and concerts conducted by maestro Carion.

The camp authorities had their say in what was done, of course, and they particularly liked music. That's why they made matters easier for 'KG' Olivier Messiaen when he started to compose one of his greatest works. In Hut 19A there was a large group of French and Belgian prisoners of war, among them Olivier Messiaen and the author of this article. And I can testify that the one we affectionately called the French Mozart was exempted from fatigue duties by the occupants of the hut themselves.

On that cold night in January 1941, squeezed onto the benches in Hut 27, we listened – some with an unexpected intensity, others irritated by unfamiliar rhythms and sonorities – to the birth of the quartet which Messiaen hoped was a 'great act of faith', and for which he wrote his own commentaries.

During this great première at Görlitz, Olivier Messiaen, who was completely imbued with chapter 10 of the Book of Revelation, provided explanatory texts at the start of each of the eight movements of his *Quatuor pour la fin du Temps*. [. . .] Working in Hut 19A, he had to battle with an environment which was hardly conducive to writing a musical masterpiece. All credit to Messiaen, then: while working on the third movement of the great quartet, called 'Abîme des oiseaux', he was surrounded by the terrible din of hammering and clanking.

If Jourdanet is correct about Messiaen working on the third movement in the camp, presumably he was revising it, since Pasquier's account of the performance in the field at Toul is surely a reliable one. Nevertheless, Jourdanet's article is a fascinating memoir, notable for its lack of sentimentality or bitterness, and it places the famous première of the *Quatuor pour la fin du Temps* in the wider context of the camp's cultural activity.

By the time the article in *Lumignon* was published in Stalag VIIIA (alongside the earliest printed commentary on the work by the composer), Messiaen had been liberated – probably thanks in part to the persistent efforts of Marcel Dupré – and was back in France. On 10 March 1941 Messiaen was able to write to Claude Arrieu from Neussargues about the joyful reunion with his family, and to tell her about his newest work:

Thank you for all the nice letters to my wife, thank you for arranging all the performances of my works, and thank you for the delicious parcel which arrived here two months ago. Here . . . because I am free! with my wife and little Pascal! in *Neussargues*! (Cantal). Do I need to tell you what joy this gives me? I am gradually getting used to family life again, in fact to life pure and simple. Apart from bronchitis with some pleural problems (now over! – I am very well), I brought back from over there a *Quatuor pour la fin du Temps* in eight movements, for violin, clarinet, cello and piano: I am very proud of it as it was written under such difficult circumstances! I think you wanted my brother's address. Poor fellow! He is still a prisoner![16]

Two days after writing to Arrieu, Messiaen was in Vichy, the capital of Laval's puppet French government. On 12 March he wrote to Claire on the headed paper of the 'Association Jeune France, sous l'égide du Secrétariat Général à la Jeunesse'. His official duties were largely administrative, but this detailed letter provides a rare glimpse of musical activity in Vichy in 1941, and the musicians working there; it also reveals something of Messiaen's anxieties for his family and his own future:

Ma Mie chérie,
Here's all the news in one go. It was delightful to be met at the station by [Daniel-] Lesur and [Maurice] Martenot. Lesur invited me to his restaurant: a very good dinner. They have found me an excellent room. Jeune France and Radio Jeunesse combined form an immense organization grouping more than 70 musicians, poets, administrative staff, secretaries etc. All these people work and sleep at the Hôtel d'Angleterre. The work involves the organization of concerts, lectures, tours, stage performances, folklore, etc., etc.

   This will also be my work: to *organize* (letters, visits, telephone calls, diplomacy, etc.). I leave this evening for St-Étienne for a performance of *Carmen* (a project which involves the new director of the Opéra de Lyon and, consequently, performances by Jeune France there!). I come back to Vichy tomorrow morning where I will meet Baudrier and Martenot.

   In principle, I will partly deputize for Lesur until 20 March, the date on which I will return to Neussargues. I need to come back to Vichy on 26 March for a tour in which I am involved as a pianist (with Auclert the composer and Marthe Bailloux the singer): I will play accompaniments, folksongs, Duparc, Lesur, as well as my own *Trois Mélodies*, *Vocalise*, and perhaps one of the *Chants de terre et de ciel*. Auclert will include my *Préludes*, his own music, some Rameau, Franck, etc. The tour will go to Grenoble, Chambéry, Gap and Valence, on 31 March, 1, 2 and 3 April. In making my arrangements with Lesur, I can substitute for him in the morning and afternoon, and practise the piano or compose during the evenings. I am going this morning to look at lodgings with a kitchen for you and Pascal, if that interests you? Life is expensive here, but it is easy to obtain things. However, it is difficult to imagine you in such a room with Pascal, who's so lively and needs so much space! On the other hand, if I agree to work here, I will only be able to come to see you in Neussargues for five or six days each month.

At Radio Jeunesse in Vichy, I can be assistant director to Lesur, for a salary of 3,000 francs per month, as well as composing incidental music for payment (for orchestra and for recording). That could start from today. There will be frequent travel, all expenses paid.

In Paris the Association de Musique Contemporaine (chamber music) brings together Triton, Sérénade, J[eune] F[rance], [Société] Nationale (all *defunct*) and gives concerts every eight days. The Trinité and other Parisian organ posts are unpaid. The École Normale is still there, and the Conservatoire is open. Cortot could give me a job at the École Normale, since that is mine by rights. But for the post at the Conservatoire, it is necessary to apply here, directly through the Minister. There are several vacant places for harmony teachers. Duruflé and Revel[17] are on their way up, but I should have more chance, being here, and with my *Leçons d'harmonie* published by Leduc. People are talking about Delvincourt[18] as a possible new director for the Conservatoire, and Dupré will be Professor of Composition. To buy music it is necessary to go to Béal (Lyon), and for working out registrations to use organs in Lyon. An appointment to the Conservatoire is obviously very significant and would mean my leaving Vichy.

What do you think of all that? [. . .] All is well with me at the moment. But I want to be with Pascal and you, or at least to see you frequently. (A secretary spoke to me just now about a small apartment where she lives with her husband and her little boy: one room, a kitchen, a small garden. The rent is 400 francs per month.) But we must not pass up the chance of a better future. I am very confused about what to do . . . give me your opinion. I will do whatever you think is best. It is *you* who will decide. Having been pining for my little ones for so long, the idea of being separated once again is unimaginable! But it is also necessary for me to earn enough to provide a more comfortable life for you. I must think too about composing (here I can do orchestration or copying chores, but long reflection is impossible!).

I await your response. Don't forget that what I want most is to stay with you and Pascal, and above all to *make you happy*. A big kiss for my little Pascal's blonde head. I kiss and adore my 'smiling star'. Do you have the patience to wait for me until 21 March?[19]

The Association Jeune France (AJF), on whose writing paper Messiaen sent the letter, was active from November 1940 until March 1942. The organization was under the energetic direction of the young Pierre Schaeffer, and it was responsible for some spectacular musical and dramatic presentations as well as a number of other cultural initiatives. Despite its name, Schaeffer's AJF is not to

68 Daniel-Lesur in 1941.

69 The Hôtel d'Angleterre in Vichy (photo: Peter Hill).

be confused with the group La Jeune France (Baudrier, Messiaen, Daniel-Lesur and Jolivet): they were two entirely separate enterprises, but potential confusion is exacerbated by the involvement of three of the Jeune France composers (Baudrier, Daniel-Lesur and Messiaen) with one of the major events mounted by the AJF in 1941. The declared aim of the AJF, stated in article 1 of its constitution, was 'to create for young people a Jeune France movement which will revitalize the great French tradition in artistic and cultural matters: theatre, music and songs, dance, plastic and architectural arts, etc'.[20] This entailed the establishment of touring groups of actors and musicians, libraries and exhibitions, and presenting 'dramatic celebrations or festivals, in which the professional performers of Jeune France and local artistic societies will work together with schools and local youth groups'.[21] Offices were established in Lyon and Paris, and with Daniel-Lesur and Martenot in charge of musical decisions in Lyon, it is hardly surprising that their close colleagues Baudrier and Messiaen were approached to provide music for the elaborate celebrations for Joan of Arc's Feast Day (11 May) in 1941, proclaimed as a public holiday by Marshal Pétain, the Head of State of the Vichy government. A third composer involved in the project was Léo Préger, a Nadia Boulanger protégé. Messiaen wrote to Claire again on the evening of 28 March; he was frantically busy, and uneasy about the future:

> Mie chérie,
> You can't imagine what joy your telegram has given me! You are going to come here . . . with Pascal . . . We can go out together, all three of us; we can go and be a little crazy in the town, see a few people, eat in the restaurant together – and we should go to the pretty park which runs alongside the Allier! But the words 'Vichy via Grenoble' quickly brought me back to reality: it is why I put you off as quickly as possible by telegram. So did you not receive my first letter? In it I told you that the concert in Grenoble and the ones which follow it will take place at the end of April (between 25 and 30 April). There are so many things in my head! I am trying vainly to copy the parts of the *Quatuor*: I have been able to recopy all of the music for *Jeanne d'Arc* and a little of my *Quatuor*, but I am constantly interrupted. [. . .] In a month's time, some of Jeune France (including Lesur) will move to Marseille; since I don't see myself staying here just for the sake of musical administration, *I will leave*. But earlier than I expected and too soon to think of Versailles. But it is likely that I will definitely leave for Paris in time for the third term of the academic year. In fact I have moved heaven and earth for the harmony job and I think it is going to happen. But I won't say any more about it, because nothing is ever certain in this rotten world, and it will be at least fifteen days before anything is definite. I have seen Mme Albert Roussel about it, and have alerted Dommange[22] and Delvincourt. Parisian

musicians are on my side; I will see Cortot again on Tuesday. Through Martenot I have seen or hope to see some people who are even higher up. [...]

I go on Sunday to Limoges to see about a possible performance of *Mireille* – and I also need to organize everything to do with *Jeanne d'Arc*. I hope to do the concert in Grenoble and so our escapade can happen. If not,

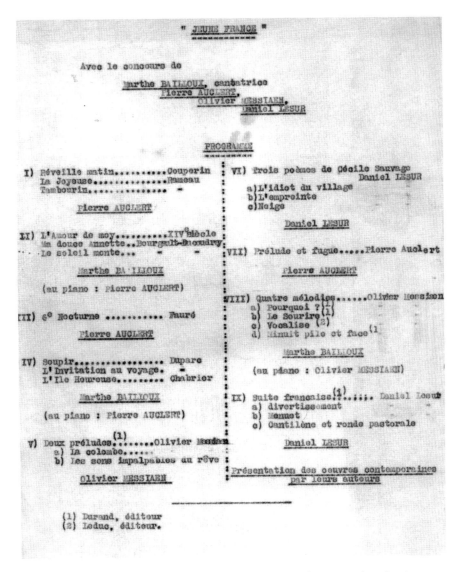

70 Programme for a concert in spring 1941 during Messiaen's time working for the Association Jeune France based in Vichy.

I will spend at least ten days at Neussargues before leaving for Paris. Another matter weighs heavily on my conscience as a result: will you come with me or not? How terrible it is swimming in all these worries! And I am dreadfully miserable on my own. If the harmony job comes to nothing and Lesur leaves for Marseille, nothing would give me the courage to stay, alone, without Mie, without Pascal and really without music, in order to be a paper-pusher. On the other hand, if they call me to Paris for the third term, I will need to ask for a passport in order to leave as quickly as possible. That will still leave us separated, perhaps for a long time? It's terrible and I no longer know what to think about it. It is obviously better that I go on my own, but – I repeat – it's terrible! For your part, try not to be as neurasthenic about it as me: you have Pascal and a lovely church very nearby to comfort you and keep you on an even keel. My only 'peace' is to copy a little (so little!) of the parts for my *Quatuor*. I could not have imagined all these separations and all these dilemmas when I looked so joyously towards France! Finally, there is good news and great hope: I will be very surprised not to get the harmony job. I've wanted it so much since before the war! Do you remember? So near to reaching the goal, I would be so ashamed . . .

So, to sum up, there is great hope for the harmony job in Paris; and there are concerts at Grenoble and elsewhere between 25 and 30 April. In any event, I want to see you, to kiss you and to hold you like my darling little child, and to play with little Pascal for at least a fortnight before Paris, if Paris it is to be. Without Paris, I'll definitely leave Vichy after Lesur's departure.

I am staying in a pension (45 francs per day for the room, lunch and dinner, wine, breakfast and tips not included). [. . .] My room is large: two windows with balconies, one to the south, the other to the west, a vast double bed, a clothes rail in a black cabinet, a wardrobe, a table and three chairs. There is a view over a small square with Italian-style white columns. The Parc des Célestins is very near, as is the Hôtel d'Angleterre, and there's an ultra-modern church twenty paces away.[23] Lesur is infinitely kind to me. I am really eating very well. Every morning I conscientiously eat the bread and cheese which you so kindly gave me. On days without meat, we have rabbit, fish, paté, etc. [. . .]

My Mie, I love you, I love you. Write me a quick note to cheer me up and think about all these things. Forgive me if I am still an egoist. I want so much to make both you and Pascal happy! And above all not to leave you! It's my life to amuse Pascal and to talk endlessly to you . . . (forgive me!). You are my dear little children. Big kisses to both of you.

Olivier – Papa
Jeune France, service musical, Hôtel d'Angleterre, Place d'Allier, Vichy (Allier).

P.S. I leave for Limoges on Sunday and will come back to Vichy on the evening of Monday 31 March.[24]

By the time he wrote this letter, it is clear that Messiaen had set to work on the music he listed in 1944 as 'Chœurs pour une Jeanne d'Arc, pour grand chœur et petit chœur mixtes, a cappella'.[25] The choruses were written for *Portique pour une fille de France*, a pageant by Pierre Schaeffer and Pierre Barbier, first performed in Lyon and Marseille on the feast of Saint Joan of Arc, 11 May 1941. The title page of the original edition describes it as a play in ten scenes, with 'composition musicale de Yves Baudrier, Léo Preger et Olivier Messiaen'. The play was declared to the Société des Auteurs et Compositeurs Dramatiques (SACD), with a note that the Marseille performance was given in the open air.[26] The preface to the play admits that preparations were very hurried: 'This text is a child of haste. It should be taken for what it is: an improvisation.' The play text includes a number of references to choirs, to music and to dance in the stage directions. According to his 1944 worklist, Messiaen composed two choruses: 'Te Deum' and 'Impropères'; both occur in complex scenes which involve a combination of music and speech. The 'Te Deum' comes in the 'Reims' scene which closes Part 1 of the play, and the 'Impropères' are the *Improperia* or Reproaches traditionally chanted during the Veneration of the Cross at the Good Friday liturgy.

The score of Messiaen's choruses has not so far been discovered, but it is almost inconceivable that no copies survive given the large performing forces which were involved. With such limited rehearsal time, the music was presumably relatively straightforward; what is evident from the indications in the play is that if Messiaen's two pieces were to be found, they might well be unperformable as independent entities, since the music and the spoken dialogue are so closely interwoven in the two scenes concerned. But Messiaen had more important things than incidental music on his mind by May 1941, and when *Portique pour une fille de France* was performed, he was already back in Paris.

During March 1941 Messiaen submitted a formal application for a post at the Paris Conservatoire, and made a copy on the headed paper of the Association Jeune France. Having explained that his application was a little late because he had only just returned from captivity in Germany, he presented his *curriculum vitae*, ending with a description of his very apt forthcoming publication:

I have currently in the press a series of *Leçons d'harmonie* to be published by Leduc. Having considerable experience as a teacher of harmony, I have written these exercises in the style of the masters of music from Monteverdi to Ravel (via Mozart, Schumann, Fauré, etc.): this collection thus has the advantage of requiring the student to examine some great musical master-pieces in order to understand different languages, to find in this work the source and application of different rules, and even to develop a personal language if any potential is there.

Applications for any government or teaching post at this time required the submission of a detailed declaration relating to the employment laws promulgated by the Vichy regime. Perhaps the most repugnant of all the initiatives from the early months of Vichy France was the first 'Statut des Juifs', the law signed by Pétain and his ministers on 3 October 1940 requiring the removal of Jews from posts in teaching, public service and the media. Messiaen was thus obliged by law to write a declaration that his father was French, that he had never belonged to any secret society, and that 'I am not a Jew, my four grand-parents are not Jewish, and there is absolutely no Jewish blood in my family'.[27] Once again, Marcel Dupré gave Messiaen the fullest support:

I wrote to Messiaen who was in the army as a sapper, even though he ought to have been working in a hospital, like all the musicians who had been called up. He replied in a desperately sad letter, saying that since I was offering to send him pocket orchestral scores, please could I send such and such works, which I hastened to do. Then the poor man was taken prisoner. [. . .] One of my colleagues said to me: 'You're the only person who can get him out of there!' 'How?' 'By going to the Kommandatur and explaining who he is.'

I took my courage in both hands and went there. I was seen by an officer, a doctor of musicology called Piersig, who said he had heard me play not only in Berlin, but just recently at my Bach recitals at the Trocadéro. I explained Messiaen's predicament to him, and he recognized his name. He rang for a secretary, asked my pardon for speaking German and gave him instructions. Ten minutes later, he handed me a piece of paper, written in French, and said: 'In ten days' time, at the latest, he will be in an office. Do exactly what it says on that piece of paper. You have a good chance of bringing him back to Paris.' Two months later we had a meeting of the governing body of the Conservatoire to choose a professor of piano and a professor of harmony. I was seated between two good friends: the pianist Yves Nat and the cellist Gérard Hekking. There was a list, typed in black, with fifty candidates on it, but all eyes were drawn to the name 'Messiaen' written in purple in the margin. He had rushed to apply the day before, explaining that he had only just come back from a prison camp (as I learnt from him subsequently). My two neighbours and I exchanged winks with dear Marcel Samuel-Rousseau sitting some way away, and in the very

71 Claire in the early 1940s.

first round things went our way. Messiaen was appointed. So it was that, on his return after years of desperation, he was given a permanent post.[28]

Messiaen returned to occupied Paris without Claire and Pascal, who had yet to obtain permission to travel from the *zone libre*. His first sight of the occupied city was vividly described by Pierre Messiaen in his book *Images*:

> The next Sunday, we took Olivier for a walk in the Bois de Boulogne. Some young Prussian lieutenants lay in wait with their monocles, their chubby pink faces and their old duelling scars. They pranced about on our lovely horses, on our beautiful lawns, then went to stuff themselves on cakes and ham in a café reserved for these men. We watched people coming back from the races at Longchamp, and it was like a carnival procession: taxi bicycles and taxi tandems pushed by men and women in shorts, ancient carts and carriages dating from the 1860s or 1880s, pulled by old nags which were nearing their thirties and were so thin that you could count their ribs, and by shaggy and conscientious old workhorses with big heavy hooves.[29]

Things had moved swiftly with Messiaen's appointment to the Conservatoire, since his first class as a teacher of harmony was on 7 May. Yvonne Loriod recalls that it included an analysis of Debussy's *Prélude à l'après-midi d'un faune* which Messiaen played from the well-thumbed miniature score that he had taken to Görlitz.[30] A few weeks later, Loriod was the first member of his class to be awarded a prize: Second Prize for Harmony.

THÉATRE DES MATHURINS
(MARCEL HERRAND - JEAN MARCHAT)
36, Rue des Mathurins, 36 — — PARIS - VIII⁰
Métro : Saint-Lazare et Havre-Caumartin — Autobus A A

MARDI 24 JUIN, à 17 HEURES

OLIVIER MESSIAEN

présente

à l'occasion de son retour en France

LA PREMIÈRE AUDITION DU

"QUATUOR POUR LA FIN DU TEMPS"

écrit pendant sa captivité.

AVEC LE CONCOURS DE

MARCELLE BUNLET, de l'Opéra

JEAN et ETIENNE PASQUIER

ANDRÉ VACELLIER

OLIVIER MESSIAEN

PRIX DES PLACES DE **10** A **30** FRANCS
— Location : , Théatre des Mathurins — —
et chez Durand, 4, Place de la Madeleine, Paris

72 Yvonne Loriod in 1941.

73 Handbill for the first performance in Paris of the *Quatuor pour la fin du Temps*, 24 June 1941.

May 1941 was a grim month in Paris, with the occupying forces exerting an ever-increasing stranglehold: on 14 May the first systematic round-up of foreign and stateless Jews took place, and later the same month (26 May), Honoré d'Estienne d'Orves, who had led one of the first clandestine missions in occupied France, was condemned to death by a German military tribunal. Cultural incursions by the occupying powers included a visit by the Berlin Staatsoper to the Opéra, with performances of Wagner's *Tristan und Isolde* on 22 and 25 May conducted by Herbert von Karajan, and a cast which included Max Lorenz as Tristan and the French soprano Germaine Lubin making an exceptionally ill-advised guest appearance as Isolde – one of many instances of her collaborationist conduct which led to her trial and imprisonment after the Liberation.

While Messiaen was in captivity, there had been some Paris performances of his music. On 8 November 1940 the Orchestre Symphonique Français, conducted by Hubert d'Auriol, performed 'Prière du Christ montant vers son Père' (from *L'Ascension*) in a 'Concert spirituel'. The same performers gave a concert on 22 December 1940, with Ginette Martenot among the soloists, in which the most intriguing aspect was the inclusion of a piece by Messiaen described as 'Oraison: ondes et orchestre', presumably an arrangement of the most famous passage from the *Fête des belles eaux*.

The Association de Musique Contemporaine (AMC) served as a kind of umbrella organization which attempted to absorb some of the activities (and the audience) of 'the Société Nationale, Triton, the SMI,[31] the SIMC, the concerts of *Revue musicale*, *Jeune France*, *Sérénade* etc'.[32] The AMC's concerts in the 1940–1 season included the première of Poulenc's *Sextuor* in its definitive version (9 December 1940), and Messiaen's *Chants de terre et de ciel* performed by Marcelle Bunlet accompanied by Simone Tilliard (23 December 1940). The AMC's committee was a broad church: Florent Schmitt was Honorary President, and other members included Auric, Delvincourt, Duruflé, Françaix, Jolivet, Münch, Poulenc and Sauguet.

Following Messiaen's return to Paris, arrangements were quickly put in hand for a concert of his music. On Tuesday, 24 June, at the Théâtre des Mathurins, he gave the first Paris performance of the *Quatuor pour la fin du Temps* with the work's original cellist Étienne Pasquier, his violinist brother Jean Pasquier, and the clarinettist André Vacellier. The page-turner was Yvonne Loriod. The concert was reviewed enthusiastically by Serge Moreux in *L'Information musicale*, though his criticism of Messiaen's spoken commentaries is a pre-echo of the hostility which erupted in the Parisian press a few years later as 'Le Cas Messiaen':

The *Quatuor pour la fin du Temps* [. . .] is the most striking piece of chamber music heard in Paris since the performance of the last quartet by Schoenberg. Why is it so striking? Because it employs a melodic and metrical language which is both original and *organized*, born of meditations on ancient Greek metre and Hindu modality. These meditations are vital to Olivier Messiaen's creative evolution and he has introduced us to them again here, going a little further this time into the enchanted jungle which flourishes in his imagination. There, he delights us with the joy of pure music. The dazzling harmonies, the imposing slow lines of hieratic intensity, the dance of unorthodox and noble rhythmic patterns, the incredible originality of invention: all these come together in this major work to astonish and delight; and even the most refractory members of the audience behaved impeccably throughout the concert.

The ejaculatory manner of the spoken introductions which preceded the performance of each of the eight movements, apart from disrupting the tonal balance of the work, surprised some and displeased many because of their tone of religious apologetics. A more technical description was expected and hoped for in the talks, not least because the audience on this occasion was made up of the musical élite of Paris.[33]

Writing in *Comœdia* (12 July), Arthur Honegger was worried that 'some may find that there is too much literature surrounding this music, and will regret it', but concluded that the *Quatuor* was 'a moving work of great beauty, denoting a musician of high aspirations'. In the pro-German *Les Nouveaux Temps* (13 July), Marcel Delannoy had far harder words: 'With Messiaen there is a fanatical subjectivity, a quasi-Luciferian arrogance in wanting to describe light. What is more, he seeks to create in his music the power of a personal miracle and then calmly announces that he has succeeded.'[34]

Messiaen was busy with teaching, rehearsals and concerts, but with his wife and son still in Neussargues, he was all on his own at the house in the villa du Danube. As he said in a letter to Claire on 26 June, he had 'not yet tried out *Les Corps glorieux* at the Trinité, and not yet given my *Quatuor* to Durand who have asked me for it. [. . .] At the [villa du] Danube the seringa is in bloom. [. . .] A very good result in the women's harmony competition [Loriod's prize].'[35] In a slightly later letter (undated), Messiaen wrote: '*Corps glorieux* sold to Leduc, and my *Quatuor* to Durand. All that and a month's salary from the Conservatoire, paid into the Crédit Lyonnais, will be for you: this money should help you [. . .] to buy music, to look after your health, and to get some treats and toys for Pascal. The Blumenthal Prize will also be for you.'[36]

The 'Échos' column in *L'Information musicale* included an unsigned article which declared: 'Jeune France is not dead. The proof is to be found in the concert on 18 July at 5 p.m. at the Hôtel de Sagonne, given by Olivier Messiaen, Daniel-Lesur, Yves Baudrier and André Jolivet. [. . .] This belated event is an opportunity to catch up with the activities of "The Four" of La Jeune France, who have some huge projects planned for the new season in October. We will also have another chance to hear the *Quatuor pour la fin des* [!] *Temps* by their leader, which was unanimously greeted as a French masterpiece after the recent concert devoted to its composer's music at the Théâtre des Mathurins.'[37] In fact only the 'Louange à l'Éternité de Jésus' was played at this 18 July concert, by Étienne Pasquier and Messiaen, along with the *Thème et variations* (Jean Pasquier and Messiaen).

On 22 July Messiaen took his pupils to the Trinité for a private performance of *Les Corps glorieux* while he was in the process of adding fingering, pedalling and registrations for the work's publication.[38] This is its earliest known performance, and it was given under fraught circumstances: Messiaen was still awaiting permission to join Claire and Pascal at Neussargues for the summer holidays; and authorization to depart for the free zone arrived only at the end of July. He returned to Paris for the start of the Conservatoire term and his duties at the Trinité on 29 September with a heavy heart, since the authorities would not yet give permission for Claire and Pascal to travel with him.

The continuing solidarity of La Jeune France was made apparent in a letter written by Jolivet to *L'Information musicale* responding to an article by Armand Machabey which lamented the current state of French music, and the lack of any obvious successor to Honegger. Jolivet's riposte is a stirring tribute to his friend Messiaen:

> M. Machabey wants to limit himself to the names of significant figures [to succeed Honegger], and I would suggest just one to him: Olivier Messiaen. Even if he is unable to hear performances, he should study the *Poèmes pour Mi* (in the orchestral version), the *Chants de terre et de ciel*, *La Nativité du Seigneur*, *Le Combat de la vie et de la mort* [*recte* 'Combat de la mort et de la vie'] and the *Quatuor pour la fin du Temps*. It is easy to examine them as all these works are published. M. Machabey should be able to notice that the 'style' is not in the least jaded, that the 'tendencies' are clearly affirmed, that 'boldness' is apparent in every bar, and that the 'magnificence' of this music preserves us from a 'long and mediocre monotony'. I am happy for these remarks to be published. Through their directness and brevity, I hope to prevent us from forming the false impression that our generation is incapable of inheriting the legacy of Rameau, of Berlioz and of Debussy.[39]

By December 1941 daily life in Paris had become difficult in the extreme: curfews were imposed and there were some days when the Métro stopped running at 5.30 p.m. Jean Guéhenno's journal for 8 December reported this and continues: 'It is 6.30 p.m. and I am watching evening fall. Not a sound, not a breath. And this is Paris!'[40] However, for Messiaen there was some good news. On 30 November 1941 he noted that 'Les Pio [his father and step-mother[41]] dined with us'. The significant word is 'us': at last Claire and Pascal had been allowed to travel from the free zone to Paris.

On 28 December 1941 Messiaen gave the seventh in a series of organ recitals by several leading players at the Palais de Chaillot. He performed works by Tournemire, Dupré and Delbos in the first half; the second was devoted entirely to his own music, including the first public performances of 'Joie et clarté des corps glorieux' and 'Combat de la mort et de la vie' from *Les Corps glorieux*. Norbert Dufourcq reviewed the recital in *L'Information musicale*:

> [Messiaen's] recent works, notably *La Nativité du Seigneur*, had led some to fear that he might have become trapped in his own system. This was not the case, and it is the sign of a great artist, coupled with a great spirit, that he is no slave to procedures. [. . .] In the second part of the concert, the composer presented and championed his own works: movements from *L'Ascension* ('Transports de joie') and *La Nativité du Seigneur* ('Les Mages'), and two pieces receiving their first performances, taken from a collection entitled *Les Corps glorieux*. [. . .] It is through his continual experiments into the opposition of ideas and of the clash of different moods that Olivier Messiaen attains the power to move us. In this respect, no musical instrument can serve him better than his own, which he plays with true virtuosity.[42]

A note at the end of Messiaen's 1941 diary referred to a forthcoming project for a play the following year: 'See Herrand again about the incidental music for a work by Euripides or a tale about the Middle Ages at the Mathurins. *I will write the music*.'

At the start of Messiaen's diary for 1942 he made notes on a project which was clearly well advanced: 'phone M. Dommange between 11 a.m. and mid-day about the *Traité*. [. . .] A *Traité* of 280 pages: it would cost 50,000 francs to engrave it all.' Messiaen spent the mornings of 9, 10 and 11 January at rehearsals for *Les Offrandes oubliées*, and the performance took place in the Salle du Conservatoire at 5.45 p.m. on Sunday, 11 January. This was an unusual event: a free concert given by the Société des Concerts du Conservatoire, conducted by Charles Münch, including works by three composers who had been PoWs. As well as Messiaen's piece, the programme featured Jean Martinon's *Stalag IX* and Jean Cocteau as narrator in the first performance of Maurice Thiriet's *Œdipe Roi*. The concert ended with a Münch favourite: Roussel's Third Symphony. Rehearsals with the Pasquiers and André Vacellier were also underway for the next performance of the *Quatuor*, and on 12 January Messiaen made a note to 'ask Loriot to turn pages for the *Quatuor*'. Here (as elsewhere in his diaries from the early 40s) he misspelled his future wife's name as 'Loriot'.

On 17 January 1942 the *Quatuor* was given in the opulent surroundings of Comte Étienne de Beaumont's home. De Beaumont (1883–1956) was a generous and flamboyant patron of the arts whose splendid Paris town house at 2 rue Duroc – built in the eighteenth century for Prince Masserano – was the location during and after the Occupation for concerts promoted by de Beaumont's Centre d'Échanges Artistiques et de Culture Française. The Count had been well known since the 1920s for his support of ballet, notably the *Soirées de Paris* in 1924, and for his magnificent annual costume balls. He was a passionate supporter of new music, and a collector of modern art, particularly works by Braque and Picasso who were both friends, as were Cocteau and Derain.

The concerts held in de Beaumont's large music room at the rue Duroc were reminiscent of music-making in the great salons half a century earlier, not least because many of the leading figures of Parisian cultural life would meet at de Beaumont's soirées. Given by Messiaen, Vacellier and the Pasquiers only a few months after the public première, this performance of the *Quatuor* was put on for the members of de Beaumont's Centre d'Échanges Artistiques. The programme included a specially printed leaflet containing Messiaen's commentaries, 'read by the composer before each movement'.[43] De Beaumont was clearly enthusiastic about Messiaen's music and suggested a commission early in 1942. The composer referred to the proposed new work in a letter of 4 June:

> Cher Monsieur,
> I have just received your cheque for one thousand francs. You are much too kind: thank you! Thank you also for having written to Dr Piertzig [Piersig];[44] I telephoned him and fixed a meeting as we wanted: we will soon see what he has to say.
>   Of course I have not forgotten your project for next winter: a work for chamber orchestra (15–20 players). Now I need to find a subject, themes, musical and instrumental ideas, and to wait for inspiration.[45]

Messiaen noted the details of this commission in his diary on 20 July: 'write a work for small orchestra (20 musicians maximum) for M. de Beaumont – with fee. To be delivered to him next January or February.' The same commission is mentioned again in October, and clearly Messiaen was serious about the work, but it seems to have come to nothing. However, de Beaumont continued to encourage Messiaen for several years.

Preparations for the publication of the *Quatuor* were well advanced by the start of February 1942. Messiaen was taking a close interest in some of the problems of printing such a complex score, and on 2 February he visited Durand in connection with the preface and the second proofs (on the same occasion he also ordered a piano-vocal score of Stravinsky's *Le Rossignol*). The first edition of the *Quatuor* was published three months later, on 15 May 1942. The paper is of unusually high quality for a wartime publication, though Durand's printing ledgers reveal that a mere 100 copies were printed.[46]

Another regular supporter of Messiaen's music was Virginie Bianchini (her surname sometimes appears as Schildge-Bianchini and later as Zinke-Bianchini). An American living in Paris – at an opulent address: 38 avenue de Président Wilson (16ᵉ) – she took private lessons from Messiaen during 1942, and her active interest in his music went back to the 1930s.[47] On 7 February 1942 Bianchini visited Messiaen to discuss plans for a concert at her house and Messiaen jotted down 'a selection of my songs with Bunlet (30 mins)'. In fact nothing was arranged until May: on 13 April Messiaen noted that he had to 'organize the programme for 3 May at Bianchini's with Bunlet. Complete the invitation form, fix and confirm the date of the concert.' By the end of April, Bunlet was unwell but Messiaen was able to replace her with the singer charmingly described in his 1942 diary as 'Mme Irène Joachim (Mélisande)'.[48] The concert took place on 3 May and Messiaen noted that 'Loriot' played some of his *Préludes* on the same occasion. Bianchini's name crops up again in connection with two other events in 1942: a recital she gave at the Trinité on 31 June, and a private performance of the *Quatuor* at her house on 2 December, by the regular team of the Pasquiers, Vacellier and Messiaen. She is perhaps best remembered for a slightly later achievement, compiling the first detailed catalogue of Messiaen's works.[49]

Messiaen noted that 'Les Pio dined with us' on 8 February; the invitation was reciprocated a week later (15 February), when Messiaen mentioned that he also picked up his father's English translation for a commentary on *Les Corps glorieux*. However, the first edition of the work contains no preface, no list of registrations, and no English text. Evidently a decision was taken not to include the planned introduction (perhaps because of paper shortages), but Leduc dealt efficiently with *Les Corps glorieux*. Second proofs were ready by mid-February (Messiaen visited the firm about these on 17 February), and the work was published at the start of June. The sheer originality of the *Quatuor* and *Les Corps glorieux* – published within the space of a couple of weeks – did not go unnoticed: in a letter to André Schaeffner written in late summer 1942, Poulenc remarked that 'apart from [Jean] Françaix and Messiaen, all the young composers are quite happy with what was done before 1914'.[50]

On 8 March Messiaen was at the Trocadéro for a performance of Honegger's *Le Roi David*, conducted by the composer, whose popularity in occupied Paris was immense – something the Nazis found acceptable since he was a non-Jew and a neutral Swiss. The next day Messiaen made a brief visit to Lévigny to stay with his aunts; he also hoped to bring back some cheese and eggs which were strictly rationed in Paris. Messiaen was to make several of these short trips to the Aube during the next couple of years.[51]

A Jeune France concert took place on 15 March at the home of Mme de Brouilly, in the avenue Foch, including two *Préludes* (nos.5 and 6) played by Loriod, and the *Thème et variations* played by Messiaen and the violinist Malvesin. A few days later (19 March) he accompanied Marcelle Bunlet in six songs at a Triptyque concert in the Salle Chopin, and provided timings for them in his diary: 'Le Sourire' (1'), 'Prière exaucée' (3'), 'Épouvante' (3'), 'Le Collier', (3'), Vocalise (4'), Résurrection (3').'

Before leaving for an Easter holiday at Lévigny, Messiaen took the proofs of *Les Corps glorieux* to Leduc on 25 March, and that same evening he and Marcelle Bunlet gave the first performance of André Jolivet's *Messe pour le jour de la paix*, a work for soprano, organ and drum, composed in 1940.[52] It must have been a relief to spend some time away in the Aube. During spring 1942, daily life in Paris was becoming increasingly threatening: on 3 March the RAF began the allied bombing of France with an air raid on the Renault factory at Boulogne-Billancourt; 27 March was an appalling day in the history of the city, as the first trainload of Jews left the vast and dismal transit camp at Drancy for Auschwitz.

Messiaen's diary (8 June) returned to a subject that had been mentioned the previous year: 'Incidental music for *Œdipe* ready for 15 June: 10 minutes of music for one ondes Martenot (the theatre has an instrument and player), composed for a fee.' *Œdipe* was mentioned again on the next two days, and presumably Messiaen was at work on the score. A dress rehearsal took place at the Théâtre des Mathurins on 19 June; a few days later the name 'Herrand' appears in the diary, a reference to Marcel Herrand, co-director with Jean Marchat of the Rideau de Paris, the company for which Messiaen composed his score. There were further rehearsals or previews during the last week of June, and the composer registered his music for performing rights with SACEM on 25 June (at the same time as *Les Corps glorieux*). The play opened on 1 July. Confusingly, it wasn't called *Œdipe*: according to contemporary listings (such as those in *L'Information musicale*) the work presented at the Théâtre des Mathurins in July 1942 was the 'tragédie' *Dieu est innocent*, written by Lucien Fabre (1889–1952). Messiaen's diary recorded that 'all three' (presumably Messiaen, Claire and Pascal) were present on the first night. While there may be some mystery about the title, the presence in Messiaen's diary of Herrand's name and the Mathurins confirms that it was indeed for this production that he wrote the music. Conclusive evidence is found in the records of the Société des Auteurs et Compositeurs Dramatiques (SACD) which show that Messiaen was registered as the composer of the incidental music for *Dieu est innocent*.[53] He was soon to use some of it again for a rather larger project. The music for *Dieu est innocent* remains to be rediscovered, but according to Loriod some of the themes in it were to reappear in *Visions de l'Amen*.[54] The play's author Lucien Fabre (sometimes given as Lucien Favre) was to work with Messiaen again in 1945, on *Tristan et Yseult*, and once more the music for it would be recycled to notable effect.

The bureacratic obstacle-course which marked musical life under the Occupation is clear from another diary entry on 8 June: '4 p.m., 52 avenue des Champs-Élysées, to see Dr Piertzig'. The precise purpose of this visit is not stated, but all those involved with the organization of concerts were required to visit 'Piertzig' (Piersig) whenever they wanted to put on a concert, providing him with details of the programme and of those who would be attending. As one of the Germans charged with the oversight and administration of music in occupied Paris at the time, he was in a position to give or withhold permission for performances of particular works, and to approve the names and addresses of those invited. Walking through the streets of Paris that afternoon, Messiaen may have been struck by a new and terrible spectacle: on the very same day, Ernst Jünger, a writer serving as a German officer in Paris, was in the same part of the city:

> In the rue Royale I encountered for the first time in my life the yellow star, worn by three young girls who passed close by me, their arms linked. [. . .] In the afternoon I saw the star again far more frequently. I consider that this is a date which will leave a deep mark, at the personal level too. A sight like this cannot but provoke a reaction. I was immediately ashamed to be in uniform.[55]

Messiaen had three tickets for the *Festival Honegger* on 3 July at the Palais de Chaillot. This was the culminating event in a series of celebrations for Honegger's fiftieth birthday: a concert conducted by the composer including *Le Chant de Nigamon*, some songs, *Pacific 231*, the Concertino for piano, and *Le Roi David*. On 10 July Messiaen dined with his father ('chez Pio') and on 13 July wrote himself a touching reminder to buy a toy for Pascal's fifth birthday, which was the next day. A few days later, virtually every corner of Paris was witness to a profoundly shocking episode: on 16 and 17 July, 9,000 policemen (including trainees) were involved in the *grande rafle*, by far the largest systematic rounding-up to date of Jews (many of them French citizens), taken from their homes all over the city. This macabre operation began at 4 a.m. on the morning of 16 July, and by the end of the next day almost 13,000 people had been placed under arrest; 7,000 of them (including over 4,000 children) were herded into the Vél d'Hiver sports stadium where they languished in squalid conditions, without food or water, for five days. Many of them were to perish in Auschwitz.[56]

Though most Parisians were unaware of the extent of the *grande rafle*, it was in the context of this appalling inhumanity that they began their summer vacations. Messiaen saw Line Zilgien on 25 July to make all the arrangements at the Trinité during the summer, and he then started his holidays. As always, this was a time for serious composing, though on 11 August (presumably at Petichet) his diary recorded more mundane matters: 'Sheets, wine, wood, milk, oil. 8 p.m. leave for Neussargues.' It was during this vacation that Messiaen later said he wrote much of *Technique de mon langage musical*, though earlier diary entries indicate that some of his ground-breaking treatise was already in existence before this date: he almost certainly used this summer to put the book into its final form.

Messiaen was back in Paris at the start of October. By the middle of the month, he was putting the finishing touches to *Technique de mon langage musical*: 'finish Traité and give it to Leduc with list of subscribers for its publication'. The explanation for this remark seems extraordinary now: so unconfident were Leduc about selling copies of *Technique* that the firm only agreed to publish it if Messiaen supplied a list of potential purchasers. Moreover, Leduc was at least the third publisher (after Dommange at Durand, and Lemoine) that Messiaen had approached. This was an important project for the composer and he did his best to promote the work in the musical press. In mid-October he sent an article to Éric Sarnette at *Musique et radio* for publication in the November issue. Entitled 'Technique de mon langage musical',[57] it includes details of the nineteen chapters that the reader would find in *Technique*, along with some explanatory remarks. The treatise was eventually published in spring 1944, in two volumes – the first containing the text, and the second the music examples.

November 1942 saw France plunged into further chaos. On 11 November the Germans occupied the former free zone in the south (including Lyon), and from then on, until August 1944, the whole country came under Nazi control. Given this unstable situation, it is not surprising to find Messiaen reminding himself on 16 November to ask Durand about the current whereabouts of one of his works: 'Telephone Durand about the manuscript score and parts of *Hymne* which are being sent to Lyon. Have they arrived?' This note by an anxious composer reveals how the performing material for the *Hymne au Saint-Sacrement* came to be lost: it was sent to Lyon in autumn 1942 and was never seen again. Two months later, on 19 January 1943, Messiaen once more noted down his concern about the work's disappearance: 'write to Jean Witkowski in Lyon about the material for the *Hymne au Saint-Sacrement*. How was it sent? Perhaps it is still with Béal?'[58] It never turned up, and astonishingly nobody – neither the publisher nor the composer – seems to have kept a copy; Messiaen reconstructed the score from memory in 1946 for performances by Stokowski in New York on 12–14 March 1947.

Between November 1942 and November 1943 the Secrétariat général des Beaux-Arts and the Association Française d'Action Artistique embarked on an ambitious project to record forty works by modern French composers. The sixth record in this series, made in December 1942, was Messiaen's *Les Offrandes oubliées* with the Orchestre Pierné, conducted by Roger Désormière. It was the first commercial recording of any work by Messiaen.[59]

A diary note during the week of 21–27 December 1942 mentions 'M. Méhu, 18–20 place de la Madeleine – Société Cinématographique Synops'. Jean-François Méhu was soon to become the administrator of the Concerts de la

Pléiade and he worked for Synops, the film company of Denise and Roland Tual. This is the earliest reference to the commission from Tual for *Visions de l'Amen*.

Messiaen's diary at the end of December provides an insight into the practical difficulties of travel. He wanted to leave for a holiday at Lévigny and noted that it was necessary to 'see the Préfecture of Police first, boulevard Chaptal. 1. M. Leclerc, 2. Mme Bourreau, 3. M. Moutarde, who makes the decision, 4. M. Nostitz, 6 place du Palais Bourbon or at the German Embassy, 78 rue de Lille (telephone number in the directory).' However, it appears that he and his family were able to spend a few days in Lévigny over the New Year (28 December–2 January).

The last few pages of Messiaen's diary for 1942 included notes on how he might go about securing the release of his brother Alain (still a prisoner of war in Germany), and some lines of music with the comment 'see the Alleluia for the 10th Sunday after Pentecost (Gregorian plainchant)'.[60]

One of the most significant musical premières given in Paris during the Occupation took place at the Concert de la Pléiade on 10 May 1943: the first performance of Messiaen's *Visions de l'Amen*. During the autumn of 1942, Denise Tual went into the Église de la Trinité early one evening and was overwhelmed by the extraordinary music coming from the organ. She determined at once to meet its composer, but was informed by the verger that such a meeting could only be arranged in writing:

> That same evening I wrote to Olivier Messiaen and received by return a very friendly reply on yellow paper, which fixed a meeting with me a few days later at the Trinité, in front of the door leading up to the organ loft.
>
> I was expecting to meet a very young and trendy ('zazou') man. I was still imagining the prewar generation of musicians, the elegance of a Désormière or the eccentricity of a Varèse. I found myself in front of an ageless man of the church. [...] He asked me to sit beside him on the organ bench. Our conversation was in hushed tones and he seemed visibly frightened. His face lit up when I told him the purpose of my visit. A commission? He beamed.

The letter 'on yellow paper' arranging their first meeting is not among Tual's papers in the Bibliothèque Nationale de France, and the surviving correspondence about *Visions de l'Amen* begins with a letter from Messiaen to Tual dated 26 December 1942.[61] This confirmed the details of the commission, though as yet the work had no title which Messiaen was prepared to make public; characteristically, he also fussed over the method of payment:

> We are entirely in agreement on all the points. I will write for you a work for two pianos; you will put it on at your third concert. I will be paid 10,000

74 24 rue Visconti, the home of Guy Bernard-Delapierre (photo: Peter Hill).

75 Guy Bernard-Delapierre, c.1960.

76 André Dubois travelling by bus in October 1954 (photo: Lipnitzki-Viollet).

francs for it and I have already received your cheque for 4,000 francs on account. (Incidentally, you sent this cheque crossed, which is perfect, but without mentioning my name as the bearer; I am not sure if I can cash it like this. Don't worry. If there is any difficulty, I will let you know.) [...] I am leaving Paris for eight days. I will not forget to take our work with me. On the contrary, I am taking my sketches to have a think about them.

By early 1943 Messiaen had re-established contact with Guy Bernard-Delapierre, and on 28 February he performed at Delapierre's house (24 rue Visconti, Paris 6e) with Marcelle Bunlet. This may well have been the event Delapierre recalled in his 1945 article as 'the most stunning of revelations ... That evening I experienced the same shock as I had as a child, hearing *Pelléas* or *Le Sacre*.'[62] Most of the start of the year was spent working on *Visions de l'Amen*. Messiaen needed to find a good piano to work on as his own 'pedalier' at the villa du Danube was hopelessly inadequate. Delapierre had a fine Bechstein in his salon, but the instrument Messiaen used most often during January and February 1943 was in the apartment of André Dubois, whose name appears several times in Messiaen's diary. Who was Dubois? His obituary in *Le Monde* in 1998 summarized an astonishingly varied career:

Born on 8 March 1903, André-Louis Dubois was an adviser to several government ministers between 1930 and 1939. He became a director of the police in 1940, before being relieved of his duties by the Vichy government and working for the Resistance. In 1954 he became préfet de police for the

Seine region and acquired the nickname 'Préfet du silence' for banning the use of car horns in the capital. He was subsequently *résident général*, then ambassador, to Morocco. In 1956 he joined Jean Prouvot's press goup, as general administrator of *Paris-Match* and *Marie-Claire*. In 1971 he became vice-president of *Le Figaro*.[63]

An enthusiastic amateur musician with a passion for new music, Dubois also crops up in connection with Poulenc (who dedicated the last of the *Chansons villageoises* to him). Over a decade later, it was during his time as Prefect of Police that he attended the crowded Paris première of Messiaen's *Livre d'orgue*. But his interest in the arts went wider than music: Dubois was a regular visitor to Picasso during the Occupation,[64] and he was on friendly terms with the playwright (and occasional prison inmate) Jean Genet.

During late February Claude Delvincourt asked Messiaen to write a test-piece for the piano *concours* at the Conservatoire that summer (the *Rondeau*), but despite this extra task, progress on *Visions de l'Amen* was swift. On 17 March 1943 Messiaen was able to announce the completion of the work in a *carte pneumatique* to Denise Tual:

> My work is finished. Here are the title and subtitles: *Visions de l'Amen* for 2 pianos. I. Amen de la Création; II. Amen des Étoiles, de la Planète à l'anneau; III. Amen de l'Agonie de Jésus; IV. Amen du Désir; V. Amen des Anges, des saints, du chant des oiseaux; VI. Amen du Jugement; VII. Amen de la Consommation.
>
> In 15 days I will have finished a first fair copy which I will give to Mlle Loriod so that we can start rehearsing together as soon as possible. I am completely at your disposal as far as the content of the programme is concerned, but this work has quite a fully developed literary and musical commentary.
>
> The work is of considerable proportions: it lasts a total of 40 minutes, almost 45! It is in a very characteristic style and should, as a result, be placed in the middle of the concert. It would be impossible to start with it. Thank you for giving me the opportunity to undertake this huge project, and to complete it.

With *Visions de l'Amen* Yvonne Loriod graduated from her previous role, so far limited to being a page-turner and performing short groups from the *Préludes*. The writing for piano 1 – Loriod's part – tells us what first caused Messiaen to be dazzled by her playing. Her passage work must have been sparkling, she was adept at juggling complexities (rhythmic canons in three layers, for example) and – a particular trademark – she had a remarkable capacity to fire off streams of rapid chords. Messiaen made no attempt to share material

77 Yvonne Loriod on the balcony of Mme Sivade's apartment at 53 rue Blanche in 1941.

78 Yvonne Loriod in 1943.

between the two pianos. Instead, the music was tailor-made for their contrasting techniques and temperaments. Loriod was assigned the bells, birdsong and other virtuoso embellishments; nonetheless, her part is musically subservient – though more difficult technically – with Messiaen playing the themes, and being responsible for the pacing of the music.

One can sense the teacher-pupil relationship almost literally in the opening 'Amen de la Création', where Loriod's glacial chords are like chips of matter floating in the void, given light and life by the recurring Creation theme rising from the depths of piano 2. This creates problems of ensemble, since piano 1 is in precise rhythmic patterns while piano 2 needs rhetorical elbow room, particularly towards the climax where the theme enlarges into grandly broken chords. Messiaen seems to have changed his mind on the best way to play this passage. In the Messiaens' 1962 recording the ensemble, though still essentially together, is clearly under strain, and the broken chords sound rushed. Later, Messiaen recommended to George Benjamin and Peter Hill that the pianos should proceed independently, simply reconnecting with each other at the start of each phrase.

Another consequence of the separation of musical material between the two pianos is that all the movements progress through accumulation. The 'Amen des Anges, des saints, du chant des oiseaux' (no.5), for example, starts simply, with the pianos in unison; later the reprise of the exposition is decorated exuberantly by broken chords and rhythmic canons. The middle section of no.5 is a rare instance when Loriod has the principal line, a medley of birdsong accompanied by dancing rhythms on piano 2. A dance of a different kind occupies the centre of no.2 (the 'Amen des Étoiles, de la Planète à l'anneau'), with the pianos this time working in tandem in a fierce depiction of orbiting planets. In the central 'Amen du Désir', the exposition has two sections, slow and fast, the second of which is a stupendous solo for Messiaen; this is repeated exactly, with the desire of Creation to be united with its Creator heightened by equally brilliant interjections on piano 1.

The final movement – 'Amen de la Consommation' – is a tour de force for Loriod, piano 1 storming the heavens in a crescendo of virtuosity. The music transforms the material of the first movement: the rather four-square Creation theme comes into its own (on piano 2), marching onwards and upwards towards Paradise, while the descant of dissonant chords becomes peals of bells deployed in a rhythmic canon. These become ever more turbulent and congested as the canon takes closer alignment, eventually modulating via modal harmonies into the pure light of A major (the home key), with descending scales – pianissimo – arranged in 6-part chords. This moment of stillness is actually the hardest test in the work for piano 1, exemplifying Loriod's priceless ability – immediately recognized by Messiaen – to play very quietly with no loss of incisiveness. The final pages are a sprint finish,

79 Rehearsing *Visions de l'Amen* in 1943.

80 Nelly Eminger-Sivade.

spiralling through volleys of chords and the Creation theme in rippling semiquavers, before erupting into carillons of glittering bells.

As soon as *Visions de l'Amen* was finished in mid-March 1943, Messiaen needed to have copies made, then to rehearse it with Loriod. At the same time, he was preparing his class for the annual harmony *concours*. He was also busy as an organist, and not just at the Trinité: the marriage of Daniel-Lesur on 30 March, at Notre-Dame-de-Grâce, was an occasion when Messiaen and Jean-Jacques Grunenwald both improvised at the organ. The copying of the score of *Visions de l'Amen* was done by mid-April, and Messiaen's diary on 14 April showed that preparations were beginning in earnest: 'Take *Amen* to Mlle Loriod at her godmother's house, 53 rue Blanche.'

Loriod's godmother Nelly Eminger-Sivade, originally from Austria, was a remarkable woman. She did much to encourage her brilliant goddaughter, putting on monthly recitals in her salon where the young Yvonne would play for invited guests: 'Honegger, Migot and Poulenc came to hear me at these concerts when I was eighteen, and I played music by Messiaen, Jolivet, etc.'[65] Nelly Sivade's husband worked as an engineer for the Parisian water company, and the couple lived in a handsome apartment, with a balcony, at 53 rue Blanche, on the west side of the street, a few hundred metres uphill from the Trinité. The first rehearsals for *Visions de l'Amen* took place on 16 April at Mme Sivade's, after dinner. The Conservatoire's Easter vacation began the next day, and Messiaen went to the Aube for a holiday: on 18 April 1943 he wrote to Tual from his aunt Agnès's house at Fuligny about the guests he wanted invited to the première of *Visions de l'Amen*, and reported progress on rehearsals:

You will find enclosed a list of 50 names and addresses. These are the people I would like you to invite to the Concert de la Pléiade on 10 May. I have included only those that are strictly necessary among the numerous pupils and friends who want to come to the first performance, and who have already spoken to me about it several times. Perhaps the hall is going to hold a larger audience than for the previous concerts as the layout is different. Since many of these people are friends of both of us, I hope you will be able to invite all of those on the list, and I thank you for doing that with all my heart.

I should also mention that my wife and son appear on the list – above all, don't forget them! It will also need to be remembered that the two pianists (Mlle Loriod and myself) and the two page-turners (because we must have two page-turners) will also require passes to get in. I thought of this because your front-of-house arrangements are draconian – and I congratulate you on that!

Forgive me for troubling you with these down-to-earth questions! I gave my manuscript to Mlle Loriod five days ago (my own copy is just finished) and we have had a first rehearsal: she already plays magnificently!

The mention of 'draconian' front-of-house arrangements in this letter is the only reference in Messiaen's correspondence with Tual to the controls which were necessary to ensure, presumably, that neither undesirable occupying Germans nor known collaborators were admitted. The first performance of *Visions de l'Amen* was originally scheduled to form part of the third Concert de la Pléiade, at the Galerie Charpentier on 3 May 1943, but a small printed invitation (which manages to misspell Messiaen as 'Messian' and Loriod as 'Loriot') announced the decision to perform the work on its own a week later, and gave the reason: 'The significance, the character and the duration of this work have led the Concerts de la Pléiade to present it in a concert which will be entirely devoted to it. *Visions de l'Amen* will be performed by Olivier Messian and Yvonne Loriot on 10 May at 17.00 hours. This invitation will be required for entry.' A private dress rehearsal for *Visions de l'Amen* took place at Mme Sivade's the day before, on Sunday, 9 May, as Messiaen noted in his diary: '14h. rehearsal at Mme Sivade's. Those present were Mme Tual, Gallimard, Poulenc, Jolivet, Samazeuilh, Honegger, Mme Messiaen.' Loriod herself recalled that after this dress rehearsal Messiaen took these invited guests down the rue Blanche to attend Vespers at the Trinité.[66]

The première itself – before an invited audience – was attended by many of the most distinguished figures in French cultural life, and photographs of the event in the Tual collection show Marie-Blanche de Polignac, Roland-Manuel, Christian Dior and Francis Poulenc among the audience.[67] According to Tual's own recollections,[68] others present included Paul Valéry, François Mauriac and Jean Cocteau. The two page-turners were Serge Nigg and René Hanicot.[69] Such was the lustre of the audiences for the Concerts de la Pléiade that they were sometimes written about not so much as musical events, but as glittering social occasions enlivening an otherwise sombre time. For example, Marcelle Auclair wrote the following in her column 'Ma semaine à Paris' for *Marie-Claire*:

81 The first performance of *Visions de l'Amen*, Galerie Charpentier, 10 May 1943.

82 The audience at the first performance of *Visions de l'Amen*, with Poulenc in the back row, third from the right.

It is thrilling to comment on the Concerts de la Pléiade which take place at the Galerie Charpentier. During this time when we get butter from the butcher, meat from the hairdresser and sugar from the shoe repairer, these fashionable concerts take place in an art gallery. It is only possible to go to them by invitation and, of course, it's a personal affront not to be invited! Madame Colette arrives on her bicycle, in her sports outfit, wearing sandals and a boater. She has cycled from Palais Royal because it's all on the flat, she confided to us.[70]

The Pléiade's programmes were innovative and imaginatively planned. In the eleven concerts given during the Occupation, premières included not only Messiaen's *Visions de l'Amen* but also Poulenc's Violin Sonata and *Chansons villageoises*, and Jolivet's *Poèmes intimes*; there were also regular performances of Stravinsky and of early French music (including an evening devoted to Rameau's *Platée*).[71] Among the most distinguished musicians at the première of *Visions de l'Amen* was Honegger. His review appeared in *Comœdia* on 15 May. It begins with a reference to the fashionable audience, before considering the work itself in some detail:

The glamorous ladies wearing hats like table-tops or multicoloured tennis racquets who provide the visual ornament at the Concerts de la Pléiade must have been rather surprised. The charming ear-ticklers of recent programmes[72] were unexpectedly replaced by a work which is long, highly individual, and densely written, eschewing the variety of orchestral timbres by restraining itself to the black and white of two pianos. And what a serious subject: *Visions de l'Amen*, seven large musical frescos with a duration of almost an hour. Nevertheless, the experience was a perfect success. I must say straight away that this work by Olivier Messiaen seems to me a remarkable one, of great musical richness and of true grandeur in its conception.

Perhaps I might discuss some details. First, the fact that it is written for two pianos lends a certain austerity. In the first piece, the same chords (augmented fourths and perfect fourths) are used with a little too much persistence. There is a certain difficulty in discerning the principal musical lines resulting from the absence of different timbres. But what does this matter given the poetic power, the constantly exalted level of the musical discourse, and the quality of the musical invention which is affirmed so impressively? The rules which the composer has invented and imposed upon himself with rigorous discipline give to the whole work a noble style with no hint of dryness.

My personal preference is above all for the 'Amen de l'Agonie de Jésus' and the 'Amen du Désir'. In the first there is an anguished theme which turns at length on the same three notes (C sharp, D, E flat) and is of extraordinary expressive intensity. In the second, a calm theme of exquisite tenderness is set, in variations, against a second motif, with a syncopated rhythm, which is ardent and passionate. [. . .] The composer himself performed the work with Mademoiselle Yvonne Loriod as his partner. Given the technical difficulty of the score, I can hardly begin to do justice to the extraordinary command of this young arist, but I do so in all sincerity.

One personal wish. I would like this work to be heard, preceded by its commentaries, at the Jeunesses musicales. That would be infinitely more interesting and useful than the parade of works which is usually served up there. In this work there are things for the young to discuss and to admire. Some will be passionate about it, while others will repudiate it, but that would give life to the world of music. Finally, we should thank the organizers of the Pléiade for having put on a work of this quality in the best possible conditions.

Following the concert, Messiaen wrote a letter to Denise Tual, thanking her not only for arranging the concert, but also for 'the opportunity to write a long and serious piece'. The second performance of *Visions de l'Amen* was a few weeks later, on 22 June, at the Salle Gaveau (again by Loriod and Messiaen). It was an event organized by Guy Bernard-Delapierre, who read Messiaen's commentaries. In the first half of the concert, Bunlet and Messiaen performed the *Poèmes pour Mi.*

In September 1943 Denise Tual contacted Messiaen again, with the offer of a further commission for the piece which was ultimately to become the *Trois petites Liturgies de la Présence Divine*. Messiaen's original plan was for another work using two pianos. He replied to Tual on 22 September:

Your letter has just reached me in Neussargues (Cantal) where I am finishing some rather hard-working holidays, mostly spent correcting the proofs [presumably of *Visions de l'Amen*]. My wife is well, and Pascal is in particularly good form: he has grown, and his neck and arms are suntanned from the fine air and the light. He is interested in a thousand different things, and runs non-stop!

Thank you for thinking of me again for your concerts. I am very grateful to you and to M. Gallimard: what kindness! My specific intention is to write a new suite for two pianos and to offer that to you. I know it is dangerous to redo something that was a success the first time round, but apart from two pianos, which I like a great deal, I am only interested in writing for a quartet or a large orchestra, neither of which is possible. Aside from the matter of a first performance, I would, however, love to hear my *Quatuor pour la fin du Temps* (violin, clarinet, cello and piano) at the Concerts de la Pléiade. I wrote it while in captivity, and it is one of my best things!

So, I agree to compose a new work for first performance at the Concerts de la Pléiade during the 1944 season. But I am not able to show it to you before 1 November, as you wanted, because I will only start getting down to work in October and will scarcely be finished by 1 May, which would fix its performance at one of your last concerts, perhaps at the beginning of June. This work will be written for two pianos, with a similar style, genre and duration to my *Visions de l'Amen*. It could be played by Mlle Loriod (I don't know of a better interpreter!) and myself, as we did last season. Finally, as this will be a considerable undertaking for me, you could pay me 10,000 francs, in two instalments, again as for last season. (Forgive, please, the implacable precision of this last sentence!)

I return to Paris on 2 October and resume my duties straight away at the Conservatoire and at the Trinité. Would you like to send me a note to say that we are in agreement about these proposals?

On 4 October 1943, two days after his return to Paris, Messiaen visited Tual's office in the place de la Madeleine; she was not there and, from the perspective of over half a century later, her absence was fortuitous, as Messiaen was obliged to write down his current thinking on the new work, on the headed writing paper of the film company Synops, run by Roland and Denise Tual. This important letter reveals that his plans had changed dramatically in the space of less than two weeks:

I came to Synops this morning in the hope of talking to you at greater length about the Concerts de la Pléiade. Having been unable to find you, I am writing you this quick note.

I have thought a great deal about the matter of your new commission. The combination of two pianos, which worked so well last year, and which I originally wanted to use again, is attracting me less now, as I am afraid of simply rewriting *Visions de l'Amen* less well.

So here is another project which supersedes the previous one: I could write a work of similar character to [*Visions de l'*] *Amen* in terms of style and subject, but it would be more complex and would also need a much greater number of performers. To begin with, I would need:
1) A reciter (a speaking male voice)
2) An ondes Martenot (this is a marvellous radio-electronic instrument, not very cumbersome, which I am sure you know about!)
3) 3 flutes
4) 3 trombones
5) A piano (a large grand piano, of course)
6) Percussion consisting of: celesta, tam-tam, cymbals and tambourine

7) Ten strings (that is to say, double string quintet comprising 2 first violins,
2 second violins, 2 violas, 2 cellos, 2 double basses).

It needs a conductor (Désormières [*sic*] would be perfect); for the reciter,
J.-L. Barrault. The piano and the ondes have very important and difficult
parts: the piano could be given to Mlle Loriod, and the ondes to Mlle
Martenot, sister of the inventor.

The work will last between 15 and 20 minutes but will not be finished
until 1 May as I need to complete the text, the music and the instrumentation. The labour involved is as much as before, so we could keep the same
arrangements, that is to say 10,000 francs, in two payments. Would you like
to send me a note saying whether this project would be acceptable?

There are fascinating differences between the plan in this letter and the work's
final form, particularly in terms of scoring. The surprises include the proposed
use of three flutes, three trombones, and, most strikingly, a narration to be spoken by Jean-Louis Barrault. Messiaen seems at this stage to have envisaged a
shorter work than the one which emerged: the duration of 15–20 minutes given
in this letter is almost half that of the finished piece.[73] Remarkably, Messiaen
included no mention of the female choir, presumably contemplating a spoken
text at this stage, rather than the sung setting which he was to begin a few weeks
later. However, a number of the suggestions made in the letter turned out as
planned: Désormière conducted the première with Loriod and Ginette
Martenot as soloists, and the eventual scoring included parts for solo piano and
ondes Martenot, percussion and strings.

On 2 November 1943 Messiaen wrote to Denise Tual, acknowledging receipt
of the first payment for the new commission, and promising to finish it by 15
April 1944. According to his note in the programme for the first performance,
composition of the *Trois petites Liturgies* began a fortnight later, on 15 November 1943 (the date which is also given on the published score). The work
was completed on 15 March 1944, a month earlier than predicted.

A note in Messiaen's diary in October 1943 had important implications for his
teaching activity: 'Organize at Delapierre's regular lessons in analysis and composition for Martinet, Nigg, Prior, Loriod, Aubut, Grimaud (one afternoon
each month).' This is one of the earliest mentions of the group which came to
be called 'Les Flèches' ('The Arrows'), who attended Messiaen's private courses
outside the Conservatoire (though Nigg, Loriod and Aubut were also members
of his official harmony class). Yvette Grimaud (b.1920) had been introduced to
Messiaen by Maurice and Ginette Martenot in 1938, and attended informal
meetings at 13 villa du Danube before the war. She recalled these as 'more than
about aesthetics, but lessons about life, as in the time of Bach or Monteverdi'.[74]
Jean-Louis Martinet (b.1912) studied privately with Messiaen, and received a

letter from him on 22 September 1943: 'To lead you and your five friends deeper into the heart of music, I have decided to arrange classes in composition and musical analysis at the home of my good friend Guy Bernard-Delapierre, exclusively for Delapierre and our little group. We will have a magnificent grand piano with unique casework. What better way is there to cement friendship?'[75]

Soon after Messiaen's return to Paris in 1941, he had started teaching private pupils, often for no fee, and he also taught groups of students at the home of Nelly Eminger-Sivade, at 53 rue Blanche. In autumn 1941 Messiaen's diary listed Virginie Bianchini, Claude Prior and Father François Florand, a Dominican priest, as pupils, with Grimaud and Martinet added in 1942, as was the Canadian organist Françoise Aubut, to whom Messiaen gave lessons in improvisation. In 1943 he started to teach Pierre Henry and Maurice Le Roux, along with Raymond Depraz and Marcel Frémiot, who worked as copyists for Messiaen. When did the 'little group' described by Messiaen start to be known as 'Les Flèches'? The name came from a calligraphic device made up of Messiaen's initials. The 'O' enclosed an 'M' with arrow heads on the two upper tips. This monogram was certainly current by June 1944, when Maurice Le Roux wrote a poem for Messiaen entitled 'Magister adest', with an attractively stylized version of the 'Flèches' symbol at the foot of the page.[76]

The private classes were established at Guy Bernard-Delapierre's house by 29 November 1943 when Messiaen analysed Honegger's *Antigone*, probably prompted by the work's Paris première which had taken place in January 1943. The venue for the class was a historic one: 24 rue Visconti had once been Racine's home (he died there, and his death is commemorated by a plaque on the wall). The following year, Bernard-Delapierre was to be the dedicatee of *Technique de mon langage musical*, a touching gesture of gratitude from the composer to a man who gave him such support during the most difficult years of the Occupation.[77] Bernard-Delapierre was born in 1907 and died in 1979. In conversation with Antoine Goléa, Messiaen said that Delapierre had introduced himself in 1940 as 'an Egyptologist'.[78] But this is only part of the story, since Delapierre was primarily a musician. While he certainly went on some archaeological expeditions, he was professionally active as a composer of film music, usually as 'Guy Bernard' (the 'Delapierre' seems to have been dropped during the 1940s). From 1942 until the 1960s he produced over forty scores for short films ('*courts métrages*').[79] In the mid-1940s he was also an impresario and agent: concert programmes given by Messiaen and Loriod at the time often included a note stating that they were represented by the Bureau de Concerts de Paris: Directeurs G. Dussurget et G. Bernard-Delapierre.[80] Loriod recalled the last time she and Messiaen went to visit Bernard-Delapierre: 'He died on 30 July 1979 at Juan-les-Pins (near Nice). My sister Jacqueline, who lived at Antibes, drove Messiaen and me over to see him a few months before his death. He asked us over to his house and took us out onto the terrace. He was very happy to see Messiaen again. He was already very ill (undoubtedly cancer) but was still writing music for films.'[81] Though contact between the two men had become sporadic, Bernard-Delapierre's name (usually shortened to 'Delap.') appeared time and again in Messiaen's diaries from early 1943 onwards, for a period of four or five years.

Messiaen's diary for 1944 opened with some jottings on the preliminary leaves about possible projects; the first of these is for an orchestral work and suggests first thoughts for what eventually became the *Turangalîla-Symphonie*:

> With the orchestra, think of the rhythmic personalities of *Le Sacre* (Danse sacrale): one rhythmic character is immobile, while the other character waxes and wanes, lives, dies, rises again. Use a kaleidoscope of chords: chords of five different combinations superimposed, then change the order of the superimposition. A theme of chords [. . .] notes grouped in a new order etc. Treat *all* the instruments of the orchestra, woodwind, *brass*, percussion and strings, in continuous staccato semiquavers. [. . .] Two speeds superimposed: one always the same, the other progressively and uniformly accelerating. The principle of the kaleidoscope: an image reflected five times, always making a simultaneous star shape, the same quintuple reflection in 20 or 30 forms (different versions of the same theme).

In fact, Messiaen began writing *Turangalîla* more than two years after these notes were made (the Preface to the score gives the starting date as 17 July 1946).[82] However, many of their ideas seem equally applicable to Messiaen's next work, *Vingt Regards sur l'Enfant-Jésus*, which at the start of 1944 had yet to be composed. *Vingt Regards*, like *Turangalîla*, has a 'theme of chords', and employs extensively the principle of balancing 'immobile' elements against those that change and develop; and the superimposition of two 'speeds' occurs in no.18 of the *Vingt Regards*, in the form of two scales of durations, one of which increases in its values as the other simultaneously decreases. Both works make prodigious use of rhythmic process, explore gamelan-like textures, and have at their centre an exuberant, life-affirming scherzo. There are also thematic links. The three-note ostinato used with mounting excitement in *Turangalîla*'s 'Développement de l'amour' is taken from the last movement of the *Vingt Regards*, and there are close similarities between the love music of *Turangalîla* and the 'theme of love' from the *Vingt Regards*. The difference, of course, is that in *Vingt Regards* the passion is spiritual, while in *Turangalîla* it is the joys of human love that are celebrated with unembarrassed abandon. Thus, where the *Vingt Regards* gravitates inwards towards rapt meditation, *Turangalîla* proceeds through hyperactive accumulation – so that even in the stillness of the 'Jardin du sommeil d'amour' (the sixth movement), the love music on strings and ondes Martenot unfolds against a background of flickering rhythmic patterns.

The same 1944 diary entry includes two other intriguing comments. The first suggests that Messiaen contemplated orchestrating some of *Visions de l'Amen* for two pianos and an orchestra with ondes Martenot:

> In the 'Amen de l'Agonie': orchestrate the three-note lament, with ondes Martenot, oboe, cor anglais, muted trumpet, flutter-tongue, strings muted. [...] Song of Paradise: smooth, singing, symphonic (see symphony by Mozart, and also rainbows, Picasso and *ffff*). Superimpose all the rhythmic canons in my *Traité* – that will make more than twelve rhythms working together, each with its own chords, on modes etc. (for two pianos and orchestra).

On the next leaf Messiaen outlined another project: 'Write a Requiem for brass instruments playing under the Arc de Triomphe for M. Edm. Lex (in six months).' At the time this came to nothing, though the idea of an instrumental Requiem found a distant echo twenty years later in *Et exspecto resurrectionem mortuorum* for winds, brass and percussion, commissioned by André Malraux, to the memory of those who died in the two world wars.

The name of the writer Maurice Toesca appears on 4 January 1944. Messiaen saw a lot of him during 1944 in connection with the music for a radio presentation of Toesca's poems on the Nativity. The result of this was to be far more extended – and vastly more significant – than was originally intended, at least by Toesca (Messiaen may already have had the ultimate form of the work in mind): instead of twelve short piano pieces to complement spoken texts by Toesca, by the end of the summer Messiaen had completed his mightiest work to date: *Vingt Regards sur l'Enfant-Jésus*.

The saga of how a modest commission became a composition more than twice the size of anything Messiaen had so far written is reflected in the work's final form. In effect, *Vingt Regards* is a giant rondo, anchored around the eight movements which employ the 'Theme of God', the most important of a number of recurring leitmotifs. The work's momentum derives from two factors. One is the way the 'Theme of God' is transformed, with each change marking one of the main staging posts in the theological journey: from God the Father and the Son (nos.1 and 5), via the convulsive energy of creation and its counterpart in the 'Spirit of Joy' (nos.6 and 10), to the events of the Nativity (nos.11 and 15) and finally to the glory of the eternal Church (nos.19 and 20). The other element in the plan was to use these movements as frames for the remaining *regards*, which are grouped in threes. In the second half, each group grows progressively in scale, reaching a climax with the celebration of Christ's coronation in the 'Regard de l'Onction terrible' (no.18).

The relationship of this rigorously executed design to Toesca's request for *Douze Regards* is that the 'independent' movements (those not containing the 'Theme of God') number twelve. To claim these as the original set of *Regards* may be too convenient, especially as Messiaen's diaries are enough to suggest that some movements may have existed earlier in a more concise form. These may well have included some of the 'Theme of God' *Regards*: 'Le Baiser de l'Enfant-Jésus' is an obvious candidate, a piece that could have been a simple lullaby, without the momentous developments that occupy its second half. Even so, there is much to be said for the theory. The 'Theme of God' *Regards* are generally on a markedly larger scale, contain the most transcendent virtuosity (nos.6, 10 and 20) and above all form the key element in a design which would have become necessary only when Messiaen decided to expand immensely beyond the confines of the original commission.

In one sense the *Vingt Regards* marks the end of an era. Aside from two much shorter organ works – the *Messe de la Pentecôte* and the *Livre d'orgue* – it was to be his last religious composition until the 1960s. Instead, the years that followed the end of the war would see Messiaen taking new paths: in the Tristan trilogy, in the 'experimental' works of 1949–50, and in the decade of birdsong (1952–62). But many of these paths begin here. One obvious expression of creative renewal comes in radical ways of writing for the piano. There is a new awareness of its percussive possibilities, in the thudding clusters and rasping cymbals of no.12, the drumming that opens no.10, or the scales of durations that cross over one another as they accelerate and decelerate (nos.16 and 18). The birdsong (nos.8 and 14) has a velocity and cutting edge far removed from its role hitherto as decorative descant, while five years before the *Quatre Études de rythme* we encounter rotating 12-note patterns (in no.20). Above all, in 'Par Lui tout a été fait' (no.6) and the 'Regard de l'Esprit de joie' (no.10) the ruthless pursuit of pattern and process drives the pianist to heroic feats of virtuosity.

In all this the presence of Loriod can be detected. Her pianistic wizardry, already tested in *Visions de l'Amen* and the *Trois petites Liturgies*, could be taken for granted; but the *Vingt Regards* – Messiaen's most ambitious work to date – was a true coming-of-age (she was indeed twenty-one at the time of its première). Loriod's influence went beyond virtuosity. As Messiaen described her, in a note added to the text of his interviews with Goléa, she was a 'unique, sublime and brilliant pianist, whose existence transformed not only the composer's way of writing for the piano, but his style, vision of the world, and modes of thought'.[83]

One of the few non-French contacts which Messiaen was able to maintain during the Occupation was with Paul Collaer in Brussels.[84] Messiaen wrote to him on 19 Febuary 1944 to express his pleasure at a forthcoming performance of the *Quatuor* and to tell him about *Visions de l'Amen*:

It is with joy that I learn you are giving my *Quatuor pour la fin du Temps* at the start of April in Brussels. I would like to come to hear this concert. Thank you. And thank you for your very kind letter.

Visions de l'Amen is still in manuscript and will be available soon [...] (this summer, I think, though engraving and printing take so much longer than they used to, because of a lack of materials and of manpower). As soon as my *Visions de l'Amen* is published I will have a copy sent to you and will be very happy if you can arrange a performance. I wonder if I could come to play it myself in Brussels at the same time as your performance of the *Quatuor*? But I don't know what the difficulties, conditions and travel expenses might be.[85]

Messiaen was being optimistic about a publication date for *Visions de l'Amen*: the first edition eventually appeared in March 1950 and all performances before then were given from copies of the manuscript. The Brussels performance of the *Quatuor* took place a few months later than originally planned, on 14 November 1944 at one of the Concerts Collaer, and the earliest performance there of *Visions de l'Amen* was given by Messiaen and Loriod in April 1946.

Early in 1944 Messiaen's *Technique de mon langage musical* was published by Leduc (the printer's date on the volume of music examples is February 1944). This was a remarkable work of self-revelation in which the composer explained his musical vocabulary, explored its origins, provided a comprehensive list of works (several of which have vanished) and evaluated his own compositions with an extraordinary system of Michelin-style stars: 'works which are characteristic of my musical language are marked with one star; very characteristic works are marked with two stars.' Among those with no stars at all it is intriguing to find two of his most popular compositions: *L'Ascension* and *O sacrum convivium*.[86]

In the Introduction, Messiaen thanked his teachers, those who had influenced him, and his most faithful interpreters. The teachers are comparatively predictable (Jean and Noël Gallon, Dupré and Dukas), as are the performers (Roger Désormière, Marcelle Bunlet, Étienne Pasquier and Yvonne Loriod); but the influences are a bewildering, glorious mixture: his mother Cécile Sauvage, his wife Claire Delbos, Shakespeare, Paul Claudel, Pierre Reverdy, Paul Eluard, two theologians – Ernest Hello and Dom Columba Marmion – birds, Russian music, Debussy's *Pelléas et Mélisande*, plainchant, Hindu rhythms, the mountains of the Dauphiné and 'all that is stained glass and rainbows'. Finally, Messiaen thanked those who encouraged him to write *Technique*, 'especially my friend André Jolivet'. There is a wide-eyed excitement and sense of wonder in these influences, with a child-like delight (and devotion) evident in many of them too. Messiaen was seldom as innocently frank again; by allowing so many of his passions and enthusiasms to tumble out in a short, readily comprehended paragraph, he was laying himself open to attack. This duly materialized in 'Le Cas Messiaen', discussed in the next chapter. The first edition carried no dedication, but this was an oversight: an English version appeared in 1956 with a dedication to Guy Bernard-Delapierre which has been included in all later editions.

Messiaen always had a fascination with the music of the Orient. On 15 March he was at Delapierre's to listen to some rare recordings of Balinese music which Delapierre may have borrowed from the Musée de l'Homme. Messiaen's enthusiasm for the music of Bali went back to 1931, when he heard a gamelan at the Exposition Coloniale Internationale de Paris;[87] this is nowhere more apparent than in the *Trois petites Liturgies*, but it is fitting that we discover him listening to Balinese music at Delapierre's house on the very day he finished the *Trois petites Liturgies* (15 March 1944 is the completion date given on the score). A letter from Delapierre also reveals that Messiaen gave him a private preview of the work that day. Writing from Vaison-la-Romaine in the Vaucluse on 31 March, Delapierre expressed his delight in characteristically generous terms:

> How often I have thought of you and your latest work, during these few days of peace and quiet. I can't tell you how much these three pieces moved me. More than ever, your music expresses everything that I hope secretly to hear one day. It seems to me that, mastering your language with ever increasing skill, you have achieved the most direct form of expression and that, throughout, the most intense feeling is that of love. Contrary to what many believe, mysticism doesn't need to involve things which are obscure or hidden. Before everything it is a song of light and of love and it seems to me that your rainbow is ever more brilliant as it reaches the skies and descends to those of us who have the good fortune to hear you, and the grace to be close to you.[88]

Messiaen's diary on 16 March, the day after finishing the work, included notes about the *Liturgies*, laying the ground for the best possible preparation before the première: 'telephone Passerone about the vibraphone and maracas; give the score to Désormière, Jolivet, Martenot (and to Delapierre)'. During the next few weeks he was very preoccupied with the new work. On 20 March he noted that all the copying of the score, parts and piano part had to be ready by 15 April. At the same time, he was about to embark on a huge new project, for solo piano: according to the title page of the score, Messiaen began the *Vingt Regards* on 23 March, though his diary suggests perhaps that work did not begin in earnest for another week or so, when he returned from a brief trip to his aunts in the Aube. He was back by 31 March, when he visited Louis Durey. The same day also included an important reference to Messiaen's new project for Toesca's radio broadcasts: 'Prepare music for the 12 *Regards*'.

While Messiaen was hard at work beginning the *Regards*, he was also trying to complete arrangements for the première of the *Liturgies*: on 5 April he gave the '*Liturgies* to Déso[rmière]', and while plans for a performance in May had by now been abandoned, Denise Tual was still hoping to perform the work at the Concerts de la Pléiade in June; Messiaen wrote to her on 21 April enclosing programme notes and insisting, as was his custom, on a precise adherence to the text as written:

> You will find enclosed all the documents for the programme of our Concert de la Pléiade (early June). First the programme proper (titles, subtitles, names of the performers) to print in large type. Then the note on the work which I have written and which can fit – printed in small type – into the format of one page of your programmes this season (recto only), or on two pages if you prefer it in larger type. In any event do not cut anything in the programme or the note because I have only included what is indispensable. And if, by bad luck, something does not suit you, please telephone me!

A photocopied score was ready by 4 May (a presentation copy survives in Tual's archives; Yvonne Loriod has another copy) and Messiaen gave the piano and ondes Martenot parts to Loriod and Ginette Martenot on 17 May. The next day he was at Delapierre's 'with Mie and Pascal', noting that they watched a film and that Messiaen played the *Liturgies* for Delapierre and André Dubois (at whose piano much of *Visions de l'Amen* had been written). On 26 May he gave the celesta part of the *Liturgies* to Yvette Grimaud.[89] Messiaen was also contemplating yet another new piano work. On 29 May he noted in his diary: 'write a piano piece for Loriod, for her three recitals in October', but by the end of the summer he had completed the monumental *Vingt Regards* which is dedicated to her.

There is a further mention of the *Regards* project on 31 May: 'Write music for Toesca, ready and orchestrated for 1 November at the latest' (the only time in the diary where there is a suggestion that the work might be scored for anything other than solo piano). Meanwhile, concert activity continued unabated. On 7 June Messiaen played the *Quatuor* at Delapierre's house, with his usual partners the Pasquiers and Vacellier (Messiaen noted that 'tout le monde' came to the performance).

Messiaen was seeing many of his pupils regularly for individual sessions (often on Saturdays) as well as at his Conservatoire class or at the classes for 'Les Flèches'. But this summer a new name appeared: on 28 June, at 9.30 a.m., 'M. Boulez (pupil of Pierre Jamet)' came to see Messiaen for the first time. He is mentioned on several more occasions during 1944, visiting Messiaen at home at least four times.[90] Boulez first attended one of Messiaen's classes for 'Les Flèches' at Delapierre's house on 8 December (Messiaen discussed Ravel's *Ma Mère l'Oye* on this occasion, and noted that the others present included Nigg,

Grimaud, Aubut, Loriod and Martinet). Boulez's then address (14 rue Oudinot, Paris 7ᵉ) appears several times, but the most delightful reference is at the back of the diary: 'Pierre Boulez [. . .] likes modern music, wants to take harmony lessons etc. with me.'

Messiaen acknowledged receipt of the second cheque in part-payment of the commission for the *Liturgies* on 15 July. His unnamed correspondent was probably Jean-François Méhu, secretary of the Concerts de la Pléiade. Messiaen also alludes to the chaotic situation in the months before the Liberation of Paris; the D-Day landings had taken place on 6 June, power supplies were at best unpredictable, and a further postponement of the première became unavoidable:

> I have now received the cheque for 5,000 francs signed by Madame Tual on behalf of the Librairie Gallimard. Thank you very much. I am very much hoping that you will perform my work at the Concerts de la Pléiade as soon as circumstances permit it. And I will leave a photocopy of my score at your office when I am passing through your district in the next few days.

The much-delayed première of the *Trois petites Liturgies* eventually took place on 21 April 1945.

In August 1944 Paris was in turmoil. The French police force was on strike; police officers took over the Préfecture at the quai des Orfèvres on 19 August and one of their first actions was to hoist the *Tricolore*, 'the first time the French flag had been flown in the capital for over four years'.[91] Street fights broke out between French *résistants* and German soldiers, with loss of life on both sides, and for a few days there was a real fear that the city might descend into urban warfare. But on the evening of 24 August a few allied tanks slipped quietly into the city and parked in front of the Hôtel de Ville. The main allied forces, led by General Leclerc's *Deuxième Division blindée*, arrived the next morning; and though the allies encountered some heavy German defence near Les Invalides, the Occupation of Paris ended on 25 August. General Choltitz signed the German surrender at the Gare Montparnasse and that same evening de Gaulle went to the Hôtel de Ville where he made his first speech since arriving in the the French capital: 'Paris! Paris humiliated! Paris broken! Paris martyrized! But Paris liberated! Liberated by herself, by her own people, with the help of the armies of France, with the support and help of all France, of fighting France, of the one France, of the true France, of the eternal France.'[92] The next day, de Gaulle led a triumphant parade down the Champs-Élysées.

Though Messiaen made no mention of these events in his appointment diary, their impact on him can readily be imagined, not least because de Gaulle was the only political leader about whom Messiaen expressed public support. Messiaen was never involved in any Resistance activity (though musicians he greatly admired were, notably Désormière), but his recollections of de Gaulle suggest a man who was both politically engaged and fiercely patriotic. In an interview published in 1973, the composer explained why he had signed a call for de Gaulle's re-election in 1965:

> As a child I witnessed the First World War and I participated in the Second. In 1940 I was taken prisoner – I was a prisoner at Stalag VIII[A], in Silesia – and this was a moment when all seemed lost to me and my companions. In our despair, a single name rose up, a name to which everyone clung, and it was that of General de Gaulle. He did not yet have the recognition which was to follow, since he was still a clandestine figure if you like. But despite all the precautions taken by the Germans, the prisoners very quickly found out about him, and put their hope in him. This was a flame which glowed in the darkness.[93]

Messiaen's support for de Gaulle was no passing matter. When asked about those who had admired the General in 1944 but later looked in new directions and changed their allegiance, he was candid:

> I think those who did not follow him were wrong – precisely because, whatever their opinions, General de Gaulle represented France. He was someone who truly loved France, who personified France, who symbolized France and who was part of French mythology.

At the time of the Liberation, Messiaen was very close to completing the *Vingt Regards* and started making arrangements for performances. On 31 August he wrote: 'For the *Regards*, see Enrich Straram at the Palais Berlitz, opposite the Paramount [. . .] or Dutilleux instead' (both working at French Radio), and 'bring together Toesca, Delapierre and Yvonne Loriod to play them the *Regards*'. On 3 September he observed that 'Barraud is in charge of putting on Toesca's *Regards* with piano pieces between the text, and under the text, on the Radio in January (five or six piano pieces in each concert): ask for payment later. Barraud will put on the first performance of the *Petites Liturgies* with the Orchestre National.'[94] There are numerous further references to the *Regards* during the last quarter of 1944. On 5 September: 'Delapierre wishes to publish by subscription a *recording* of the *Regards* by Loriod.' The next day Messiaen jotted down plans for the spring, including '*Regards* in two concerts given by Loriod'. According to the first edition of the work, he completed it on 8 September. Three days later, on 11 September, two entries suggest that he was wasting no time in introducing it to friends: 'telephone Toesca, Loriod and Delapierre to play them the *Regards*' and, below this, an appointment at 2.30 p.m. the same afternoon, 'at Delapierre's with Toesca, André Dubois and Loriod to play the *Regards*'. On 3 October Messiaen telephoned Jacques Chailley to arrange a time to play them to him and noted that 'Toesca wants to produce a deluxe edition of the *Douze Regards*, with music, text, and illustrations by Rouault and Picasso'. Sadly, this project which would have brought together Messiaen and two of the century's greatest visual artists never came to fruition.[95]

Étienne de Beaumont was hoping to put on the first performance of the *Vingt Regards*. On 11 October Messiaen noted that 'M. de Beaumont has asked for the *Regards* for his first concert (organized by Bourdariat)'. And on 14 October the composer 'phoned Désormière to tell him that my *Vingt Regards* are finished!'

But while Messiaen had by now completed a vastly more ambitious work than the one originally envisaged, Toesca was still eager to have at least some of the new pieces to accompany his poems. On 31 October an intriguing event is noted in connection with this: '*Cut* the Regards so that they can be used in Toesca's piece, and try out the *cut version* for him and Delapierre. I give a fragment of my manuscript for reproduction in Toesca's publication.' Underneath this there is a note: 'Play the *Vingt Regards*, *complete*, at the Conservatoire for my pupils and at Delapierre's.' On 2 November he telephoned Dutilleux about the work, and showed it to Capdevielle (head of chamber music at French Radio) a week later. An entry on 16 November included further mention of the cut version: 'Look at the cut version of the *Regards* and the texts, for the *Studio d'essai*, with Bourdariat, Toesca and Delapierre.'

The Théâtre la Bruyère was the venue for the earliest public performance of a movement from the *Vingt Regards*. This was at a concert billed (in English) as a 'Musical Evocation [...] A French Pianist Yvonne Loriod plays Modern French Music [...] Reserved Show for Allied Forces.' The handbill for the concert only mentioned works by Debussy and Ravel, but Loriod recalled the whole programme: two preludes by Debussy, Ravel's *Gaspard de la nuit*, and music by Messiaen: nos.5, 3 and 8 of the *Préludes* and the *Rondeau* played by Loriod; and 'Le Baiser de l'Enfant-Jésus' from the *Vingt Regards* played by Messiaen himself.[96] By the following month Messiaen was seeking a publisher for the work and visited Leduc to discuss possibilities (which came to nothing). He rehearsed the *Regards* with Loriod at Mme Sivade's house on 15 December and four days later, on 19 December, Loriod played two *Regards* in a Triptyque concert devoted to music by La Jeune France, held at the Conservatoire: this was the first performance of 'Regard de l'Esprit de joie' and the second of 'Le Baiser de l'Enfant-Jésus'. The year ended with a plan to present the complete work with detailed commentaries. On 28 December Messiaen outlined his scheme: 'give the *Regards* in private (at Mme Sivade's or Mme de Polignac's) in four concerts, played by Loriod with *technical explanations* by me'.

'Le Cas Messiaen' and the Tristan trilogy
1945–1948

Messiaen was in a dark mood at the start of 1945: his self-confidence was at a low ebb, and he was concerned about Claire's deteriorating health. Guy Bernard-Delapierre wrote some heartfelt words of encouragement to him on 15 January 1945:

> Your visit this morning gave me great joy and great pain: joy because it is a manifestation of your friendship which is priceless to me, and pain because it hurts me to see you so distressed. I have spent the day at my piano, playing through *La Nativité* and *Les Corps*. Your music is one of the four or five manifestations of art and of the spirit in which I believe with all my strength, and with all my heart. I said enough to you this morning about how I would do everything to enable people to know your music and to love it. You know that, and I don't need to tell you that my loyalty to you, and to your music, will endure until I die. You have written, and you continue to write, everything that I could have hoped to express if I had such a gift or the technical ability. There are some weeks when we do not see each other, but I swear to you that your music is always in me, and that I speak about it ceaselessly with my friends. Even so, you sometimes feel lonely and disheartened. It seems monstrous to me that you could lose confidence in yourself, and in those who, like me, love you and admire you with all their hearts. Do you not sense these feelings around you, and how much we are looking forward to what you are going to give us? I beg you, write, create always. You don't just belong to yourself any more: you belong to us, and to all those who put their hopes in you and who will discover your music later. We need you. And I urge you not to attach any importance to the fact that your music is not played as much now as it sometimes has been. It's simply a case of the present circumstances. [. . .]
>
> I dare not hope that my friendship will be able to give you comfort, but it would be the greatest joy for me to play the humblest part in the construction of your work, that of a friend who believes in you and in what

83 The 'Thème d'Amour' from Messiaen's incidental music to *Tristan et Iseult*, reproduced in the programme for the first night at the Théâtre Edouard VII, 22 February 1945.

84 Messiaen and Loriod, c.1945.

you do, and who will reassure you in your hours of doubt. [. . .] As soon as circumstances allow, the whole world must hear your music.[1]

On 2 February, from 5 p.m. until midnight, Messiaen was at the Palais de Chaillot for an unusual commission: he had been asked to provide improvised music for Lucien Fabre's play *Tristan et Yseult* and it had been decided to record the music on the organ. That these improvisations were very carefully planned becomes clear from the lavishly produced programme book for the play's gala opening at the Théâtre Edouard VII on 22 February. This is an unusually handsome publication including a facsimile of Eluard's poem *À celle dont ils rêvent*, an article by Loys Masson (dated March 1943) about Concentration camps, several reproductions of Alain Cuny's set designs, and a facsimile of a page from Messiaen's score. Headed 'Tristan et Yseult: Thème d'Amour', it is scored for organ (with registrations supplied). Messiaen was never someone to let a memorable idea go to waste, and this theme is none other than the great cyclic melody which dominates *Harawi* (notably in 'Bonjour toi, colombe verte' and 'Adieu'). It is fascinating to rediscover the original incarnation of this haunting music, harmonized precisely as it is in *Harawi*, composed and performed several months before Messiaen began writing the earliest work in his 'Tristan' cycle.

Messiaen and Loriod were involved in a whirl of concert activity at the end of March 1945, including concerts on three consecutive days. On Saturday, 24 March both of them appeared in the Société Nationale concert; Loriod was on the programme as a composer, playing her own *Trois Mélopées africaines* for flute, ondes Martenot, piano and drum with Ginette Martenot, the flautist Jan Merry and the percussionist Jacques Boucher. Messiaen was present to accompany Marcelle Bunlet in songs by Claire Delbos and Raymond Depraz. The following afternoon (a Sunday) saw Loriod and Messiaen at the Schola Cantorum for a concert organized by the Mouvement Artistique Évolutif where they performed *Visions de l'Amen* with spoken commentaries by the composer. By far the most important of these concerts was at the Salle Gaveau on Monday, 26 March. This was the first major Messiaen première since the Liberation of Paris: the *Vingt Regards sur l'Enfant-Jésus*. For this occasion Messiaen prepared a small four-page leaflet containing 'Commentaires par l'auteur' and at the concert he read these before each piece.

Clarendon [Bernard Gavoty] in *Le Figaro* took issue with the spoken commentaries, as well as with the music itself, in a review which is more notable for its vituperation than for the quality of its critical judgment:

> I want this 'regard' to be lucid and free of facile mockery. The abysmal commentaries by Messiaen are more than enough, and one might mistake a transcription of them for a parody. [. . .] Let's stick to the music, though it's hardly any kinder to do so. What do we find there? An ambitious plan: to express the inexpressible. Critical sense is abandoned. An erudite composer who is a prisoner of his own system, attempting to translate the sublime utterances of the Apocalypse through muddled literature and music, smelling of the hair-shirt, in which it is impossible to detect either any usefulness or any pleasure.
>
> There is a persistent contradiction here: like a lunatic curator of a vanished museum, the composer announces marvels when he speaks, but which the piano immediately refutes. There's not a hint of tenderness in this suite of 'regards' upon the Infant-God. To evoke the eternity of the stars, a great gaggle of chords, immobile to the point of nausea, then rearing up in sudden convulsions. Is this heaven? No, it's purgatory.

Though critics had already expressed reservations about Messiaen's commentaries on his works, this article can perhaps lay claim to be the first shot in what soon became known as 'Le Cas Messiaen', the war of words which continued in the French musical press for the next couple of years, much to the composer's distress. Two principal issues were at stake in this debate. First, there was the literary quality and relevance of Messiaen's commentaries: some critics found the mixture of theology and musical theory an unwelcome distraction from the music itself; second, and perhaps more fundamental, concerns were expressed about the characteristic traits of Messiaen's music. Specifically, was the sound-world of his compositions really appropriate to 'religious' music? And was his much-discussed system a vital part of his originality, or a theoretical yoke which hampered true creativity? Clarendon's own part in this affair was ambivalent, since he changed his mind a few months later after hearing a broadcast of the *Trois petites Liturgies*. But the sentiments expressed in his review of the *Vingt Regards* were to be echoed by some – and repudiated by many others – in numerous articles over the months to come.

Another detractor declared his hand a few days later. Fred Goldbeck, in an article entitled 'Perils of Ingenuity' (*Le Temps présent*, 6 April), criticized the rhythmic aspects of Messiaen's system, as exemplified in the *Regards*: 'The distortion of metre is done according to a rigorously algebraic method, by adding or subtracting fragments of note values. According to the composer this "makes the rhythm limp along delightfully". In reality, it wrings the neck out of any rhythmic life; rhythm is impetus and energy, and however delightful it may be, you dance badly with a limp.' Goldbeck then moved on to attack another aspect of Messiaen's musical language, as described in *Technique de mon langage musical*, and he mocked the composer with a Gaudi-like architectural analogy: 'Imagine, for a moment, such a system applied to architecture: a cathedral façade with its arches "passed through a distorting prism", next to corkscrew-shaped doric columns; flying buttresses made of nickel chromium tubes; an asymmetrical pagoda instead of a steeple, and here and there, in the alcoves, some traditional religious statues. But while this would be completely unsuitable for a church, it could work very effectively as the set for a Surrealist ballet.'

Messiaen was hurt by critical assaults of this kind: they sought to undermine not only the theoretical foundations of his music, but even to cast doubt on the genuineness – the 'sincérité' – of his music. It is unsurprising that he never felt quite the same about the musical press after 'Le Cas Messiaen', even though many critics were firmly on his side. Roland-Manuel, writing in *Combat* (3 April), was clearly more sympathetic to Messiaen's vision in the *Vingt Regards* than some of his colleagues:

Olivier Messiaen has gathered under this title a series of piano pieces of a dazzling and magnificent diversity of style and expression, the coherence of the whole being assured by three important themes which serve to unify this vast meditation on the childhood of Christ at just the right moments. It is what used to be called a 'cyclic' work in the good old days of the Schola Cantorum.

However, it seems to me that the best way to characterize Messiaen's art is to place it at the extreme opposite to that of academicism. This musician's entire output proclaims the supremacy of things spiritual. It is as far away as possible from the sentimental austerity of the Franckists, and closest to the sensual delights of sound, as if the most concentrated musical material, the richest, and the finest, is – in his eyes – the best way to translate the ineffable splendours of the spiritual world. [. . .] Everything which an impressionist sensuality uses to express earthly delights, Olivier Messiaen devotes to the praise of the divine. [. . .] A music critic hesitates to comment on the spiritual content of the message, or on the value of a system which is very much our composer's own. [. . .] It is enough for today to pay homage to a very great musician who proclaims himself triumphantly in the *Vingt Regards sur l'Enfant-Jésus*, as well as to his magnificent interpreter, Mlle Yvonne Loriod, who plays this astoundingly complex music as if it were born spontaneously under her fingers.

Claude Chamfray, writing in *Arts* (6 April), explicitly welcomed Messiaen's commentaries, seeing in them a real value in explaining the music: 'Olivier Messiaen presented this complex work himself, with words and phrases which, like his music, were charged with feeling and poetry. He shows again here what has already been demonstrated beyond doubt, that in his music everything is symbolic and can be explained.' Marc Pincherle, in *Les Nouvelles littéraires* (12 April), was more sceptical: '[Messiaen] increasingly inhabits a phantasmagorical universe to which we do not have a key [. . .] every [symbol] is quite enigmatic for us, and he translates these into a highly individual musical language into which we must be initiated by his printed and spoken commentaries. They don't sit well together.' But Pincherle had more positive things to say towards the end of his article, even if he wasn't wholly convinced:

Now I am running out of space and I have only made negative criticisms: don't conclude that there is nothing to admire. Uninitiated I may be, but in many places I was grabbed by flashes of brilliance or by moments of pervasive sweetness, by the sheer jubilation of *Noël*, by the explosion of *L'Esprit de joie*, where the horns and harps of Paradise try out some jazz. Nevertheless, I hope very much that Messiaen will come back down to our planet, and that he will soon give us a work to applaud which needs nothing except the music, seeking a path to the All-Powerful by its musical virtues alone. That was Bach's way, a pretty good model after all.

Jean Wiéner (in *Ce Soir*, 4 April) was enthusiastic, describing the work as a 'masterpiece [. . .] of the most overwhelming grandeur and the highest musical worth'. Wiéner leaves his sole reservation until the last sentence: 'Only one element of this piece puzzles me: the use of transcendental piano writing in the manner of Liszt serving as the clothes for a work which is so inward, so intimate and so spiritual.'

Yves Baudrier's review in *Volontés* (11 April) provided a perspective on the work from a fellow-member and co-founder of La Jeune France. His enthusiasm perhaps got the better of him when he suggested that 'we can already single out some incomparable triumphs which should be on every piano tomorrow' (referring to the 'Première Communion de la Vierge' and 'Regard de l'Esprit de joie'), but he made a telling point about Messiaen's unusual position in the music of the time, seemingly emphasizing the distance between Messiaen and the schools of Neoclassicism and Serialism:

> For those who expect to find passionate emotion in music, a new fervour, and who have open minds, the music of Messiaen is an unhoped-for source of nourishment in our age. For those who hope for an art of musical games, who only have a taste for the ingenuity of forms, Messiaen could well appear treacherous, such is the vehemence with which he proclaims – in a singularly effective way – the right of music to be violently emotional, the vehicle for a fiery inner life.

At the same time as the extensive press coverage of the *Vingt Regards* was appearing in spring 1945, Messiaen was preparing for his next important concerts. The first of these was *Les Corps glorieux* at the Palais de Chaillot on 15 April. This was only the second performance of the complete work (the première, also played by Messiaen, had been on 15 November 1943 at the Trinité), and according to the programme, it was 'presented and introduced' by Norbert Dufourcq. A venomous review by Claude Rostand appeared in *Carrefour* (21 April). Rostand began by praising Goldbeck's article in *Le Temps présent* (quoted above), then launched an attack of his own: 'We know that M. Olivier Messiaen likes to wrap up his works in elaborate gobbledegook, as if they are not enough by themselves! [. . .] But if he speaks to me about "Birds which swallow some blue", I will answer him simply with the five letters which made Général Cambronne famous.'[2] But Rostand didn't stop there. He continued: 'The case of M. Messiaen, musically speaking, is a curious one: in his work there are the most beautiful things and the most sordid', and he objected to 'the musty smell of pious congregations and the images of slimy bigots' which he found in the music. This was one of the most scathing attacks on Messiaen at the time, and it is a credit to the composer that he later forgave Rostand, and to the critic that he recanted in print, on more than one occasion. While Rostand felt that there had been some legitimate criticisms, he 'particularly regretted the way in which these were said, in the heat of the battle'.[3]

The first performance of the *Trois petites Liturgies de la Présence Divine* took place at the Salle du Conservatoire on Saturday, 21 April 1945, in a concert which also included the premières of Milhaud's *Quatrains valaisans* and Poulenc's *Un Soir de neige*, both performed by the Chorale Yvonne Gouverné conducted by Fernand Lamy. Messiaen later noted many musicians, artists and writers in the audience. Among the musicians were Arthur Honegger, Andrée Vaurabourg (Honegger's wife), Georges Auric, Francis Poulenc, Henri Sauguet, Roland-Manuel, André Jolivet, Claude Delvincourt, Lazare Lévy, Marcel Ciampi, Jean Wiéner, Irène Joachim, Maurice Gendron, Guy Bernard-Delapierre and Jean Roy; the artist Georges Braque was present, as were the poets Paul Eluard and Pierre Reverdy. Several of Messiaen's pupils attended the concert, including Pierre Boulez, Serge Nigg, Jean-Louis Martinet and Pierre Henry. Jean Cocteau was also in the audience, as Bernard-Delapierre revealed in his 1945 'Souvenirs sur Olivier Messiaen'. Cocteau's reaction to the work is perhaps surprising:

'There's nothing more to be said after that,' proclaimed Cocteau, whom I would not have thought likely to appreciate this music. 'It's Genius.' Poulenc, who sincerely admires Messiaen's music, spoke of Byzantine art and of Rouault. Honegger applauded wildly. Many musicians, deeply moved, were silent, because the sudden revelation of this masterpiece, in a Paris liberated only a few months earlier and still learning slowly to live again, took on the importance of a great event.[4]

Messiaen was delighted by the performance. He sent a warm note of thanks to Denise Tual three days later:

I have never had such a fine performance, given in such favourable conditions. Désormière was marvellous, unforgettable, and each soloist, and all the orchestra and choir, were beyond praise. This concert cost you a great deal of effort from every point of view, and so my gratitude is still greater. It was too beautiful and I am not worthy of all that. Thank you with all my heart.

The première of the *Liturgies* provided an opportunity for more lively debate in the French press of 'Le Cas Messiaen', though as with the *Vingt Regards*, there were many favourable reviews of the work. In *La Revue musicale*, Suzanne Demarquez described the *Liturgies* as 'a dazzling success'.[5] Poulenc was also enthusiastic, and a few days after the concert wrote to Paul Collaer in Brussels: 'Messiaen has just given a marvellous work at La Pléiade, *Trois Liturgies* for chorus and small orchestra which you should do next winter.'[6] A few weeks later (25 June) he told Collaer that the 'Messiaen remains the event of the winter, which is well deserved'.[7]

Two reviews are worth quoting at length: those by Roland-Manuel and Jean Wiéner. Roland-Manuel, a friend and disciple of Ravel, wrote about the première in *Les Lettres françaises* on 29 April 1945, making some telling points about Messiaen's musical language:

Under the title, both modest and forbidding, of *Trois petites Liturgies de la Présence Divine*, Messiaen presents us with three mystical poems [. . .]. It must be admitted that this mystagogic literature, this Balinese orchestra and the commentary in the programme seem at first to be a suspicious mixture, just the thing to antagonize even the most well-intentioned listener. Our music has had trouble in ridding itself of the empty phrases of art and religion, and of the apparatus of the picturesque-exotic. So we are delighted to find them united and combined in the work of a composer who has so many loyal and committed disciples.

The music which is, I think, the most lucid and the most direct that Messiaen has ever composed, immediately converts us to his viewpoint, because of its irresistible quality of authenticity. This surprising language seems to become natural and necessary.

Does it matter to us that Messiaen borrows his instrumentation from Bali, then makes it his own, and delivers to us a message which is at once personal, overwhelming and new? Does it matter that in the final 'Psalmodie' some of the percussion writing recalls the sonority and the distinctive rhythms of Stravinsky's *Les Noces*? The spirit which enlivens these two works is completely different. But I think it is in the second part of the work, 'Séquence du Verbe: Cantique Divin', where the magic and the power of this work shine out in their clearest and purest form. It is the simplest and most marvellous song of triumph.

Messiaen here reveals the true secret of his power, which his liking for the worst literature and picturesque mystagogy are completely unable to obscure: it is the secret of a musician, a born melodist, who knows from instinct and from experience that rhythm and tonality are joined by the deepest roots; that the basis of harmony is consonance. But his ear has an acuteness which is second to none – it is the ear of an acoustician – and it guides him in the art of capturing and arranging the fleeting sounds of partials, directing them towards their poles of attraction. Despite appearances, Olivier Messiaen is much more the master of harmony than the slave of counterpoint.

The composer and pianist Jean Wiéner had been one of the most enterprising proponents of new music in the early 1920s (his 'Concerts Wiéner' included the first Paris performance of *Pierrot Lunaire*), and he played in a hugely popular two-piano duo with Clément Doucet. His recollection of the first performance of the *Trois petites Liturgies* tries to get to the core of Messiaen's aims as a composer:

> What gives value to a work of art is its authenticity; and to create that authenticity, above all, conviction and belief. This needs to be kept in mind if one is to welcome new masterpieces; it is necessary to desire, to facilitate, to encourage and to love enthusiasm. [. . .] I say all this because of the criticism and reproach expressed by some people about the first performance of the *Trois petites Liturgies de la Présence Divine*. [. . .] Messiaen's music is a music of love. And all this love is expressed in a completely new language: new from the point of view of sonority [. . .] and new from the point of view of rhythm. Messiaen's rhythmic system is completely individual and of true richness; it is more Hindu than Stravinskian and includes more suppleness than violence.
>
> One feels in this music all the affection which Messiaen has for *Pelléas*, all his harmonic theory which was already evident fifteen years ago, all the interest he has in poets (above all in Eluard and Reverdy, as I know), all his knowledge of plainchant. But one feels [. . .] that all this is at the service of his faith. In the end, it is a blaze of stained glass, an extravaganza of sound and light, a sumptuous work, a work of glory, which arrives fully formed. All that, however, comes to us straight from the simple heart of Messiaen, from his humility, from his truthfulness.[8]

So far so good. But Messiaen often recalled the scandal which erupted in the press about the *Liturgies*, and a year on from the première, the *Revue musicale de France* (1 April 1946) published an anthology of critical opinion compiled by Messiaen's old friend Daniel-Lesur:

> No work since *Le Sacre du printemps* has unleashed such a furore. If duelling was still in favour we should undoubtedly now be mourning the violent death of several critics and music lovers, anxious to have their say. [. . .] The main complaint against Messiaen in general and the *Petites Liturgies* in particular is their lack of religiosity. Precisely!
>
> 'The spirit of this work ought to be religious, to judge by the title and the words,' writes Roger Blanchard in *Mondes*; 'but the music does not lead us to a mood of contemplation by reason of its multifariousness: meditation is followed by jazzy uproar, and that in turn by easy-on-the-ear passages which sometimes remind us of a charming operetta finale. In short, far from ascending in a fine continuous line towards the ethereal spheres, the work follows a downward curve and heads unerringly towards the prosaic world which it ought to eschew.'

Such, however, is not the view of M. Marc Pincherle who, on the contrary, claims in *Les Nouvelles littéraires*: 'The harmonic mobility and the complexity of some of the melodic lines bring out, by means of contrast, the persistence of certain figurations, so that the result for the listener is an impression of escape, of entry into a celestial world which accords with Messiaen's intentions and indicates that he has succeeded in fulfilling them.'

Guy Bernard-Delapierre, replying to a 17-page article by Bernard Gavoty on the 'Messiaen affair' in the Catholic magazine *Études*, proclaimed: 'The same people who blame Messiaen for revealing the nuts and bolts of compositional techniques are no more supportive over what they call his mystical excesses. Faced with charm, heightened sensuality and, ultimately, physical delirium, some of them speak of curses and sorcery, like Bishop Cauchon faced with the replies of Joan of Arc. All that is fearfully suspect to certain people, who forget that art transfigures and purifies everything when it consists of love, greatness and sincerity.'

Fearfully suspect, at any rate, to Claude Rostand, the critic of *Carrefour*, who sees in Messiaen's 'current manner' nothing but 'lies and sacrilege'. This is what M. Rostand actually says: 'the *Petites Liturgies*, this work of tinsel, false magnificence and pseudo-mysticism, this work with dirty nails and clammy hands, with bloated complexion and unhealthy flab, replete with noxious matter, looking about anxiously like an angel wearing lipstick', and further on (writing about the *Quatuor pour la fin du Temps*): 'here we find the earliest manifestations of that vulgar, strident sensuality which has subsequently burst fully upon the world, bespangled with the most appalling sacred jargon imaginable'.

But here comes Yves Baudrier rushing into the arena, lance in hand, a pure and fearless knight brandishing a formidable irony, courtesy of the weekly magazine *Arts*: 'I am under no illusions about the literature with which Messiaen adorns his music, any more than I am about that with which Messrs Hell, Claude Rostand, Gavoty and Kaldor surround the composer's work. Both express the naïve language of faith; the first good faith, the second bad, as is obvious to the meanest intelligence.'

Finally, M. Claude Rostand has no hesitation in stating: 'The truth is, the Messiaen affair is not concerned with music but with psychopathology. This composer, who wishes to pass himself off as a revolutionary, brings nothing important to music that has not already been said, from Massenet to Roane [*recte* Raoul] Moretti.'[9] We know of no better way to counter this than with the view expressed by Lily Maurice-Amour in *Heures nouvelles*: 'This work of Messiaen, bold in construction, infused with the lively, coloured poetry of the great ages of mysticism, and vibrant with faith and love, brings with it something truly new. It derives from no school, and provokes no comparisons. Through the richness and density of its expression, it shines with such a bright light as to enter at once into the ranks of the great works of French music.'

And now, let everyone retire to their tents to meditate in silence on the fragility of human judgments and opinions.

During April 1945 Messiaen found himself embroiled unwittingly in another hullabaloo, this time about Stravinsky, whose orchestral music was comprehensively covered in a series of seven concerts at the Théâtre des Champs-Élysées. One of these, conducted by Manuel Rosenthal, included the *Danses concertantes* and *Four Norwegian Moods*. It was disrupted by booing and hissing from younger members of the audience, readily identified as 'messiaeniques', with Pierre Boulez as their ringleader. Boulez later told Antoine Goléa that he and his friends were simply 'protesting against the neoclassical works of Stravinsky'.[10] But since the protesters were all from his harmony class, Messiaen was bound to become involved, and to be the target of criticism for his pupils' conduct.[11] Moreover, Messiaen's friend Jolivet had also launched a scathing attack on Stravinsky. In his article 'Assez de Stravinsky' in *Noir et blanc* (4 April), Jolivet declared that Stravinsky 'had taught us nothing, in terms of rhythm, or in terms of melody, orchestration or form' and objected to such extensive coverage of Stravinsky's works.[12] Poulenc immediately leapt to Stravinsky's defence, in 'Vive Stravinsky' for *Le Figaro*, where he also defended Messiaen's position:

> I would not attach the slightest importance to all this yelling, if it didn't risk a backlash, creating a misunderstanding around a musician of great distinction whom I admire profoundly: Olivier Messiaen. It is a fact that some of his disciples hissed the *Danses concertantes* in a slightly timid way, and then the *Suite norvégienne* [*Four Norwegian Moods*] in a premeditated way. Messiaen, I am certain, has too much integrity and too much intelligence not to see the foolishness of all that, and to advise his pupils to adopt a more dignified attitude.[13]

Messiaen wrote to Poulenc on 19 April, thanking him warmly for a 'frank, direct and chivalrous article, in which you so kindly defended me [...] I feel less alone now that you have spoken up for me.'[14] A month later Messiaen tackled the issues head-on in 'Querelle de la musique et de l'amour', an article which appeared on the front page of *Volontés* (16 May 1945):

> Yes, they are all quarrelling! For aesthetic reasons, for mere aesthetic reasons, they are quarrelling! There are some who are for Stravinsky, some against Stravinsky, and they are not even capable of analysing the 'rhythmic characters' – whether moving or stationary – in *Le Sacre* or *Les Noces*. André Jolivet

is a great composer and my pupils Serge Nigg and Martinet have never booed anything. So what is this all about? Are we talking about neoclassical music? This movement has produced its masterpieces: Stravinsky's *Symphony of Psalms* and some works by Hindemith, for example. It has been useful too, like Schoenberg and Alban Berg, like polytonality: everything has its uses. But down with those false revolutionaries who say: 'We are the new music' just because they have shifted a few bass lines in a Donizetti cavatina into the wrong place!

Stravinsky is a huge genius; when it comes to it, his name is no more than a pretext in this affair.

After Stravinsky, Honegger and Bartók, we are waiting for a composer who is not neoclassical but who is so profoundly and brilliantly revolutionary that his style will one day be called *classical*. Several French and foreign composers have tried to fill this role: they are the precursors of this astonishing genius. When will he appear? In 20, 50, 70 years? What a burden of influences, hesitations, reappraisals, blind alleys, hopes, experiments and partial successes will rest upon his shoulders! Because it will be from all of us that he will be born: he will be our conclusion, I was on the point of saying our *Amen*.

There is so much that is dry and inhuman in contemporary music! Will our innovator be revolutionary only in his language? It seems almost certain that he will also bring new love. And not these blocks of despair, these uninhabited planets, but Love with a capital L, Love in all its forms: of Nature, of Woman, of Childhood, and above all Divine Love. And not brutality, sensuality and bloodshed without reason or heart, but Pity, Piety, Purity and the pure joy of the spirit with Charity and Hope.

I have been placed in the centre of this quarrel. Could a composer be found who is more solitary, more wretched, more uncertain of himself and of others, and further from the intrigues, selfishness and unreasonableness of this world? But they have picked on me so that they can harass me. I have had only two stars shining in my darkness: my faith and my music. They have painted these with their vile colours. The stained glass window of rhythms and modes constituted precisely the qualities of *Les Corps glorieux*, and the absence of a tonal background or of strongly marked rhythms and metre was intended to bring me nearer to Him who is beyond space and time. And even if my music is the source of violent displeasure, even if my life is far, very far from the Divine Love that I adore, I nonetheless imbued my notes with a little celestial tenderness. I did that in my bitterness, in my unworthiness – but I am sure I did it! But that is found shocking. No, that is not acceptable. The middle-class father allows his children to come home in the middle of the night without explanation, but that they should be dying of love, that's not normal.

What did Beethoven do to be the greatest of all? He loved, he suffered, and his music speaks from his heart.

My dear detractors, leave Stravinsky in peace, his fame has no need of us. Stop tormenting André Jolivet, the admirable composer of *Mana* and the *Danses rituelles*. Don't accuse my poor students unjustly. And if some of the young – without telling me beforehand – manifest their enthusiasm or their disapproval too noisily, be glad of their passionate feelings, signs of a more generous and humane generation. And pray with me to the years, the days and the minutes that they may make haste to bring before us that innovator, that liberator who is so impatiently awaited: the composer of Love.

In spite of the controversy surrounding the premières of the *Vingt Regards sur l'Enfant-Jésus* and the *Trois petites Liturgies de la Présence Divine*, and the quarrels about Stravinsky, Messiaen found himself more in demand than ever, often performing his works in semi-private gatherings in the houses of Étienne de Beaumont, Guy Bernard-Delapierre and others. The second half of May 1945 shows this kind of activity at its most intense. On Monday, 14 May Loriod and Messiaen played *Visions de l'Amen* at the home of Henry Gouïn, 4 avenue Milleret de Brou (16ᵉ); the next evening, at 7.30 p.m., Messiaen was at Delapierre's house, 24 rue Visconti, to accompany Marcelle Bunlet in the *Poèmes pour Mi* and *Chants de terre et de ciel*. Friday, 18 May found Messiaen at Étiennne de Beaumont's town house for the third complete performance of the *Vingt Regards*, played by Loriod.[15] The following week there were more concerts, including the *Quatuor pour la fin du Temps* on 25 May, at another of Delapierre's private concerts in the rue Visconti, played by the usual team of the Pasquiers, Vacellier and Messiaen. Messiaen ended this extraordinarily busy fortnight with a performance of *La Nativité du Seigneur* at the Trinité on 29 May.

At about the same time, Messiaen made extensive corrections to the *Préludes* for a second edition (issued in July 1945). A number of errors in the original edition had been introduced at a late stage as a result of some less-than-meticulous editing by Lucien Garban, one of Durand's most experienced proofreaders. Garban (1877–1959) was a lifelong friend of Ravel, whose proofs he usually corrected with the greatest care, but his approach to Messiaen seems to have been less painstaking.

Messiaen's major project for the summer of 1945 was a new song-cycle: *Harawi*. On 15 May he responded to a request from the Conservatoire, noting in his diary the need to 'give an answer about the oboe *concours* at the Conservatoire'. Messiaen did indeed write a piece for that year's oboe competition, and according to Loriod it was reworked almost at once as 'L'Amour de Piroutcha', the fifth song in *Harawi*. Messiaen and his family left Paris for their summer holidays,

85 Messiaen's notations of music from the Solomon Islands, 1976.

spent at Grenoble, on 17 July. Most of the summer was taken up with composing *Harawi* and by 17 September it was finished, Messiaen noting that day that he needed to 'copy *Harawi*'.

Was it the furore in the press about his commentaries which led Messiaen to remain virtually silent about *Harawi*? The published score contains no commentary on the work, and the earliest performances had programmes which provided just the titles of the songs. Its significance as the first work in his 'Tristan trilogy' is implicit in the subtitle ('Chant d'amour et de mort'), and this was something Messiaen was happy to discuss, connecting the song-cycle with the *Turangalîla-Symphonie* and the *Cinq Rechants*. While an explicit musical connection to the Tristan story was never mentioned by Messiaen, the facsimile of a fragment from his earlier incidental music for Lucien Fabre's *Tristan et Yseult* (February 1945) provides just such a link, since the 'Thème d'Amour' in the music for the play became, a few months later, the great recurring love theme in *Harawi*.[16] The coincidence is intriguing. It seems that Messiaen's incidental music may have given him not only *Harawi*'s main musical idea but the song-cycle's theme of irresistible, fatal love. Moreover, the 'Thème d'Amour' has what is for Messiaen a most unusual provenance. It was taken from the collection of Peruvian folk melodies edited by Marguérite Béclard d'Harcourt and Raoul d'Harcourt[17] – an unlikely source for Tristan music, until one remembers that the Quecha 'harawi' is a type of song depicting lovers destined to be united only in death.[18]

When discussing *Harawi* with Antoine Goléa, Messiaen was at pains to play down his interest in folk music.[19] The diaries, however, show that Peruvian melodies figured in Messiaen's composing plans for some years after *Harawi*. None of these projects came to anything, although folk music from another part of the world – Papua New Guinea – features in the two *Île de feu* pieces from the *Quatre Études de rythme*, written five years later. Messiaen discussed Peruvian melodies with his class in 1949, and returned to the subject in later courses when the class also studied music from Hungary, Japan and Mongolia. It was probably around this time (the late 1940s and early 1950s) that Messiaen compiled the chapter on 'Le Folklore mondial' for the *Traité*,[20] and in 1956 he wrote the Preface to a Canadian folksong anthology by the d'Harcourts.[21] His interest evidently continued: a manuscript dating from 1976 contains extensive transcriptions made from recordings of songs and instrumental melodies from Papua New Guinea, Bali and the Solomon Islands.[22]

The 'Thème d'Amour' melody is the most obvious of a number of borrowings from the d'Harcourt volume.[23] Messiaen's version is close to the original, but his alterations – detaching the tune from its pentatonic mode by sharpening the second and sixth notes (F to F sharp, C to D flat) – have an extraordinarily potent effect. At the theme's first appearance (in the second song) the lovers' greeting already carries a sense of doom. In the songs that follow, dark forces crowd in, so that even the enchanting dialogue between the lovers in the fifth song ('L'Amour de Piroutcha') is menaced by images of decapitation ('Coupe-moi la tête, doundou tchil') and death ('amour, la mort'). Altogether the music of *Harawi* has a ferocity and desperation not found elsewhere in Messiaen. Even the birdsong seems pursued by demons, at one with the grimly obsessive ostinati and with the disciplined wildness of the dance movements ('Doundou tchil' and 'Katchikatchi les étoiles').

By far the most revealing comments from Messiaen himself on *Harawi* came in his interviews with Antoine Goléa:

> At the time I wrote [*Harawi*] I was a great reader of Pierre Reverdy and Paul Eluard, and also a very good book by André Breton on Surrealism and paint-ing.[24] It is thus an almost entirely Surrealist work, apart from some images borrowed from the mountains of the Dauphiné (because I have never seen the Andes *cordillera*), and certain Peruvian Surrealist phrases such as the 'green dove'. The dove is a symbol for a girl in Peru, and the colour green represents spring.[25]

Messiaen's two previous song-cycles had both been autobiographical. Is *Harawi*? Certainly it is, and similarly intense and private. In *Harawi* the sym-bolism of a young woman and of springtime would seem to indicate that he was composing a kind of love poem to his young muse, Yvonne Loriod. This was definitely Goléa's view:

> In reality separated from his wife who had to live for many years in a nurs-ing home, Messiaen remained joined to her until her death by the sacra-ment of marriage. He was overwhelmed, however, by a love of unique force and depth, which precisely mirrored the legendary love of Tristan and Yseult, or, much closer to our own times, the passion which Wagner and Mathilde Wesendonk felt for each other, a passion which finds its artistic transfiguration in Wagner's *Tristan*. Messiaen [. . .] lived throughout these years, blazing and pure, joined only in spirit and communing through music alone with the object of his passion.[26]

But some evidence suggests a different interpretation. The onset of Claire's illness came much earlier than was previously believed,[27] and worrying signs of mental disorder had been apparent since at least 1943. The condition had its ups and downs: in 1946 Claire attended the wedding of Messiaen's cousin, Albert Guéritte, and during the service she was well enough to play the violin in the minstrels' gallery in the church at Ville-sur-Terre, near Fuligny, with

86 Pascal and Claire smiling,
mid-1940s.

Messiaen accompanying her on the harmonium. But in 1945, as a result of increasingly chaotic conditions at the villa du Danube brought on by Claire's forgetfulness, Messiaen requested Delapierre to organize a studio where he could work without distraction, although he seems not to have used it. The first published account of Claire's illness was by Goléa, who found Messiaen understandably reticent:

For a long time [Messiaen] kept these terrible things hidden, and when questioned about his wife he limited himself to responding vaguely that she was ill, and that she had been, before her illness, a very fine artist; then, later, unable to hide the truth, he spoke of her as a saint, because of her long and painful martyrdom.[28]

Photographs of Claire in the 1940s show her isolated and confused. The Messiaen family's bewilderment is reflected in a poignant document in Pascal's child's handwriting:

To darling Mummy
As a house-warming for our little place in Neussargues, we are planning a little party which will, I hope, be full of an atmosphere of 'joy and friendship' (the motto). I intend to make you laugh a little and you will be entertained. It is essential that we are happy. The revels will commence at 8.15, dinner at 8.45, the evening gathering at 9.15, and bedtime at 9.45. We are to respect the motto 'joy and friendship', Mummy – I hope the spirit of our motto will last a long time. If I haven't mentioned 'obedience', that's because, if you love your mother, you obey her.[29]

By 1945 – the year in which *Harawi* was composed – Messiaen must have been greatly concerned that his beloved Mi was slipping away from him into a world of her own. Seeing Claire as the subject of *Harawi* explains the work's mood of almost unbearably passionate lament. The parting of the lovers comes not at the end but at the midpoint of the cycle, in the seventh song, 'Adieu', the words accompanied by the second appearance of the love theme: 'Farewell, green dove, / Farewell, limpid pearl.' But for Messiaen death was not the end, and in the ninth song ('L'Escalier redit, gestes du soleil'), the lovers are reunited, as the music celebrates ecstatically:

Death is there, my green dove.
Death is there, my limpid pearl.
Death is there.

We sleep far from time
In your glance.
I am dead.
The water will pass over our heads,
Sun-guardian.
The fire will consume our breath,
Love philtre for two voices.
Our glances from one end to another
Seen by death.
Let us invent the love of the world
To seek us, to weep for us,
To dream of us, to find us [. . .]

In the song that follows – 'Amour oiseau d'étoile' – serenity is at last regained, in music that achieves the stillness of the slow meditations of the *Vingt Regards*. The song was inspired by Roland Penrose's painting *Seeing is Believing* (or *L'Île invisible*) which Messiaen saw reproduced in the Swiss art journal *Formes et couleurs*. Penrose (1900–84) was a British Surrealist artist whose work was exhibited in Paris before the war, though Messiaen never saw the original painting.[30] The composer described the picture as showing 'two male hands stretched out, then a woman's head upside down; continuing upwards, her hair spreading out, her brow, her eyes, her face, her neck, but the rest of the woman is missing, or rather she is continued in the sky or in the stars'. This powerful imagery clearly affected Messiaen deeply, since his next sentence explains that the picture's importance went beyond one song, being 'the symbol for the whole of *Harawi*'.[31]

In the final lines of 'Amour oiseau d'étoile' the lovers are depicted beyond space and time: 'Far from the scene hands are singing / Star, increased silence of the sky. / My hands, your eye, your neck, the sky.' The words describe the woman in Penrose's painting. It is surely no coincidence that, at the same time, they echo the love song to Claire that opened *Chants de terre et de ciel*: 'Your eye of earth, my eye of earth, our hands of earth [. . .] / Star of silence to my heart of earth, to my lips of earth.'

Messiaen's diaries during summer 1945 show that he was not only preoccupied with *Harawi*. On 22 July he jotted down some ideas: 'Make some classifications of tempo' (possibly some early thoughts about the *Quatre Études de rythme*) and 'write *Paradis* for orchestra – with chasms above and below, waves of colour, teeming depths, shivering heights, sparkling, which the orchestra tears apart and throws open'.

Messiaen also turned his thoughts to the teaching of composition, and specifically to the post of composition professor at the Conservatoire. He outlined the situation in his diary during August: Roger Ducasse had gone, and Henri Busser was staying on for one more year. Milhaud had been sounded out by Delvincourt and had accepted, but was unable to start for another year, and Tony Aubin would cover classes in the meantime. As for Messiaen's chances, he wrote: 'They criticize me not only because of my age, but above all for forcing my pupils to imitate my music and to confine them to Messiaen. *Defend myself* on this point.' He resolved to keep his application alive, in case there might be a chance of taking Busser's place. On 15 September he noted that he would write to Delvincourt, outlining 'what I would intend to teach in the composition class', a comprehensive curriculum for aspiring composers:

> Rhythm, melody, harmony, development, melody-writing, through individual sessions with me; detailed analysis at the piano of modern and older works: all styles and forms from antiquity and the exotic up to the various contemporary schools, passing through the Middle Ages, the sixteenth century, and all the classics and romantics; instrumentation and orchestration, then correction of works by students, expanding their knowledge of literature, art, science, etc. Push them as far as possible to compose music which has life and which sings, *respecting their individuality*.

It was another eighteen years before Messiaen was appointed to the post of composition teacher at the Conservatoire, but here he has already prepared a blueprint for the courses he started in 1963.

Back in Paris at the end of September, Messiaen handed over the full score of a new work which Henry Barraud had commissioned a few months earlier for French Radio: the *Chant des déportés*, a short piece for large orchestra and massed unison voices, written during the summer as a break from intensive work on *Harawi*.

By 10 October he was already contemplating his next large project – 'Write a symphonic work for Koussevitzky' – and plans soon crystallized into what would become the *Turangalîla-Symphonie*. In a letter dated 23 March 1980 to Klaus Schweitzer, Messiaen documented the order in which he composed the symphony: 'The order of composition was as follows: I first wrote movements I, IV, VI and X. Then the three rhythmic studies called "Turangalîla" 1, 2 and 3. Then no.II. Then the large development which is no.VIII. And I finished with no.V.'[32] Though Messiaen didn't say as much to Schweitzer, it is probable that he followed his custom of composing the work complete in short score, only then turning his attention to the orchestration.

Meanwhile, to the composer's irritation, 'Le Cas Messiaen' continued to reverberate in the press. Clarendon reviewed a broadcast of the *Liturgies* in *Le Figaro* on 4 October 1945, six months after his hostile review of the *Vingt Regards*:

Without denying a single word that I wrote here on 3 April last, I concur joyfully with the view that some passages in this work are real summits. [. . .] At such moments in the second movement, and throughout the third, we reach the extreme heights of ecstasy: there Messiaen transports us to the limits of music and of silence, as if at the threshold of eternity.[33]

The same month Clarendon, under his real name Bernard Gavoty, published a long and largely hostile article in the journal *Études* entitled 'Musique et mystique: Le "Cas" Messiaen'. Bernard-Delapierre immediately produced a vigorous riposte for *Confluences*: 'Le Cas Messiaen devant la pensée Catholique orthodoxe'; and Messiaen's publisher Gilbert Leduc joined the fray with his 'Réponse à Monsieur Bernard Gavoty'. This is a staunch defence of the composer, his innovations, his sincerity and his quest to discover new means of musical expression. Messiaen was always grateful for Leduc's support, and in a speech in 1973 he recalled the episode:

[*The Liturgies*] had been an immense success – and (no one will ever know why) all the critics launched themselves at me and heaped insults upon me! (The uproar went on for long afterwards; for more than ten years critics in France and elsewhere emptied their waste-paper baskets over my head.) But, in 1945, you decided to take action. You defended my cause against one of my most persistent attackers in a pamphlet that has become famous – I have kept a dozen or so copies and I often read your words with emotion. Your courageous and noble attitude surprised many people at the time: for my part, I have never forgotten it.

On 26 September 1945 Béla Bartók died in America after a long illness. Pierre Boulez recalled that Messiaen's earliest classes for 'Les Flèches' had included analyses of the violin sonatas, string quartets and *Music for Strings, Percussion and Celesta*,[34] and Messiaen's obituary tribute, published in *Images musicales*, demonstrated how much he admired the Hungarian composer:

Béla Bartók is dead. A few years before the war, in London, at the ISCM Festival, I met him with some like-minded friends. He was an extremely elegant man, cultivated, with a quiet speaking voice: a piercing gaze, white hair, and a pale, aristocratic head which stays long in the memory. His biographers tell us that he studied at the Conservatory in Budapest where he was later to become a Professor of Piano. There, he was influenced by contact with works by Wagner and Strauss. He became a passionate defender of Debussy in Hungary (there are still some traces of Debussy in *Duke Bluebeard's Castle*). Without actively linking himself to Schoenberg and the atonal school, his

87 Programme for the first performance of Messiaen's *Chant des déportés* at the concert on 2 November 1945 in memory of those 'morts pour la France'.

experiments were similar. His counterpoint is full of minor seconds to the point of asphyxiation – a link with Schoenberg and with the quarter-tone composers Ivan Wyschnegradsky and Alois Hába. But the great force behind Bartók is his native land, its songs and its dances. [. . .] It is perhaps in the *Music for Strings, Percussion and Celesta* that Bartók's genius finds its greatest expression. A new way of using the celesta, the xylophone and the piano;[35] unprecedented writing for the strings, divided into two orchestras, with unexpected glissandi and pizzicati; free neume-like rhythms, a harmonic language composed almost exclusively of minor seconds and augmented fourths; a mixture of tonal, modal, atonal and extremely chromatic writing in the cyclic returns of the principal theme; a fascinating fan-shaped fugue (in which successive entries, alternating between the two string groups, lead towards either light or darkness); and a third movement in the form of a bridge (that is to say, a centre surrounded by four pillars, two to the left and two to the right), where the theme slithers in as wistful and distant little fragments, between each section, among the gypsy fury of the appoggiatura figures and the rustling silk of the chords in trills.

Béla Bartók is dead. He was a man alone, apart, like all great visionaries. He takes with him the secret of his solitude. [. . .] But let us admire this secret world, this unique and precious mind, and the pure sounds of the music which outlives him.[36]

On 2 November Manuel Rosenthal conducted the first performance of the *Chant des déportés* in the Palais de Chaillot. This occasion, described on the programme as 'In memoriam: concert à la mémoire des déportés politiques morts pour la France', also included music from Debussy's *Martyre de Saint-Sébastien*, Henry Barraud's *Offrande à une ombre* (in memory of Maurice Jaubert, killed in battle in 1940) and Fauré's Requiem. The Fauré was conducted by Maurice Hewitt, who had recently returned from captivity in Buchenwald. Jean Wiéner's review included praise for Messiaen's new work:

It was an emotional experience for me to listen to the performance of the *Chant des déportés*, written in their honour by Olivier Messiaen. A sort of heroic and tender deformation of the *Chant du départ*, this short blast of music, imploring yet glorious, is at once pitying and joyful. This *Chant des déportés* oozes genius, like everything which comes from Messiaen.[37]

This was the work's only performance until its rediscovery in the archives of Radio France during autumn 1991.

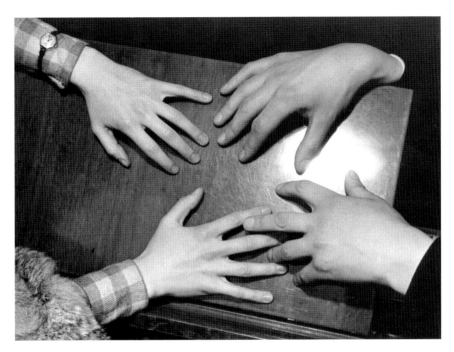

88 The hands of Loriod and Messiaen, 1947.

Messiaen went to hear Loriod play Bartók's Second Piano Concerto at the Théâtre des Champs-Élysées on 15 November 1945,[38] with the Orchestre National conducted by Manuel Rosenthal. Messiaen reviewed the concert for the magazine *Lumière de la ville*. As well as discussing the music (describing it as 'definitely one of Bartók's best works [...] which surpasses human possibilities and thus is called genius'), he goes on to praise the soloist:

> Yvonne Loriod deserves the highest praise. Having accomplished the extraordinary feat of learning the work by heart in eight days, she gave us a performance of incredible precision, energy and resonance. Yvonne Loriod understands and penetrates what she plays to such an extent that she could be said to bring it into the world. [...] Such pianists are rare, but we need them: they enlarge the musical firmament.[39]

Just before Christmas, Messiaen and Loriod travelled to London for a series of concerts and broadcasts between 20 and 23 December: *La Nativité du Seigneur* at St Mark's, North Audley Street, at 6.30 p.m. on 20 December was followed by a play-through of *Visions de l'Amen* to an invited audience at the BBC starting at 8.45 p.m. the same evening. Back at St Mark's the next day, Messiaen played music by de Grigny, Bach, and his own 'Combat de la mort et de la vie' before joining Loriod for a private performance of *Visions de l'Amen* at Felix Aprahamian's house in Muswell Hill. Messiaen and Loriod returned to Paris on 23 December and the year ended with a broadcast of the *Liturgies* for French Radio on 28 December.

During March 1946 Messiaen was concerned with fixing the first performance of *Harawi*. He wrote to the administration of the Concerts de la Pléiade about what was intended to be its third Messiaen première:

> I am completely in agreement about the date [paper missing] in May, in the hall of the old Conservatoire at 9 p.m., for our Concert de la Pléiade. I am writing by the same post to Marcelle Bunlet to tell her that this date is confirmed and that there are no others possible. She will certainly be in agreement (since she is free in May). I agree too about the arrangements: 10,000 francs for Bunlet. For me nothing, out of gratitude to La Pléiade! [...] My work *Harawi* lasts one hour and a quarter, enough to fill a concert. I have refrained from any commentary.

The absence of commentary on *Harawi* is surely a most eloquent silence – as we have seen, this was a work which explored some of Messiaen's most intimate thoughts. The planned concert never took place. Despite the evidence of this letter that arrangements were quite advanced, *Harawi* was instead given its private première by Marcelle Bunlet and Messiaen at Étienne de Beaumont's house on 26 June (see below).

The evening of 8 March found the composer and Loriod in the unlikely but glamorous venue of Schiaparelli's fashion house in the place Vendôme to perform *Visions de l'Amen*.[40]

On 21 March Messiaen embarked on a two-day train journey to Prague. The Czech Minister of Culture, Mojmír Vaněk, had hatched an imaginative scheme to arrange a football match between France and Czechoslovakia which would provide the finance for performances of the *Trois petites Liturgies* and *Visions de l'Amen*. Vaněk was a man of considerable courage: he was arrested when Russia invaded in 1948 and spent the next eighteen years in prison, before eventually settling in Switzerland. The concert took place on 27 March and consisted of *Visions de l'Amen* (Loriod and Messiaen) and the *Liturgies* – sung in Czech[41] with Loriod and Martenot as soloists, and Jaroslav Krombholc conducting a choir and orchestra from the Prague National Theatre. It was repeated the next evening. Messiaen and Loriod then travelled from Prague to Vienna, playing *Visions de l'Amen* in the small hall of the Konzerthaus (2 April); Loriod performed the *Vingt Regards* in the salon of Universal Edition (6 April) for an audience which included the firm's progressive director, Alfred Schlee. The next day, 7 April, Messiaen performed the *Quatuor pour la fin du Temps* at the Musikverein, with Austrian musicians including the clarinettist Friedrich

Wildgans, a former member of the Staatsoper orchestra who had been arrested by the Nazis in 1939, and who served as director of the Vienna Musikhochschule in 1945–7. A brief return to Paris was followed almost at once by a trip to Brussels: *Visions de l'Amen* was played by Messiaen and Loriod on 16 April for the Tribune Franco-Belge at the Galerie Georges Giroux (with Bernard-Delapierre presenting the work[42]), and there was a repeat performance of the *Liturgies* under Paul Collaer on 20 April.

While Messiaen was in Brussels, *Le Figaro littéraire* published two long articles on consecutive Saturdays (13 and 20 April). 'Y-a-t-il un "Cas Messiaen"?' included reponses from several leading composers and critics. The introduction summarized the issues as follows:

> Some reproach Messiaen, an artist inspired by his Catholic faith, for the sensual dynamism and the 'whiff of sulphur' [i.e. of heresy] in his music. They say this is incompatible with the 'mysticism' which Messiaen himself denies. Others declare that his melodic invention owes too much to Massenet, or even to insipid religious songs ['cantiques saint-sulpiciens']. Traditionalists criticize the revolutionary or extremist aspects of his music, while revolutionaries cannot forgive him for his sense of tradition. Many hold against him the 'mystico-poetic' commentaries, philosophical, literary or technical, with which he surrounds his works, as well as the texts which he writes himself, like the words to his vocal music. Finally, a lot of concert-goers have a passionate admiration for Messiaen and are not afraid to call him a musical genius.

The first contribution was a generous tribute from Honegger: 'There is controversy about Messiaen in the same way that there is controversy every time an outstanding personality arrives on the musical scene. [...] My opinion: the *Petites Liturgies* is a magnificent work and stands beside others like the *Regards sur l'Enfant-Jésus* or *Visions de l'Amen*. The man who wrote these is a great musician.' Poulenc, too, admired the music, but not the theoretical apparatus: 'While I heartily disapprove of Messiaen's writings, as well as the "recipes" in his composition treatise – the only useful recipes, I think, are those for cooking – I would not deny for one moment the pre-eminent place this musician holds today. His incomparable organ works contain passages of absolute beauty. If there is a Messiaen controversy it is about aesthetic rather than musical issues, since he is indisputably a born musician.'

Claude Delvincourt, director of the Paris Conservatoire and the man who had appointed Messiaen to his teaching post there, began with words of sympathy: 'Beethoven, Wagner, Debussy: none of these incited, before their thirty-fifth birthdays, the sort of very well-publicized controversy stirred up by those who want to assassinate the composer of the *Petites Liturgies*. I hope he has the inner strength to resist this roller-coaster.' Delvincourt did not believe there was any 'Cas Messiaen' and added that to focus on the 'mystico-literary hotchpotch' of Messiaen's commentaries (he found them 'intolerable') risked missing the real point: works which 'demonstrate an importance and musical value which are sufficiently eloquent by themselves'. Fred Goldbeck proposed a fresh point of departure for the composer, suggesting that Messiaen should reinvent himself as a kind of spiritual Surrealist. All the characteristics Goldbeck found so disconcerting would

> make for a perfectly valid style if Messiaen could accept that he has within him a talent for the *grotesque* in music, which he despises perhaps because of a romantic notion of serious-mindedness. So I wish that the composer of the *Petites Liturgies* could find a Diaghilev to commission from him a ballet based on Hieronymus Bosch: the temptresses of St Anthony enclosed within the iridescence of a soap bubble, a demoniac aviary full of feathered porcupines and herons wearing spectacles; a Devil Musician whose back turns into the page of an antiphonal, and another, reading from it, whose nose becomes a trombone. Here's the best place for Messiaen's harmonic rainbows, his jumbles of birds and his favourite rhythms which he calls non-retrogradable because they're the same backwards as forwards.

Little could Goldbeck have guessed that a couple of years later Messiaen was indeed to be commissioned to write a ballet based on Bosch's *The Ship of Fools*, or that Bunlet and Messiaen were only weeks away from giving the first performance of a song-cycle which was partly inspired by a Surrealist painting. The other contributors to 'Y a-t-il un "Cas Messiaen"?' were generally agreed about Messiaen's importance and largely uninterested in the so-called controversy.[43] Was the 'Cas Messiaen' simply an illusory controversy whipped up by Gavoty and Goldbeck in April 1945, and sustained for a year or so in the musical press? Certainly René Dumesnil of *Le Monde* thought so, and though he eventually weighed into the argument, he kept silent until December 1945, believing the affair to be of no interest to the wider musical public.[44] While its worst excesses had greatly hurt the composer personally, the brief summing-up by *Figaro littéraire* answered the question posed in the title of its articles with a decisive 'no':

> We believe that this enquiry has exploded the myth of a 'Cas Messiaen'. Almost all the replies describe Messiaen as a very great musician of our time.

The majority are also in agreement about rejecting all the literature and commentaries which the composer or certain bumbling exegetes place around his works, and concur that these do the music a disservice.

One other writer entered the debate at the time, though not in *Figaro littéraire*. The short-lived (and confusingly named) *Revue musicale de France* lasted barely a year, but in its issue of 15 April 1946 it published 'Messiaen ou le surréel en musique' by the erstwhile Surrealist Ernest de Gengenbach (1903–79),[45] whose earlier publications included a rare pamphlet, *Surréalisme et christianisme* (privately printed for the author in 1938), which would surely have interested Messiaen. Gengenbach was not a musician, but offered some intriguing ideas in conversation with the composer, using avowedly Surrealist vocabulary (such as 'merveilleux' and 'dépaysement') in connection with Messiaen's music. One notable feature of their discussion is Messiaen's easy familiarity with Surrealist concepts and terminology.

If I had to define Messiaen, I would not hesitate to say that Olivier Messiaen is the Surreal in music. Up to now there have been Surrealist poets, painters and sculptors, but as yet no Surrealist composer. Through your music, you respond to a cherished wish of the Surrealists: the element of the fantastic ['merveilleux'], and you grant their urgent desire, their longing for a sense of being disconcerted by unfamiliarity ['dépaysement']. But the method you use to achieve this, through prayer and contemplation, the Surrealists rejected, and considered an abomination. That explains their failure. [. . .] Your music is *Surrealist* music because it draws its inspiration from elements of the fantastic in Christianity ('merveilleux chrétien') to which access is granted thanks to the loving prayer of a soul who resonates, like a harp, under the fingers of the Artist, of the Poet par excellence; of the Word, Creator of sound, of words, of colours.

Messiaen's response shows a thorough knowledge of the writings of André Breton and other Surrealists:

I don't know if I possess the gifts of mystical mediation or of artistic thaumaturgy [miracle-working] which you so kindly bestow on me. But if you define Surrealism as a mental vantage-point ('point de l'esprit') where visible natural realities and invisible supernatural realities are no longer in opposition to each other and where they cease to be perceived as contradictions, then I am a Surrealist composer. The disciples of André Breton [. . .] wanted passionately to have on earth a state of the beyond. It did not occur to them to have that through faith. In a present eternity, I glimpse infinite life unbounded by Time and Space.

Part of this answer is an uncanny allusion to Breton's *Second Manifeste du surréalisme* (1930) which declared that the Surrealists were striving to attain 'a mental vantage-point from which life and death, the real and the imaginary, past and future, communicable and incommunicable, high and low, will no longer be perceived as contradictions'. Messiaen was expressing these thoughts at just the moment when he was also getting ready to give the first performance of his most explicitly Surrealist work, *Harawi*.

Messiaen always had Marcelle Bunlet in mind for *Harawi*. On the contents page of the first edition, the voice is specified in unusual detail: 'grand soprano dramatique; registre plûtot médium et grave, malgré quelques *si* aigus en force' ('a strong dramatic soprano voice; mostly in the medium and low register, despite some forceful high Bs'), and in conversation with Antoine Goléa, Messiaen said that he 'wrote this work thinking of the voice of Marcelle Bunlet, who is a dramatic soprano. However, while *Harawi* demands a brilliant upper register from the singer, the influence of Peruvian folk music led me to ask equally for her to have a warm lower register, powerful and sonorous.'[46] Goléa asked if the ideal voice for *Harawi* was that of a Brünnhilde (such as Bunlet), and Messiaen replied that his requirements were still more particular: 'sadly, there are few singers, even Wagnerian ones, who combine the two qualities of the upper and lower registers that are needed'.[47]

Harawi was given its first performance, at a private concert, by Marcelle Bunlet and Messiaen on 26 June 1946, at Étienne de Beaumont's home (2 rue Duroc). The invited audience was given a handsome programme, printed on fine paper, with a cover design by Picasso of the Three Graces. Messiaen provided no commentary, but just the title and list of songs reproduced in a facsimile of his handwriting. Loriod was Messiaen's page-turner, and Claire was in the audience. The next day (27 June), Bunlet and Messiaen were in Brussels for the first public performance of *Harawi*, arranged by the *Tribune Franco-Belge* at the Galerie Georges Giroux, 43 boulevard du Régent, and the following evening they repeated the work in Antwerp.

A fortnight later, Messiaen was in London and gave the British première of the *Quatuor pour la fin du Temps* at Goldsmiths' Hall on 10 July, as part of the 1946 ISCM Festival. The players originally announced were the usual team of Messiaen, the Pasquiers and Vacellier, but a slip inserted into the programme announced two personnel changes: the clarinet was played by Henri Akoka – one of the few times he played the work apart from the famous première in Görlitz – and the cellist was Charles Bartsch.

Messiaen's diary for 1946 contains numerous notes about his largest undertaking to date – the *Turangalîla-Symphonie*. For instance, in Petichet on 14 August he commented: 'write the third piece for orchestra (the fast finale in

F sharp will become the fourth movement)', but Messiaen's thoughts during the summer were not only on *Turangalîla*: on 27 August he wrote: 'Compose a Credo for choir and orchestra, emphasize the words: creator of things *invisible*, and other similar ones: *light from light*, etc.' This may have been part of a larger projected work for which the only evidence seems to be a mention in the diary: 'Symphonie théologique (for large orchestra)'.

By 30 August yet another plan was in his mind, this time for an innovative ballet score in which not only pitches but also durations and timbres would be developed according to serial principles. This is a remarkable concept for Messiaen to be articulating, albeit in a private note to himself, as early as 1946, several years before the composition of the *Quatre Études de rythme*. The *mise-en-scène* has decidedly Surrealist elements:

> Large orchestra: write a ballet on Time. It is night on stage; a dancer – a man completely still – the creation of Time – an angel with a rainbow halo enters, with a fearsome head, eyes rolled upwards to the beyond, no body, two Greek columns ablaze instead of legs. A hand which emerges from the clouds – the sun and a rainbow surrounding the head – a hallucinatory figure – when it appears, the man dances: it is Time, then the man *stops still*: the end of time. He stands with his arms stretched out, not moving. Chords and resonances like those in my *Quatuor*, and a serial theme giving a series of twelve notes and a series of timbres, one timbre for each note, and one duration and nuance for each note. Develop timbres, durations and nuances according to the principles of serialism. [. . .] Think of the star which opens the well to the Abyss.

On 4 September Claire and Pascal left for the Monastery of Ste-Claire at Cimiez in Nice, while Messiaen remained alone in Petichet until 18 September. Then he travelled to Romans to spend a couple of weeks with Germaine Sauvage, his aunt 'Tatin', before returning to Paris on the night of 2–3 October. He was straight away plunged into correcting the proofs of the *Vingt Regards* for Durand, and checked the manuscripts of *Harawi* and *L'Ascension* (in its orchestral version), both of which were soon to be published by Leduc. At about the same time, he wrote or revised the prefaces for the printed scores of *Visions de l'Amen* and the *Vingt Regards*. In the midst of all this activity, and concerts including *Visions de l'Amen* and the *Quatuor*, Messiaen found time in November to send his reconstructed score of the *Hymne au Saint-Sacrement* (now called simply *Hymne*) to the publisher Broude in New York.

On 9 January 1947 Messiaen noted that 'Raynaud is copying the *Trois Tâla*', evidence that movements 3, 4 and 5 of *Turangalîla* were not only composed but also orchestrated by this date. On 13 January Bunlet and Messiaen gave a private performance of *Harawi* in Paris, at the home of Mme de Prévot,[48] and a week later, on 20 January, they gave the first public performance of *Harawi* in

89 Messiaen and Pascal in
March 1947.

France, at the Salle des Fêtes in Mâcon, preceded on this occasion by seven
Regards played by Loriod. In February and March Messiaen travelled abroad,
first to Holland (giving *Visions de l'Amen* at the Amsterdam Concertgebouw on
17 February), then to Italy, for concerts in Turin, Florence and Rome; while
Messiaen was in Italy, Leopold Stokowski conducted the first performance of
the reconstructed *Hymne* in New York (12 March).

Messiaen's piano music appeared on record for the first time in 1947
when Pathé released 78 rpm discs of Loriod playing 'Le Baiser de l'Enfant-Jésus'
from the *Vingt Regards* (PDT 113), and three *Préludes* (PDT 132).[49] His
reputation outside France was growing too. In May he visited England again,
going first to Cambridge for *Visions de l'Amen* at the Faculty of Music on the
afternoon of 14 May, and a recital by Loriod at St John's College that evening.
But the major event on this trip was the first London performance of the *Trois
petites Liturgies* at the Wigmore Hall at 3 p.m. on 18 May, followed by a performance for the BBC at 9.15 p.m. the same evening. The conductor was Roger
Désormière with Yvonne Loriod and Ginette Martenot as the soloists. At the

end of June Messiaen and Loriod were in Vienna: the *Vingt Regards* played by Loriod in the Kammersaal of the Musikverein, and performances of *Visions de l'Amen* in Vienna and Innsbruck.

On 16 July Messiaen set out for Petichet in order to devote two months of intensive work to *Turangalîla*. Back in Paris on 23 September, the composer, assisted by Loriod, played the symphony to Koussevitzky in his suite at the Hôtel Raphaël. But on the evidence of Messiaen's diaries, the form of the work was still fluid: movement titles, and indeed the title of the whole work, were not finalized.

It is clear that *Turangalîla* was not composed according to a pre-existing plan, but evolved gradually. As we have seen, the work began as a four-movement symphony. The 'Introduction' sets out two of the cyclic themes (the 'statue' and 'flower'), following this exposition with a densely woven passage of rhythmic rotations. Superimposition of a different kind comes in the next movement, a scherzo with two trios, in which the material for all three sections is gathered together for the climax. The music from the second of the trios is then developed in the slow movement – eventually to be called 'Jardin du sommeil d'amour' – a love theme set against birdsong descants that are sharp and brittle on the piano, languorously even on the woodwind. The Finale (originally called 'Sonata') is a headlong toccata whose second theme is a further variant of the love music, climaxing in an ecstatic apotheosis.

This relatively conventional four-movement plan was superseded by Messiaen's next step, the addition of the three 'Turangalîla' movements, predominantly slow, or moderately paced, and concerned with complex patterns of rhythm and timbre. (These movements were known at first as 'Tâlas', but are not to be confused with the *Trois Tâla*, one of the selections from *Turangalîla* originally sanctioned by Messiaen, which comprised movements 3, 4 and 5 of the finished work.) The balance of fast and slow music was redressed in 'Chant d'amour 1', whose heady mixture of fast and slow – exuberance and rapture – was then amplified and surpassed in 'Développement de l'amour'.

In notes at the end of the 1947 diary Messiaen took stock of the work so far. The first plan was for a ten-movement work, in which the eventual Finale was to be used twice, in the middle and again (in varied form) at the end. At about the same time Messiaen devised a nine-movement version, this time with the Finale appearing only once:

Titles and subtitles for the *Symphonie-Tâla*
  1. Introduction (old first movement)
  2. Ist Tâla
  3. Chant de rêve (old second movement)

    4. 2nd Tâla

    5. Sonata (old fifth movement)

    6. Chant de tendresse (old fourth movement)

    7. Chant de passion (old eighth movement)

    8. 3rd Tâla

    9. Kheyâla–Mâruta (old third movement)

  10. Finale (use the old fifth movement again, in perpetual semiquavers by the whole orchestra *fff*)

or 9 movements:

  1. Introduction

  2. Chant de rêve

  3. 1st Tâla (with birdsongs on the piano)

  4. Chant de tendresse

  5. Kheyâla–Mâruta

  6. 2nd Tâla

  7. Chant de passion

  8. 3rd Tâla (with ondes and clarinet only, using rhythmic series)

  9. Finale (the old fifth movement orchestrated *fff*)

Order: *Bien.*

The eventual solution involved composing one more movement, 'Joie du sang des étoiles', which has the same galvanizing effect at the heart of the work as the 'Regard de l'Esprit de joie' in the *Vingt Regards.*

It is interesting that even at this advanced stage of composition (1947) only the first and last of the ten movements had their definitive names. The overall title, *Turangalîla*, was also arrived at after these movement lists for a *Symphonie-Tâla* were made. *Turangalîla* was chosen for its sound as well as for its meaning; taken together, the two halves of the word express the overflowing energy of the music and Messiaen's fascination with time and rhythm – '*turanga* has a sense analogous to our use of tempo', he told Goléa; while *lîla* refers to the 'life-force, the game of creation, rhythm and movement'.[50]

Messiaen started his class in Analysis and Aesthetics – new subjects at the Conservatoire – in November 1947, so he had a particularly busy autumn at the Conservatoire: for the new course, there were two classes of three hours each per week, on Tuesdays from 4.30 p.m. to 7.30 p.m. in the Salle Pugno, and on Thursdays from 2 p.m. to 5 p.m. in the Salle Cherubini. He also continued to teach his harmony classes for three sessions of three hours each, on Mondays, Wednesdays and Fridays, in the Salle Pierné.

Turangalîla dominated Messiaen's thoughts at the start of 1948, and for the first time in his diary, Messiaen gave the work, and several of the movements, definitive titles:

For the Symphony: do not forget the dedication to Koussevitzky. Call the eighth movement Développement de l'amour. Call the three little Tâla: Turangalîla I, Turangalîla II, Turangalîla III. Call the two love songs: Chant d'Amour I, Chant d'Amour II. Call the Symphony *Turangalîla-Symphonie.*

After a trip to Budapest in January (where Messiaen and Loriod met Kodály), the analysis class started up again at the Conservatoire, and on 1 February Messiaen was in Orléans for an unusual performance of *Visions de l'Amen*. His partner on this occasion was Janine Coste,[51] perhaps the only time Messiaen played the work in public with a pianist other than Loriod. On 14 February 1948 there was a public rehearsal for a work billed as *Trois Tâla* (movements 3, 4 and 5 of *Turangalîla*), followed by the première the next day. The Orchestre de la Société des Concerts du Conservatoire was conducted by André Cluytens. According to Loriod,[52] it was after the rehearsal that Boulez went backstage and made his notoriously wounding remarks about the work to Messiaen (witnessed by the Chilean composer Acario Cotapos), an exchange which was to fracture the relationship between teacher and pupil for a few years.[53] Critical reaction to the *Trois Tâla* was mixed. 'Y.H.' [Yves Hucher] in the *Guide du concert* reported that 'at the Société des Concerts, the *Trois Tâla* by Messiaen caused quite a stir. This is a difficult work, with its complex and confusing rhythms, its ultra-modern sounds, and its extraordinary orchestral writing. But Messiaen is a man on the move.'[54] Curiously, Clarendon was mostly indifferent: in *Le Figaro*, he described the music as based on ideas which were 'banal, or at least without surprises', though he admitted that it might be 'of some interest as a document of the exotic. What we take as revolutionary discoveries may be no more than a record of distant civilizations.'[55] Fred Goldbeck reviewed the work in *Le Figaro littéraire* under the headline 'La symphonie, elle aussi, va au cinéma' ('The symphony goes to the movies too'):

Olivier Messiaen's *Trois Tâla* ('Hindu rhythms') recalls the cinema screen. [...] Everything here is games with prisms, montage, slow-motion, speeding-up, zooming in on motifs which grow, or shrink, or are caught by surprise. And it is rich in elements of the exotic and the documentary (in the percussion), and the scientific (ondes Martenot). [...] This listener finds it all like an extraordinary musical toy, complicated, polyphonic and polyrhythmic. To be candid, he finds here both softness and violence, magic at every level, and an almost irresistible lashing of the senses.[56]

The first performance of *Trois Tâla*, and the others which followed, were strictly provisional. At no point did Messiaen consider these three movements to be anything other than fragments, but hearing them in concerts enabled

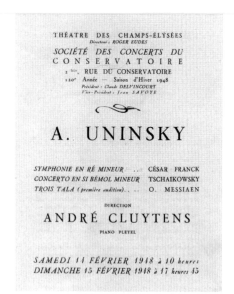

THÉATRE DES CHAMPS-ÉLYSÉES
Directeur : ROGER EUDES

SOCIÉTÉ DES CONCERTS DU
CONSERVATOIRE

2 ᵇⁱˢ, RUE DU CONSERVATOIRE
120ᵉ Année — Saison d'Hiver 1948
Président : Claude DELVINCOURT
Vice-Président : Jean SAVOYE

A. UNINSKY

SYMPHONIE EN RÉ MINEUR .. CÉSAR FRANCK
CONCERTO EN SI BÉMOL MINEUR TSCHAIKOWSKY
TROIS TALA (première audition).. . . O. MESSIAEN

DIRECTION

ANDRÉ CLUYTENS

PIANO PLEYEL

SAMEDI 14 FÉVRIER 1948 à 10 heures
DIMANCHE 15 FÉVRIER 1948 à 17 heures 45

90 Programme for the first performance of *Trois Tâla* (later to become movements 3–5 of the *Turangalîla-Symphonie*) on 14 and 15 February 1948.

him to judge the effect of the highly original orchestration. In a letter to Karl Schweitzer of 23 March 1980, Messiaen was firm: 'The *Trois Tâla* never existed. Through the publisher Durand I forbade the improper use of this title. Besides, I have never been of the view that my *Turangalîla* should be split into separate pieces. So this title should not be used, as it is misleading.' It is interesting to see how Messiaen's views evolved after the symphony had some thirty years of performance history behind it; in the 'note' to the first edition of the score (1953), the composer was more flexible about incomplete performances. While he stressed that the work had been 'conceived as a *whole*' and that performances should be 'complete and without interruption', he then proposed various shorter options, including movements 3, 4 and 5 (the *Trois Tâla*), adding that 'this selection is the best and has already been performed on many occasions'.[57]

On 13 March 1948 Messiaen was at the Trinité to play for *Les Matins du monde*, an 'oratorio' for two reciters and spoken chorus by the poet Roger Michael. First given on 10 March at the Salle Chopin by spoken voices alone, the Trinité performance by the 'Feux Tournants' company was enhanced by extensive organ improvisations by Messiaen. The first edition of the text (Paris, 1950) included 'Notes de travail pour l'accompagnement musical' by Messiaen. These offer a rare glimpse of his careful planning for such extemporizations. He played a 'Prélude', 'Interlude' and 'Final' and his notes supply some details of the music itself:

Prélude: Roger Michael, like Picasso, has his own vision of the world. He wants to recreate it, but to do so in his own way, direct and forceful, like a great artisan, a master mason from the Middle Ages. [. . .] I have chosen as my principal theme a broad unison melody played *fortissimo*, a thunderous S.O.S. A rhythmic canon, and its conflicting note values, represents disorder. Swollen and muffled reeds for the revolt. Big staccato chords followed by a panic in semiquavers represent destruction.

Interlude: I like this passage above all for its phonetic richness and its poetry. It is the 'first night'. After the creation of the birds and the beasts. [. . .] A mysterious alternation in staccato notes like drops of water. A solo on the 16-foot Quintaton based on my opening S.O.S theme, now transformed, distant and tender. Birdsong on some piquant mixtures. A time of love and of calm.

Final. [. . .] I build up a crescendo of joy as bells proclaim the renewal of the earth. All the earlier ideas reappear, join together, clash, run into each other, confident, dynamic. The poem ends magnificently:

> Earth! Earth! Shout your name!
> Like the sailors of Columbus
> Drunk on laughter, drunk on life
> Carried naked by the wind on the open sea
> Before their chances of greatness.

Then Roger Michael, poet–musician–architect falls silent. The earth is rethought, renewed, recreated. It only remains for the organ to add its own formidable comments, the S.O.S. theme flying overhead, now glorified by the notes in the bass.

The second half of 1948 was spent working flat-out on completing *Turangalîla* and then making a fair copy. On 26 July Messiaen noted that the 'Symphony was finished today', and on 31 July: 'copy the Symphony out in ink'. Things evidently didn't go quite as smoothly as this suggests, since at the start of his 1949 diary Messiaen wrote: '9 December 1948: Symphony finished and *good* ['bien'] from all points of view.'

Experiment and renewal
1949–1952

What did Messiaen plan after *Turangalîla*? The answer – a very surprising one – had come earlier in 1948, in the Paris newspaper *France-Soir* (28 March). The article is indicative of public interest in Messiaen's work, one of a series in which the newspaper interviewed French men and women with growing reputations abroad. The author, Robert de St Jean, admitted to knowing little about his subject, and made the best of his ignorance by concentrating on Messiaen's supposed eccentricities. Nonetheless, the portrait that emerges is surprisingly informative. We learn something of what Messiaen was like, his working methods, and the importance to him of birdsong; and he talked freely about future plans, in a way that would become unthinkable in later years. The most intriguing piece of news came at the end, with the revelation that Messiaen was planning an opera, astonishing in view of the assertions he made thirty-five years later, in the wake of *Saint François d'Assise*, that he had never had the gift or desire to write a dramatic work:

> We are at the Conservatoire in the rue de Madrid. Through a closed door one can hear the plaintive sound of a violin playing scales. I am waiting for Olivier Messiaen, whom I've never seen, and I'm wondering what will enable me to recognize him. He is organist of the Trinité: won't that mean a thin face, lowered gaze, bitter lips? But he's also professor of harmony at the Conservatoire, and that inevitably involves long hair, doesn't it?
>
> At last he's here. The long hair is there, but the facial expression, in this man of 40 [*recte* 39], remains very fresh and very open, with glimmers of childlike gaiety, sometimes, in his eyes.
>
> Do you know, I say to him, that the American critics are talking a lot about you and that the gossips tell all sorts of extraordinary details about you? They say that for three months a year you lead a hermit's life in the mountains, walking in bare feet and letting your beard grow; that you call your son Pilule and your wife Mi, this name of a note fitting perfectly, after all, the wife of a musician? [...]

I think, says Messiaen, that all these tall stories came into being the day it was known that Serge Koussevitzky had commissioned from me a symphony for the Boston orchestra.

No. Your reputation in the United States (which is equalled only by that of Darius Milhaud) has spread like a trail of powder since the Liberation. In their first articles on Paris freed from the Germans, American reporters rushed headlong to tell their readers that the Eiffel Tower remained intact, that Picasso was painting women with three eyes in the rue des Grands-Augustins, that ladies' hats were in the shape of a helix, and that a new composer had emerged: Olivier Messiaen. You have also been identified, to the correspondents of *France-Soir* in central Europe, as the latest revolutionary in French music. But hasn't any revolutionary at the outset undergone influence, and which masters do you recognize as having left their mark on your work?
– The birds.
– Excuse me?
– Yes, the birds: I've listened to them a lot, when lying in the grass, pencil and notebook in hand.
– And to which do you award the palm?
– To the blackbird, of course! It can improvise continuously eleven or twelve different verses, in which identical musical phrases return. What freedom of melodic invention, what an artist!

But birds are not the only inspirations for Olivier Messiaen: the creator of *Harawi*, a song of love and death, still pays tribute to Claude Debussy, and to the Hindus.

I believe, explains Messiaen, that we remain very ignorant from the point of view of rhythm, and that it will need several centuries before our ears have been completely educated.

I ask Messiaen if he grew up in a family of musicians. Certainly not! His father was a teacher of English, and his son, now aged 10, is interested only in biology!

When I was a boy, I built with my brother a little cellophane theatre in which we would enact all of Shakespeare. The tragedies were our favourites, as were tales of the extraordinary, by Edgar Poe, for example. You must realize that if I also devise the subject matter of my musical works, it's because I remember many marvellous stories learned in childhood: stories of the fantastic, fairy tales, tales of supernatural adventures. People are mistaken when they write that I seek originality at all costs in my chosen themes and in my commentaries. It's not true. And it's also incorrect, he adds, laughing, that my music, as one critic has claimed, is the work of a man who never washes! [. . .]

I live for the summer, he adds, when I get back to my little lake near Grenoble! For the holidays remain the only time in the year that I can work for myself.

It's there that you live the life of a hermit, so picturesquely described on the other side of the Atlantic?

And in their imagination. I've done only half of the symphony promised for Koussevitzky, and so I've still lots to do. The work will last an hour and a half.

Do you work on it in Paris?

Impossible. [. . .] I make notes in Paris, between my teaching, my weddings and funerals, and when I really get down to the task, at the start of my holidays, I advance along a road already prepared. After the symphony I shall write an opera.

On what subject?

I don't yet know, but what I do know with certainty is that I shall find a theme – I'm sure of it – and the work will happen. There's a childhood idea that still haunts me, and I set great store in keeping my word!

Having so confidently publicized his intentions, what caused Messiaen to change his mind and abandon the opera? And why did Messiaen's music, from the late 1940s, so radically alter course? The usual explanation to the second of these questions is that Messiaen decided to follow the achievement of *Turangalîla* with a period of experiment. It was to be many years before he would again write music on the scale that had become normal in the 1940s, in works like *Visions de l'Amen*, *Vingt Regards* or *Turangalîla*. Instead, Messiaen now added a third Tristan work, the *Cinq Rechants*, far more concise than its two predecessors, and for modest forces, twelve solo voices. This economy becomes even more marked over the next three years, during which the music would be exclusively for solo instruments: *Cantéyodjayâ* and *Quatre Études de rythme* for piano, and the organ pieces *Messe de la Pentecôte* and *Livre d'orgue*. Solo instruments, especially the ones Messiaen himself played, were the obvious medium for experiment, particularly as performers were finding his music forbiddingly difficult to play (see below).

The idea that these works are 'experimental' finds plenty of support in the notes Messiaen made in his diaries. As early as 1945 he was planning to extend serialism to tempo ('Faire des séries de tempo').[1] The following year, when Messiaen planned a ballet on the subject of Time, the techniques envisaged (as noted earlier) exactly foreshadow *Mode de valeurs et d'intensités* and sections of *Île de feu 2* (both from *Quatre Études de rythme*): 'a serial theme giving a series of twelve notes and a series of timbres – one timbre per note – one duration and one nuance per note'. Messiaen instructed himself to 'develop timbres, durations and nuances along serial principles'. He was consciously looking for ways to enlarge his language: 'Look for melodic motifs, chords, rhythmic figures from beyond my language, make myself a little dictionary', and in 1947 made plans for a set of 'études rythmiques'.

Messiaen's new direction has another explanation, however. A month after Messiaen finished *Turangalîla* Claire's health took a turn for the worse. In January 1949 she underwent a hysterectomy. Perhaps for fear of the effect of general anaesthetic on her brain, the operation was performed with an epidural, at the time blamed for a drastic further deterioration in her memory. Despite three weeks in hospital there was no investigation of her mental condition. On her discharge (30 January) Claire was cared for by Messiaen's father, Messiaen being absent throughout February with several concerts abroad. Indeed Messiaen and his wife would now lead increasingly separate lives. Claire spent long periods on her own at Neussargues; when she was in Paris life was rendered acutely difficult by her erratic behaviour. Messiaen was also anxious about his manuscripts, which he considered giving away (the autograph of *Visions de l'Amen* went to the Conservatoire) as the only way of keeping them safe. He also began to deposit drafts of work-in-progress with his bank (a practice which he continued for the rest of his life). Above all, it was difficult for Messiaen to find the order and peace necessary to compose. His whole life was a battle to make time for composing, and when he did have time, as in the summers at Petichet, he liked to work without interruption, all day and far into the night. This was now impossible. The achievement of *Turangalîla*, given these circumstances, had been heroic, but it could not be repeated. From now on music had to be composed in short bursts, where and whenever the opportunity arose.

It is against this tragic background that *Cinq Rechants* has to be understood. The published score dates the work to December 1948 – in other words a month before the operation that set the seal on Claire's decline. This seems early, coming so hard on the heels of *Turangalîla*; nonetheless, *Cinq Rechants* must have been finished by early February when Messiaen received payment

91 Claire, Messiaen and Pascal in the late 1940s.

from the work's publisher, Salabert. In later accounts Messiaen seems to have been confused about the chronology of his music at this time, hardly surprising with so many works overlapping one another. Yet the chronology is important if we are to make sense of the dazzling speed with which Messiaen's thought was moving forward in 1949. Besides *Cinq Rechants*, the other puzzling dates concern *Mode de valeurs* (composed, according to the score, at Darmstadt in 1949) and *Cantéyodjayâ* (Tanglewood, 1948). The latter date is certainly wrong: Messiaen simply mis-remembered the year of his first visit to Tanglewood, which in fact took place in July and August 1949 (though Messiaen was so convinced by his error that he went to the trouble of re-dating several of his Tanglewood photographs). It is especially important to have an accurate dating for *Mode de valeurs*, the work that famously put into practice Messiaen's new ideas about organizing rhythm, dynamic and attack. Messiaen was at Darmstadt at the time the piece was supposed to have been composed, in June 1949, but he was there for only three days, and had a performance to give, of *Visions de l'Amen*. The probable explanation is that *Mode de valeurs* was conceived (and perhaps sketched) at Darmstadt, but finished in the early autumn. Messiaen then (in July) borrowed the same principle when composing *Cantéyodjayâ*, which contains one passage that looks and sounds very much like a prototype for the *Mode de valeurs*. Messiaen's note for Loriod's recording of *Cantéyodjayâ* confirms the point: 'one finds a mode of durations, of pitches, of dynamics, the first at this date!'[2]

Significantly, the score of *Cinq Rechants* (like that of *Harawi*) has no explanatory introduction, apart from brief notes for the performers. The last of these reads: 'The work is a song of love. This word alone is sufficient to guide the singers in the interpretation of the poem and the music.' The title is a homage to Claude Le Jeune's *Le Printemps*, a work repeatedly used by Messiaen in his class:

> In *Le Printemps* the couplets are called *chants*, the refrains *rechants*. Melodically [*Cinq Rechants*] derives from two sources: the *harawi* or *yaravi*, a love song from the folk music of Peru and Ecuador; and the *alba*, a medieval song of the dawn, in which an unearthly voice warns the lovers that the night of love will finish.[3]

The *alba* calls to mind not only the troubadours and trouvères of the Middle Ages but Brangäne's dawn song in Act 2 of *Tristan*, which Messiaen described to Goléa as the 'most beautiful page in Wagner: the sublimation of the descant; I refer to the calls of Brangäne which hover above the loving couple'.[4]

In his account in the *Traité*,[5] Messiaen identified five symbols of love in his poem. Three of these – relating to Tristan, Orpheus and Bluebeard – were myths enshrined in operas known by Messiaen since childhood. In addition, Messiaen invoked the terrible sight of Perseus with the severed head of Medusa (echoing images of decapitation in 'L'Amour de Piroutcha' and 'Katchitkatchi les étoiles' from *Harawi*), and of Vivian and her lover, Merlin, whom she imprisons in a magic bubble of air. The imagery of this 'bulle de cristal' is also visual, inspired by the central panel of Bosch's allegory *The Garden of Earthly Delights* in the Prado; another image, of the lovers in flight ('les amoureux s'envolent'), comes from one of Messiaen's favourite painters, Marc Chagall.

The myths of Tristan, Orpheus and Bluebeard all hinge on a single step which, once taken, is irrevocable. In Tristan, for example, the defining symbol is the love potion, obliquely invoked in the line that concludes the third *Rechant*: 'tous les philtres sont bus ce soir' ('all the love potions have been drunk this evening'). But not surprisingly it was Bluebeard, and especially Dukas's *Ariane et Barbe-bleue*, which most haunted Messiaen. The subject, incidentally, continued to obsess him. In a later diary (1952) we find these cryptic notes:

Bluebeard has only one woman – the seven women are different aspects of the one: 1. purity; 2. genius (artistic) and intellect; 3. pleasure (dressing up); 4. childishness (granddaughter); 5. maternal love; 6. mysticism – suffering, drive for suffering; 7. sensuality. It is the woman who kills one of her characteristics each time she opens the door (fleshly union).

The text of the first *Rechant* shows the pattern of 'chants' and 'rechants' – which follows Le Jeune – and the interleaving of the poem in French with a second text in an imaginary language, with Sanskrit consonances, and syllables 'chosen for their aptitude in stressing the music'. All the principal symbols (except Perseus, who figures only in the final *Rechant*) are present:

Introduction
hayo kapritama la li la li la li la ssaréno

Rechant
les amoureux s'envolent
Brangien dans l'espace tu souffles
les amoureux s'envolent
vers les étoiles de la mort

tktktk ha ha ha soif
l'explorateur Orphée trouve son cœur dans la mort

Couplet
miroir d'étoile château d'étoile
Yseult d'amour séparé
bulle de cristal d'étoile mon retour

Rechant
les amoureux etc.

Couplet
miroir d'étoile etc.
Barbe Bleu(e) château de la septième porte

Rechant
les amoureux s'envolent etc.

Coda
hayo kapritama la li la li la li la ssaréno

Who then are these lovers? In view of what we now know about Claire, it seems impossible not to interpret the *Cinq Rechants* as an expression – albeit sublimated, and in heavily disguised Surrealist code – of Messiaen's agonizing predicament. Where *Harawi* was a passionate elegy to Claire, in the *Cinq Rechants* the image of the fateful step, the love potion, the seventh door, all point to Loriod. Antoine Goléa had no doubt of this, though he was too tactful to question Messiaen directly:

> I stopped myself saying out loud what I quietly thought, namely that *Tristan et Yseult* is essentially a story of tragic love, because illegitimate in the Christian sense of the term. Obviously, the opposite can happen: the man can be tied by the sacrament of marriage, and find a maiden who is still free in his path.[6]

It is clear that Goléa's views on the *Cinq Rechants* were his own and not Messiaen's: there is little doubt that Messiaen would have toned down the account had he had the opportunity. The proof of this came in 1989 when Messiaen was sent the draft of a chapter on the *Cinq Rechants* by Michèle Reverdy (apparently unpublished). Reverdy's analysis – which followed Goléa's closely, at times almost word for word – was meticulously amended by Messiaen, who deleted what he called 'several observations on the frankly carnal side of my music'; these included phrases such as 'the lovers attain the supreme delight' and 'this is the calm that follows the orgasm'. We may take it that what remains in Reverdy's interpretation did have Messiaen's approval. Reverdy identified a progression through the five poems. The first is an exposition of the main symbols, the second the betrothal of the lovers. The central *Rechant* 'glorifies the total union of the lovers' and its coda borrows a theme of love from the *Turangalîla-Symphonie* – 'tous les philtres sont bus ce soir'. The fourth *Rechant* celebrates the fulfilment of love. Finally, Reverdy saw the work as ending on a note of hope, with the lovers transcending death, and she quoted Messiaen: 'the beloved stands above time, while, very mysteriously, her eyes travel, into the past, into the future'.[7]

The stunning originality of the *Cinq Rechants* presented singers with unprecedented challenges; even Messiaen seems to have had doubts about the work's feasibility, as the following account by Marcel Couraud shows. Couraud recalled his first encounter with the music, when it was still a work-in-progress:

> The *Rechants* is a unique work in the sense that it is like nothing else in the contemporary polyphonic repertoire: technical demands, aesthetic, atmosphere, everything is absolutely new, and that includes its difficulty, which makes everything written up until then seem like child's play. I remember the evening Yvonne Loriod and Messiaen brought me the work in its raw state: four hands intertwined at the keyboard brought to life the twelve voices that I was trying to decipher from the thousands of sketches littering the music desk. A work was born from the genius of this amazing composer who, at a stroke, turned choral writing on its head and put everything back into the melting pot: in short, it was a moment of history, like *Pelléas* or the *Sacre*, a masterstroke, perhaps never to be repeated.
>
> It was on me that the responsibility would fall of bringing this terrifying work to life! Messiaen was worried that he had gone beyond what voices could manage and would play over this or that passage, asking: 'Is that possible?' I suspect I was not entirely honest that evening, because the problem was this: either the work would be performed as Messiaen had written it, or else it would never be heard in a concert hall, because this was not music that could be tinkered with. Despite my anxieties, I gave Messiaen my reassurance.
>
> Some months later I had on my desk a clean score, carefully engraved by Rouart. I read and reread the score, trying initially to ignore the difficulties and concentrate simply on the music, and then, being a practical person, I made an attempt to identify the difficulties. [. . .]
>
> I soon worked out that to achieve this I should need something like forty rehearsals. So I got my group together and handed each of them a copy of this daunting score. There was the expected storm of protests and the wildest adjectives flew round the room: impossible, crazy, ridiculous and so on. Once the fury abated, I simply said: 'The work will be performed, as arranged, on the specified date.' Each of them left hurriedly, weighed down by these fifty pages dedicated to the Ensemble Vocal Marcel Couraud!
>
> Patiently, work began as I had planned. I isolated groups, brought them together again, took one or two solo voices, went back to ensemble work, wanting as I did to keep individual and collective work on the go at the same time. The rhythms caused serious difficulties and each singer understandably

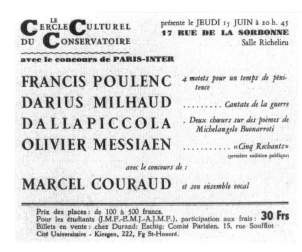

92 Handbill for the first public performance of the *Cinq Rechants*, at 17 rue de la Sorbonne, Paris, 15 June 1950.

found it hard to 'defend' their melodic line against their neighbour's! Throughout a fortnight of unremitting labour I had the continual feeling of being lost in an endless tunnel with no way out. Where was this hesitant progress taking us? Messiaen too was anxious and wanted to attend; doggedly, I reassured him and begged him to wait. What could he have done while I was still trying to fit the pieces of the puzzle together? Then, suddenly, we all began to feel that the piece was becoming familiar; each of us began to escape from our fears, to feel more confident in our parts and, at last, the music broke through, sweeping away the initial hostility. Continual patience and an exhausting and tyrannical regime had conquered the notes: Messiaen could now attend. [...]

I shall never forget the day when we sang the *Cinq Rechants* to their composer – in the museum of the Conservatoire, because we could not find a studio!

Messiaen listened, reassured and, I think, even surprised. Bar followed bar and Messiaen made no changes to my interpretation. That was my best reward![8]

Messiaen's home life was thrown into turmoil during the early months of 1949 because of Claire's perilous state of health. But he was obliged to continue his public appearances. Throughout January there were performances in Paris, notably Bunlet singing the *Poèmes pour Mi* with the Orchestre National under Désormière on 20 January at the Théâtre des Champs-Élysées. On 23 January Jean Witkowski conducted the *Trois petites Liturgies* in Lyon, with Loriod and with the young Serge Baudo – who became, in the 1960s, a leading champion of Messiaen's music – as one of the percussionists. On 28 January Messiaen accompanied the singer Gabrielle Dumaine in the *Poèmes pour Mi* at a concert for the 'Cercle France-Outremer' with spoken commentaries by Roger Michael, with whom Messiaen had collaborated on *Matins du monde* (and who was soon to become one of Claire's carers). Messiaen had commitments in Baden-Baden where a concert on 6 February in the Kurhaus included the *Trois Tâla*, again conducted by Cluytens with Loriod and Ginette Martenot as the soloists.

On 15 February *Harawi* was published by Alphonse Leduc in two versions: a deluxe edition of 100 numbered copies signed by Messiaen, and an unsigned edition of 200 copies. Both had pictorial covers depicting a pair of birds on the front and a single bird on the back. Four days later, Messiaen left for Barcelona where he played *Visions de l'Amen* with Loriod on 24 February. The following night Eduardo Toldra conducted a performance of the *Trois Tâla*. Loriod recalled that it was 'an immense success: the public threw their hats, programmes and flowers onto the stage!' The same artists repeated the work in Madrid on 28 February, enabling Messiaen to visit the Prado that morning. Returning to Paris, Loriod played two gigantic solo works on 7 and 9 March at the old Conservatoire: *Iberia* by Albéniz and the *Vingt Regards*, both of which Messiaen had recently analysed in his Conservatoire classes. A broadcast improvisation on 18 April made a deep impression on one of the leading literary figures of the time, Julien Green (1900–98). In his diary that day he wrote a brief but evocative account:

> Heard an improvisation by Messiaen. Music which one could say was composed *after* the end of the world. It is of monstrous beauty, opening up immense caverns where rivers flow, where piles of precious stones glitter. We do not know where we are – in India perhaps. The composer was playing on the organ of the Trinité. Never have the vaults of this hideous edifice heard more disturbing sounds. Occasionally I had the impression that hell was opening, suddenly gaping wide. There were cataracts of strange noises which *dazzled* the ear.[9]

On 7 June John Cage came to Messiaen's class to play his works, and was back a week later to hear Loriod play the *Vingt Regards*. On 18 June Loriod and Messiaen made their first recording of *Visions de l'Amen* (for the Dial label [10]). Despite primitive sound, this performance has a more pioneering spirit, with generally brisker speeds and less polished ensemble, than the later Loriod–Messiaen recording for Véga. The recording had to be made in a single afternoon, and that same evening Messiaen needed to be at the Trinité by 10 p.m. to record *Le Banquet céleste* and three pieces from *La Nativité* for the BBC. The next day he set out for Baden-Baden with Loriod, for a radio recording, and for a concert performance of *Visions de l'Amen* in Darmstadt on 23 June.

Messiaen returned to Paris for only the briefest of stays, since he was about to make his first visit to the United States. On 27 June 1949 he sailed from Le Havre on the *De Grasse*, one of the ships of the Compagnie Générale Transatlantique (French Line). The ship's newspaper included a photograph of him with a fellow-passenger, the violinist Angel Reyes: 'Musicians get together: Mr Olivier Messiaen, composer, with

93 Messiaen on board the S.S. *De Grasse*, with the violinist Angel Reyes and Mrs Reyes.

PAQUEBOT "DE GRASSE"
COMMANDANT CHARLES PERRIN

A 17 HEURES DANS LE SALON   AT 5 P.M. IN THE LOUNGE

CONCERT

AU PROFIT DES ŒUVRES DE MER
TO THE BENEFIT OF THE SEAMEN'S FUND

AVEC LE CONCOURS DE :

Angel REYES   Olivier MESSIAEN
VIOLONISTE   COMPOSITEUR

Maître de Cérémonie :
Monsieur F. HEYBERGER

Orchestre Pierre BAËTZ

Dimanche 3 Juillet 1949.   Sunday, July 3rd, 1949.

PROGRAMME

I.   Egmont (ouverture)......... L.V. Beethoven
        Orchestre Pierre BAËTZ

II. a) Adagio du Concerto en Sol   Mozart
     b) Final de la Sonate........   Franck
        Angel REYES - Olivier MESSIAEN

III. Improvisation
        Olivier MESSIAEN

IV. Dans les steppes de l'Asie
        centrale ....   Borodine
        Orchestre Pierre BAËTZ

94 Programme for the concert in which Messiaen took part on 3 July 1949, on board the S.S. *De Grasse*.

Mr Reyes, violinist, and Mrs Reyes.' On Sunday, 3 July Messiaen and Reyes participated in an on-board concert for the benefit of the 'Œuvres de mer', a seaman's charity. The printed programme shows that they played the Adagio from Mozart's G major Violin Concerto and the Finale from Franck's Sonata; Messiaen then played an improvisation on the piano. According to an article in *Newsweek*, Messiaen put his days at sea to good use:

On his way across the Atlantic last week to visit the United States for the first time, Olivier Messiaen got terribly seasick. Unlike most sufferers from *mal de mer*, however, Messiaen had a solution. Being a composer, he took his mind off his ailment by whipping out his stubby blue lead pencil (without which he feels lost) and working out the sketches for some pieces for organ. While these notations served their purpose, the most important score which Messiaen brought to this country was a ten-movement, one-hour-and-a-half symphony which Serge Koussevitzky commissioned and which will be given its world première in Boston sometime during the 1949–50 season.

The report in *Newsweek* went on to discuss the meaning of the title *Turangalîla*, the extent to which Messiaen was a 'figure of controversy' in France, his plans for teaching analysis at Tanglewood ('Messiaen expects to follow his Paris pattern'), and finally a 'human interest' closing paragraph, with the subheading 'Birds and Long Hair':

Messiaen is content with his work as a composer and organist and has never been tempted, like some composers, to take up the baton. During most summers, Messiaen lives at Grenoble and does his major composing there. He likes it, he says, because of the birds: 'That is my great hobby – collecting the songs of the birds I hear there. Especially at night they are fine and varied. The birds and I have been friends for a long time now. We know each other, but I am no St Francis in talking to them, you understand. I just listen and take down what they have to say. I have an enormous notebook filled with their songs. I like the song of the sea, the song of growing things – all the songs of creation I love. But bird songs and a singing rhythm are my great speciality in life.' Messiaen also likes Grenoble, he admits, because 'everyone wears their hair long – like me'.[11]

De Grasse arrived in New York on 6 July, and Messiaen made the nine-hour journey to Tanglewood the same day. He stayed there at the house of Douglas Francis, appropriately enough the organist of the Trinity Church in Lenox, Mass. According to Messiaen, Francis was a charming man who spoke French and was an excellent chef; he later became a monk in a Protestant community.

The programme book for the Berkshire Festival included an appreciation of Messiaen by the composer Virgil Thomson, whose conclusion is all the more impressive because the article is objective and clear-sighted:

Messiaen is a fully-fledged romantic. Form is nothing to him, content everything. And the kind of content that he likes is the conclusive, the ecstatic, the cataclysmic, the terrifying, the unreal. That the imagery of this should be derived almost exclusively from religion is not surprising in a church organist and the son of a mystical poetess, Cécile Sauvage. What is a little surprising in so scholarly a modernist is the literalness of his religious imagination. But there is no possibility of suspecting insincerity. His pictorial concept of religion, though a rare one among educated men, is too intense to be anything but real. Messiaen is simply a theologian with a taste for the theatrical. And he dramatizes events with all the sangfroid and all the elaborateness of a man who is completely at home in the backstage of religious establishments.

I once described this religio-musical style as the determination to produce somewhere in every piece an apotheosis destined at once to open up the heavens and to bring down the house. Certainly the latter action is easier to accomplish in modern life than the first. And certainly Messiaen has accomplished it several times in the *Liturgies*. The success of the accomplishment is due to a natural instinct for making music plus the simple sincerity of his feelings. These are expressed moreover through a musical technique of a great complexity and considerable originality. The faults of his taste are obvious; and the traps of

95 Tanglewood, 1949. Serge Koussevitzky (wearing a straw hat) is seated in the centre, with Messiaen (left), and Aaron Copland and Leonard Bernstein (right).

mystical programme-music, though less so, are well-known to musicians, possibly even to himself. Nevertheless the man is a great composer. One has only to hear his music beside that of any of the standard eclectic modernists to know that. Because his really vibrates and theirs doesn't.[12]

At Tanglewood a busy schedule had been arranged for Messiaen, with a programme of teaching and concerts every day. On 24 July Messiaen attended a performance of the *Quatuor*. The following day he improvised in public at Trinity Church, and on 29 July he played *Turangalîla* on the piano to Koussevitzky and Bernstein. In the final concert of the Berkshire Festival (14 August), Koussevitzky conducted *L'Ascension*.

Messiaen had eight composition pupils, each of whom had one lesson a week lasting an hour and a half. He gave a course of analysis, cramming into six seeks all the repertoire he had taught at the Conservatoire over the previous two

96 Messiaen's class at Tanglewood, 1949.

years: Hindu and Greek rhythms, Mozart, Stravinsky (*Le Sacre du printemps*), Debussy (*Pelléas, La Mer, Prélude à l'après-midi d'un faune*), Ravel's *Ma Mère l'Oye, Vingt Regards*, and so on. The class was visited by a correspondent from the *Berkshire County Eagle*:

Messiaen, who lists Mozart, Debussy, Stravinsky, Villa-Lobos and a colleague, André Jolivet, among his favorite composers, admits that his creations are hard to play. But he's not so sure they're hard to understand. 'Most listeners have a strong impression of my music', he says. 'The rhythmic innovations are so dramatically striking that one's reaction is rarely tepid.' [...] In class the bespectacled, casually dressed composer sits at the piano with his students grouped around him. His explanations of the subject matter are punctuated by frequent demonstrations on the instrument. [...] One of the theories he imparts to his pupils is that certain rhythmic groups have a character of their own – much as human beings have character. He thinks of rhythmic groupings as changing during the course of a composition, developing their characters as do the protagonists of a play. [...] Messiaen emphasizes, however, that the principles behind his music were not discovered by reason alone and then used as the basis of his work. The act of composition came first. 'The principles came instinctively, almost physically,' he says. 'I analyzed them later.'[13]

As well as the concerts and teaching, Messiaen was also busy correcting proofs of the *Cinq Rechants* and of *Visions de l'Amen* (the latter was to appear in print for the first time in March 1950). The only time Messiaen could find for composing was early in the morning, in the classroom where he taught, and 'in the company of an excellent Steinway'.[14]

The air of being on holiday, of composing for the fun of it, makes *Cantéyodjayâ* unique in Messiaen's output, and its coruscating wit brilliantly lays the ghost of the ill-conceived *Fantaisie burlesque* of 1932. If music is a symptom of a composer's state of mind, then the overflowing invention of *Cantéyodjayâ* shows Messiaen in rude psychological good health. The other reason for the work's exuberance is that in *Cantéyodjayâ* the old and the new Messiaen collide. The first three episodes, for example, juxtapose the 'theme of chords' from *Turangalîla*, an *alba* in the manner of the *Cinq Rechants*, and finally the section in 'mode de valeurs' technique that put into practice the theoretical ideas he had been sketching in his diaries. Musical ideas were cheerfully recycled from Messiaen's immediate past, so that *Cantéyodjayâ* became a sort of marshalling-yard for material assembled from *Turangalîla* and the *Cinq Rechants*, and subsequently distributed through the music of the 1950s (one motif even reappeared in Messiaen's final work, the *Concert à quatre*). A particularly fruitful quarry was *Turangalîla*'s 'Jardin du sommeil d'amour', whose languid descants are utterly transformed so that, in Messiaen's new style, they bristle with purpose.

Messiaen himself never performed *Cantéyodjayâ* in public, although the *Quatre Études de rythme* – which pursue in more specialized ways the trail blazed by *Cantéyodjayâ* – became for several years the cornerstone of his solo piano repertoire.[15] Messiaen's dislike of *Cantéyodjayâ* is hard to explain. As Loriod put it: 'It's an unpretentious virtuoso piece and Messiaen didn't like it much. However, it's certainly fun to play!'[16] It is true that Messiaen regarded *Cantéyodjayâ* as a rhythmic study and that in later life he also became ambivalent about the other rhythmic studies, the *Quatre Études*, whose importance (as he told Peter Hill) had been disproportionately exaggerated. Even at the time Messiaen had doubts about *Cantéyodjayâ*. He kept putting off making a fair copy, which was only done in 1952 (the work was published in 1953); and the first performance did not take place until 23 February 1954, when it was given by Loriod at the Petit Théâtre Marigny in the second of the new Domaine Musical concerts.

Messiaen finished *Cantéyodjayâ* on 15 August (1949). In his remaining few days in Tanglewood he began *Neumes rythmiques*, a second étude to go with *Mode de valeurs*. After returning to France (his ship, the *Île de France*, arrived at

Le Havre on 27 August), Messiaen delayed joining Claire at Neussargues until 13 September, probably using the time to finish the two études. The immediate spur to composing these had been a request from Durand for some 'easy pieces' for piano. Though primarily studies in composition, they are anything but easy to play.

Two documents have recently been published which shed light on *Mode de valeurs et d'intensités*. The first of these is Messiaen's analysis, included in the *Traité*, and as the preface to the second edition of the score (Durand, 2000). This shows that the music, which might be thought to be a matter of moment-by-moment intuition on Messiaen's part, results from what in fact is a perfectly lucid and understandable strategy. Essentially, what Messiaen does is to exploit and contrast two possible uses of his modes. The first is to deploy them as scales, as far as possible in the order given in the preface. The opening operates in this way: where there are changes to the 'expected' note, these are to avoid octave doublings, or perhaps other inappropriate harmonies (though a rather charming quirk of the piece is the way the occasional tonal triad is allowed fleetingly to form). The middle part of the piece takes the second approach, in which the modes are chopped into small fragments, which Messiaen rotates like an ostinato. At one point, for example, the lowest line sets up a rotation using just three pitches; as it does so, a game of *fortissimos* is played out between all three layers. The end brings together these two ways of using the material. After a long restatement of the lowest layer, this time in retrograde, the top mode is heard complete while the other two layers rotate shorter figures. Fittingly, the final sound is bottom C sharp, the longest, loudest and lowest note.

The other key document is Messiaen's recording of the *Quatre Études*, which he made in May 1951.[17] In *Mode de valeurs* Messiaen's playing is unexpectedly dance-like, a world away from the rigorous style in avant-garde music pioneered in the 1950s by such pianists as the Kontarsky brothers, or indeed by Loriod. The snag is that Messiaen simply side-steps one of the main pianistic problems, that of holding down keys at points where the three lines diverge beyond what the hands can stretch. The only way to get round this (apart from using an assistant and effectively turning the étude into a duet) is through a deft use of the middle pedal, which, according to Loriod, was not on the piano used for Messiaen's recording. Whatever the reason, his liberal use of the right sustaining pedal has the effect of reducing the carefully calculated durations to a wash of sound. Nor is Messiaen much more successful at differentiating dynamics (the other main challenge for the pianist), so that the 'game of fortissimos', described earlier, has very little effect. Much of Messiaen's playing in the remaining études is magnificent, however. Interestingly, the *Quatre Études* was the only solo piano work which both Messiaen and Loriod recorded for disc. A comparison shows that while at times Loriod clearly follows Messiaen's approach (she too uses pedal extensively in *Mode de valeurs*), in general she goes about things very much in her own way. An example of their widely differing musical personalities (of which Messiaen was well aware, and which he had consciously exploited in the piano parts of *Visions de l'Amen*) is the opening to *Île de feu 1* in which Loriod's immaculate brilliance contrasts with Messiaen's impulsive and grandly rhetorical playing. Loriod recalled that Messiaen was exhausted by the recording, which took place on a single day (20 May 1951). Without the benefit of editing, he had to repeat each piece in its entirety many times, and in the 'drumming' coda of *Île de feu 2*, with its *moto perpetuo* of repeated notes, the strain is clearly audible. The consequence was a bad attack of cramp, which took several weeks to wear off.

Much of Messiaen's time in autumn 1949 was spent making the final arrangements for the première of *Turangalîla* and doing battle over who should play the solo piano part. There was no argument about the *ondiste*, Ginette Martenot, since nobody in the United States could play the instrument; but Loriod's engagement was much more precarious as American concert managers felt it would be a simple matter to find a local pianist to take on the part. With matters still not completely resolved, Messiaen and Loriod embarked for New York on the *Île de France* on 10 November, arriving in New York six days later. When Stokowski conducted the *Trois petites Liturgies* in Carnegie Hall on 17 and 18 November, the ondes was played by Ginette Martenot, but the piano part was given to the orchestra's resident pianist, Leonid Hambro. Messiaen and Loriod were both present in the audience and found it a depressing occasion: the ondes was hidden behind the percussion section, while the piano part was virtually inaudible. Thanks to Koussevitzky's intervention, it was agreed – at

97 Messiaen and Leonard Bernstein rehearsing the *Turangalîla-Symphonie*, Boston, December 1949.

last – that Loriod should play the piano part in *Turangalîla*. Messiaen and Loriod, with Ginette and Maurice Martenot, caught a train to Boston on 19 November. Ten rehearsals had been set aside for the *Turangalîla-Symphonie* and the work was given its first performance at Symphony Hall, Boston, on 2 December, with Yvonne Loriod, Ginette Martenot and the Boston Symphony Orchestra, conducted by Leonard Bernstein. Loriod also found time on 30 November to play the *Vingt Regards* at Koussevitzky's home, for a small audience which included Bernstein. And while he was in Boston, Messiaen visited Walter Piston's class at Harvard to give an analysis of *Turangalîla*.[18]

On 8 December Messiaen and Loriod played *Visions de l'Amen* at the Institut Français in New York, with John Cage present in the audience. Two days later (10 December), New Yorkers had the opportunity to hear *Turangalîla* for the first time (with the same artists as the première), in Carnegie Hall. Messiaen's last engagement in New York was a purely social one: dinner with Varèse and his wife on 15 December. The next day, he set sail for Cherbourg on the *Queen Mary*, arriving there on 22 December. On Christmas Eve he was back at the Trinité playing a half-hour selection from *La Nativité* for a radio broadcast, and on 27 December he registered *Turangalîla* with SACEM.

Late in 1949 Messiaen was also making plans to compose for the organ. The extra pages at the end of the diary were used to devise a piece for organ with voice, setting a text by Tagore,[19] that recalls *Mode de valeurs*, with the organ's three manuals each having a distinct timbre. Messiaen's ideas then develop into a 'Livre d'études rythmiques' for organ: 'Use very long durations [. . .] create modes of timbres, modes of resonances; with superimposed Hindu rhythms.' At the same time, he made a note to look out old sketches for organ pieces and improvisations.

The significance of these jottings is that they show how music which would eventually become two separate works – the *Messe de la Pentecôte* and the *Livre d'orgue* – was conceived initially as one. This helps to explain why the *Messe de la Pentecôte* – which Messiaen maintained was based on twenty years of improvising – contains passages of highly calculated rhythm which seem anything but improvisatory. In the *Messe* the two types can be heard side by side in the second movement, 'Offertoire'. The piece opens with three Hindu rhythms, developed as a trio of 'rhythmic characters'. Later a short 'scale' of durations is developed through three simultaneous permutations. In between these sections, however, comes a rhapsodic monody, based on melodic patterns from *Turangalîla*, the 'Jardin du sommeil d'amour', from which so much of the *Cinq Rechants* and *Cantéyodjayâ* had been derived. The fourth movement, 'Communion', is especially saturated with self-quotation. Most of the references are to the Tristan works and to *Cantéyodjayâ*, though at one point there is a sideways glance (a passage of birdsong) to the exactly contemporary *Île de feu 1*. The rapt, closing phrase of the fourth movement returns to the

98 Messiaen, Ginette Martenot, Loriod and Günter Wand, Cologne, May 1950.

99 Messiaen working at Petichet, 1950.

music of the *Cinq Rechants* and the harmonies that accompany 'Tous les philtres sont bus ce soir'.

A project from this time, which Messiaen unfortunately never fulfilled, was to have been another collection of piano pieces, a 'Surrealist gallery (or gallery of monsters)', inspired by Bosch, Goya, Max Ernst, and Grünwald's Isenheim Altarpiece. As well as his 'freakish monsters', Messiaen passionately admired Grünwald's handling of Christ's resurrection: 'Christ didn't rise up; he wasn't raised up; suddenly he was alive again. And to express this total change, Grünwald used light: a sort of rainbow forms between Christ and the trailing shroud. [. . .] The effect is stunning. I've often tried, in vain, to reproduce this in my music.'[20] Messiaen, incidentally, always considered a knowledge of other arts important for his students. A few years later (in 1958) he introduced a novel examination: students were shown slides and required to identify paintings from details. Needless to say, the class was mystified, and the innovation was quickly abandoned.

The *Messe de la Pentecôte* was composed during 1950, and finished on 21 January 1951, still under its original title, 'Messe du Saint Esprit'. Messiaen gave the first performance of at least two movements at the Trinité, on 13 May 1951, during one of the Masses for Pentecost Sunday. In the May issue of the Trinité's parish magazine, he introduced his new pieces to the parishioners:

For the midday Mass, reserved for modern music, I have composed two pieces specially: an offertoire and a sortie. The offertoire comments on the words 'Les choses visibles et invisibles' ('All things visible and invisible') which we recite each Sunday in the Creed, and which are applied perfectly to the kingdom of the Holy Spirit, an inner kingdom of invisible grace. The sombre colours of the registration, the construction with 'rhythmic characters', the alternation of the 16-foot bassoon which growls in the extreme bass, with the piccolo and tierce making the sounds of distant bells in an extremely high register, depict the workings of grace. The sortie, entitled 'Le vent de l'Esprit' ['The wind of the Spirit'], uses a text from the Acts of the Apostles: 'A powerful wind from heaven filled the entire house' (taken from the Epistle of the day). A fortissimo, at first very violent, rises up in rapid swirls, like a chorus of larks as a symbol of joy.[21]

Two further organ masses were planned, but never written, one for Palm Sunday and Holy Week, the other for Easter Sunday and Eastertide. Messiaen's notes described 'the power of the darkness' and the apparition of Christ to Mary Magdalene: 'et Marie dit: Rabboni' – 'Mary saith unto him, Rabboni, which is to say, Master' (John 21:16). Both ideas would come to fruition more than thirty years later, in the *Livre du Saint Sacrement*.

Throughout the first part of 1950 Messiaen was active as a pianist. With Gabrielle Dumaine he performed *Harawi*, and Claire's tiny song-cycle *Primevère*. He also recorded three of the *Vingt Regards* for broadcast in the United States. But the main event of the year for Messiaen was the first performance in France of *Turangalîla* (conducted by Désormière), which took place at Aix-en-Provence on 25 July. The venue was outdoors, the Théâtre de l'Archevêché, and the weather was so ferociously hot that the musicians rehearsed in shirtsleeves and were issued with colonial-style sunhats. Goléa recorded his impressions of Messiaen at a rehearsal:

Silent, concentrated, intensely attentive, Messiaen followed the rehearsal, speaking only when Désormière asked his advice or opinion; only once, in the middle of an extraordinary sonic eruption, did I hear him murmur (as I was next to him): 'It needs a little more from the maracas.'[22]

There was no shortage of controversy after this performance. Poulenc described the scene in a letter to Milhaud dated 6 September:

At the end of Messiaen's *atrocious Turangalîla-Symphonie*, in the place de l'Archevêché, in front of an astonished crowd, Roland [-Manuel] and Arthur [Honegger] set upon each other; as for Georges [Auric] and me, that was a real drama. Georges was green, still unwell from a mixture of flu and a frozen melon, and I was red as a beetroot. For seven minutes we said dreadful things, Georges defending Messiaen, while I was at the end of my tether about the dishonesty of this work, written to please both the crowd and the élite, the bidet and the baptismal font, all in the awful tradition of Dukas and Marcel Dupré. People surrounded us as if they were at a cock-fight.[23]

100 Messiaen's class at the Conservatoire, 1952. The group includes the composer (centre), Loriod and Mme Christiane de Lisle (right), Pierre Tallec (behind de Lisle) and Karlheinz Stockhausen (behind Messiaen).

It was in the summer break following this performance that Messiaen finished the two *Île de feu* pieces, which complete the set of *Quatre Études de rythme*. Messiaen's interest in Papua ('Papouasie') – the 'isle of fire' of the title – stemmed from his friendship with Pierre Tallec, a former French official in Papua. Tallec was a frequent visitor to the organ loft at the Trinité as well as to Messiaen's class (he can be seen on the edge of a photograph of Messiaen and his students taken in 1952). Messiaen used the brilliant and exciting *Île de feu* pieces, whose themes are from Papua,[24] to frame the more abstract *Mode de valeurs* and *Neumes rythmiques*. *Île de feu 1* returns to the refrains-and-episodes of *Cantéyodjayâ*, and to a similar freewheeling virtuosity. *Île de feu 2* is the summation and climax of the 'mode de valeurs' technique: a 'row' of twelve sounds is systematically transformed, unfurling like a fan (or 'scissors', as Messiaen calls it in the diaries). The technique is an obvious precursor of the elaborate numerical processes developed by Boulez in *Structures*, which was started the following year. Strangely the *Quatre Études* – which were to make Messiaen (temporarily at least) a figurehead of the avant garde – received their première not in Darmstadt or Donaueschingen, but in Tunis (6 November 1950), in the course of an extended tour of North Africa by Messiaen and Loriod. The frankly miscellaneous programme was typical. In another concert, excerpts from *Visions de l'Amen* were paired with Beethoven's Fourth Piano Concerto. A week later the tour had moved on to Algeria; in Rabat Messiaen recorded the *Quatre Études* for radio, having to work at night since the studio was immediately above the main post office. Not surprisingly, when Messiaen returned to France he was exhausted and in poor health, suffering from jaundice.

The *Livre d'orgue* was the last of the major pieces from this period of Messiaen's life to be composed in short sections, as time permitted. Three of the movements were written in Paris, three others in the mountains of the Dauphiné and at Petichet, ostensibly in the summer of 1951.[25] The difference of place is significant. In one way the *Livre d'orgue* was the culmination, at least for the time being, of the years of rhythmic experiment. Many of its techniques followed directly from the *Quatre Études* or the *Messe de la Pentecôte*. For example, the idea of 'personnages rythmiques' ('rhythmic characters') is taken to extraordinary levels of complexity, and the fan-shape developments of *Île de feu 2* and *Turangalîla* are refined so that the fan not only 'opens', but also closes, by starting at the edges and moving inwards. These fans were not just mathematical conceits, but were seen by Messiaen as deriving from nature: 'When butterflies are enclosed in their chrysalis, their wings are folded and stick one against the other; the pattern on one is thus reproduced in the opposite direction on the other. Later, when the wings unfold, there will be a pattern with colours on the right wing which mirror those on the left'.[26] Despite the complexity of the structures for which it is renowned, the *Livre d'orgue* is also the work in which Messiaen flings open the door on nature – nature as experienced directly in the wild. 'Les Mains de l'abîme', the third movement, was composed 'while contemplating the meandering of the Romanche River through the terrifying mountain pass of the gorges of the Infernet. It's a truly impressive chasm; I wanted at the same time to pay homage to the sensation of vertigo it imparts and, symbolically, to the two gulfs of human misery and divine pity'.[27]

Nature and number combine in the final movement, 'Soixante-quatre durées'. The immediate model was the final toccata of the *Messe de la Pentecôte* ('Sortie') in which the lower two layers have scales of durations, moving in opposite directions to one another, while a descant on the upper manual flies free in a jubilant chorus of skylarks. Another source for 'Soixante-quatre durées' was a preliminary idea (noted in July 1950) for *Île de feu 2*. This was for an immense mode of durations, one for each note of the piano; by Messiaen's calculations there were eighty-five of these, a quaint indication of the antiquity of the pianos he was accustomed to, rather than the standard eighty-eight keys of the modern concert instrument.

In 'Soixante-quatre durées', the result of using scales of durations that are much longer than those in the 'Sortie' is that note values become correspondingly extended, and correspondingly difficult for the listener to perceive. Another consequence is that, compared with the 'Sortie', the overlay of birdsong seems estranged from the inexorable working-out of the scales, an effect beautifully described by Gillian Weir: 'The unbroken succession of chords create slowly shifting patterns of light that form a stark backdrop for the strange and remote calls of birds; there are two extended flurries, as they are disturbed and

101 Programme for the first performance of the *Quatre Études de rythme*, given by Messiaen in Tunis on 6 November 1950.

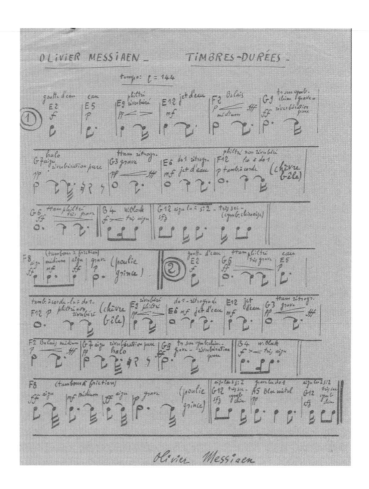

102 A page from Messiaen's graphic score for *Timbres-Durées*.

beat their wings in agitation, while the accompaniment flows gravely on, dispassionate, detached.'[28] Messiaen later defended himself against the charge of obscurity – with indignation to Goléa, and with a more measured argument to Samuel. The problem for the listener was that of distinguishing between durations, particularly in the absence of a sense of regular pulse: 'We are average-sized creatures of medium height and, alas! of average thinking capacity. [. . .] So we perceive very long durations with difficulty, and the very tiny durations, which can contrast with the long durations, with still greater difficulty.'[29] This problem of perception would be allowed to rest, but only for the time being: it was a challenge to which Messiaen would return with a vengeance eight years later, in *Chronochromie*.

In the early months of 1952 Messiaen temporarily put aside the *Livre d'orgue* in order to compose two short works. In March he ventured into wholly unfamiliar territory, with a composition for tape, *Timbres-Durées*. This piece of *musique concrète* was a collaboration with Pierre Henry (who had studied with Messiaen in the early 1940s); Messiaen selected the sounds and composed the rhythmic framework, while the realization for tape was done by Henry. *Timbres-Durées* was performed twice, on 21 and 25 May 1952, at concerts presented by French Radio. Messiaen contributed two notes to the programme. The first is a general preamble, giving his thoughts on the future of music:

Music – in the sense of harmony – has now reached a ceiling. There are no longer musicians of the twentieth century who will break through this ceiling. We must wait two or three hundred years at least for a renewal of music in this sense. On the other hand, some elements of music – duration, timbre, attack, dynamic, and especially rhythm, which has for so long been neglected – are, in our time, reintroduced. If I am in a large way responsible for this state of affairs, I must pay homage to the prophets who pointed the way – the way which leads from Varèse to Boulez by way of Webern, Jolivet, John Cage and myself. *Musique concrète* belongs quite naturally in this line of research into developing new musical resources.

Messiaen's note on his own piece is more modest:

Being entirely a novice to *musique concrète*, I present today an unpretentious study in rhythm, without any 'musical' sonority. Here is an analysis of it. There are 24 sequences, and in each sequence there are four rhythmic characters (A, B, C and D). 'A' contains 11 prime numbers designed to generate new permutations at each repetition. 'B' (Hindu *dhenki*) undergoes various transformations [...] and combinations of these transformations. 'C' is a non-retrogradable rhythm developed by interpolation and extrapolation. 'D' (Hindu *ragavardhana*) increases by a demisemiquaver in duration each time: these are filtered and reverberated, using recordings of water droplets and fountains.[30]

By the time *Timbres-Durées* was performed in May, Messiaen had stepped decisively in another direction. These early months of 1952 form one of the most fascinating phases of his life. Put simply, a battle was going on between head and heart, between the number theory which had been his obsession, and the call of the wild. The latter had never been far away: even when his music was at its most esoteric, a Dyonisiac rage was never far below the surface, erupting, for example, in the rampaging codas of the *Île de feu* studies.

In this context *Le Merle noir* is a modest but significant hint at what was to come. Commissioned as a test piece for the flute examination at the Conservatoire, it was composed quickly in March 1952 (not 1951, the date given by Messiaen). *Le Merle noir* has two main sections, which are repeated in varied form, with a virtuoso coda to end. The first idea of this simple design consists of a cadenza of birdsong (for the flute alone) which is significantly more realistic than anything Messiaen had yet attempted. The second idea, a slow melody, is clearly not birdsong, but the score gives no indication of what it represents. A clue is that the tune comes from the 'Jardin du sommeil d'amour' in *Turangalîla*, so this may be Messiaen's attempt to evoke the bird's habitat. Equally, it may be his way of presenting the emotion which birdsong produces when recollected in tranquillity; these moments of private reflection would later become integral to Messiaen's greatest bird essay, the *Catalogue d'oiseaux*.

In the end the need for fresh air became irresistible. A month after composing *Le Merle noir*, Messiaen set off for a short trip to south-west France. The object was a tutorial in ornithology from a noted expert, Jacques Delamain. Delamain was a producer of the brandy that still carries his name, but he was widely known as the author of a number of popular books on birds. One edition of the most famous of these, *Pourquoi les oiseaux chantent*, included in its preface this account by Messiaen:

> How I met Jacques Delamain is very simple. My publisher, Alphonse Leduc, who owned a property in Charente not far from Delamain, talked to him about my endeavours. Some time later, Jacques Delamain wrote to me: 'Come, I'm expecting you.' His home, at Branderaie de Gardépée, was, I seem to remember, a large two-storeyed house. I had a bedroom on the first floor with a vast balcony on which I could settle down with my music paper from four in the morning, and take down birdsong at the break of day without disturbing anyone.

The house was situated at the centre of an immense garden in which Jacques Delamain had had a variety of species planted which attracted all kinds of birds. [...] I had already, for a long time, devoted myself to not-

103 Gardépée, near Cognac, the home of Jacques Delamain (photo: Peter Hill).

104 The abbey of Châtre, near Gardépée (photo: Peter Hill).

ing more or less accurately the songs of birds, but without knowing which of them I was writing down. [...] Jacques Delamain had used his spare time to study birds, and had become over the years an amateur who was recognized and respected by experts. And if his books are not strictly speaking scientific, they are none the less completely accurate, ornithologically speaking. It is he who taught me to recognize a bird from its song, without having to see its plumage or the shape of its beak, or its flight, so that I no longer mistook a blackcap for a chaffinch or a garden warbler![31]

Loriod visited Gardépée for the first time in 1957. Forty years later she recorded her impressions:

I retain such a happy memory of a favoured spot where Messiaen took me one day on the road behind Garde Épée [Gardépée] which leads to the church of Châtre. A façade which he much admired; and on the way he took down lots of birdsongs. I was driving a Renault 4, and he took me to Chassor (where Delamain had taken him to hear some doves), before going back to stay the night at a little hotel in Jarnac. It was a sort of pilgrimage.[32]

The April 1952 visit to Delamain enables us to modify another date, that of '1951' given by Messiaen for the *Livre d'orgue*. The score describes the birdsong of the fourth movement ('Chants d'oiseaux') as having been collected at several locations, one of which is Delamain's garden at Gardépée.[33] Thus this movement, probably the last to be written, cannot have been completed before April 1952. The point is confirmed by the close resemblance between the sections for blackbird here and the flute cadenzas in *Le Merle noir*. In both pieces the birdsong writing breathes a new authenticity; in the *Livre d'orgue*, Messiaen even hints at the passing of time by ending with a long solo for the nightingale.

The re-dating of *Le Merle noir*, and of the completion of the *Livre d'orgue*, both from 1951 to 1952, reveals the logic in Messiaen's development in the early 1950s. The *Livre d'orgue* now emerges as the furthest point of this kind of experiment, but also as a work that pointed the way forward. The watershed came in the spring of 1952: after then, technical theorizing played a lesser role. Instead, Messiaen turned from number to nature, for reasons he explained in a note introducing the *Catalogue d'oiseaux* in 1959:

In melancholy moments, when my uselessness is brutally revealed to me, [...] what else is there to do except search for the true face of Nature, forgotten somewhere in the forest, in the fields, in the mountains, on the seashore, among the birds?[34]

The French première of the *Livre d'orgue*, given by Messiaen at the Trinité on 21 March 1955, has gone into legend. The recital, under the auspices of the Domaine Musical, was organized by Boulez, who expected about fifty people and had arranged for the audience to be admitted through a small side door. In the event there was a huge crush, with Messiaen barely able to force his way into the church, and with André Dubois, the préfet de police, there in a private capacity as a Messiaen admirer, losing two overcoat buttons in the fray.[35]

Birdsong into music
1952–1959

The idea of a work for piano and orchestra had been in Messiaen's mind for some time. The first jottings date from July 1950, when Messiaen planned a concerto for two pianos and orchestra. A year later (12 June 1951), in response to a request from Günter Wand, conductor of the Gürzenich Orchestra in Cologne, this double concerto now included a large chorus singing wordlessly; the orchestra (a pointer to the later *Oiseaux exotiques*) would be of wind and percussion, without strings. Both plans specify a huge mode of durations, in the manner of 'Soixante-quatre durées' from the *Livre d'orgue*.

If that is the sort of piece Heinrich Strobel envisaged when he commissioned Messiaen to compose a work for the 1953 Donaueschingen Festival, he was in for a surprise. By the end of August 1952 Messiaen's ideas had moved on. The piece was now going to be a 'Piano Concerto (birdsongs)'. Initially, however, some ideas were still derived from Messiaen's immediate past: Peruvian

105 Messiaen, Loriod and Boulez at Darmstadt, looking at the *Quatre Études de rythme*, 1951.

106 With Rudolf Albert and Gabrielle Dumaine in Munich for a performance of the *Poèmes pour Mi*, 25 January 1952.

melodies as in *Harawi*; the percussion combining rhythm and timbre as in *Timbres-Durées*; and a 'mode de valeurs' using a row of twelve notes. The big change was the idea of incorporating the birdsongs that Messiaen had been collecting, inspired by his studies with Delamain. Messiaen specified an instrumentation for piano and woodwind (piccolos, flutes, clarinet and bass clarinet) allied with a trio of keyboard percussion (xylophone, celesta, glockenspiel), the birdsong melodies all to be superimposed on one another. Thus simultaneously was born the sound of Messiaen's orchestral birds and the way they were combined into great birdsong polyphonies.

It was after the visit to Delamain in April 1952 that Messiaen began to collect birdsong systematically, in specially designated music manuscript notebooks. These *cahiers* were to become an ornithological and musical journal, which Messiaen kept for the rest of his life. In all there are some two hundred volumes, ranging in length from a few pages to a hundred or more, filled not only with birdsong, but with musical sketches of all types. Very often, in fact, the first inspiration for Messiaen's works came to him outdoors, among the birds, and can be found in a little memorandum, or occasionally in a rough musical sketch. The *cahiers* are full of words as well as music: descriptions of the unfamiliar landscapes of Japan or Utah, a storm in the mountains, the colours of dawn and sunset. Here is Messiaen in 1977 recording the precise effect of sunrise on the lake at Petichet, a sight he had seen hundreds of times, but still found marvellous:

> 25 July: radiant weather. At 7 a.m. the sun arrives and rises from behind the Grand Serre. Towards 8 a.m. the sun picks out a great line in the water, and highlights the ripples. This gives a shimmering of light against the darker lake. At 9 a.m. the lake is pale blue, and the sun picks out the little droplets of water and the green reeds: the droplets sparkle, brilliant with light.

A *cahier* was always at the ready. When a tawny owl pierced the night at Petichet, Messiaen used words to try to pin down its elusive timbre: 'The overall effect is astoundingly bright and wild – it suggests the voice of a woman or child calling for help – or super-amplified double-bass harmonics . . . the wail and final glissando like an ondes Martenot or the siren of a boat drawing away into the distance.' In Paris Messiaen came across a flock of turkeys in a street market off the rue Jouffroy-d'Abbans, not far from the Conservatoire: 'Large fowl (bigger than a goose) – its plumage is rather pretty: the overall effect is light pearly-grey – the feathers are brownish, flecked with small white lozenges – the general appearance is thin and pretentious – the cry is horrible, silly, piercing, fortissimo.' One of the earliest *cahiers* records a parrot, which belonged to the Belgian poet Maurice Carême.[1] Loriod recalled that the bird had a repertoire of two expressions: 'Attention à la marche' and 'Tu es bon comme l'amour'. Even at this early stage in his researches, in April 1953, Messiaen was recording timbre by having the parrot squawk in four-part harmony.

The *cahiers* began in May 1952, when Messiaen spent four days in the forest at St-Germain-en-Laye (14, 15, 18 and 20 May). As well as notating birds individually, Messiaen was already attempting to capture polyphonies of birdsong: in a notation made on 18 May at 8 p.m. ('coucher des oiseaux') a medley of birdsong was inscribed on three staves, and the phrases for the song thrush are recognizably similar to the same bird's appearance in *Réveil des oiseaux*. Back in Paris Messiaen noted birdsong at home ('dans mon jardin') and in the Parc Monceau. On 2 June he returned to St-Germain-en-Laye for an especially rewarding day during which he recorded a long solo by a robin which was to appear in *Réveil des oiseaux*. On 12 June Messiaen returned to Gardépée where he spent three days with Delamain. By now he had started to supplement markings of tempo, dynamic and articulation with verbal notes. The song of the wren, for example, is 'silvery, very rapid, pearly'; the golden oriole 'like a very large flute, almost a horn'; the crow 'raucous, powerful, sneering, sarcastic'. A charming depiction of turtle-doves, cooing in three-part harmony, is characterized as 'very slow, tender, with the timbre of a flute flutter-tongue'. The first *tutti* of *Réveil des oiseaux*[2] brings together the robin noted at St-Germain-en-Laye on 2 June (played by the solo piano) with the dawn chorus at Gardépée on 14 June – a blackbird on a solo violin, a second robin (celesta) and a golden oriole (horns).

107 Messiaen's notation of Maurice Carême's parrot, 1954.

108 Birds noted by Messiaen in the forest of St-Germain-
en-Laye. The robin ('rouge gorge') was later used in *Réveil
des oiseaux*.

During winter 1952–3 progress on *Réveil des oiseaux* was slowed by unusually heavy demands on Messiaen's time. No fewer than three recent works
(*Turangalîla*, *Cantéyodjayâ* and the *Livre d'orgue*) were being prepared for
publication. Loriod volunteered to help, and found herself with an unequal
share of the task: the proofs of *Turangalîla*, as well as those of *Cantéyodjayâ*.
Messiaen made frequent visits to monitor her progress (Loriod had set herself
a daily target of six pages) either at the home of her godmother, Mme Sivade,
or at her parents' house in Colombes, just outside Paris. Besides proof-reading,
Messiaen was exceptionally busy as a performer: in the early months of 1953 he
gave several performances of *Visions de l'Amen*, and also of the *Quatre Études*.
The latter was useful repertoire, enabling Messiaen to earn fees to pay the costs
of travelling abroad to hear his music. In Bremen Messiaen gave an unusual
concert at which he played two song-cycles, *Poèmes pour Mi* and *Harawi*, with

a baritone (Bernard Lefort); in view of the amount of transposition that must have been necessary, it is interesting that in later life Messiaen refused Durand permission to publish some of his vocal music in different keys. He also found time to participate in a revival, in Ghent, of Roger Michael's *Matins du monde,* improvising incidental music on the organ. On 23 April 1953 Messiaen gave the world première of the *Livre d'orgue,* inaugurating the new organ at the radio station of Südwestfunk in the Villa Berg in Stuttgart. There was further evidence of Messiaen's reputation abroad: *Turangalîla* was performed on 12 June under Rudolf Albert in Munich (where Messiaen was honoured by the Bavarian Academy of Fine Arts); Walter Goehr, another of the small band of loyal foreign conductors, directed the British première of *Turangalîla* in London (a BBC studio broadcast on 26 June[3]); and for the third year running, Messiaen was invited to Darmstadt, where he repeated his performance of the *Quatre Études,* this time as part of the opening concert of the summer course.

Another notable date in 1953 came on 5 May when Loriod gave a private concert at the home of Suzanne Tézenas (29 rue Octave-Feuillet, 16ᵉ), beginning at 10 p.m. Loriod's programme included Bach's C minor Partita, four of Messiaen's *Regards,* the first two movements of Boulez's Second Piano Sonata and two pieces from Albéniz's *Iberia.* Among the audience were Boulez, Jean-Louis Barrault, Madeleine Renaud, Antoine Goléa, the Comtesse de Polignac and Henri Michaux. It was a significant evening, serving as an important precursor to the Domaine Musical concerts which began the following year.[4]

These demands left little time for Messiaen to be with his family. At Easter he was too busy with concerts to leave Paris. The fifteen-year-old Pascal was sent to London to improve his English, while Claire left the villa du Danube for what was to be the last time, and went alone to Neussargues. There she seems to have remained, since in July Messiaen was obliged to take Pascal with him to the summer course at Darmstadt.

It was after the première of the *Livre d'orgue* in April 1953 that Messiaen found time to resume intensive birdsong research. He installed himself in the Hôtel de l'Aigle d'Or, at St-Germain-en-Laye, in order to set out early into the forest to hear the dawn chorus. Messiaen must have been conscious that he was setting his music on an entirely new course, and for once he seems to have needed reassurance, calling on Loriod to join him on 3 May; Loriod recalled their 'grande émotion' late that evening in the train back to Gare St-Lazare.[5] Another sign of her value to Messiaen (and perhaps of his uncertainty) was that he showed her the music of *Réveil des oiseaux* before it was finished. This was wholly exceptional; normally Messiaen kept his music strictly private until finished in every detail. In early June Messiaen paid a first visit to what was to become a favourite haunt, the Moulin d'Orgeval, near St-Germain-en-Laye.[6] Here he noted the songs of thrushes, blackbirds, greenfinches, warblers, and a golden oriole that continued singing until 9.30 at night. The dawn chorus of 4 June was 'unforgettable'. In years to come Messiaen would be shadowed by Loriod operating a tape recorder (enabling detailed revisions), but he always maintained the value of noting birdsong direct from nature:

> I make one notation on the spot with all the variations, and my wife makes a tape recording which is less varied than mine, but which captures everything exactly. Then I make a second notation from the tape recorder which is more exact but less artistic. [. . .] So I always have my two notations, one exact and one more artistic, and I mix the two.[7]

Messiaen must have worked on *Réveil des oiseaux* with extreme rapidity, as by the time he left for Darmstadt in July the score was almost ready. On 15 July Messiaen wrote to Strobel attaching a programme note to be translated into German 'without changing anything (add nothing, take nothing away)'. With characteristic thoroughness Messiaen gave all the names of the birds in German, excepting 'la bouscarle' (Cetti's warbler) for which, unable to find the German word, he used the Latin name. Messiaen's letter concluded with a sentence that seemed to show that he regarded the birds as the true composers of *Réveil des oiseaux*, with himself merely the transcriber: 'Don't include any biography, or any personal or musical information with my analytical note: I'm anxious to disappear behind the birds.'

Back in Paris, Messiaen now had to prepare the material for *Réveil des oiseaux* with a deadline of mid-September. In August no copyist was available, so he and Loriod set about the work together, though not before she had attacked the dirt and disorder of the villa du Danube. While Messiaen made a fair copy of the score, Loriod worked on the solo piano part; the copyist (back from holiday) created the orchestral parts. All was done by 15 September when Messiaen personally took the material by train to Donaueschingen. Once the material was ready, Loriod could begin practising *Réveil des oiseaux*, which by now she must have known inside out. After only a week she invited Messiaen to hear her play the work. This she did from memory and (as she remembered) almost without fault. To her dismay Messiaen was anything but pleased: 'There are no mistakes, but that's nothing like it. You haven't got the timbres of the birds.' Loriod decided to conduct some research of her own, and asked her mother to drive her out to the forest around Orgeval in the small hours of the morning so that she could experience the dawn chorus at first hand. The next rehearsal found Loriod contrite (she had completely revised her interpretation) and Messiaen apologetic. Her reading was now 'much more authentic, and I apologize as it's my fault; I should have put some onomatopoeics in the score to help pianists'.[8] As a result, when Messiaen came to prepare the work for publication he spared no effort to make his ornithological intentions clear to performers.

The preface contains a list of all the birds used in the piece, in order of appearance, and translated into five languages, together with a descriptive essay tracing the course of the music from midnight to midday. In the score each birdcall is identified, along with onomatopoeic equivalents: 'goudilio (golden oriole), tikotikotikotiko (nightingale), zip, zap (chiffchaff)', and so on. Recalling Loriod's experience, Messiaen has special advice for the soloist: 'As the pianist is called on to imitate the sounds of a great number of birds in the cadenzas, I recommend walks in the woods, in spring, especially early in the morning, to get to know the birds themselves.'

A further sign of the care that Messiaen took with *Réveil des oiseaux* is that the solo part appeared with comprehensive fingerings; again Messiaen turned to Loriod for help, though normally the fingerings in published scores of Messiaen's piano music are by the composer. The published score had a triple dedication: to Loriod, for her fingering and for her brilliant playing; to the memory of Jacques Delamain (who had died earlier in 1953); and to 'the birds of the forest'.

The première of *Réveil des oiseaux* took place at Donaueschingen, conducted by Hans Rosbaud, on 11 October 1953. The reception was a disappointment: the audience seemed indifferent, and the birdsong met with incomprehension.

After this setback came disaster. The neighbours at Neussargues had become concerned about Claire's disturbed behaviour, and on 25 October Messiaen left hurriedly for the Cantal to bring his wife back to Paris, placing her temporarily in a nursing home. He then returned to Neussargues to retrieve Claire's three cats. A fortnight of tests and observation followed. 'See Dr Maillard about Mie', Messiaen wrote in his diary. 'Buy her books, sweets, socks.' The first tests were for cancer – 'examination of the back of the eye, electrical examination. There is wasting of the tissues – no tumour or lesion.' On 19 November Messiaen took Claire to the Salpetrière Hospital, famous at the time for its neurological research, where she remained for several days of investigations. On 2 December he recorded the results: 'a slow-moving condition, progressive infection destroying the cerebral convolutions. [. . .] [Medication] to prevent the spread of the condition. She has been ill for a very long time – may still live for many years.' The devastating diagnosis was 'cerebral atrophy, incurable'.

On 18 December Simone Loriod, Yvonne's mother, arrived from Colombes to help Messiaen take his wife to a nursing home at La Varenne. Smiling vacantly, Claire was sick in the car, and on arrival allowed herself to be put to bed.[9] Four days after Claire's admission to a home, Messiaen had to endure the French première of *Réveil des oiseaux*, played uncomprehendingly (Loriod recalled) by the Orchestre National under his former pupil, Maurice Le Roux.

In terms of Messiaen's personal life 1954 was bleak. The diary is dotted with entries reflecting his constant anxieties for Claire, for the welfare of Pascal, and even for his own health. In February he suffered agonizing leg pains, and he had

109 Messiaen, Michel Fano and Pierre Boulez in March 1954 (photo: Lipnitzki/Roger-Viollet).

trouble with his teeth (as he did all his life), exacerbated, he believed, by the prison camp diet.

On Sunday afternoons Messiaen would visit Claire at La Varenne, after playing in the morning at the Trinité. At first he hoped to renew her interest in life, bringing her crayons and paints and getting her violin mended. Later in 1954 (starting on 19 September) Loriod took to accompanying him; they found that with two of them to support her, Claire could manage a short walk. She could recognize her visitors, greeting them with a smile, but was unable to speak. (The *cahiers* that went everywhere with Messiaen accompanied him even to La Varenne, where he made several notations of robins.) To add to Messiaen's woes, the boiler at the villa du Danube, always troublesome, broke down. While it was out of action Messiaen lodged Pascal with Pio, not merely for his son's well-being but also in the hope that Pascal's grandfather would help with his studies.

In the spring came double tragedy: Claude Delvincourt, Director of the Conservatoire, was killed in a car crash on his way to Rome; a month later (6 May) Line Zilgien, Messiaen's deputy at the Trinité, died of cancer. Delvincourt's successor at the Conservatoire was Marcel Dupré. The appointment of his old teacher must have been welcome, but it meant change and thus extra work. At the start of the autumn term Dupré called Messiaen to a meeting at which he announced that his class would take a new direction, as a 'Classe de Philosophie musicale', and that each student would be required to submit a thesis. Even playing at the Trinité had its vexations. Loriod recalled that admirers would find their way up to the organ loft, hampering Messiaen's preparation of his registrations and making it difficult for him to follow the service. On Pentecost Sunday (6 June), Messiaen found forty people crammed around the organ console.

As the *cahiers* for 1954 reveal, Messiaen was hard at work, on a project so vast that it eclipsed anything he had yet attempted. The first inkling of what he was up to came in a note made on the evening of 6 October 1953 in the Black Forest near Baden-Baden. Underneath a sketch of the cry of the tawny owl ('vociféra-tion douloureuse et lugubre') are the words 'for the piano', followed by a long list of birds classified according to habitat:

Birds of the high mountain: chough
Birds of the vineyards: linnets, ortolan bunting

Night birds: tawny owl
Tropical birds: shama, Indian minah, white-throated laughing thrush
Sea birds: curlew
Birds of the reeds and ponds: great reed warbler
Birds of the pine woods: willow warbler, great tit
Birds of the cornfields and open sky: lark
Birds of orchards and woods: song thrush
Birds of gardens and woods: blackbird, robin
Birds of the oak trees: golden oriole
Birds of gardens and parks: blackcap, garden warbler, starling, chiffchaff
Birds of the copses: robin
Birds of the woods: green woodpecker, great spotted woodpecker

With this encyclopedic project in view, there are signs, by the summer of 1954, that Messiaen was starting to direct his birdsong sketches towards specific musical ends. One of the first of the *Catalogue d'oiseaux* to be conceived was 'Le Loriot' (golden oriole), a piece that opens with a solo for the oriole, followed by a short dawn chorus. In an embryonic sketch (dated 20 June 1954) the phrases for the golden oriole are already remarkably similar to the finished piece, although just a single line, without the colouring harmonies in the pianist's right hand that would be added. For the dawn chorus, Messiaen devised a time chart that showed when birds stopped and started, and how the soloist, the oriole, fitted with the complex medley of overlapping songs.

Throughout summer 1954 Messiaen paid visits to the forest around Orgeval. In the autumn, particularly when the recalcitrant boiler at villa du Danube was giving trouble, he took to visiting Loriod's new apartment in the rue Marcadet where he would use her gramophone to listen to discs of tropical birds. He also began to frequent the bird markets of Paris, noting the minahs and shamas that would sing in *Oiseaux exotiques*.

By the end of 1954 Messiaen's researches had evolved into an idea for a work. The plan was to combine birdsongs with Balinese rhythms, and to score the music for chorus, a 'gamelan' (two xylophones, vibraphone, celesta, two glockenspiels), an arsenal of metallic percussion (gongs, cymbals, tamtam, bells) along with woodwind and a solo piano. Apart from the choir, the instrumentation clearly points to *Oiseaux exotiques*. Very possibly the commission – which came from Boulez – had already arrived when Messiaen made this note, and early in 1955 Messiaen recorded in his diary that he had confirmed the instrumentation with Boulez, and that the first performance would be at a Domaine Musical concert.

Composition was again delayed by Messiaen's work as a performer. On 4 January 1955 he broadcast with Gabrielle Dumaine several songs from *Harawi*.

110 A dawn chorus notated at Orgeval, 20 June 1954.

There were performances of *Visions de l'Amen* (at Orléans) and the *Quatre Études de rythme* (Munich), and in March Messiaen gave the French première (described earlier) of the *Livre d'orgue*. Messiaen showed extraordinary dedication in preparing his concerts. On 3 October 1955, for example, he gave a performance of *Chants de terre et de ciel* with the English soprano Adèle Leigh. Messiaen had been approached, on her behalf, by his old friend Felix Aprahamian, and agreed to the concert only with some reluctance: 'Having concerts and trips abroad, I was thinking of coming back to Paris just before my first class at the Conservatoire, on Tuesday 4 October. The piano part of *Chants de terre et de ciel* is *very difficult*. I need a fortnight to work at it and I would have to come back around 15 September, just for that. Moreover the balance between voice and piano is tricky. Would we have enough time in four days before the concert?'[10] Messiaen's point is borne out by the fact that in the previous year (1954) he had set out for Vichy on 1 September, allowing himself nearly a fortnight to rehearse *Harawi* with Marcelle Bunlet, in spite of the numerous performances they had already given.

111 Hans Rosbaud, Zurich, 1954.

Behind the public success lay the agony of Claire's decline; she was now incontinent, and it fell to Messiaen to purchase the necessities to cope with this. At least the weekly visits to La Varenne were made easier because Loriod had learned to drive and had purchased a small car. There was another way in which Loriod's Renault proved a godsend: with her help Messiaen was now able to range further afield – and to remote areas – in search of birdsong. The first of these expeditions (in June 1955) was to the Sologne region, south of Orléans, with its network of ponds and lakes. Here among the marshes Messiaen found the reed warblers whose virtuosity he would celebrate in 'La Rousserolle effarvatte', the long central piece of the *Catalogue d'oiseaux*; he spent two nights in Loriod's car in order to hear their nocturnal song. A week later (28 June) he and Loriod went by train to Grenoble, but in the high mountains around La Grave the weather was cold and to Messiaen's chagrin no birds were to be heard. They returned via Petichet where Loriod's first impressions so enchanted her that she offered to return in the summer to keep house for Messiaen and Pascal.

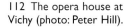

112 The opera house at Vichy (photo: Peter Hill).

In the event the summer holiday was not an unqualified success. Loriod was horrified by the primitive facilities, and in particular the lack of mains water. There was a simple pump that required forty-five minutes of strenuous exercise in order to fill a tank in the attic. The tank was filthy, home to a colony of bats, and it seemed to Loriod a miracle that the Messiaen family had escaped serious infection. Moreover, with Messiaen shut away in his study, Loriod found herself in the company of Pascal, now aged eighteen. The young man was fractious, understandably so, given his father's single-minded dedication to work. Messiaen's only relaxation was

a short swim in the lake at the end of the morning, and after lunch an hour's siesta. Supper was served after Messiaen had finished work, often as late as eleven o'clock at night. The sole variation in the regime came with excursions to the mountains, but these were serious expeditions, with Messiaen filling his *cahier* with impressions and notations of birdsong.[11]

Throughout the summer of 1955 Messiaen worked at collecting birdsong for his great project. In the peaks of the Écrins (to the east of Petichet), he recorded the 'high-pitched and strident rattling' of the Alpine chough. On 25 July he watched a buzzard: 'immense grey silhouette. It flies in circles at a great height, then descends, still circling, describing vast orbits in space. It drops out of its glide and takes a fish from the water, immediately flying off.' In Grenoble Messiaen made notes on the acrobatic flight of a flock of swallows. As usual, place, date and time of day were carefully recorded. '14 July, 8 p.m., on the right the Téléférique and Fort Rabot, at the end, by the town hall and the belfry of St-André, in the garden, scarlet cannas, pink hortensias [. . .] geraniums, pansies, thousands of blue, purple and pink violets, some zinnias adding a striking note of orange. Coming out of the belfry of the old church, a ballet of swallows, criss-crossing the sky in curves, crosses, stars, flowers – all kinds of shapes.' In September Messiaen made his first trip to the coast at the far end of Brittany, filling pages of his notebook with musical representations of the waves, and the foaming wake of the boat taking him from Brest to the island of Ouessant (Ushant).

Back in Paris Messiaen was beset by anxieties for his family, and was suffering from painful gallstones, for which he was prescribed a strict diet (no wine, no eggs). Another trial was uncertainty as to whether Durand would continue to publish his music. No doubt the firm was wary of taking on works in Messiaen's new birdsong style, after the lack of interest in *Réveil des oiseaux*. Even his pupils were causing Messiaen to feel demoralized. Alexander Goehr, who was in Messiaen's class during this time (1955–6), drew a touching portrait of Messiaen's feelings of isolation:

> Face to face with his sometimes obstreperous students and opinionated hangers-on, he was even reduced to tears. We sat in silence for long periods, especially after an aggressive attempt by one of us to argue with him. Here were we, before one of the most perfect musicians of our times, combative and argumentative, in tense, unbroken silence. And he would say, 'Gentlemen, let us not argue like this. We are all in a profound night, and I don't know where I am going; I'm as lost as you.'[12]

Antoine Goléa, who began his interviews with Messiaen in March 1956, visited him at the villa du Danube and recorded this description:

113 Messiaen at Perros-Guirec, Brittany, in September 1955.

Messiaen is a man of extraordinary delicacy, of moving timidity, of exquisite courtesy. What rather embarrassed him, as he asked me in, was the untidiness of the house; he lived at that time alone with his son, who was still at school, and without any help he looked after the house and the housekeeping. I had already learnt something of his troubles from some of his pupils. The most intractable of the duties which he shouldered was lighting the boiler for the central heating, in the course of winters which were harder in the north of the Buttes-Chaumont than anywhere else in Paris. I knew also that snow and ice sometimes blocked his front door, exposed directly to the north wind, and that his pedal piano had been destroyed by damp. The truth was that he had no 'home', that he usually left his lodging very early in the morning, returning only late in the evening, and that he ate most meals out.[13]

It is puzzling that Messiaen should have allowed the best part of 1955 to elapse before beginning the composition of *Oiseaux exotiques*; according to the score the work was composed quickly, between 5 October 1955 and 23 January 1956. The dates are misleading, however. The first birds for *Oiseaux exotiques* to appear in the *cahiers* were a shama and a Red Cardinal which Messiaen noted at the home of a Mme Billot (who owned a collection of tropical birds) on 18 May 1954. The shama ('brassy timbre, brilliant') is virtually identical to its appearance on the trumpet in the finished work.[14] Messiaen described the Red Cardinal in detail: 'The voice is brilliant and pearly. The oscillations resemble a nightingale when quiet, and the drumming of a great spotted woodpecker when loud. Certain strophes are somewhat like the song thrush.' In the piano cadenzas of *Oiseaux exotiques*[15] Messiaen simplified the Red Cardinal's song, reducing it to three elements: arpeggios, staccato attacks preceded by grace notes, and a tremolo which he dramatized with a crescendo and diminuendo.

Almost all the birdsong in *Oiseaux exotiques* derived, however, from recordings. Over the winter of 1954–5 Messiaen created a *cahier* specially devoted to Mexican and North American birds. The order in which the latter appear in the *cahier* matches six 78 rpm records, released under the title *American Bird Songs* by Comstock Publishing in 1942.[16] Because he was working from recordings rather than direct from nature, Messiaen was able to notate several versions of individual birdsongs, refining the detail each time. As the *cahier* proceeds, these notations become in reality musical sketches. A spectacular example is the wood thrush, with its sunburst of E major harmony, whose progress from primitive notation to finished score can be seen on p.216.

Altogether, *Oiseaux exotiques* shows Messiaen moving to a new and far less self-effacing relationship with birdsong. Whereas in *Réveil des oiseaux* Messiaen had truth to nature as a priority, in subsequent works of the 1950s the musician gradually gained the upper hand over the ornithologist. Harmony, in particular, became a potent force in Messiaen's 'style oiseau'. In *Réveil des oiseaux*, individual lines were almost always monodic;[17] in *Oiseaux exotiques* a much richer and more varied effect is created, such as the not-quite-parallel ripplings of the

114 The evolution of the music for the wood thrush in *Oiseaux exotiques* from (*a*) the first birdsong notation to (*b*) the sketch and (*c*) the finished score.

arpeggios of the Red Cardinal. The other new element is drama. The birds in *Réveil des oiseaux* had not been lacking in character, as the adjectives scattered throughout the score show: 'joli, poétique'; 'un peu irrité'; 'autoritaire et incantatoire'; but Messiaen was tied to his midnight to midday plan, and so to the sequence of events in nature. In *Oiseaux exotiques*, without a programme to follow, Messiaen was able to move his material around at will, to maximum dramatic effect.

The first performance of the work was arranged for 10 March, and on 31 January Messiaen and Loriod began hurriedly copying the orchestral material. Rehearsals began on 1 March, at the home of Suzanne Tézenas, and the première (10 March) took place at the Petit Théâtre Marigny (made available by Jean-Louis Barrault), the sort of small auditorium for which the work was expressly designed, as the preface to the score makes clear. Rudolf Albert conducted the orchestra of the Domaine Musical, with Loriod as the piano soloist. Messiaen noted the timing in his diary: 13 minutes and 10 seconds.

Alexander Goehr was in the audience at the first performance. He remembered being particularly resistant to the idea of Messiaen's birds:

I could not imagine how one could, as it were, compose from nature without falling into bathos, analogous to Strauss's *Sinfonia domestica* or Honegger's *Pacific 231*. Messiaen retorted, in answer to my ignorant tittering, that for his part he certainly would not take me for a walk in the forest, as my giggling would upset the birds. But I had to realize the superficiality of my view when it came to the première at Boulez's Marigny concerts of *Oiseaux exotiques*. [. . .] The students in the class asked Messiaen to talk about the new work, which he immediately refused to do. [. . .] He arrived at the following class with an even larger mountain of books than he normally brought with him. These turned out to be ornithological treatises of various sorts, and the lecture, lavishly illustrated at the piano, was a factual description of the countries of origin, habitat, physical appearance and song of a large number of birds. Some pages contained Red Cardinals, Blue Popes and a 'Singer from South America' which, as I recall, aroused some mirth among us. However, when the performance came, we realized he had taken us at our word, and provided us with what he thought an appropriate introduction to his new work. [. . .] But he could not really be drawn about the music itself. I was bowled over by the piece then (as I am now), not only because of the extraordinary colours and the masterly instrumental writing, but also, more conventionally, by the continuity and form, which seemed quite original. To this day, few commentators have paid attention to the way in which the dawn choruses, consisting of many different and overlapping parts, have been built up rhythmically and harmonically, and no wonder, because here technique at the highest level hides technique. You hear the final harmony and the balancing combinations of voices, but you cannot say how it's done. Questions about such matters elicited no response at all from Messiaen.[18]

The concert in which *Oiseaux exotiques* had its first performance (alongside music by Gabrieli, Stravinsky, Henze and Barraqué) was recorded and released by Véga, with a cover designed by Miró. Véga's enterprising director, Lucien Adès, was quick to realize the significance of the programmes that Boulez was devising. Later in March there were sessions to record music by Boulez (*Le Marteau sans maître*) and Messiaen (*Vingt Regards*). Two other record companies were interested in his music. One was the Club Français du Disque for whom (on 8 and 9 May) Messiaen recorded the *Quatuor* with André Vacellier and the Pasquier brothers. A few days later he began the considerable task of recording all his organ music for Ducretet-Thomson. The sessions, which took place at the Trinité, were spread over seven days between 14 May and 22 June. Finally at the end of June there were five extra sessions held in the evening and at night, presumably to patch passages which had been disturbed by traffic noise.

Shortly after the first performance of *Oiseaux exotiques* Messiaen and Loriod left Paris by car for a second visit to the Sologne area. The bird life was again rich, and Messiaen refined his jottings with nuances and accents, while noting precise indications of habitat which would find their way into 'La Rousserolle effarvatte'. In June Messiaen telephoned the bird sanctuary of the Camargue to ask permission to make a visit. (The director was Jacques Penot, who would later help Loriod with preparing the volume of the *Traité* devoted to birdsong.) The result was a long trip, in July, during which Messiaen for the first time notated the birds of Provence and the Mediterranean coast. Among these were the blue rock thrush and short-toed lark which would have leading roles in the *Catalogue d'oiseaux*. At Les Baux (near Arles) Messiaen discovered a landscape which would become a favourite, filling his *cahiers* with notations made at dawn and sunset.

On 14 July Messiaen and Loriod set off for Paris, travelling via the Forez, an area on the north-eastern slopes of the Massif Central. There, on the road to St-Sauveur-en-Rue, they heard a woodlark, in an episode noted in the *cahier* that would be exquisitely evoked in 'L'Alouette lulu':

Edge of the road – umbrella pines, acacia, chestnuts [. . .] hazels, firs, ferns, maize in green chandeliers with Lilliputian clusters of corn – purple foxgloves, opening their red-violet finger-stalls to let one see inside the corolla, white, flecked with blood [. . .] a magnificent panorama of mountains: misty, smoky clouds, rising from the valley and wreathing the fir trees opposite [. . .] after the rain, a wonderful rainbow extends a semicircle of colour over the whole landscape.

As well as the shimmering, chromatic descents of the woodlark's song, Messiaen's *cahier* recorded a flock of yellowhammers, a skylark, the tinkling of a stream, and the sight of two species of owl:

> Eagle owl: two large plumes of feathers, incorrectly called 'ears', give it the physiognomy of a great cat. Its great wingspan deployed in flight. Breeches of beige feathers. Magnificent breast, light russet and beige-grey, flecked with maroon. [. . .] Its eyes are marvellous: very black, shining, surrounded by an immense orange circle, they appear widened as if in terror before some vision of the beyond, like those of the Delphic Sybil (Michelangelo's ceiling of the Sistine Chapel). [. . .] A magnificent long-eared owl suffering horribly, almost crucified, nailed by its wing to a post.

After his return to Paris at the end of the summer break (6 September), Messiaen made his second trip to Ouessant. For ten days he filled the pages of his notebooks with seabirds, the sketches identifiable as the music of 'Le Courlis cendré' ('The Curlew'), the haunting final piece of the *Catalogue*. The most exciting page of this expedition comes, however, at the very end, when – to judge from the spidery handwriting – Messiaen was in the boat or the train on his way home. At the top of the page is the final laconic gesture of 'Le Courlis cendré', the splash of surf. Messiaen now started to think about another piece in progress, 'Le Loriot' ('The Golden Oriole'). First he jotted down the two chords that would open the piece, framing the oriole's first solo. Below this, to the left, he wrote a fragment of the oriole's song, exactly as notated on 20 June the previous summer, but this time with a descant of shadowing harmonies. He now devised harmonies for 'L'Alouette lulu' ('The Woodlark') and sketched a few chords to represent 'night'. The first jotting was primitive, but the second attempt formed a sequence virtually identical to the penultimate page of the printed score, complete with chromatically descending octaves in the bass and a cadence on a chord of B flat major. In tiny handwriting Messiaen chased this line of thought, and sketched a blueprint for the whole piece: the chorale of the opening, the more agitated middle section (with a note to add a nightingale between the chord progressions) and the lingering cadences on B flat major that bring the piece to a close. This whole page marked a further advance in the re-establishing of harmony in Messiaen's language, with the uses we see here: background colour, the harmonization of birdsong, and (as in 'L'Alouette lulu') the shaping of the musical form.

By early 1957 Messiaen had composed six pieces of the *Catalogue*, and had given photocopies to Loriod. On 30 March, at a Domaine Musical concert, she gave a performance of these as 'Extracts from the *Catalogue d'oiseaux*'.[19] After some indecision (evident from the diary) the following order was chosen: 'Le Chocard des Alpes', 'L'Alouette lulu', 'La Chouette hulotte', 'Le Loriot', 'L'Alouette

115 A page from Messiaen's fair copy of 'L'Alouette lulu', with later revisions.

calandrelle' and 'Le Courlis cendré'. This formed a sort of skeleton of the *Catalogue* as it eventually became (there are thirteen pieces in all), with the opening and closing pieces in place, and 'L'Alouette lulu' and 'La Chouette hulotte' adjacent but the wrong way round. A further piece – 'La Rousserolle effarvatte' – had been composed, but had been given to Loriod too late for her to learn; in fact, 'La Rousserolle effarvatte' would be revised and considerably enlarged later in the year.[20] Messiaen's original timing for the piece (noted in his diary with customary care) was 17 minutes; the revised version lasts over half an hour. The six pieces were warmly received in a review by Suzanne Demarquez:

> Messiaen, no doubt freed long ago from principles and theories, seems to me to have followed the advice of Debussy, who found it more worthwhile to admire a sunset than to go to a concert. He has travelled by day and night from the Alps of the Dauphiné to the island of Ouessant, by way of the Crau. He has listened to numerous birds of which we know nothing [...] and he has translated [their] songs for us thanks to his knowledge of the piano, from which he draws hitherto unimagined sonorities, thanks also to Yvonne Loriod, that fairy with the magic fingers.[21]

This early state of the *Catalogue d'oiseaux* reflected Messiaen's ornithological knowledge to date. Only one piece came from southern France – 'L'Alouette calandrelle', which had been collected near Les Baux – and none from the Mediterranean. It is interesting to note that the music written so far was all comparatively straightforward in design. Of the six pieces played by Loriod on 30 March, 'Le Chocard des Alpes' and 'La Chouette hulotte' had a static strophic architecture; 'L'Alouette lulu', 'L'Alouette calandrelle' and 'Le Courlis cendré' were each ternary, with an excitable middle section. Only 'Le Loriot' had an evolving structure, which followed the progress of the sun from dawn to midday. It is impossible to determine the original form of 'La Rousserolle effarvatte', the seventh piece to be composed, since it was to be revised so extensively before its first performance.

Messiaen seems to have conceived the *Catalogue* as a huge (perhaps open-ended) work, quite different from the organized symmetry of its final form: the diary contained further lists of bird pieces to write, including fifteen that were never composed. In later life Messiaen said that he had enough material for a second *Catalogue* but had never found the time to write it. During the early months of 1957 Messiaen's health was poor, and he had X-rays of the stomach and gall-bladder (where stones were found); a rigorous diet was ordered, with no wine, eggs or oil, and only boiled vegetables and peeled fruit. Too ill to teach, he remained at home, using the time to begin composing 'La Bouscarle', a piece whose fluid construction made it a watershed in the *Catalogue*'s evolution.

In April the simmering dispute with Durand came to a head. Messiaen believed that his publishers were not exerting themselves to promote *Réveil des oiseaux,* and he began to doubt their support for his music. Frequent entries in the diaries show him undecided whether to offer *Oiseaux exotiques* to Durand or elsewhere; at a meeting with Durand's directors, the Raveau brothers, he was accused of sharp practice by concealing the work's existence.

For the sake of his health Loriod persuaded Messiaen to take a holiday at Orgeval. So successful was this that they decided to extend the break and travel south to the country round Gardépée. On the way they visited Chartres, where Messiaen noted the cries of jackdaws perching on gargoyles with 'enormous lions' heads and eyes bulging like frogs'. Inside the cathedral, at 7.30 on an April evening, the north rose window glowed with light: 'the other windows are darkening – the tree of Jesse still appears *blue*! – each piece of stained glass is a precious stone that glimmers in the darkness'. At Gardépée Messiaen's composing was helped by the discovery of a number of 'bouscarles' (Cetti's warblers), whose abrupt and authoritative calls he used in the music as refrains. It may well have been on this trip that he decided on the geographical setting of 'La Bouscarle', on the banks of the Charente, which flows near the Delamain estate.

After the return to Paris, the diary confirmed a rift with Durand. Messiaen turned instead to Alfred Schlee, a director of Universal Edition, and a long-time admirer of Messiaen, who had published *Cantéyodjayâ*; Schlee came at once from Vienna to Paris and met Messiaen at the Hôtel Montalembert (3 May). Messiaen noted the agenda: 'Score of *Exotiques* – discuss the material, the cost of photocopying – the Véga disc – take him home – bring programmes – discuss the English and German translations.' Messiaen proposed that instead of preparing the score in Vienna, the engraving should be done by Buchardt (whose workshop was at 21 villa Chaptal in Levallois, a suburb in the north-west of Paris); he had worked on *Turangalîla* and engraved most of Messiaen's subsequent music until the mid-1960s. Buchardt had trained an assistant, Germaine Robert, and after Buchardt's death she engraved several of Messiaen's most complex scores, including *La Transfiguration* and *Des Canyons aux étoiles. . .*

In late June 1957 Messiaen travelled south to the Hérault, the region around Perpignan, which he explored in the company of an erudite ornithologist who became a friend, Henri Lhomond. Messiaen never forgot his first sight of the rocky coastline near Banyuls on a brilliant sunny day. The *cahier* recorded the scene: the arid countryside with its cypresses, agaves and tamarisks, and below the jagged cliffs the herring gulls, their white wings flashing in the sun. Between 22 and 27 June the *cahier* teemed with notations that would find their way into the three pieces from the *Catalogue* with this Mediterranean setting: 'Le Merle bleu', 'Le Traquet stapazin' and 'Le Traquet rieur'. Messiaen's excitement is palpable in the rapid handwriting and in the ecstatic impressions of the changing light:

The sea is silvery, mirroring from below the blue, grey and mauve of the sky, and the white clouds. In the distance the glory of the sunlight mingles with mist, partially lighting up the sea, and making some of the cliffs turn gold or pink.

[9 a.m.] The sea is blue, sapphire, ultramarine, the light magnificent – a Thekla lark is singing above a plateau with cypress, vines, etc.: its flight is like a butterfly, trembling with joy, or like a skylark.

The sky is ablaze, red-purple above the mountains – little by little darkness spreads over the sea; the first star appears.

After several days of birdsong notations came four pages of sketches for 'Le Traquet stapazin', on the last of which is the chorale which represents the sunset at the end of the piece. Judging by the handwriting, these sketches are spontaneous notes, made in the field, yet they are already marvellously close to the finished score; in his haste Messiaen employed a shorthand of figures and letters to indicate how the details would fit together.

Moving inland (28 June), Messiaen came to the Cirque de Mourèze, the setting for 'Le Merle de roche'. The chaos of rock formations caused Messiaen's imagination to run riot:

A man, head lowered, hands tied behind his back, crouched on a staircase, in a horrible attitude [...] a diplodocus, long neck, erect lizard's head, the remainder of the enormous body drags behind the wall! Chimera! Sphynx! Armies of hooded ghosts who advance slowly! A gigantic medieval warrior – an enormous monkey [...] a convoy of phantoms bearing a dead woman, her hair hanging down [...] Assyrians, a giant galloping horse!

While in the Hérault, news reached Messiaen that his father had died suddenly at Orange on 26 June. Messiaen at once took the train to Orange, then to Paris for the reading of the will and signing of papers. In the aftermath of Pierre's death, Messiaen hoped that it would be possible to find the missing manuscript of his mother's *Livre d'amour*, but in the event nothing was discovered. Messiaen had once asked his father about its whereabouts and had received such an angry response that he suspected his father had destroyed Cécile's work.[22] After Cécile's death Pierre had married Marguérite Élie, who came from Orange. They had a son, a half-brother to Messiaen, some twenty-five years his junior; a second son died in infancy in 1934, and is buried in the cemetery at Lévigny. The Paris address of Pierre and Marguérite, at 44 quai Henri IV, was also home to Alain, who occupied rooms at the top of the house.

The summer of 1957 at Petichet saw two improvements. A Gaveau grand piano had been purchased (from a silk manufacturer in Lyon) together with a

116 Pierre Messiaen in 1955.

new water pump with which to fill the bat-infested tank in the attic. Messiaen had his own crowded agenda: 'Finish the piano pieces [. . .] finish the *Traité du rythme*. [. . .] Talk about retrograde and contrary motion in nature.' The grandest undertaking here was Messiaen's vast *Traité*, a project which he planned in detail but left unfinished at his death four decades later; the composition for the summer was probably the reworking of 'La Rousserolle effarvatte', which more than doubled in length. Messiaen was thrilled with the new piano, which he used not only for composition but to play for enjoyment (Ravel's *Gaspard de la nuit*, for example); Loriod's piano practice was still limited to the brief periods when Messiaen went for his daily swim.

In November Messiaen arranged for Claire to be moved to a new home, run by Catholic nuns, at Bourg-la-Reine; earlier in the year he had been horrified to discover that she was malnourished. The transfer was effected by Messiaen with the aid of Loriod and her car, as he noted in the diary: 'two suitcases, undersheet, black skirt, toilet things, sheets purchased by Yvonne. Pay La Varenne, and the advance for November to Bourg-la-Reine. An exquisite welcome from the Sisters there.'

Early in 1958 Messiaen continued to be dogged by ill-health and he was increasingly reliant on Loriod's support: 'Yvonne to my house to do the housework', he noted on 6 January. He was too unwell to travel to Rome for *Réveil des oiseaux* (conducted by Rudolf Albert), but managed to continue both his teaching and his visits to Claire. On 23 January Loriod came to his class to play the revised version of 'La Rousserolle effarvatte'. At the première two days later, at a Domaine Musical concert, the work was warmly received, notably by Boulez, and by Walter Goehr, whose passionate performances of *Turangalîla* Messiaen greatly admired. In early February Messiaen was in

117 Igor and Vera Stravinsky with Robert Craft, listening to the *Trois petites Liturgies*, Scuola di San Rocco, Venice, 20 September 1957.

118 Messiaen with Cardinal Roncalli (the future Pope John XXIII), Venice, 1957.

Berlin for a triumphant *Turangalîla* under Hans Rosbaud, though a few days earlier, when Messiaen had performed the *Livre d'orgue*, the audience had been hostile.

At the end of March 1958 came the spring break, and Messiaen and Loriod embarked on an ambitious birdsong-collecting tour, travelling south through central France, via Issoire, Saint Flour, the Gorges du Tarn, Millau and Béziers to Banyuls. So fruitful was their stay that in late May Messiaen returned alone to Banyuls, enchanted anew by the scenery of Cap Béar and Cap Rederis. As soon as the summer term had finished, Messiaen set off south with Loriod, this time to research the birds of the Causse, even disregarding the recording sessions for the *Cinq Rechants* that were taking place in Paris. On 26 June Messiaen and Loriod arrived at Mont Aigoual, the highest peak in the Cévennes:

Towards Point Sublime – terrible storm: after the storm flashes of lightning splinter the sky in zigzags – distant thunder – an immense vista of mountains wooded with pines! Fields! A chasm! We are above some jagged cliffs! 6.25 p.m. Storm of wind! . . . a black storm comes out of the sky: the clouds rise from the valley towards the tops of the mountains like the smoke of a fire! 7.30 p.m. Point Sublime: immense view! Chasm, abyss! Near me a plateau, fields, pine woods, box trees! At the bottom of the chasm, the wayward meandering of the Tarn, the green waters. Curves, angles, lines, fantastically opposed geometries of all the summits – at the bottom, on the right, the Roche Aiguille! Below, the Cirque des Baumes! [. . .] Nearby a sort of castle of red rock, with keep, loopholes, battlements! In front of us, on the other side of the gorge, an enormous rock: red ochre, orange, with torrents of black ink falling from the top of the rock! The clouds race, driven by the wind!

[27 June] Arrived on Mont Aigoual around 7.15 p.m. Howling wind that makes notes and chords. On our descent, a forest of firs with the robin noted above – after the wind, delightful rain! A forest of pines! [. . .] From time to time the clouds and banks of fog disperse and give a glimpse of an immense panorama, with thirty or forty mountains on three levels, some black, others green, the furthest away in full sunlight. The fragments of panorama suddenly lit up resemble a picture by Max Ernst – the effect is very surreal!

By now Loriod accompanied birdsong expeditions with a tape recorder. On one occasion she heard a 'whistling' cry which she recognized as a curlew. Messiaen was at first sceptical but when he heard the tape conceded that she was right. She attributed her new-found ornithological expertise to his music:

'If you hadn't notated it so clearly in the piano piece I've just learned, I wouldn't have recognized it!'

Pascal had announced his intention to marry his fiancée, Josette Bender, and Messiaen gave written permission. The wedding took place on 2 August 1958; Messiaen, though invited, was not present. It seems clear that a rift had opened between father and son, though the reasons can only be guessed at. Given the difficult circumstances of Claire's long illness, it is probable that Messiaen felt he had worked round the clock in order to provide for his son as best he could, while Pascal felt as if he had been brought up without the emotional support – or even the company – that he craved. But whatever the explanation, and Messiaen's own misgivings, he bought the couple an apartment, at 62 boulevard de Belleville, Paris 20^e, and they became regular visitors to Petichet during summer vacations.

At Petichet Loriod was having some success in bringing a modicum of comfort and convenience. She bought a cooker, and persuaded Messiaen to sanction repairs to the roof, a proper track to lead to the garage, and best of all, mains water.

Messiaen went to Brussels on 13 September, where he lectured at the Philips Pavilion, designed for the World Fair by Le Corbusier and Xenakis, and attended *Réveil* conducted by Bruno Maderna. His lecture, published as the *Conférence de Bruxelles*, was an important statement of his views on rhythm, on time, on the inspiration of nature, and on the future of music (he singled out his former pupils Boulez and Stockhausen as 'two musicians of genius').[23] The last act of the summer was to show Loriod the new pieces for the *Catalogue d'oiseaux*, 'Le Merle de roche' and 'Le Traquet rieur'.

Much of the early part of 1959 was taken up with preparations for the first complete performance of the *Catalogue d'oiseaux*, billed as a concert to celebrate Messiaen's fiftieth birthday which had fallen on 10 December 1958. Loriod had six new pieces to prepare, as well as the seven she had already performed. Among the last to be finished was 'La Buse variable', a homecoming, as the buzzard's orbiting flight surveys the meadows of Petichet. The première took place on 15 April at the Salle Gaveau. Loriod accomplished her epic feat (the work lasts close on three hours) with just a single interval (after 'La Rousserolle effarvatte'). Messiaen had introduced the *Catalogue d'oiseaux* in an article entitled 'La Nature, les chants d'oiseaux', published in the *Guide du concert*:

Nature, birdsong! These are my passions. They are also my refuge.
    In melancholy moments, when my uselessness is brutally revealed to me, when every musical language, whether classical, exotic, ancient, modern or ultra-modern, seems to me reduced to being merely the praiseworthy result of patient research, without anything behind the notes to justify so much

labour, what else is there to do except search for the true face of Nature, forgotten somewhere in the forest, in the fields, in the mountains, on the seashore, among the birds?

For me, it is here that music lives: music that is free, anonymous, improvised for pleasure, to greet the rising sun, to charm one's mate, to tell all the world that this branch and this meadow belong to you, to put an end to all disputes, bickering and rivalry, to work off the excessive energy born of love and *joie de vivre*, to articulate time and space and join with your neighbours in constructing rich and improvised counterpoint, to solace your fatigue and to say farewell to another portion of life as the evening falls.

Rilke wrote these magical words: 'Music: the breath of statues, the silences of paintings, the language where all languages end . . .'! Birdsong exists on a plane beyond that poet's dream. It exists most certainly beyond the composer who is trying to note it down. No matter! Ornithology is a science; and like every science it entails labour and difficulties.

It is some 30 years now since I began noting down birdsong. My first transcriptions are scattered through my earliest works. Unfortunately I had no experience at the time and did not always know to which bird I should attribute this or that song. Subsequently I asked the advice of specialists in the field and learnt a great deal in the course of guided walks. [. . .]

Once I had done that, I was able (no transformation or pun intended) to fly with my own wings. And so each spring, armed with pencils, rubbers, manuscript paper, drawing paper and an enormous pair of binoculars, I visit a different province of France in search of my teachers.

This is how I wrote the *Catalogue d'oiseaux* for solo piano, which Yvonne Loriod will play for the first time on 15 April in Paris. It is an open-ended work. If death does not put an end to my activity, this first catalogue will be followed by a second and perhaps by a third. [. . .]

Everything is accurate: the soloist's melodies and rhythms, those of its neighbours, the counterpoint between the two, the responses, ensembles and moments of silence, and the correspondence between the song and the time of day.

Transcribing the timbres was especially difficult, particularly on the piano: we all know that timbre comes from the greater or lesser number of harmonics, so I had to resort to unusual combinations of notes. On the other hand, because of its wide range and the immediacy of its attack, the piano was the only instrument capable of speaking at the great speed and in the very high registers called for by some of the more virtuosic birds, such as the woodlark, the skylark, the garden warbler, the blackcap, the nightingale, the song thrush, the sedge warbler and the reed warbler. The piano was also the only instrument that could imitate the raucous, grinding, percussive calls of the raven and the great reed warbler, the rattling of the corncrake, the screeches of the water rail, the barking of the herring gull, the dry, imperious sound, like tapping on a stone, of the black-eared wheatear, and the sunny charm of the rock thrush or the black wheatear.

All these remained engraved on my memory with such poetic force that I was unable to turn them into music without emotion. But let there be no mistake! The birds alone are great artists. It is they who are the real composers of these pieces! If at times the musical quality drops, it is because the composer out in the countryside has broken cover clumsily, or made a disturbing noise by crunching his feet on the gravel, turning a page, or snapping off a dry branch.[24]

Once again the critical applause was led by Suzanne Demarquez, whose review appeared in the *Guide du concert* on 1 May:

Messiaen, armed not with a hostile gun but with manuscript paper and pencils, spends nights among the pools of Sologne, watches dawns and sunsets on the rocks of the Côte Vermeille, and contemplates the mighty battle of the elements around the Isle of Ushant. He does this not only so that he can meticulously note down a solo from the reed warbler, the 'abrupt, brief' call of the black-eared wheatear ('a Spanish grand seigneur going off to a masked ball'), or the 'slow, melancholy tremolos' of the curlew, but also to describe their habitat, paint its colours, capture its atmosphere at each hour of the day and night, and give it life through the activities of its winged denizens. And he does all this with the aid simply of a piano! I should add that he has found in his incomparable interpreter Yvonne Loriod, to whom the work is dedicated, an irreplaceable collaborator. Dressed like the brilliant golden oriole, her near homonym, 'gold with black wings', Yvonne, with her amazingly accurate fingers, chatters, chirps, strokes and teases the piano from its twittering heights down to its booming depths 'of terror', and gives us a film of unknown landscapes from which all human presence is firmly excluded. Needless to say, composer and interpreter joined in taking the applause.

After triumph came tragedy. Messiaen visited his wife on 19 April and found her unchanged, but three days later Claire was dead. A brief diary entry recorded her passing: 'Mi died 22 April at 10 in the morning.' 24 April: 'placed in her coffin at 14.45. Give the news to Pascal, Alliet [Messiaen's dentist and a close friend], Marguérite and Alain.' There is no record of who attended the funeral, which took place on 25 April at 9 a.m. at the church of Bourg-la-Reine, followed by interment in the cemetery.

Outwardly life went on as normal. On the day of the funeral Messiaen kept an afternoon appointment with the singer Colette Herzog and her pianist Jacqueline Bonneau, who were rehearsing the *Chants de terre et de ciel*. Goléa, who was present, and knew about Claire's death, recorded the occasion:

> The rehearsal was to have taken place at 4 p.m. but the day before Colette Herzog [. . .] received a phone call from Messiaen who begged her, with exquisite courtesy and repeated apologies, to postpone the rehearsal by one hour. As it happened, the following day Messiaen arrived at 5.10 p.m., and apologized again. [. . .] Messiaen was late for the rehearsal because of his wife's funeral. He had come straight from the cemetery. He didn't talk about it, of course. His face was extremely pale, but also seemed to show a sort of deep peace. He seemed calm, serene, relaxed; he gave the impression of arriving from another world. Having made his apologies, he at once began the rehearsal, and worked for two hours with Colette Herzog and her pianist in the most rigorous and concentrated way.[25]

That evening Messiaen went to the Gare de l'Est to meet Loriod, who was returning from Karlsruhe unaware of Claire's death. She remembered him pale but with a firm voice: 'Something terrible has happened: Claire has died, on Wednesday; I've just come from the burial. [. . .] You must not leave me, you who are young and so full of life.'[26]

Messiaen's declaration confirmed what had been unsaid for years. Initially, Loriod's regard for him had been that of an adoring pupil: admiration for his music, for the way he kept faith in himself in the face of setbacks, and, on a human level, for his solicitude towards Claire. Messiaen's increasing dependence on her throughout the 1950s had been almost comically mundane, with Loriod as unpaid proof-reader, driver and even cleaner. These were ways to repay what she saw as her debt to Messiaen, who had done so much to foster her career. They were in love – an 'impossible love' as Loriod put it – but they were not lovers; they needed frequently to escape from one another, to resist the temptation to defy the moral precepts of their shared faith.[27]

As for Messiaen's feelings, one need only look at his music. For nearly twenty years, since their first meeting, every major work (bar those for organ) had been for solo piano or had given the piano a virtuoso role. In the early days, Messiaen sometimes used to misspell Loriod's name, referring to her in the diaries as 'Mlle Loriot' ('Loriot' is the French for 'Golden Oriole'). In the *Catalogue d'oiseaux* Messiaen seized the opportunity to turn his mistake into an act of homage. 'Le Loriot' – the pun must have delighted Messiaen – has the most gorgeous timbre and plumage of any bird in the *Catalogue*, and in the music that accompanies the sunrise, a scintillating duet for garden warblers, the piece reaches a surpassing peak of virtuosity. As the birds fall silent in the luminous E major of midday, the music goes into a sort of trance, meditating on the oriole's harmonies; meanwhile, slowly ascending in the left hand are the chords from the *Cinq Rechants* that accompany the words 'Tous les philtres sont bus ce soir' ('All the love potions have been drunk this evening'). The meaning could hardly be clearer.

Public controversy, private happiness
1959–1963

One consequence of Claire's death demanded Messiaen's immediate attention and was to cause the next four years of his life to be poisoned by anxiety, time-wasting paperwork and expensive consultations with lawyers. Claire's financial affairs had effectively been frozen for six years, and these now had to be unravelled. Claire and Messiaen were married under a contract of 'réduit aux acquis'. Under the terms of the contract Messiaen had no share of his wife's property; moreover, everything acquired since their marriage in 1932 had to be shared with her family. In 1954, shortly after Claire had gone into a nursing home, Messiaen visited the Delbos family lawyer to acquire power of attorney over Claire's finances. A meeting with the same lawyer a week after Claire's death brought the unwelcome news that all accounts, including Messiaen's own, would have to be frozen while the estate was being sorted out.

Messiaen's summer break in 1959 was a long one, from early July to mid-September. The transition from city to rural life was especially sweet. At 4 a.m. on 7 July Messiaen noted a long solo by a nightingale in his *cahier*. His health improved, owing (Loriod believed) to copious quantities of milk, fresh from a nearby farm. For once Messiaen allowed himself some time off. Always keen to explore, he and Loriod made expeditions deeper into the mountains than before, and on 12 July they drove via mountain roads as far as La Clusaz, near Annecy. Two days later, they took the cable car to the Aiguille du Midi opposite Mont Blanc, a trip vividly evoked in Messiaen's *cahier*:

119 An Alpine picnic with Loriod's Renault.

> Deep swathes of immaculately white snow. Below is an immense snowfield. Mont Blanc is lost in cloud. Great rocks, weirdly eroded into a thousand geometrical forms. In sunlight the snow is intensely white and luminous, alongside snow with a bluer tinge. Tumbling rocks set up ricochets with prolonged echoes in the chasms. Two choughs, with red feet and little grey and red horizontally-striped wings, hover and twist uneasily.

Their movements, and the sudden noises of the falling rocks, contrast with the awesome silence and stillness.

Another trip was to the Col d'Iseran (the source of the River Isère) where they found ptarmigan and snowfinches among the snowdrifts; the descent was awkward, bumping down into Val d'Isère on two flat tyres.

There was work to be done, however – notably the commission from Heinrich Strobel for an orchestral work (which would become *Chronochromie*), due for delivery on 1 June the following summer; Messiaen recorded the deadline in his diary, stressing the urgency with an exclamation mark. Entries in the diary show Messiaen feeling his way towards the work's central idea, although the title had yet to be invented. His notes refer to a 'series': this was to become the permutating scale of durations, the rhythmic material of the piece which meshes with birdsong and with inanimate sounds of nature – most memorably the wind and the rushing of Alpine torrents. The *cahiers* for 1959 have examples of Messiaen's fascination for wild water. In March, in the Jura, he made notes on a waterfall known as the Cascade de l'Éventail:

120 Sketch made on 3 August 1959 for the sounds of a waterfall in the Gorges de la Bourne used in *Chronochromie*.

A series of eight overhangs, some close together, others well apart, over which the fall of the water creates a deafening din. A monumental castle of water! On the right, the stream is so powerful that it forces itself into a single giant swathe. A cloud of droplets extends a further 500 metres in a cascade of white water. The torrent bounces off the mossy rocks, twisting and boiling – green, gold and white. The turbulence is like a thousand tiny beings in peril, like white flames, horses' manes, Pharaoh's army drowned in the Red Sea. A huge curtain of water: solemn, sumptuous, majestic, a dizzying staircase. The tremendous noise of the water is an enormous turbine of uninterrupted sound, with thousands of upper and lower harmonics. It's like a chord of a thousand notes circling in every register, particularly the bass. Then there are the resonances from the rocks, which set up other rhythms and sounds, with higher counterpoints from the little waves and droplets.

On 3 August Messiaen made a musical sketch in his *cahier* of water racing through the Gorges de la Bourne. The notes are almost identical to passages in the opening and closing sections of *Chronochromie*, marked 'le torrent'. A footnote in the score explains the instrumentation: 'The sound of the water turning is given mainly to the violas and cellos. [. . .] The bassoons, bass clarinet, tuba and pizzicati on the double bass should be heard only intermittently. The trills are merely vapour and confusion.'[1]

Chronochromie's pattern of Strophe, Antistrophe and Épôde had been used before, in 'Le Chocard des Alpes' (*Catalogue d'oiseaux*), a piece with a similar ruthless virtuosity. By the summer of 1959 Strophe I had already been composed. According to notes in Messiaen's diary, both the Antistrophes and the Épôde would be 'like the Strophe', and would be framed symmetrically by a Prologue and Epilogue. Eventually the Épôde was to become quite distinct, the boldest and most complex of Messiaen's birdsong polyphonies to date, with the birds flying free from the trellis of 'interversions' (permutations) in a mêlée of solo strings. The Strophe and Antistrophe acquired variants, giving a final form of seven sections: 'Introduction', 'Strophe I', 'Antistrophe I', 'Strophe II', 'Antistrophe II', 'Épôde' and 'Coda'. In his original idea for the Introduction, Messiaen was already thinking of Japan, a gagaku decorated by Japanese birdsong. The gagaku idea was postponed – to be revived in the mesmeric fourth movement of the *Sept Haïkaï* – but the Japanese birds remain.

Messiaen's first title for *Chronochromie* was 'Postlude'. The possible significance of this odd title is that he may have planned the work as a coda to the *Catalogue d'oiseaux*, a conclusion to the great cycle of bird compositions he had outlined during October 1953 in the Black Forest. It would be fascinating to know more about how *Chronochromie* evolved. Certainly it has close affinities with the *Catalogue*, which would be closer still if Messiaen had adhered to his original idea of finishing with a solo for the nightingale – it may well be that Messiaen imagined a nocturnal farewell to his epic project, with the music fading into the night, rather like the end of 'L'Alouette lulu'. Another piece from the *Catalogue* with which *Chronochromie* has much in common is 'Le Traquet stapazin', a favourite of Messiaen's, to which he drew particular attention in his article 'La Nature, les chants d'oiseaux'.[2] Two passages in 'Le Traquet stapazin' seem especially influential: the springy trampolining of the Orphean warbler is very close in style to the chorusing birdsongs of *Chronochromie*, while the chorale in the closing pages – something that would become a feature of Messiaen's music in the 1960s – is taken up as a framing device of monumental power in *Chronochromie*'s Introduction and Coda. What makes *Chronochromie* stand apart from the *Catalogue* is the complex of rhythms, a structural backbone of a kind completely absent in the *Catalogue*; there, numerical schemes are only ever used as local colour. The renewal of Messiaen's interest in rigorous organization links *Chronochromie* back to the works before *Réveil des oiseaux*, and particularly to the *Livre d'orgue*. The astonishing 'Épôde' was a completely original departure, which trumped the more orderly polyphonies of *Réveil des oiseaux* and *Oiseaux exotiques*.

The autumn of 1959 opened with an unusual concert in Berlin. Herbert von Karajan, who normally gave contemporary music a wide berth, had taken upon himself to conduct *Réveil des oiseaux*, cushioned safely by a Bach Suite and Beethoven's Seventh Symphony. Finding the score hard to understand, and unable to trace a recording, Karajan asked Loriod to play the work through at the piano, saying that he would pick up the music by ear and conduct without the score. The performance (on 23 September) had a disastrous reception, and Messiaen hardly dared go backstage to offer his congratulations. He found the conductor, however, in great spirits, embracing the startled composer with the words: 'Thank you – at last, thanks to you, my first scandal!'[3] Another concert was to have far-reaching consequences. Messiaen travelled to Perugia for a performance of the *Trois petites Liturgies* (29 September) conducted by Marcel Couraud. This part of Italy was new to Messiaen, and Couraud acted as his guide, taking him and Loriod on a tour of Assisi.

In October 1959 Messiaen prepared a new edition of *Le Banquet céleste*. The main purpose of the revisions

BERLINER
PHILHARMONISCHES ORCHESTER
KONZERTSAAL DER HOCHSCHULE FÜR MUSIK

MITTWOCH,   DEN 23. SEPTEMBER 1959, 20.00 UHR
DONNERSTAG, DEN 24. SEPTEMBER 1959, 20.00 UHR
FREITAG,   DEN 25. SEPTEMBER 1959, 19.30 UHR

I. PHILHARMONISCHES KONZERT

DIRIGENT
HERBERT VON KARAJAN

SOLISTIN
YVONNE LORIOD

JOHANN SEBASTIAN BACH   SUITE NR. II IN H-MOLL
                        FÜR ORCHESTER
                        OUVERTÜRE
                        RONDEAU
                        SARABANDE
                        BOURRÉE I II
                        POLONAISE
                        MENUET
                        BADINERIE
         SOLOFLÖTE   MATHIAS RÜTTERS

OLIVIER MESSIAEN   RÉVEIL DES OISEAUX FÜR PIANO
                        UND ORCHESTER (ERSTAUFF.)

LUDWIG VAN BEETHOVEN   SYMPHONIE NR. VII A-DUR OP. 92
                        POCO SOSTENUTO – VIVACI
                        ALLEGRETTO
                        PRESTO
                        FINALE (ALLEGRO CON BRIO)

KONZERTFLÜGEL: STEINWAY & SONS

121 Programme for the concerts in Berlin, 23–25 September 1959, in which Herbert von Karajan conducted Messiaen's *Réveil des oiseaux*.

was to emphasize the extreme slowness of the tempo. As well as many additional registrations, the note values were doubled (from semiquaver to quaver) with a new tempo marking (to replace the former 'Extrêmement lent'): 'Très lent, extatique (*lointain, mystérieux*)'.

Another editorial task was revising the *Catalogue d'oiseaux* for publication. Originally Loriod agreed to review all the metronome marks and fingerings, only to find that any changes she made were meticulously re-checked by Messiaen, and not infrequently changed back to the original. Messiaen's additions, made in pencil on the ink fair copy, are a fascinating glimpse of the composer clarifying and refining his conception.

The 1959 manuscript of the *Catalogue d'oiseaux* contained dynamics, but only general indications of tempo ('Vif', 'Un peu vif', and so on), and no pedal marks. It is interesting that Messiaen had fully worked out the fingerings, however; on the amended manuscript a few of these are altered, rare instances where he must have accepted Loriod's recommendations. Some of Messiaen's revisions were straightforward. On the first page of 'Le Chocard des Alpes', he simply added pedal and metronome indications, and a description of the music's character, 'Implacable et massif'. In 'Le Merle bleu', however, he inserted a detail that clears up a possible misunderstanding. The 'swifts' (in bar 3) are left at *mf* – their cries must be glimpsed, as it were, through the crash of bass resonances – but the added 'strident' ensures that their character is anything but reticent. The opening page of 'Le Loriot' shows the importance of these later changes, made in the light of hearing the music in performance. Not only is the use of pedal and *una corda* new, but Messiaen adjusted the tempi of the opening two ideas (the background chords and the oriole's solo) so that they are more sharply contrasted. Another new thought was to terrace the right-hand and left-hand chords in the first bar (and elsewhere) with different dynamics: here it is the upper chord that is quieter. A significant touch was the addition of accents to emphasize the E major triad within the oriole's song. At the start of 'L'Alouette lulu' Messiaen took great pains to define a beautiful but elusive effect: again the background chords are given layered dynamics, but the problem was that the birdsong must somehow be lively, yet quiet or distant. To this end Messiaen reduced the dynamics (from *mf* to *p*), gave a description of the woodlark's character ('poetic, liquid, unreal'), and, to make doubly sure his intentions could not be misunderstood, added a footnote: 'The virtuosity of the woodlark must remain unreal: like a voice which falls from the stars . . .' Messiaen's revision of the tempo is intriguing. As with 'Le Loriot', the background chords become slower and the birdsong faster, but this time so that their tempi are actually related (semiquaver = 63, quaver = 126). This linking of the music's foreground and background is unusual; normally in the *Catalogue* Messiaen kept musical elements sharply distinct from one another – indeed there is only one similar instance, in the opening music of 'L'Alouette calandrelle'. It is striking that what seems fundamental to the musical idea – a calm, hypnotic unity of tempo – should have been arrived at only at this late stage.

Messiaen's first ornithological *magnum opus* was now behind him, but there was to be no slackening in his birdsong researches. Exactly when Messiaen acquired a gramophone for the villa du Danube is unknown, but he certainly had one by 1959, when his teaching schedule mentioned 'audition de disques chez moi'. In February 1960 he acquired a new system, installed by the ornithologist Jean-Claude Roché, with 'un pick-up de grand qualité [. . .] pour entendre des disques d'oiseaux'. In April Messiaen continued his researches, returning to Brittany, for the first time since 1956, to visit the bird sanctuary of the Île de Rouzie. He was ferried in a small boat to the island where he was left for the day, finding a paradise of bird life, as he recorded in his diary: 'crowds of gannets, gulls of all kinds (especially herring gulls), puffins, shag, razorbill, rock pipit, oystercatcher'. What ensued became one of Messiaen's favourite anecdotes. The birds seemed unafraid of their visitor, and notebook in hand Messiaen recorded not only their songs but also details of their flight, behaviour, nest-building materials, and so on. At one point he slipped on the rocks and gashed his leg, so that the precious *cahier* became spattered with blood as well as with seawater. His last notations were recorded at 5.50 in the afternoon. By now the light was fading, and the incoming tide – which Messiaen had failed to notice – had covered the shoreline where he had landed. Thoroughly lost, it was the birds (so Messiaen believed) who now came to his aid, flying ahead and indicating the way through the gloom. At last he heard distant shouts and, hurrying forward, he encountered the boatman who, having raised the alarm, had come ashore to search for him. Returning to the boat, Messiaen found the sea channel illumined by the lights of patrol launches.

The composition of *Chronochromie* continued over the winter of 1959–60. The first reference to the title came in a progress report to Strobel on 11 May 1960: 'The work I'm writing for Donaueschingen will have the following title: *Chronochromie*. This is a better title than the one I gave it originally [Postlude] and I think you will like it more. It's a word invented by me, coming from the Greek: Chronos meaning time, and Chrôma meaning colour, which come together to mean Colour of Time. The music is completely finished. I just have some pages to orchestrate.'[4] In fact, the piece was not finished until 26 August. Messiaen then returned hurriedly to Paris from Petichet in order to make a fair copy of the full score, and to supervise the copyists who had been engaged to make the orchestral parts. It was clearly impossible to deliver all the music as promised by 1 September, so instead the copyists began with what Messiaen considered most difficult, the virtuoso percussion parts and the solo strings of the 'Épôde'. They must have worked with astonishing speed, because by 12

September Messiaen was able to take these to the conductor, Hans Rosbaud, at Baden-Baden. The remaining material was delivered, again by Messiaen in person, on 24 September. Thereafter he was content to leave preparations to Rosbaud, returning only for the final rehearsals, two days before the first performance on 16 October. Whereas there had been an indifferent reception in 1953 for *Réveil des oiseaux* – Messiaen's previous commission for Donaueschingen – for *Chronochromie* the audience was vociferous, both for and against.

The first performance in France took place a year later, at the Besançon Festival on 13 September 1961, given by the Orchestre National under Georges Prêtre. Again opinion, both in the audience and among the critics, was sharply divided. Bernard Gavoty ('Clarendon') in *Le Figaro* reported that, as at Donaueschingen, it was the younger members of the audience who were most hostile: 'At 53 Messiaen is again a revolutionary figure: that's something to console him.' Gavoty explained the work as operating on two levels:

> Nature is present to humanize the intellectual workings, and the sounds of the natural world colour the arbitrary divisions of time. This explains the title of the work, split into seven sequences that reproduce, in enlarged form, the traditional triad of Greek poetry. [...] Nothing is haphazard, all is the fruit of calculation and observation. As Messiaen told me, on the very morning of the concert, explaining his music with angelic patience: 'Six months of research, two years of orchestration: please let us not speak of chance or improvisation.' So, what happened in the concert? The opposite of what the composer anticipated. Like Goethe's sorcerer's apprentice, betrayed by his own spells, Messiaen has become the victim of excessive calculation. The minutely-detailed organization simply gave the impression of chance. The screen of multicoloured orchestral timbres masked the colours of the instruments, just as the seven colours of the prism blend together into white light. An excess of brilliance turned everything to grey. So many durations, subtly interleaved, ended by obliterating all sense of rhythm. All those birdsongs, lovingly transcribed and scrupulously varied, gave the impression that we were trapped in a mad aviary.

Messiaen was also interviewed by Robert Siohan for *L'Express*:

> 'What are you', I asked the composer of this strange music, 'a realist or an impressionist?'
> 'Both at once.'
> 'Obviously, it is not a question of descriptive music, seeking to imitate the

voices of nature – though in your sketchbooks you endeavour to note these with scrupulous accuracy – but of a transposition, a stylization.'

'That's certainly my purpose. After all, isn't all music, like poetry or any art, always a form of stylization?'

'And your title – *Chronochromie* – literally "colour of time".'

'That's indeed the exact translation. *Chronochomie* is above all a technical term. But it is also, from the poetic point of view, a sun-drenched protest against twelve-tone music.'[5]

Claude Rostand's article in *Le Figaro littéraire* (September 1961) explained his conversion from Messiaen detractor to admirer and apologist:

Formerly one could sometimes regret in Messiaen an excess of dubious melodies, whose origin was not always far from Massenet. One could also sometimes regret excesses of sound, with flashy, overloaded effects, not always in perfect taste, which left an impression of turn-of-the-century orientalism. All this came to an end some fifteen years ago. Olivier Messiaen then headed towards an art that is infinitely more spare, less indulgently voluptuous, and which, while still keeping his taste for refinement and for complexity, is more sober, and has a livelier edge, more clarity of line. The *Quatre Études de rythme*, the *Livre d'orgue*, the *Messe de la Pentecôte*, *Oiseaux exotiques* are in this vein, in which a drive for rigour has happily come to replace the earlier sensual swoonings.

'Bataille pour *Chronochromie*', Rostand's headline, grabbed the attention, and like his colleagues he devoted much space to addressing the music's difficulties. He even canvassed the views of the orchestra, whose response was not encouraging: 'We're very keen to master all the technical acrobatics required – which we're confident of doing well – but what the hell does it all mean?' Unlike Robert Siohan, who maintained that Messiaen was 'not in any way a Romantic' and argued that the music demanded a more 'Oriental' approach from listeners, Rostand sought to make the work intelligible by emphasizing its descriptive side:

It seems that with his two latest works, the *Catalogue d'oiseaux* and this recent *Chronochromie*, Olivier Messiaen arrives at a compromise, at a new balance. Less exclusively 'theoretical' – but just as deliberately and rigorously constructed – these two works allow the reappearance, in an almost imperceptible filigree, of the old impressionist heritage, which is part of Messiaen, as it has been in most musicians of the French tradition since the 16th century. [. . .] As in most of his works, the composer has used here on a large scale melodic and sonic material borrowed from birdsong, for which he has long been criticized. Messiaen is by adoption a man of the Dauphiné: he loves and fears its mountains, which are both so beautiful and so terrible, the Meije massif before which he so often composes, dizzy in front of its sheer cliffs and avalanches of scree, among the raucous, ferocious and shrill cries of mountain birds. I am not saying that these are the images the composer wants to evoke in a work like *Chronochromie*, which pursues much more abstract goals. But to those who ask 'What does it mean?' one can reply that *impressions* of this kind certainly exist deep within a score like this. And it is there that one finds the presence of a human being, no matter how scientifically and rigorously the work may be constructed. For, however bold or experimental the character of some of his works, Messiaen never loses this feeling of humanity.

Since 1961 was a year without major deadlines, Messiaen could afford the luxury of a three-week spring break, in which he and Loriod travelled across southern France, from the Dordogne to Provence, as well as a further week in May when he went by himself to the Hérault to stay with his old friend, the ornithologist François Hüe. It was shortly after returning to Paris after the first of these trips that Messiaen and Loriod set a date for their marriage. The decision was taken on 25 April, two years almost to the day since Claire's death. Although they must have been aware that their union would hardly come as a surprise to the outside world, they decided for the time being to keep it a secret. The façade would be maintained for a further three years, and it was only in 1964 that Messiaen moved house permanently to join Loriod in the rue Marcadet.

Why the secrecy? To Messiaen and Loriod two years was a decent interval that showed respect for Claire's memory; but they felt longer was required if all possibility of gossip was to be avoided. Paradoxically, the fact that their lives and work had been intertwined for so long made it easier to keep the marriage clandestine. Moreover, for the time being they were content to live apart. Loriod's apartment was too small for them to share, as was the villa du Danube. Messiaen was in no position to sell up, since under the terms of Claire's estate the house belonged as much to Pascal as to Messiaen. Messiaen and Loriod also wondered how two musicians could work in the same home without disturbing each other. The eventual solution was to expand at the rue Marcadet. The opportunity arose in the summer of 1961 when another studio apartment, adjacent to Loriod's, came up for sale.[6] Further purchases over the years enabled them to isolate Messiaen's composing from Loriod's practising. In 1963 the Messiaens bought a third apartment, situated on the floor above the two they already owned.[7] This became Messiaen's studio, and during the course of the year sound-proofing and shelves were installed to Messiaen's specifications. The room where he composed had magnificent wallpaper based on designs by the nineteenth-century English bird artist John Gould.

122 Messiaen's home from the early 1960s until his death, rue Marcadet, Paris, 18e (photo: Peter Hill).

The months leading up to the wedding in July were crowded. In May Messiaen returned from his week of birdwatching in the Hérault in time to coach organ students at the Conservatoire who were preparing the *Verset pour la fête de la Dédicace* to play at the *concours* for which Messiaen had composed the piece. This took place on 13 June and among the *premiers prix* was Raffi Ourgandjian, a young Lebanese organist who had been brought up by Messiaen's old classmate, Elsa Barraine. Messiaen also had the annual duty, which came round each May, of playing for the First Communion Mass, for the children of the parish of the Trinité, and for the girls attending the nearby Lycée Jules Ferry.

Wedding rings were purchased – rather indiscreetly, from a jeweller in the rue Blanche, the street where Loriod used to live with her godmother, and beside the Trinité – and the legal documents were drawn up. The marriage contract was a prudent one: 'séparation des biens'.[8] Finally, at the end of June, Messiaen had the pleasure of his first visit to Portugal, where he witnessed five thousand people at the Coliseu in Lisbon applauding *Réveil des oiseaux*. The occasion was organized by Madalena Perdigão, who would later commission *La Transfiguration*.

The civil wedding took place at the Mairie of the 18th arrondissement on 1 July 1961. The religious ceremony came two days later, not at the Trinité, but at the Église Sainte-Geneviève-des-Grandes-Carrières, in the rue Championnet, five minutes walk from the rue Marcadet. The witnesses were Gaston Loriod (Yvonne's father), and Jacques Charpentier, the gifted composer who had studied with Messiaen in the 1950s. The tiny congregation comprised Loriod's mother and her two sisters, Pascal and Josette, and Danièle, the wife of Jacques Charpentier. The occasion was kept as simple as possible. Even the tradition

123 Jacques Charpentier and Messiaen in the early 1960s.

124 Recording *Visions de l'Amen* for Véga at the Petit Théâtre Marigny, March 1962.

where the couple are greeted at the entrance to the church was dispensed with, rather to the dismay of the officiating priest, Abbé Aubin, and the service was without music (Loriod remembered Messiaen saying, 'We won't bother an organist'). However, during the Mass an uninvited guest – a blackbird – perched on the roof and sang thrillingly in what the married couple took to be a sign of benediction. The wedding breakfast was at a Chinese restaurant near the Opéra.

At Petichet a new and slightly larger garage was constructed, with enough room for Loriod to install an upright piano and to use it as a makeshift studio, shared with the Renault 4. The local planners insisted the building was of an appropriately traditional design, since the site was historic. The main road bordering the Messiaens' property was the Route Napoléon, and Laffrey was the spot where the Emperor had persuaded the forces sent to arrest him to defect to his colours.[9]

The schedule for autumn 1961 gives an idea of married life for the Messiaens. The main event of October was a performance of *Turangalîla* at the Théâtre des Champs-Élysées (10 October), followed by several days recording the work for Véga in the uninspiring surroundings of the Salle des Fêtes at Puteaux. The performers were the Orchestre National under Maurice Le Roux with Yvonne and Jeanne Loriod as pianist and *ondiste*. Immediately afterwards Loriod left for Baden-Baden to give the première of Boulez's *Structures*, livre II, with Boulez himself on the other piano. Messiaen had by now completed correcting the first proofs of *Chronochromie* (this must have occupied him during the summer break at Petichet) and he now took the score to Buchardt, the engraver. The Messiaens were together on 26 October when they dined with the Milhauds in order to discuss a visit to Colorado, where Milhaud's seventieth birthday was going to be celebrated at the 1962 Aspen Festival; he invited Messiaen and Sauguet to the Festival, 'as polar opposites of French music'.[10] At the end of October Messiaen began work on editing the recording

125 Aural tests by Messiaen.

126 Petichet. In the foreground is the garage constructed in 1961 where Loriod practised the piano (photo: Peter Hill).

of *Turangalîla*; on 23 November he recorded an interview with Claude Samuel to be included with the discs of *Turangalîla*, and two days later took part in a public debate on contemporary music with Antoine Goléa.

Meanwhile, Messiaen's classes at the Conservatoire had resumed on 2 October. During the three months to Christmas he had twenty-eight teaching days, discussing music by Rameau, Scarlatti, Beethoven (the 'Pathétique' Sonata), Falla, Albéniz and Debussy (the *Préludes*), and as usual in the autumn he prepared pupils for the written exams after Christmas, teaching harmony, history, fugue and 'general culture'. This was a characteristically eclectic mix of repertoire for his classes, which Messiaen had been teaching at the Conservatoire for two decades, during which he had nurtured some of the most creative musical minds of their generation. Loriod was in the first class in 1941, and Pierre Boulez and Pierre Henry joined in 1944; Jean Barraqué attended as an *auditeur* in 1947–52, as did Karlheinz Stockhausen in 1951–2, Iannis Xenakis in 1951–4 and György Kurtág in 1957–8. During the 1950s, others who attended as registered members of the class included Gilbert Amy and Alexander Goehr, while occasional visitors included Peter Maxwell Davies and Mikis Theodorakis. It is worth underlining the international scope of the students, not only from francophone Belgium and Canada, but also from Spain, Great Britain, Argentina, Lithuania, the USA and Japan.[11]

On 4 December Messiaen left the keys of the villa du Danube with Pascal, with instructions on how to get the boiler repaired during his absence. There followed a gruelling tour of Switzerland. At Lausanne Messiaen gave a lecture, and Loriod two performances of *Oiseaux exotiques*. At Winterthur (13 December) he lectured on 'Musique et ornithologie', illustrated by Loriod playing excerpts from the *Catalogue d'oiseaux*. The following night she performed a marathon programme, with 'La Rousserolle effarvatte' sandwiched between *Réveil des oiseaux* and *Oiseaux exotiques*. The next day (15 December), at Neuchâtel, Loriod's recital consisted of the four Fantasias by Mozart, six of Debussy's *Études*, the 'Première Communion de la Vierge' and 'Regard de l'Esprit de joie', and 'La Rousserolle effarvatte'. The Messiaens returned to Paris the same evening in time to take the train to Strasbourg for a performance of *Visions de l'Amen* the following day (16 December).

Not surprisingly, Messiaen was discovering that the price of success was less and less time for his own work. The last year had seen *Turangalîla* recorded, and *Chronochromie* had been prepared for publication; but in terms of composing he had completed only one short work (the *Verset* for organ) in the fifteen months since finishing *Chronochromie*. Nonetheless, he was constantly thinking about future works, as jottings in the diary reveal. One of these, at the start of the diary for 1962, explains why Messiaen had spent so much time in April and May 1961 in the south of France researching birdsong: 'Write a concerto for piano, xylophone and flute, on the birds of the Hérault.' Technical details then follow: 'The brass and strings will play a series of durations and timbres, in symmetrical permutations, and rhythmical characters [personnages rythmiques]. The woodwind and the three soloists play birdsong.' The planned triple concerto was in response to a commission from the Ministry of Culture for a work to celebrate the Debussy centenary in 1962. Originally the commission had specified a concerto for organ and orchestra, but Messiaen had other ideas, and by December had renegotiated the terms with Amable Massis, General Inspector for Music at the Ministry. The triple concerto would last fifteen minutes, and Messiaen's fee was to be 500,000 AF. However, the same page of the diary also recorded another project: 'Concerto for ten players, for piano, nine instruments and string orchestra. One principal soloist (the piano) with nine subsidiary soloists (flute, xylophone, bells, clarinet, oboe, bassoon, trumpet, horn, trombone) and plenty of strings.' At the end of the diary for 1961 came a brief note that would have momentous consequences: 'Write an *action sacrée* for large choir and large orchestra – like a liturgical service (see Bach's Passions and B minor Mass – see the services for Palm Sunday and for Holy Saturday, etc.). Compose my own graduals, hymns, Alleluias, etc. Write a work for choirs and orchestra on the Transfiguration.'

Living apart had become a trial. At the start of 1962 the Messiaens explored the possibility of extending the villa du Danube by building on an adjacent plot. Plans reached an advanced stage, but the sale of the land fell through. There was more gloom, with Messiaen's diary detailing his mounting legal expenses. A glimmer of hope was the promise of a final settlement of Claire's estate in October 1962.

Publicly, Messiaen's star was firmly in the ascendant, with *Chronochromie* enjoying a *succès de scandale*. The first performance in Paris took place at the Théâtre des Champs-Élysées (13 February 1962). The audience arrived scenting blood, and the commotion at the end amounted to 'un scandale inimaginable'.[12] Messiaen even had the disagreeable experience of being waylaid afterwards by a member of the audience, incoherent with rage. One senior critic, René Dumesnil, went so far as to liken the reception to the notorious première of *Le Sacre du printemps*, which by coincidence had taken place in the same auditorium nearly half a century earlier. The protests began when, in a pause between sections, a single stentorian voice called for mercy, and the unrest became so bad that the conductor, Antal Dorati, did well to steer the music to its conclusion without mishap. At the end Messiaen's appearance on stage if anything increased rather than abated the storm, but as Dusmenil observed, 'M. Messiaen is used to such demonstrations, and seemed unperturbed'.[13] Other orchestras and conductors were quick to take up the challenge. Boulez conducted *Chronochromie* at Munich, his début conducting a Messiaen piece. Before the concert Messiaen gave a lecture that included a spirited rebuttal of criticisms:

Up to now, whatever the tastes of different audiences – conservative, avant-garde or a mixture of the two – the reactions have been extremely violent. At the work's fifth performance, in Paris, the hubbub was so loud and long that it exceeded the most pessimistic predictions. I'm not going to launch myself into a 'defence and illustration'. I will try merely to present the work to you, and at the same time to explain the reason for all this commotion.

First of all there is the rhythm. Within the 'macro-time', which is represented by the seven linked sections of the work, is embedded the detail of the 'micro-time', deriving from the counterpoints of birds and the permutations of the thirty-two chromatic durations. The differences between the large durations which make up the 'macro-time', and especially the differences between each of the thirty-two chromatic durations, would doubtless be perceived by those from the East (especially by those accustomed to these subtleties): they remain hardly perceptible to Western ears. And although working with numbers appeals to those modern musicians who are avid for rigorous structures, 'musical mathematics' repels and annoys the lay public. Then again, avant-garde musicians who prefer chance (in the form of irrational values) to the rigour of permutations of durations won't find what they're looking for.

Next the birdsong. Old and young agree in saying that the songs of birds are impossible to note down, that birdsong is not art, that it is demeaning for man and his dignity to prostrate his intelligence in front of the mysteries of Nature. The rift here is between urban man and the man of the woods. The audience at concerts comes from cities – and I am offering the music of fields and vineyards, of the sea and the mountain, of the open sky and the forests.

A third misunderstanding concerns the colours. Neoclassicists expect clear tonal cadences, while old-fashioned dodecaphonists miss the greyness of the 'series'. And when I speak quite straightforwardly of resonant harmonies being 'purple flecked with orange and red and surrounded with violet', they look at me smilingly as if this were a dangerous illusion. However, these connections between sound and colour are not a purely subjective phenomenon: I myself feel them intensely – and I know, having had the experience, that others also feel them. No matter that there may be a few differences of detail between the different feelings of different individuals: 'the scents, colours, sounds harmonize' well before science may verify and codify them.

The final cause of outrage – and by no means the least – is freedom, and the opposition between rigour and freedom. My permutations of durations are rigorous, my birdsongs are entirely free. Rigour is implacable, but so too is freedom. Mingling them together shocks audiences of all persuasions. And when in the 'Épôde' a vast counterpoint of birds in eighteen real voices unfolds simultaneously, with all these freedoms tangled, the apparent disorder of inextricable sounds is the last straw for the audience, and provokes shouts and tumult.

Freedom! Doubtless we're afraid of this word. In the end it is freedom which triumphs in my music. And if I had given a title to this modest talk, perhaps I would have called it: 'a plea for freedom'.[14]

During the early 1960s Messiaen was becoming noticed by the wider world beyond music. In 1959 he was nominated an Officier of the Légion d'Honneur and over the years he was subject to regular promotion. Photographs tend to show that formality and ceremonial made Messiaen ill at ease, and the expense of the elaborate regalia could be considerable. When it fell to Messiaen to introduce Xenakis as a member of the Académie des Beaux-Arts he had to spend 6,000 francs on the requisite robes, and Messiaen was horrified to discover that these were 'new' not 'old' francs, multiplying the cost a hundred times. Nonetheless, Messiaen's formal visiting card is evidence of his serious appreciation of honours and distinctions, and there was cause for pride since his music had genuine admirers among senior government figures such as Pompidou, Malraux and Chirac.

In the early months of 1961 Messiaen was the subject of public lectures by Harry Halbreich and by Claude Rostand, the latter as part of the 'Hommage à Messiaen' at the École Normale. Messiaen appeared on television, interviewed by his sternest critic, Bernard Gavoty, alongside a performance of the *Trois petites Liturgies* conducted by Couraud.[15] In March he was awarded a Grand Prix du Disque for Loriod's recording of the *Catalogue d'oiseaux*. Messiaen was also granted the accolade of an interview for *Paris-Match*, which appeared in the same issue as a feature on Robert Kennedy. Some atmospheric but rather contrived photographs were taken for this: a number of birds were purchased, and despite Messiaen's protests that they would die in the cold, were released as background to a shot of Messiaen perched in a tree; the gloomy interior of the villa du Danube was enlivened by importing two enormous paintings by Robert Delaunay, loaned by his widow, Sonia. When the article was published (10 March 1962) these were spotted by the Inspector of Taxes for the 19th arrondissement, who repeatedly harried Messiaen to explain why he had not declared them to the authorities.[16]

Messiaen's international reputation was underlined by the invitation to tour Japan in the summer of 1962, his first visit outside Europe since the première of *Turangalîla* in the USA in 1949. The organizer of the tour, Mrs Fumi Yamaguchi, came in person to Paris, in June 1961, to discuss the details.

Throughout the early months of 1962 Messiaen prepared for his trip to Japan, accumulating recordings of native birds, many presented to him by Japanese former pupils. Departure was on 19 June. This was Messiaen's first experience of flying, and he was fascinated by the landscapes unfolding beneath.

> Flight over Greenland, Grant Land, the Baffin Sea, the Beaufort Sea. Deep blue sky, full sun, *no night*, always *midday*. Flight at altitude of 12 kilometres (at 200 kilometres per hour[17]). Marvellous sea of clouds. Then blue open sea, icy, with ice fields, the ground frozen and wrinkled. Valleys and chasms, some red, others white with snow. Glaciers of immaculate whiteness! *Impression of eternal solitude*, like the first morning of Creation. Kilometre after kilometre (hundreds of them!) of mountains and abysses, of *eternal snow* – sublime. The Alps multiplied by 10,000!!! No trace of life![18]

127 Mme Fumi Yamaguchi at the villa du Danube, June 1961.

In Tokyo the Messiaens were overwhelmed by their reception. They were embraced by former pupils, and given celebrity treatment, with teams from television and radio in attendance; and for once Mount Fuji was not shrouded in cloud, traditionally a good omen. The schedule was crowded with rehearsals, concerts, receptions and press conferences, but the organizer, Mrs Yamaguchi, had taken to heart Messiaen's plea for time to explore the sights and the countryside. The first full day (21 June) was given over to a reception and press conference, followed by a short concert, but the next three days were spent on the nature reserve at Karuizawa, just beyond the outer suburbs of Tokyo, and it was here that Messiaen laid the foundations for the sixth movement of the *Sept Haïkaï*, 'Les Oiseaux de Karuizawa'. Heat and humidity were intense. Messiaen was guided by two former pupils: Sadao Bekku who acted as interpreter, and Mitsuaki Hayama whose job was

128 At Tokyo airport, 20 June 1962.

129 Japan 1962: notating birdsong.

130 Musical sketches for four clarinets made at Karuizawa, Japan, 24 June 1962.

to spray the mosquitoes. A television crew (from NHK, the Japan Broadcasting Corporation) padded silently in their footsteps. In the *cahier*, birdsong notations jostle with Messiaen's first impressions of the Japanese landscape and ideas for a new work:

Maple-trees, which in autumn have blood-red leaves. Very sharp outline of mountains, with lots of little peaks in perspective, on several planes, much adorned with trees whose foliage is shaped like parasols. For a work about

131 Seiji Ozawa, Loriod and Messiaen at a rehearsal for *Turangalîla*, Japan, July 1962.

132 *Turangalîla* in Tokyo, July 1962: Reiko Honsho learning to play the ondes Martenot with Yvonne Loriod's assistance.

Japan: use a rhythmic plan based on odd numbers with permutations; also use gagaku, nô, bunraku.

23 June, 6 p.m. Grassy terrain, bare mountains. The Ô-yoshikiri bird twirls in the sky (dry sound like a piston), gets excited (a noise like torn silk) – score for three horns, rasping and brassy, high-pitched and loud, in chords; then the noise of an engine accelerating and slowing down, like a lathe, or an aircraft landing – all this makes one complete strophe.

7 p.m. We're climbing very high on the mountain. Birch-trees, pines. Behind the volcano, an astonishing landscape: in front of us the dark crater continuously pouring out smoke in a sort of great white and grey cloud thick with lava. To one side there are thickets, young pines, marvellous wild azalea bushes, vivid pink, red and bright vermilion. The gold of the sun as it sets between the peaks.

7.30 p.m. The eruption of the volcano (Mount Asama) in 1788 created an immense expanse of black rocks, taking fantastic forms: wizards, monsters, jackals, lions. Night falls. The path is marked out with stone lanterns which lead to a red Buddhist temple. The jumble of rocks extends over a vast area with its stones forming jagged Gothic arches. A pagoda, in which hangs the bell of the temple. Alone in the darkness, the rocks and the Yotaku, a type of nightjar.

133 Fr Ernest Goossens, Hiroshima, 1962.

8 p.m. In the silence of the night the Ruribitaki and the Yotaku, which repeats up to a hundred times the same mournful note – kyo, kyo, kyo – with

the timbre like a bell, a wood-block, a sneeze, a slap. In the darkness the Yotaku is wonderful!

Messiaen immersed himself in Japanese life and culture:

> I tried to live like a true Japanese. I forgot about my music, and the concerts, and I began with the cuisine. In spite of my stomach problems (which never troubled me during the trip), I ate all the fourteen or so courses usually served at each meal. [...] There is the famous Sukiyaki, made with red onions, and extremely fine vermicelli like angel's hair, and piles of little pieces of bread. Then the tempura: fried fish and shellfish and aubergines. I ate stretched out on the tatami, or even on the ground. I went about in slippers rather than shoes.[19]

Rehearsals for *Turangalîla* began on 26 June, in Tokyo. The conductor was the young Seiji Ozawa, who directed 'with faultless technique, and extraordinary rhythm and passion'.[20] There was a stormy start when it was discovered that there was no keyed glockenspiel (the part had to be played by two percussionists with sticks) and no trumpet in D. The ondes Martenot was played by the orchestral pianist Reiko Honsho, who fortunately proved adept at mastering this unfamiliar instrument, while Loriod played the piano part. The Messiaens were charmed, at the lunch break, by the picnic prepared for them by the orchestra, consisting of 'cold meats accompanied by very salty seaweed in a little basket filled with ice'.[21]

Messiaen took every opportunity to immerse himself in Japanese music and theatre. He bought a number of books and recordings of gagaku, and on 30 June he and Loriod attended an evening of koto.[22] Most of the following day, after Mass, Messiaen was at a performance of nô theatre: 'It's essential to prepare for this, and I had done so. I understood the texts, which I had read in advance in French, and I delighted in the music, the steps, the slowness of the movements, and the extraordinary cries of the players of the tsuzumi.'[23]

The performance of *Turangalîla* took place on 4 July, followed two days later by *Visions de l'Amen*. On 7 July Messiaen gave an interview for Japanese television on his impressions of the country, followed by an evening of bunraku, traditional Japanese puppet theatre. After several days recording *Turangalîla* for television, there was time for more sightseeing and birdwatching. The Messiaens visited Kamakura, with its Shinto temple and great image of Buddha, then went by train to Fuji and the lake of Yamanaka, which was to inspire the third piece of the *Sept Haïkaï*, 'Yamanaka-Cadenza'.

After returning briefly to Tokyo for a performance of kabuki, Messiaen and Loriod took the train to Osaka:

Right at the beginning of the journey, after leaving Tokyo: the sea (blue-green!). On the other side is Mount Fuji, dominating the undulating flanks of other mountains, dominating the clouds that cover these mountains: lonely, noble and majestic. Astonishing landscape of hills, clothed with Japanese pines with twisted branches. Paddy-fields whose mirrors of water and thousands of green shoots adorn the valleys and reflect the sky, all laid out in terraces which divide the hills in the foreground with their sumptuous staircases. Contrasting patterns of the hills, pines, rice-fields, tea plantations. At 7 p.m., the sun: a great red disc. 7.30 p.m., the sad and sombre blue of the sky: the mountains are black – here and there silhouettes of pines are still visible. 8.30 p.m., complete darkness.

At Nara Messiaen found the setting for the second piece of the *Sept Haïkaï*, visiting the Buddhist temple and the park with its stone lanterns, stags, hinds and fawns.

The journey now took them to Hiroshima. Apprehensive at what they would find in the shattered city, the Messiaens were enchanted when they were greeted on the station platform by a choir of young girls singing in French.[24] Their host was a Belgian priest, Fr Ernest Goossens. Under his guidance they carried the bouquets with which they had been welcomed and placed them at the memorial to the dead. He then showed them the church, in which all the furnishings – altar, pews, organ – had been a gift from somewhere in the world. As they sat in the nave a recording of Fauré's *In paradisum* started to play, reducing them to tears. That afternoon they took a boat to Miyajima, where Messiaen admired the Shinto temple and the red arch of the torii, celebrated in the fifth piece of the *Sept Haïkaï*, and indeed illustrated on the front cover of the score:

The sea: salty smell, of seaweed and of water, and the scent of a grove of pines. Large red *torii* in the sea. Marvellous red and white Shinto temple, maze of rooms, corridors, columns of red wood. Dark interior of the temple where the divinity is hidden (principal room), and the other temple (which one cannot see) with the invisible true God, behind the red *torii*, in the sea and the sky. Monstrous stone lions defend the temple – stone lanterns on the path beside the sea – the mountains velvety with pines. Sunset above the temple. From a distance one can see the *torii* against the evening clouds, orange, red, pink, violet. At night one can just make out the *torii* in the darkness – a full moon, gold and silver, with a hazy red halo, veiled by a thin strip of completely black cloud.[25]

Father Goosens told them of how he had tried to stay with his Japanese parish during the war, but he had been interned as a foreigner. After the war, in his efforts to rebuild the community, he had organized first a choir, and then a concert series at the Queen Elisabeth Institute, which he had built. It was there (21 July) that the Messiaens gave their recital; later, engulfed by flowers, they autographed dozens of programmes, and even the lids of the pianos. A courtesy that Messiaen particularly noted was the incense placed behind the pianos to freshen the atmosphere in the absence of air-conditioning. The departure from Hiroshima was unforgettable, with the children's choir running down the platform, still singing as the train pulled away.[26]

On 24 July the Messiaens flew to Denver for the Aspen Festival. Arriving worn out by jetlag and by the intense emotions aroused by Japan, Loriod had to cope with a week packed with concerts, as well as serving on the jury for the piano competition. The concerts took place in a sort of circus tent, with audience all round the performers, and the canvas flapping noisily in the wind.[27] With Walter Susskind conducting, Loriod played *Réveil des oiseaux*, *Oiseaux exotiques*, and Milhaud's *Cinq Études*. In addition she gave a marathon solo recital with excerpts from Debussy's *Études*, Boulez's Sonata no.2 (movements 1 and 2), Jolivet's *Mana*, a group of *Regards*, and six of the *Saudades* by Milhaud. The third and final leg of this world tour was the shortest, a visit to Montreal where they repeated the repertoire used in Japan, with the addition of some Mozart (the A major Sonata, K331 and the G major Concerto, K453).

134 Messiaen and Milhaud, Aspen, July 1962.

Arriving in Paris on 16 August, the Messiaens departed at once for Petichet. There Messiaen threw himself into his work, and using the notations gathered in Japan began to compose. Although *Sept Haïkaï* is profoundly marked by Messiaen's impressions of Japan, some characteristics of the music spring directly from *Chronochromie*. There is the same interest in rigorously ordered rhythm, the layers moving with apparent independence of time as well as timbre, and again a wild profusion of birdsong. The latter, as with *Chronochromie*, is more finely controlled than at first appears. Comparing the *cahiers* with the score shows that although the Japanese birdsongs were incorporated almost exactly as Messiaen first jotted them down, there were numerous subtle transpositions in mid-phrase that reveal his acute attention to the way they sound together.

Messiaen's cultural tourism had none of the gentle Orientalism of, say, Debussy's *Pagodes*; and although *Sept Haïkaï* was a work for Debussy's centenary, there is no mention of him in the dedications at the front of the score. What seems to have most impressed Messiaen in Japan – and what gives *Sept Haïkaï* its unique sound – is the stern, hieratic quality of the architecture, music and theatre. The work is flanked by a short Introduction and Coda, complex rituals played out with austere formality, and corresponding to the 'guardian kings that frame the entrance to Buddhist temples'.[28] Between these is a series of 'sketches' of Messiaen's most vivid memories of Japan: the park at Nara, the virtuoso birdsong collected on the slopes of Mount Fuji ('Yamanaka-Cadenza'), a gagaku from the Imperial court, the *torii* at Miyajima bathed in the colours of sunset, and finally (before the Coda) the longest movement, 'Les Oiseaux de Karuizawa'. Representative of the piercing, edgy timbres Messiaen found in Japanese music is the central 'Gagaku': 'This music contains a melody that is surprising to European ears, played by a small, primitive oboe: the hichiriki. Its sound is extremely vinegary and it is doubled badly by other instruments which add flourishes and don't stick to the same modes. These false doublings are both extremely disagreeable and at the same time expressive.'[29] In *Sept Haïkaï* the hichiriki is imitated by the trumpet ('noble, religious, nostalgic'),[30] and given a nasal edge by the doubling of two oboes and cor anglais. The melody moves with a sort of reptilian indifference against three other similarly enclosed layers: bells and gongs, piccolo and E flat clarinet in parallel, acidly dissonant intervals, and astringent chords on strings, *sul ponticello* and without vibrato, in imitation of the Japanese shô.

Commissions were coming in thick and fast. There were at least three of these at the time. The earliest of them, a request from the City of Paris for a work commemorating Debussy, Messiaen hoped to fulfil with his new Japanese piece, *Sept Haïkaï*. This necessitated a further re-negotiation of the original agreement, and on 1 December Messiaen wrote to Amable Massis in somewhat defiant tone:

> You gave me a commission for a work for piano, percussion and small orchestra. The work is now very advanced although not quite finished: there are still several pages of orchestration to do. Re-reading the official wording of the commission I note that [. . .] it does not say that the work must be in the style of Debussy (and in any case it was never my intention to deliver a pastiche), but only that one should take note of the fact that the work is for Debussy's centenary. I am therefore entirely within the rules.

The second commission was from Heinrich Strobel, for what would become *Couleurs de la Cité céleste*. The new work was discussed at a dinner party on 13 December 1962 attended by the Messiaens, Suzanne Tézenas, Strobel, and Boulez, who had recently conducted a triumphant concert (31 October) of contemporary classics to celebrate ten years of the Domaine Musical: Stockhausen's *Kontrapunkte*, Berio's *Serenade*, *Oiseaux exotiques*, and *Le Marteau sans maître*. Messiaen noted some preliminary thoughts on the new piece: 'For Strobel, compose *Fragment from the Apocalypse*. Re-read the Apocalypse, and find a language for leitmotifs, applied to the main ideas, characters, symbols and colours of the Apocalypse.'

The Messiaens left for Argentina on 17 June 1963. The trip began inauspiciously: at Montevideo in Uruguay, their Boeing 707 overshot the short runway and became embedded in the grass, necessitating an emergency evacuation. Disorientated, the Messiaens asked for a taxi to Buenos Aires and had to be reminded that they first had to cross the seventy or so miles of the estuary of the River Plate. In the Argentine capital, Alberto Ginastera had assembled a class of composers, to whom Messiaen delivered an esoteric-sounding course on Greek and Hindu rhythms, while Loriod taught a group of pianists. There were concerts, with *Visions de l'Amen*, selections from the *Vingt Regards*, *Oiseaux exotiques* (conducted by Rafael Frühbeck de Burgos),[31] and a recital of Messiaen's works by the piano class. The Messiaens heard their first native birds on a tour in a horse-drawn carriage. A longer trip was made into the pampas near Navarro, where Messiaen noted two birds, the hornero and benteveo, which would figure in *Couleurs*.

Returning to Paris on 10 July, Messiaen needed to begin work on *Couleurs*. A week was spent catching up on correspondence and packing for Petichet: Messiaen's luggage included 'the new chords discovered for *Haïkaï*'. Suddenly Loriod fell ill, and was admitted to hospital (18 July) where she was given two blood transfusions. Visiting-time was at 6.30 in the evening. Messiaen arrived with a transistor radio and three balls of wool (according to Loriod the same three that he had given to Claire in hospital in 1949, and which had remained all these years unused). Loriod was much too ill for knitting. On 25 July she had a hysterectomy, and the Messiaens were now faced with the fact that they would never be able to have children. On 30 July Loriod's condition worsened when she suffered an embolism. Between visits to the hospital Messiaen began to compose.[32] Loriod's recovery was slow and she was discharged only on 31 August. The Messiaens left for Petichet at once, taking a train to Grenoble and then a taxi to the house. While Messiaen composed, Loriod spent her convalescence correcting the orchestral material of *Sept Haïkaï* and learning the solo part on her piano in the garage.

Messiaen's classes resumed on 2 October. The following day he took the score and orchestral parts of *Sept Haïkaï* to Boulez. Rehearsals began on 22 October. The première, on 30 October, was a considerable success; while some of the audience protested, Messiaen felt that he had found a brilliant interpreter in Boulez.[33]

On 25 October, less than a week before the première of *Sept Haïkaï*, Roger Désomière died at his home in the rue Caulaincourt, after over a decade as an invalid. Messiaen was always profoundly grateful for Désormière's support from the mid-1930s onwards, and in a moving tribute to the conductor ('Absence et présence de Roger Désormière'), he linked two of his most gifted advocates:

In terms of orchestral conducting, there is certainly a filiation between Désormière and Boulez. What I must first say loud and clear is that Boulez is more than the continuation of Webern, the follower of the three Viennese, and so on. He is firstly a composer of genius, the most lucid and the most profoundly intelligent of the twentieth century. He is also an extraordinary conductor. Now, it is certain that the first advice given to Boulez by Désormière was decisive. [. . .] The external differences in their conducting – absolutely precise stick technique with one, the expressiveness of hands alone with the other – aim for the same result: complete effectiveness with an orchestra. [. . .] It is undeniable that 'Déso' has now left us for good. His soul undoubtedly contemplates now a more radiant light than our own [. . .] but he will certainly know who his spiritual son is here below. [. . .] It is thus that absence has become presence.[34]

The first inspiration for *Couleurs de la Cité céleste* predated the approach from Strobel by more than two years. It stemmed from a note in the diary for September 1960 made just as Messiaen was finishing *Chronochromie*: 'Write a work on "La muraille multicolorée".' This 'wall of many colours' referred to the penultimate chapter of the Book of Revelation, with its description of 'a wall great and high. [. . .] And the building of the wall of it was of jasper [. . .] and the foundations of the wall of the city were garnished with all manner of precious stones. The first foundation was jasper; the second, sapphire; the third, a chalcedony; the fourth, an emerald. The fifth, sardonyx; the sixth, sardius; the seventh, chrysolyte; the eighth, beryl; the ninth, a topaz; the tenth, a chrysoprasus; the eleventh; a jacinth; the twelfth, an amethyst.'[35]

For the first time in many years Messiaen was contemplating a major religious work, and one on a recurring theme in his music, the Apocalypse. Explicitly religious subjects had been conspicuous by their absence in Messiaen's recent output, although of course for him the bird pieces of the 1950s stood equally as an expression of faith, as a celebration of God's creation. Nonetheless, a decade had passed since the *Livre d'orgue* (1952), and nearly twenty years had passed since the last religious work written for the concert hall (the *Vingt Regards* in 1944). Perhaps it is no coincidence that *Couleurs de la Cité céleste* came from a time when Messiaen had found happiness and stability. A more specific impulse, however, may have been the *Verset pour la fête de la Dédicace*, composed in December 1960, shortly after Messiaen's first idea for *Couleurs*. The *Verset* used birdsong as a foil to sections of plainsong, one of which – the Alleluia for the Feast of the Dedication – is found in *Couleurs*.

The commission from Strobel gave Messiaen the opportunity to realize the work he had conceived in 1960. A snag was that the commission specified a very unusual instrumentation, including a trio of xylophones (or, as Messiaen interpreted it, keyboard percussion) and a trio of trombones. After some thought, Messiaen saw that this could tie in with his existing idea for a work on the Apocalypse: 'I had accepted but was very unhappy, for I couldn't see how I was to use these instruments. Finally, after long reflection, it occurred to me that trombones had an apocalyptic sound, so I re-read the Apocalypse looking for quotations from it.'[36] From extensive notes in Messiaen's diary it appears that deciding on the instruments to go with those required by Strobel was far from easy. The first plan was for solo piano with brass (4 trumpets, 4 trombones), a trio of pitched percussion (xylophone, vibraphone and xylorimba), with cencerros (and perhaps also crotales), bells and tam-tams. Messiaen noted in his diary a version almost identical to this (with marimba replacing xylorimba) which was agreed with Boulez, who was to conduct the work.[37] The next step was to reduce the role of the piano – it replaced the xylophone in the trio of pitched percussion – and to add woodwind: piccolo, oboe, cor anglais, piccolo clarinet, clarinet, bass clarinet, contrabassoon. The third and final line-up was a synthesis and simplification of the first two. The piano was once again soloist; there are 10 brass, adding 2 horns to the trumpets and trombones; in the trio of pitched percussion the original vibraphone is replaced by marimba; and the rest of the percussion is streamlined to cencerros, bells, 4 gongs and 2 tam-tams.

Messiaen's intention in *Couleurs de la Cité céleste* was a glimpse of eternity: 'The work never finishes, never having truly begun.'[38] The timelessness of *Couleurs* is very different from that in the *Sept Haïkaï*. There Messiaen's think-ing was overwhelmingly linear, the layers seemingly indifferent to one another, their freedom set into relief by the inscrutable working out of rhythmic processes (a famous earlier precedent for this was the 'Liturgie de cristal', the first movement of the *Quatuor*). *Couleurs* belonged to a more recent tradition, beginning with *Cantéyodjayâ* and continued in the *Catalogue d'oiseaux*. In 'La Bouscarle' (from the *Catalogue*) the many strands of the music are woven together, appearing intermittently on the surface of the music at different stages in their life cycle. Messiaen described *Couleurs* in similar terms, as being like a play with different characters and subplots superimposed.[39]

The material of *Couleurs* was exceptionally rich. The birdsong, for example, came from Messiaen's continuing exploration, reflected in the *cahiers* from the early 1960s, of birds from distant parts of the world. *Couleurs* contained five birds from New Zealand, five from Brazil, three from Venezuela, one from Canada, and two from the Argentinian pampas. In the *cahiers* pride of place was given to notations of the bell bird (from New Zealand) which in *Couleurs* is shared between clarinets, piano and keyboard percussion against an appropriate backdrop of resonances on bells, cencerros and gongs. The birds play their part in symbolizing Messiaen's vision of the Apocalypse – 'extraordinary, extrava-gant, surrealistic and terrifying'[40] – which can be heard, for instance, in the shriek of the Brazilian araponga. The four Alleluias provided a specific religious source. It is interesting that one of Messiaen's first ideas for *Couleurs* – jotted in the diary during the period in August 1963 when Loriod was in hospital – was for an alleluia, arranged in a *Klangfarbenmelodie*, with successive notes played by bells, piano and horn.[41] The most frequently used Alleluia (for the eighth Sunday after Pentecost) is a brisk fanfare, with jangling gongs and cencerros, while the Alleluia of the Blessed Sacrament is an extended chorale, used to close the two halves of the work. The music of *Couleurs* is at its most dramatic when it makes direct reference to the Bible. In one such passage the upbeat is a flashing figure on the piano – marked in the score 'the star that has the key of the abyss' – followed by a plunge into the depths on gongs and tam-tam.[42] The source for this passage is one of five quotations from Revelation in the preface: 'And the fifth angel sounded, and I saw a star fall from heaven unto the earth: and to him was given the key of the bottomless pit.'[43]

Colour is paramount here: 'The form of the work depends entirely on colours. The melodic and rhythmic themes, the complexes of sounds and timbres evolve in the manner of colours.'[44] The descriptions in the *cahiers* demonstrate that for Messiaen colour was as much a passion as timbre. In *Couleurs* he even went so far as to design the cover of the printed score himself, cutting out orange lettering and sticking it on a blue background. Messiaen was also a collector of semi-precious stones, and talked knowledgeably to Claude Samuel about their properties. Jasper crystals, for example, were 'not only endowed with all the colours of the rainbow but translucent. [. . .] I've tried to get into my work the colours mentioned in the Apocalypse, and I don't think I've ever gone so far with the sound-colour relationship. [. . .] The brass should, so to speak, "play red"; the woodwinds should "play blue", and so forth.'[45]

135 Messiaen with his collection of crystals.

All this creates a difficulty for listeners and performers who cannot 'hear' colour as Messiaen did. Perhaps our best hope of grasping something of Messiaen's experience is in the moments of stillness, when colour chords merge slowly, like a stone turned in the light.[46] Messiaen's final thought, at the end of the preface to the score, is to stress the union of form and colour. The work 'turns on itself, lacing its temporal blocks, like the rose window of a cathedral with its brilliant and its invisible colours'. Like the *torii* at Miyajima opening onto the unseen temple, or indeed like Messiaen's own music, stained glass offers a glimpse of the beyond.

An establishment figure?
1964–1969

Messiaen's move to the rue Marcadet was finally accomplished early in 1964, almost three years after he and Loriod were married. In February his books, music, paintings and furniture were transported across Paris from the villa du Danube, and he and Loriod went to Gaveau's to choose an upright piano for his new composing studio. Then on 27 April Messiaen and his son signed the papers which brought to a conclusion the long-running saga of Claire's will.

Messiaen at last found serenity in his domestic circumstances after twenty years clouded by the tragedy of Claire's illness and the legal uncertainties in the aftermath of her death. It is no coincidence that the decade which now followed was to be one of resplendent achievement. The works of this period contain three of Messiaen's most important commissions – *Et exspecto resurrectionem mortuorum*, *La Transfiguration de Notre-Seigneur Jésus-Christ* and *Des Canyons aux étoiles. . .* – as well as the largest organ work since the 1930s – *Méditations sur le mystère de la Sainte Trinité* – and a monumental retrospective of his *style oiseau* in *La Fauvette des jardins* for solo piano.

The settled calm of home life also encouraged Messiaen to make a more systematic collection of his musical sketches and important papers. Very likely the forming of an archive shows Loriod's influence. As we shall see, in the years to come she would devote more time to assisting Messiaen, while after his death she would undertake the formidable task of setting his papers in order, editing some of the unpublished music, and preparing for publication the seven volumes that make up Messiaen's *Traité* on composition.

The first works to demonstrate Messiaen's new policy were *Et exspecto* and *La Transfiguration*, for both of which Messiaen retained meticulously the letters received from the commissioning body and carbon copies of his replies. This correspondence provides an unprecedented insight into the way his compositions evolved.

Et exspecto resurrectionem mortuorum set the seal on Messiaen's rise to becoming a figure of national importance. The first intimations came in October 1963 when Messiaen noted down some preliminary thoughts following an approach from no less a person than André Malraux, de Gaulle's

Minister of Culture: 'Commission from *Malraux*: a sacred work for the dead – chorus, large orchestra, brass – to be performed at the Sainte-Chapelle, at Notre-Dame de Chartres etc. Ready for June 1964.' In a note at the back of his 1963 diary, he jotted down a slightly fuller version of this plan:

> Malraux commission: write a work for *choir* (300 singers) and *brass* (50 players) – see the Mass by Machaut, for the *dead* (a De profundis?).

The official request for the work was sent to Messiaen on 15 November 1963, originally offering a fee of 5,000 F, though Malraux subsequently increased this to 9,000 F.

One consequence of this prestigious project was the unsuccessful attempt by René Dommange to lure Messiaen back into the Durand stable:

> Durand: M. Dommange wants to publish the *Malraux commission* – very long, chorus, large orchestra, lots of brass – Dommange agrees to all of that. He also wants to publish my works for piano and for small orchestra.

The Malraux commission was for a major national commemoration. Robert Siohan, Inspector General for Music (who, almost thirty years earlier, had conducted the première of *L'Ascension*), wrote to Messiaen on 24 April, requesting a progress report on the composition and underlining its intended purpose: 'I need hardly tell you that M. André Malraux attaches the greatest possible importance to your name being associated with the solemn national occasion'. The next day (25 April), Messiaen replied with some details of his work, which was now starting to take on a more recognizable form:

> Following our conversation about the recent commission by the Minister, André Malraux, for a musical work written to the glory of the dead of two World Wars, I am able to clarify certain points:
> 1. The work will be delivered at the end of 1964.
> 2. It will be a work for an orchestra of brass instruments, concerning the Resurrection of the Dead.
> [. . .] Once I have finished my work, I will take personal charge of the arrangements for photographing the score and the copying of orchestral material. When I deliver the work, I would ask, at the same time as the commission fee, for reimbursement of the photographic and copying expenses.

A note in Messiaen's diary for June 1964 contained some further thoughts: he had changed his mind about the length of the work (the 'very long' of March had become '10 minutes'), and he had already devised a title:

A work about the Resurrection of the Dead – Et exspecto resurrectionem mortuorum . . . for very large brass orchestra – see plainchant, [. . .] chords, birds from Africa and Amazonia. Must be delivered by 15 November 1964 with the material copied. [. . .] The work will be performed in public on the occasion of the commemoration of the anniversaries of 1914 and 1944.

On 27 June Messiaen reminded himself to 'prepare everything for the Malraux commission' and the same day he and Loriod left for their summer vacation. At Petichet, Loriod was busy not only looking after all domestic matters, but also composing cadenzas for several Mozart piano concertos: she was to perform a Mozart cycle (22 concertos) with the Lamoureux Orchestra in seven concerts during November and December; Boulez, Bruno Maderna and Louis Martin were the conductors.

Messiaen started work in earnest on *Et exspecto* in early July. Émile Biasini, an administrator at the Ministry of Culture, wrote to Messiaen on 22 September with the news that Malraux wanted the new work to be performed at a solemn celebration in Chartres Cathedral during October in honour of the writer Charles Péguy, killed in action in 1914. Messiaen reacted with dismay to this impossible new deadline. In a letter to Malraux dated 6 October, he explained his position in detail:

I have received in quick succession three letters: the first from Monsieur Biasini, the second from Monsieur Robert Siohan, and the third from Mademoiselle Moreau, requesting delivery at the beginning of October for your commission. [. . .]

I am sorry, because it would have been a great joy for me to participate in this ceremony [for Charles Péguy]. Unfortunately I promised you this commission for the end of 1964, which to my mind means around Christmas. I continue to promise you that it will be finished by Christmas.

Here is the story of the commission. Having the good fortune to be a Catholic, and a strong believer, I have taken the subject in its loftiest sense and have thus written five pieces on the *Resurrection of the Dead*. These pieces are scored for a large orchestra of woodwind (full) and of brass (very full, ranging from a piccolo trumpet in D to a bass saxhorn). To this is added metallic percussion (bells, gongs and tam-tams). In all, 40 players.

I spent the summer in the High Alps in order to work in peace, and for three months I spent ten hours a day on orchestration. The music is completely finished. The first, second and third pieces are orchestrated, as is half of the fourth. Thus, all that is left to do is the remainder of the fourth movement and all of the fifth. It is impossible to perform such a work in fragments, and in any event once I have finished, it is still necessary to allow three weeks for the copying of the orchestral material.

I therefore expect to be able to show you the finished score around 25 December, and the copied orchestral material at the end of January.

I would certainly have finished sooner if I had treated the work as an ordinary commission. But it seemed to me that the nobility of the subject required this majestic and powerful orchestration, suitable for a cathedral, and even for the open air. If I have written five pieces instead of one, it is because the quotations from Scripture on which they are based required such a structure, as did the formal balance of the work. I will write to you as soon as I have finished.

Another obstacle to early completion of the new work was that the autumn was busy with concerts, notably the première of *Couleurs de la Cité céleste* by Loriod, Boulez and the Domaine Musical for Heinrich Strobel's Musiktage in the Stadthalle, Donaueschingen, on 17 October, then Loriod's marathon series of Mozart concertos throughout November and December. The last of these, on 19 December, was conducted by Boulez (there were three concertos on the programme: K491 in C minor, K482 in E flat major, and K488 in A major), and a few days earlier, on 16 December, Loriod and Boulez had also given the French première of *Couleurs de la Cité céleste* at the Domaine Musical concerts in the Odéon.

Messiaen showed *Et exspecto* to Malraux on 11 February 1965[1] and on 21 February he wrote to Biasini at the Ministry of Culture announcing the work's completion, and revealing publicly the definitive title for the first time:

The commission for Monsieur André Malraux has been finished since the beginning of January, as promised. I have had the score photographed and I showed it to Monsieur Malraux on 11 February. The copying of the orchestral material is under way, and the copyist has assured me that it will be finished by 20 March. As my presence at the first performance is absolutely essential, I should tell you that on account of concerts of my works abroad, my frequent travels, and the examination period for Conservatoire classes, it is desirable that the orchestral rehearsals and the first performance of the work should take place either between 26 April and 8 May, or between 26 May and 5 June.

Monsieur Malraux would like the first performance to take place in the Sainte-Chapelle in Paris, and he has asked Monsieur Siohan to make all the necessary arrangements. I am also meeting Monsieur Maurice Werner (concert organizer) the day after tomorrow to ask him (at M. Malraux's request) for an estimate of the expenses which are likely to be involved in such an event.

The work is called *Et exspecto resurrectionem mortuorum* (and obviously it is dedicated to the Resurrection of the Dead). It comprises five movements and lasts about 20 minutes.[2] [. . .] We need to settle quite an important matter. Of course my publisher has no involvement at the time of the first performance: every organization which commissions a new piece has the absolute right of the première. It is also understood that after the first performance in France, I have the right to give my work to my publisher and to organize other performances in France and abroad. Please be so kind as to confirm all this in writing.

On 2 April Biasini wrote to Messiaen about the arrangements that were in hand to pay the commission fee into the composer's bank, and stated that Malraux wanted to reserve the first three performances, after which Messiaen was free to give the work to his publisher. A few weeks later, on 27 April, Messiaen wrote to Monsieur Trapenard at the Ministry, with detailed instructions for the printing and distribution of invitations to the private first performance, then just over a week away:

> Given the cramped dimensions of the Sainte-Chapelle, and the presence of 40 musicians, I think that 150 invitations and 150 separate sheets will suffice, to be distributed as follows: 40 for the musicians (who would not otherwise be able to get in), two for the conductor Serge Baudo, two for Robert Siohan, two for Monsieur Werner, fifty for the personal guests of Monsieur André Malraux, and fifty-four which I would ask you to send to my home address, for myself, my family, my publisher, and some pupils and friends.
>
> Here is the form of words for the invitation: '. . . invites you to attend the first performance (private) of the work by Olivier Messiaen: *Et exspecto resurrectionem mortuorum* for orchestra of wind, brass and metallic percussion – 40 players under the direction of Serge Baudo – which will take place in Paris at the Sainte-Chapelle on Friday, 7 May 1965 at 11 o'clock in the morning.'

The front of the programme begins with the words 'In homage to the dead of two World Wars'. This was the explicit intention of the commission, but Messiaen was uneasy about the memorial aspect of the work, preferring to focus on the concept of eternal life. By the time the score was published by Leduc in February 1967, Messiaen's preface contained no reference to the war dead, stating only that 'this work was commissioned by André Malraux'.

Messiaen noted some details of the private première at the Sainte-Chapelle in his diary: 'In the audience, M. and Madame Malraux (very moved, both in tears), Siohan and his wife, pupils from my class, Yvonne, Pascal and Josette, 150 guests. A marvellous performance with the reflections of the sun in the blue and the red of the windows, and all that resonance! It was broadcast on the radio.' Messiaen also spotted the irony in the way the event was funded: the expenses of the performance were 'met by war veterans, paying a concert

136 The Sainte-Chapelle, 6 May 1965, at a rehearsal of *Et exspecto*.

association which was collecting on their behalf.' A more complete list of those who were present at the performance was written down by Loriod: old Conservatoire friends such as Elsa Barraine, Jean Langlais, Daniel-Lesur and Gaston Litaize, and pupils such as Jacques Charpentier, Jean-Pierre Guézec, Paul Méfano and Iannis Xenakis. There, too, were Mme Sivade and Mme Tézenas, Gilbert Leduc, Gabriel Dussurget, Messiaen's copyist Raymond Cremers, and Jean Bonfils, his regular deputy at the Trinité.

The second performance took place in Chartres Cathedral on 20 June 1965. Loriod recalled the tight security for the event:

> The cathedral was being guarded by hundreds of police officers, since the President of the Republic was arriving the next day. All the musicians had to be issued with passes to get into the cathedral, as did the cameramen who were going to record the concert. The organization was complex because, in general, churches are not able to provide enough lighting for a concert and it was necessary to bring in music stands with individual lights, like those is the pits of opera houses.

Messiaen gave a vivid description of the day itself in his diary:[3]

> Everyone was in their place by 9.15 a.m. The Archbishop and his retinue were in the south crossing, de Gaulle and his retinue in the north crossing, and the public in the nave. The orchestra was in the chancel, between the two altars: the bells, gongs and tam-tams on the steps of the old altar, the brass and woodwind lower down, towards the new altar, then the conductor. De Gaulle arrived and the Solemn Mass began. It was the Office of Corpus Christi. At the end of Mass, at 10.30 precisely, the A flat of the contrabassoon and saxhorn, assisted by the third tam-tam, started to play. Suddenly the immense nave was filled by a vast and overwhelming presence.

After the performance Messiaen was warmly congratulated by de Gaulle. The composer seldom expressed any interest in politics, but his admiration for Charles de Gaulle led him to sign an appeal in support of the General's re-election in the autumn of 1965. It was perhaps the only instance of Messiaen voicing a political opinion in public. He later gave an interview for the de Gaulle memorial volume of the journal *L'Herne*, in which he explained the reasons behind his support for a man whom he regarded not so much as a political leader but as a symbol of France itself (see p.140).

Messiaen's composing activity during the second half of the 1960s was dominated by a single large-scale work, for instrumental soloists, chorus and orchestra. *La Transfiguration de Notre-Seigneur Jésus-Christ* was commissioned in 1965 by the Calouste Gulbenkian Foundation of Lisbon, as a memorial to its founder; it was eventually given four year later, at the thirteenth Gulbenkian Music Festival, on 7 June 1969. The work developed considerably during the four years Messiaen spent composing it, becoming his grandest utterance to date, and a precursor, in terms of sheer monumentality, of *Saint François d'Assise*. Messiaen's fascination with the subject was initially fired by a sermon which he heard at Petichet on the Transfiguration as the encapsulation of Christ who is the True Light. He first mentioned the idea of a 'work for chorus and orchestra on the Transfiguration' at the end of his diary for 1961. But this reference and a few isolated sketches were all that seem to have existed before 1965.

The surviving sketches for *La Transfiguration* are a remarkable record of the work's evolution.[4] As is clear from Messiaen's letters to Mme Maria Madalena de Azeredo Perdigão at the Gulbenkian Foundation in Lisbon, the work was initially planned in nine movements. The early sketches are mostly on two staves, with only occasional ideas about orchestration. Written in pencil, they reveal that some movements were renumbered while work was in progress. The following chart shows the original numbering of these sketches where it has been possible to establish what this is – Messiaen's use of the eraser is one of the more tantalizing features of his work-in-progress. Confusingly, the autograph title page of these mainly two-stave sketches calls them 'Transfiguration / Brouillon / d'orchestre'. A slightly later photocopied short score (c.1965–6) is also in nine movements and on the title page a note in Messiaen's hand mentions that the work comprises 'les 9 pièces' and that 'toute l'œuvre au complet est *Bien*'. The table below shows how movements from the original nine-movement plan were relocated in the definitive state of the work.

Initial nine-movement plan (c.1966)	Definitive version (1969)
La Transfiguration	*La Transfiguration de Notre-Seigneur Jésus-Christ*
1. Récit Évangélique	1. Récit Évangélique
2. Candor est lucis aeternae	2. Configuratum corpori claritatis suae
4. Christus Jesus, splendor Patris	3. Christus Jesus, splendor Patris
3. Récit Évangélique	4. Récit Évangélique
7. Quam dilecta tabernacula tua	5. Quam dilecta tabernacula tua
	6. Candor est lucis aeternae
	7. Choral de la Sainte Montagne
6. Récit Évangélique	8. Récit Évangélique
	9. Perfecte conscius illius perfectae generationis
5. Oraison	10. Adoptionem filiorum perfectam
8. Récit Évangélique	11. Récit Évangélique
	12. Terribilis est locus iste
9. Final	13. Tota Trinitas apparuit
	14. Choral de la Lumière de Gloire

From the middle of 1965 onwards, the genesis of *La Transfiguration* is vividly documented in the correspondence between Messiaen and Mme Perdigão of the Gulbenkian Foundation – an exchange which had occasional moments of irritation and anxiety on both sides, but which provides an unusually detailed account of the progress of one of Messiaen's most important works.[5]

Mme Perdigão wrote to Messiaen on 9 June 1965 with a request for a new work to be written for the 1966 festival, in memory of Calouste Gulbenkian. This extremely tight deadline gave Messiaen less than a year before the planned first performance:

> We are commemorating this year the tenth anniversary of the death of our founder, Calouste Sarkis Gulbenkian, and we wish to mark this occasion by commissioning a musical work in his memory, not of a funereal character, but above all celebrating the generosity of Calouste Gulbenkian. We would like a symphonic work, preferably with chorus, which would last either 45 minutes to fill half of a concert, or one hour and a quarter for an entire concert. The governing body of the Foundation has allocated to us a sum equivalent to two million old francs.[6] Would it be possible for you to do us the great honour of composing this work? We would like to give the world première in our next festival, in May–June 1966. It would therefore be necessary for us to receive the manuscript by the end of February 1966. But if this is too soon, we might be able to put back the date of the performance.

Messiaen replied just over a week later, on 17 June, accepting the commission and providing some details of his first thoughts about the work:

> I agree to write a work for the commemoration of the 10th anniversary of the death of Calouste Gulbenkian. [. . .] I will write a work lasting about 45 minutes which will form the second half of a concert. This work will be written for five soloists, large orchestra and mixed chorus. The five soloists will sometimes play alone, and in quintuple cadenzas (so there will be nothing to orchestrate during these passages). The orchestra [. . .] will need to have at least 80 players, for a good balance between the orchestra and the choir. The choir will be [. . .] about 100 singers in all.
>
> The choir will vocalize without words. This will allow me to use more effects of sonority and rhythm (and will avoid my having to write [. . .] a poem in French, translating it into Portuguese, adapting the translation to the accents of the music, etc., etc.).
>
> I have already thought about the names of the five soloists. We should ask for the following: for the flute, Severino Gazzelloni (an Italian flautist of

international renown); for the piano, Yvonne Loriod (my wife, whom you already know, a marvellous pianist who is a specialist in my music, of international renown); for the cello, Mstislav Rostropovich (the Russian cellist of international renown, one of the greatest cellists of our time!); for the clarinet, Guy Deplus (an admirable French clarinettist who is a specialist in my music); and for the marimba, Jean Batigne (one of the famous percussionists from Strasbourg). [...] I accept the fee of 2 million old francs. [...] For the festival in May–June 1966, it won't be necessary to have the work completed by February 1966. I will try to have it finished for 1 March. [...]

The idea of a work for multiple instrumental soloists, chorus and orchestra was already in place, but it was to last just forty-five minutes, with a wordless choir. Mme Perdigão's next letter, sent from Lisbon on 18 June, contained a suggestion about the text which Messiaen was to take up with enthusiasm: 'I wanted to suggest that you might use a poem in Latin which could be sung easily by a Portuguese chorus and would be universally understood. It seems to me that such an option would greatly simplify matters.'

In a letter sent on 24 June, Mme Perdigão raised a question which was to prove surprisingly intractable: 'I am curious to know who you are going to suggest as the conductor.' Messiaen replied on 8 July, suggesting six names, 'all excellent, but given here in order of preference, as far as my music is concerned'. They were Pierre Boulez, Bruno Maderna, Michael Gielen, Seiji Ozawa, Constantin Iliev[7] and Serge Baudo. The proposed date of the première also turned out to be problematic, as Messiaen explained in a letter written on 31 October. Having spent much of the summer at work on the piece, he provided a great deal of information about its overall plan at the time (nine movements rather than the eventual fourteen), his progress on the composition, his decisions concerning the choice of texts, and, for the first time, a title:

Regarding the conductor, I saw Boulez in Scotland and he isn't free on 4 June. Yvonne Loriod saw Gielen in Stockholm and he isn't free on 4 June either. A few days ago Maderna conducted one of my works in Paris with Yvonne Loriod as soloist and we talked to him about Portugal, but he isn't free on 4 June.

So, I suggest an excellent young French conductor, and a fine musician [...], Serge Baudo. He conducted the first performance of my *Et exspecto resurrectionem mortuorum* in front of General de Gaulle and André Malraux at the Sainte-Chapelle in Paris and at Notre-Dame de Chartres. [...]

Regarding publicity, the cover of the programme and the leaflet, I cannot agree to the use of quotations of musical themes. First, they are given without harmonies, without orchestration, in the form of melodic embryos:

that is incomprehensible and pointless for the public and critics alike. Moreover, it will hamper my work: the thought of other people reading my themes before I have finished is completely unbearable for me. I am sorry.

Now I come to the work itself. Apart from a fortnight for the Edinburgh Festival in Scotland, I have been able to work every day without interruption, throughout July, August and September, since I was in the mountains, alone with my wife, and in complete peace and quiet. The work comprises nine sections. I wrote nos.1, 2, 3, 4, 6, 7 and 8. Then I wrote the fifth movement, which was finished at the start of October. I am in the process of completing the ninth and last movement, which should be finished shortly. There will be a few interruptions owing to the preparations for my class and concerts in Liège, Brussels, Dijon and Metz, but I can already promise you that *all the music* will be finished at the end of November and that I can start the orchestration at the start of December. That will take me until 1 April at the earliest, 15 April at the latest.

We remember the dead by their most saintly qualities, and those who were good people on earth will become one day the 'glorious body' in heaven. There is a moment in the life of Christ when this glory was shown to us and promised to us: the Transfiguration. So I have written a work on the Transfiguration: *La Transfiguration*. My chorus sing without words, but they also chant with words, to Latin texts drawn from the Gospel of St Matthew, from the Psalms, from St Paul, from the Book of Wisdom, from St Thomas Aquinas, and from the Office for the Feast of the Transfiguration. You can announce the title and the subtitles as follows:

La TRANSFIGURATION by OLIVIER MESSIAEN

Nine meditations on the Transfiguration of Christ, for five instrumental soloists, mixed chorus and large orchestra.
Written in memory of Calouste Gulbenkian, and commissioned by Mme Azeredo Perdigão on behalf of the Gulbenkian Foundation, for the 10th anniversary of the death of Calouste Gulbenkian.

Still the matter of finding a conductor proved impossible: Serge Baudo was booked to conduct the first performance of Milhaud's opera *La Mère coupable* in Geneva during June 1966 (the première was on 13 June) and was unavailable for the concert in Lisbon. Messiaen wrote to Mme Perdigão about this on 17 November, proposing Manuel Rosenthal instead; he also suggested a programme and provided full details of the forces required for *La Transfiguration* (the duration of which had lengthened from an original plan of 45 minutes to 1 hour 15 minutes):

Regarding the conductor, I have just telephoned Serge Baudo. [. . .] He has confirmed that it is impossible to change the date of the première of the Milhaud opera, so he has to say no to us. So now I suggest Manuel Rosenthal. [. . .] He has just given a sensational performance of my *Turangalîla-Symphonie* in Liège, with fabulous success. [. . .] He is a remarkable conductor and a friend, so I would be very happy to work with him. [. . .]

For the programme on 5 June, we spoke a little hastily the other day. I suggest the following solution which I think is better:

Couleurs de la Cité céleste (duration 17′)
Louange à l'Éternité de Jésus (8′) from my *Quatuor pour la fin du Temps*
Interval
La Transfiguration (1 hour 15′)
A total of 1 hour and 40 minutes of music. [. . .]

P.S.: *Everything* is saved! I've just had Rosenthal on the telephone. He is free on the dates proposed and he is delighted to conduct *La Transfiguration*. You cannot imagine how much pleasure this gives me. Let's hang on to this marvellous conductor and, above all, not make any more changes!

While Messiaen was relieved to have found a conductor (or so he thought), he also had to line up the most elusive of the soloists. Mstislav Rostropovich wrote from New York on 19 December agreeing to play the cello part: 'It was with great joy that I learned you had composed a work for my instrument, the violoncello. I want you to know that it would be a great honour for me to have the pleasure of playing one of your works, regardless of the performers or ensemble involved.'

On 7 February 1966 Mme Perdigão wrote to Messiaen, confirming that *La Transfiguration* would be played by the orchestra of the ORTF, conducted by Rosenthal, and that he could now finish the work in a more tranquil frame of mind. She added that Philips were planning to record the work on the two days following the première:

I was relieved to hear, at last, from the French Embassy that the Orchestre Philharmonique of the ORTF, conducted by Manuel Rosenthal, will give the first performance of your work. No doubt you have already heard this good news which will, I think, enable you to finish your work in peace. All the soloists have accepted and have written to tell me that they are available. Before sending them contracts I need to write to M. Rosenthal since you have now told me about rehearsing the soloists in Paris. This was news to me, as up to now there has been no question of holding rehearsals anywhere except Lisbon.

But don't worry any more. Everything will now go very well. [. . .] The concert will be on 5 June at 9.30 p.m. We have asked all the musicians to remain in Lisbon on 6 and 7 June for the recording by Philips. The Foundation will of course pay your first class travel and your hotel expenses. Would you like to stay in the Hotel Tivoli like last time?

All this has been difficult to arrange, but at last all is done.

Mme Perdigão was being unduly optimistic. She spoke to Messiaen on the telephone on 14 March and learned that difficulties had arisen over rehearsal arrangements with the ORTF, that Rosenthal had threatened to withdraw from the performance unless more rehearsal time was scheduled, and, most alarmingly, that Messiaen might not finish the work in time. She sent a letter to the composer by express post the next day:

After our telephone conversation yesterday which dismayed me, as you can imagine, I want once again to clarify some points concerning the presentation of your work *La Transfiguration* at the closing concert of the Tenth Gulbenkian Festival of Music. With regard to this, I enclose a photocopy of a letter sent to me by Mr Robert Bréchon, director of the Institut français in Portugal, which confirms what you have told me, which is that the problems raised by M. Rosenthal have been resolved by the ORTF. [. . .]

a. The ORTF has accepted Mr Rosenthal's requirements.
b. Mr Rosenthal thus has no valid reason for breaking the agreement he has made with the Gulbenkian Foundation and with you personally (see your letter of 17 November 1965).
c. The Gulbenkian Choir has set aside all the rehearsals from the month of April onwards in order to devote itself to learning your work.
d. The instrumental soloists requested by you, including the Percussions de Strasbourg, have accepted the invitations we have sent them. [. . .]

If, to our great regret and despite everything, you stand by your decision not to present *La Transfiguration* at our next festival, I will be obliged to ask you to confirm in writing the reasons which prevent you from finishing the work in time, so that I can present these to our governing body.

Messiaen responded on 19 March, complaining about the tight deadline (to which he had agreed in the first place), and the constant changes in arrangements for the concert and recording. It was, he explained, force of circumstances which obliged him to put off the first performance. He also gave a remarkable progress report on the state of work in the spring of 1966, one that has moved on somewhat from that outlined in his letter of 31 October 1965, not least the identification of structural weaknesses:

> The decision [to delay the performance] is not mine to make as we are faced with a situation which distresses me even more than it does you: I have fallen ill and aged ten years. The deadline was too short for such a monumental commission, and everything has conspired to prevent me finishing. And the fact of the matter is that I have not finished.
> You will acknowledge the following facts:
> 1. Philips has pulled out of the recording.
> 2. The soloists have still not received any contracts.
> 3. Mr Erlanger has refused to make any grant.
> 4. The conductor has been changed more than ten times.
> 5. Mr Rosenthal alone hung on bravely for as long as he could, before having to withdraw. [...]
> When Serge Koussevitzky commissioned my *Turangalîla-Symphonie* he gave me six years: two for researching, two for composing and two for the orchestration. For a work which is just as massive, you have given me nine months. I worked ceaselessly during the three months of the summer, when I was alone and peaceful in the mountains; since October I have returned to my class, my pupils, concerts abroad, recordings . . . and an enormous post-bag. Moreover, I have turned down four other commissions in order to do yours. It would have been a tour de force to have completed even half the work under these circumstances. I should explain to you that I have made a first sketch, with music and Latin words, which in many places consists of just the melodic line alone. To go more quickly, I am putting to one side my search for counterpoint, harmonies, orchestral timbres. Between October and December I have written the music for the ninth movement, and when I wanted to undertake the orchestration, I had to start with all these little scraps which consist of just a melodic line. In part, they are finished, but since most of the music has yet to be orchestrated, I would only be able to deliver a representative fragment. Moreover, in the course of my work I have discovered a formal imbalance: the piece lacks a development at the centre and a true finale. There are two pieces to add for which I have written no music at all yet. [...] So I do not want to pull out, but *circumstances force me to pull out.*

By the autumn of 1966, a new plan emerged: to perform the work in 1969, with Pierre Boulez conducting. Boulez wrote to Yvonne Loriod from Baden-Baden on 9 September cautiously agreeing to conduct, but only on certain conditions which were related to his ongoing battle with French officialdom in the mid-sixties and, especially, his well-publicized objections to the appointment of Marcel Landowski as head of the governing body for new music. This was to precipitate Boulez's resignation from the Domaine Musical, the publication of his article in the *Nouvel Observateur* denouncing the French minister of culture ('Why I say NO to Malraux'), and some extremely hostile reactions to these outbursts from the French press. Notable among these was Clarendon in *Le Figaro*, who decried Boulez's 'Hitlerian methods'.[8] So it was a bad moment to ask Boulez to work with a French orchestra, not least because one of his proposals to the Ministry of Culture had been to reorganize the five Paris orchestras into two flexible groups. In his letter to Loriod, Boulez made specific reference to his current thinking on French cultural policy:

Portugal in June 1969 might be possible, though only the first half, but not with a French orchestra. I refuse now to tour abroad with a French orchestra. If you can find a way of arranging things with, for example, the BBC or one of the German Radio stations, preferably Hamburg or Baden, that would suit me perfectly, especially an arrangement with the BBC (or the orchestra in Brussels, which is excellent). It isn't that I find the Orchestre National to be no good, quite the opposite, but after all the stories about Landowski, I do not want to set foot in a French organization. You know me very well, so you realize that I keep my promises![9]

By December 1966 Messiaen had solved the structural problems identified a year earlier, and *La Transfiguration* had grown considerably, reaching its final number of fourteen movements, divided into two seven-movement parts – 'septenaries' – and requiring six soloists instead of the five previously mentioned. On 18 December Messiaen wrote to Mme Perdigão about this, though he was distressed that she had not responded to a letter sent six weeks earlier. He was, however, delighted to report a discussion with Boulez about possible performing forces for the première:

Having returned from concerts in Germany and Czechoslovakia, I was expecting to find an answer to my letter, which I sent over a month and a half ago. I am astonished to find nothing. Many serious issues need to be considered:

My work now comprises fourteen sections, divided into two times seven, with the interval after the seventh. It takes a whole concert. It still requires a very large orchestra, a mixed chorus of 100 people, and six soloists: flute, Severino Gazzelloni; clarinet, Guy Deplus; xylo and marimba for the same player; and another marimba (these three instruments played by two of the Strasbourg percussionists, perhaps Jean Batigne and Georges Van Gucht);

piano solo, Yvonne Loriod; cello solo, Mstislav Rostropovich, who has agreed to play the part.

I have just spoken at length to Pierre Boulez, who was conducting my *Oiseaux exotiques* in Germany, and my *Chronochromie* in Brussels. Boulez is in London (England) from 21 May to 21 June 1969. He suggests coming to Portugal to conduct my work, between these two dates, with the best English orchestra, which he will be conducting at the time: the London Symphony Orchestra (LSO). Since Boulez arranges his calendar three or four years in advance, I would ask you to write to him *immediately*. [. . .] Several people who were present at the last festival in Lisbon have told me that since the centenary of Calouste Gulbenkian's birth falls in 1969, it would be preferable to delay the first performance of my work until 1969, and that you are of the same view.

I will finish my orchestration by January 1968 as planned, but it would be useful for us to have more than a year to deal with copying the orchestral material, chorus parts and parts for the soloists, and to correct these copies, as well as to have time for all the rehearsals.

Please be so kind as to do the following:

1. Let me know if you are in agreement with all these points, and in particular whether you would prefer 1968 or 1969 for the first performance.

2. Write to Pierre Boulez and the London Symphony Orchestra as quickly as possible.

3. Make arrangements with all the soloists, especially with Rostropovich, whose diary is very full. [. . .]

137 Messiaen and Boulez, Domaine Musical, Théâtre de l'Odéon, January 1966 (photo: Lipnitzki-Viollet).

138 Boulez, Loriod and Messiaen, recording *Couleurs de la Cité céleste*, 1966 (photo: Leloir).

Mme Perdigão responded just after Christmas, on 30 December, and she raised some practical difficulties with the arrangements proposed by Messiaen:

I was pleased to hear that Pierre Boulez has agreed to conduct *La Transfiguration* at the Gulbenkian Music Festival in 1969 with the London Symphony Orchestra. There are, however, some problems to resolve:

The date: I am going to insist to the governing body that the project must be postponed until 1969 and to give your reasons for this.

The orchestra: there has always been an issue of the first perfomance being entrusted to a French orchestra. Even if this idea is modified, the question of giving the performance of *La Transfiguration* to the London Symphony Orchestra poses difficulties with regard to rehearsals with the soloists (where will they take place? in London? in Lisbon?) and also with regard to the subsequent commercial recording of your work. On this last point, it would be preferable, I think, to ask a radio orchestra which is better used to the working conditions required for a recording.

I am, however, going to write immediately to Monsieur Boulez for reassurance that he accepts the plan in principle and I will think at the same time about the problems I have just outlined to you. As far as the London Symphony Orchestra and the soloists are concerned, I will write to them as soon as the problem of the date is definitively resolved, which I hope will be in the very near future.

139 Ozawa conducting *Sept Haïkaï* with Loriod at the piano, Besançon, 15 September 1966.

At the start of 1967 Messiaen went to several meetings of the committee which oversaw the foundation of a major new orchestra, the Orchestre de Paris, which was to succeed the Orchestre de la Société du Conservatoire. Other members of this committee included Jolivet, Dutilleux, Daniel-Lesur and Messiaen's pupil Serge Nigg, as well as Marcel Landowski (president of the new orchestra), André Malraux and Charles Münch. The orchestra's inaugural concert, conducted by Münch, was given in the Salle Pleyel on 14 November 1967.[10]

Messiaen's involvement demonstrated his increasing acceptance by the musical establishment: following the success of *Et exspecto*, he was becoming a more significant figure in French cultural politics. In 1966 he had been appointed – at last – Professor of Composition at the Conservatoire, and in April 1967 Pierre Belfond published Claude Samuel's *Entretiens avec Olivier Messiaen*. Later in the year (in December) he was elected to the Académie des Beaux-Arts of the Institut de France. The French establishment had accepted one of the nation's most original creative voices as one of its own.[11] This kind of recognition changed little in his working routine. At the Trinité he was increasingly frustrated by newer trends in French liturgical music (he particularly loathed the psalms and canticles by Joseph Gelineau), but he was almost always at the organ for First Communion and Confirmation Masses (when the latest songs would usually be used), as well as for Sundays and Feast Days.

In June 1967 Messiaen and Loriod went to Oxford, where Lina Lalandi had organized a series of concerts to celebrate Messiaen's music for that year's English Bach Festival. As well as organ recitals by Gillian Weir and Raffi Ourgandjian, highlights of this busy week included Charles Brück conducting *Turangalîla* (28 June), *Chronochromie* (29 June), and the *Sept Haïkaï* and *Couleurs de la Cité céleste* (30 June), Loriod and Messiaen playing *Visions de l'Amen* (1 July), and the complete *Catalogue d'oiseaux* played by Loriod with

140 Seiji Ozawa, Henri Dutilleux, Charles Münch and Messiaen at Besançon, 15 September 1966.

141 *Le Mystère de Dieu*, an evening at the Trinité on 23 November 1967, when Messiaen played improvisations which were subsequently developed into the *Méditations sur le mystère de la Sainte-Trinité*.

commentaries by the composer (2 July). Back in France, Michel Garcin of Erato suggested some new recording projects to Messiaen, including *Harawi* with either Régine Crespin or Martina Arroyo, but, sadly, nothing came of the idea. Messiaen's teaching commitments, touring, and his involvement in government committees meant that his first serious chance to carry on with *La Transfiguration* was not until early July. At this stage in the composition, it was details of timbre, of figuration and of orchestration which he was thinking about, as he noted in a diary entry at the end of June:

> In T[ransfiguration], especially in 'Terribilis' and in the third and fourth 'Récit Évangélique', use *speeds* ['allures']: undulations with differing rhythms, faster and slower trills with rhythms and chords of colours; *blocks* ['masses']: the same sonority multiplied by itself in different octaves. During the pauses, change timbres, change harmonies, evolving into complex sustained chords. Low sounds pianissimo, with speeds and blocks, high sounds in rapid counterpoint with hundreds of wild staccato notes in rapid demisemiquavers, pizzicato, or the sound of xylophones, or the sound of rain, or the crashing of rocks, or crackling of burning wood etc. [...] Choral voices superimposed in complex sonorities pianissimo, with mouths closed and open.

These vivid ideas were incorporated into *La Transfiguration* during the work's orchestration. A dramatic example can be found by comparing the short score[12] and the finished full score of the fourth 'Récit Évangélique' (movement 11). In the short score there is no indication of the trills on small bells (grelots) and luminophone which shimmer beneath the choir at the words 'dixeritis visionem donec Filius' (figure 6), or of the elaborate rhythms in the tubular bells, temple blocks, gongs and tam-tams in the music which opens this movement. Here Messiaen is using the process of orchestration not merely as a chore, but as an opportunity to refine and to elaborate his initial ideas.

On 23 November 1967 the Trinité celebrated its centenary with a special event billed as *Le Mystère de Dieu*. Monsignor Charles, famous for his sermons at the Sacré-Cœur, was invited to preach, and Messiaen provided a series of improvisations, which he planned with even greater care than usual, so much so that some of his sketched outlines for these improvisations were to be developed to form part of his next great organ cycle. Yvonne Loriod recounts a snatch of conversation between Messiaen and the Monsignor about a practical matter:

> Mgr Charles: How will I know when your improvisations are finished?
> Messiaen: My wife can switch a light on and off, or even better, I will finish each improvisation with the song of the yellowhammer: seven repeated

142 Messiaen playing the organ at the Trinité, 23 November 1967 (photo: Rancy).

notes, followed by a long held note, which you'll recognize easily.

This delightful idea was preserved in the work which partly evolved from these improvisations: the *Méditations sur le Mystère de la Sainte-Trinité*. But composing this had to wait until *La Transfiguration* was finished, and it was nearly two years later, in the summer of 1969, that Messiaen was finally able to devote himself to this new organ project.

There had been attempts to stage *Turangalîla* as a ballet going right back to the European première at the Aix-en-Provence Festival in 1950. On that occasion Messiaen was approached by Hubert Devillez, who worked for the French tax authorities, but whose ambition was to have a ballet scenario accepted by the Paris Opéra. In about 1952 Devillez drew up an outline for *Turangalîla* which was rejected by the Opéra on the grounds that it was too lurid, though only after two possible choreographers had been mentioned (Serge Lifar and Léonide Massine).

On 22 June 1960 the Hamburg Opera put on a ballet based on the third, fourth and fifth movements of *Turangalîla*, choreographed by Peter van Dyk, who was just starting to work as a choreographer while still dancing for Lifar at the Paris Opéra (it was perhaps Lifar who gave him the idea for a *Turangalîla* ballet). The three scenes are listed in the programme as 'Solitude', 'Chant d'amour' and 'Danse joyeuse', and in his programme note Antoine Goléa described the ballet as 'a choreographic symphony without plot'. Messiaen did not attend the performances and, according to Loriod, he was unhappy about the project.[13]

Plans for a *Turangalîla* ballet at the Opéra wouldn't go away. In spring 1964 Messiaen saw Georges Auric (Director of the Opéra) and the great dancer and choreographer Janine Charrat. His diary on 20 April included a fairly detailed account of their meeting, though for the time being there was no further progress: 'See Auric with Charrat. Establish the symbolism and choreography, and discuss a conductor, set designer and costume designer. Charrat wants to be the choreographer. Coloured projections, turning movements, a fateful statue, flowers, a man killed by a falling block, the lovers in rings of glass, several couples in circles turning in combined movements, fire, pairs of stars, pairs of fantastic birds, a multiplicity of imprecise symbols, without plot, marvellous colours.'

In autumn 1967 plans for *Turangalîla* at the Opéra were resuscitated, but with a different choreographer: on 27 November Messiaen went to see Auric and Roland Petit at the Opéra, and he was persuaded that with Petit as choreographer the ballet might work. Various names were mentioned in connection with the set designs, including Marc Chagall, though the eventual choice was the great Surrealist painter Max Ernst. Manuel Rosenthal was chosen to conduct, and a tape of a broadcast performance by Rosenthal and the Orchestre National was used for the rehearsals.

The first performance of Roland Petit's *Turangalîla*, on 21 June 1968, was a considerable success. Manuel Rosenthal conducted, and Yvonne and Jeanne Loriod were the soloists. But the embittered and persistent Devillez had come back into the picture while the production was in rehearsal: he proposed legal action against the Opéra for not using his scenario. The theatre and Durand both dismissed his claims, and Petit simply tore up the letters; Devillez was thus left with nobody to prosecute apart from the hapless composer. Messiaen took advice and was assured that it was an open and shut case, and so it seemed, though – incredibly – Messiaen went on to lose.[14]

In his programme note for the first performance, Roland Petit wrote about his meetings with Messiaen over the ballet, and reported the composer's initial reaction:

'Nobody in the world will dance to my music', exclaimed Olivier Messiaen twenty years ago when I told him that I wanted to stage a ballet based on *Turangalîla*. Since then, he has refused the suggestions of several choreographers. But I did not forget *Turangalîla*. This winter I tried once again to persuade Messiaen. To my great surprise, he said yes. Since I had to work on a ballet abroad, I took a tape recording of *Turangalîla*, some sheets of paper and drawing pencils, and I wrote a libretto. I then had another meeting with Messiaen. He told me that he, too, had written a libretto. We looked at each other a little suspiciously: which one of us would be the first to describe the ballet to the other? I let Messiaen have priority – and he had exactly the same ideas as mine!

For Messiaen, as for me, *Turangalîla* is a ballet without a story. A great wave of love, and a quest for the absolute, which can only be reached after death. *Turangalîla* thus meets *Tristan et Iseult*. The ballet comprises ten movements. [. . .] No stories, and choreography which is often 'horizontal' – more slid than danced, with the dancers lying on the stage, evoking movements from Far Eastern dance.

The production received widespread attention, and it was reported by Ossia Trilling in *The Times* (27 June 1968), a review which suggests that Petit achieved just what he set out to do with his 'horizontal' choreography:

The most exciting feature of the opulent choreography is the way in which the intricate balletic pattern is made to form and re-form on the shiny reflective groundcloth. Petit's rhapsodic style lends itself ideally to the score and the formalized groupings remind one sharply that the floor is not only a surface to dance on with the feet but the background for endless and complex variations on which the human rump and other parts of the body can be placed to graceful aesthetic purpose.

The shape of the choreography and its present style no doubt derive from the etymology of the title, which in Sanskrit conveys a whole series of notions from love song to rhythmic movement, and the ten sections are ingeniously strung together to make a single plastic poem, a hymn to love, to life and to death, and all the other passions that the human form is capable of stimulating in the aware spectator.

Messiaen was delighted with this production, and described it in glowing terms to Almut Rössler in 1983: 'That was absolutely excellent, the work of Roland Petit. In itself, my music isn't suitable to dancing. I wouldn't have thought it could be used as a ballet, but then I found it very good. It was performed only once and will never be performed again because of a lawsuit between me and the author of the "story".'[15]

Messiaen continued to work on *La Transfiguration* well into 1968 – a year which saw dreadful scenes of violent unrest between students and police on the streets of Paris. On 29 June 1968 Messiaen wrote to Mme Perdigão informing her about his extremely busy schedule at the time, and referring to these traumatic events of May–June 1968 in Paris, which had greatly disrupted his work on the closing stages of *La Transfiguration* as well as rehearsals for the *Turangalîla* ballet. Messiaen's letter also included a further progress report on *La Transfiguration*, as well as some of his customary worries about soloists. Boulez was now out of the picture for the première, and the work was to be played by the newly formed Orchestre de Paris:

Thank you for all your letters. My numerous concerts abroad, as well as those of my wife, and all the recent events have turned my calendar upside down. Now I must leave for England, and the new term at the Conservatoire has been rearranged for 1 September instead of 1 October. So I need to work for you ceaselessly, away from Paris, during July and August. [. . .]

My work is now very advanced and I have no more than three large sections to orchestrate out of fourteen, which will take about six months. [. . .]

I am working for you every day and this work will certainly be the largest work I have ever written, in terms of length and performing forces.

On 5 July 1968 Mme Perdigão replied to Messiaen:

I completely understand that recent events have thrown your diary into chaos and I wish you all the best for the work which still remains for you to do in order to finish *La Transfiguration*.

1. First of all, I must ask you when you think you will be able to send us the vocal parts, so that we can organize the rehearsal schedule for the Gulbenkian Chorus. Concerning this I must not forget to say how pleased I am that you accept our point of view about the collaboration of the Gulbenkian Chorus which will now definitely be involved in the first performance of your work.

2. We are delighted that Mme Yvonne Loriod is able to play the piano solo part in Portugal as we have always thought of her as the person to do this.

By 30 September Messiaen reported that just two movements (nos.12 and 13) remained to be orchestrated and that the rest of the work was finished. In November he predicted with confidence that work would be completed in January 1969.

On 23 February he wrote to Mme Perdigão:

I am writing to announce some great news: my work is completely finished. To be exact, it was finished on 21 February, the day before yesterday. [. . .]

As I have already explained, I have for the moment taken on all the expenses of copying, photocopying and printing which will amount to more than 2,000,000 old francs. I will sort out reimbursement of all these expenses with my publisher, after the first performance.

I think I now deserve the rest of my payment. You can send it whenever you like. (I actually deserve a great deal more than was agreed, given that I have worked for four years instead of the one which was intended. I leave that for you and your husband to consider . . . and forgive me for speaking so frankly about these material questions!)

I think it better if nobody attends the rehearsals in Lisbon, neither friends nor critics and others, except the dress rehearsal on 7 June, if Serge Baudo gives his consent.

I do not want to give a talk at the Gulbenkian Cultural Centre in Paris on a work which has not yet been heard: that would be harmful.

On 15 March Messiaen wrote again to Mme Perdigão, irritated at the lack of any response to his letter, but reporting that the performance material for the whole of the first septenary was now photocopied and bound, and that he had given this to Pierre Salzmann, who was to train the Gulbenkian Chorus for the première. Messiaen suggested that Salzmann should return to Paris on about 14 April in order to go through the score of the second septenary and take the material back to Lisbon. Messiaen then turned to the matter of choir rehearsals: 'I must insist on a minimum of 30 rehearsals for the choir alone', adding that without that many 'we will never get there', and pointing out that this schedule only amounted to about two rehearsals for each of the fourteen movements.

While the first half of 1969 was mostly concerned with the forthcoming première of *La Transfiguration*, there were also a number of concerts: on 24 January Gaston Litaize gave a broadcast recital entirely devoted to the music of his old classmate: *Le Banquet céleste*, *Apparition de l'Église éternelle* and the whole of *La Nativité*. Messiaen was delighted (noting Litaize's 'magnificent playing' in his diary). On 30 January he jotted down some preliminary thoughts for a new commission for the 1971 Royan Festival – never realized – to write a work for Couraud's choir: 'Voices: spoken, sung, noises and onomatopoeia, with two sets of bells, two flutes, three trombones, bass trombone, onde, piano, gongs and tam-tam.' Always loyal to his friends in La Jeune France, Messiaen went to see Auric on 16 February to ask for a small prize from the Institut for Yves Baudrier, who was living in poverty; Auric agreed to award Baudrier the modest sum of 1,000 francs. Despite numerous appointments with copyists (preparing the material for *La Transfiguration*), Messiaen was able to go to Rome on 25 February, and over the next few days recorded a busy tourist itinerary in his diary. On 26 February: 'saw the Coliseum, the Forum, the Capitol' and two days later 'the Farnese gardens, orange trees with fruit on them, Japanese cherry trees, mimosas, palms, cypresses, umbrella pines'.

Back in Paris, on 10 March Messiaen was at the Trinité for a special Mass in memory of Berlioz (who had died almost exactly a hundred years before, on 8 March 1869). His diary recorded what must have been a notable occasion: 'I play an introit and sortie *fortissimo*, and improvise on themes by Berlioz.' Henri Dutilleux was present, and recalled that Messiaen improvised on the opening unisons of the 'Évocation' (Scene XII) from *La Damnation de Faust*.[16] On 16 March he played for a Confirmation Mass, performing triumphal opening and closing voluntaries, and doing the best he could with the accompaniments to the jaunty choruses which the children sang. (Loriod recalled these with amusement: 'Some of them, like *Oui, oui, oui, Jésus, compte sur moi*, were catchy, with the "ouis" being real shouts of joy which could raise the roof. But others were absolute horrors of word-setting, with soppy melodies and harmonies so feeble that Théodore Dubois would be weeping up in heaven!')

At the end of April 1969 there was a minor crisis when Serge Baudo flew to Lisbon, only to discover that his scores for *La Transfiguration* had not travelled with him. They turned up a few days later in Dakar, having been misrouted by the airline, but it was a worrying moment for all concerned, especially as there were only a few weeks to go before the première. Rehearsals for the orchestra began in Paris on 27 May (at the Gaieté-Lyrique theatre) and five days and nights of intensive work ensued. 1 June, a Sunday, was a busy one for Messiaen, as his diary records: after 7 a.m. Mass at Sainte-Geneviève-des-Grandes-Carrières, and voting at 8 a.m. (in the first round of the Presidential elections – Georges Pompidou was the eventual winner), the Messiaens took a flight to Lisbon later that morning, then a train to Coimbra at 2.10 p.m., in order to be there for a concert that evening, when Loriod played nine *Regards* and Marcel Couraud conducted the *Cinq Rechants*. The same programme was repeated in Lisbon the next night, and on 3 June the final rehearsals for *La Transfiguration* began.

On the night of the concert itself, 7 June, in the spectacular Coliseu, there were alarums backstage when Rostropovich failed to appear. Mme Perdigão phoned his hotel room and was told there was no reply. Not one to give up easily, she went to his hotel and made her way to the great cellist's room only to find him in bed with a fever, the result of food-poisoning. After five years of patient negotiations, arrangements and numerous rearrangements, Mme Perdigão was sympathetic but firm: Slava must get up at once; she would take his cello and music in her car, and he should follow in a taxi as soon as possible. Knowing nothing of all this, the vast audience was becoming restless at the delayed start, but eventually an ailing and feverish Rostropovich arrived, and the performance began. Despite Rostropovich's fragile state of health, the work was a triumph. Nine thousand people applauded for half an hour at the end, and Messiaen's reaction was even more enthusiastic than usual – as was his use of exclamation marks when he noted in his diary a 'succès absolument formidable!!!!!'

The empty pages in Messiaen's diary for August 1969 are testimony to time spent in Petichet on creative activity, but at the end of the month he travelled to Iran for a few days of concerts and sightseeing. The Messiaens arrived in Tehran by plane on 30 August. On 2 September the Orchestre National de France under Bruno Maderna gave an open-air concert at Persepolis including Mozart's Piano Concerto K503 (with Loriod) and *Et exspecto resurrectionem mortuorum*. Whenever Messiaen was abroad for performances of his music, he took every opportunity to notate birdsong, and this trip was no exception: on the afternoon of 4 September he wrote down 'the song of a bird soloist, similar to a rock thrush or black wheatear? Sunset. Golden glory among the columns.' Messiaen was unsure of the bird's identity at the time, and its song appeared in no.7 of the *Méditations* as 'oiseau de Persépolis' (he later identified it as a

143 Loriod and Maria Madalena de Azeredo Perdigão, with Messiaen in the background, 2 June 1969.

bulbul). The Messiaens returned to Paris on 7 September and Messiaen took the opportunity to try out some of his new work on the Trinité organ. After a visit to Ghent for a performance of the *Liturgies* on 13 September, the Messiaens were back in Petichet two days later and remained there until 29 September. Composition of the *Méditations sur le Mystère de la Sainte Trinité* was completed by the end of this stay. Back in Paris, on 10 October, he had the manuscript photocopied. The première was planned well in advance (in Messiaen's diary for 1970 there is already a note that it would be 'in Washington on 20 March 1972').

A more pressing concern was the first performance in Paris of *La Transfiguration*. This took place at the Palais de Chaillot on 20 October. It was the climax of an entire day of Messiaen-related events, beginning with a recital by Loriod at 12.30 p.m. in the Chaillot's small Salle Gémier (five pieces from the *Catalogue d'oiseaux*). At 4.30 p.m. a film of the Chartres *Et exspecto* was shown,[17] followed at 6.30 p.m. by a performance of the *Quatuor pour la fin du Temps*. *La Transfiguration* was given at 8 p.m. with the same soloists and conductor as at the Lisbon première.

144 The first performance of *La Transfiguration de Notre-Seigneur Jésus-Christ* at the Coliseu, Lisbon, 7 June 1969.

At the start of November, Messiaen remembered the death of Claire ten years earlier: on 2 November, with melancholy appropriateness – this was Claire's birthday as well as the feast of All Souls – he went to the cemetery of Bourg-la-Reine to place an inscription on her grave. The bizarre Devillez affair rumbled on with a hearing at the Palais de Justice about the *Turangalîla* ballet on 1 December. But there were more pleasant distractions too. On 8 December 1969 Messiaen was present at the sessions for *Visions de l'Amen* played by Katia and Marielle Labèque – their first commercial recording. Still in their teens,[18] the two sisters played the work with tremendous youthful passion and energy under the composer's enthusiastic supervision. The venue for the recording was the Salle Adyar, in the 7th arrondissement, the striking art nouveau building in the square Rapp belonging to the Theosophical Society.

145 With Katia and Marielle Labèque, recording *Visions de l'Amen* in December 1969.

146 Messiaen notating a blue rock thrush, Rome, 7 May 1970.

At the end of April 1970 the Messiaens went to Italy for concerts and a few days of sightseeing in Milan and in Assisi – a visit which was to have enduring consequences. As well as hearing birdsong, he also attended Mass in the Basilica of Saint Francis (where the saint is buried) and made careful notes on the frescos in his diary.

La Fauvette des jardins ('The Garden Warbler'), a majestic supplement to the *Catalogue d'oiseaux* and Messiaen's longest single movement for solo piano, took up much of summer 1970. Before setting off for Petichet that year, a particularly extensive list of things to take away filled his diary. This included material related to the *Traité* and the proofs of *La Transfiguration*; he also packed scores of several piano works including Debussy's *Préludes* and *Études*, Jolivet's *Mana* and Milhaud's *Saudades do Brasil* along with orchestral works by Ligeti and Penderecki, theological and ornithological books, and records of birdsong. In fact, the inspiration for *La Fauvette des jardins* was in his own garden at Petichet: at 4 o'clock in the morning on 6 July he notated a 'grand solo' by a garden warbler, and he did the same again the next day. This productive summer idyll was interrupted by an important event: the Messiaens travelled to London for the British première of *La Transfiguration*. This was on 17 July at the Royal Albert Hall as the opening night of that year's Proms. The conductor was Serge Baudo and the soloists included Loriod and Maurice Gendron. Messiaen noted in his diary: '4,000 people in the hall – a formidable success!!!' The day before, Messiaen was presented with an honorary degree by the Royal Academy of Music and the Messiaens were also able to savour the delights of London's Chinese and Indian restaurants before returning to Paris on 18 July and Petichet the next day. Serious work on *La Fauvette des jardins* began again, though Messiaen also took the time to note some minor revisions to the tempo and expression marks in *La Transfiguration* in the light of the London performance.

A constant flow of new ideas was noted in Messiaen's diary, as on 31 July when he jotted down a scheme for a piano concerto:

Write a concerto of the mountains (piano and orchestra):
  I. Le grand Serre et Le Galibier
  II. Persépolis et les tombeaux des rois perses
 III. La Jungfrau et Le Trommelbach

While this remained only a plan, the sheer grandeur of the music of *La Fauvette des jardins* suggests a similar kind of homage to landscape. Indeed, as with many of the pieces in the *Catalogue d'oiseaux*, the music is as much about the setting for the birds as the birds themselves. For *La Fauvette des jardins* the scene has a particular significance, being nothing less than the view over which Messiaen gazed from his studio at Petichet, down to the Lac de Laffrey and up the far side to the 'bald-headed' summit of the Grand Serre. Strangely, the *Catalogue* had lacked a full celebration of this spectacular landscape; the two pieces that took place in or around Petichet had rather specialized subjects, 'Le Chocard des Alpes' being set high above the snowline, and 'La Buse variable' taken up with an undignified scrap between the buzzard and a flock of marauding crows.

Also overdue was a piece dedicated to the garden warbler, a bird of such virtuosity that in his *cahiers* Messiaen had to devise a unique mode of notation, cramming down the notes – without indicating rhythm, timbre or dynamic – as the only way he could keep pace with the torrent of song.

As in the two largest pieces from the *Catalogue* – 'La Rousserolle effarvatte' and 'Le Traquet stapazin' – the piece follows a complete day, from the darkness before dawn to nightfall. Unlike them, however, it has no depictions of sunrise and sunset. Instead, the passing of time is measured more subtly by the music of the lake, as it mirrors the changing colours of the sky, or reflects the trees at the water's edge and the 'green-gold' of the mountain. This progress reaches its culmination in one of Messiaen's most inspired pages, a slow chorale ('calm, ecstatic'), with the lake basking in the full light of afternoon.

The emphasis on colour extends to the song of the garden warbler, which carries the music forward in a series of immense and inexhaustibly varied solos. Again the approach is quite different from that of the *Catalogue*. In 'Le Loriot' the warbler's song had been used as decoration, adorning the rising of the sun in a frenetic blur. In *La Fauvette des jardins* Messiaen's concern is with richness of timbre, and he sacrifices speed (the tempo is markedly more spacious) to allow the harmonies space to speak, especially at the many cadences. The effect Messiaen wanted from the pianist can be seen in the indications added by him and by Loriod to the manuscript score from which she studied the piece (markings in her handwriting that have Messiaen's authority are annotated 'O. dixit'). These stress the weight, depth and variety of tone required, and the eloquent style of performance: the sequence on the final page, for example, is marked 'majestic and overwhelming climax [. . .] the memory [of the lake], always very

147 Loriod and Messiaen with her parents, Simone and Gaston, at the Gorges de la Bourne near Petichet, 1970.

slow and solemn – don't hurry!' Similarly, Messiaen told Peter Hill to resist the tendency to play this very taxing music like an étude: the solos for the garden warbler were to be 'always "easy", relaxed and cantabile'.[1]

Though the Messiaens returned to Paris on 22 September, it was only for a week. On 27 September they dined at the Critérion restaurant with Yvonne's parents and her sister Jacqueline – a reunion which was to have a special poignancy – and two days later, on 29 September, they flew to New York for the start of a six-week tour of the USA and Canada, with an itinerary which necessitated criss-crossing the continent. In Calgary on 6 October they were shocked to hear of the sudden death of Loriod's mother, Simone. To make matters worse, the tour schedule made it impossible to return to Paris to attend the funeral.

It was during this visit that a commission from Alice Tully for a new work was confirmed. Messiaen asked if it would be possible for him to seek inspiration amid some of America's greatest mountain landscapes rather than among the skyscrapers of Manhattan. The impresario Herbert Breslin, who took care of the practical aspects of this commission on behalf of Mrs Tully, agreed to arrange a trip to Utah at a good time of year for the scenery and for the birdsong – a journey which the Messiaens took in 1972.

Back in Paris, another commission had been proposed. Messiaen noted in his diary on 15 December: 'a *Symphonie théologique* for Solti and the Orchestre de Paris.' Nothing came of the plan, but just before Christmas, on 22 December, Messiaen put down some early thoughts on the commission for Alice Tully: 'Work on the Tully commission for New York. Duration: 20 minutes, to be finished by 1 October 1973, the copying and photocopying to be paid for by me. Performance in April 1974. A total fee of 4 million old francs, with 10% for Breslin. Orchestra of 43 players and solo piano.' This was a modest estimate: while the details of the scoring remained largely the same, the Tully commission was to become Messiaen's longest orchestral work, lasting ninety minutes.

On 28 January 1971 Katia and Marielle Labèque gave a concert performance of *Visions de l'Amen*, following their recording for Erato. The concert took place at the new Espace Pierre Cardin – an ambitious arts centre just off the Champs-Élysées conceived by the leading fashion designer who was also an enthusiastic supporter of the arts. Loriod recalled that Cardin himself designed striking new outfits for these two beautiful and brilliant sisters – colourful tops (one in yellow, the other in purple) and black silk trousers – and that the pianos were placed, unusually, at the extreme left and right of the stage.[2]

Messiaen's pupil Jean-Pierre Guézec died at the age of thirty-six on 9 March, and at the 1971 Royan Festival, less than a month later, a musical tribute was paid to this young composer. On the morning of 6 April, the first half of the memorial concert was presented as a *Tombeau de Jean-Pierre Guézec*. Eight composers had written pieces for solo instruments: Gilbert Amy (for flute), André Boucourechliev (clarinet), Marius Constant (double bass), Georges Couroupos (oboe), Betsy Jolas (cor anglais), Alain Louvier (bassoon), Iannis Xenakis (cello) and Messiaen, whose piece was for solo horn. Messiaen made a fair copy as early as 20 March (noted in his diary), so his response to Guézec's death was not only deeply felt but immediate. An autograph manuscript has the title *Pièce pour cor (à la mémoire de Jean-Pierre Guézec)*,[3] and this piece was to find its final home – with the new title 'Appel interstellaire' – as the sixth movement of *Des Canyons aux étoiles*. It was first played at the Royan concert by Daniel Bourgue.

148 Messiaen at Royan in 1971.

In mid-May Messiaen and Loriod were in Florence for a concert at the Maggio Musicale, but they also took time to visit the Convent of San Marco to look at the frescos painted around 1440 by Fra Angelico (whose name is circled twice in Messiaen's diary). Messiaen was overwhelmed by these, and bought several prints of angel musicians which he put on the wall of his study in the rue Marcadet. On the way home, the couple stopped in Milan, where Messiaen was delighted to be able to climb onto the roof of the cathedral (as he had done the previous year) and to marvel at the extraordinary statues. He also took time to note the details of a drink he enjoyed: 'Drank a cocktail of orangeade – orange, pineapple, strawberry – in enormous round glasses (like punch glasses or the monsters which hold a litre of beer).'

Back in Paris, there was a nostalgic reunion of all four composers of La Jeune France at the ORTF on 2 June, for a broadcast discussion with Pierette Mari. The next morning, wearing his Academician's robes, Messiaen was at Saint-Sulpice for a sombre occasion: the funeral of his beloved teacher Marcel Dupré, who had died on 30 May. On the evening of 5 June Messiaen set out for Munich, where Rafael Kubelík was preparing performances of *La Transfiguration*.

It was not until the end of June that Messiaen was able to get back to work on the Tully commission. In his diary he listed what he needed for the summer: 'The commission from Mrs Tully must be ready before 31 March 1974 – music finished, orchestration finished, the score photocopied and the orchestral material copied. Take books on astronomy, books and my notes on the birds of the USA, books on Utah, Arizona and [unspecified] Islands.' By 8 July plans had advanced considerably, with a diary entry outlining in severely abstract terms what was to become the work's third movement ('Ce qui est écrit sur les étoiles. . .') along with some more general thoughts, and a working title: *Transmutations*, for piano and orchestra:

149 Marcel Dupré and Messiaen at the Institut de France, 15 May 1968 (photo: Rancy).

150 Messiaen and Rafael Kubelík behind the gongs after a rehearsal for *La Transfiguration* in Munich, June 1971.

151 Loriod, Messiaen and Josette, summer 1971.

For the Tully commission:

Méné: Weighed – Transmutations, with the same musical material: high or low, fast or slow, *ff* or *pp*, slurred or detached, undulating slowly or trilled.

Tekhel: Counted (the numbers) – divisions of duration, retrograde rhythms from the centre to the extremes, from the extremes to the centre, rhythmic personalities, rhythmic canons, permutations.

Oupharsin: Divided (superimposed tempos, different tempos together, glissandos, irrational note values [. . .] etc.).

Transmutations for piano solo and orchestra.

Beyond that, there is little in the diary to record Messiaen's progress on the work, but the evidence of empty pages indicates that he was able to devote himself almost entirely to the new composition without distractions. Apart from visits from Pascal and Josette at the end of July, and from Loriod's father and sister for a week in August, it was a summer during which plenty of creative work could be done.

The fair copy of the *Méditations sur le mystère de la Sainte-Trinité* had been finished and during late October Messiaen worked at the Trinité on registrations. On 8 November he gave a private performance of the work for the organist Almut Rössler, who was to give the first European performance in June 1972.

On 29 November the Messiaens travelled to Annecy for two performances of *Visions de l'Amen*, preceded by three *Regards*. Loriod recalled that the first of these concerts was during the afternoon, for schoolchildren, with explanations of the work by Messiaen: 'The children were excited by the music and some of them started to dance in the wide central aisle – silently of course.'[4]

The second performance was given that evening, and the programme was repeated over the next few days at Chambéry and then at Dole (in the Jura). On the day of the Dole concert, the train in which they were travelling stopped unexpectedly, and Messiaen noted the display which the natural world put on for them:

> Feast of the Immaculate Conception, 8 December, on the train. Stopped in open countryside near Auxonne because of an accident in the restaurant car, causing a delay of one and a half hours. For more than five minutes we were able to watch a completely white sun, visible with the naked eye (through a grey sky), then it became bright violet (lilac purple) and occasionally there were shafts of violet sunlight, then a grey-black sky covered it, and all that remained was pink light beneath the clouds.

Messiaen's diary for December recorded those to whom he was sending gifts of money: his aunt Tatin ('Tantique'), and two composers he admired, both living in straightened circumstances: Yves Baudrier and Ivan Wyschnegradsky.

Early in 1972 Leduc stopped work on an edition of the solo horn piece in memory of Guézec, since Messiaen had now decided that he wanted to include it in his new work for Mrs Tully. On 11 March the Messiaens flew to Washington, where the composer gave the first performance of the *Méditations* at the Basilica of the Immaculate Conception on 20 March. He spent many hours at the organ, experimenting with its immense array of sonorities very different from those of the Trinité instrument; but rehearsal times needed to fit around the numerous Masses at this National Shrine, so Messiaen was usually at work from 7 a.m. for a few hours, and then during the late evening. He gave a press conference on 18 March to introduce the work, and the première itself – before an audience of 3,000 – was preceded by a half-hour recital on the basilica's carillon.

152 Messiaen with Gilbert Leduc, 1972.

Antal Dorati conducted the US première of *La Transfiguration* in Washington on 28 March, followed by two further performances there, and one at Carnegie Hall, New York, on 2 April. This was Easter Sunday and Messiaen was delighted: 'All of the Westminster Choir (young men and women) were dressed in long red robes!!! A magnificent effect!!! at all four concerts of T[ransfiguration] and for the 125 choristers!' Two days after the Carnegie Hall concert, the Messiaens played *Visions de l'Amen* at Hunter College, then travelled to Appleton, Wisconsin, for a repeat performance on 6 April. On 7 April they flew to San Francisco. This turned out to be a dramatic trip: a

153 Messiaen at the organ of the Basilica of the Immaculate Conception, Washington DC, 20 March 1972 (photo: Robert G. Heittman).

violent blizzard forced the small plane to land at Milwaukee and the passengers had to battle through a tornado to reach the airport buildings, where a four-hour delay was cheered by a meeting with the pianist James Avery, who had been to several of the Messiaens' concerts in the previous few days. In Berkeley they were looked after by the pianist Joaquín Nin-Culmell, whom Messiaen had not seen since the 1930s.[5] A recital by Loriod on 9 April in Berkeley was followed by a few days in Pasadena for *Visions de l'Amen* on 12 April; but this was a visit which had a significant bonus for Messiaen when he was taken by the space scientist Paco Lagerstrom to a nearby canyon to see (and notate) Mockingbirds and other birds native to the West Coast. On 13 April the couple arrived in Los Angeles, where Messiaen was able to see Zubin Mehta to discuss *Et exspecto*. The following day it was back to France, but only for a short stay. According to Loriod, Messiaen had thrown himself on the mercy of Raymond Gallois-Montbrun, the Conservatoire's director, for permission to be absent for a second trip to the USA.[6]

The couple flew to Washington on 26 April for the recording of *La Transfiguration* conducted by Dorati. They stayed at the Watergate Hotel, in a self-catering apartment where Loriod was able to do the cooking. During the stay, the Messiaens met Gillian Weir, who was going to give the British première of the *Méditations*. She recalled the meeting in her diary:

Sunday April 30. What a day. Set off for the Shrine at 9.30, in time for the 10.30 meeting arranged with Messiaen. Last night the clocks were set forward, and they must not have known, as they didn't arrive till 11.15 and made no mention of it. They are simply incredible people, I fell in love with both of them immediately. [. . .] I was sick with fright at meeting him, especially having to manage in French. [. . .] They were both unbelievably natural and friendly; they simply don't seem to realise how fantastically famous they are. [. . .] After only a few minutes he started talking about the new piece; I was wondering how to approach it, but he started right in, and incredible though it seems, they really seem to appreciate my playing it, rather than the reverse. [. . .] Messiaen was saying that he himself would copy the piece and send it to me by June 1st! [. . .] I was so thrilled, and tried to thank him, but charming Loriod joined him in saying no, no, we must thank you for playing his music. She always referred to him simply as 'Messiaen'. [. . .] He spoke excitedly about the *trompette en chamade* [organ stop] at the Shrine, and somewhere else – he is, of course, completely a Romantic. [. . .] He warned that it [*Méditations*] is extremely difficult; I wish I had thought to ask whether it is more difficult than the other works and in what way. [. . .] M. said that the plates won't be ready for final correction until January, and he doesn't expect the work to be published for over a year. [. . .] She is adorable, and so is he; I don't see how anyone could resist falling in love with both of them. Certainly they are so happy together that they restore one's faith in love itself. She directs him and affectionately gets him about; he patters after her, 'taking care of her' in that endearing, half-worried way that older men often – no, sometimes have, because it is too fragilely affectionate to happen very often.[7]

Once the recording sessions were finished, the Messiaens flew to Utah for a trip which was to have far-reaching creative consequences. Arrangements had been made for an extended trip to some of America's most dramatic scenery which would serve as Messiaen's inspiration for the Tully commission. After spending the night of 1 May in Salt Lake City, the Messiaens were taken on the four-hour drive to Bryce Canyon. For three days there, Messiaen filled numerous notebooks with birdsong notations. He carefully noted in his diary what he saw and heard:

2 May: Brown-headed Cowbird and Yellow-headed Blackbird.

3 May: Robin. At Fairyland View (near the entrance to the canyon): Red-shafted Flicker, Steller's Jay. Rainbow Point, Penderosa Point. At Agua Canyon: Cooper's Hawk. At Bryce Canyon Bridge: Clark's Nutcracker and Grey-headed Junco. At Sunset Point – magnificent – great columns of

154 Messiaen at Bryce Canyon, May 1972.

bold red and orange, awe-inspiring entrances and mysterious chasms – an amphitheatre – 7 km on foot in the Canyons.

4 May: 6.20 a.m.: Robin. From 10 a.m. until 1 p.m. on foot to Sunset Point. See the view from above, then descend into the valley and climb up again on the sandstone paths – Sublime!!! Evening: Brown-headed Cowbird. Bought a rock of copper sulphate from Arizona.

5 May: 5.20 a.m.: Pygmy Owl. 10.30 a.m.: Dixie National Forest – Western Bluebird, Robin, Cowbird, Western Meadowlark. 5 p.m. descent into Bryce Canyon, from Sunrise Point to Queens Garden. Rocks reaching into the sky.

6 May: 7 a.m.: Western Meadowlark.

On 7 May the Messiaens went to Cedar Breaks and the next day they were driven to Zion Lodge, stopping on the way in Springdale, where Messiaen bought rocks and crystals. At Zion Lodge they stayed in one of the chalets and Messiaen made an excited note in his diary about a walk in the forest on 9 May: 'Suddenly there was a fortissimo chorus of Nutcrackers, very noisy and very excited, calling to each other from the mountain tops! A symphony of whirling sounds, with crescendos and diminuendos with the entry of the chorus *fff*! A truly joyous commotion as each bird wanted to add its own chattering to join in this unbelievable symphony, so loud that the mountains seemed to shake.' The stay in Zion Park was brief, just two days, since the Messiaens needed to set out for Los Angeles on 10 May. A car journey across part of the Nevada Desert was followed by a flight from Las Vegas to Los Angeles, where the composer attended Zubin Mehta's rehearsals and concert (12 May) of *Et exspecto* before returning to Paris.

During the last week of May and the start of June, Messiaen spent a great deal of time at the Trinité preparing for his Erato recording of the *Méditations*, made between 29 May and 3 June. On this last date he was at the organ for a quite different purpose – the Profession of Faith by the girls from the Lycée Jules Ferry – as well as for their Mass the next day. On 7 June the Messiaens left for Düsseldorf where Almut Rössler gave the first European performance of the *Méditations* (10 June). Back in Paris, Alain Périer had found a publisher for his forthcoming book on Messiaen and visited his former teacher on 13 June for the first of numerous interviews. On 17 and 18 June, Felicity Palmer and Pierre Boulez (with the BBC Symphony Orchestra) recorded the *Poèmes pour Mi* in London, but Messiaen remained in Paris because of an obligation to play for a Profession of Faith, this time by the boys of the Lycée Condorcet. Given how busy Messiaen was, his commitment to these celebrations of the faith of young people is particularly touching.

There had been little time for any composing, so it was with relief that Messiaen and Loriod were able to leave Paris for Petichet at the end of June. Just before setting out, he listened to the tapes of the *Méditations* sessions and was delighted with the results ('C'est magnifique!!!'). Messiaen got down to work on *Des Canyons* without delay, and his diary on 10 July revealed some of the sounds he was imagining for the new work: 'use temple blocks and clouds of pizzicato'. A list in his diary of things to take to Petichet revealed that his reading that summer included a book on the life of Christ by Romano Guardini, books on astronomy and on the birds of the USA, Canada and Africa. Loriod recalled that for some relief from composing, he also took copies of Ravel's piano pieces to play. He had been asked to write a short work for the Conservatoire (a test piece for flute) and noted in his diary 'say yes or no before 20 August', though in the end this piece was unwritten. Despite working on *Des Canyons*, Messiaen was able to spend some time in his garden. Loriod recalled that he was an inveterate reader of the plant catalogues issued by Delbard, and he was able to choose colours and shapes which could inspire him. This summer saw a good deal of new planting, duly noted by the composer in his diary:

155 Messiaen in the garden at Petichet, 1973.

Red roses, yellow roses, orange roses, red begonias, red hortensias, red and purple fuchsias, red and white fuchsias. By the upper cottage: deep purple petunias, striped purple and white ones, red geraniums, purple verbena. Next year we'll have thujas [a kind of conifer] at the upper cottage and at the house delphiniums, deep blue, pale blue and mauve larkspur.

On 5 August, the day before the Feast of the Transfiguration, Messiaen was delighted to receive printed copies of the first septenary of *La Transfiguration*. And while he worked on *Des Canyons*, Loriod spent much of the summer learning *La Fauvette des jardins*. By 10 August she had memorized this immensely complex piece and played it to Messiaen that day. Messiaen travelled to Romans by train to have dinner with his aunt Germaine ('Tantique') on 27 July. He was extremely fond of her, and the end of the summer was clouded by her illness and death: on 3 September Messiaen visited Germaine in hospital and she died at 9 p.m. that evening. Her funeral took place on 13 September and she was buried in the Sauvage family grave at Grenoble.

At the end of September Messiaen made a careful note of some small changes in the requirements for music during Masses at the Trinité which

included scope for extensive improvisation at the midday Mass (two improvised 'versets' after the first and second readings as well as improvised Offertory
and Recessional pieces). His notes are evidence of the humility with which he
approached his duties at the Trinité, and his willingness to tailor his improvisations – whether in 'classical' or 'modern' style – according to the wishes of the
clergy:

1. Mass at 9.55 a.m.: classical music. Play without a break from the end of
Mass until the start of the 11 o'clock Mass.

2. Mass at 11 a.m.: classical music. Improvisation on the large organ, then
singing by the choir. Play without a break from the end of Mass until the
start of the midday Mass.

3. Mass at 12 noon: play verset after the first reading. Kyrie plainchant
sung, Gloria in French sung. Psalm spoken, play a short verset after the
second lesson. Offertory and Sortie: organ.

Since his election to the Académie des Beaux-Arts in 1967, Messiaen had taken
his duties as an Academician as seriously as time permitted. At the start of
October he was appointed chairman for the coming year – necessitating regular
attendance at the Wednesday meetings, wearing his full Academicians' robes. As
well as delivering speeches to honour members of the Institut who had died that
year, Messiaen made the most of his position by mobilizing a campaign to prevent the destruction of the concert hall at the Palais de Chaillot. Built for the 1937
Exposition, it was particularly close to the hearts of a number of Academicians,
some of whom had been involved as young men in the design, construction and
decoration of the building, or, like Messiaen, in the celebrations which had
formed part of the Exposition programme.[8] Coincidentally on 16 October, at the
cinema in the Palais de Chaillot, the documentary film *Olivier Messiaen et les
oiseaux* was shown. Denise Tual and Michel Fano had worked on this during the
previous couple of years and it contained some particularly valuable footage of
Messiaen's class at the Conservatoire; it was shown in several other Paris cinemas
over the coming weeks.

Messiaen's next important première was on 7 November, when Yvonne
Loriod gave the first performance of *La Fauvette des jardins* at the Espace Pierre
Cardin. This was part of a concert devoted entirely to Messiaen's music: Marius
Constant and the Ensemble Ars Nova played the *Sept Haïkaï* (with Loriod),
then came *La Fauvette* and finally *Et exspecto resurrectionem mortuorum*. A
week later, on 15 November, Messiaen chaired the annual meeting of the Institut; he paid tribute to members who had died, and the session ended with a
concert (extracts from *The Firebird* and *Petrushka*) in celebration of the cente-

nary of Diaghilev's birth. At the end of the month he was at the Trinité to take part in a Mozart concert: on 30 November the church's choir sang the *Ave verum* and the *Coronation Mass*, and Messiaen improvised in the style of Mozart.

In Marseille on 13 December Messiaen and Loriod played *Visions de l'Amen* and he recorded that it was 'the 106th performance we have given of the *Amen*. Packed House. Great success!!!' Back in Paris, Messiaen had the manuscript of *Des Canyons* photographed on 19 December, which suggests that the complete short score was finished by then as well as some movements being fully orchestrated. The year ended, as usual, with Midnight Mass (preceded by a recital) at the Trinité. On Christmas Day the Messiaens went to Mass at the Sacré-Cœur, before going to the rue Blanche to wish Mme Sivade a Happy Christmas. The end of the diary contains notes on large-scale proposals, including 'a choral-orchestral work, for the BBC (50 minutes) for 1977 or 1978. Boulez to conduct. Write a work for large orchestra for Pierre Dervaux and the Orchestre Symphonique de Québec for 1977.'

On 8 and 9 February 1974 Loriod recorded the *Sept Haïkaï* for Erato with the Ensemble Ars Nova conducted by Marius Constant, and *La Fauvette des jardins* on 6 March. On 10 March Messiaen visited the copyist Raymond Cremers and took with him scores of movements 1, 2, 3, 4, 6 and 9 of *Des Canyons* so that Cremers could start work on preparing the orchestral parts. On 24 March Messiaen's diary provides evidence of his characteristic generosity as he noted that he had sent Wyschnegradsky a cheque for 150,000 AF to help the impoverished composer to save his quarter-tone piano.

Méditations sur le mystère de la Sainte-Trinité was published by Leduc on 3 April and Messiaen sent copies to a number of organists, including Almut Rössler, Gillian Weir, Ferdinand Klinda, Xavier Darasse, Raffi Ourgandjian, Louis Thiry, Jean-Jacques Grunenwald, Gaston Litaize, Jean Langlais, Pierre Cochereau, Jean Bonfils (his regular deputy at the Trinité), and his old school-friend Maurice Poté in Nantes. Darius Milhaud was also sent a copy.

Easter Monday (23 April) was the start of a trip to London (Messiaen noting that he needed to remember to take the Luminophone). Things got off to a bad start when the taxi which had taken them to the Gare du Nord drove off with their luggage still in the boot. A comical scene ensued. Despite frantic shouting and waving by both Messiaens, the taxi disappeared into the distance. They asked the police if anything could be done and the officers on duty escorted them to a police car which took them down to the station to try to trace the driver. The mind boggles as to what any bystanders would have made of the sight, as a seemingly respectable couple were taken away in a police car. But it was to no avail and the police advised them to take the train to London so as not to miss the concert the next day. The police drove them back to the Gare du Nord. In London the following morning Loriod was taken to find a shop which could lend her a concert dress. Not so Messiaen, since no tails in his size could be found: at the Queen Elizabeth Hall that evening, before playing *Visions de l'Amen,* he gave a short speech in which he told an amused audience the story of the taxi and the disappearing suitcase. In the first half, Loriod had played *La Fauvette des jardins,* and the evening was noted in Messiaen's diary as an 'extraordinary and wonderful triumph for the whole concert!!!' The next day Messiaen heard Nicholas Kynaston playing *L'Ascension* and the *Messe de la Pentecôte* at Westminster Cathedral. On 26 April two words are surrounded by a frame: 'Valise retrouvée!!!' The taxi driver had seen nothing of their gesticulations at the Gare du Nord and had started a three-day break immediately afterwards. On returning to work, he noticed a mysterious suitcase. After ensuring that a message was got through to the Messiaens, he took the suitcase round to the rue Marcadet where it awaited their return. In London, Loriod appeared as piano soloist in a borrowed speckled-blue dress for *La Transfiguration* at St Paul's Cathedral on 27 April with the Orchestre National de France and BBC Chorus conducted by Marius Constant. Returning to Paris the next day, the Messiaens and their lost suitcase were finally reunited.

Messiaen was in Vienna for a performance on 7 June of *La Transfiguration* at the Konzerthaus, conducted by Miltiades Caridis. The Austrian percussionists broke the much-travelled Luminophone while they were taking it apart to see how it worked. Messiaen noted that he would need to 'have the Luminophone repaired', but in fact it had had its last outing: it never worked again and even François Dupin, the distinguished player who was principal of the Orchestre de Paris at the time, could not coax any life back into the instrument.

On 19 June Maurice Poté, whose friendship dated back to their schooldays in Nantes, asked Messiaen to be godfather to his newly born daughter Aline. He was to be a supportive and generous godparent. The same day, he went to Mont Saint-Aignan, near Rouen, to attend the wedding of his former pupil Didier Denis. In Paris the Messiaens went on 25 June to dinner at Jacqueline Loriod's for a celebration of Gaston Loriod's eightieth birthday, and on 27 June they left for the summer in Petichet. The stay began with a visit to the mayor to arrange the purchase of two plots in the cemetery at Saint-Théoffrey in Petichet, one for Messiaen and one for Loriod. This transaction was duly completed on 11 August (at a cost of 500 francs). As in the previous year, a vigorous programme of planting and of purchases from the Delbard seed catalogue is recorded in Messiaen's diary. Loriod has likened Messiaen's passion for plants to Monet's. Though Petichet was on a very much smaller scale than Giverny, the care with which both the artist and the composer selected flowers, and the thought which subsequently went into planting them, certainly have points of similarity. Loriod wrote that 'it is impossible to deny the relationship of Messiaen with Claude Monet, in their love of combinations of colours, their choice of flowers, and through the harmonies which Messiaen chose in his music.'[9]

Messiaen was hard at work on the orchestration of *Des Canyons*, but he continued to take his daily swim in the lake. A trip to the Col du Galibier, one of the main passes into Savoie, on 8 July had some perilous moments on the way home when the Messiaens encountered a series of small avalanches, one of which blocked the road. But they went back to the Col du Galibier ten days later, a sunny day, and the occasion when Loriod took the memorable photograph of Messiaen sitting on a rock at the summit, reading Thomas Merton.

A visit to a neighbour, Madame Avril, on 26 August brought back memories of thirty years earlier: during the summer of 1945, Messiaen visited M. and Mme Avril, to work on some of the most complex passages in *Harawi* (presumably they had a good piano he could use). Another recollection of the 'Tristan' trilogy came a few days later, on 9 September, when the Messiaens went to the Grottes de Sassenage, which had impressed Messiaen on a visit while composing the *Turangalîla-Symphonie*. These grottos are an extraordinary natural wonder – legend has it that the formations of crystalline semi-precious stones were made from Melusine's tears when they dried (as early as 1790 the Abbé de Lescat provided a scientific explanation, but this charming legend persists). There was one piece of immensely sad news during the summer: the death of Jean Barraqué on 17 August. He had been one of Messiaen's favourite pupils as well as one of the most original.

They returned to Paris on 28 September and Messiaen was back at the Trinité on 30 September and teaching his first class of the year at the Conservatoire on 1 October. His diary entry for 3 October recorded that he would 'buy two books on Saint Francis: 1. *Cantique des créatures* by E. Leclerc et 2. *Le pauvre d'Assise* by Monseigneur Pézéril'. Messiaen had known Daniel Pézéril for many years: when the composer lived in the villa du Danube, Pézéril had been the parish priest at the nearby church of Saint François d'Assise. Between 5 and 9 October Loriod recorded a number of Messiaen's works for piano as part of Erato's planned complete recording: in five days she taped the *Vingt Regards*, *Cantéyodjayâ*, and three smaller pieces: the *Fantaisie burlesque*, *Rondeau* (with which she had won her *premier prix* at the Conservatoire in 1943) and the *Pièce* in memory of Dukas. *Des Canyons* was well on its way to completion, and on 12 October Messiaen took Cremers two further movements which were now orchestrated ('Cedar Breaks' and 'Bryce Canyon'). From 14 October until 2 November the Messiaens were on tour in the USA. As well as concerts, Messiaen had a meeting with Frederic Waldman on 25 October to discuss arrangements for the première of *Des Canyons*, which Waldman was to conduct. At Dartmouth College in New Hampshire, the Messiaens were joined by Felix Aprahamian for a few days. Together they looked at the College's copy of

Audubon's famous *Birds of America,* and on 1 November Loriod gave the first performance in America of *La Fauvette des jardins* before she and Messiaen played *Visions de l'Amen.*

Back in Paris, on 23 December the Messiaens had a visit from Marc Denayer and his grandfather, Jean Sencie. A tragic story lay behind this – one to which the Messiaens responded with generosity. The summer storms and landslides, which had almost stranded them on a trip to the Col du Galibier, had caused a major accident on the road between Vizille and Laffrey: a Belgian coach came off the road and crashed into the river Romanche. Thirty-eight people died and there was only one survivor: a thirteen year-old boy called Marc Denayer, who lost his parents in the crash. Deeply touched by this event, the Messiaens sent a note to the hospital and also established contact with the boy's grandfather. As a result, the young Marc became a kind of godchild to the Messiaens and they supported him financially through the rest of his school years. Marc flourished. He married and became the father of two boys.[10]

Messiaen performed his usual duties at the Trinité during the Christmas period, but was also very busy finishing *Des Canyons* and writing the analytical notes for the first performance. As usual, the end of his diary for 1973 contains some private thoughts on projects: 'The end of the opera: chorus, bells, skylarks – all together!' – a reference to *Saint François d'Assise* which was gradually taking shape in his mind. A BBC commission is mentioned too: 'a *long* – important – work for orchestra, or soloists and orchestra or chorus and orchestra, one and a half to two hours long – first performance by the BBC in 1976 [. . .] 1,500 pounds.' And Messiaen was clearly contemplating a new organ work as well: 'Write for organ: 1. pieces based on improvised *versets*; 2. a *fortissimo* piece on Greek rhythms (with *fff* chords) [. . .] 3. Postludes on the altar at Isenheim (could write seven or more).'

The condition of the organ gallery at the Trinité was giving Messiaen cause for concern and he wrote to Père Guinchet on 6 January 1974:

> As you know, there are two rooms behind the organ at the Trinité. One of them has blue and white windows which are completely smashed. In this room the cold wind blows ferociously, chilling not only the organ console, but especially the bellows, the mechanics and the pipes. I don't want to play the old man and to moan about draughts. But I urge you to think about the organ, which is a masterpiece by Cavaillé-Coll, one of the best instruments in Paris and in France, and which is worth a considerable fortune. For the good of the organ, I would ask you to stop the cold wind blowing in through the room on the side of the rue de Cheverus.[11]

Loriod recalled that the problems were not only broken windows, but also ripped-up parquet and a constant risk of damage to the organ. The culprits were thought to be the members of a scout group that met in the large room behind the organ gallery and used it for discos.

The diary continues to record progress on *Des Canyons*. By the end of February 1974 Raymond Cremers had copied the orchestral parts of the first nine movements, and two months later, on 30 April, Messiaen went to Argenteuil to collect photocopies of the full scores of the first ten movements (the orchestration of two movements was still to be finished). On 11 May Alice Tully came to dine with the Messiaens and she took away the scores of the ten completed movements.

The contemporary music group L'Itinéraire had been founded by Tristan Murail with Michaël Lévinas, Gérard Grisey and Roger Tessier in 1973. All four had been Messiaen pupils at the Conservatoire and Murail had a particular interest in novel keyboard instruments and played the ondes Martenot. L'Itinéraire was soon to become the most important forum for *musique spectrale*, but on 23 April at Notre-Dame-des-Blancs-Manteaux it put on a concert which included a performance of the *Fête des belles eaux* given by a sextet led by Jeanne Loriod, with Murail as one of the other players.[12] A little under a month later, on 20 May, Messiaen was in Neuilly for a demonstration of the latest version of the ondes Martenot. He was very enthusiastic about it and immediately placed an order.[13] From another instrument maker, Monsieur Larivière, Messiaen commissioned a new instrument: the Geophone (filled with thousands of tiny lead pellets) which he called for in the score of *Des Canyons*. This cost 1,200 francs to make, and Messiaen took it with him wherever the work was being performed.

Early in June, Messiaen took a nostalgic trip to see his aunts and cousins in the Aube. After the Mass for Pentecost in Bar-sur-Aube, Messiaen and Loriod drove a short distance north for a reunion, which Messiaen recorded in his diary: 'Saw Aunts Madeleine and Agnès [. . .] Went to Fuligny to Agnès's house.' There were strong emotional links with this house and Messiaen's youth: it was here that he was welcomed after the death of his mother and where he was to spend many summer holidays. The day ended with dinner at Lévigny attended by a number of Messiaen's relatives.

On 9 June Messiaen played for a televised Mass at the Trinité (on this occasion he improvised in a 'modern' style, according to his diary), and the next day he left with Loriod for Nice. They visited the recently opened Chagall museum[14] on the morning of 11 June and played *Visions de l'Amen* there at a concert that evening. The setting could hardly have been more appropriate for the work, since the small but spectacular auditorium in the museum is dominated by a magnificent stained-glass window by Chagall depicting the Creation.

Messiaen was back in Paris by 20 June for his last class of the year at the Conservatoire – Maurice Martenot came to give another demonstration of the latest version of his instrument. Two days later, on 22 June, Darius Milhaud died. The Messiaens had seen him in Geneva only a month earlier, and there was real sadness at this news: Loriod had been in Milhaud's class for two years at the Conservatoire (held in Milhaud's apartment at 10 boulevard de Clichy) and she recalled with affection his generosity of spirit and his unforgettable sense of humour, adding that 'he radiated joy and serenity, despite being wheelchair-bound for so many years'.[15]

Des Canyons was still not finished and this was the most pressing task for the summer in Petichet. While Messiaen got down to completing the last two movements, Loriod checked the orchestral parts which Cremers had produced. There were some memorable outings as well, especially one on 29 July when the Messiaens took Marc Denayer for a day out at Mont Blanc. Messiaen noted in his diary that on the return journey they 'watched the sunset on Mont Blanc, where the snow changed from orange, to pink, then mauve'. But the most remarkable sighting was the 'Gypaète' – the Bearded Vulture – which he described as 'extraordinary, powerful, immense!! With baggy trousers of white feathers on his legs, a black patch on his eye, and a tousled white head of hair, like an ageing hippie or a Romantic poet.'

From 30 July until 3 August Messiaen was back in Paris for meetings about *Des Canyons*, to sort out orchestral parts with Cremers and scores with the photocopying firm. He also went with Loriod to collect the newly made Geophone, which proved its effectiveness on the journey home: Loriod recalled it 'making a splendid crescendo as the car went round every corner'.[16]

156 Maurice Martenot demonstrating the new model of ondes Martenot to Messiaen's class at the Conservatoire, 20 June 1974.

Frederic Waldman, who was to conduct the première of *Des Canyons*, came to Petichet on 11 August to discuss the new work, which was by now all but complete. Messiaen spent a whole day talking to Waldman about detailed matters of tempo and expression, and about the rehearsal schedule.

Back in Paris on 30 September, Messiaen put the finishing touches to *Des Canyons*. He made photocopies of the twelfth (and last) movement, and gave a copy to Cremers for making orchestral parts. Tempo markings were reviewed following the sessions with Waldman, and during October Messiaen set about finalizing these. On 7 October there was a rare night out at the theatre: a performance of *À la fin était le Bang* by Messiaen's old friend René de Obaldia. At the end of October a visit to Madrid for performances of *Turangalîla* (on 19 and 20 October) gave Messiaen a chance to go the Prado, and he noted in his diary that he 'saw all the Goyas, the Murillos, and *The Garden of Earthly Delights* by Hieronymus Bosch'.

November was given over almost entirely to *Des Canyons*. According to his diary, Messiaen took 'the material for movements 11 and 12, and the Geophone with a special document for the customs' in his luggage for the flight to New York. When the Messiaens arrived there on 2 November, the precious instrument and the scores and parts were collected for Waldman, and the next morning, after Mass at the Lady of the Skies church in the airport, Messiaen and Loriod flew straight to Los Angeles for two concerts conducted by Zubin Mehta.[17] They were back in New York in time for the start of rehearsals for *Des Canyons* on 11 November. The Messiaens were guests in Mrs Tully's box for a recital by Horowitz at the Metropolitan Opera on 17 November, and they met the great pianist afterwards. Two days later, *Des Canyons* was played complete for the first time at a rehearsal, and Messiaen, Loriod and Michel Béroff celebrated this with a Japanese meal at the Rock Garden of Tokyo on 56th Street.

The world première of *Des Canyons aux étoiles. . .* took place on 20 November in Alice Tully Hall at New York's Lincoln Center. It was given by Yvonne Loriod, Sharon Moe (horn) and the Musica Aeterna Orchestra, conducted by Frederic Waldman. Messiaen, as usual, noted his reaction: 'Very fine performance! Brilliant! Moving! A unanimous, tremendous and extraordinary success!!! Packed house!!'

This sucess is not surprising given the radiant splendour of the score. Though scored for a comparatively small orchestra (solo piano, solo horn, full woodwind, a modest brass section, extensive percussion and thirteen string players), the dimensions are epic, and the musical language has a grandeur which is a match for the magnificent landscape it seeks to evoke.

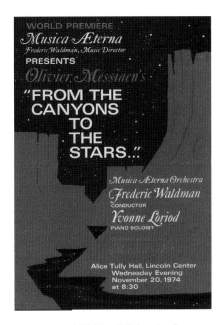

157 Handbill for the first performance of *Des Canyons aux étoiles. . .* at Alice Tully Hall, New York, 20 November 1974.

The instrumentation was a consequence of the commission: the Musica Aeterna Orchestra was founded by Waldman in 1961 with financial support from Alice Tully, and the first performance took place in the hall that bears her name: opened in 1969, Alice Tully Hall has a seating capacity of just over 1,000 and is regularly used for chamber music.

Des Canyons is in twelve movements, divided into unequal parts: the First Part, movements 1–5; the Second Part, movements 6 and 7; and the Third Part, movements 8–12. There are three solo movements – two for solo piano, no.4, 'Le Cossyphe d'Heuglin' ('The White-browed Robin'), and no.9, 'Le Mocqueur polyglotte' ('The Mockingbird'); and no.6 for solo horn, 'Appel interstellaire', which, as we have seen, began as a memorial to Jean-Pierre Guézec); but otherwise the instrumental forces are deployed to dazzlingly colourful effect, with, for example, some highly innovative swirling effects played on a trumpet mouthpiece in no.5, 'Cedar Breaks et le Don de Crainte' ('Cedar Breaks and the Gift of Awe'), and in no.11, 'Omao, Leiothrix, Elepaio, Shama'.

The longest movement, no.7, 'Bryce Canyon et les rochers rouge-orange' ('Bryce Canyon and the Red-orange Rocks'), was directly inspired by Messiaen's long walks in its stunning scenery, as he explained in his preface to the score:

> Bryce Canyon is the greatest marvel of Utah. It is a gigantic amphitheatre formed of red, orange and violet rocks, in fantastic shapes: castles, square turrets, rounded towers, natural windows, bridges, statues, columns, whole towns and the occasional black bottomless pit. From above, we may gaze in wonder at this spectacular forest of petrified sand and stone [...] or, if we descend to the heart of the gorge, we may wander though its magical architecture.[18]

The result is a movement which seems to blaze with a sense of the marvellous. Its formal lucidity is due in part to a memorable refrain of brass and woodwind chords which represent – according to the score – the great red-orange rocks themselves. Messiaen's instrumentation throughout *Des Canyons* is fabulously resourceful, and despite the moderate forces the full *tuttis* sound massive. The work makes extensive use of glowing major triads, and after the monumental majesty of Bryce Canyon, there is a slow movement, 'Les Ressuscités et le chant de l'étoile Aldébaran' ('The Resurrected and the Song of the Star Aldebaran'), an ecstatic reverie which is reminiscent – in terms of mood, decoration, and harmonic language – of the sixth movement of *Turangalîla*, although Messiaen achieves a sense of enchantment in *Des Canyons* with greater economy and the most delicate colouring. The work ends, aptly, with one of Messiaen's most memorable hymns to Creation: 'Zion Park et la Cité céleste' ('Zion Park and the Celestial City'): a brass chorale, intercut with bells and with brilliant birdsong cadenzas. That the splendours of nature represent those of Eternity is underlined by Messiaen's description of the closing cadence: 'Over a chord of A major (immutable like Eternity) on the strings, the bells ring out their resonance with the ultimate joy.'[19]

After the première of *Des Canyons*, the Messiaens were guests of honour at a post-concert dinner given by Mrs Tully, though before going to the meal they took the scores, the orchestral parts and the Geophone back to the hotel for safe-keeping.[20] The couple returned to Paris on 22 November and Messiaen turned his mind to other projects: on 28 November he wrote 'work on the *Traité*, chapter on birdsong, and look again at India with Alain Daniélou's book';[21] and he resolved to 'correct *Fête des belles eaux* and offer it to Durand' (though he seems not to have done this). On 29 November he jotted down some more thoughts about a new project for his own instrument: 'write *versets* for the organ (look for new *combinations* of timbres – look for new language)'.

On 20 December André Jolivet died. That evening, the three surviving members of La Jeune France paid tribute to their old friend on Radio France. The funeral was at Sainte-Clotilde on Christmas Eve (there was music by Jolivet, and Rostropovich played unaccompanied Bach). Afterwards the Messiaens took Hilda Jolivet back to their flat for a meal, though Messiaen also needed to prepare for Midnight Mass at the Trinité and the recital which preceded it. After Christmas, Messiaen wrote a short tribute to Jolivet, reflecting on thoughts that occured to him at the funeral:

I am always struck by the change which takes place straight after the death of a great man, in the hearts and minds of those who knew him. Details vanish, and the true figure emerges, with all the force of its destiny, its interior beauty manifested at last. This was how André Jolivet seemed to me, from the first notes of his marvellous *Incantation* for solo flute, during his funeral at Sainte-Clotilde. And I see this now in all his best works: the symphonies, the concertos, *Mana*, *Épithalame*. André Jolivet had a particularly strong sense of the sacred. Sacred in his ecstatic lyricism, sacred in his incantatory repetition, sacred in his exploration of time and space in sound. From the start of the extraordinary *Danses rituelles*, when the gong and the tam-tam punctuate the phrases of the alto flute, a sense of the sacred is present in us and around us. And it remains present, through the formidable 'Danse du Héros' until the final lament, passing through the very moving 'Danse nuptiale'. There is something awesome there, which suggests the grandeur of the Druids and the Sibylls approaching the Gift of Awe and Wonder in the face of the Divine, the source of Christianity. Hearing this solemn music now, we encounter the truth of one whom we loved and whose place we can henceforth measure precisely.[22]

'Messiaen, faites-moi un opéra'
1975–1978

I didn't feel I had the gift, and that's what I told Rolf Liebermann, general manager of the Paris Opéra, when he wanted to give me a commission. He then invited me to the Élysée Palace and, ceremoniously, at the end of a dinner, in the presence of Georges Pompidou, he said to me: 'Messiaen, you will write an opera for the Opéra de Paris!' I couldn't refuse in front of the President of the Republic.[1]

The first sign that Messiaen was planning an opera came in a diary entry on 1 July 1971: 'Give Liebermann a reply to the Opéra de Paris (with an opera for 1975!!!).[2] *Urgent.*' Messiaen had also been approached by the Ministry of Cultural Affairs; the initiative had come from President Pompidou, who may have seen theatrical potential in Messiaen's music when he attended the ballet production in 1968 of *Turangalîla.* Later in July 1971 Messiaen started to think seriously about the suggestion. There is no indication at this stage of a subject, but already Messiaen had in mind a vast orchestra, augmented by coloured light projections; the text was to be mainly declaimed, by actors in speaking roles amplified through loudspeakers. The dinner attended by the Messiaens at the Élysée Palace took place on 28 September, with Liebermann and Duhamel also present. One can imagine the conspirators waiting with bated breath for Messiaen to make some response, but in fact the evening (with 'delicious food', Loriod remembered) passed off without any mention of the opera. Nonetheless, the next day Messiaen had a meeting with Liebermann, and another followed a week later; some outline agreement must have been reached because on 15 October Messiaen told himself to 'find a subject and write the libretto for an opera'. The notes at the end of the diary for 1971 sketch five scenes from the life of St Francis:

1. La Joie parfaite
2. La Règle at les vertus
3. Le Prêche aux oiseaux

158 Teaching at Tanglewood in 1975.

4. L'Ange au violon et les Stigmates

5. Le Cantique et la mort

By February 1972 Messiaen and Liebermann had reached agreement. The commission (for a fee of 100,000 francs) was for a 'large-scale opera to be performed at the Palais Garnier [i.e. the Opéra] for its centenary on 5 January 1975'. Messiaen was still thinking of a work that would be largely spoken: 'Make the singers speak: one, two or three singing voices for the more important characters over a wordless chorus accompanying spoken passages. Use chorus, with several ondes Martenot in the chorus.' He was by no means completely settled on *Saint François*. Another subject was from the Bible, 'The Pilgrims at Emmaus' (Luke 24:13–35). Again the main roles were to be spoken, and again the concept was highly stylized: 'A static drama in four simultaneous tableaux – four scenes together. Scene 1, on the left: the pilgrims walking. Scene 2: the continuation of their journey. Scene 3, in the middle: the inn. Scene 4: a chorus of angels who fill in the empty scenes as the story moves along.' The difficulty of this subject for Messiaen would have been the representation on stage of Christ. He had long had the ambition to write a Passion or Resurrection of Christ, 'but I thought I wasn't worthy of it and, above all, that such images aren't presentable on stage, except in the case of works conceived in faith and innocence, like those popular Oberammergau performances.'[3]

The plan for an opera for 1975 lapsed, overtaken by the commission from Alice Tully for *Des Canyons aux étoiles. . .* The invitation must have remained open, however, but it was not until 1975 that Messiaen was able to give the project his attention. The first page of the diary for 1975 included three quotations from the *Imitation of Christ*, suggesting that Messiaen was reflecting on the 'perfect joy', to which Francis aspires, and which is the theme of the opera's first scene. 'Let me rest in You, above all other creatures; above health, honour and glory, power and dignity'; 'Knowledge that comes from heaven, through the influence of grace, is nobler than that acquired by the work of the human spirit. Jesus Christ is the way, the truth and the life'; 'For, to live as a true Christian and to be sure of salvation, it is necessary to begin by renouncing and dying oneself.'[4]

In the first three months of 1975 Messiaen's time was filled by following a world tour of *Turangalîla*, conducted by Ozawa, with different orchestras in Europe and the United States; there were some thirty performances, most of them attended by Messiaen. He noted with approval the characteristics of Ozawa's conducting, his fast tempi, and the way he was efficient as well as 'passionate and sublime'. Messiaen had particularly happy memories of San Francisco, where Ozawa took him on a systematic tour of the Asian and Polynesian restaurants. A favourite Japanese recipe was copied down: 'Miso:

soup (fish juices, warm, little squares of white soya pastry) – tempura – fried prawns – fried courgettes and aubergines, other fried fish, soya sauce.'

Despite his absences from Paris, Messiaen's teaching continued undiminished. Since his appointment as Professor of Composition (in 1966), Messiaen had greater freedom in his choice of works, and as a result his teaching concentrated more than before on contemporary scores. In January 1975 the class analysed music by Ligeti (*Ramifications, Aventures, Nouvelles Aventures, Requiem*); in February Boulez's *Le Marteau sans maître*, and (to coincide with Ozawa's Paris performances) *Turangalîla*; April was devoted largely to *Tristan*. In the summer term Messiaen discussed music by Berio (*Circles, Sequenza 3*), Penderecki (*Dies Irae*) and Xenakis (*Metastasis, Pithoprakta*), together with the *Sept Haïkaï*, noting in his diary: 'Listen to discs of Japanese birds, to gagaku, to the recording by [Marius] Constant, take in postcards of Japan, analyse the whole work.'[5]

Messiaen was making plans for a trip later in the year to New Caledonia. The island, one of the few remaining French colonies, lies just north of the tropic of Capricorn, some 1500 kilometres from the coast of Queensland. Long and narrow, it has at its southern end a small island, the Isle of Kounié (also known as the Isle of Pines), giving the shape, as Messiaen put it, of an exclamation mark. Messiaen had been in correspondence with Albert Tonnelier, a pharmacist in the capital, Nouméa, and an expert ornithologist, and on 17 April Messiaen had a visit from a colleague of Tonnelier who brought him a tape of indigenous birdsong; Messiaen began to study and notate the birdsong (the diary of 8 May

159 Prix Salabert: Ivo Malec, Lukas Foss, Iannis Xenakis, Mme Salabert, Messiaen and Claude Samuel, 22 December 1975.

mentioned 'the Oiseau-Moine and Notou of New Caledonia'). On 2 June he purchased air tickets to New Caledonia; a new project was clearly in view, but Loriod knew from experience that it was better not to ask questions.

The summer break was decisive. On 16 June Messiaen reminded himself to pack 'everything for composing the opera and for the opera libretto'. At Petichet he made detailed notes on the birds of New Caledonia:

Fan-tailed gerygone: *small*, with a white circle around the eyes. The plumage is olive-grey, whitish underneath. Lives in forests and gardens, in the treetops. Its nest is a ball of cotton and lichen, with a side entrance. The song is high, rapid, staccato – very sharp like a spiky piccolo, a celesta, glockenspiel or crotales. First type of song: groups of three notes, ending with a group of two (two anapaests and one iamb), followed by variants. [. . .] Second type of song: at first the bird hesitates, in a Bacchic rhythm, then throws itself into rapid staccato groups of seven or eight notes, repeated several times.

The Messiaens flew to New Caledonia on 18 September. In preparation for the tropical forest, Messiaen had equipped himself with a new pair of boots and an enormous 'cowboy hat',[6] together with binoculars, recording tape and books on birds. He also packed a copy of St Francis's *Fioretti*, the Prayers of St Francis, Thomas Merton's *Monastic Peace* and the libretto of the opera so far written. The flight was a trial for Messiaen but he revived immediately on arrival: 'I have a good remedy for fatigue. As soon as I hear birdsong [. . .] I'm cured! I listened to the birds and was wild with joy.'[7] Albert Tonnelier, Messiaen's guide, took them at once to the forest of Thi. The next day, after attending Mass (at Notre-Dame-de-Vœu in Nouméa), they visited Mount Koghi. Later Messiaen made further notations of the birdsong from the recordings made by Loriod:

Second notation of a fan-tailed cuckoo from Mount Koghi (21 September at 4 p.m. and 5.30 p.m.). The first song, which is the less common of the two, ascends in steps, with a crescendo; the song is loud and very bright. The anacrusis is always spiky, and the long note is preceded by a brief tremolo. [. . .] The second song is very commonly heard, often alone, without the first. The timbre is still loud and bright, but less bold and more liquid. The tempo is also a little quicker – one descends faster than one climbs! [. . .] This cuckoo is popularly known by the apt name of *gammier* [scaler]. The ascending song is not immediately followed by the descent; generally one hears the latter on its own. On Mount Koghi I heard only the second song. On the Isle of Pines I heard both songs, separated from each other by a 15-second interval. The rising song always came first, but there were six or seven ascents for each descent. 22 September: Eopsaltria (yellow-bellied robin). 1. very high whistling – piccolo, violin harmonics; 2. water gurgling – temple block, trill on the tambourine; 3. flute-like timbre – woodwind chords rich in harmonics.

On 24 September the Messiaens moved to a ranch in the countryside, accompanied by Tonnelier and two American ornithologists. The latter, to the Messiaens' dismay, were intent on shooting pigeons; these were 'not grey like our horrible Parisian pigeons, but green, a marvellous emerald green, covered with a silky, moss-like down, delightful to pet'.[8] The scenery and the bird life were extraordinary:

4.30 p.m. The road is through a forest of niaouli. Frightful potholes: the jeep climbs, descends, crosses rivers. Lantana bushes, sweet-basil (smelly leaves, with marvellous peppery scent), and trees which have delicious fruit like a mango. Everywhere there are niaoulis, with white trunks, writhing white branches, and small glossy green leaves shaped like spearheads, reminiscent of eucalyptus. Saw a kingfisher; very large, blue plumage with yellow underneath – magnificent! 6 p.m. Sunset red over the mountains. We return in darkness, the jeep bouncing over the potholes. In the moonlight the white of the niaoulis makes them look like phantoms. 25 September: nine kilometres from La Foa. Ate a fruit salad. Corossol: a large fruit with green skin and dark prickles, prepared with sugar and rum. Tastes like lychees. The fruit is the size of a melon; the inside is white with black pips. The pulp is white and mossy, like a bridal veil.

Back in Nouméa, Messiaen visited the local museum where he noted the 'tribal drums with ancestral heads – petroglyphs', while Loriod practised on the hotel's piano. In the evening, with Tonnelier, they dined on fish, watching with fascinated horror as the Americans roasted their green pigeons. On 29 September the Messiaens flew to the Isle of Pines:

In the sea are little coral islands. The sea is blue and green, emerald and jade green, shining like opals! The blue is intense, like precious stones, or the first reflection of the opal! [. . .] Our bungalow is built like a Melanesian hut, with a round, pointed roof held up by logs and covered with a thick thatch made from the bark of the niaouli. Between the bungalow and the beach are bamboos of various heights, like organ pipes. Out to sea the blue is like sapphire, or emerald green with violet patches. There is a hissing sound as the waves break, white like the manes of an army of horses. The sand is very white and fine, like talc; it forms into a solid surface, like cement. When swimming in the sea one sees alternating bands of pale green and mauve;

where the water is shallow, the reflections of the sun create a honeycomb of light. [...] Found an extraordinary flower: cluster of 25 to 30 husks shaped like olives [...] glossy white with a pink tip. When the olive opens it reveals a yellow, red, and wine-coloured flower inside, with a white pistil, like a candle.

The Messiaens passed an idyllic week, swimming in the sea and gorging on sea food. The colours were extraordinary: 'The meeting of these green pigeons, red leaves, white trees, and the violet sea is absolutely amazing. They're the colours of dreams and madness.'[9] A note from Pascal reminded them that Paris in the autumn was rather different: 'Here there's no coral lagoon, no white niaoulis, just rain on the plane trees.'[10] Messiaen started to fill the *cahiers* with ideas for his opera:

Add various poetic expressions in all the Scenes: see Reverdy, Eluard, Claudel, etc.[11] Talk about brother space and brother time, and what has to be transformed (see several quotations from St Paul). For the Sermon to the Birds, add birds from Japan, Utah, and tropical birds, especially from New Caledonia: these are not Italian! They come from afar, from seas beyond the seas (as in the Psalm: 'And let the islands applaud!'). Talk of the green birds (green pigeons), violet leaves (of the bougainvillea) and red leaves (poinsettia).

For the Angel's theme (at 'ton cœur'): tonal harmonies, *pianissimo*, on the strings. Add a counterpoint on the temple block for the moment when the Angel stops, and above this a counterpoint for xylophone and glockenspiel (like the water drops in Pierre Henry's *Voyage*).

Loriod hired a Mini-moke and they explored the Isle of Pines. In the Grotte d'Oumagna Messiaen noted a bird's hooting, magnified by the echoes of the cave: 'Barn owl (Tyto alba lifuensis) – *No!! It must have been a pigeon*, perhaps at the end of its strophe.' On the evening of 2 October the Messiaens were taken on a tour of protected forest. Again the birds were marvellous: friarbird, yellow-bellied robin, and in the small hours of the morning, a kingfisher. The final expedition was to Gadji, and its forests of banyans, coconut palms and Kohu trees. Loriod had taken dozens of photographs and filled four reels of tape. While recording the gerygone she used an ornithologist's trick of recording the song, then replaying it so that the bird senses a rival and is provoked into a second burst of song.[12] The final evenings, now back in Nouméa, were spent with Tonnelier reviewing the contents of the tapes:

Third notation of birds from the forest of Gadji (3 October at 5 p.m.). Kingfisher: the call is sharp and piercing – ensemble of woodwind with piccolo, piccolo clarinet and trumpet in D. Friarbird: high horn, with harmonics on violins and cellos. Striated starling (a kind of blackbird) – solo flute. Friarbird: a carillon of woodwind chords with xylorimbas, bells – and *resonances*! – as though the bird is singing in a vast empty cathedral. Yellow-bellied robin: liquid, flowing, laughing. Woodwind chords, and 32 violins playing cluster glissandi (with temple block on the second note of each group, triangle on the third). First version. Bar 1: flute-like, trumpeting, brilliant. Bar 2: like the sound of water, gurgling. Bar 3: whistling! Bar 6: gurgling (like bar 2) but more melodically shaped. Bar 7: whistling! Last three notes: brilliant, triumphant, *fff*!

It was only after the visit to New Caledonia that Messiaen decided to commit himself to the opera, five years after it had first been mooted. In November he wrote (twice circling the entry): 'Begin Opera – at least the libretto!!!' (Even so, Messiaen continued to keep Liebermann waiting: the contract was finally signed on 25 April 1976.) On the next page of the diary, in faint pencil, comes a tiny fragment – 'fragile stream, fragile stars' – anticipating the description of the robin's song in Scene 6 of the opera: 'a quick, light melody, a fragile stream, as if one were unthreading most precious pearls'.

Messiaen's diary for 1976 was as crowded as ever, and the first opportunity to work uninterrupted on the libretto had to wait until the mid-term break from the Conservatoire in February. Eager to find time for composing, Messiaen was none the less unhappy about the prospect of retirement from the Conservatoire, and was relieved to find that he had a further year: 'I take my class and draw my salary until 30 September 1978; after that it's retirement – yes.' To add to his anxieties Messiaen became ill at the end of February, on a visit to Vienna. Viral hepatitis was diagnosed and a gallstone found which necessitated a strict diet. By the end of March Messiaen had sufficiently recovered to take a short holiday in Greece. After visiting the Acropolis, the Messiaens drove to Delphi, via Corinth and Mycaenae. Messiaen admired the outdoor theatre at Epidaurus (and its acoustics) but in general was more interested in nature than classical remains. '25 March. Road from Corinth to Mycenae: Orphean warbler. At Mycaenae: eucalyptus, orange trees, lemon trees, black-headed bunting, rock bunting. [. . .] Delphi: sublime landscape!!! Cretschmar's bunting and a blue rock thrush.' There are pages of notes in this vein: 'Saw the temple of Apollo (chaffinch). Saw the theatre and the stadium (booted eagle, blue rock thrush, goldfinch).' Everywhere the blue rock thrush was a recurring theme, and its songs, noted and recorded in Greece, found their way into Scene 3 of the opera, after the curing of the Leper, where the scoring is for xylophone, xylorimba and marimba: 'It's a sort of Balinese music, but with triumphal accents and a whole dusting of trills in the strings and cymbals.'[13]

160 Messiaen in 1976.

161 Signing autographs after *Visions de l'Amen* at the Théâtre de la Ville, Paris, in 1976.

162 Notating a blackcap at the Carceri, Assisi, June 1976.

Messiaen put the finishing touches to the libretto in early June 1976, fittingly during a week spent in Assisi and Florence. Many of the notations in the *cahiers* were made at the hermitage of the Carceri, which was chosen by Messiaen as the setting for St Francis's Sermon to the Birds in the opera:

4 June. Climb from Assisi to the Carceri. Magnificent countryside. On the left are olive trees with bright silvery leaves! [. . .] Large tree where Francis preached to the birds: it's an evergreen oak. Opposite is where Francis struggled with the Devil. [. . .] On the road near the Carceri, a robin; in the court-yard of the Carceri, a blackcap. The blackcap has a very bright timbre, powerful, quite flowing, legato and joyful. A clock strikes one, followed by a bell chiming twenty times (the summons to the refectory) – this inspires the blackcap to sing again, a series of strophes.

Messiaen took great trouble over the blackcap's song: 'I transcribed thousands [. . .]; for each warbler solo I had to invent chords on each note in order to translate the special timbre, which is very joyous and very rich in harmonics.'[14]

After the Carceri the Messiaens visited the Basilica in Assisi:

Saw the tomb of St Francis in the crypt of the Lower Basilica, along with the tombs of the Brothers. In the Upper Basilica are the frescos by Giotto. On leaving, there was a magnificent carillon, a real concert of bells! At the convent of San Damiano the garden has marvellous flowers. The church is simple and very dark. The refectory is of bare stone, with wooden tables and benches along the walls. A vase of flowers marks the place of St Clare.

163 Messiaen's notation of a blackcap at the Carceri, 4 June 1976.

5 June. Saw the great Basilica of La Verna; in the great ambulatory are frescoes depicting the entire life of St Francis. Attended Mass at the Chapel of the Stigmata – a magnificent Christ, twisted in suffering, and a very fine statue of St Francis, also in pain, on his knees. 5.30 p.m. Sasso Spicco: a great overhang of rocks, a wooden Cross. Far above, against the sky, trees. Frightening wind! The rocks are piled chaotically, shaped like the teeth of a dragon!

In Florence Messiaen spent several hours at the monastery of San Marco making notes on the paintings by Fra Angelico:

6 June. Fra Angelico's *Annunciation*. The Angel kneeling before the Virgin wears a mauve (bright violet-pink) robe, the material falling in long folds. Gilded breast-plate; the middle part of the sleeve and the top of the Angel's back are gold. The wings are half-opened and have blue and white stripes, with red for the border. Fair hair. The face has an inviting smile. The halo is gold, like a transparent plate raised behind the head. [. . .] Fra Angelico's *Last Judgement*: on the right (that is to say the left as one looks at it) the elect in Paradise; in the middle is Christ, on the left (or the viewer's right) are the damned in Hell. The gateway to Paradise is a great golden portal. The angels form a circle and dance with the saints, their feet scarcely touching the ground. The angel embracing a Dominican has a mauve (pale red-violet) robe; the halo is large, a full circle, gilded, the wings are golden, with green and maroon eyes, like the eyes of a peacock's feather.

In the opera the Angel's costume was copied from Fra Angelico's *Annunciation*. From the outset, Messiaen decided to base the libretto on contemporary accounts of St Francis's life. Where possible he used St Francis's own words, drawing principally on the *Fioretti*, the *Considerations on the Holy Stigmata* and the *Canticle of Brother Sun*:[15] 'The poem [i.e., the libretto] has no literary pretensions. It exists only to inspire the music and I frequently changed words to suit my melodic lines and to provide the singers with good vowels. I cut out a lot, retaining only the broad lines of my subject. I chose what could contain colour, a sense of mystery and birdsong.'[16]

The opera begins – as in the 1971 sketch – with a scene about 'perfect joy'. This is the starting point for Francis's spiritual journey. 'At the beginning, he's Francis. Then, little by little, he becomes Saint Francis, and even Super-Saint Francis.'[17] Scene 1 takes the form of a dialogue between Francis and Brother Leo, based partly on chapter 8 of the *Fioretti*. The comment by the chorus, that reinforces Francis's teaching and closes the Scene, is taken from St Mark's Gospel (8:34): 'Whosoever will come after me, let him deny himself, and take up his cross, and follow me.' The gloomy refrains of Brother Leo are derived from Ecclesiastes (12:3): 'I am afraid on the road, when the windows grow large and fade away.' Brother Leo's other symbols of doubt, besides the darkening windows, are tropical flowers:[18] 'when the leaves of the Poinsettia no longer turn red', and 'when it is going to die, when it no longer has scent, the Tiaré flower'. The Tiaré had particularly struck Messiaen when he had seen it in Tahiti, on the way home from New Caledonia, as noted in his diary: 'white, scent of lilies and jasmine, even stronger and sweeter when made into floral necklaces'.

In Scene 2 ('Laudes'). Francis sings in praise of God, quoting from verses four to seven of the *Canticle of Brother Sun*, giving thanks for 'Brother Wind', 'Sister Water', 'Brother Fire' and 'Mother Earth'. The only part of the Scene in which the words are Messiaen's own comes after the service, when St Francis is left alone in prayer.

The episode of 'Le Baiser au lépreux' (Scene 3) is found in the *Fioretti* and in the account of Francis's life by Thomas of Celano. This is a key scene in the opera, and presents the one element of the story conspicuously missing from the 1971 outline. The Leper is both the opportunity for which Francis prayed in Scene 2, and a serious obstacle, who confronts Francis's acceptance of suffering with scorn. The Angel's appearance in this scene is Messiaen's invention, and for the Angel's words to the Leper he drew from the Bible: 'Your heart accuses you [. . .] but God [. . .] is greater than your heart' (1 John 3:20). The Leper repents of his rage towards the Brothers' charity and Francis draws near, using the words of the *Prayer for Peace*: 'Where there is sadness may I sing of joy!' Messiaen described the moment of the embrace as a double victory: not only is the Leper healed, but 'Saint Francis also is cured of his fear!'[19] In the aftermath of the Leper's miraculous cure, the orchestra resounds with the songs of the blue rock thrush that Messiaen had collected at Delphi. The Leper's physical appearance is based on the figure of St Antony in Matthias Grünwald's *Isenheim Altarpiece*, and St Francis himself on the frescos attributed to Cimabue (painted c.1280) and attributed to Giotto (c.1290) in the Basilica of S. Francesco, Assisi: 'Saint Francis must be rather small and of humble appearance. He has a small thin reddish beard. Reddish hair, tonsure and earth-coloured robes must differentiate him from the other Brothers.'[20]

There are obvious parallels between Scene 3 and Scene 7, 'Les Stigmates', but the difference, in Scene 7, is that Francis willingly approaches his ordeal, as he prays to receive the Stigmata (the imprint of the five wounds of Christ's Passion). Musically, the ominous darkness which opens the scene borrows from the *Catalogue d'oiseaux*, using the calls of the owl and the jostling dislocations of the 'mode de valeurs' technique as in 'La Chouette hulotte'.

There is also a symmetry between Scene 2, 'Laudes', and the final scene of the opera, 'La Mort et la Nouvelle Vie'. Francis's dying words take up once more the *Canticle*, begun in Scene 2, and now concluded with the verse composed by St Francis in 1226 shortly before his death: 'Be praised, my Lord, for our sister Death.' At the end of the opera, Brother Leo's lament returns to the imagery that Messiaen gives Francis in his prayer at the close of Scene 2: 'He is gone [. . .] like a teardrop of clear water which falls slowly from a flower's petal. He is gone like a butterfly, a golden butterfly which flies from the Cross to pass beyond the stars.'

'L'Ange voyageur', Scene 4, which begins Act 2, serves as an interlude, standing apart from the central theme of Francis's spiritual journey. The Angel's interrogation of the Brothers comes from the *Fioretti*, though the issue there (an obscure dispute about the eating of meat) is upgraded by Messiaen to a discussion of Predestination. The point of the scene is to contrast the otherworldliness of Francis (offstage at prayer) with the arrogant bluster of Elias, the archetypal bureaucrat, a caricature that is Messiaen's revenge, perhaps, on the pen-pushers who had plagued him. As Messiaen observed, this slice of life, with ordinary people behaving ordinarily, has a place in the opera similar to the tavern scene in *Boris Godunov*.[21] The Brothers are characterized musically by birdsong. The earnest Bernardo is introduced by the New Caledonian friarbird, Elias with the notou (New Caledonian pigeon) and with the rasping, exasperated accents of the reed warbler. The gerygone of the Angel is used here for its 'mocking' quality.[22]

'L'Ange musicien', Scene 5, recalls an image that Messiaen remembered from his youth, when he owned an edition of the *Fioretti* with this episode illustrated by a Maurice Denis engraving.[23] The scene is described in a passage from St Francis's *Considerations*: 'An Angel appeared to him [. . .] holding a viol in his left hand and a bow in his right hand. [. . .] At once, such a beautiful melody invaded Francis's soul [. . .] that [. . .] he wondered whether, if the Angel had drawn the bow down again, his soul would not have left his body owing to the unbearable loveliness of the music.'[24] The words of the Angel express a belief that was central to Messiaen's thinking: 'Dieu nous éblouit par excès de Vérité. La musique nous porte à Dieu par défaut de Vérité' ('God dazzles us with an excess of Truth; music carries us to God bypassing that Truth'). The point was discussed at length in Messiaen's conversations with Samuel: 'The arts, especially music but also literature and painting, allow us to penetrate domains that are not unreal, but beyond reality. For the Surrealists, it was a hallucinatory domain; for Christians, it is the domain of faith. [. . .] Now, I think music, even more than literature and painting, is capable of expressing this dreamlike, fairy-tale aspect of the beyond – this "surreal" aspect of the truths of faith. It's in that sense that music expresses the beyond with its absence of truth.'[25]

Messiaen followed the music of heaven with the music of the skies, in the ornithological tour de force of 'Le Prêche aux oiseaux'. The libretto adheres to the outline of the sources, but the details are Messiaen's, especially in the charming way that the birds of New Caledonia invade the ornithology tutorial given by Francis to Brother Masseo on the birds of Umbria:

> Saint Francis: A song of praise! An exclamation mark! An island like an exclamation mark! [. . .] An island in the seas, beyond the seas. Where the leaves are red, the pigeons green, the trees white, the sea changes from green to blue and from violet to green like the reflections of an opal. For we must have the birds of the islands as well, in order to answer the vows of the Psalm: Let the islands applaud!
> Brother Masseo: How do you know all this?
> Saint Francis: I have seen it in a dream.

St Francis gives pride of place to the remarkable fan-tailed cuckoo that so intrigued Messiaen by appearing to sing scales in reverse, descending before ascending. This impression was later corrected by Tonnelier who discovered, after Messiaen's return to Paris, that the effect was produced by two birds duetting, one with a descending call, the other ascending. Messiaen, however, stuck with the original interpretation, which he adapted into a metaphor for the resurrection in the words he gave to St Francis: 'We also, after the resurrection, will climb the stairs of heaven, while appearing to descend.' In the passage that prefaces St Francis's Sermon, Messiaen declared unambiguously his belief in the privileged role of birds in creation, with an allusion to Keats: 'Everything of beauty must come about from Liberty, the Liberty of glory. Our Brothers the birds await the day . . . that day when Christ will reunite all creatures: those of the earth, those of the sky!'[26]

According to Messiaen *Saint François d'Assise* took four years to compose and four years to orchestrate.[27] The diaries tell a different story. On 15 August 1976, Messiaen wrote to Yves Baudrier: 'I am working hard on a new commission.'[28] That summer the diary shows an unprecedented ninety-four days free from appointments. By the time Messiaen returned to Paris (2 October) four of the scenes were already complete in short score, Messiaen reminding himself to add bar numbers and timings. In order of composition, the finished scenes were: Scene 4 ('L'Ange voyageur'), Scene 2 ('Laudes'), Scene 3 ('Le Baiser aux lépreux') and Scene 5 ('L'Ange musicien').[29] Messiaen was already thinking about practical details. He planned to make an appointment with Liebermann to propose the idea of reserving three of the boxes at the Opéra for the ondes Martenot and two sets of bells, and 'to show him the work done so far, in order to obtain the first payment'.

At the end of the diary for 1976 there are three pages of notes detailing instrumentation, the type of singer needed for the Angel, the positioning of the chorus, the number and type of ondes Martenot (Messiaen originally envisaged four), the need for seven flutes and a large chorus. The scenery would have gauzes, mirrors and coloured projections of paintings by Delaunay and Kandinsky. Who would produce, and who would conduct ('Boulez or Ozawa')? Messiaen's urgency was understandable given the need to stage the opera before Liebermann's term of office came to an end in June 1980. The timetable (Messiaen described the dates as 'imperative') was to finish the music and orchestration by January 1979, prepare the vocal score by November, and the orchestral material by the following April.

As well as his usual duties at the Conservatoire and at the Trinité, Messiaen – contrary to his usual practice in Paris – was hard at work composing, still with extraordinary speed. Two more scenes ('La Croix' and 'Les Stigmates', Scenes 1 and 7) were ready for photocopying on 16 February. On 30 March Messiaen came home after teaching all morning at the Conservatoire, then hurried to Guy Moquet Métro station on his way to an appointment at the Institut. Just before the station he tripped and fell heavily, breaking his glasses and inflicting a deep gash on his right ankle. Passers-by called the local pharmacist, who helped Messiaen hobble up the rue Marcadet to the Rothschild Clinic. His face was badly cut and bleeding, needing stitches on the eyebrows, nose and lips; unfortunately, in dealing with these obvious injuries, the serious wound to the leg was overlooked. Loriod recalled returning from her class at the Conservatoire to find her husband unexpectedly at home and barely recognizable. His greeting was characteristic: 'Quick, fetch the car: I must go to the orchestral rehearsal of *Couleurs*.' At the concert that evening he appeared on stage, alarmingly disfigured, to thank the conductor Michel Tabachnik and the pianist Michel Béroff.

Messiaen's Aunt Agnès died in January 1977. The Messiaens drove to Fuligny for her funeral (26 January). On 1 April they travelled to the Aube again, to visit Aunt Madeleine. Messiaen noted birdsong (the Aube being in Messiaen's view the best location in France for larks), but the continuing problem with his ankle finally forced him to return to Paris on 6 April and to cancel his playing at the Holy Week services. An immediate operation was decreed, but Messiaen refused to stay in hospital on account of a meeting (8 April) with Ozawa. That was a comfort, at least, with Ozawa accepting Messiaen's invitation to conduct the opera. The operation (11 April) success-

164 With Aunt Agnès and Aunt Madeleine, Lévigny, summer 1974.

165 Messiaen reading Thomas Merton at the summit of the Galibier, 14 September 1977.

fully dealt with the dead tissue on the ankle, but the long-term result was to be a succession of leg ulcers that plagued Messiaen for the rest of his life. He stayed at home, working when he felt able to on the opera, and going out only for the daily dressing of the wound at the clinic two hundred metres up the street. The treatments were excruciating, with a daily application of disinfectant to the deep wound. By the beginning of May Messiaen was back at the Conservatoire, analysing *Die Walküre* with his class. The surgeon was pleased with the way the wound was healing, and Messiaen resumed playing, travelling to Poitiers to perform *Visions de l'Amen*. He attended Mass at the Sacré-Cœur, noting the sermon by Mgr Charles, and the 'brilliant improvisations on the organ by Daniel Roth!'

At Petichet there were plans to enlarge the accommodation by constructing an upper house beside the lane that leads off the main road. Building began at the end of June, just as the new piano (a Bösendorfer) arrived: in due course it had to be winched through a first-floor window, an operation all the more perilous because of the steep slope of the ground. From his new music room Messiaen looked directly down to the lake, over the top of the trees at the bottom of the garden. His delight at the view was evoked in his diary: 'Sun and light mist – it's very fine and calm – the alder opposite my window is covered with dewdrops which shine in the sun like diamonds! Along the line of my gaze, each dewdrop is a miniature rainbow which passes through violet, blue, to green, and from orange yellow to red – the dark violet petunias are marvellous!!'

Messiaen had left to the last the two largest scenes in the opera, 'Le Prêche aux oiseaux' (Scene 6) and 'La Mort et la Nouvelle Vie' (Scene 8); nonetheless, he was confident enough of progress to take with him to Petichet outsize manuscript paper so that the task of orchestrating could begin. On 6 October 1977 the short score of the opera was complete. Messiaen's diary read: 'Telephone Liebermann to show him the finished opera.' The music, lasting four hours, had taken just fifteen months to compose. Messiaen now had the same amount of time for the orchestration if it was to be done by January 1979. This was not going to be long enough, as Messiaen's agenda for the meeting with Liebermann made clear: 'Talk about 1980–81, or 1982 [. . .] discuss the title, the singers, sets, costumes.' Messiaen wondered if Liebermann might extend his directorship; if not, would the contract for the opera remain valid? During their meeting, which took place at the rue Marcadet on 15 November, Liebermann first learned the subject of Messiaen's opera. He must have been indiscreet, because news of the work was broken on the radio, much to Messiaen's dismay.[30] But Liebermann persuaded Messiaen to stick to the plan to perform the opera in 1980. He now aimed to finish the orchestration by October 1979. In the end, however, the schedule would be hampered by the celebrations for Messiaen's seventieth birthday – which claimed his time for most of the second half of 1978 – and any hope of meeting the deadline was finally scuppered by the breakdown in his health at the end of the year.

Messiaen was determined to end his teaching in style (he was to retire in June). Much of January was taken up with a complete analysis of *Pelléas*, and in February and March the class studied *Siegfried*. As well as discussions of student compositions there was a demonstration on the tuba and contrabass tuba (by Fernand Lelong) and a talk by Tristan Murail ('*Mémoire/Érosion* – marvellous!!!'). In the last week of the spring term Messiaen turned to more old favourites: Greek metres, Adam de la Halle, Le Jeune's *Le Printemps*, and madrigals by Monteverdi and Gesualdo.

At the end of May there was a family reunion when the Messiaens, together with Jeanne Loriod, were in Nice for a performance of the *Trois petites Liturgies*, staying at the home of Loriod's sister, Jacqueline. Rehearsals took place in the Musée Biblique Marc Chagall, in the recital hall lit by Chagall's stained glass. Guy Bernard-Delapierre lived nearby in Antibes, in a large house filled with the treasures collected during a lifetime. The Messiaens were shocked to find that Delapierre was living in disarray, his mind still alert but his body in sad decline.

In May and June the main work of Messiaen's class was *Götterdämmerung*, though there was time for discussion of *Le Sacre* and of contemporary works (by Penderecki, Dutilleux, Pierre Henry, and *Chronochromie*). The analysis of *Götterdäm-*

merung was finished on 14 June. In his final week Messiaen gave the class a course in plainchant. The last class was on 19 June 1978: 'Saw and listened to gagaku, [. . .] Benjamin's harmonies, a work by [Erzebet] Csik. The students gave me a present of the facsimile sketches of *Pelléas* – [Jean-Michel] Bardez has knitted a scarf for me in violet, orange, green.' Messiaen had taught continuously for thirty-seven years. To his great distress, not a single member of the Conservatoire hierarchy came to say goodbye. Messiaen had certainly been something of an independent spirit during his long career, but that was probably why he had presided over the institution's most productive class since Fauré's. The failure of the Conservatoire's director, Raymond Gallois-Montbrun, to note Messiaen's retirement was an inexplicable lapse.

The second half of 1978 was packed with world-wide concerts and celebrations in honour of Messiaen's seventieth birthday. In late June there were preparations in Paris for the forthcoming tour of Japan – *La Transfiguration* (with the choir of Radio France), *Les Offrandes oubliées*, *Réveil des oiseaux* and *Chronochromie*. Rehearsals were disrupted by the absence of the conductor, Lorin Maazel, who was elsewhere in Paris recording the soundtrack for Joseph Losey's film of *Don Giovanni*. On 24 June Messiaen left for Petichet, taking with him 'everything for Scene 4'. Leaving Petichet in the care of Pascal and Josette, the Messiaens flew to Tokyo on 11 July along with the singers and musicians of the Orchestre National. After an emotional reunion with former pupils, and garlanded with flowers, they arrived at their hotel where to Messiaen's delight the

167 Messiaen's class at the Conservatoire in 1978. George Benjamin is sitting on Messiaen's right.

168 Messiaen dining in Kyoto, 22 July 1978.

music piped throughout the building was of birdsong. Maazel had by now learned the score of *La Transfiguration* and the performance (15 July) at the NHK Hall was 'brilliant'. Other concerts followed, and the last performance of *La Transfiguration* in Kyoto was 'even more beautiful than in Tokyo'. Characteristically, Messiaen reminded himself to 'collect the Luminophone' after the concert. Loriod's recital, with five of the *Regards* framing *La Fauvette des jardins*, was given on a Yamaha ('the best piano I ever played', she recalled). Messiaen awarded his wife six exclamation marks, then devoted space to the colours on display – Loriod's blue dress, the violet seats, the brown-yellow walls, orange screens, and floral decorations of mauve, blue and pink hortensias.

By 25 July the Messiaens had returned to Petichet. During the summer he finished the orchestration of Scene 4 and began work on Scene 2. He was too busy to travel to Utah for the naming of Mount Messiaen, but noted the occasion in his diary: '5 August. In the morning the naming of Mount Messiaen – unveiling of the plaque on the rock. In the evening, a performance of my *Quatuor pour la fin du Temps* by students of the Aspen Conservatory, a showing of the film by Denise Tual, *Messiaen et les oiseaux*, an exhibition of photos by J.S. Carter on southern Utah.'

There now began (2 October) an extended tour of North America, with concerts in Boston, Cleveland, Detroit, Philadelphia and Montreal. The diary records the details of this gruelling tour, with at one point the rueful comment 'I was present for everything'. During a few days without engagements in New York, the Messiaens attended Mass at St Patrick's Cathedral and had the pleasure of meeting Julie Whitaker, the schoolteacher from Utah who had organized the naming of Mount Messiaen. Zubin Mehta conducted *Les Offrandes oubliées*, *Oiseaux exotiques* and *Et exspecto* at a Friday afternoon concert in Avery Fisher Hall, at which he had warned Messiaen to expect an audience of elderly ladies with lapdogs. The reception, however, was 'a miracle: they took off their gloves and applauded.' Peter Serkin took advantage of Messiaen's presence in New York to play him the *Vingt Regards*. On 12 November the Messiaens flew to Washington, and with Rostropovich they were received at the White House by President Carter and his wife. Rostropovich conducted *L'Ascension* and *Oiseaux exotiques*, and after each of the four performances he presented Loriod with a differently coloured spray of flowers.[31]

The Messiaens returned to Paris (on Concorde) on 18 November, just in time for the start of the French birthday celebrations. The first concert (19 November) was introduced by Jean-Louis Barrault and included *Visions de l'Amen* played by the brilliant team of Jean-Rodolphe Kars and Michel Béroff. On

169 Messiaen, Loriod, President Jimmy Carter, Rosalind Carter and Rostropovich at the White House, 14 November 1978.

21 November Messiaen attended a ceremony with speeches at the Ministry of Culture, leaving Paris by road at 4.30 p.m. in order to be in Bordeaux that evening. The next day Messiaen was in great pain. A prostate operation was needed; he spent two nights in hospital, where a catheter was inserted, while Loriod fulfilled engagements (*Turangalîla*) at La Rochelle and Bordeaux. Messiaen was transferred by air to Paris, and spent a week at home awaiting admission to hospital, trying to carry on as normal. He went to Mass and confession at the Sacré-Cœur, a rehearsal and performance of *La Transfiguration*, to rehearsals of *Turangalîla*, and to a performance of the *Catalogue d'oiseaux* by a team of young pianists. Only on 30 November did Messiaen capitulate, cancelling attendance at a concert of works by former students.

From 1 December Messiaen was in hospital at the Cochin. Loriod shuttled between rehearsals and the hospital, sleeping in Messiaen's room on a folding chair, much to the disapproval of the medical authorities. The operation was performed early on 5 December. That evening Loriod returned from playing *Réveil des oiseaux*, still in her concert dress, carrying her music together with bouquets of flowers, to find that her husband had listened to the broadcast and so was able to conduct their usual post mortem.

For Messiaen, fretting at the lack of progress on *Saint François* and the prospect of several weeks of convalescence, the tributes in the press and the letters from well-wishers had a double edge. All anticipated the early completion of his opera. Yves Baudrier wrote with hopes for a speedy recovery and for 'new strength, for we are expecting everything, now that you are completing the orchestration of *Saint François*'.[32] Bernard Gavoty, in his review of the Messiaen festivities for *Le Figaro*, awaited 'the opera – *Saint François d'Assise* – which [Messiaen] is finishing orchestrating'.[33]

On 10 December, the day of Messiaen's seventieth birthday, Loriod performed *Des Canyons*, the occasion marked by a speech from Pierre Boulez (who was the conductor) in which he gave an affectionate and acute portrait of his former teacher:

Olivier Messiaen was to have been with us for his seventieth birthday today. He is still in hospital after an operation, but I know that he is listening to the broadcast of this concert, and so I want in these few words to convey to him our thoughts and affections, all the warmer for his absence. [. . .]

Were it not for the fear of being taken for a bad punster I would add that 'composer' is exactly the right word for Messiaen, in that it suggests the word 'composite'. His personality resembles some great baroque building: he fascinates us by the diversity of his options and the elaborate simplicity of his choices. Beneath the very real complexities of his intellectual world he has remained simple and capable of wonder – and that alone is enough to win our hearts.

Olivier Messiaen, I know that you are listening to me and I want to repeat to you the gratitude and the affection that we all feel for the example you have never failed to set both as a composer and as a teacher. We thank you for *your* adventure, which has also become ours, and we wish you a speedy recovery so that you may continue to share that adventure for many years to come. Happy birthday![34]

'Brother Messiaen at the Opéra'
1979–1983

Saint François took five-and-a-half years to orchestrate. Messiaen worked methodically, scene by scene, first making an orchestral draft, then a fair copy. One advantage of the opera no longer being a secret was that he could recruit Loriod to help, and early in 1978 she began work on arranging a vocal score. Among Messiaen's first appointments after convalescing from his operation was a meeting at the offices of Leduc (2 March) where he gave a presentation on *Saint François* and explained the sources for the libretto. It was an emotional occasion. Leduc agreed to publish the opera and to pay the costs of copying.

One of the most important documents to do with *Saint François* is the manuscript of Messiaen's short score. In essence this must be what Messiaen had presented to Liebermann in November 1977. However, the manuscript shows that the music was subject to considerable further revision, and it is clear that some of the more complex sections – the birdsong in Scene 6, for example – were far from complete in 1977.

170 Messiaen's drawing (12 April 1980) of the tree at the Carceri under which St Francis preached to the birds.

Messiaen began orchestrating *Saint François* in the order in which the music had been composed, beginning with Scene 4. His first change was to the scene's title page, crossing out 'La visite de l'Ange' and substituting 'L'Ange voyageur'. Revisions to the short score can be seen from the different styles of handwriting and the use of ink or pencil. The music is in Messiaen's large 'fair copy' style, with small but neat indications of the outline of the instrumentation. Later Messiaen added much more detail. A case in point is the phrase for the New Caledonian notou, originally scored for horns. Markings made on the short score show Messiaen thickening the harmonies with a trumpet and bassoons, and picking out the bass line on the ondes Martenot. In the final score he goes further, adding oboes and a cor anglais, and giving a shimmer to the notou's repeated chord with trills on flutes and clarinets.

The whole of the central part of Scene 4, from the entry of the Angel until after the exasperated departure of Brother Elias, is hurriedly written, indicating a wholesale later revision. Within this there are yet further changes in the form of inserted pages; very surprisingly it was only at this late stage that Messiaen devised a key element of the scene, the music that announces the entrance of the Angel – a jerky fanfare in the style of Japanese nô theatre,[1] with a piercing sonority for high oboes and clarinets. More inserted pages come at the entrance and exit of Brother Elias ('Why am I always being disturbed?'): in both places Messiaen added solos for what he calls the 'fitful rhythms' of the reed warbler.[2] Another significant change is to the music of the gerygone, in the passage where the Angel 'seems to dance without touching the ground'.[3] The full score has *pizzicati*, with additional syncopated chords, probably to enhance the persistent and 'mocking'[4] tone of the gerygone's song, which is played by a solo piccolo.

Scene 5, 'L'Ange musicien', contains, as one would expect, some of the opera's most extraordinary instrumental effects. Francis's quotation from St Paul, 'Autre est l'éclat du soleil' ('There is one glory of the sun', 1 Corinthians 15:41), is conceived in the short score as an austere sonority for four solo instruments: flute, oboe, cello and bassoon. In the full score the sound is refined with the utmost delicacy, with staccato 'water droplets' for two ondes Martenot and crotales, and subtle doublings on clarinet and another flute. For the music of the kestrel, which alerts Francis to the Angel's approach, Messiaen added the bizarre effect of a contrabass tuba playing with a bassoon reed, an 'atrocious screeching – high approximate sounds';[5] 'from a contrabass tuba this is rather unexpected; I even manage to have it play a genuine theme of two or three notes.'[6] Several minor changes arise from simple practicalities: making the singers more audible, or helping to give them the note at the start of a phrase. An example is at the Angel's 'Dieu nous éblouit par excès de Vérité' ('God will dazzle us with an excess of Truth'), where a preliminary chord on the vibraphone was added, with the consequence of altering the whole shape of the phrase. Where the Angel prepares to play the viol, the short score goes straight into an orchestral sketch: glissando harmonics on upper strings, with keyboard percussion and bells, and the chorus supported by lower strings. The only addition in the finished full score is 'a solo double bass, playing on two strings with either the metal screw button of the bow or a triangle rod, while the instrumentalist muffles the fundamentals: this produces a tremolo of harmonics and results in some high-pitched sounds akin to water droplets'.[7]

In Scenes 6 and 7, a high proportion of the short score consists of orchestral sketch, written in a comparatively untidy way. There is evidence in the *cahiers* that much of the music for these two scenes was conceived well after the supposed completion of the short score in October 1977. Preliminary notes for Scene 7, made at Saarbrücken on 9 July 1978,[8] show that Messiaen's ideas were only just forming: 'Ensemble of cluster glissandos which move at different speeds – see Bali, gagaku, [Boulez's] *Pli selon pli*, Xenakis, Ligeti'. The clusters can be found in the manuscript of the short score, which at this point is a very full orchestral sketch, hardly differing from the finished score. On the same page of the *cahier* is a rather fuller sketch for the infliction of the Stigmata: a stalking figure on the brass, with an accelerando and crescendo, and a huge accented chord, borrowing the notes of the harmony with which the Angel hammers on the monastery door in Scene 4. Originally Messiaen intended each staccato chord to synchronize with the inflicting of each wound, an idea subsequently abandoned; in the finished score the chords were transferred to accompany the words of the chorus, 'C'est Moi'.[9]

Messiaen used the same June 1978 *cahier* to plan the birdsong at the end of Scene 6: 'After the Blessing – birdsongs for 3 xylophones (larks), another lark harmonized on the woodwind, a counterpoint of New Caledonian white eye [zostérops] on the violins, a blackbird harmonized on the violas, and a carillon of bells – all played together.' The same sheet of the *cahier* contains an outline of music to describe the birds flying away in the shape of a Cross: 'See the end of *Erwartung* (or *Wozzeck*) and Xenakis.' In the event the birds were not portrayed in this way, but more simply and more impressively, through a sequence of rising chords.[10]

One of the most striking differences between the short score and finished work is Messiaen's invention of birdsong played 'outside the tempo'. The short score shows the actual moment when this occurred to Messiaen, when the orchestral introduction to Scene 6 – scored for xylophone, xylorimba and marimba – is crossed out. In the final score this music is reinstated, and overlaid with a medley of birdsong, played *hors tempo*. This inspiration came very late in the process of orchestrating the opera. None of the orchestral sketches in the short score contains any *hors tempo* music. Moreover, a note at the top of the short score for Scene 6 indicates that the whole scene had already been thoroughly revised and approved: 'All checked and *good* [. . .]: Yes.'

171 The opening of Scene 4 of *Saint François d'Assise* in Messiaen's short score.

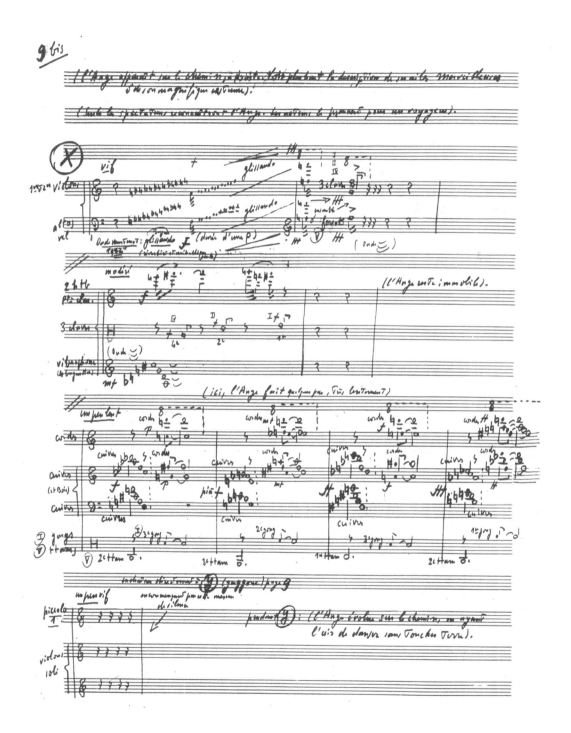

172 The apparition of the Angel in Scene 4 of *Saint François* in Messiaen's short score. This was a later addition.

173 The music of the Angel in Scene 5 of *Saint François* in Messiaen's short score.

174 A sketch for the 'hors tempo' music in Scene 6 of *Saint François*.

Messiaen may well have started the orchestration of Scene 4, 'L'Ange voyageur', as early as the summer break of 1977. The bulk of the work on this and on Scene 2, 'Les Laudes', was done the following summer at Petichet, from late June to the end of September, although neither was fully finished until March 1979. Meanwhile, Messiaen had begun the orchestral sketch of Scene 3 ('Le Baiser au lépreux') on which he worked in January 1979, while confined to bed recovering from his operation. He was still aiming to have the opera ready to be performed, as agreed, in June 1980, before the end of Liebermann's tenure as Director of the Opéra. To this end Messiaen asked the copyists to give priority to the vocal parts, which would be needed for rehearsal before the orchestral material. However, by April 1979, with only three of the shorter scenes ready, it must have become clear that there was little chance of the opera being ready. On 11 May Messiaen went to hear a double-bill of *Oedipus Rex* and *L'Enfant et les sortilèges* at the invitation of Bernard Lefort, who was to be Liebermann's successor. Messiaen had known Lefort for years, as a distinguished baritone, with whom he had performed the *Poèmes pour Mi* and *Harawi*. Lefort outlined a solution which would enable at least a partial fulfilment of the agreement with Liebermann: give *Saint François* as 'Four Franciscan Scenes' (Scenes 2–5) and postpone a complete première. Messiaen was much relieved when Liebermann – very honourably – vetoed the suggestion of an abridged performance, and gave Messiaen three more years to finish the opera: 'Liebermann rejects the solution of four scenes – and I finish for 1983 – yes.' Though Lefort and Liebermann had acted impeccably, the episode seems to have sown seeds of disquiet in Messiaen's mind, and over the next four years his relations with the management of the Opéra remained clouded by suspicion.

Part of the reason for the slow progress in orchestrating *Saint François* was that Messiaen viewed the opera as a *Gesamtkunstwerk* over which he was to have total control; originally he even wanted to direct the staging himself.[11] Notes in Messiaen's diary show his minute concern with details of the entire production. In 1979, for example, he was worrying away at the problem of where to put all the instrumentalists, and in particular the three ondes Martenot (the original plan had been to place one of these at the back of the theatre, among the audience). He was also thinking about whether the chorus should be on- or offstage in Scene 7, 'Les Stigmates'. Then there was the entry of the Angel in Scene 5 for which Messiaen imagined a staircase on wheels; in the end the designer, Sandro Sequi, devised a less hazardous solution, the Angel appearing on a bridge above the stage.[12]

At least Messiaen was content to delegate the casting of the principal roles to Lefort: in December 1979, at Lefort's suggestion, he went to the Opéra for *Les Contes d'Hoffmann*, in which he heard Kenneth Riegel and Christiane Eda-Pierre, who would take the roles of the Leper and the Angel. Messiaen was enthusiastic about both singers. Riegel came to the rue Marcadet

(17 December) to try out the music of Scene 3 ('The Kissing of the Leper') and to Messiaen's delight accepted the role. In the event Lefort's tenure was shortlived, and it was his successor, Massimo Bogianckino, who was left to negotiate Messiaen's demands. Messiaen's vastly augmented woodwind, brass and percussion sections (and the three ondes Martenot) were not negotiable, but Bogianckino managed to reduce the strings and drastically prune the chorus, from 500 to 100.[13]

By the end of 1979 Scenes 2, 3, 4 and 5 had been orchestrated, and Messiaen had begun work on 'Les Stigmates', noting ideas in his diary: 'Use Swanee whistles (as in Ravel's *Sortilèges* and Xenakis's *Terretektorh*). At the beginning, use the three ondes for the Owl. After that, during the choruses, all the violins doing glissandos in harmonics in 32 real parts (written aleatorically), and also the three ondes doing little glissandos (mixed with the aleatoric writing).'

During 1980 Messiaen's life became increasingly reclusive as he dedicated himself to working on the opera. For the most part he stayed at home, forgoing trips abroad to hear his music; he even absented himself from a press conference at the Opéra, attended by representatives of La Scala who were interested in staging *Saint François*. One event Messiaen did not miss was the visit to Paris of Pope John Paul II, when he was part of a vast crowd that converged on Notre-Dame ('I was on my feet for five hours'). He admired the Pope's sermon, and was struck by the effect of the welcoming fanfare as it clashed with the peal of bells: 'orchestration of Scene 8: use ensemble of brass *fortissimo* with double carillon of bells'.

In March 1980 Messiaen dined with the clergy of the Trinité, reminding himself to take along three bottles of wine and a cake. During the evening it was suggested that Messiaen write a booklet about the organ. He was also asked to give a recital in December 1981 to celebrate his fifty years at the Trinité. Messiaen duly wrote the booklet, but proposed a recital in 1984 or 1985, noting in his diary that 'I shall be able to give the first performance of a work by me for organ'; this is the first indication of the future *Livre du Saint Sacrement*. The postponement of the recital may have been due to worries over a finger in Messiaen's right hand: after X-rays he was prescribed manipulation of the head, neck and shoulder, possibly an early sign of the arthritis which was to plague his last years. The diary records several visits to the Opéra (*Boris Godunov*, *Die Frau ohne Schatten* and *Dardanus*), and in April Messiaen heard José Van Dam (who was being considered for the role of Francis) in Gounod's *Faust*. On 24 April Van Dam came to the rue Marcadet. Messiaen read through the libretto and Loriod played the music of Scene 3. She remembered Van Dam as very shy, sipping tea but refusing strawberries ('they irritate the throat'). Messiaen noted in his diary that Van Dam had the necessary range, and 'will sing the Canticle of the Sun easily – he is in agreement to sing the role of St Francis'.

By April 1981 Scene 7, 'Les Stigmates', was largely finished. Messiaen rewarded himself with a spring holiday in Assisi, departing on 5 April after playing for the Easter services. His excitement is apparent from notes in his *cahier* and diary:

9 April: morning at the convent of San Damiano. Saw the garden of the cloister, then at Rivortorto the two stone huts of the first community reconstructed from the church, followed by the tiny church of the Porziuncola in the middle of Santa Maria degli Angeli. Mass at the Basilica. 10 April at Pian d'Arca: fine sunny weather! Strong wind! The Sermon to the Birds is commemorated by a small altar with an inscription: 'In this place St Francis sang God's praises, and urged the birds to thank God for enabling them to multiply peacefully, for the streams, mountains and valleys, and for trees in which to take refuge and build nests, and for their *marvellous songs* – and let the birds announce to the world the good Word and Divine Providence.' – very approximate translation!!! Towards Montefalco (4.30 p.m.) a blackcap (*capinera* in Italian) and a mistle thrush (*tordela*) – very pretty countryside.

11 April. Greccio, where St Francis founded the first crèche. Midday, in the forest near the convent: robin, wren and great tit. 5.30 p.m., at the convent of Fonte Colombo. Visit to the convent with Brother Giorgio (a Franciscan). Grotto where St Francis fasted forty days before establishing his order. In the convent: a robin; in the forest: a blackcap. 12 April: on foot in Assisi. Visit the church of St Clare. Sun! lovely fine weather. Then from 11.30 a.m. to 7.30 p.m. at the Carceri (robin and blackcap). Took numerous notes on the large evergreen oak for the set of the Sermon to the Birds.

During the years of working on *Saint François*, Messiaen noted in his diary the details of a number of commissions, none of which he accepted. The first of these came in October 1976 when the Messiaens visited the Abbey of Montserrat after performing *Visions de l'Amen* in Barcelona:

Saw the Father Abbot, Brother Gregori Estrada (organist, musicologist, specialist in medieval manuscripts); saw the gardens, trees, marvellous rocks in sugarloaves in the countryside; heard a robin. The brothers have given me a disc of their children's choir, and a book on the birds of Catalonia. Write for Montserrat a *Salve Regina*, for a choir of children singing in three parts, in a simple style, with soprano voices ranging from C to G – about fifty children.

Daniel Barenboim asked for a ten-minute work for the Orchestre de Paris, and Marcel Couraud, who had directed over two hundred performances of the

Cinq Rechants, requested a piece for the Chorale Marcel Couraud. Even a commission from Rostropovich came to nothing, though Messiaen did get as far as making a few notes:

> Compose three or four very short pieces, very well contrasted, for cello and orchestra. See the *Prelude* no.18 [in F minor] by Chopin: this could form a recitative of forceful motifs for cello solo, punctuated by dry fortissimo chords on the orchestra. Write a second piece with gently descending melodic movement, a piece of charm (with ensemble of flutes etc.), together with a very slow movement, with a solo on the cello supported by trombones – and a finale, *fortissimo*, 'vif'.

In the second half of 1980 work proceeded steadily: Scene 7 was finished on 23 June, and a week later, at Petichet, Messiaen began Scene 8. In terms of public appearances the busiest month of an otherwise quiet year was December. Messiaen travelled to Brussels to receive the Croix de Commandeur de l'Ordre de la Couronne; among the speeches was 'a marvellous poem (referring through symbols to all my works) by Henri Pousseur'. On 16 December he heard Van Dam at the Opéra in *Der fliegende Holländer*. Van Dam came to the rue Marcadet and received copies of Scenes 2, 3 and 7, which were now ready in vocal score. On Christmas Eve, at the Trinité, Messiaen accompanied choruses from Handel's *Messiah*. The following year, 1981, opened with a reunion at the rue Marcadet, with the entire Loriod family – Jacqueline, Jeanne and their husbands, together with Jacqueline's three children and grand-daughter Eléonore. A day later Messiaen visited another relative, Michel Guéritte (the grandson of Messiaen's Aunt Madeleine), to discuss audio-visual effects:

> Marvellous!!! This is exactly what's needed for the opera; projections on a large screen (five metres high), placed behind the stage, which can be raised or lowered. These are called 'dioramas' – perfect for the *flights of birds*, for *stained glass*, for the *final light* and for the *Cross*. One can also project a Cross in the auditorium with laser beams.

Progress on the opera now became agonizingly slow. Scene 8 took the whole winter of 1980–1, and it was not until June 1981 that Messiaen was ready to begin the challenge of orchestrating 'Le Prêche aux oiseau*x*' (Scene 6). Messiaen was worried about his health: he had a sore throat, the ankle injured in 1978 was painful, and he needed sleeping pills. He also complained of an irregular heartbeat and saw a cardiologist (whose verdict, however, was reassuring), and as always his eyesight was troublesome. By autumn 1981 the task of orchestration was alarmingly behind schedule. Messiaen's diary shows that he planned to continue work on Scene 6 until Christmas, and then turn to making the fair

175 La Sauline.

176 Messiaen and Loriod playing Scene 4 of *Saint François d'Assise*, 14 May 1982.

copy of Scene 5. Still the work fell behind, with Depraz, the copyist, worried about the lack of new material. The crisis came in December. Loriod recalled that Messiaen was subdued and exhausted, unable to decide what to do; he was prone to fits of weeping, and was convinced the opera would never be finished.

At this point Loriod offered to help, in a way that was without precedent: she suggested that she should take the job of finishing Scene 5 – transferring Messiaen's orchestral sketch into fair copy – while he continued with Scene 6. It says much for Messiaen's desperation that he agreed. He was also lucky to have a doctor (Dr Bernachon) who mixed medical advice with doses of common sense; according to Loriod, the doctor urged Messiaen to take daily exercise, if only to go to the post or walk to the hairdresser. The very next day Messiaen noted in his diary an appointment for a haircut, and he resumed the practice, begun in 1980 while the organ at the Trinité was being overhauled, of climbing the hill to Montmartre to attend evening Mass at the Sacré-Cœur.

Another new interest was the purchase in 1981 of a second country retreat. Much though the Messiaens loved Petichet, it had several disadvantages: the distance from Paris, the Alpine climate which meant the house was snowbound for much of the year, and the fact that it was known to so many friends, pupils and admirers, who were liable to call and interrupt Messiaen's work. They decided to search in the Sologne region, just north of Bourges, only two hours drive from Paris, and a happy hunting ground on earlier birdsong trips (the setting, for example, of 'La Rousserolle effarvatte' from the *Catalogue*). Brochures from estate agents began to arrive. One particularly caught Messiaen's eye: 'House in a hamlet, near the forest of Vouzeron. 85 million old francs. Birch-trees, oaks, aspens, copses, rhododendrons, 2 hectares. Large house: living room, kitchen, 3 bedrooms, tout confort, phone, electric heating.' Characteristically, it was the grounds that most interested Messiaen. Unlike Petichet, which for much of the time had to look after itself, the garden had been carefully tended:

> Sauline (the place is known as La-Lœuf-du-Houx). At the entry to the wood on the north side: cotoneaster. At each corner of the house: four small shrubs (thujas) in pyramid shapes. In front of lawn: thuja (dark green); in front of the sitting-room: red geraniums; on the lawn: pink rhododendrons; and in the wood: hornbeams, birch, beech, oak, with ferns, starry ferns, mushrooms. In the undergrowth are brambles, honeysuckle, autumn ferns, all red: marvellous!!! In the centre of the wood is an immense silver birch (this is the biggest tree in the wood). At the southern end of the lawn is a thuja from Arizona – pale green, blue-shaded – and an American oak, like a maple, with red leaves.

Messiaen decorated this diary entry with drawings of leaves. In early summer the garden would be a riot of colour: 'Magnificent foxgloves, cascades of red-violet with little bells. Brown Indian carnations, red sage with its long carnival nose, a flowerbed of magnificent begonias, and above all, Busy Lizzies in all their orange and purple-mauve hues.'

The sister of the vendor turned out to be a close friend of Jacqueline Loriod, a coincidence which confirmed Messiaen's belief that his choice was guided by providence. The purchase was completed on 6 June 1981, and the Messiaens' first act was to plant a weeping willow in honour of the property's name, La Sauline, and to remind them of the lakeside at Petichet. Loriod had chosen three new pianos for the house, a Bösendorfer grand and two Rameau uprights. The living room, paved with Italian flagstones, had a warm acoustic and was large enough to hold an audience of seventy. Its main purpose, however, was to act as a recording studio, since Messiaen's plan was to record the whole opera, with himself singing and Loriod at the piano, and to distribute cassettes to the singers.

The Messiaens moved into La Sauline on 26 October 1981, having shopped for furniture at Galéries Lafayette in Paris. The Bösendorfer arrived the following day, and Messiaen, as usual with a new piano, sat down to play Debussy's *Reflets dans l'eau*. Petichet would continue to be the summer home, but between October and June the Messiaens used La Sauline as often as possible for short breaks. They attended Mass at Neuvy (six kilometres away) and to their amazement found that they were recognized by the priest, Père René Bobineau, who had been a fellow prisoner at Görlitz. Messiaen was delighted by the coincidence, but asked Père Bobineau to keep the Messiaens' presence in the locality a secret.

The emotional crisis in December 1981 proved a turning point. Once his feelings – about whether the opera would ever be finished – were out in the open, Messiaen started to feel better. Early in the new year he agreed to a visit by all Loriod's relations, and attended a concert by her pupils, pleased to note that the pianist who played 'Le Merle bleu' wore a dress of exactly the right shade of blue. Loriod had been working to good effect and by the end of January she had copied all of Scene 5. The Messiaens spent a week at La Sauline. Loriod recalled Messiaen's greater optimism, helped by sunny weather and the garden radiant with birdsong. In March Messiaen travelled to Luxembourg to hear the *Méditations* played by Louis Thiry, *Vingt Regards* (Loriod), and *Turangalîla* conducted by Louis de Froment. The concerts were 'marvellous' and the diary speckled with exclamation marks. Best of all, Messiaen was turning his thoughts to new composition. Initially his plans were modest, an indication of how low his self-confidence had sunk. Instead of taking up one of the orchestral commissions that had come his way, Messiaen returned to an idea he had had in 1980, for a series of études for organ. He reminded himself to look for musical ideas by listening to the improvisations he had recorded in 1977 to go with recitations (by Gisèle Casadesus) of poems by Cécile Sauvage. He now began to make notes on his improvisations at the Trinité: on Easter Saturday he improvised on 'the walls of water from the passing through the Red Sea – très bien'.

In March 1982 Messiaen had a number of meetings with Ozawa, who was in Paris to conduct *Tosca*. Ozawa came to the Trinité (13 March) and then accompanied Messiaen to the rue Marcadet where he heard Scenes 3 and 8, and was given scores of Scenes 5 and 8, and a cassette of Scene 3. In early April Ozawa returned in the company of Jean Laforge, the chorus-master, and was given home-made recordings of Scenes 2, 3 and 4 ('très bien') and Scene 7 ('pas très bien'). On 5 April Ozawa received a cassette of Scene 8; this must have been unsatisfactory because Messiaen and Loriod re-recorded it at La Sauline later in April. The diary is busy with engagements: the première of Daniel-Lesur's opera *Ondine* at the Théâtre des Champs-Élysées; on the radio there were broadcasts of the *Sept Haïkaï* and *Couleurs de la Cité céleste*, with Pierre-Laurent Aimard as soloist, and at the Evian Festival Loriod played *Oiseaux exotiques*. Messiaen went to Beauvais to hear Jennifer Bate play *La Nativité*: 'very beautiful stained glass – the highest vault in the world!!!' In June a milestone was passed with the declaration of *Saint François* to SACEM.

At the end of May 1982, at La Sauline, Messiaen finished orchestrating Scene 1. By July he was immersed in orchestrating the second and larger 'concert of birds' from Scene 6. The task was physically exhausting, and for two weeks Messiaen spent most of each day on his feet leaning over outsize sheets of manuscript paper. On 6 July he was appalled to learn that Bogianckino planned to make cuts in the opera. Messiaen wrote at once refusing permission, but the weeks passed without reply. The 'concert of birds' was finished on 26 August. Still anxious about developments in Paris, the Messiaens went to Turin where Messiaen, Berio and Penderecki received awards. Messiaen was disappointed to find that the Holy Shroud was not on display: 'I believe in it, because it seems to me not like a miracle but like a natural phenomenon. At Hiroshima bodies of the victims were found etched on the walls. In the same way the Resurrection was like an atomic explosion: Christ rose at a stroke and his image was imprinted on the Shroud.'[14]

Messiaen heard from Bogianckino on 14 September. His letter must have been conciliatory, because a month later (18 October) Messiaen recorded a satisfactory meeting: 'Bogianckino and Sequi [the designer] came to rue Marcadet – NO MORE CUTS.' Almost certainly the Opéra administration was fearful that an opera that had taken over five years to orchestrate must be immensely long, and would pass the magic hour of midnight when union regulations demanded overtime, an unthinkable expense in view of the vast number of musicians. Messiaen remained implacable: the opera would be played in full or not at all.[15]

In autumn 1982 Messiaen was in poor health. On 10 October he cancelled his playing at the Trinité: his back was painful, he was spitting blood, and had a high fever. Dr Bernachon diagnosed bronchitis and ordered an X-ray of the lungs. Messiaen entered hospital for five days of tests, during which (Loriod recalled) he begged the doctors to be allowed to leave and continue his work. He decided for the time being to continue with Scene 6 in draft form, postponing making a fair copy. By late October Messiaen was better, and recorded sleeping three nights in succession without pills.

In November the roles of Brother Massée and Brother Bernard (Georges Gautier and Philippe Courtis) were cast. Messiaen was delighted with both singers. Loriod remembered that the interpretation of Courtis in particular would cause Messiaen to incorporate many new nuances in the score. Courtis accepted the role on 18 November: 'He is marvellous!! We played him the whole of Scene 4 – it's *yes*.' The diary is full of such meetings:

30 November. Sandro Sequi came to the rue Marcadet with the scene painter Giuseppe Crisolini-Malatesta. We discussed positionings and practicalities, and whether to lower the curtain after each Scene. Spoke to them about the Leper: it's he who dances (not a dancer!), as he tears off his sores and leaps for joy – there must be lighting on St Francis at the same time. 3 December at the rue Mardadet: Michel Philippe (Brother Léon) and Robert Grenier (understudy for Brother Bernard). 5 December: Liebermann at 5 p.m., here – give him the *Sigle*.

177 Messiaen in Jerusalem, 1983.

This tiny piece, a *Sigle* (or 'acronym'), for flute solo, was composed by Messiaen at Liebermann's request. The music lasts about thirty seconds, and was recorded by Alain Marion on 16 December for Erato. The fragment would be re-used in the seventh movement of *Éclairs sur l'Au-delà*.

Messiaen headed the diary for 1983 with words from the *Imitation of Christ*, sung by the chorus at the end of Scene 7 of *Saint François*: 'Is there nothing so hard that one must not bear it for eternal life?' The year began with a bereavement, the death of Loriod's godmother, Nelly Sivade: the funeral took place at Père Lachaise on 19 January. The fair copy of Scene 6 was finally finished at La Sauline in February. Loriod recalled that Messiaen at once started to sleep better, and the diary noted the flowers planted in the garden, and a visit to the church at nearby Nançay to admire a statue of St Francis. Back in Paris there were almost daily visits to the photo-copying shop: 160 vocal scores were needed for the chorus, bound at Messiaen's insistence in a different colour for each Scene, and these were ready only just in time for the first rehearsal on 1 March. At a high-level meeting on 21 April with Bogianckino, Sequi and Crisolini-Malatesta, Messiaen noted the tension between management and Ozawa, who was demanding no fewer than twelve full rehearsals.

A break came with Messiaen's first visit to Israel, in May, where he received a prize from the Wolf Foundation, shared with Vladimir Horowitz and the Israeli composer Josef Tal. The Messiaens visited Bethlehem, the Mount of Olives and Gethsemane. At Petichet (from 7 July) the Messiaens worked against the clock proof-reading the material. Loriod was finishing the vocal score of Scene 6, using Messiaen's short score, which she covered with finger-ings, arranging the music for two pianos in order to sacrifice as little of the birdsong as possible. Messiaen approved the vocal score and they recorded Scene 6. The opera was at last finished on 22 August. The relief was stupendous: Loriod remembered a tame dormouse, galloping about the attic as if in celebration.

Rehearsals for *Saint François* began at the Opéra on 6 September. Kent Nagano had been recruited as assistant conductor on Messiaen's recommendation. He had first come to Messiaen's attention in the summer of 1980, when he sent Messiaen a tape of the *Poèmes pour Mi* performed by students at Berkeley, as part of a cycle of Messiaen's orchestral music. For months Nagano heard nothing, then was astonished to receive a long letter of congratulation with detailed comments. He sent more tapes, each receiving meticulous criticism. Messiaen suggested coming to California in person, offering the services of Loriod as piano soloist. The upshot was that Nagano organized a performance of *La Transfiguration* in May 1981. At the first rehearsal it seemed embarrassingly obvious that he had overreached himself. Preliminary rehearsals had not gone well, and now, with Messiaen present, the choir seemed unable to sing more than a few bars without breaking down. Nagano decided to begin by running through one of the movements:

> Sure enough, after three bars, major disaster. We continued for another couple of bars, and finally limped through the movement. I looked at Messiaen's face but he said nothing: he was really quiet, staring at his music. I asked 'What should we do now?' and he said, 'Well, maybe we should go on.' So we went through the whole piece, and when I spoke to him afterwards I said, 'The choir is having a difficult time, but we have scheduled a few more extra rehearsals.' And he replied, 'Yes, it's quite difficult.' But somehow Messiaen's presence was such a serious fear-generating factor that the choir became animated and demanded even more rehearsal time. And to cut a long story short, within three days they learned the piece, amazingly well.[16]

178 With Kent Nagano for *La Transfiguration* in Hilversum, June 1983.

Despite Nagano's apprehensions Messiaen was touched by the obvious dedication of the musicians and thrilled by the performance (the diary is bursting with compliments). He was also enchanted by the surroundings at Berkeley: 'Trees with red flowers, like red brushes! Also eucalyptus! Palm trees! Roses, hortensias, petunias! Trees with blue violet flowers: Jacaranda!! Red rhododendrons, and red and violet bougainvilleas!!!' Nagano, for his part, was charmed by the way Messiaen autographed hundreds of posters as a way of raising money for the orchestra.

In Paris Nagano found himself housed in the spare 'studio' (acquired in 1980), temporarily free of its collection of ondes Martenot, which, labelled and insured, had been delivered to the Opéra. Nagano had imagined that Messiaen would live in some style, and was astonished by the comparative simplicity of the Messiaens' accommodation. On arrival he was presented with an enormous key that unlocked one of the Spartan communal lavatories, one to each floor, all that were thought necessary when the apartments were built between the wars. The Messiaens for their part marvelled at Nagano's diet, which seemed to consist solely of yoghurt and Coca-Cola.

Messiaen was unwell. There were traces of blood in his urine, and he believed he had cancer. He had an electrocardiogram on 19 October and saw Professor Steg at the Cochin Hospital. As Nagano recalled, the feeling that *Saint François* would be his swansong had haunted Messiaen all along:

> Messiaen told me that his life's work was finished – 'I've lived to write *Saint François* and I feel that I'm not going to write any more' – and he said this in such a way that I felt he was referring to the end of his life. You have to remember that I was a true Californian, so of course I tried to lighten up the situation, saying 'C'mon Olivier, it can't be that bad'. He didn't find this amusing at all: 'No, no, I'm serious. I feel something is happening. I tell you honestly, Kent, if I live long enough to hear the first orchestral rehearsal I'll be happy.' Then after the first rehearsal Messiaen said, 'I just wish I could see a rehearsal on stage.' So we got into the opera house and did the first rehearsal on stage, and I breathed another sigh of relief, but Messiaen said, 'You know if I could hear just one complete run-through of my opera then I'll know it's been created'. We had the dress rehearsals, and then the first performance, and Messiaen not only survived but by the end was in remarkably good health.[17]

Dr Bernachon was amazed by the transformation: 'I must confide to you', he wrote to Loriod, 'that I had a lot of anxiety for the health of your husband. My worries were only lifted when I saw him radiant on the steps of the Opéra.'[18]

Messiaen had no time to give in to depression. Musicians and singers came every day to work with him at the rue Marcadet. He gave interviews to *Le Figaro*, *Matin* and *Paris-Match*. He bought tickets for friends, colleagues and pupils, seeming not to have thought of asking for complimentary tickets. There were constant practical problems to be solved. One of these was how to get the chorus on stage for the start of Scene 5 without undue disruption and noise. Bogianckino's first solution was to reverse the order of Scenes 5 and 6. Another battle seemed about to erupt, but fortunately Sequi intervened with an alternative which struck Messiaen as ingenious and beautiful: to keep the chorus in the dressing room and relay the singing through loudspeakers. A whole day (6 November) was spent installing platforms above the orchestra pit. There was a rush to buy tickets, as *Le Quotidien de Paris* reported: 'At the box office, seats are selling like those for performances by the greatest singers of the century. The other day there were even disorderly scenes in the queue for the ticket booths.'[19] The diary recorded Messiaen's exhilaration as the production began to take shape: 'Soloists and chorus with sets and costumes – saw the marvellous costume of the Angel.' The dress rehearsal was on 26 November, a Saturday. On Sunday Messiaen played as usual at the Trinité, and arranged for his fourth ondes Martenot to be transported to the Opéra as a spare.

In the diary entry for the première (on 28 November) Messiaen allowed himself a moment of satisfaction – 'Triumph!!! Packed house!!!!!' – before characteristically turning to details, recording the timings of the three acts, and a list of friends, former pupils and musicians who were present: Almut Rössler, Jennifer Bate, Michèle Reverdy, Roger Muraro, Felix Aprahamian, Henri Dutilleux, Madeleine Milhaud, Iannis Xenakis and his wife, Marcelle Bunlet, George Benjamin, Karl-Anton Rickenbacher and his wife, Maurice Le Roux, Marius Constant, Pascal and Josette, Jacqueline Loriod, René de Obaldia, Raymond Depraz, Betsy Jolas, Denise Tual, Harry Halbreich. If the critical reception was at times less than convinced, particularly among foreign reviewers (the French press was respectful), Messiaen comforted himself with the increasing enthusiasm of the audiences during the opera's eleven performances, culminating in the last night (18 December): 'The whole audience stood to applaud for twenty minutes!!! Colossal success!!!!!!' Messiaen explained to Samuel that he had learned to live with adverse criticism:

> As far as the press goes, I read numerous articles, in French, English, Italian and German; some were very laudatory, others not. A few journalists wrote articles almost as malicious as those for my *Petites Liturgies*, although in more respectable turns of phrase. Because I'm older, because I devoted eight years of work to my opera, they may not have attacked me head-on, but attack me they did nevertheless. All things considered, I told myself that these attacks proved I had preserved a certain youthfulness.[20]

Inspiration regained
1984–1987

How could Messiaen follow *Saint François d'Assise*? Thirty-five years earlier, when arriving at a similar milestone, the completion of *Turangalîla*, he had looked confidently to the future. *Saint François* was not only three times the length of *Turangalîla*, but had involved years of anxiety, with Messiaen battling to ensure his work was staged as he had conceived it. At seventy-five it was hardly surprising that Messiaen should feel empty. On the day of the opera's première, 28 November 1983, *Libération* reported him as saying: 'Twilight has arrived. I have finished. I will never compose anything else.'[1]

There was plenty for Messiaen to do in retirement. The score of the opera had to be prepared for publication: there were revisions to make, mistakes to be corrected, and a new fair copy of Scene 5 – the scene that had been copied by Loriod – which it was a point of honour for Messiaen himself to complete. Two other projects were to dominate the diaries for the next four years. One was his attempt to interest publishers in his mother's *L'Âme en bourgeon*, the other Messiaen's fervent wish for *Saint François* to be released on CD. The performances of the opera had been recorded by ORTF, and both tape and video were available to Messiaen. On 7 January he had a meeting with Maurice Fleuret at the Ministry of Culture to request a grant; he also tried to interest EMI, offering to subsidize the deal by personally buying 500 CD sets. Both approaches came to nothing.

No doubt these rebuffs affected Messiaen's spirits. Loriod recalled that by the end of January he was in deep depression, exhausted and unable to eat or take exercise. This complete collapse was shortlived, however. Concerts in Israel had been scheduled in April, and Messiaen set about preparing for the trip in the usual way, studying birdsong recordings and writing to local ornithologists. Better still, he was making preparations to compose, the first actual composition – as distinct from orchestration or revision – for several years. For a ten-day break at La Sauline at the end of February Messiaen's diary noted that he packed his full composing tool-kit. The planned work was for organ, a 'Livre d'orgue': 'Take all my sketches, the big box of colour chords and birdsongs, the briefcase with Greek metres and deçi-tâlas, a book of plainchant, the Bible, *Imi-*

179 Snow at La Sauline, 1984.

tation of Christ, Urs von Balthasar, my improvisations on *L'Âme en bourgeon*, the plan of the organ at the Trinité, books on the Rose, on flowers, on stained glass, music paper, pencils, etc.'

Messiaen's account of how the *Livre du Saint Sacrement* was conceived came in the last interview of his life, given in January 1992:

> My post as a church organist obliges me to improvise. My wife records me, and I review my improvisations, listening very critically. But one day something happened: it was Holy Thursday, when the Church commemorates Christ's institution of the Eucharist. I had three minutes to fill, and that's how I came to play a piece that seemed at first to be nothing special: a very simple Bacchic[2] rhythm, a commonplace first inversion chord, [...] but when I listened again I suddenly realized that this was unlike my other improvisations. I think I was inspired by the moment, moved by the service, which was very beautiful. I rewrote this piece, gave it the title 'Institution de l'Eucharistie', and I began to compose the *Livre du Saint Sacrement* [...] this was more than a year after *Saint François*.[3]

'Institution de l'Eucharistie' is eighth in the final order of the eighteen movements that make up the *Livre du Saint Sacrement*, and is exactly as Messiaen describes it. Holy Thursday in 1984 fell on 19 April, some fourteen months after the orchestration of *Saint François* was finished. Messiaen's diary for the day records: 'Improvisations: très bien. Played a chorale by Bach: *O Mensch, bewein' dein' Sünde gross*.'

Messiaen's charming anecdote concealed a far more complex story. The idea of a work on the Blessed Sacrament had been simmering for some years. Originally, as we have seen, Messiaen planned some modest pieces for organ, études based on his improvisations: that was in 1980. By 1981 a vastly more ambitious project was under consideration, a *Prière au Saint Sacrement*, with a movement for each of the feast days of the liturgical year. A sketch of the 'Institution de l'Eucharistie' records that in fact the improvisation on which this piece is based was given on Holy Thursday 1981, not 1984. In 1982 Messiaen was again thinking about organ studies for which he devised titles: 'Études on complementary colours, on grace notes, and on light and dark'. The same entry in the diary mentioned 'a series of pieces on the Blessed Sacrament' and a piece about the miraculous parting of the Red Sea.

By 1984 Messiaen was back with the idea of a 'Livre d'orgue'. The first piece to be composed (at La Sauline, in February) is a survivor from the original idea for a set of études, a brilliant toccata entitled 'La Visitation et la joie de Jean Baptiste'. By early March Messiaen was making photocopies of the sketches for what he still called his 'organ pieces'. A definite commission was now in view: 'Write a work for organ for Ray Ferguson [Ferguson paid

180 Sketch for 'Institution de l'Eucharistie' made on Holy Thursday 1981 and later used in the *Livre du Saint Sacrement*.

for the commission] to be given its première at the Festival of the American Guild of Organists by Mme Almut Rössler on the gigantic organ at Detroit (USA) in July 1986.' Undated notes show Messiaen turning his 'Livre d'orgue' into a work on the Sacrament of the Eucharist, its Mysteries illuminated by episodes from the Old Testament: 'Pieces for organ: add 1) crossing of the Red Sea (two walls of water to right and left), 2) rainbow after the flood, and 3) Absence and Presence of Jesus (as in *Points de repère* by Urs von Balthasar).'

Many of the ideas for the *Livre du Saint Sacrement* were inspired by Messiaen's second trip to Israel (31 March–14 April 1984). The first few days were spent in Tel Aviv, where Loriod gave performances of *Vingt Regards* and *Réveil des oiseaux*. The sightseeing that followed was a revelation. The first place the Messiaens visited was Gethsemane:

5 April. Coming down from the place where Jesus wept and prophesied the destruction of Jerusalem. In the Garden of Olives some of the trees are several hundred years old, with huge trunks. This is where Christ sweated blood! Beautiful church, where a Franciscan brother greeted us, and gave us two pieces of the rock on which Jesus prayed in agony, and some olive leaves. He is Brother Bertrand, a Canadian, friend of Gilles Tremblay [a Messiaen pupil]. Gethsemane: the name comes from 'gat shemanim', meaning olive press. Eight of the trees are a thousand years old, offspring of the trees that sheltered Jesus at prayer. Saw the Mourning Chat (oenanthe lugens) and Desert Lark (Ammomanes deserti), and a buzzard attacked by a kestrel.

6 April. 11.15 a.m. Desert of Judea. Sun and heat, with a warm wind. Blue sky, brilliant light. In the foreground large hills with very white boulders. A few trees, and then a great expanse of desert, grey and white – silence. The Desert Lark has a marvellous voice, liquid and limpid, high in the sky and the silence. Marvellous landscape of crumpled sand-dunes, rippling like waves.

For 'La Manne et le pain de Vie', use the mountains of Judea and the Desert Lark and the Desert Chat. Contrast between the contours of the mountains (low, *pianissimo*) and the quick, high birdsong. Then use brighter colours and the Common Garden Bulbul for the sermon on the Bread of Life. For the manna the taste changed, so change the colours. Make a contrast with the piece entitled *Les Ténèbres* by a piece called *Lumière*: 'He who follows me shall not walk in darkness but in the light of life.'

For 'Les Deux Murailles d'eau': Moses and the Hebrews escaped from the Egyptians, by passing on foot through the Red Sea, between two walls of water to right and left; so we pass from the evils of this life to the joys of Heaven.

6.20 p.m. Jericho. Heat and strong wind. In the garden, among the cypress and orange trees, a Common Garden Bulbul; also the cries of a kingfisher and kestrel. The garden is part of a Greek Orthodox monastery, built in a cleft in the rock, and is tended by a Bedouin who looks after the fruit trees. When the sluice gate is opened the little depressions around the trees are filled with water. Beyond the farm are Bedouin tents. On the left a landscape of cypresses and yellow dunes, on the right the terrible yellow-grey mountain.

The mountain where Christ fasted for forty days, repelled the temptations of the devil, and was saved by three angels. Awesome! Grandiose!

On 8 April the Messiaens attended Mass at the church of the Dormition in Jerusalem. Two nights were spent in a kibbutz near the Dead Sea. Above the kibbutz was a 'monumental yellow mountain, weathered into a stairway'. In the village, Messiaen noted the barbed wire ('to ward off leopards'), the profusion of flowers (roses, poinsettias, hibiscus), the baobab trees, and 'everywhere the presence of the Dead Sea, blue and green':

9 April. Midday. On a high plateau: below, on the left, is the Dead Sea, the blue of the sky merging into the blue of the water. The rock is black, brown, yellow, red-pink, grey. [. . .] Cries of the fan-tailed raven – rolling, sliding, strident, wild. At Engeddi, tropical flowers and trees beside the dried-up river of David. Saw a little lynx (like a large squirrel) and a sand partridge.

The visit to the Dead Sea had to be cut short because Loriod began to suffer dizziness from the low altitude. Her indisposition meant an early return to Paris: the flight from Tel Aviv (14 April) was delayed for three hours, but on arrival Messiaen at once went out to hear a performance of the *Sept Haïkaï* conducted by Lionel Friend. Tactfully he kept away from the Trinité so as not to deprive his deputy, Bonfils, of his scheduled services.

In May Messiaen was the principal speaker at the induction of Xenakis as a member of the Académie des Beaux-Arts at the Institut. Messiaen, speaking in his full Academician's robe, recalled the electrifying impression made on him by his first encounter with Xenakis:

Cher Ami,

Today marks our second official meeting.
    Our first meeting was a less impressive occasion. It was late one afternoon, at the Paris Conservatoire. I had just finished my class and was getting ready to leave, when someone pushed open the door and came in. I had a sudden shock! Before me stood a hero, the bearer of a glorious scar, but radiant with an internal light. It was Iannis Xenakis! The tragic smile, greedy for knowledge, the noble forehead and the piercing gaze gave me to understand immediately that the man I was looking at was out of the common run, *not like the others*!

He told me that he wanted to be a composer. When I found out that he was Greek, that he had studied mathematics and that he was working as an architect with Le Corbusier, I told him, 'Keep going with all that! Be Greek, be a mathematician, be an architect, and out of it all make music!' Without realizing it, I had just given an almost exact definition of the music he was to write. [. . .]

On the question of the connections between music and architecture, I will say only that the preparatory sketches for the extraordinary clouds of glissandi in *Metastasis* (for an orchestra of solo strings with xylophone, wood block, and a few woodwind and brass) were the same sketches that underlay the building of the Philips Pavilion in Brussels. For a single creative artist to be able to bring together an orchestral work and an architectural one in the same geometrical pattern was something new in the history of music, and few are the intelligences of today capable of bringing off such a synthesis! [. . .]

Some years ago I was in the little village of Lauterbrunnen in Switzerland, and I was intending to take the téléférique up to the top of the Jungfrau to admire the eternal snows at my leisure. But a thick fog descended on the mountains and the valley, so someone suggested I might go and see the waterfalls at Trümmelbach. This is a vast underground torrent that cascades into a terrifying succession of pools, eroded from the rock. The noise of the water rushing and swirling between the rocky walls is an enormous, deafening fortissimo, but it's possible to listen to it for a long time without getting tired: this fearful noise is full of harmony and its resonances seem to be always changing. I listened to this torrent for a long time. And suddenly, a comparison sprang into my mind: I cried out, 'It's Xenakis!'

My dear friend, I cannot leave a great Greek composer without addressing him with a 'dithyramb'! Allow me to be slightly irreverent towards Stéphane Mallarmé and modify one of his best-known poems in your honour:

As one whom our 'Immortals' finally turn into himself,
The Composer with his naked sword stirs up
His times – astonished are they not to have known
That 'sounds' reached triumph in this unknown voice!

They, with a start like some foul Hydra hearing long ago
The Angel, gave a purer meaning to the tribe's discourse,
Proclaimed aloud the magic potions drunk
From the 'probabilities' of some dark mixture.

The earth and skies are both hostile, alas!
If no thoughts carve out a bas relief
To decorate Iannis Xenakis in his brilliance

(A solid block fall'n from some obscure catastrophe),
May 'his music' at least here set its boundaries
Against black flights of blasphemy in future disarray.

(Rearranged from *Le Tombeau d'Edgar Poe*)

Work on the *Livre du Saint Sacrement* continued at extraordinary speed. Much was done at La Sauline in May, interrupted by the annual service of Confirmation at the Trinité. Messiaen took advantage of the return to Paris to fix the registrations for nine of the pieces. By mid-June the number of pieces had risen from ten to fifteen:

Livre du Saint Sacrement

June 1984 version	Final version (pieces added later in italics)
1. Adoro te	1. Adoro te
2. La Manne et le pain de Vie	2. La Source de Vie
3. La Source de Vie	3. Le Dieu caché
4. Les Ressuscités et la lumière de Vie	4. *Acte de Foi*
5. La Transsubstantiation	5. Puer natus est nobis
6. Le Dieu caché	6. La Manne et le pain de Vie
7. Les Ténèbres	7. Les Ressuscités et la lumière de Vie
8. L'Apparition du Christ à Marie-Madeleine	8. Institution de l'Eucharistie
9. Les Deux Murailles d'eau	9. Les Ténèbres
10. Institution de l'Eucharistie	10. La Résurrection du Christ
11. La Visitation et la joie de Jean Baptiste	11. L'Apparition du Christ à Marie-Madeleine
12. Prière avant la communion	12. La Transsubstantiation
13. Prière après la communion	13. Les Deux Murailles d'eau
14. Puer natus est nobis	14. Prière avant la communion
15. La Résurrection du Christ	15. *La Joie de la grâce*
	16. Prière après la communion
	17. *La Présence multipliée*
	18. Offrande et Alléluia final

Messiaen seems to have regarded the fifteen-movement version of the work (June 1984) as finished, and began to make a fair copy. The title page, listing the order of the movements, is remarkable for how little it resembles the eventual finished work. In the June 1984 order the work was very much a *Livre*, traditionally a loose collection of pieces rather than a cycle, quite different from *Les Corps glorieux*, for example, in which there are thematic links between movements, or from the inner cohesion of the *Méditations*. The plan in June was to interleave meditations on the mysteries of the communion with scenes from the Gospels. The only surviving Old Testament depiction was the miraculous parting of the Red Sea ('les deux murailles d'eau'), a prophecy of the presence of Christ in the broken halves of the Host at communion. Very likely this spectacular piece – in particular the 'snatched' arpeggios which represent 'les vagues dressés' ('the towering waves') – was intended to be the culmination of the first half of the work.

A feature of the June 1984 version was that Messiaen followed only fitfully the order of events in the Bible. Jesus's sermon on the Bread of Life (no.2 in the June order) looked forward to his Resurrection; 'Les Ténèbres' (no.7) evoked the darkness at the Crucifixion, and the next piece the appearance of the risen Christ to Mary Magdalene. At this point, however, the June version departed from chronology, and backtracked to the beginning of the Gospel story. 'La Visitation et la joie de Jean Baptiste' (no.11) is explained by its accompanying quotation: the joy is that of Elisabeth, on learning that she has conceived.[4] The penultimate movement represented the Nativity ('Puer natus est nobis') and the work ended with the glory of Christ's Resurrection.

Messiaen may have sensed that the *Livre du Saint Sacrement* needed more work. He sketched a sixteenth piece – 'La Présence multipliée' – in September, but otherwise concentrated on the fair copy of Scene 5 of *Saint François*. During the autumn Messiaen was cheered by the visit of Martine Guéou, from Benin, whom the Messiaens had 'adopted' fifteen years before but whom they had never met. Another new acquaintance was the Chinese composer Chen Qigang, who was to study on a regular basis with Messiaen for several years. On the radio there was an exceptional performance of the *Poèmes pour Mi* conducted by Boulez with Phyllis Bryn-Julson: 'Marvellous!!! Absolute precision, perfect rhythm, beautiful voice, ample, liquid, warm lyric soprano.' The rehearsal confirmed Messiaen's low opinion of the discipline of French orchestras. Boulez was so incensed by extraneous chatter that he walked out, resuming (after anxious negotiation by the management) with the ominous words: 'I will come back once but not a second time.'

In December Messiaen set about giving the *Livre du Saint Sacrement* a thorough revision. The clearest problem was a musical one, that of the final movement – 'La Résurrection du Christ' – which though impressively massive was too short to be conclusive. The obvious candidate to replace it was 'La Visitation et la joie de Jean Baptiste'. A preliminary fair copy of 'Visitation' (probably made in March 1984) showed that Messiaen made a major revision, rejigging the order of material so as to create the threefold sequence that gives energy and direction to the heart of the piece. It is interesting that even at this early stage Messiaen had already worked out precise details of fingering and registrations. Although 'Visitation' was an ideal conclusion musically, theologically it was in the wrong place. Messiaen solved the problem very simply, at the stroke of a pen, by changing the title to 'Offrande et Alléluia final': the music's joy was no longer that of Elisabeth but of all the Saints.

Putting 'La Résurrection du Christ' earlier enabled Messiaen to assemble the Gospel scenes in chronological order. From there it was a simple step to see that they would work best not scattered through the work but placed consecutively. In the finished order the opening movements (1–4) are a prelude, acts of adoration before communion; numbers 5–11 follow events in the life of Jesus; and numbers 12–18 contemplate the mysteries of the Sacrament. Musically, the outer sections needed bolstering, and this was done with the addition of 'Acte de foi' (no.4) and 'La Présence multipliée'. The final inspiration was to fill the gap between the prayers before and after communion with 'La Joie de la grâce', one of Messiaens's most ecstatic birdsong creations, composed exclusively using the birds he had heard in Israel and Palestine.

Throughout the winter of 1984–5 Messiaen spent evenings at the Trinité, working on the registrations of the *Livre du Saint Sacrement*. There were further abortive attempts to secure a new publication of *L'Âme en bourgeon*, but one major task, at least, was brought to a conclusion: Messiaen finished the fair copy of Scene 5 of *Saint François d'Assise* on 19 February. On 1 March Messiaen noted: 'Have given Mme Rössler a bound photocopy of the new organ work.' He contacted Ray Ferguson in Detroit, and on 20 March completed the formality of registering the *Livre du Saint Sacrement* with SACEM.

Messiaen at once turned to a commission that had been on the table for more than a year. The eventual work, the eight-minute *Un Vitrail et des oiseaux*, though Messiaen's most modest orchestral piece to date, was to bring him close to despair. The tortuous genesis of its composition – ironically coinciding with some of Messiaen's greatest public triumphs – is worth following through all its stops and starts. The story illustrates Messiaen's paralysing loss of self-confidence, a loss that makes the crowning achievement of his last years, *Éclairs sur l'Au-delà*, heroic and indeed miraculous.

The commission for *Un Vitrail* had come from Boulez, who wanted a work for the Ensemble Intercontemporain (EIC) to mark Messiaen's eightieth birthday in 1988. The first approach was informal, in a conversation that took place in late January 1984; Messiaen at once noted in his diary: 'For Boulez, *Vitrail* for Mary, Queen of Peace – two or three pianos, and small orchestra, lots of colours.' Evidently the 'retirement' announced by Messiaen in December 1983 was to be short-lived. Further notes show Messiaen planning a work for two piano soloists – Loriod and Pierre-Laurent Aimard – an ensemble of wind and brass, some strings, and an enormous percussion section (including xylophone, glockenspiel, vibraphone, celesta, and the Eoliphone and Geophone). A more modest line-up, but one which now included two ondes Martenot, followed receipt of a letter from the EIC's adminstrator, Brigitte Marger (28 February), listing the instruments available to the Ensemble.

Notes made in Messiaen's *cahier* while he was in Israel and Palestine in April 1984 reveal ideas that would have had a unique place in his output had they been realized. The work was to be called *Le Vitrail de l'Assomption*, scored for three pianos and three singers (soprano, contralto and tenor) with woodwind and percussion, without strings or ondes Martenot:[5]

> For the two flutes, various birdsongs; for the xylorimba, a motif with tremolos, also using birdsong. On the bass clarinet a trill, as low as possible – see *Réveil des oiseaux*. For the three singers, a chord in second inversion, *pianissimo*. Above, a flute solo (birdsong). In the bass, a cluster, *pianissimo*. In the middle, muted trumpet and two horns in chords (mode 3) – it's the singers who colour the held chord (see *Jeanne d'Arc au bûcher* by Honegger). For the three pianos: see the *Sonata for two pianos and percussion* by Bartók, and the concertos for 2 and 3 pianos by Mozart (also études by Chopin and Debussy, and the *Second Sonata* by Boulez). The singers vocalize on sustained chords. They also speak. The text has quotations from the Song of Songs and the Book of Wisdom. [...] See also the 'Litanies of the Virgin', dedication to the 'Queen of Peace' (as in Medjugorje) and the women clothed in sunlight in the Apocalypse (see the book by Hello: *Paroles de Dieu*).

Reading between the lines, it is clear that Boulez sensed Messiaen's difficulties. The commission was perfectly judged: a short work, for a reasonably distant date, prestigious, and for superb performers. Once he had Messiaen's acceptance, Boulez lost no time in indicating that a shorter time-scale would be desirable, with a first performance in 1987 or even 1986. The reason for this became clear a few months later, in July, when Brigitte Marger wrote formally asking if the composition of the new work could be brought forward. She now gave a specific date – January 1986 – so that the EIC would have time to rehearse the work with a view to including it in a tour of major cities in the United States in February and March. In October Marger wrote again, having received no reply. A week later (25 October) Messiaen answered in the negative:

> I have at home several sacks with hundreds of letters to which I have not yet replied. After searching, I have retrieved your letter of 16 July last. Having worked for eight years exclusively on an opera, I find myself with several commissions that I haven't yet been able to complete. Out of affection for Pierre Boulez, it's essential to me that I give him a successful work. It seems to me impossible to have everything finished, including the

copying of the score and the parts, to be able to rehearse by January 1986. I think it therefore wiser to plan another programme for the tour by the EIC of the USA.

The next entries on *Vitrail* came at the start of 1985. In February Messiaen reminded himself to 'start the commission for Boulez', but although Loriod remembered him devising harmonies for the new piece, work on *Vitrail* was sidelined by more pressing concerns. As well as putting the finishing touches to the *Livre du Saint Sacrement,* there was much to be done preparing *Saint François* for publication (the spring break at La Sauline was given to revising metronome markings). On 22 April Messiaen delivered the fair copy of the *Livre du Saint Sacrement* to Leduc. (Earlier in April Messiaen had attended the funeral of Gilbert Leduc, the publishing firm's long-standing director.) The following months were too full of comings and goings for settled work on composition. There was the Glenn Gould piano competition at Toronto, where Messiaen was a member of the jury, concerts conducted by Nagano in Los Angeles, and a week in Italy. Messiaen's notes show the highlight of the summer to have been the coinciding of their stay in Venice with the visit of Pope John Paul II – from their hotel window the Messiaens had a grandstand view of the Pope's ceremonial arrival, proceeding up the Grand Canal amid a flotilla of gondolas.

Arriving at Petichet (8 July 1985), Messiaen began work at once, but not on the commission from Boulez. Under cover of correcting proofs, he was composing for the piano, music which would become a set of short pieces, the *Petites Esquisses d'oiseaux*. These are 'sketches', both in terms of their relatively miniature scale, and because they have the simplicity and finesse of a pencil drawing. Messiaen's previous ornithological piano work, *La Fauvette des jardins* (1970), had been a summary of all his techniques, with every aspect vividly coloured: the mountains, the lake (the scene is the view at Petichet), sunrise and sunset. In the *Esquisses* only one bird is used in each piece, and the inessentials are stripped away, leaving solo birdsong, supported by brief chorales of colour chords which serve to open up new perspectives on the song. Though composed at Petichet, the *Esquisses* reflect Messiaen's contentment at La Sauline; the place had become an ideal retreat, and for a time he even considered living there permanently. The birds of the *Esquisses* are the common garden species Messiaen watched from the music room window at La Sauline – blackbird, song thrush and skylark, with three of the six pieces for the robin. The robin, after its leading role in Messiaen's first major bird piece, *Réveil des oiseaux*, had played an unaccountably small part in his music, never having a 'title role', though memorable for exquisite appearances in 'Le Loriot' and 'La Bouscarle' (*Catalogue d'oiseaux*) and as the 'fragile stream' from *Saint François*. The memory of these shimmering waterfalls must have been Messiaen's point of departure, especially as one of the last pieces to be composed for the *Livre du Saint Sacrement* – 'Acte de Foi' – has a virtually identical cascading hand-over-hand descent.

During summer 1985 Loriod had reason to be concerned about Messiaen. Arthritis was beginning severely to affect his spine, he was perpetually tired, and he seemed lacking in self-belief. The obligations of fame were never-ending. At La Sauline, in late September, Messiaen worked on three speeches, to be given in Japan in November as a result of being nominated a winner of the Inamori prize (one of the speeches would be published by Leduc as the *Conférence de Kyoto*). Then, to Loriod's astonishment, Messiaen suddenly revealed a new and finished work for piano, the *Esquisses*. It was a Sunday morning, after they had returned from Mass at Bourges Cathedral. She recalled his diffidence as he sat at the piano ('I'm tired, I can no longer write, the pieces are not very good'),[6] and her excitement at finding in their spareness a completely new style, with a new kind of pianism, 'poetic and sublime'.

Despite Loriod's encouragement, Messiaen was completely stuck with the commission for Boulez. He now took the unprecedented step of trying to abandon the work altogether, contacting Boulez to ask if he could be released from their agreement. By way of compensation Messiaen offered the *Esquisses* as a replacement. Boulez's response came swiftly (23 October), a nice blend of sympathy and insistence:

> Brigitte Marger has told me that in a moment of discouragement – at least I hope it's only a moment – you've given up writing a work for the Ensemble. I am truly sorry. We would of course be ready and willing to ask Yvonne to play the new piano pieces which you have written for her. But I would like all the same for you to reconsider your decision. The Ensemble and I very much wish to give a first performance, and in addition to the première to play it in various tours abroad.
>
> Once you have decided, let me know what you are able to do. But I've no doubt myself that you'll find a way of overcoming this obstacle and write for us the work which you have promised and to which we will devote ourselves.[7]

Boulez's letter must have done the trick, but during autumn 1985 there was little immediate prospect of finding time for sustained work. A week was spent in Bremen, crowded with concerts and lectures, culminating in a performance of *Et exspecto*, under Nagano, of 'extraordinary solemnity and grandeur'. On 7 November the Messiaens flew to Osaka for the Inamori prize-giving. Messiaen noted in his diary every detail of the elaborately choreographed ceremony, which extended over three days. One of the speeches was given by Henriette Roget, a fellow-student fifty-five years earlier in the organ class at the

181 Loriod and Messiaen in Japan, 1985.

Conservatoire, and the pianist for whom he had composed the *Préludes* (see page 27). She had moved to Japan in 1979 and lived in Tokyo, where she taught the piano. While in Japan, Messiaen took the opportunity to re-experience the delights of the gardens: 'Silence, and marvellous colours, with green pines and red maples – pools and the sound of a little waterfall.'

182 Ozawa and Messiaen after a performance of three scenes from *Saint François d'Assise*, Tokyo, 12 March 1986.

The following year, 1986, was an *annus mirabilis* for concerts. Between March and July the Messiaens travelled to Japan, Berlin, Boston, New York, Vienna, the Bath Festival, Rome, and finally to Detroit for the première of the *Livre du Saint Sacrement*. In the autumn they went to Bonn (where the Beethoven–Messiaen Festival gave an all-but-complete cycle of Messiaen's music), followed by an incessant round of concerts all over Europe. Hardly a note of music was composed. In January Messiaen tried to make progress with the Boulez commission, toying with ideas for the title – 'Vitrail en fleur . . . amaryllis . . . Carpathian campanula' – but these sketches were 'laboured attempts' according to his diary, which also mentioned commissions, none of them fulfilled: a piece (unspecified) for Japan, a Gloria to celebrate the visit of the Pope to Lyon Cathedral ('In French, unaccompanied, for a congregation of 3,000 people'), and a work for violin and small orchestra. One tiny request Messiaen did answer was from Marc Bleuse, the Director of the Conservatoire, to write a 'chant donné' in the style of Mozart for a harmony examination.

The cornerstone of the concerts in the first half of 1986 was a world tour of Scenes 3, 7 and 8 of *Saint François*. Messiaen's collection of ondes Martenot (as well as his Geophone) travelled the world in the wake of Ozawa as he moved across continents and from one orchestra to another. In Tokyo (12 and 13 March) the soloists were Japanese, and the performances were semi-staged in the Catholic Cathedral:

Very good acoustic. The actors are in costume: St Francis and the others dressed as Franciscans, in chestnut-coloured robes with belts of rope, the leper in white with a horribly made-up face. The Angel has a long white robe. She sang (up in the organ loft) standing on the organ console, behind the conductor – she was very frightened! Lighting: a Cross, twenty metres high at the end of the church. Present: the Archbishop, the Ambassador, Takemitsu, Mayuzumi, all my ex-pupils and Yvonne's – 2,000 people. Before the concert, the priest (a Japanese Franciscan) gave a sermon on St Francis. I signed hundreds of programmes and discs.

The most important concert of 1986, however, was the première in Detroit (1 July) of the *Livre du Saint Sacrement*, given by Almut Rössler in the Metropolitan Methodist Church. Messiaen noted that the audience (all supplied with a detailed programme book) numbered 2,000, composed of organists from the American Guild of Organists. The august gathering caused Rössler to have an attack of nerves, but her performance was judged 'very fine' and the success 'brilliant'. Messiaen, however, was putting a brave face on what had been a difficult occasion. The church was acoustically dead, and the audience, sweltering in the summer heat, became restive as the performance was dogged by a persistent cipher on the organ.[8] To be heard in its true colours the work had to await Rössler's next performance, at the Johanneskirche in Düsseldorf (1 November).

The *Livre du Saint Sacrement* was introduced to a vast and appreciative London audience in Westminster Cathedral by Jennifer Bate (7 October 1986). It was at this performance that Peter Hill (who had begun a recording of all the music for piano) was introduced to Messiaen and invited to Paris. The first of their meetings took place in December, recorded in Hill's diary:

Arrived early, of course, and spent half an hour on a bench in children's playground (in the Square Carpeaux) opposite the house. Inside very dark, and one creaks slowly up to the fifth floor in ancient lift. Turn left, as instructed in M's letter, and there indeed is the front door. Surprised to be received by Messiaen alone (no sign of Yvonne Loriod). Inside I perch on an odd-looking folding chair, which immediately collapses! Messiaen almost as embarrassed as I am. He makes a short, prepared speech – 'I am a French composer, but not a French impressionist' – the point being that the performer needs to be clear and exact. When I play ('Le Merle bleu') the first ten minutes are an ordeal: the acoustic is utterly dead, and Messiaen keeps up a blizzard of instructions. Suddenly the atmosphere relaxes and he allows me to play long chunks without interruption, and becomes smiling and constructive. Very solicitous, and offers whisky and (fortunately) tea. Obviously pleased when I ask about birds: does passable birdsong imitations and goes off to fetch little ornithological guides. Laughs at himself about the fact that he sees birds as human personalities. Fascinating also on colour: he explains (in 'Le Loriot') the gold of the sun, and gets me to bring out the left hand G sharp (in the E major chord) so that it sounds brassy, 'like a trombone'. He wants me to explore colour within chords, to bring out certain inner notes, and demonstrates this on the piano. Altogether an absolutely *passionate* (not 'abstract') musician: everything has to be 100 per cent vivid, and really *be* the birds, places, etc.

The last turning point of Messiaen's life came in 1987. He at last regained the confidence to compose, and at the same time realized his ambitions to see *Saint*

183 Messiaen with Felix Aprahamian, Peter Hill and George Benjamin after the British première of the *Livre du Saint Sacrement*, played by Jennifer Bate, at Westminster Cathedral, 7 October 1986 (photo: Malcolm Crowthers).

François d'Assise on CD and his mother's poetry back in print. Good news had come the previous August (1986) with a sudden breakthrough over the recording of *Saint François*, thanks to the initiative of Eric Alberti, who played in the Opéra orchestra. Alberti planned to form a company (Cybelia) and issue on CD a recording edited from the broadcast tapes. Financially the plan was viable thanks to an agreement with the orchestral players that they would be paid only when and if the discs made a profit. Messiaen cut short his summer break at Petichet and hurried back to Paris to supervise the editing. A provisional edit was ready by January. On 8 January he 'listened to *Saint François* in entirety. They've tightened the chording of the chorus in Scene 7.' 12 January: 'Alberti telephones this morning. Ozawa wants to listen to the Radio tape: if he agrees, Van Dam will agree. The others have agreed.' The main stumbling block was Ozawa who, despite Messiaen's passionate desire for the recording to be released, took several months to make up his mind. On 6 February Messiaen went to the Opéra for a performance of *Elektra* with Ozawa conducting, and there was a meeting afterwards at which Messiaen tried to get his consent. By 1 March Alberti and Guy Chesnais were 'doing the corrections required by Ozawa. Then they will both leave by plane for Boston, with the master tape and my eight orchestral scores to obtain Ozawa's immediate consent.' Meanwhile Messiaen was also aware of Nagano's version, recorded the previous September at a concert performance in Utrecht. By the end of April, Alberti reported that Ozawa was in agreement. Messiaen was still apprehensive, however, and in May noted: 'In June Ozawa comes to Paris. Then Alberti will see him with Chesnais, get him to listen to the corrected tape and get his "yes" for the disc.' All was well, and Messiaen's agony over. Ozawa and Messiaen met to make the final edits, and on 22 June listened to and approved the entire opera.

By 1987 three years had passed since Boulez had given Messiaen the commission for a new orchestral work. Meanwhile, the première of the *Petites Esquisses d'oiseaux* took place, as Boulez had promised, at a concert by the Ensemble Intercontemporain (25 January), a little incongruous in a programme which included *Couleurs de la Cité céleste*, Stockhausen's *Mixtur*, and music by Berio and Xenakis. The occasion was glittering: Messiaen noted that he was seated between Mmes Chirac and Pompidou, and that Loriod's playing was 'marvellous and brilliant'.

By Messiaen's standards the early months of 1987 were comparatively quiet. He received the Grand-Croix of the Légion d'Honneur from his old admirer Jacques Chirac, now Prime Minister, attended a performance in Nantes of the *Trois petites Liturgies* (with a choir of children) at which he was presented with 'a gold medal with my name and the coat-of-arms of Nantes', and went to the Sorbonne to hear a paper on women's poetry that mentioned Cécile Sauvage. A particular pleasure was a visit to England in March. At the Royal Academy of Music Messiaen found the standard of performance high: 'The English love Messiaen and work hard.' He gave a masterclass on the *Vingt Regards*, followed by dinner with his old friend Felix Aprahamian, who always served him unusual and delicious food. In Paris (25 and 26 March) there was a splendid *Et Exspecto* conducted by Boulez. Messiaen noted that the gongs (so important in the final movement) were played by François Dupin, a percussionist he much admired.[9]

It was during these early months of 1987 that *Un Vitrail et des oiseaux* was finally composed. In the end Messiaen found the answer to his problems in simplicity. *Un Vitrail* is an affectionate revisiting of familiar musical imagery: the nightingale, as pioneered in the *Catalogue d'oiseaux*, played by a trio of key-

184 Messiaen with Bernadette Chirac, February 1987.

board percussion, the brilliance of a garden warbler assigned to the piano, and the blackcap presented in the mellifluous, richly harmonized style in which it appears in *Saint François*. The melody of the chorale, which acts as a frame for the simple block structure, comes from the more distant past, one of the melodies (from *Turangalîla*) that had been reworked in the *Cinq Rechants* and *Cantéyodjayâ*: Messiaen would use it again in the *Concert à quatre*. *Un Vitrail* was composed and orchestrated in less than three months. Messiaen took the score to be photocopied on 27 March, and on 7 April Depraz started to copy the orchestral material.

Un Vitrail was declared to SACEM on 4 May, and a week later Messiaen handed a copy of the score to Boulez.

The summer break of 1987 was delayed a fortnight by Messiaen festivities in Avignon, including a course of teaching at the Centre Acanthes. On 7 July Messiaen gave a class of analysis on the *Trois petites Liturgies* and in the evening attended the performance at the Église St-Pierre conducted by Nagano, who had asked Messiaen to write an opera for Lyon. There were classes by Loriod and by Messiaen, and a complete performance of the *Catalogue d'oiseaux* given by a team of young pianists, all pupils or ex-pupils of Loriod (the central piece, 'La Rousserolle effarvatte', was played by Roger Muraro). The fortnight's climax was *Turangalîla*, given outdoors, in front of the Palais des Papes. Despite a menacing sky, a large audience gathered for what proved to be a performance they would never forget:

Deplorable acoustic. Wind (the Mistral), music stands blown over, music carried away above the orchestra by the wind. They begin, the wind calms a little: four movements are completed, but with only half the orchestra playing, the players on the inside of each desk holding down the music. Some heavy drops of rain. Nagano turns to the audience: 'Shall we go on?' 'Yes.' Flashes of lightning. Jeanne [Loriod] raises her hands: she has received an electric shock. She stops. Yvonne tries to press on, but suddenly waterspouts burst over the orchestra and audience. Sauve qui peut!! Jeanne takes her keyboard under her arm, running for the wings. All the pianists present at the concert can be seen rushing towards the grand piano to push it under cover. Admirable and touching behaviour! In ten minutes Avignon turns into a sea, like a beach drowned by the tide, with blocked drains and the sirens of fire engines (powerless to do anything, however). The storm lasts several hours

185 Messiaen with Georges Hirsch and Henri Dutilleux in 1987.

186 With Claude Helffer and Sigune von Osten during a recording of *Harawi* in December 1987.

before the Flood (of Biblical proportions) susbsides and people can risk wading through the water without the danger of being knocked over.

It must have been shortly after arriving at Petichet (22 July) that Messiaen had a momentous communication from Zubin Mehta. His reply is dated 2 August:

> I shall soon be 79, and I have to fulfil two other commissions for large orchestra, to say nothing of my ceaseless travelling for concerts abroad. I feel very well and I hope that I will still be in good health in 1992–93. At all events, I will try to write a work worthy of you and the orchestra, but it is impossible to tell you so long in advance what will be its duration and instrumentation. So a little later we will have to decide the material details of the commission. Whatever happens, you can count on me, it's yes!

One of the two commissions mentioned by Messiaen in his reply to Mehta (the other, a work for piano and orchestra for Salzburg, was never fulfilled) was a work for the Orchestre de Paris and Boulez, for the Festival d'automne in 1989. In August, despite dismal weather, and saddened by the death of his Aunt Madeleine at the age of ninety-five, Messiaen set to work in determined fashion to clear his path for the New York commission. As with *Un Vitrail*, he composed *La Ville d'En-Haut* at speed; by September a draft score of the work was complete and Messiaen embarked on the fair copy.

187 Yvonne and Jeanne Loriod with Messiaen, recording the *Trois petites Liturgies*, Prague, December 1987.

Meanwhile the recording of *Saint François*, apparently safely on course, was suddenly derailed by the news, on 30 September, that the sponsor, the tobacco firm Morris, was withdrawing support. Messiaen was not to be baulked at the last moment:

> Alberti no longer has a backer. It's costing him 95,000 NF. Write him a cheque for this sum in the name of Cybelia – get a letter of agreement from Moines [Messiaen's accountant] and ask for 20 complete discs of *Saint François* – and repayment in 2 years. 6 October: Telephone Alberti – give him as an advance a cheque for 10 million old francs. At 6.45 p.m. meet Alberti at the artists' entrance of the Palais Garnier – I've given him a cheque.

Perhaps in anticipation of the release of the discs of *Saint François*, Messiaen bought himself a new hi-fi system that was to sit in the music room, on the fifth floor at the rue Marcadet, under a silk cover of oriental design.

On 16 October Mehta came to Paris to direct *Les Offrandes oubliées* and had a meeting with Messiaen about the commission for New York. The conversation acted as a tonic. Three days later (31 October) he was at La Sauline. The weather was sunny, and notes in the diary for the new work jostle with observations of nature:

> Take books on astronomy, on painting. The same music can change in substance by being high or low, *fortissimo* or *pianissimo*, very fast or very slow. Pack the cassettes of New Zealand birds. Devise harmonies, rhythms, melodies for the *Prélude à l'Apocalypse*. In the woods heard jays and a robin!! On the lawn, saw a green woodpecker – the top of the

188 Jeanne and Yvonne Loriod, Prague, December 1987.

189 Messiaen and Pascal.

head and the neck are bright red, with a greenish-grey cloak; underneath, the bird is yellowish-white, with a very long pointed black beak. It hops heavily . . . heard the owl.

At the end of November Messiaen spent a day checking the CDs of *Saint François*, drawing a line under the project – 'All is well.' More loose ends were tied up in a crowded day just before Christmas. Messiaen went to SACEM to declare *La Ville d'En-Haut*, then took to Leduc the corrected proofs of the *Petites Esquisses d'oiseaux*, and the score of *La Ville d'En-Haut*. The day ended with an evening at the Centre Pompidou, organized by the publisher Pierre Archimbaud to mark the publication of Cécile Sauvage's *L'Âme en bourgeon*; Messiaen gave a talk about his mother and Gisèle Casadesus read her poetry. Messiaen sent out copies of the book, including one to Pascal who wrote from Neussargues where he was spending Christmas:

> Thank you for the beautiful volume which we received a few days before leaving. I wanted to thank you by phone but you were out. Naturally I threw myself on the Preface. I've learned more about my grandmother in ten minutes than in fifty years. What a beautiful Christmas present![10]

Illuminations of the Beyond
1988–1992

Messiaen did not take long to begin the commission for Zubin Mehta. At the end of October 1987, at La Sauline, he was working on the harmonies for the opening movement, which at this point was simply called 'Prélude'. Several aspects of what was to become *Éclairs sur l'Au-delà* were already in place: it was clear from the books that Messiaen took with him to La Sauline that astronomy was to be an important element, as well as Biblical texts, in particular the Book of Revelation, and birdsong.

By the beginning of 1988 Messiaen's ideas had advanced. The working title was now 'Paradise'. The 'Prélude' had become 'Apparition du Christ glorieux', and was to be a chorale scored for brass. Messiaen seems to have been planning a work with seven movements. As with the *Quatuor,* the ending would be a slow movement, 'Le Christ, lumière du Paradis', at this stage called 'Song of the Lamb'.

Fairly early in the composition of *Éclairs* Messiaen drew up a plan, which he amended as he went along. The work was to have two birdsong movements: 'Un Oiseau des arbres de Vie' and 'Un Autre Oiseau des arbres de Vie': eventually these were combined in the ninth movement, 'Plusieurs Oiseaux des arbres de Vie'. For this, Messiaen had in mind an infinite tree, representing Christ, with the elect gathering its fruit and singing like birds; in the finished score, the songs of twenty-seven species are shared by eighteen players from the upper woodwind: 3 piccolos, 6 flutes, an alto flute, and 8 clarinets (6 in B flat, 2 in E flat). The instruments play freely *hors tempo* ('outside time'), each entering on a cue from the conductor, in the technique introduced in Scene 6 of *Saint François*, and continued in *Un Vitrail et des oiseaux*. Providing the players follow Messiaen's dynamic markings, the effect is anything but haphazard. Individual lines emerge surprisingly clearly, and there is the great advantage that they can

190 With Peter Hill at the BBC Maida Vale studios, 23 January 1988 (photo: Malcolm Crowthers).

be shaped with a natural-sounding flexibility which Messiaen always wanted[1] but which is so hard to achieve in the tightly co-ordinated birdsong ensembles of his earlier orchestral music.

Another set of notes from early in 1988 is an outline of the seventh movement, 'Et Dieu essuiera toutes larmes de leurs yeux': 'For "Paradise": endless trill in the heights. Woodwind melody in descending chords, like a divine caress, broken by silence – repeated several times.' The finished movement begins just as Messiaen describes, with the trill and then the 'caress' of chords, which modulate in colour as they are handed down through the vast woodwind section. Three tiny gestures follow: a pair of chords on horns (echoed by low flutes) hint at a fanfare, and are echoed again by the same harmony on muted cellos, with above them a fragment of birdsong. The effect is like a distant suggestion of the forest in Wagner's *Siegfried*, with the horn call, and the 'forest murmurs' traced in the high trill. Wagner's 'woodbird', to continue the parallel, comes in the short middle section, a joyous blackbird played by a solo flute. The passage for flute already existed: it was the *Sigle* that Messiaen had composed in December 1982 as a gift for Rolf Liebermann, which is transposed up a tone in *Éclairs* in order to fit with the D major harmony of the horn call. The movement is extraordinary: understatement is not a word normally associated with Messiaen, and it is necessary to go back to the second of the *Trois Mélodies* (1929) to find music that is quite so spare and distilled.

A more recent precedent came in the *Petites Esquisses d'oiseaux* (1985), where Messiaen's birdsong style, so forceful and dramatic in the *Catalogue d'oiseaux*, was refined to an exquisite transparency. *Éclairs* is a vision of Paradise quite distinct from the many other examples in Messiaen's work. There is nothing remotely like the heaven-storming finale of *Visions de l'Amen*, for example, where the faithful march towards the Heavenly City surrounded by peals of bells and torrents of virtuosity. Such directness is foreign to *Éclairs*: instead, each movement is intended to give a sidelong glimpse of eternity, as Messiaen explained in his last published interview, which took place in January 1992:

> I imagined myself in front of a curtain, in darkness, apprehensive about what lay beyond: Resurrection, Eternity, the other life. [. . .] I try simply to imagine what will come to pass, which I can sometimes perceive in 'éclairs' ['flashes' or 'illuminations']. I speak of course of Christ, who will be the light of the resurrected: they will shine with the light of Christ.

At first Messiaen wanted to call the work 'Déchirures sur l'Au-delà' – 'déchirures' meaning the parting of a curtain – but feared confusion because of the word's other meaning of 'tearing'.[2]

A trip to New York in January 1988 (to hear *Turangalîla* conducted by Mehta) gave Messiaen the opportunity to discuss details of the commission with the management of the New York Philharmonic. Mehta conducted three performances of *Turangalîla*, the opening concerts of a year in which Messiaen's eightieth birthday was celebrated all over the world. While in New York, Messiaen visited the Natural History Museum to see the dioramas of birds of the Pacific. He also had dinner with Alice Tully (who had commissioned *Des Canyons*) at her sumptuous Manhattan apartment. Messiaen was dazzled by his hostess's collection of antiquities, noting in his diary the figurines from Egypt and the Cyclades, and a Hittite head of a bull picked out in gold leaf. Even more impressive was the tureen of caviar, accompanying the aperitifs, into which guests were invited to dip a silver spoon the size of a small shovel.

191 Messiaen and his eightieth-birthday cake, Nantes, 9 February 1988.

In January Messiaen's thirty complimentary copies of the Cybelia recording of *Saint François* arrived. It had taken four years to reach this moment: the diary records a single word: 'Marvellous!!!' On the following day (20 January) another labour was brought to its conclusion when Messiaen transported to Leduc the nine boxes containing the opera's autograph score. There followed three days in London for a concert that included *Chronochromie* and a work by Messiaen's pupil George Benjamin (*Ringed by the Flat Horizon*). Even with performers vastly experienced in his music (the BBC Symphony Orchestra conducted by Boulez), Messiaen took the trouble to attend the preliminary rehearsal at the BBC's Maida Vale Studios, and during the coffee break could be seen expressing his concerns to Boulez about the intonation of the orchestra's celesta. The next leg of the birthday year was to Nantes, Messiaen's childhood home during an important phase of his musical development, when he was taught by Jean de Gibon and introduced to Debussy's *Pelléas et Mélisande.* Nantes did its former citizen proud: the Mayor unveiled a plaque, there was a lecture by Claude Samuel, and an 'extraordinary performance' of *Turangalîla* conducted by Marc Soustrot. Still more amazing was the birthday cake, a collective achievement of the patissiers of Nantes in the form of a grand piano in chocolate, with icing sugar sculpted into pink and green birds.

Messiaen prepared with his usual thoroughness for the six-week tour of Australia, which took place in May and June 1988, and corresponded with a number of Australian ornithologists. One of these, Ivan Kinny, sent Messiaen his own notations of birdsong, and commended the musical possibilities of the Australian Butcher Bird: 'The bird is carnivorous and gets its name because of its practice of making a larder, impaling its prey on a thorn or

192 Receiving the Grand Prix du Disque for *Saint François d'Assise*, Hôtel de Ville, Paris, 15 February 1988. Jacques Chirac, Marcel Landowski, Bernadette Chirac, Messiaen, Christiane Eda-Pierre (photo: Desmarquest).

193 Loriod and Messiaen in February 1988.

194 With Harold Bradley in Sherbrook Forest, 3 June 1988.

wedging it in the fork of a tree to eat later. There is a grey variety (cracticus torquatus) and a black-and-white species (cracticus nigrolatus), which are among the finest bird singers. Their calls are very tuneful and diatonic and the sound is bright and pure, like a flute.'[3] The trip to Australia was very nearly cancelled owing to the ill-health of Messiaen's brother, Alain, who was suffering from Parkinson's disease, and could no longer look after himself. Alain was a difficult patient, accustomed to living alone in squalid conditions, and the attempt to care for him at the rue Marcadet proved hopeless. It was only at the last minute that a place was found in a nursing home; among the final diary entries before Messiaen's departure for Sydney was a note to send a cheque as advance payment.

In Australia the schedule of concerts allowed Messiaen time for three expeditions to gather birdsong. The first was a visit to Sherbrook Forest, near Melbourne, home of the Australian lyrebird. Messiaen was already intent on giving an important role to the lyrebird in the new work.[4] He recorded the search for this elusive bird in his *cahier*, mingling descriptions of the forest with ideas for music:

30 May. Mountain ash: tree with an enormous trunk, 70 metres tall – they live two or three hundred years. Pine trees, and eucalyptus, with white trunks, curved branches and a canopy of scented leaves. The bare patches of black earth are where the lyrebird *dances*! In the nuptial ceremony the lyrebird raises its tail feathers above its head, forming two symmetrical curves – like a lyre – and at the same time it dances and sings!! [. . .] Heard the white-backed magpie, Australian ground thrush, Eastern whipbird and the lyrebird.

Orchestration for 'L'Apparition de la Cité céleste': to imitate the sound of the wind use trilled clusters on all the strings, with upward glissandi on the Eoliphone; use bells with temple block and glockenspiel, and glissandi (from one extreme to the other) on xylorimba, coinciding at the end of the glissando with the whip – for the whipbird – with cluster glissandi on all the strings. Use three piccolos to coincide with the whip.

Theme on the piccolo (*forte*), with xylorimba and six temple blocks, broken by a harmonized theme (one chord per note) for clarinets and oboes staccato. Each string soloist plays a different birdsong. Emerging from this confusion are the xylorimba, piccolo, flute, oboe and clarinet.

Write a complete plainchant *Kyrie eleison*, for brass, with an incessant carillon on two peals of bells, with varied rhythms, together with a different birdsong on each woodwind instrument.

1 June at 11 a.m. saw the golden whistler and white-naped honeyeater. Marvellous play of light and shade. Giant ferns, four to six metres high, form the undergrowth of the forest, the eucalyptus towering above them. The sunlight strikes marvellously into corners of the forest. Strong scent of eucalyptus. Here and there the enormous trunks of the mountain ash. Saw a grey fantail, Eastern whipbird, Eastern yellow robin, honeyeater. Large glade of grass flecked with pink. Sun and blue sky through the eucalyptus leaves. Saw the territory of the wombat, a sort of little bear, very powerful. Saw a robin and a white-throated tree creeper. We walk on a narrow path. To the left is a gorge filled with ferns, to the right a pond – the water is russet-green, reflecting the colours of the landscape.

12.20 p.m. Crossing the path a male lyrebird: it's big! – larger than a pheasant. The tail is very long, and from a distance appears black. On the way back saw a large tree covered in pink, with droplets on each leaf shining in the sun. After the brilliance of the light a plunge into darkness, as the giant ferns form a tunnel around the vehicle.

In the afternoon returned twice to Sherbrook Forest on foot. The huge eucalyptus have a deep hole at the base where a man could live – like

195 Messiaen's notations of the Superb lyrebird, made at Tidbinbilla, 11 June 1988.

the tree in which Ariel imprisoned the witch Sycorax (who was freed by Prospero) in *The Tempest* by Shakespeare. The lyrebird selects a clean patch for its dance, where the earth has not been disturbed. The sun's rays fall on the bird's lyre and on its dance, like a spotlight in a theatre. Saw the nest of a lyrebird, on a bank of reddish earth one-and-a-half metres high.

2 June. Rose at 5.30 p.m. Around 8 a.m. heard a solo by the lyrebird. Then went to a part of the forest where there are little waterfalls. A little ravine in which water flows between black moss-covered rocks: 'turning' sounds of the

water and wind. Saw a man, almost naked, running alone in the forest ('jogging'), and an elderly lady ornithologist looking for nests. Our driver is a Herculean figure with a red beard: he only needs a spear or sword to play Siegmund or some other primeval hero. Spent the morning with the ornithologist Harold Bradley, his wife Isobel, and the interpreter, Anna Murdoch.

In the shadow of the stands of eucalyptus, which seemed like some giant outdoor cathedral, the lyrebird's ritual suggested to Messiaen the Heavenly City preparing herself as the bride of Christ. The image gave him the title of the third movement of *Éclairs*, 'L'Oiseau-lyre et la Ville-fiancée'. Its music is based largely on notations made at Tidbinbilla, near Canberra, where on 11 June Messiaen heard three Superb lyrebirds singing in concert for an hour. The effect, as Loriod recalled, was overwhelming:

> [The] remarkable, luminous song is extremely varied and carries over great distances. Extending over several registers, it is composed of iambs (short–long), rapid wide-ranging slides, rolls, ascents to repeated notes. It can leap in three notes from high to low and back, make a swell on a held note followed by a cry on two notes, flung from low to high, and sing a long strophe of twenty notes, changing register with each note. In this song, by turns whistling, fluting, grating, radiant, brassy and disjunct, the sounds of water mix with imitations of other birds (the lyrebird is also called 'Master Mimic') with a prodigious virtuosity and range of dynamics and attacks. Three lyrebirds singing together can fill a forest with the trumpeting, joyous colours of an entire orchestra.[5]

Finally, in the forest at Tamborine Mountain (south of Brisbane) Messiaen heard another species of lyrebird, the Albert lyrebird; the name intrigued Messiaen, and he looked it up and recorded his findings: 'lyrebird of Prince Albert, husband of Queen Victoria, Queen of England'.

The experience of Australia and its birds had a decisive impact on *Éclairs*. Messiaen changed his original plan in order to make room for the Superb lyrebird heard at Tidbinbilla, deleting a piece that he had already completed in short score on the Tui bird from New Zealand. Changes to the eighth movement, 'Les Étoiles et la Gloire', may also have been made in order to include birds from Australia. The earlier title – 'Journey among the stars' – sounds like a space Odyssey, and suggests that stars rather than birds were its subject-matter. In its finished form the movement became not only the longest but the most turbulent in *Éclairs*, with a counterpoint between the implacable rhythms of the stars and the extravagant, gestural birdsong. The contest is resolved in the final unison hymn to the Highest, which is all the more tremendous for being the first time the whole orchestra is heard together. The birdsong is chosen for its brilliance: as well as the Albert lyrebird there is the equally assertive Mallee ringneck (also from Australia), birds from Papua, New Guinea, and, from Europe, the garden warbler, with only the gentler cadences of the blackcap and Orphean warbler by way of contrast.

The subtlety with which Messiaen uses his vast orchestra – enormously augmented because of the scoring of the birdsong – crowns a lifetime's obsession with the nuances of timbre. An example of Messiaen's exactness is the opening of the fifth movement, 'Demeurer dans l'amour'. The halo of string sonority is minutely defined, with the supporting harmony played by solo strings without mutes, while the melody – *legatissimo, molto legato* – is given to all sixteen first violins, of which six (but only six) play with mutes. At the opening, the melody is poised weightless and apparently motionless, but imperceptibly flexes and develops towards a searing climax, with the first violins driven up to a seemingly impossible high G sharp.

The marvellously extended and deceptively natural melodic lines of *Éclairs* – especially in the slow music of the first, fifth and final movements – crown another of the passions of Messiaen's life, and even surpass the intensity and beauty of the slow movements of the *Quatuor*. The flowering of melody in *Éclairs* stems from the renewal of Messiaen's love for the music of Mozart. In 1987 Messiaen published his collected analyses of the concertos (*Les 22 Concertos pour piano de Mozart*). Then, at the end of 1989, in the middle of composing *Éclairs*, Messiaen received a commission from Marek Janowski, stipulating (as Messiaen noted in his diary) a work 'for small orchestra in the spirit of Mozart', to be performed on 5 December 1991, the bi-centenary of Mozart's death. Within a week Messiaen had devised a title: *Un Sourire*.

It was while Messiaen was in Australia that his health suddenly became perilously fragile. On 1 June, during the trip to Sherbrook Forest, he had a momentary blackout, falling heavily while alone in his hotel room. Messiaen noted the fall in his diary, but kept it to himself and continued the schedule as planned. Back in France the blackouts continued. On 3 July, at La Sauline, Messiaen fell in the bath, catching his head against the taps, and was found by Loriod lying under a stream of scalding water. He was treated in hospital at Vierzon, where a range of tests proved inconclusive: the heart was sound, and the blackouts were attributed to a fault in the inner ear which caused loss of balance. Messiaen seemed to recover, working steadily on *Éclairs*. At Petichet there was a family reunion, with Pascal, Josette and Jacqueline, and time to listen to music – *Saint François*, *Die Walküre* and *Siegfried*, and a televised performance of *Götterdämmerung*. Loriod had installed handrails and a telephone to link the upper and lower houses. It was just as well, because Messiaen was struck by a spate of further blackouts. After a particularly bad fall, on 10 September, Messiaen was ferried back to Paris by ambulance and spent a fortnight in hospital. He used the time to note birdsong from cassettes that had just arrived from Malaysia after a lengthy correspondence with the Malaysian Nature Society in Kuala Lumpur. The transaction had been hampered by the complexities of the currency and perhaps by the language barrier (Messiaen's original spelling has been preserved):

> I'm writing to you for the forth time. I am always willing to buy the three 45 minute tapes of Singapore (and South-East Asia) birds's song. Thank you very much for your last letter. About the three tapes' price, you indicated 27 Ringgit. But the international Post-Office orders muste be in Sterling Pounds; and nobody knows here what's the change between Ringgit and Sterling Pound. Anyway I send you by Post-Office Order the equivalent in Pounds of 300 french francs; it would be quite enough. As soon as you'll have got my Post-Office order, it will be very kind of you to send me the three tapes. Thank you by advance.

Messiaen was discharged from hospital on 26 September. Two weeks later he was well enough to spend a day at the Erato studios editing the recordings of *Poèmes pour Mi* and *Chants de terre et de ciel* by Maria Orán and Loriod. He began practising the organ kept in the apartment on the fourth floor at the rue Marcadet, and on 16 October resumed his duties at the Trinité, playing music by Clérambault and de Grigny: the only ill effect was 'tired feet'. The principal event in the autumn of 1988 was the première of *Un Vitrail et des oiseaux* on 26 November, in a packed Théâtre des Champs-Élysées: 'Marvellous performance!!! Boulez: precise, vital, tremendous. Yvonne: dazzling technique, brilliant! The EIC: marvellous virtuosity, beautiful sound!!!' A week of concerts in London in early December reached a climax with a complete performance of *Saint François*, staged at the Royal Festival Hall on Messiaen's eightieth birthday. The difficulties of the venue were overcome by an ingenious set that included a footbridge, enabling the singers to stand above the orchestra.[6] Again Messiaen was overjoyed: 'Nagano marvellous!!! Very good orchestra!! Ondes T[rès] B[ien] – Production by Rennison excellent – costumes very fine, pretty set – a fifteen-minute standing ovation!!!' The birthday year concluded with a happy ceremony at the Trinité on Christmas Day. All the clergy at the church 'came up to my organ loft to wish me happy birthday. The Curé gave me a 19th-century medal showing the church of the Trinité. Jean Leduc was present at the Mass and brought me the first copy of the *Conférence de Kyoto* in French and Japanese – and on the cover a superb colour photo of the *torii* at Miyajima.'

At the start of 1989 Michel Guy, who had commissioned *La Ville d'En-Haut*, came to the rue Marcadet to receive the score: Messiaen reminded himself to provide 'tea, sugared almonds and petits fours'. This was the year of Loriod's retirement from the Conservatoire, and on 11 March Messiaen attended her

196 Loriod and Messiaen outside the Trinité, c.1990.

final class audition. On 21 March Messiaen shared a recital at the Trinité with the Chorale Grégorien du Conservatoire de Louis-Marie Vigne: 'I improvise on the plainsong texts for Holy Week. Stations of the Cross – six to nine minutes of improvisation between each one.' The church was packed for the occasion, with at least four distinguished organists present – Susan Landale, Gaston Litaize, Daniel Roth and Thomas-Daniel Schlee – as well as Mme Pompidou and Mme Chirac. A week later Messiaen received the Prix Paul VI from Cardinal Lustiger at a ceremony at Notre-Dame. A large sum of money was involved which would go to a cultural organization nominated by the prizewinner. Messiaen broke with tradition by nominating Médecins sans Frontières, to further the charity's work in Afghanistan.

Messiaen's health continued to be fragile. He underwent a neurological examination at the American Hospital in Neuilly, and was having difficulty climbing on stage to acknowledge applause, as he ruefully noted in the diary. Despite the constant claims on his time, work on *Éclairs* proceeded with none of the self-doubt that had plagued *Un Vitrail*. In June 1989 Messiaen revised the penultimate movement, 'Le Chemin de l'Invisible', and a month later, at Petichet, the work of orchestrating began. By October Messiaen was ready to write to Mehta with news of *Éclairs*, and he had also finished the draft score of *Un Sourire*, the commission for Janowski. In November he was well enough to accompany a tour, by the BBC Symphony Orchestra and Boulez, during which the first performances of *La Ville d'En-Haut* were given. The première took place at the Salle Pleyel on 17 November 1989. The diary noted a gratifying reception and the 'tremendous success' of another work in the programme, Boulez's *Le Visage nuptial*. Messiaen accompanied the subsequent tour to Milan, London and the Huddersfield Festival. At Huddersfield he met John Cage, forty years after Cage's visit to Messiaen's class: 'John Cage talked about his prize (the Inamori) in Japan, and told us how he had arrived at Kyoto in a pullover with no smart clothes, and the Japanese decided that as he was so fond of Japan he had to receive the prize in a kimono! After the concert a little reception and John Cage congratulated me!'

Messiaen spent the first days of 1990 at La Sauline working on 'Les Étoiles et la Gloire', reminding himself to add a tuba to the unison chorale that ends the movement. By early February he had orchestrated the final movement, 'Le Christ, lumière de Paradis', and by late March had completed the third movement, 'L'Oiseau-lyre et la Ville-fiancée'. In April work on *Éclairs* had reached the stage of making fair copies of the orchestral drafts, a task that would occupy Messiaen for over a year. On 10 May 1990 came the news that Alain had died.

Loriod remembered Messiaen visibly shaken, but still completing his daily quota of orchestration. This was an inflexible rule; he once told Peter Hill: 'I am like Richard Strauss. If I don't finish a page every day I don't get any supper.' Alain's funeral was on 16 May.

At Petichet, in summer 1990, Loriod found herself for once without proofs to correct, and turned instead to the annual task of issuing cheques to the fifty or so charities supported by the Messiaens. Letters received by Messiaen testify to his generosity. A matter of priority was supporting his two churches – repairs to Saint-Théoffrey (at Petichet) and the soup kitchen run by the Trinité. He sent donations (often unasked) to old friends or colleagues who were facing adversity through illness or old age, and sponsored numerous 'orphans' from different parts of the world. On more than one occasion complete strangers – musicians who had fallen on hard times – received substantial sums. Messiaen's goddaughter, Aline Poté, received such a large cheque as a present for her eighteenth birthday that in her letter of thanks she mentions receiving professional advice to invest the money wisely:

> I confess I was speechless, and had to re-read your letter several times before its meaning sunk in. Your letter touched me deeply, even overwhelmed me, both for the immense present and for the many good wishes accompanying it. I don't know whether I am worthy of either. I hope to see you soon in Paris, and find rather better words to thank you again. We think and pray a lot for the difficulties you have with your health.[7]

Messiaen was equally generous with his time. Although it was ten years since he had retired from the Conservatoire, he faithfully attended performances of works by former pupils and was always ready to help performers who were working on his music. In the early months of 1988, for example, the diary recorded meetings with the pianist Carl-Axel Dominique to work on the *Catalogue d'oiseaux*, a concert by students tackling the *Sept Haïkaï*, and the *Vingt Regards* performed by a team of Loriod's pupils. Messiaen was a particular admirer of the young pianist Roger Muraro. In January 1989 he attended a recital at the Salle Gaveau at which Muraro played the *Préludes* and 'La Rousserolle effarvatte', and the following month heard him in the Tchaikovsky First Piano Concerto. In May, though only a few days after cracking three ribs in another heavy fall, Messiaen attended a Messiaen masterclass given by Muraro to students at the Conservatoire. Peter Hill found to his surprise that Messiaen placed no time limit on their sessions, which began in the late afternoon and could continue beyond midnight. Messiaen seemed genuinely interested in new approaches, and though strict over detail made no attempt to impose a 'standard' interpretation.[8] And he was quick to show his appreciation:

197 Aline Poté, Messiaen's goddaughter, in 1985.

after a gruelling but productive session on 'La Rousserolle effarvatte' Hill found himself leaving the rue Marcadet with a bottle of champagne that Messiaen had tucked in his briefcase.

Messiaen also paid the closest attention to recordings of his music. Martha Argerich must have been delighted by the letter of thanks that she received from Messiaen in May 1991. What she could not have known was that the letter was based on pages of closely written pencil notes:

> I have just listened to the CD of my work *Visions de l'Amen* which you have recorded with Alexandre Rabinovich. It is absolutely marvellous. Your extraordinary technique allows you to take very rapid tempi that never seem too quick because balanced by well-judged rallentandos. The pleadings of number 3, 'Amen de l'Agonie de Jésus', are extraordinarily expressive, the 'Amen du Désir' has marvellous contrasts, and the last Amen, 'Amen de la Consommation', is quite simply amazing. Your partner is admirable too, and he follows you with exemplary fidelity in the sudden changes of tempo which your genius demands.

The summer break in 1990 was interrupted by a fortnight in Israel for a series of performances of *Turangalîla* conducted by Zubin Mehta. At the airports Messiaen now had to use a wheelchair, but would not be parted from the briefcase that contained his scores, his numerous spectacles, and the copy of the *Imitation of Christ* that travelled everywhere with him. At the concerts Messiaen for once was in a critical mood; his diary noted that the performances were error-strewn: a clarinettist picked up the wrong instrument, tempi were too fast, the percussion was too loud, and in the final concert there were 'mistakes by the orchestra in each of the ten movements'. That autumn Messiaen attended a production at the Châtelet of Dukas's *Ariane et Barbe-bleue*. He was not one to tolerate a lack of fidelity to the stage directions, and along with Elsa Barraine, another Dukas pupil, he found himself irritated when the scene in the castle cellars was transposed to the roof of a block of flats.

A sign of Messiaen's continuing loss of mobility came in October, when he returned to playing at the Trinité and found to his delight that the staircase to the organ loft had acquired a handrail: 'The banister paid for by a grant from the City of Paris – it's there!! Ropes, like those on a ship, very thick, are fixed to the wall by metal rings a metre apart!!'

Towards the end of copying *Éclairs* Messiaen started to plan further compositions. The idea of writing one or more concertos for favourite musicians had been in Messiaen's mind for many years. He had wanted to compose an oboe concerto for Heinz Holliger since the day in 1984 when Holliger played the *Vocalise*, demonstrating the technique of circular breathing to produce an unbroken line. In 1989 Messiaen was considering a work for oboe and harp,

198 Messiaen at La Sauline.

for Holliger and his wife Ursula. Then, in January 1990, Messiaen had a meeting with Georges Hirsch, Director of Opéra Bastille, at which Hirsch suggested that Messiaen write a work for the Opéra Bastille orchestra and its new musical director, Myung-Whun Chung. In May, Loriod appeared in a concert with Chung, performing *Couleurs de la Cité céleste* and *Un Vitrail et des oiseaux*. Messiaen was amazed by the conductor: 'Chung is marvellous, extraordinary.'

Initial ideas for the *Concert à quatre* came in the diary at the end of June 1991, among lists of things to pack for Petichet: 'Write a *concerto* for solo oboe, one cello, piano (or harp?) and orchestra.' Messiaen's plans for the work reflected his current passions. He was delighted to discover in the spring that a golden oriole had taken up residence in the woods at La Sauline, and the *cahier* for May is filled with its song: 'Golden oriole. The timbre is flute-like, whistling, gliding, golden, rich in harmonics, loud and bright, in a major key. It sang from 10.30 a.m. to 11.30 a.m., first by the gate (*mezzo forte*), then in our wood, very close by (*fortissimo*), then on the way to La-Lœuf-du-Houx (*piano* and *pianissimo*).'

Messiaen was still absorbed in the music of Mozart, and Peter Hill, who came for a rehearsal at the end of April, found him studying the score of *The Marriage of Figaro*. In September 1991 Messiaen noted a broadcast of *Apollo et Hyacinthus*, composed when Mozart was eleven, and in October he went to the Opéra to hear *Idomeneo*.

A few days after the first mention of the *Concert* came a more detailed note. The major change is the addition of a flute soloist – Messiaen had wanted to write a concerto for Catherine Cantin (principal flautist at Opéra Bastille) since 1989:

1st movement (Vif): Rameau or Scarlatti – with the Kokako from New Zealand.

2nd movement (Un peu vif): Two angels and a golden oriole. Susanna (oboe) and the Countess (cello) – sections are marked off by the golden oriole in the woods (the one at La Sauline).

3rd movement (Lent): 'Vocalise', see the Vocalise in A major. Score the beginning for oboe – at the reprise for oboe and cello in octaves.

4th movement (Vif): Use the Riroriro from New Zealand.

See Wolfgang Rihm, from Frankfurt. Tutti: cluster, then bass drum (rhythms!!!) – see also Rameau and Scarlatti.

For the flute: use the blackcap from La Sauline – for oboe: mistle thrush – for piano: garden warbler – for cello: find something characteristic.

200 With Fr Gaillard at Saint-Théoffrey, Petichet, 1991.

However, much of the early summer was taken up with *Éclairs sur l'Au-delà*, which was completed on 27 July 1991. Despite Messiaen's precarious health, and a number of falls, the time at Petichet was idyllic. Messiaen worked on the *Concert à quatre*, and in fine weather lunch was taken in the garden with visitors and their children: Pierre-Laurent Aimard and his wife came with their son Antoine (Messiaen's godchild), Roger Muraro with his son, and Martine, the 'goddaughter' from Benin, introduced her daughter Peggy.

On 1 October, back in Paris, Messiaen photocopied the drafts of the *Concert*. The main event of the autumn was a month-long festival of Messiaen's music in Austria. Messiaen attended only the first ten days of the festival, hearing *Turangalîla* in Vienna, followed by several concerts in Linz organized by Thomas-Daniel Schlee. For once, a première took place which Messiaen did not attend: the *Pièce pour piano et quatuor à cordes*, which Messiaen had composed in a few days in February, was performed for the first time in Vienna on 19 November in honour of Alfred Schlee's ninetieth birthday. Instead, Messiaen was at La Sauline working on the *Concert* where he took all the birdsongs noted at La Sauline in 1989–90 and those from the summer at Petichet, together with the 'large orange notepad' of birdsong from Singapore, New Zealand and Australia.

201 With Marie-Astrid, daughter of Thomas-Daniel Schlee, Linz, 26 October 1991.

The première of *Un Sourire* (5 December) was a disappointment. The reception was polite, and Loriod felt that the audience had missed the point. A month after the performance, Messiaen outlined his image of Mozart to Jean-Christophe Marti: 'I love and admire Mozart. I didn't try, in my homage to him, to imitate his style, which would have been idiotic. I said to myself: Mozart always had many enemies. He was hungry, cold, almost all his children died, his wife was ill, he knew only tragedy. [. . .] And he always smiled. In his music and in his life. So I too tried to smile, and I composed *Un Sourire*, a little piece lasting nine minutes, without pretentiousness, which I hope . . . smiles!'[9]

Any suggestion that Messiaen was making an elegiac farewell in *Un Sourire* can be discounted. The diary for December is so congested that at times it is indecipherable. Messiaen attended the rehearsals and performance in Paris of *Des Canyons* conducted by Nagano, and the very next day (10 December) was in Munich to hear Lothar Zagrosek conduct Scene 6 of *Saint François*. He gave a lunchtime recital at the Trinité, and at the Christmas services rounded off his playing with 'Puer natus est nobis' from the *Livre du Saint Sacrement*. The last concert of the year – and the last that Messiaen would ever attend – was at Radio France on 23 December, with Zagrosek conducting the *Trois petites Liturgies*.

Messiaen was making plans to add two further movements to the *Concert à quatre*. One of these, probably to be the finale, was a fugue with four subjects, one for each soloist. The other piece was to include two cadenzas: 'See Dutilleux, and the orchestration by Marius Constant of Ravel's *Gaspard de la nuit*. Use the grouse and the song thrush from the forest of La Frasse. For the Arctic Loon, use cello and double bass; use the bow on the body of the instrument: see the pages with special effects for strings in *Saint François* and in *Des Canyons*.' The song of the Arctic Loon was the final entry in Messiaen's last *cahier*: the notation, with the song in five subdivisions, is as detailed and vivid as ever: 'a) a shriek; b) halting, strange; c) a heart-rending plea; d) a deep growling; e) a desperate cry, like the scream of a murdered woman!!! (use motifs in clusters).'

After Messiaen's death, the work of finishing the four existing movements of the *Concert* was undertaken by Loriod, in consultation with Heinz Holliger and George Benjamin. The first movement was complete, apart from the scoring of the second half, which was a simple task given that the music follows the events of the exposition. The second movement, based on the *Vocalise* of 1935, had been fully orchestrated (Messiaen's photocopy was dated 25 November 1991). The scoring is a delicate enhancement of the original, and while the melody is given mainly to the oboe there are moments of charming interplay, as when the line is handed from one soloist to another just before the reprise, where the oboe and cello play in octaves. In the third movement, also entirely finished by Messiaen, the cello comes to the fore, with a solo based on the lyrebird. The

202 The first page of Messiaen's orchestration of the 'Vocalise' for the *Concert à quatre*.

fourth movement needed the most attention, although it was complete in short score (with indications of orchestration) and had been thoroughly checked by Messiaen: 'Completely reviewed – *good* in terms of sonority, durations and dynamics.' As well as following Messiaen's instructions for orchestrating the movement, Loriod made significant additions based on notes found among Messiaen's sketches. One of these was to turn the reprise of a section for the golden oriole into a mellifluous dialogue between the woodwind and the soloists; another was to add decorations to the final version of the theme, including a brilliant chordal descant for the piano. Just before this passage Loriod interpolated a substantial cadenza, with the soloists playing *hors tempo* using a miscellany of songs from the *cahiers*: one of these is the song thrush collected in the Forêt de la Frasse in 1964 that Messiaen had planned to use in the unwritten fifth movement.

Messiaen drew up a meticulous schedule for 1992, listing in the diary all performances of his works, the concerts he planned to attend, and the deadlines for proof-reading. He took a close interest in preparations for the Salzburg production of *Saint François*, and there are pages of notes recording names, places and rehearsals:

3 August: pack for Salzburg, the 8 orchestral scores and 8 vocal scores of *Saint François* and all the other works of mine that are being played at Salzburg, together with the complete writings of St Francis and the relevant photos (the Angel's costume, the portrait of St Francis, the birds), and something to work on between performances. Take a rehearsal schedule and the Geophone. Esa-Pekka Salonen will be at Salzburg from the 3 August to rehearse the chorus. To Salzburg by car (Yvonne, me and Régine Serra [Messiaen' secretary]) – via Grenoble, Geneva, Zurich. The Festival will pay for the hotel (I pay for Régine); meals are at our expense.

All this planned activity could not disguise the inexorable decline in Messiaen's health. He was losing blood, and the customary end-of-year break at La Sauline was cancelled. On 8 January he saw a urologist at the American Hospital who recommended an immediate operation: Messiaen refused on the grounds of urgent work. He was fretting about *Saint François*: 'Send the lady who designs the costumes and Peter Sellars the photo of Fra Angelico's Angel. Sellars has the vocal scores,[10] the recordings by Ozawa and Nagano and the libretto.' In what proved to be his last interview, with Jean-Christophe Marti, Messiaen was on good form, talking not only about the opera but about all his recent music, and even the forthcoming première of *Éclairs*.[11] On 26 January he played at the Trinité for the last time ('improvisations T[rès] B[ien]'). The operation, a minor procedure, was performed successfully on 30 January, but the following day Messiaen's back became acutely painful. He came home on 6 February and worked on the *Traité*, but within a week had to return to hospital for more tests. Up to this point the pain had been attributed to arthritis: now cancer was diagnosed. He was allowed home on 18 February: unable to go upstairs to his composing studio on the sixth floor (where the sketches of the *Concert* lay on his desk), he worked on the birdsong volume of the *Traité*.

Messiaen was unaware that he was suffering from cancer, and on 18 March dictated a letter to Zubin Mehta looking forward to the première of *Éclairs*:

> I am absolutely desolate and in despair at not being able to attend the rehearsals and two concerts (24 and 25 March) of the *Turangalîla-Symphonie* with the Berlin Philharmonic under your direction. Alas! After two spells in hospital, and successful surgery, I am suffering from terrible pains in the back which prevent me from getting up or lying down, and rule out travelling. On doctor's orders my wife, Yvonne Loriod, has to stay with me all the time, so I am sending you as piano soloist one of the most remarkable performers of my piano music, Roger Muraro, who I can assure you will play marvellously. [. . .] A big thank-you in advance. [. . .] I hope you have been able to glance at the enormous score of *Éclairs sur l'Au-delà . . .* on which I

203 The last photograph of Messiaen, at rue Marcadet on 25 March 1992.

have worked hard over the last four years. I very much hope to be recovered in two months and plan to leave for New York around 26 October to be present at all the rehearsals of the work and at the three concerts. [...] I'd be much obliged for the exact dates of your rehearsals, as well as the times and places.

On 19 March Muraro came to the rue Marcadet to work on *Turangalîla*, and the next day Messiaen telephoned Leduc to refuse permission for the 'horrible design' for a programme of *Saint François*. Two days later he managed to attend Mass at the Sacré-Cœur, and even to cast his vote in the local elections. The next few days were spent making notes on the recording of *La Transfiguration* conducted by Reinbert de Leeuw. The last photographs of Messiaen were taken on 25 March when he received the German Ambassador who had come to confer the Braunschweig prize. By the end of the month the pain was so bad that Messiaen was unable to leave his bed. On 31 March Hans-Ola Ericsson came to show Messiaen his new recording of the organ music; Messiaen was touched to note that Ericsson had gone to the trouble of including photographs of the birds from Israel and Palestine.

Messiaen was obliged to cancel an appointment with Peter Hill and wrote on 3 April – in firm handwriting – to explain his state of health:

Bien cher Ami,
Please excuse me for being unable to keep our appointment on 21 March. I heard in a letter from George Benjamin that all the concerts at the Opéra Bastille went well, with large audiences and considerable applause. George also told me that you and he played my *Visions de l'Amen* magnificently, and that you both enjoyed a huge success. Thank you and bravo! I've tried several times to phone you, always without making contact.

I should explain that after an operation and two spells in hospital I am suffering from pains in my back, with stabbing pains in my sides. These affect me for half an hour every time I change position, so it is impossible for me to go outdoors or to any public gathering. My apologies once again.

Messiaen was now too weak to attempt the steps of the Sacré-Cœur, and on 12 April attended Mass at Ste-Geneviève, the nearby church where he and Loriod had married in 1961. Two days later Messiaen was taken to the American Hospital. There his doctors conferred and recommended surgery, in case a further deterioration in his spine should lead to paralysis. Returning home, Messiaen was unable to lie down, and worked at his desk checking the tempi for *Éclairs* which he had promised to send Mehta. On 16 April there were two

J'ai essayé plusieurs fois de vous téléphoner, toujours sans résultat...

Il faut que vous sachiez qu'à la suite d'une opération chirurgicale et de deux hospitalisations, je souffre de douleurs dans le dos, avec des "coups de poignards" dans le flanc droit et dans le flanc gauche. Cela me prend pendant une demi-heure à chaque changement de position, il m'est donc impossible d'aller dans la rue ou à des réunions publiques. Pardonnez-moi encore...

Avec toutes mes félicitations, mes remerciements, et mes grandes amitiés.

Olivier Messiaen

204 Part of Messiaen's letter to Peter Hill, 3 April 1992.

entries in the diary: 'Trinité: Holy Thursday by me [crossed out]: by Bonfils – yes. At 11, Houllé (Éditions Leduc) brings me Scene 4 of *Saint François*. It's *appeared*, yes – *done*!' It is easy to imagine Messiaen's delight at seeing the first volume of his *magnum opus* in print. On 18 April he noted: 'Father Franck Hara (African priest from Ste-Geneviève) came to the rue Marcadet to hear my confession.' The next day, at Ste-Geneviève, Messiaen attended Mass for the last time. He was admitted to the Beaujon Hospital in Clichy on 21 April, 'at 9 a.m., with an empty stomach'.

The last entry in Messiaen's diary was on 22 April: 'Operation by Professor Deburge – two pins in the top of the back to support the collapsed vertebrae.' The operation, which lasted three hours, took place that evening. Loriod kept vigil in Messiaen's room. On 24 April he received a lengthy telephone call from Père Kars, and saw Pascal and Josette for the last time. On 26 April, a Sunday, he received communion. On the Monday morning attempts were made to measure him for a brace to support his back. In the early evening Messiaen started to cough blood into his handkerchief. Everything then happened quickly. Nurses rushed to help, while Loriod ran to find Messiaen's doctors: they attempted resuscitation but were unable to save him. Loriod remembered having lost track of the time. Outside darkness had fallen, and she noticed that the watch on Messiaen's bedside table had stopped at 8.30 p.m. It was the evening of 27 April 1992.

Messiaen was buried a short distance from his house at Petichet, in the tiny churchyard of Saint-Théoffrey which looks across to the mountain of the Grand Serre. The headstone, in the shape of a great white bird, bears a quotation from *Harawi*: 'Tous les oiseaux des étoiles' – 'All the birds of the stars'.

Among the many tributes paid to Messiaen, none was more heartfelt than the farewell of Pierre Boulez, when he addressed the audience at the Châtelet the evening after Messiaen's death:

> I want to dedicate this performance of *Pelléas et Mélisande* to the memory of Olivier Messiaen. This is a work for which he felt a true passion: in his harmony class, at the Conservatoire, and later, in his analysis class, *Pelléas* returned regularly in his teaching, always presented with affection and exceptional sensitivity. I benefited from the care of the Maître in all his early years of teaching, and I shall always be grateful to him for enabling me to discover, literally, such a masterpiece.
>
> My hope was that he might see this production, and that he would recall the pupil I once was all those years ago. Destiny decreed otherwise. But he will be in my mind throughout this evening, and I hope you will be able to share this memory which is so dear to me.

205 The headstone on Messiaen's grave in the churchyard of Saint-Théoffrey, Petichet (photo: Peter Hill).

Notes

Childhood and the Conservatoire: 1908–1929

1. Details about the place of Messiaen's birth are to be found in *Mémoires de l'Académie de Vaucluse*, septième série, tome v (1984), pp.50–61, which publishes the speeches given by Canon Durand and by Messiaen when he was awarded the Grand Prix of the Académie de Vaucluse in Avignon. The site of his birth was, according to Messiaen (p.60), 'a modest house in the Chemin de l'Arrousaire'; Canon Durand supplies the additional information (p.51) that this house 'disappeared, alas, under the bombs of the last war'. The Avignon website (http://www.avignon.fr/fr/culture/histoire/celebre.php) states that Messiaen was 'born on the corner of l'Arrousaire and the Boulevard Sixte-Isnard (his house was destroyed during the bombing of 1944)'.
2. The church's baptismal register gives the date of birth erroneously as 9 December.
3. The version of *L'Énergie fauchée* in Musée des Beaux-Arts, Troyes, is 175 mm tall by 121 mm wide. The museum's inventory no. is 20.7 RE1565. We are extremely grateful to Chantal Rouquet, Conservateur des Musées d'Art et d'Histoire, Troyes, for providing detailed information about this sculpture.
4. Much of the information about the Messiaen family and Fuligny has been kindly supplied by Mme Albert Guéritte, in Lévigny, during two visits to her by the authors in 2003. On 23 April 1946 she married Albert Guéritte, the youngest of the four sons of Madeleine (*née* Messiaen) and Paul Guéritte. Olivier Messiaen and Claire Delbos played the music at the wedding.
5. Samuel 1967, pp.24–5; Samuel 1986, pp.34–5. The 'rather odd farm' where Messiaen's aunts Agnès and Marthe lived was near the Mairie, in the rue du Moulin, on the left side of the road heading eastwards out of Fuligny.
6. Letter in MA.
7. Mistral won the Nobel Prize for Literature in 1904. Information about Cécile Sauvage's early encounters with Mistral and Pierre Messiaen is taken from Jean Tenant's preface to *Œuvres de Cécile Sauvage* (Paris, 1929), p.vi.
8. On the face of it, this seems a feeble objection, since military service was compulsory for all young men in France.
9. Quoted in Massin 1989, p.24. The source of this letter is uncertain: it is not to be found among those printed in Sauvage 1929.
10. Léon Daudet: 'La première . . . parce que la plus vraie', *L'Action française*, 8 November 1928. Daudet (1867–1942) was the editor, with Charles Maurras, of the right-wing daily newspaper *L'Action française*.
11. Tenant, in Sauvage 1929, p.x, confirmed by Cécile's letters from Ambert dated '1910' at the end of the same volume (pp.333–8), and by the numerous references to the landscape of the area in *Le Vallon*. Samuel 1999, p.433, gives the date of the move to Ambert as 1912.
12. Messiaen gave the place and date of Alain's birth as Grenoble in 1912, in his undated text 'Cécile Sauvage: Poète, 1883–1927' (typescript in MA). It is possible that Cécile spent the last part of her pregnancy at the home of her surgeon brother André, before returning to Ambert.
13. See Tenant, in Sauvage 1929, p.xii.
14. O. Messiaen: 'Discours pour la cérémonie du 20 janvier 1984 à Grenoble', typescript of Messiaen's speech when he was made an honorary citizen of the city (copy in MA).
15. Massin 1989, pp.38–9.
16. Samuel 1967, p.123.
17. See Samuel 1967, p.122.
18. Yvonne Loriod, personal communication.

19. See Samuel 1967, p.123.
20. Samuel 1967, p.10. In Samuel 1986, p.19, Messiaen added that 'its indecisive style and naive form make me smile'. This childhood work was recorded by Yvonne Loriod and issued in her set of Messiaen's complete piano works for Erato. In 2005 a short film about the piece was issued as a supplement to Roger Muraro's DVD of the *Vingt Regards* (Accord 476 7190).
21. Samuel 1967, p.19.
22. Samuel 1967, p.19.
23. Samuel 1967, p.19.
24. Pierre Messiaen's translations of Shakespeare came later: the first volume (*Les Comédies*) was issued in 1939, followed by a second in 1941 (*Les Tragédies*) and a third in 1943 (*Les Drames historiques et poésie lyrique*). All three volumes were reissued in 1948–9.
25. Pierre Messiaen's translations included Blake's *Songs of Innocence* (Saint-Étienne, 1934), Milton's *Paradise Lost* (Paris, 1951 and 1955), poems by Walt Whitman (Paris, 1951) and Emily Dickinson (Paris, 1956), and two large anthologies: *Théâtre anglais, Moyen-Âge et XVIᵉ siècle* [Marlowe, Dekker, Heywood, Ben Jonson, Webster et al.] (Paris, 1932, repr. 1948), and *Les Romantiques anglais* (Paris, 1955).
26. Rössler 1986, p.72.
27. Sauvage 1929, p.338.
28. See Poté 1978, p.95.
29. *Presse-Océan*, 6 January 1970.
30. Messiaen refers to 'les demoiselles Véron' (Samuel 1986, p.118). Mlle Marie Véron (10 rue de Flandre, Nantes) is listed as one of the 'artistes et professeurs: piano' in the *Annuaire des artistes et de l'enseignement dramatique et musical: 1923* (Paris, 1923), p.1250.
31. Gontran Arcouët is also listed in the 1923 *Annuaire des artistes*. He appears as a piano teacher at the École Nationale de Musique in Nantes, and under 'Auteurs, compositeurs, chefs d'orchestre' as well as 'artistes et professeurs: piano'. His address is given as 61 boulevard Lelasseur, Nantes.
32. Apart from his musical studies, Messiaen attended the Lycée Clemenceau, where his father was teaching. Maurice Poté (*Presse-Océan,* 6 January 1970) noted that Messiaen was in the 'classe de 7ᵉ de François Farineau'.
33. *Écho du Pays de Redon*, 26 January 1952.
34. Autograph draft letter, no date [?late 1919]. Private collection, England.
35. Bruyr 1933, p.125.
36. She was also a friend of Fauré, who dedicated the fourth song of *Le Jardin clos* ('Je me poserai sur ton cœur') to her.
37. Claude-Jean Launay, preface to Cécile Sauvage: *Œuvres complètes* (Paris, 2002), p.19.
38. See, for example, the chronology in Samuel 1967, p.217.
39. In other words at the start of the academic year 1920–1. This information was kindly communicated to us by Stephen Broad, Glasgow.
40. The certificates for all the prizes listed are preserved in MA.
41. This prize was awarded on the recommendation of the Conservatoire's director 'to a student who had obtained three *premiers prix*, but not just any three: one had to be in fugue, harmony, piano accompaniment (including score-reading and improvisation) or organ and one, interestingly, in the history of music' (Nichols 2002, p.187).
42. Falkenberg was a pupil of Massenet. He wrote a treatise, *Les Pédales du piano* (Paris, 1892), which Lockspeiser thought might have influenced Debussy's views on pedalling. See E. Lockspeiser: *Debussy: His Life and Mind*, vol.2 (Cambridge, 1978), pp.46–7.
43. See *Annuaire des artistes* (Paris, 1923), p.38. This gives the set work ('Mendelssohn, Prélude et Fugue op.35') and also lists Messiaen among the prizewinners.
44. Jean Gallon (1878–1959) was a pupil of Lenepveu (composition), Lavignac (harmony) and Diémer (piano). He enjoyed some success as a composer, but it was above all as a harmony teacher that he had the most lasting influence. He taught Duruflé and Dutilleux as well as Messiaen, and his classes were innovative: Gallon was the first harmony teacher to include Debussy, Ravel and Fauré in his curriculum. His brother Noël (1891–1965) was also a pupil of Lenepveu and Lavignac, and his piano teachers were Risler and Philipp. He won the Prix de Rome in 1910, and in 1914 collaborated with his brother on the score for the ballet *Hansli le Bossu*, choreographed by Ivan Clustine and given its première at the Paris Opéra on 22 June 1914. Noël became a teacher of solfège at the Conservatoire in 1920, and in 1926 took over the class in counterpoint and fugue. See *The New Grove Dictionary of Music and Musicians,* 2nd edn (London: Macmillan, 2001), vol.9, pp.479–80.

45. From 'Texte sur Noël Gallon', typescript in MA. Henri Dutilleux, who studied fugue with Noël Gallon in the early 1930s, was also present. The first half of the programme was devoted to works by Gallon, and the second half included Dutilleux's *Ainsi la nuit* and two of Messiaen's *Vingt Regards*.
46. Information from Stephen Broad, Glasgow.
47. Quoted in Nichols 2002, p.184.
48. Pierre Messiaen, autograph letter to Olivier and Alain Messiaen, 2pp., dated Paris, Tuesday morning, 6 September [1927]. Photocopy in MA.
49. Bruyr 1933, p.127.
50. 'Certain mot murmuré / Par vous est un baiser / Intime et prolongé / Comme un baiser sur l'âme. / Ma bouche veut sourire / Et mon sourire tremble.' From 'Primevère', *Œuvres de Cécile Sauvage* (Paris, 1929), p.213.
51. George Benjamin, personal communication.
52. Letter in MA.
53. Marcel Dupré: *Souvenirs*, unpubd typescript, dated 'Noël 1956', p.97.
54. Information from Stephen Broad, Glasgow.
55. The Widor was played at the organ *examen* on 10 May 1929. At the *concours* on 31 May, Messiaen was the last of the six candidates to play (the others included Langlais and Litaize). Each student played three improvisations (on plainsong, on a fugue subject, and a free improvsation on a theme) and the set piece, a 'Fugue in D' by Bach. Messiaen's *premier prix* was a unanimous decision by the eight members of the jury (information from Roger Nichols).
56. Messiaen's own list of works in *Technique de mon langage musical* (Paris, 1944), vol.1, p.64, gives 'Fuligny, Aube, 1929' for the *Préludes*; he gives a completion date of 'Paris, 1930' for the *Diptyque* and *Trois Mélodies* (pp.65–6), but it is likely that work began in 1929.
57. Photocopy of typed transcript in MA.

The Trinité and marriage: 1930–1934

1. *Guide du concert*, 17 January 1930, p.420.
2. Massin 1989, pp.44–5.
3. Rössler 1986, p.140. The orchestral *Banquet* remains unpublished.
4. See, for instance, his letter to Claude Samuel dated 14 July 1986, published in Samuel 1999, p.175.
5. In 1997 Yvonne Loriod found the manuscript of Messiaen's organ work *Offrande au Saint Sacrement*, and it is possible that other unpublished works will come to light in due course.
6. They are noted in the *Bulletin semestriel des Amis de l'Orgue*, December 1929, p.2.
7. 'Accompanied by his teacher Paul Dukas [. . .] Olivier Messiaen played his first work, *Préludes* for solo piano, on 28 January 1930 at Durand et Cie.' Durand 1969, p.77.
8. This was the 515th concert of the Société Nationale de Musique.
9. Speech given in Tokyo, November 1985, as part of the ceremony at which Messiaen was presented with the Inamori Prize. Autograph MS in MA.
10. Georges Dandelot (1895–1975) came from a musical family. His father Arthur founded an important concert agency in Paris. Known primarily for his harmony teaching, at the École Normale de Musique from its foundation in 1919, and at the Paris Conservatoire from 1942, he was also a prolific composer. Perhaps his most important work was the oratorio *Pax*, composed in 1935. His teachers included several who were later to teach Messiaen: Jean Gallon, Caussade, Emmanuel, Widor and Dukas. He was also an accomplished athlete. Five of Dandelot's solfèges were included in *Vingt Leçons de solfège modernes* (Lemoine, 1935), in which five by Messiaen were also published.
11. Dandelot is presumably referring to the second prelude played on this occasion, i.e. 'Le Nombre léger'. It is not clear why only six of the eight *Préludes* (nos.2–6 and no.8) were played at this performance, but more remarkable is that the first complete public performance of the *Préludes* did not take place until 15 June 1937, at the École Normale, when all eight were played by Bernadette Alexandre-Georges.
12. *Le Monde musical*, 31 March 1930.
13. The first page is illustrated in Périer 1979, p.23.
14. Mari 1965, pp.17–18.

15. Samazeuilh 1930, pp.475–7.
16. Specifically, the Prix Lepaule (given to a student who has produced a particularly remarkable work during the year), the Prix Eugénie-Sourget-de-Santa-Coloma (given to a first-prize winner in composition, piano or singing), one of the prizes awarded by the Fondation Yvonne-de-Gouy-d'Arsy, and one from the Fondation Fernand-Halphen. Details are given in Conservatoire 1930.
17. Tournemire 1989, p.80. During his last years as a student at the Conservatoire, Messiaen became acquainted with Tournemire; he performed some of Tournemire's organ works, and occasionally deputized for him at Sainte-Clotilde before being appointed at the Trinité. On 25 April 1932 Messiaen was one of seven young organists to perform pieces from Tournemire's *L'Orgue mystique* in a concert at Sainte-Clotilde (see Tournemire 1989, p.84).
18. Stravinsky's performance was first issued on Columbia LFX 179–181.
19. A tantalizing remark. George perhaps heard the very young Messiaen at the Paris Conservatoire.
20. *Les Nouvelles littéraires*, 26 February 1931.
21. BNF Musique, N.L.a.86. See also Simeone 2001a.
22. Such was its lack of commercial success that Durand did not need to reprint the work until forty-five years later. Relatively few performances followed in the wake of the première.
23. *Le Courrier musical*, 15 April 1931, pp.261–2.
24. The manuscript is in BNF Musique, Cons. D. 8038.
25. Paul Arosa was the son of Achille Arosa, Debussy's godfather, after whom the composer was named.
26. *Le Ménestrel*, 10 July 1931, pp.303–4, from which the subsequent quotations by Bertrand are also taken.
27. 1907–93; like Messiaen, Desportes was a pupil of Dukas, Emmanuel and the Gallon brothers. She was a prolific and successful composer.
28. *Le Courrier musical*, 15 July–1 August 1931, p.461.
29. Jaquet-Langlais 1995, p.64.
30. Marcel Dupré: *Souvenirs*, unpubd typescript, dated 'Noël 1956', p.98.
31. The autograph manuscript of Quef's score for *La Vie de Jésus*, one of the earliest film scores (composed the same year as Saint-Saëns's *L'Assassinat du Duc de Guise*), is in BNF Musique. See Robertson 1995, p.132.
32. All the correspondence relating to this appointment was formerly in the parish archives of the Trinité. It is now in MA and published in Simeone 2004b.
33. Jaquet-Langlais 1995, p.64.
34. Jaquet-Langlais 1995, p.65.
35. Bruyr 1933, pp.124–31.
36. A puzzling reference. Ravel's Piano Concerto in G major was first published by Durand in December 1931, and the first performance was on 14 January 1932. The interview with Bruyr is dated October 1931, so presumably Messiaen had seen an advance copy of the work at Durand.
37. This is particularly extraordinary given that the Straram Orchestra was recording the *Symphony of Psalms* on the day before giving the première of Messiaen's *Les Offrandes oubliées*.
38. Original letter in the possession of Marie-Louise Jaquet-Langlais; copy in MA.
39. The letters from Messiaen to Claude Arrieu quoted here are in BNF Musique, N.L.a.27. See also Simeone 2000b.
40. This information was noted on Messiaen's baptismal records at Saint-Didier, Avignon.
41. Jaquet-Langlais 1995, p.71.
42. Messiaen, disc notes for Accord 461 645–2.
43. *Technique* (1944), vol.1, p.67.
44. Halbreich 1980, p.348.
45. *Bulletin trimestrielle des Amis de l'Orgue*, no.14, June 1933, p.9.
46. Désormière also worked for Diaghilev's Ballets russes (1925–9), then as conductor of the Société de Musique d'Autrefois, an appointment which enabled him to explore the French Baroque repertoire. From the mid-1930s he was conductor of both the Orchestre Symphonique de Paris and the Opéra-Comique. From Satie to Boulez (*Le Soleil des eaux*) and Dutilleux (Symphony no.1), Désormière demonstrated a passionate commitment to contemporary music, until a stroke in 1952 left him incapacitated for the last decade of his life.
47. *Technique* (1944), vol.1, p.4. The other 'most devoted interpreters' were 'Marcelle Bunlet (singer), Étienne Pasquier (cellist) and Yvonne Loriod (pianist)'.

48. See *Technique* (1944), vol.1, p.65. Messiaen lists the movements: Kyrie, Gloria, Credo, Sanctus, Agnus [Dei], the five conventional sections of the Ordinary of the Mass.
49. The École Normale de Musique was founded in 1919 by Alfred Cortot and Auguste Mangeot. Teachers in the institution's early years included Pablo Casals, Paul Dukas (before his appointment to the Conservatoire), Wanda Landowska and Nadia Boulanger.
50. The chronology in Samuel 1967 gives the date as 1936; but in Samuel 1986 (p.193), Messiaen stated that 'from 1934 to 1939, I taught a piano sight-reading course at the École Normale'; then again, in his autobiographical entry for the Bordas *Dictionnaire de musique* (1970), the composer gives the date of his appointment as 1932, which seems to be supported by such evidence as there is. See also Boivin 1995, p.28, note 1.
51. In 1928 the length of compulsory *service militaire* was reduced to 12 months. Messiaen was obliged to live for much of the time in a barracks. He was able to obtain exemptions to perform his duties at the Trinité and for other important occasions. French National Service has a long and complex history (see: http://www.nithart.com/servmifr.htm). It was finally abolished in 1997 and the last conscripts left the French army in 2002.
52. The small organ, or *orgue de chœur*, was (and is) situated near the sanctuary in the Trinité, and is used to accompany the choir.

La Jeune France: 1935–1939

1. Fig.114 (p.325) in the Durand study score.
2. John 1:5.
3. Presumably a reference to the whole of Act Two.
4. Undated letter from Messiaen to Dukas (probably 31 January, 5 or 11 February 1935). This letter was offered for sale in the November 2003 online catalogue of Les Autographes, Paris, item 203 (http://www.lesautographes.com). We are grateful to Thierry Bodin for permission to reproduce this letter. It is frustrating that Messiaen does not mention who sang Ariane at the performance he attended, since the part was performed by both Germaine Lubin and Marcelle Bunlet. The latter was to become one of Messiaen's most important interpreters.
5. Robert Siohan (1894–1985) was active as a composer and conductor before becoming an important figure in French cultural politics. He chaired André Malraux's commission on the problems of music in France (1962), which led, among other things, to the foundation of the Orchestre de Paris. In his role at the Ministry of Culture in the 1960s he had contact with Messiaen over the commissioning of *Et exspecto resurrectionem mortuorum*.
6. By 1944 Messiaen seems to have regarded *L'Ascension* as relatively atypical: in *Technique* (1944), vol.1, p.67, it is not awarded any of the *Guide Michelin*-type stars given to 'characteristic' works (one star) and 'very characteristic' works (two stars).
7. According to the programme for the inaugural concert on 28 May 1935, the new stops were: *Récit*: Bourdon 16′, Cymbale (3 ranks), Nazard; *Positif*: Principal 8′, Cor de nuit 8′, Nazard, Tierce.
8. At the Salle du Conservatoire Russe, 26 avenue de Tokio.
9. At the Salon des Tuileries, 235 boulevard Raspail.
10. Private collection, London.
11. Messiaen, disc notes for Accord 461 645–2.
12. The nine pieces are by Tony Aubin, Elsa Barraine, Manuel de Falla, Julien Krein, Gabriel Pierné, Joaquín Rodrigo, Guy Ropartz, Florent Schmitt and Messiaen.
13. The pianist and composer Joaquín Maria Nin-Culmell was born in Havana in 1908 and died on 14 January 2004. He came from a remarkable family and is the brother of the writer Anaïs Nin and son of the Cuban composer and pianist Joaquín Nin. Nin-Culmell was trained in Paris, where he was a pupil of Dukas, and he later studied with Manuel de Falla before settling in the USA.
14. Georges Migot (1891–1976) is now a somewhat forgotten figure. He was a pupil of Widor and Maurice Emmanuel at the Paris Conservatoire. A man of extraordinary versatility, he was not only a composer but also a talented artist and writer. After returning from World War I badly wounded, he exhibited his paintings at two of the leading private art galleries in Paris (those of Georges Petit and Marcel Bernheim). As well as composing in smaller forms, Migot also wrote a series of oratorios on the life of Christ. His *Premier Livre d'orgue* was praised by Messiaen in a review for *La Revue musicale*, no.182, March 1938, p.228.
15. Jolivet 1978, p.83.

16. Jolivet 1978, p.84.
17. 'Thanks to Paul Le Flem and Varèse, Jolivet was familiar with the Second Viennese School, Bartók, etc., and he guided his friends. These young musicians often met at our house to look at every work possible, especially the most recent.' H. Jolivet: 'André Jolivet', in *Zodiaque*, no.119, 1979, p.15.
18. For more details of La Spirale and a listing of its concert programmes, see Simeone 2002b.
19. Éditions Costallat/Lucien de Lacour (Paris, 1946). The pianist who gave the première of *Mana* was Nadine Desouches.
20. A famously improbable earlier instance was the encore of the 'Pie Jesu' from Fauré's Requiem at the Trocadéro in 1900.
21. Yvonne Loriod, personal communication.
22. Trinité 1995, p.89.
23. *La Nativité du Seigneur: Neuf Méditations pour orgue par Olivier Messiaen (édité chez Alphonse Leduc en quatre fascicules). Extraits de presse* ([Paris], c.1937–8).
24. Review for *La Revue hebdomadaire*, quoted in *Extraits de presse*.
25. Massin 1989, p.172.
26. O. Messiaen: 'Maurice Emmanuel: Ses Trente Chansons bourguignonnes', *La Revue musicale*, no.206, 1947, pp.107–8.
27. Brothier 1954, pp.5–6.
28. For more details of La Jeune France and a listing of its concert programmes, see Simeone 2002b.
29. Brothier 1954, p.7.
30. André Cœuroy (1891–1976) was a French critic and musicologist with wide-ranging and progressive interests. His books include early studies on jazz (*Le Jazz*, with André Schaeffner, 1926), on the importance of recording (*Le Phonographe*, 1929, and *Histoire de la musique avec l'aide du disque*, 1931), and on broadcasting (*Panorama de la radio*, 1930).
31. BNF Musique N.L.a.15, 208.
32. BNF Musique N.L.a.15, 211.
33. Roy 1962, p.326.
34. Auric, Sauguet and Le Flem, quoted in Périer 1979, pp.39 and 41.
35. Honegger 1951, pp.168–9.
36. Poulenc 1954, p.113.
37. Poulenc 1954, p.114.
38. Chimènes and Massip 1998, p.18.
39. Evidence for this comes from entries in Messiaen's diaries.
40. *Poèmes pour Mi*, no.1, 'Action de grâces'.
41. *Poèmes pour Mi*, no.2, 'Paysage'.
42. *Poèmes pour Mi*, no.9, 'Prière exaucée'.
43. Winner of a *premier prix* for organ at the Paris Conservatoire in 1928, Noëlie Pierront was an enthusiastic exponent of modern repertoire and was admired by Tournemire (who dedicated no.49 of *L'Orgue mystique* to her), Jehan Alain, Messiaen and others. She was organist of Saint-Pierre-du-Gros-Caillou in Paris.
44. Simeone 1998a, p.20.
45. See the review by Claude Arrieu in *Le Monde musical*, 31 March 1937.
46. 'Les Auditions du mardi de la Revue musicale', unsigned review, *La Revue musicale*, no.174, May 1937, pp.291–2.
47. Halbreich 1980, p.327. In summer 1937 Abbé Brun spoke at the prestigious conference on sacred music given as part of the 1937 Exposition. His subject, aptly enough, was 'Le Clergé et la musique d'église'.
48. In the private collection of Nigel Simeone.
49. *Technique* (1944), vol.1, p.65.
50. Copy in MA.
51. Information kindly supplied by Jacques Tchamkerten, Geneva.
52. *Revue internationale de musique*, vol.1, no.1, March–April 1938.
53. Programme for L'Itinéraire, Notre-Dame des Blancs-Manteaux, Paris, 23 April 1974, with Jeanne Loriod and her 'Ensemble d'instruments électroniques'. Messiaen's note on the *Fête des belles eaux* is a facsimile of his handwritten text.
54. Programme for L'Itinéraire, 23 April 1974.
55. The recording of Bunlet and Messiaen in Debussy's *Cinq Poèmes de Baudelaire* and *Harawi*

was made at the Opéra de Vichy on 13 September 1954. It has been issued on CD by INA Mémoire Vive IMV 044.

56. We are grateful to Claire Obolensky of the Société Philharmonique de Bruxelles for this information.
57. Simeone 1998a, p.25.
58. *Musical Times*, December 1938, p.925.
59. Olivier Messiaen: 'Autour d'une parution', *Le Monde musical*, 30 April 1939, p.126.
60. The 'Amis' who actually hosted concerts of music by La Jeune France included Mme Jean Imbert, the Comte et la Contesse B. de Montesquiou-Fezensac, M. et Mme Edme Sommier, and Mme La Duchesse de La Rochefoucauld. See Simeone 2002b, pp.24–5 and 32–3, and Chimènes 2004, pp.552–3.
61. Olivier Messiaen: 'Autour d'une œuvre d'orgue', *L'Art sacré*, April 1939, p.123.
62. Massin 1989, p.152.
63. Yvonne Loriod, personal communication.
64. Jaquet-Langlais 1995, p.114.
65. One of Claire's pet-names for Messiaen. His mother had called him 'Zivier'.
66. Presumably a brand-name for a toy (unfortunately our enquiries to Samaritaine and BHV have yielded no more definite results). On the evidence of surviving family photographs, it is likely to be either a horse on wheels or a pedal-car (Pascal was photographed pushing the former and driving the latter). The pedal-car is perhaps more likely as its correct size would be more important, and Claire is clearly concerned about a good fit.
67. Copy in MA.

Messiaen's war: 1940–1944

1. *L'Orgue*, nos.40–1, December 1939–March 1940, p.31.
2. BNF Musique N.L.a.27.
3. This would have been *Les Comédies* (1939), the first volume of Pierre Messiaen's translation to appear.
4. Letter in MA. A few weeks later, on 7 March 1940, Dupré inscribed a pocket score of Stravinsky's *Petrushka* and sent it to Messiaen at the front, where it joined the remarkable mobile kit-bag library of scores.
5. Copy in MA.
6. Trinité 1995, p.91.
7. Copy in MA.
8. See Myriam Chimènes: 'Alfred Cortot et la politique musicale du gouvernement de Vichy', in Chimènes 2001, esp. pp.35–7.
9. *Interlude*, c.1945, p.7.
10. In a fine piece of detective work, Rebecca Rischin has discovered a good deal about Hauptmann Brüll, as well as pinpointing the one occasion when Messiaen appears to have named him, in an interview with Leo Samama in 1991, subsequently issued on videotape (Rischin 2003, pp.28–30). Rischin's admirable study contains a great deal of further information about the genesis and early reception of the *Quatuor pour la fin du Temps*.
11. 'Let There Be Light', *Everyman*, BBC Television, 1988.
12. Goléa 1960, pp.61–3.
13. Despite his avoidance of wearing ties wherever possible, Messiaen was a modest but stylish dresser before the war. His taste in shirts and sweaters was sometimes quite flamboyant in the 1930s and 40s. In later life he developed an enthusiasm for Hawaiian shirts.
14. Lauerwald 1999, pp.21–3.
15. From the programme in MA, reproduced in Schlee and Kämpfer 1998, p.225.
16. BNF Musique N.L.a.27.
17. Pierre Revel was a Dukas pupil and can be seen in the same group photograph of the class as Messiaen (see p.19, ill.21). As Messiaen predicted, Revel became a harmony teacher at the Conservatoire.
18. Claude Delvincourt (1888–1954) studied law before going to the Paris Conservatoire, where his teachers included Boëllmann, Busser and Widor. Severely wounded in World War I, he became director of the Conservatoire at Versailles in 1931, and of the Paris Conservatoire in 1941. His appointment of Messiaen was not without controversy. It was made 'despite much comment', according to Alain Louvier, who was himself a former director of the Conserva-

toire and Messiaen pupil. See Alain Louvier: 'Claude Delvincourt', *The New Grove Dictionary of Music and Musicians*, 2nd edn (London: Macmillan, 2001), vol.7, p.188. Delvincourt died in a car crash while on the way to Rome to attend the first performance of his String Quartet.

19. Copy in MA.
20. Chabrol 1990, p.165.
21. Chabrol 1990, p.166.
22. René Dommange, the Managing Director of Durand et Cie, had been involved in politics since at least 1932 when he became a député (member of parliament). An eager supporter of the Vichy government, on 7 July 1940 he was one of the signatories to a motion in favour of collaboration and in support of an authoritarian, non-parliamentary regime. He remained a faithful supporter of Pétain and became president of the Comité d'Organisation des industries et commerces de la musique in 1942. See Anne Latournerie: 'Aux sources de la propriété intellectuelle: Quelques clés pour une lecture politique et culturelle des batailles du droit d'auteur', published online at: http://www.freescape.eu.org/biblio/article.php3?id_article5109#nb16
23. The church of Notre-Dame-des-Malades, sometimes known as St-Blaise (the older church to which it is adjacent) stands in the place d'Allier. It was indeed 'ultra-modern' in 1941: a striking art deco building, completed in 1935. The large campanile was added in the 1950s.
24. Copy in MA.
25. *Technique* (1944), vol.1, p.65.
26. Though declared to the SACD, no copy of the printed text of the play, or any of the music was submitted. Our thanks to Florence Roth, SACD, Paris, for this information.
27. Copy in MA.
28. Marcel Dupré: *Souvenirs*, unpubd typescript, dated 'Noël 1956', pp.126–7.
29. P. Messiaen 1944, pp.340–1.
30. Yvonne Loriod, personal communication.
31. The SMI had in fact disbanded in 1935.
32. From the manifesto printed in *L'Information musicale*, 22 November 1940, p.30.
33. *L'Information musicale*, 11 July 1941, p.759.
34. Delannoy, however, appears to have been the only critic to mention the similarity between the 'Louange à l'Éternité de Jésus' and the *Fête des belles eaux*.
35. Quoted by Yvonne Loriod-Messiaen in OMR.
36. Quoted by Yvonne Loriod-Messiaen in OMR. The Florence Blumenthal Prize was awarded annually by the Franco-American Foundation.
37. *L'Information musicale*, 11 July 1941, p.757.
38. Information from Messiaen's diary.
39. *L'Information musicale*, 24 October 1941, p.207.
40. Guéhenno 1968, p.255.
41. Pierre Messiaen married his second wife, Marguérite, a few years after Cécile's death.
42. *L'Information musicale*, 23 January 1942, p.644.
43. Copies of the programme and the leaflet with the commentaries are in Nigel Simeone's collection.
44. Fritz Piersig (1900–78) worked at the Propaganda-Staffel in Paris from 1940. He spent most of his life in Bremen where he was a critic and musicologist.
45. Letter from Messiaen to Étienne de Beaumont, 4 June 1942. Pierpont Morgan Library, New York City (Morgan Collection, Music Mss. and Letters, record ID 118708); we are grateful to the library for permission to use this letter, and to Rigbie Turner for kindly providing a copy.
46. See Simeone 1998a, pp.70–3.
47. On 16 May 1938 she played 'Transports de joie' and three movements from *La Nativité* in a concert of contemporary French organ music given for the American Guild of Organists at St Mary the Virgin, 139 West 46th Street, New York.
48. Messiaen's description is both charming and apt, since Irène Joachim (1913–2001) is best remembered now for her portrayal of Mélisande on the recording conducted by Désormière (recorded in Paris during 1941 and issued on twenty 78 rpm discs in 1942) with other singers from the Opéra-Comique, where she was a principal from 1939 until 1956, and where she attracted immediate attention as an outstanding Mélisande in the theatre (she had studied the role with Mary Garden, the first Mélisande). Her voice was much lighter than Bunlet's, but she was greatly admired by Messiaen.
49. *Olivier Messiaen: Compositeur de musique et rythmicien. Notice biographique, catalogue détaillé des œuvres éditées* (Paris, 1949).

50. Buckland 1991, p.130.
51. Bar-sur-Aube, a few miles to the south of Lévingy and Fuligny, is on the main Paris–Basel line.
52. See Jolivet 1993, p.45. The performance took place at the Franciscan Chapel, 7 rue Marie-Rose, Paris 14ᵉ.
53. Personal communication from Florence Roth, SACD, Paris.
54. Yvonne Loriod, personal communication.
55. Jünger, quoted in Ousby 1999, p.185.
56. See Jackson 2000, p.218.
57. O. Messiaen: 'Technique de mon langage musical', *Musique et radio*, November 1942, pp.253–4.
58. Béal was the leading Lyon music dealer, who presumably acted as Durand's agent.
59. See Philippe Morin: 'Une nouvelle politique discographique pour la France', in Chimènes 2001, pp.253–68, and disc notes by Philippe Morin and Jean-Charles Hoffelé for Dante LYS 310. Désormière's recording of *Les Offrandes oubliées* (AA6) is extremely rare and at the time of writing (2005) it has yet to be reissued.
60. The celebratory spirit of plainchant alleluias had an enduring attraction for Messiaen; see, for instance, the use of the Alleluia for the 8th Sunday of Pentecost twenty years later, in *Couleurs de la Cité céleste*.
61. BNF Musique, Rés. Vm. dos. 70. All the letters from Messiaen to Tual and Méhu quoted below are in this dossier. For transcriptions and translations of all the letters from Messiaen to Tual in this dossier, see Simeone 2000a.
62. Bernard 1945, unpaginated.
63. 'André-Louis Dubois', *Le Monde*, 18 November 1998.
64. In 1998 the Musée Picasso, Paris, was given a wash-drawing in black ink by Picasso from Dubois's estate. Showing a ram's head on one side and two sheep's heads on the other, it is dated 26 March 1943.
65. Yvonne Loriod, personal communication.
66. Yvonne Loriod, personal communication.
67. Photographs of the concert are included in the Tual dossier, BNF Musique, Rés. Vm. dos. 70.
68. D. Tual: *Itinéraire des Concerts de la Pléiade*, in BNF Musique, Rés. Vm. dos. 70.
69. It has sometimes been suggested that Pierre Boulez was one of the page-turners for this concert, but he did not arrive in Paris until Autumn 1943. Nigg and Hanicot were both in Messiaen's class at the Conservatoire. As Boulez himself told Roger Nichols, he turned pages for the vibraphone player at the first performance of the *Trois petites Liturgies* (see Nichols 1986, pp.167–70).
70. Undated cutting in BNF Musique, Rés. Vm. dos. 70.
71. For a full account of these concerts and a complete list of programmes, see Simeone 2000a.
72. Living composers represented in the previous concerts had included Auric, Françaix, Poulenc, Stravinsky, Émile Damais and Michel Ciry.
73. Désormière's recording, made at the time of the 1945 première, has a duration of 30 minutes, and most later performances and recordings are several minutes longer.
74. Yvette Grimaud, quoted in Jean Boivin 1995, p.44.
75. Boivin 1995, p.47.
76. Letter in MA.
77. For some reason the dedication did not appear on the first edition, but it is present in all subsequent editions.
78. Goléa 1960, p.60.
79. See Lacombe and Porcile 1995, pp.151–2.
80. While Bernard-Delapierre moved on to other areas of activity, Gabriel Dussurget was to become a distinguished artistic administrator, founding the Aix-en-Provence Festival in 1948. Dussurget died, aged 92, on 28 July 1996.
81. Yvonne Loriod, personal communication.
82. See also Goléa 1960, p. 82.
83. Goléa 1960, p. 147.
84. Paul Collaer (1891–1989) founded the Pro Arte concerts in Brussels in 1921 with the aim of promoting performances of contemporary music. In 1937 he took up a post at Belgian Radio, which enabled him to nurture not only new music but also the works of early Baroque masters. He enjoyed friendships with numerous musicians, including Ansermet, Auric, Bartók, Berg, Dallapiccola, Désormière, Falla, Hindemith, Honegger, Messiaen, Milhaud, Poulenc, Prokofiev, Roussel, Satie and Stravinsky. See Wangermée 1996.

85. Wangermée 1996, pp.371–2.
86. In the worklist of the revised single-volume edition of *Technique de mon langage musical* (Leduc, 2001), p.111, *L'Ascension* has acquired two stars. *O sacrum convivium* remains starless.
87. There is a copy of an undated *Programme de la musique et des danses exécutées par une troupe de danseurs et danseuses de l'île de Bali* from the 1931 Exposition in MA.
88. Copy in MA.
89. A Messiaen pupil, Yvette Grimaud was also an outstanding pianist who gave the first performances of four piano works by Pierre Boulez: *Notations* and *Trois Psalmodies* (dedicated to Grimaud) on 12 February 1945; the public première of the First Piano Sonata in 1946; and the Second Sonata on 29 April 1950. See Jameux 1991, p.32.
90. Messiaen's diary records that Boulez visited on 10 July, 7 August, 23 September and 6 December.
91. Ousby 1999, p.291.
92. De Gaulle 1970, pp.439–40.
93. 'Des paroles d'esprit: Entretien avec Olivier Messiaen', in *Charles de Gaulle* (Paris: L'Herne, 1973), pp.44–6.
94. Henry Barraud (1900–97), was director of music programmes for the RTF in 1944–8. In 1948 he became director of the 'chaîne nationale' (which broadcast classical concerts, opera, theatre and programmes about literature). He was also active and successful as a composer.
95. Eventually Toesca's poems were published as *La Nativité* in 1952, with original illustrations by Michel Ciry, a distinguished artist who had also studied composition with Nadia Boulanger.
96. Yvonne Loriod, personal communication.

'Le Cas Messiaen' and the Tristan trilogy: 1945–1948

1. Letter in MA.
2. 'Les cinq lettres de Cambronne' is a French euphemism for 'merde'.
3. Rostand 1957, p.8, note 2; see also Rostand 1952, pp.56–8.
4. Bernard 1945, unpaginated.
5. *La Revue musicale*, no.198, February–March 1946, p.70.
6. 27 April 1945. Wangermée, 1996, p.385, note 8.
7. Wangermée 1996, p.384.
8. Jean Wiéner: 'À propos d'une première audition d'Olivier Messiaen', quoted in Massip 1996, pp.15–16.
9. Raoul Moretti (1893–1954) was a composer of light music, including chansons, operettas, and film scores for directors such as René Clair and Abel Gance. See Colpi 1963, p.316.
10. See Goléa 1958, pp.9–11.
11. Messiaen went round to Manuel Rosenthal's dressing-room after the concert and apologized (information from Roger Nichols).
12. Chimènes 1994, p.595, letter 45–12, note 9.
13. Chimènes 1994, p.586, letter 45–5, note 1.
14. Chimènes 1994, p.586.
15. Loriod had given the second complete performance, on 29 April at Nelly Sivade's house in the rue Blanche, to a small invited audience that included Auric, Delvincourt, Désormière, Honegger, Ibert, Poulenc, Sauguet, Tcherepnin and Fr Florand. See OMR, and Chimènes 1994, p.586.
16. See Simeone 2002d.
17. Marguérite Béclard d'Harcourt and Raoul d'Harcourt: *La Musique des Incas et ses survivances* (Paris: Paul Guenthner, 1925).
18. *Traité*, vii (2002), p.66.
19. Goléa 1960, pp.148–9.
20. *Traité*, vii, pp.53–94. The dating of the chapter is supported by the footnote on p.53.
21. Marguérite Béclard d'Harcourt and Raoul d'Harcourt, eds.: *Chansons folkloriques françaises au Canada: Leur langue musicale* (Québec: Presses universitaires Laval, 1956).
22. Unpublished manuscript in MA.
23. For a full discussion see Griffiths 1985, pp.126–7.
24. Possibly a reference to Breton's *Second Manifeste du surréalisme* (Paris, 1930) which Messiaen knew well, as is clear from his discussions wth the Surrealist Ernest Gengenbach (see pp.167–8).

25. Goléa 1960, p.155.
26. Goléa 1960, p.156.
27. It was not until 1997, five years after Messiaen's death, that an authoritative account was made public. This came about when the draft of an article by Lionel Couvignou, *Un arc-en-ciel théologique*, was submitted to Yvonne Loriod for her comments. In her reply she wrote: 'What I know from OM's own lips is that from the start of the marriage (in 1932) Claire had several miscarriages before bringing Pascal into the world. After the war, even as early as 1943, her health declined, and after an operation she began to lose her memory. The epidural was blamed for having started the deterioration, but in reality it must have been either a hereditary trait or an atrophy of the brain. This meant that she had to be placed in a nursing home. She was gentle, smiling, but totally dependent.' Copy of Loriod's letter in MA.
28. Goléa 1960, pp.150–1.
29. Copy in MA.
30. See Davidson 2001, p.51 and p.62 note 52. The author reports that it was lost during World War II and, according to Penrose himself, was not found after the war.
31. Goléa 1960, pp.155–6.
32. This was a response to Schweitzer's request for information about *Turangalîla* for his monograph on the work (Schweitzer 1982).
33. Gavoty 1990, pp.53–4.
34. Pierre Boulez: 'Rétrospective', *L'Artiste musicien de Paris*, 64ᵉ année, nouvelle série, no.14, 1966, p.8; Eng. trans. in Boulez 1986, p.405.
35. A telling reference given Messiaen's own writing for celesta, piano and another tuned percussion instrument (vibraphone) in the *Trois petites Liturgies*.
36. Olivier Messiaen: 'Béla Bartók', *Images musicales*, no.2, 19 October 1945, p.[4].
37. Jean Wiéner, unidentified press cutting, December 1945.
38. Apparently at least two other pianists – Monique Haas and Samson François – were unwilling to learn the work in the time available. Yvonne Loriod, personal communication.
39. Olivier Messiaen: 'Le 2ᵉ Concerto de Béla Bartók', *Lumière de la ville*, 18 December 1945, p.25.
40. Elsa Schiaparelli (1890–1973) was one of the most brilliant and original fashion designers of the 1930s, famous for her use of 'shocking pink'. Her friends including the artists Cocteau and Dali, both of whom made designs for her. Her Paris salon (closed during the war) reopened in 1945, but she never quite recaptured the extraordinary exuberance of her earlier designs. She retired in 1954.
41. Yvonne Loriod, personal communication. The programme for this 'VIᵉ concert de l'Association Tchécoslovaquie–France' is bilingual (Czech and French).
42. Information from the original programme.
43. They included Bernard-Delapierre, Roland-Manuel, Louis Beydts, Max-Pol Fouchet, Henri Barraud and Fr François Florand O.P.
44. See Boswell-Kurc 2001, esp. pp.56–7. This important dissertation is by far the most thorough exploration of 'Le Cas Messiaen'.
45. According to the BNF Catalogue général, the correct form of Gengenbach's name is Ernest Gengenbach. His pseudonyms included Ernest de Gengenbach (as here), Jean Genbach (a name he used as one of the contributors to the Surrealist journal *La Révolution surréaliste*), and Jehan Silvius.
46. Goléa 1960, p.157.
47. Goléa 1960, p.157.
48. We have been unable to find any information about Mme de Prévot.
49. 'La Colombe', 'Le Nombre léger' and 'Les Sons impalpables du rêve'.
50. Goléa 1960, p.84.
51. At the Conservatoire, Janine Coste was in Messiaen's harmony class from 1942 and was a piano pupil of Marcel Ciampi. She died young, of cancer, not long after this performance of *Visions de l'Amen* (Yvonne Loriod, personal communication).
52. Yvonne Loriod, personal communication.
53. According to Jameux 1991, p.33, Boulez told Messiaen that the work made him 'vomit'. Jameux claimed that this violent reaction was largely because of the ondes Martenot, an instrument Boulez detested but knew well – having played it first at the Folies-Bergère and then for the Renault-Barrault company (see Jameux 1991, p.17).
54. *Guide du concert*, vol. 28, nos 23–5, 12, 19 and 26 March 1948, p.254.
55. Clarendon: 'Les Trois Tâla d'Olivier Messiaen', *Le Figaro*, 18 February 1948.

56. Fred Goldbeck: 'La Symphonie, elle aussi va au cinéma. . . Henri Sauguet choisit la tragique et Olivier Messiaen organise la magie', *Le Figaro littéraire*, 21 February 1948.

57. *Turangalîla-Symphonie*, Durand et Cie, 1953. In the revised edition of the score, published in 1992, there is no mention of allowing selected movements to be performed.

Experiment and renewal: 1949–1952

1. This contradicts what Messiaen later told Goléa: 'At the time of my *Mode de valeurs* [1949] I had the idea of a series of attacks; and since then Boulez has added series of tempo and series of sound-complexes' (Goléa 1960, p.248). Strictly speaking, Messiaen is right, since neither *Cantéyodjayâ* nor the *Quatre Études* contain any rigorous organization of tempo; indeed they are the last of Messiaen's works for piano not to use metronome marks. But the idea of applying serial writing not only to pitch but also to other 'parameters' was clearly Messiaen's.

2. Messiaen, disc notes, reprinted in Accord 465 791–2.

3. Couraud, disc notes for Erato STU 70457.

4. Goléa 1960, p.177.

5. *Traité*, ii (1995), p.152.

6. Goléa 1960, p.150.

7. Copy of typescript in MA.

8. Marcel Couraud: 'Première audition', article dated 'Paris, December 1953', in *La Musique et ses problèmes contemporains*, Cahiers de la Compagnie Madeleine Renaud–Jean-Louis Barrault, deuxième année, troisième cahier (Paris, 1954), pp.104–6.

9. Typed copy of this extract in MA.

10. Reissued on CD by FMR Records in 2003, FMRCD120–LO403.

11. *Newsweek*, 18 July 1949, p.67.

12. Programme book for Berkshire Festival at Tanglewood, Thirteenth Program, 14 August 1949, pp.22–3. Thomson's article was originally published in the *New York Herald-Tribune*.

13. *Berkshire County Eagle*, 13 July 1949.

14. Messiaen, disc notes, Accord 465 791–2.

15. As well as the *Quatre Études* Messiaen also gave occasional performances of a few pieces from the *Vingt Regards* – a selection that avoided the most virtuoso numbers – and the fifth of the *Préludes*, 'Les Sons impalpables du rêve'.

16. Hill 1995, p.297.

17. Reissued on CD by FMR Records in 2003, FMRCD120–LO403.

18. For an extensive anthology of reviews of the first Boston and New York performances of *Turangalîla*, see Simeone 2002d, pp.105–25.

19. Tagore's 'Megher pore megh'. See *Traité*, vii, pp.73–6.

20. Samuel 1994, p.44.

21. O. Messiaen: 'Orgue', *La Trinité: Journal paroissial*, May 1951, p.3.

22. Goléa 1960, pp.78–9.

23. Chimènes 1994, p.695. For other European critical reactions to *Turangalîla*, see Simeone 2002d, pp.123–5.

24. See *Traité*, vii, pp.73–6.

25. Each movement in the published score is dated '1951'.

26. Samuel 1976, p.44.

27. Samuel 1994, p.119.

28. Hill 1995, p.366.

29. Samuel 1994, p.118.

30. Recording made available to the authors by François Donato and Bernard Bruges-Renard of the Groupe de Recherche Musicale.

31. Copy in MA.

32. Yvonne Loriod, letter to Jean-Pierre Valion, Gardépée, dated 18 February 1995. Copy in MA.

33. 'After a stay in Charente with the ornithologist Jacques Delamain, I wrote my *Réveil des oiseaux* (1953), for piano and orchestra, and the "Chants d'oiseaux" from my *Livre d'orgue*.' *Guide du concert*, 3 April 1959, p.1093.

34. *Guide du concert*, 3 April 1959, p.1093.

35. Goléa 1960, p.208.

Birdsong into music: 1952–1959

1. Carême (1899–1977) was the poet of Poulenc's song-cycle *La Courte paille*, composed in 1960.
2. Fig.17 in the score.
3. The first concert performance in London took place a year later, at the Royal Festival Hall on 12 April 1954. Walter Goehr was again the conductor, with Ginette Martenot and Loriod as the soloists, and the London Symphony Orchestra.
4. The first public concert of the Domaine Musical took place at the Petit Théâtre Marigny on 13 January 1954. The organization was largely the brainchild of Pierre Boulez who wanted to develop concerts at which the most daring contemporary music would be performed. Financial support came from Suzanne Tézenas (who became President of the Domaine Musical), Jean-Louis Barrault and Simone Volterra (Director of the Théâtre Marigny), and artistic advice from Pierre Souvtchinsky and André Hodeir. The theatre was made available by the Barrault-Renaud company, for which Boulez had been musical director since 1946, after a short stint as *ondiste* of the Folies-Bergère (see Jameux 1991, p.17).
5. Yvonne Loriod, personal communication.
6. Orgeval is a village 11 km (7 miles) from St-Germain-en-Laye. The Moulin d'Orgeval is close to the site of a ruined abbey.
7. Roger Nichols, unpublished interview with Messiaen, 1978.
8. Yvonne Loriod, personal communication.
9. Yvonne Loriod, personal communication.
10. Simeone 1998b, p.47.
11. Yvonne Loriod, personal communication.
12. Goehr 1998, p.56.
13. Goléa 1960, p.17.
14. Fig.12 in the score.
15. The piano solos at figs.5 and 7.
16. The authors are grateful to Robert Fallon for drawing their attention to this source.
17. The sole exception is the mistle thrush whose motif on oboes, clarinets and trumpet is paralleled by what Messiaen calls a 'resonance': eight-part chords played quietly by violins and violas.
18. Goehr 1998, pp.49–50.
19. In fact the programme announced 'Sept pièces pour piano (1957) [. . .] extraites du *Catalogue d'oiseaux*', but 'La Roussserolle effarvatte' was not finished in time.
20. Messiaen had already had the idea of placing 'La Rousserolle effarvatte', the longest piece, just before the shortest, 'L'Alouette calandrelle'; though not performed at the concert, it was listed there in the programme for 30 March 1957.
21. *Guide du concert*, 12 April 1957.
22. Yvonne Loriod, personal communication.
23. *Conférence de Bruxelles* (Paris, 1960), p.6.
24. *Guide du concert*, 3 April 1959, pp.1093–4.
25. Goléa 1960, pp.151–2.
26. Yvonne Loriod, personal communication.
27. Yvonne Loriod, personal communication.

Public controversy, private happiness: 1959–1963

1. See *Chronochromie*, fig.17.
2. *Guide du concert*, 3 April 1959, p.1094.
3. Yvonne Loriod, personal communication.
4. Letter in MA.
5. *L'Express*, 21 September 1961.
6. The price was 2,940,000 AF.
7. The sale was completed on 3 March 1963 for a price of 47,000 NF.
8. According to this type of French marriage contract, there is no jointly owned estate. Each partner remains sole owner of his or her property before the marriage, and of earnings and other revenue during the marriage.
9. In March 1815 Napoleon escaped from exile on Elba. He landed on the French coast at Golfe Juan near Cannes and travelled from there via Grasse, Digne-les-Bains and Gap to Grenoble. The 'Route Napoléon' traces this historic journey through the Alps.

10. Milhaud 1995, p.244.
11. For lists of those who attended Messiaen's classes from 1941 to 1978, see Boivin 1995, pp.409–32.
12. Yvonne Loriod, personal communication.
13. *Le Monde*, 15 February 1962.
14. From an unpublished lecture by Messiaen given in Munich on 29 March, the day before Boulez's performance of *Chronochromie*. Text in MA.
15. The programme was transmitted on 2 March 1961.
16. The photographer was Izis (1911–80), whose real name was Israelis Bidermanas. He was a Lithuanian who settled in Paris and set up a photographic studio. He published several collections, including *Paris des rêves*, *Le Monde de Chagall* and *Le Paris des poètes*.
17. This is clearly incorrect. Air France started its polar route from Paris to Tokyo in 1958 and the cruising speed (depending on the aircraft used) was between about 500 and 800 kph (or 300 to 500 mph).
18. Messiaen, unpublished pencil notes made in Japan, in MA.
19. Messiaen, typescript, 1964, in MA.
20. Messiaen, typescript, 1964, in MA.
21. Yvonne Loriod, private communication.
22. Gagaku is a form of Japanese court music. The koto is a Japanese long zither which is used in gagaku and other traditional music of Japan.
23. Messiaen, typescript, 1964, in MA. Tsuzumi are hourglass hand drums used in nô theatre.
24. Messiaen, typescript, 1964, in MA.
25. Unpublished pencil notes in MA; these formed the basis of the description in the *Traité*, vii, pp.21–2.
26. Messiaen, typescript, 1964, in MA.
27. Messiaen, typescript, 1964, in MA.
28. Footnote in the score of *Sept Haïkaï*, p.1.
29. Messiaen, typescript, 1964, in MA.
30. Score of *Sept Haïkaï*, p.46.
31. Messiaen, typescript, 1964, in MA.
32. On 19 July at 7.45 p.m., presumably on his way home from visiting Loriod in hospital, Messiaen sketched in his diary a remarkable page which anticipated figs.58–61 of *Couleurs de la Cité céleste*.
33. Any dissent must have been marginal since none was mentioned in a wholly complimentary review by Robert Siohan in *Le Monde* (2 November 1963).
34. Olivier Messiaen: 'Absence et présence de Roger Désormière', in Mayer and Souvtchinsky 1966, pp.127–33.
35. Revelation 21:12 and 18–20. See also *Traité*, vii, p.21.
36. Samuel 1994, p.138.
37. Messiaen's diary, 13 July 1963.
38. Preface ('Première Note de l'Auteur') to the score.
39. Preface ('Première Note de l'Auteur') to the score.
40. Samuel 1994, pp.138–9.
41. See fig.58 in the score of *Couleurs*. The literal meaning of *Klangfarbenmelodie* is 'sound-colour-melody'.
42. See figs.27–31 in the score.
43. Revelation 9:1.
44. Preface ('Première Note de l'Auteur') to the score.
45. Samuel 1994, p.139.
46. For example at fig.11, where three chords are labelled successively 'yellow topaz, bright green and crystal'. This passage makes an interesting comparison with similar passages in the *Catalogue d'oiseaux*, such as the 'blue sea (soft, harmonious, contemplative)' in 'Le Merle bleu'.

An establishment figure? 1964–1969

1. Noted in Messiaen's diary.
2. Serge Baudo's 1968 EMI recording, supervised by Messiaen, lasts about 27 minutes. Boulez's 1966 Erato recording, also supervised by the composer, lasts approximately 30 minutes.

3. A similar account appeared in the preface to the published score, issued by Leduc in February 1967.
4. The sketches for *La Transfiguration* discussed here are in MA.
5. The complete surviving correspondence about *La Transfiguration* is published in Simeone 2004a.
6. Though new francs had replaced old francs in 1960, it was still common to quote the old currency – Messiaen himself did so into the 1970s. 2,000,000 old francs converted to 20,000 new francs (100 old francs = 1 new franc). In 1965 there were approximately 12 francs to the pound or 4.5 francs to the US dollar.
7. Iliev was a Bulgarian conductor whose performances of *Turangalîla* in December 1963 had greatly impressed Messiaen.
8. Jameux 1991, pp.138–9.
9. Letter in MA.
10. The programme consisted of Debussy's *La Mer*, the first European performance of Stravinsky's *Requiem Canticles* and Berlioz's *Symphonie fantastique*.
11. Messiaen's formal installation took place a few months later, on 15 May 1968, when he gave a speech on the life and work of the artist Jean Lurçat. On 23 August 1967 the Académie des Beaux-Arts took the decision to reduce the number of places for artists, and Lurçat's place (Fauteuil XIV of Section I) was not filled after his death in 1966. As part of the same reorganization in August 1967, the Académie increased the number of seats for composers, and Messiaen was thus the first occupant of the newly created Fauteuil VII of Section V (Composition musicale). He was succeeded on his death in 1992 by the conductor and composer Marius Constant.
12. Photocopy in MA.
13. There was one connection which was to yield spectacular results. The General Manager of the Hamburg Opera was Rolf Liebermann, a long-time Messiaen admirer. After his move to the Paris Opéra, Liebermann commissioned *Saint François d'Assise*.
14. On 21 October 1971 *Le Figaro* published an article headed 'Conflit entre musicien et librettiste'. This mentioned that Messiaen in an incautious moment had once written to Devillez saying 'your synopsis is perfect. I accept it entirely'. This was the basis of the claim against Messiaen, who was obliged to pay Devillez 20,000 francs as compensation for a share in their 'joint work' despite the fact that there had never been any contract between the two. It was a sorry end to a long-running saga.
15. Rössler 1986, p.132.
16. Roger Nichols, personal communication.
17. This was presumably the film made during the rehearsal on Saturday, 19 June 1965, the eve of the performance. The film was originally broadcast by the ORTF on 11 November 1965. A copy on videotape is preserved in BNF (Tolbiac).
18. The Labèque sisters were born at Hendaye in the Basque country, in 1950 (Katia) and 1952 (Marielle).

Splendours of nature: 1970–1974

1. Note made by Messiaen on Peter Hill's copy of the score.
2. Yvonne Loriod, personal communication.
3. Photocopy in MA.
4. OMR, p.350.
5. Nin-Culmell's association with Messiaen went back to 1936, when he gave the first performance of *Le Tombeau de Paul Dukas*.
6. Yvonne Loriod, personal communication.
7. Gillian Weir, unpublished typescript.
8. Sadly, this campaign ended in failure and the concert hall at the Palais de Chaillot fell into disuse.
9. OMR, p.387.
10. Yvonne Loriod, personal communication.
11. Copy in MA.
12. See pp.75–6 above for the programme notes written for this concert by Messiaen and by Maurice Martenot.

13. Eventually Messiaen was to buy four of these instruments, at 5,000 francs apiece, each equipped with the additional metal loudspeaker.
14. The formal title of the museum is Musée National Message Biblique Marc Chagall.
15. Yvonne Loriod, personal communication.
16. OMR, p.408.
17. The programme, given twice, consisted of *Les Offrandes oubliées*, *Poèmes pour Mi* (with Felicity Palmer), *Réveil des oiseaux* (with Loriod) and *Et exspecto resurrectionem mortuorum*.
18. Preface to the score of *Des Canyons* (Paris: Leduc, 1978), p.16.
19. Preface, p.19.
20. The Paris première of *Des Canyons* was given almost a year later, on 29 October 1975 at the Théâtre de la Ville, by Loriod, Georges Barboteau (horn) and the Ensemble Ars Nova under Marius Constant. The British première was a couple of weeks later on 12 November at the Royal Festival Hall, London, with Loriod, Alan Civil (horn) and the BBC Symphony Orchestra under Pierre Boulez. At the end of the concert, Boulez presented Messiaen with the Gold Medal of the Royal Philharmonic Society.
21. Probably a reference to Daniélou's *La Musique de l'Inde du Nord*, published in 1966.
22. Typescript in MA, dated 3 January 1975.

'Messiaen, faites-moi un opéra': 1975–1978

1. Samuel 1994, p.207.
2. Rolf Liebermann (1910–99) was something of a catch for the Paris Opéra. After working for Swiss and German radio stations, he served as General Manager of the Hamburg State Opera from 1959 to 1973 and developed the company's contemporary repertoire (23 first performances, of which 21 were new commissions). His seven seasons at the Paris Opéra were marked by strong casting and included the world première of Berg's *Lulu* in its complete three-act version in February 1979. Liebermann was also active as a composer of operas, including *Leonore 40/45* (Basel 1952) and *Penelope* (Salzburg 1954). His Concerto for Jazz Band and Symphony Orchestra (Donaueschingen 1954, conducted by Hans Rosbaud) was an early attempt to combine jazz with twelve-tone techniques.
3. Samuel 1994, p.209.
4. *Imitation of Christ*, book 3, chapters 21, 31 and 16.
5. Diary.
6. Yvonne Loriod, personal communication.
7. Samuel 1994, p.228.
8. Samuel 1994, p.229.
9. Samuel 1994, p.229.
10. Letter in MA.
11. Messiaen did not draw on any of these writers for the eventual libretto.
12. Samuel 1994, p.229.
13. Samuel 1994, p.226
14. Samuel 1994, p.237. The chords for the blackcap's song must have been composed later, because in the *cahiers* the notations of the blackcap are all monodic.
15. In this respect Messiaen adheres to the policy already apparent in the outline of the opera sketched in 1971.
16. Olivier Messiaen: 'Saint François d'Assise', essay in the programme book for the first complete performance in Britain (10 December 1988).
17. Samuel 1994, p.214.
18. Samuel 1994, p.218.
19. Marti 1992, p.16.
20. O. Messiaen: 'Saint François d'Assise' (10 December 1988).
21. Samuel 1994, p.216.
22. Samuel 1994, p.230.
23. Samuel 1994, p.230.
24. Brother Ugolino di Monte Santa Maria: *The Fioretti, Part Two: Considerations on the Holy Stigmata – Second Consideration in St Francis of Assisi* , in *Omnibus of Sources* (Chicago, 1973), pp.1443–4.
25. Samuel 1994, p.233.

26. The passage in question, attributed by Messiaen to the *Ode on a Grecian Urn* (Samuel 1994, p.238), is in fact from the opening lines of *Endymion*:

> A thing of beauty is a joy for ever:
> Its loveliness increases; it will never
> Pass into nothingness; but still will keep
> A bower quiet for us, and a sleep
> Full of sweet dreams, and health, and quiet breathing.

27. Samuel 1994, p.216.
28. Letter in MA.
29. Samuel 1994, p.216.
30. Information supplied by George Benjamin, who at the time was a student in Messiaen's class at the Conservatoire.
31. According to Loriod, it was Rostropovich's custom to send Messiaen a bouquet of roses whenever he performed one of his works.
32. Letter in MA.
33. *Le Figaro*, 24 December 1978.
34. Boulez 1986, pp.418–20.

'Brother Messiaen at the Opéra': 1979–1983

The chapter title is taken from the headline of a review in *Les Échos*, 2 December 1983.
1. Samuel 1994, p.227.
2. Samuel 1994, p.218. This is one of three types of music that are used to characterize Elias, all prefigured in the orchestral introduction to Scene 4. The other two are glissandi for strings and trombones, and the music of the notou, described by Messiaen as 'a gloomy sounding pigeon from New Caledonia' (Samuel, p.218).
3. Stage direction.
4. Samuel 1994, p.230.
5. Direction in the full score.
6. Samuel 1994, p.232.
7. Samuel 1994, p.234.
8. See figs.23, 27 and 31.
9. See figs.38–40.
10. Fig.127.
11. Samuel 1994, p.247.
12. Samuel 1994, p.232.
13. Samuel 1994, p.219.
14. Marti 1992, p.11.
15. Alex Ross, personal communication.
16. Alex Ross, personal communication.
17. Alex Ross, personal communication.
18. Letter from Dr Bernachon to Loriod, 20 April 1984, in MA.
19. *Le Quotidien de Paris*, 20 November 1983.
20. Samuel 1994, pp.248–9.

Inspiration regained: 1984–1987

1. See also Marti 1992, p.17: 'I thought I'd said everything, that I'd now stop composing'.
2. Originally a Greek and Latin metrical foot consisting of short–long–long syllables.
3. Marti 1992, p.17.
4. 'And she spake out with a loud voice [. . .] And whence is this to me, that the mother of my Lord should come to me? For, lo, as soon as the voice of thy salutation sounded in mine ears, the babe leaped in my womb for joy.' Luke 1:42–4.
5. The full details of the scoring for *Le Vitrail de l'Assomption* were: 3 pianos, 3 singers (soprano, contralto and tenor); piccolo, 2 flutes, alto flute, oboe, cor anglais, piccolo clarinet, 2 clarinets, bass clarinet, bassoon, contrabassoon; trumpet, 2 horns, trombone, tuba; xylorimba, bells, glockenspiel (with sticks), crotales, wood block, 6 temple blocks, 3 gongs, 2 tam tams.
6. Hill 1995, p.301.
7. Letter in MA.

8. Hill 1995, p.380.
9. Dupin (d.1994) had supervised the making of the Geophone and Luminophone for Messiaen. Dupin's *Lexique de la percussion* was published in 1971 and Messiaen consulted it frequently when composing.
10. Letter in MA.

Illuminations of the Beyond: 1988–1992

1. See Hill 1995, p.278.
2. Marti 1992, p.18.
3. Letter in MA.
4. The *cahier* shows that Messiaen had a provisional title for the movement to feature the lyrebird's song – 'L'Apparition de la Cité céleste', later changed to 'L'Oiseau-lyre et la Ville-fiancée'.
5. Programme note by Yvonne Loriod-Messiaen for the first performance, translated by Gerald Levinson.
6. The designer was Mark Wheeler.
7. Letter in MA.
8. See Hill 1995, pp. 273–82.
9. Marti 1992, pp.17–18.
10. This must refer to photocopies of Loriod's handwritten vocal scores.
11. Marti 1992, p.18.

Bibliography

1. Primary Sources

i. Messiaen Archives, Paris [MA]
The archives of Olivier Messiaen and Yvonne Loriod-Messiaen have been our principal source.
  They comprise an unparalleled collection of documents including:

Messiaen's diaries from 1939 until his death in 1992
Autograph sketches and drafts of some works
Photocopies of autograph mss
Letters to the composer (sometimes with copies of his replies)
Articles by Messiaen (mss and typescripts)
Speeches and scripts by Messiaen (mss and typescripts)
Commentaries by Messiaen on his works (mss and typescripts)
Informal working notes, records of meetings and telephone conversations, and other ms documents
Books and articles about Messiaen
Concert programmes
Various other documents including posters, Conservatoire certificates and miscellaneous papers
Photographs

In addition to these sources, Yvonne Loriod-Messiaen also provided us with typed transcriptions
  of passages from Messiaen's diaries, to which she has added her own annotations: 'Olivier Messiaen: Relevé des concerts, des classes et des èvènements de la vie d'Olivier Messiaen notées au
  jour le jour sur ses agendas depuis 1939' [OMR]

ii. Bibliothèque Nationale de France, Département de la Musique [BNF Musique]:
Cahiers de notation des chants d'oiseaux
Letters from Messiaen to Claude Arrieu
Letters from Messiaen to Nadia Boulanger
Letters from Messiaen to André Cœuroy
Letters from Messiaen to Denise Tual and others about the Concerts de la Pléiade

iii. Other collections
The Pierpont Morgan Library, New York City
Felix Aprahamian, London
Thierry Bodin, Paris
Marie-Louise Jaquet-Langlais, Paris
O.W. Neighbour, London
Roger Nichols, Kington, Herefordshire, UK
The collections of the authors
Other private collections

2. Books and Articles

I. By Olivier Messiaen (arranged in chronological order)

'L'Ascension' [unsigned article], *Le Monde musical*, 28 Feb 1935, pp.48–9

'L'Émotion, la sincerité de l'œuvre musicale [. . .]', privately printed, Paris, 1936 or earlier [a small slip of paper, printed on one side only, distributed by Messiaen at performances of *La Nativité du Seigneur* and other works]

'La Nativité du Seigneur', *Tablettes de la Schola Cantorum*, Jan–Feb 1936, 2pp., unpaginated

'La Nativité du Seigneur', *Le Monde musical*, 30 April 1936, pp.123–4 [ends with an enthusiastic review of an organ recital by Guy Lambert]

'Ariane et Barbe-bleue de Paul Dukas', *La Revue musicale*, no.166, May–June 1936, pp.79–86

'Musique religieuse', *La Page musicale*, 19 Feb 1937, p.1

'Derrière ou devant la porte?. . . (Lettre ouverte à M. Eugène Berteaux)', *La Page musicale*, 26 Feb 1937, p.1

'L'Orgue', *Le Monde musical*, 31 March 1938 [review of *Sept Chorals-Poèmes pour les Sept Paroles du Christ en croix* by Charles Tournemire, the *Premier Livre d'orgue* by Georges Migot, and *Ave Maria, Ave Maris stella* by Jean Langlais]; repr. in Tournemire 1989 (see section II below), p.86

'Le Premier Livre d'orgue de Georges Migot', *La Revue musicale*, March 1938, p.228

'Un Spectacle Darius Milhaud', *Syrinx* [Brussels], March 1938, pp.25–6 [review of *Esther de Carpentras*]

'L'Orgue mystique de Tournemire', *Syrinx*, May 1938; repr. in CD notes for Accord 205342 and Accord 206002.

'Contre la paresse', *La Page musicale*, 17 March 1939, p.1

'Autour d'une parution', *Le Monde musical*, 30 April 1939, p.126

'Autour d'une œuvre d'orgue', *L'Art sacré*, April 1939, p.123

'Le Rythme chez Igor Stravinsky', *La Revue musicale*, no.191, June 1939, pp.91–2

'De la musique sacrée', *Carrefour*, vol.1, no.4, June–July 1939, p.75

Contribution by Messiaen to: M.F.J. [Miramon Fitz-James]: 'Les Amis de l'Orgue et la guerre', *L'Orgue*, nos.40–1, Dec 1939–March 1940, pp.30–8 [contains reports from various organists serving in the French armed forces, all identified by their initials; the first, on p.31, is from 'soldat pionnier d'infanterie O.M.']

'Quatuor pour la fin du Temps', *Lumignon: Bi-mensuelle du Stalag VIIIA*, no.1, 1 April 1941, pp.3–4

'Technique de mon langage musical', *Musique et radio*, vol.33, no.386, Nov 1942, pp.253–4

'Sur mon traité de composition', *Comœdia*, 5 Dec 1942, pp.1 and 4

Technique de mon langage musical (2 vols, Paris: Alphonse Leduc, 1944; new edn in one vol., Paris: Leduc, 2001)

'Querelle de la musique et de l'amour', *Volontés*, 16 May 1945, p.1

'Béla Bartók' [obituary], *Images musicales*, 19 Oct 1945, p.[4]

'Le 2ᵉ Concerto de Béla Bartók', *Lumières de la ville*, 18 Dec 1945, p.25

'L'Inspiration musicale', *Opéra*, 19 Dec 1945, p.10

'Réponses à une enquête', *Contrepoints*, no.3, March–April 1946, pp.73–5

'Concert Line Zilgien (Concert de La Revue musicale)', *La Revue musicale*, no.201, Sept 1946, p.267

'Introduction au *Mana* d'André Jolivet', in André Jolivet: *Mana* (Paris: Éditions Costallat/Lucien de Lacour, 1946); printed in Fr. and Eng., trans. Pierre Messiaen and Rollo Myers

'Maurice Emmanuel: Ses Trente Chansons bourguignonnes', *La Revue musicale*, no.206, 1947, pp.107–8

'Notes de travail pour l'accompagnement musicale de *Matins du monde* à l'église de la Trinité', in R. Michael: *Matins du monde* (Paris: Bordas, 1950), pp.109–12

'Orgue', *La Trinité* [parish newspaper], May 1951, p.3 [Messiaen's introduction to the *Messe de la Pentecôte* for parishioners]

'Hommage à un Maître disparu: Jean de Gibon', *Écho du Pays de Redon*, 26 Jan 1952

Preface to Marguerite Béclard d'Harcourt and Raoul d'Harcourt, eds.: *Chansons folkloriques françaises au Canada: Leur langue musicale* (Québec: Presses Universitaires Laval, 1956)

Conférence de Bruxelles, prononcée à l'Exposition Internationale de Bruxelles en 1958 (Paris: Alphonse Leduc, 1960); in Fr., Ger. and Eng.; first pubd in Ger. as 'Musikalisches Glaubensbekenntnis', *Melos*, Dec 1958, pp.381–5

'Isaac Albéniz *Iberia*', disc notes [c.1958] for Véga C30A127 and C30A128

'La Nature, les chants d'oiseaux', *Guide du concert*, no.229, 3 April 1959, pp.1093–4

Preface to 'Experiences musicales: Musiques concrète, électronique, exotique', *La Revue musicale*, no.244, 1959, pp.5–6

[Hommage à Roger Désormière], *Les Lettres françaises*, no.1001, 8 Oct–6 Nov 1963, p.11

Situation artistique et sociale du musicien en 1964 (Institut de France, Académie des Beaux-Arts, Communications 20 mai–25 novembre 1964) (Paris: A. and J. Picard, 1964)

Disc notes [c.1964] for Jacques Charpentier: *Études karnatiques* (extraits), Club National du Disque CND 58

'Matière-lumière, espace-temps, son-couleur. . .', *Preuves*, no.179, Jan 1966, pp.39–41

'Absence et présence de Roger Désormière', in Mayer and Souvtchinsky 1966 (see section II below)

'Hommage d'Olivier Messiaen aux artistes de l'orchestre', *L'Artiste musicien de Paris*, 64ᵉ année, nouvelle série, no.14, 1966, pp.15–17

Notice sur la vie et des travaux de Jean Lurçat [. . .] lue à la séance de mercredi 15 mai 1968 (Paris: Institut de France, 1968)

Hommage à Suzanne Balguerie (n.p., Imprimerie d'Allier, ?1968) [incl. reminiscence by Messiaen on p.6]

'Olivier Messiaen', in *Dictionnaire de la musique*, ii. *Les Hommes et leurs œuvres*, ed. Marc Honegger (Paris: Bordas, 1970), pp.819–20

Preface to Albert Roustit: *La Prophétie musicale dans l'histoire de l'humanité* (Roanne: Horvath, 1970)

Preface to Françoise Gervais: 'Étude comparée des langages harmoniques de Fauré et de Debussy' *La Revue musicale*, no.272, 1971, pp.7–8

Discours pour la réception de M. Marc Saltet: élu membre de la section d'architecture en remplacement de M. Charles Lemaresquier [. . .] 23 mai 1973 (Paris: Institut de France, 1973)

Discours de M. Olivier Messiaen, Président, Institut de France, Académie des Beaux-Arts, séance publique annuelle du 14 novembre 1973 (Paris: Institut de France, 1973)

'Des paroles d'esprit: Entretien avec Olivier Messiaen', in *Charles de Gaulle*, ed. Michel Cazenave and Olivier Germain Thomas (Cahiers de L'Herne, no.21; Paris: L'Herne, 1973), pp.44–6

Preface to Marcel Dupré: *Recollections* (Melville, NY: Belwin-Mills, 1975) [written specially for the Eng. edn]

Preface to Jean-Michel Bardez: *Pulsations: Rythmes à frapper* (Paris: Rideau Rouge, 1976)

Conférence de Notre-Dame prononcée à Notre-Dame de Paris le 4 décembre 1977 (Paris: Alphonse Leduc, 1978)

Arts–Sciences alliages: Iannis Xenakis, Olivier Messiaen, Michel Ragon, Olivier Revault d'Allonnes, Michel Serres, Bernard Teyssèdre (Paris: Casterman, 1979)

Les Grandes Orgues de l'église de la Sainte-Trinité à Paris (Paris: [Église de la Sainte-Trinité], Oct 1980)

Preface to Pierre-Yves Artaud and Gérard Geay: *Flûtes au présent: Traité des techniques contemporaines sur les flûtes traversières, à l'usage des compositeurs et des flûtistes* (Paris: Jobert, 1980)

'Évocation de Cécile Sauvage', *Annales de Haute-Provence*, vol.50, no.291, 1ᵉʳ semestre 1981, pp.114–18

Secours pour la remise de la Croix de Commandeur de l'Ordre National du Mérite à Gaston Litaize, unpublished typescript, dated 23 Nov 1981, 4ff., in MA

Preface to Maurice Emmanuel: *L'Histoire de la langue musicale* (Malakoff: Laurens, 1981)

Preface to Francine Guiberteau: *Dichrostachys: Pièces pour orgue* (Paris: Combre, 1983)

Preface to Jean-Paul Holstein, Pierre-Yves Level and Alain Louvier: *Musique à chanter pour les classes de formation musicale* (9 vols, Paris: Alphonse Leduc, 1983–6) [Messiaen's preface is printed in each vol.]

Discours pour la cérémonie du 20 janvier 1984 à Grenoble, unpublished typescript, 3ff., in MA

Discours prononcés dans la séance publique tenue par l'Académie des Beaux-Arts présidée par M. Albert Decaris, Président de l'Académie, le mercredi 2 mai 1984 pour la réception de M. Iannis Xenakis (Paris: Académie des Beaux-Arts, 1984), pp.9–11; repr. in Mâche 2001 pp.83–6

Preface to Anne Le Forestier: *Olivier Messiaen: L'Ascension* (Cahiers d'analyse et de formation musicale, vol.1; Paris: Alphonse Leduc, 1984), p.i

'Réponse de Monsieur Olivier Messiaen' (see section II below [Académie de Vaucluse 1984])

Disc notes [c.1984] for Alain Weber: *D'Après Wols*; Alain Louvier: *Houles*; Didier Denis: *Cinq fois je t'aime*, Inédits ORTF 995040 [in Fr. and Eng.]

'L'Intuition du premier jour', *Éclats, Boulez* (Éditions du Centre Pompidou, Paris, 1986), pp.6–7

'Obstacles', in *20ᵉ siècle: Images de la musique française* ed. Jean-Pierre Derrien (Paris: SACEM et Papiers, 1986), pp.168–72

Preface to Denis Joly: *Variations pour piano (ut dièse mineur); Deux mélodies* (Saint-Étienne: Académie Musicologique du Forez, 1987)

Preface to Jeanne Loriod: *Technique de l'onde électronique, type Martenot. Volume I: Le Clavier* (Paris, Alphonse Leduc, 1987), pp.ii–iii; in Fr. and Eng. [preface dated 'Mai 1982']

Preface to Cécile Sauvage: *L'Âme en bourgeon* (Paris: Séguier Archimbaud, 1987), pp.7–15

Les 22 Concertos pour piano de Mozart (Paris: Séguier-Archimbaud-Birr, 1987)

['Le Basson français'], untitled typescript, March 1988, 1f., in MA

Conférence de Kyoto [12 Nov 1985] (Paris: Alphonse Leduc, 1988); in Fr. and Japanese (trans. N. Tamamura)

Preface to 'L'Itinéraire', *La Revue musicale*, nos.421–4 [quadruple issue], 1991, p.[7] [preface dated '1974']

Traité de rythme, de couleur et d'ornithologie (7 vols, Paris: Alphonse Leduc, 1994–2002)

'Jean Langlais: Messe solennelle (analyse par Olivier Messiaen)', undated ms, facs. in Jaquet-Langlais 1995, p.163

II. By other authors

[Académie de Vaucluse:] 'Remise du Grand Prix de l'Académie: Allocution de Monsieur le chanoine [Georges] Durand [. . .] Réponse de Monsieur Olivier Messiaen [. . .] Allocution de Monsieur Jean Keller', *Mémoires de l'Académie de Vaucluse*, septième série, tome v, 1984, pp.50–68

Annuaire des artistes et de l'enseignement dramatique et musical 1923 (32ᵉ année) (Paris: Office Général de la Musique, 1923)

Pascal Arnault (with Nicolas Darbon): *Messiaen: Les Sons impalpables du rêve* (Paris: Millénaire III, 1997)

L'Artiste Musicien de Paris, 64ᵉ année, nouvelle série, no.14, 1966 [Messiaen issue: 'L'Hommage à Olivier Messiaen de Arthur Haneuse, André Boucourechliev, Pierre Boulez ('Rétrospective'), Martine Cadieu, Claude Samuel; Hommage d'Olivier Messiaen aux artistes de l'orchestre', pp.1–17]

Guy Bernard[-Delapierre]: 'Souvenirs sur Olivier Messiaen', *Formes et couleurs* [Lausanne], nos.3–4, 1945, unpaginated, [10]pp., incl. facs. of *Vingt Regards* and *Visions de l'Amen*

Jean Boivin: *La Classe de Messiaen* (Paris: Christian Bourgois, 1995)

Lilise Boswell-Kurc: *Olivier Messiaen's Religious War-Time Works and their Controversial Reception in France (1941–1946)* (Diss., New York University, 2001)

Pierre Boulez: 'Olivier Messiaen: An Essay [. . .] written expressly for this program', programme book for the Cleveland Orchestra's *An Informal Evening with Pierre Boulez*, Severance Hall, Cleveland, 5 Dec 1970, unpaginated

—: *Orientations*, trans. Martin Cooper (London: Faber, 1986), esp. pp.404–20

Jean Jacques Brothier: *La 'Jeune France': Yves Baudrier, André Jolivet, Daniel-Lesur, Olivier Messiaen* ([Paris:] Les Amis de la Jeune France, [1954])

José Bruyr: 'Olivier Messiaen', *L'Écran des musiciens, seconde série* (Paris: José Corti, 1933), pp.124–31

Sidney Buckland, ed. and trans.: *Francis Poulenc 'Echo and Source': Selected Correspondence, 1915–1963* (London, 1991)

Véronique Chabrol: 'L'Ambition de "Jeune France"', in *La Vie culturelle sous Vichy*, ed. Jean-Pierre Rioux (Brussels, 1990), pp.161–78

Myriam Chimènes: 'Geneviève Sienkiewicz et Francis Poulenc: Correspondance inédite', in Josiane Mas, ed.: *Centenaire Georges Auric–Francis Poulenc* (Montpellier: Centre d'étude du XXᵉ siècle, Université Paul-Valéry, 2001), pp.239–85

—: *Mécènes et musiciens: Du salon au concert à Paris sous la IIIᵉ République* (Paris: Fayard, 2004)

—, ed.: *Francis Poulenc: Correspondance, 1919–1963* (Paris: Fayard, 1994)

—, ed.: *La Vie musicale sous Vichy* (Brussels: Éditions Complexe, 2001)

— and Catherine Massip, eds.: *Portrait(s) de Darius Milhaud* (Paris: Bibliothèque Nationale de France, 1998), esp. p.18: D. Milhaud: 'Je sens terriblement le poids de mes quarante-cinq ans. . .'

Henri Colpi: *Défense et illustration de la musique dans le film* (Lyon: Société d'édition de recherches et de documentation cinématographiques, 1963), esp. pp.303–4, 363 and 382–3

Conservatoire national de musique et de déclamation année 1929–1930: Distribution des prix pour le cours d'études de l'année 1929–1930 (Paris: Imprimerie Nationale, 1930)

Maurice Croizard: 'Paris siffle et applaudit le même soir Olivier Messiaen', *Paris-Match*, no.674, 10 March 1962, pp.62–71 [incl. 8pp. colour photos by Izis]

Audrey Ekdahl Davidson: *Olivier Messiaen and the Tristan Myth* (Westport, CT: Greenwood, 2001)

Christopher Dingle: 'Charm and Simplicity: Messiaen's Final Works', *Tempo*, no.192, April 1995, pp.2–7

René Dumesnil: *La Musique en France entre les deux guerres 1919–1939* (Geneva: Milieu du Monde, 1946)

[Durand et Cie:] *Centenaire des Éditions Durand & Cie: 1869–1969* (Paris: Durand, 1969)

Georges Durand: see [Académie de Vaucluse]

Herbert Eimert: 'Olivier Messiaen: Mystiker und Musiker', *105. Niederrheinisches Musikfest in Wuppertal: Jahrbuch 1950* (Wuppertal: J.H. Born, 1950), pp.53–8

Joël-Marie Fauquet: 'Correspondance inédite: Lettres d'Olivier Messiaen à Charles Tournemire', in Tournemire 1989

François Florand, O.P., ed.: 'Problèmes de la musique sacrée', *Cahiers de l'Art sacré*, no.6, 1946, esp. pp.37–42: 'Chronique parlée' [Roland-Manuel, Daniel-Lesur, Yves Baudrier and Florand, incl. discussion of Messiaen]; and pp.43–5: Florand: 'Les *Trois petites Liturgies* d'Olivier Messiaen'

Robin Freeman: 'Courtesy towards the Things of Nature: Interpretations of Messiaen's *Catalogue d'oiseaux*', *Tempo*, no.192, April 1995, pp.9–14

Charles de Gaulle: *Discours et messages: 1. Pendant la guerre, juin 1940–janvier 1946* (Paris: Plon, 1970), pp.439–40

Bernard Gavoty: *Chroniques de Clarendon: Au bonheur des soirs (1945–1981)*, ed. Jacques Longchampt (Paris: Albatros, 1990)

Ernest de Gengenbach: 'Messiaen ou le surréel en musique', *Revue musicale de France*, 15 April 1946, pp.1–3 and 18

Alexander Goehr: 'The Messiaen Class', *Finding the Key: Selected Writings*, ed. Derek Puffett (London: Faber, 1998), pp.42–57

Antoine Goléa: 'Les Festivals de musique en 1950', *Almanach de la musique 1951* (Paris: Éditions de Flore, Gazette des Lettres, 1950), pp.57–65, esp. p.62

—: *Esthéthique de la musique contemporaine* (Paris: Presses Universitaires de France, 1954)

—: *Rencontres avec Pierre Boulez* (Paris: René Julliard, 1958)

—: *Rencontres avec Olivier Messiaen* (Paris: René Julliard, 1960)

—: *Vingt ans de musique contemporaine I: De Messiaen à Boulez* (Paris: Seghers, 1962)

Paul Griffiths: *Olivier Messiaen and the Music of Time* (London: Faber, 1985)

Jean Guéhenno: *Journal des années noires (1940–1944)* (Paris: Gallimard, 1968 edn)

Nicolas Guillot, ed.: *Roger Désormière, 1898–1963: Actes du colloque, Vichy, septembre 1998* (Paris: Comité pour la célébration du centenaire de la naissance de Roger Désormière; Musée de la Résistance Nationale, 1999)

Harry Halbreich: *Olivier Messiaen* (Paris: Fayard, 1980)

Peter Hill: 'For The Birds', *Musical Times*, Sept 1994, pp.552–5

—, ed.: *The Messiaen Companion* (London: Faber, 1995)

André Hodeir: *La Musique depuis Debussy* (Paris: Presses Universitaires de France, 1961), esp. pp.81–103: 'Olivier Messiaen'

Arthur Honegger: *Incantation aux fossiles* (Lausanne: Éditions d'Ouchy, 1948), esp. pp.95–100: 'Olivier Messiaen'

—: *Je suis compositeur* (Paris: Conquistador, 1951)

Interlude: The Story of British Prisoners of War in Stammlager VIIIA at Görlitz in Lower Silesia, Germany (London: printed by Partridge and Cooper, c.1945)

Julian Jackson: *France: The Dark Years, 1940–1944* (Oxford: Oxford University Press, 2000)

Dominique Jameux: *Pierre Boulez*, trans. Susan Bradshaw (London: Faber, 1991)

Marie-Louise Jaquet-Langlais: *Ombre et lumière: Jean Langlais, 1907–1991* (Paris: Combre, 1995)

Jean-Noël Jeanneney: *L'Écho du siècle: Dictionnaire historique de la radio et de la télévision en France* (Paris: Hachette, rev. edn 2001)

Robert Sherlaw Johnson: *Messiaen* (London: J.M. Dent, rev. edn 1989)

André Jolivet: Catalogue des œuvres (Paris: Gérard Billaudot, 1993)

Hilda Jolivet: *Avec André Jolivet* (Paris: Flammarion, 1978)

Alain Lacombe and Francis Porcile: *Les Musiques du cinéma français* (Paris: Bordas, 1995)

Hannelore Lauerwald: *In fremdem Land. Kriegsgefangene in Deutschland am Beispiel des Stalag VIII A Görlitz* (Görlitz: Viadukt 1997)

—: 'Er musizierte mit Olivier Messiaen als Kriegsgefangener', *Das Orchester*, Jan 1999, pp.21–3

Guy de Lioncourt: *Un témoignage sur la musique et la vie au XXme siècle* (Paris: L'Arche de Noé, 1956)

Jacques Longchampt: *Le Bon Plaisir: Journal de musique contemporaine* (Paris: Plume, 1994), esp. pp.32–49: 'Olivier Messiaen' [reviews from *Le Monde*]

Yvonne and Jeanne Loriod: ['Témoignage'], *Les Cahiers Boëlmann–Gigout*, nos.4–5, 1999–2000, pp.102–4

Armand Machabey: 'Olivier Messiaen', *Portrait de trente musiciens français* (Paris: Richard Masse, 1949), pp.127–30; rev. version of article in *L'information musicale*, 22 May 1942

François-Bernard Mâche, ed.: *Portrait(s) de Iannis Xenakis* (Paris: Bibliothèque Nationale de France, 2001), esp. pp.83–6

Béatrice Marchal-Vincent: *L'Œuvre poétique de Cécile Sauvage (1883–1927)* (Diss., University of Paris 4, 1995)

Pierrette Mari: *Olivier Messiaen* (Paris: Seghers, 1965)

Jean-Christophe Marti: 'Entretien avec Olivier Messiaen', *Saint François d'Assise: Libretto, Analyse, Kommentare, Dokumentation* (Salzburger Festspiele, 1992), pp.8–18; repr. in disc notes for Deutsche Grammophon 445 176–2

Brigitte Massin: *Olivier Messiaen: Une poétique du merveilleux* (Aix-en-Provence: Alinéa, 1989)

—: *Les Joachim: Une famille des musiciens* (Paris: Fayard, 1999)

Catherine Massip, ed.: *Portrait(s) d'Olivier Messiaen* (Paris: Bibliothèque Nationale de France, 1996)

Denise Mayer and Pierre Souvtchinsky, eds.: *Roger Désormière et son temps: Textes en hommage* (Monaco: Éditions du Rocher, 1966)

Pierre Messiaen: *Images* (Paris: Desclée de Brouwer, 1944)

Klaus Metzger and Rainer Riehn, eds.: *Musik-Konzepte 28: Olivier Messiaen* (Munich: Edition Text + Kritik, 1982)

Darius Milhaud: *My Happy Life*, trans. Donald Evans, George Hall and Christopher Palmer (London: Marion Boyars, 1995)

Roger Nichols: *Messiaen* (London: Oxford University Press, 1975)

—: 'Boulez on Messiaen: Pierre Boulez in Conversation with Roger Nichols', *Organists' Review*, August 1986, pp.167–70

—: *The Harlequin Years: Music in Paris, 1917–1929* (London: Thames and Hudson, 2002)

[Opéra:] 'Olivier Messiaen: *Saint François d'Assise* au Palais Garnier', *Opéra de Paris*, 1 Nov 1983, pp.2–17 [special number of the Paris Opéra's house magazine, incl. tributes to Messiaen and a long interview]

Ian Ousby: *Occupation: The Ordeal of France, 1940–1944* (London: Pimlico, 1999)

Bénédicte Paulaux-Simonnet: *Paul Dukas ou le musicien-sorcier* (Geneva: Éditions Papillon, 2001)

Alain Périer: *Messiaen* (Paris: Seuil, 1979)

Roland Petit: *J'ai dansé sur les flots* (Paris: Bernard Grasset, 1993)

Anthony Pople: *Messiaen: 'Quatuor pour la fin du Temps'* (Cambridge: Cambridge University Press, 1998)

François Porcile: *La Belle Époque de la musique française: Le temps de Maurice Ravel (1871–1940)* (Paris: Fayard, 1999)

—: *Conflits de la musique française (1940–1965)* (Paris: Fayard, 2001)

Maurice Poté: 'Couples de musiciens, couples de génies', *Couple et couples* (Cahiers de l'Académie de Bretagne, vol.15; Nantes, 1978), pp.92–5

Francis Poulenc: *Entretiens avec Claude Rostand* (Paris: René Julliard, 1954)

Michèle Reverdy: *L'Œuvre pour piano d'Olivier Messiaen* (Paris: Leduc, 1978)

—: *L'Œuvre pour orchestre d'Olivier Messiaen* (Paris: Leduc, 1988)

Rebecca Rischin: *For the End of Time: The Story of the Messiaen Quartet* (Ithaca, NY: Cornell University Press, 2003)

Martial Robert: *Pierre Schaeffer: Des 'Transmissions' à 'Orphée'. Communication et musique en France entre 1936 et 1986* (Paris: L'Harmattan, 1999), esp. pp.41–75

David Robertson, ed.: *Musique et cinéma muet*, Les Dossiers du Musée d'Orsay, no.56 (Paris, 1995)

Almut Rössler: *Contributions to the Spiritual World of Olivier Messiaen with Original Texts by the Composer* (Duisburg: Gilles und Francke Verlag, 1986)

Claude Rostand: *La Musique française contemporaine* (Paris: Presses Universitaires de France, 1952), esp. pp.52–72: 'Le Groupe de La Jeune France'; Eng. edn as *French Music Today* (New York: Merlin Press, 1955), pp.33–80: 'La Jeune France ("Young France")'

—: *Olivier Messiaen* (Paris: Ventadour, 1957)

Jean Roy: *Présences contemporaines: Musique française* (Paris, Nouvelles Éditions Debresse, 1962), esp. pp.361–84: 'Olivier Messiaen'

François Sabatier: 'Bérenger de Miramon Fitz-James et Olivier Messiaen', *L'Orgue*, no.224, 1992, pp.5–11

Saint François d'Assise: Messiaen, L'avant-scène opéra: Opéra d'aujourdhui, no.4 (1992)

Claude Samuel: *Entretiens avec Olivier Messiaen* (Paris: Pierre Belfond, 1967); Eng. edn as *Conversations with Olivier Messiaen*, trans. Felix Aprahamian (London: Stainer and Bell, 1976)

—: *Olivier Messiaen: Musique et couleur. Nouveaux entretiens avec Claude Samuel* (Paris: Pierre Belfond, 1986); Eng. edn as *Music and Color: Conversations with Claude Samuel*, trans. E. Thomas Glasow (Portland, OR: Amadeus, 1994)

—: *Permanences d'Olivier Messiaen: Dialogues et commentaires* (Arles: Actes Sud, 1999)

—: *Olivier Messiaen (1908–1992): Les couleurs du temps. Trente ans d'entretiens avec Claude Samuel* (Paris: Radio France, 2000)

Cécile Sauvage: *Tandis que la terre tourne* (Paris: Mercure de France, 1910 [*L'Âme en bourgeon* is printed on pp.115–79]; repr. Paris: Librairie Séguier, 1991)

—: *Le Vallon: Poèmes* (Paris: Mercure de France, 1913)

—: *Œuvres*, preface by Jean Tenant (Paris: Mercure de France, 1929)

—: *L'Âme en bourgeon*, preface by Olivier Messiaen (Paris: Libraire Séguier Archaimbaud, 1987)

—: *L'Œuvre poétique*: see Marchal-Vincent 1995

—: *Œuvres complètes*, introduction by Claude-Jean Launay (Paris: La Table Ronde, 2002) [despite the title, this edn does not print Sauvage's complete works]

Thomas Daniel Schlee and Dietrich Kämpfer: *Olivier Messiaen: La Cité céleste – Das himmlische Jerusalem. Über Leben und Werk des französischen Komponisten* (Cologne: Wienand Verlag, 1998)

Klaus Schweitzer: *Olivier Messiaen: Turangalîla-Symphonie* (Munich: Wilhelm Fink Verlag, 1982)

Nigel Simeone [1998a]: *Olivier Messiaen: A Bibliographical Catalogue* (Tutzing: Hans Schneider, 1998)

— [1998b]: *Bien Cher Félix: Letters from Olivier Messiaen and Yvonne Loriod to Felix Aprahamian* (Cambridge: Mirage Press, 1998)

— [2000a]: 'Messiaen and the Concerts de la Pléiade: "a kind of clandestine resistance against the Occupation" ' *Music & Letters*, vol.81, no.4, Nov 2000, pp.551–84

— [2000b]: 'Offrandes oubliées: Messiaen in the 1930s', *Musical Times*, winter 2000, pp.33–41 [incl. letters from Messiaen to Claude Arrieu]

— [2001a]: 'Offrandes oubliées 2: Messiaen, Boulanger and José Bruyr', *Musical Times*, spring 2001, pp.17–22 [incl. letters from Messiaen to Nadia Boulanger]

— [2001b]: 'Music Publishing in Paris under the German Occupation', *Brio*, vol.38, no.1, spring/summer 2001, pp.2–17

— [2002a]: 'The Science of Enchantment: Music at the 1937 Paris Exposition', *Musical Times*, spring 2002, pp.9–17

— [2002b]: 'Group Identities: La Spirale and La Jeune France', *Musical Times*, autumn 2002, pp.10–36

— [2002c]: '*Vingt Regards sur l'Enfant-Jésus*', booklet notes for Steven Osborne recording on Hyperion CDA67351–2 (2002), pp.3–15

— [2002d]: 'An Exotic Tristan in Boston: The First Performance of Messiaen's *Turangalîla-Symphonie*', in *King Arthur in Music*, ed. Richard Barber (Woodbridge: D.S. Brewer, 2002), pp.105–25

— [2004a]: 'Towards 'un succès absolument formidable': The Birth of Messiaen's *La Transfiguration*', *Musical Times*, summer 2004, pp. 5–24

— [2004b]: '"Chez Messiaen tout est prière": Messiaen's Appointment at the Trinité', *Musical Times*, winter 2004, pp. 36–53

Marcelle Soulage: 'Une œuvre d'Olivier Messiaen: L'Ascension', *Les Amis de St François, Revue trimestrielle de doctrine, de littérature et d'art*, nouvelle série, vol.4, no.4, Oct–Dec 1963, pp.154–7

Charles Tournemire (1870–1939) (L'Orgue: Cahiers et mémoires, no.41; Paris: Association des Amis de l'orgue, 1989)

[Trinité:] *Olivier Messiaen, homme de foi: Regard sur son œuvre d'orgue* (Paris: Trinité Média Communication, 1995)

Robert Wangermée, ed.: *Paul Collaer: Correspondance avec des amis musiciens* (Liège: Mardaga, 1996)

Virginie Zinke-Bianchini: *Olivier Messiaen: Compositeur de musique et rythmicien. Notice biographique, catalogue détaillé des œuvres éditées* (Paris: L'Emancipatrice, 1949)

III. Selected newspaper reviews of Messiaen's works, shorter articles and interviews (arranged in chronological order)

Jacques Janin: 'Les Grands Concerts', *Ami du peuple du soir*, 4 March 1930 [review of the *Préludes*]

Joseph Baruzi: 'Société Nationale de Musique (1er mars)', *Le Ménestrel*, 7 March 1930, pp.110–11 [review of the *Préludes*]

Suzanne Demarquez: 'Société Nationale, 1er mars', *Le Courrier musical*, 15 March 1930, p.194 [review of the *Préludes*]

Georges Dandelot: [review of the *Préludes*], *Le Monde musical*, 31 March 1930

Gustave Samazeuilh: 'Le Concours de Rome 1930: Ce qu'il pourrait être – ce qu'il est', *Le Courrier musical*, 15 July–1 Aug 1930, pp.475–7

J.V.: 'Un lauréat du Conservatoire', probably from *République de l'Isère*, undated cutting, ? summer 1930 [report of Messiaen's success at the Conservatoire, with a *premier prix* for organ and another for composition]

[Unsigned:] 'L'Édition musicale', *Les Tablettes de la Schola Cantorum*, Nov 1930, p.8 [review of the pubd scores of *Trois Mélodies*, *Préludes* and *Diptyque*]

Marcel Belviannes: 'Société Nationale de Musique (14 février)', *Le Ménestrel*, 20 Feb 1931, p.84 [review of *Trois Mélodies*]

Paul Le Flem: 'Six premières auditions [. . .] *Offrandes oubliées* de Messiaen', *Comœdia*, 23 Feb 1931

Florent Schmitt: [review of *Les Offrandes oubliées*], *Le Temps*, 24 Feb 1931

Joseph Baruzi: 'Concerts Straram (19 février)', *Le Ménestrel*, 27 Feb 1931, p.95 [review of *Les Offrandes oubliées*]

André George: [review of *Les Offrandes oubliées*], *Les Nouvelles littéraires*, 28 Feb 1931

Édouard Schneider: 'Concerts Straram', *Le Monde musical*, 28 Feb 1931 [review of *Les Offrandes oubliées*]

Simone Plé: 'Les Concerts: Société Nationale (14 février)', *Le Courrier musical*, 1 March 1931 [review of *Trois Mélodies*], p.154

A. Febvre-Longeray: 'Concerts Straram (19 et 26 février)', *Le Courrier musical*, 15 March 1931, p.186 [review of *Les Offrandes oubliées*]

Guy Chastel: 'Concerts Straram: *Les Offrandes oubliées* de M. Olivier Messiaen (1re audition)', *Les Amitiés*, March 1931, p.268

Joseph Baruzi: 'S.M.I. (25 mars)', *Le Ménestrel*, 3 April 1931, p.155 [review of *La Mort du Nombre*]

Simone Plé: 'Société Nationale (28 mars), S.M.I. (25 mars)', *Le Courrier musical*, 15 April 1931, pp.261–2 [review of *La Mort du Nombre*]

Georges Dandelot: 'S.M.I.: *La Mort du Nombre* de O. Messiaen', *Le Monde musical*, 30 April 1931, p.136

Paul Bertrand: 'Concours de Rome', *Le Ménestrel*, 10 July 1931, pp.303–4 [review of *L'Ensorceleuse*]

Gustave Samazeuilh: 'Le Prix de Rome', *Le Courrier musical*, 15 July–1 Aug 1931, p.461 [report on Concours de Rome and *L'Ensorceleuse*]

Robert Brussel: 'Les Concours de Rome: Musique', unidentified newspaper, summer 1931 [incl. mention of Messiaen]

[Unsigned:] 'À 22 ans M. Olivier Messiaen est nommé organiste de l'église de la Trinité', *Le Matin*, 9 Oct 1931

P. Lamblin: 'Organiste de la Trinité à 22 ans: Une conversation avec M. Olivier Messiaen', *L'Intransigeant*, 18 Oct 1931 [interview]

Pierre Beautour: 'Le Nouvel Organiste de la Trinité', unidentified Nantes newspaper, autumn 1931

Alfred Bruneau: [untitled review of *Les Offrandes oubliées*], *Le Matin*, 7 Dec 1931

Charles Tournemire: 'Société des Concerts du Conservatoire', *Le Courrier musical*, 15 Dec 1931, p.594 [review of *Les Offrandes oubliées*]

Louis Aubert: 'La Semaine musicale', *Le Journal*, 16 Dec 1931 [review of *Les Offrandes oubliées*]

Claude Altomont: 'Cercle musical de Paris (22 novembre)', *Le Ménestrel*, 2 Dec 1932, p.490 [review of *Préludes* and *Thème et variations* ('Une pièce pour violon')]

M[arcel] B[elvianes]: 'Société Nationale (14 janvier)', *Le Ménestrel*, 20 Jan 1933, p.25 [review of *Thème et variations*]

Claude Altomont: 'Orchestre Symphonique de Paris, Dimanche 12 février', *Le Ménestrel*, 17 Feb 1933, p.69 [review of *Le Tombeau resplendissant*]

M[arcel] B[elvianes]: 'S.M.I. (8 février)', *Le Ménestrel*, 17 Feb 1933, p.70 [review of *Fantaisie burlesque*]

[Unsigned:] [untitled review of *Les Offrandes oubliées*], *Le Nouvelliste de Lyon*, 27 Feb 1933

Georges Dandelot: 'S.M.I.', *Le Monde musical*, 28 Feb 1933 [review of *Fantaisie burlesque*]

Tristan Klingsor: [review of *Le Tombeau resplendissant*], *Le Monde musical*, 28 Feb 1933

F.D.: 'Les Concerts symphoniques à Paris', *Le Courrier musical*, 1 March 1933, p.113 [review of *Le Tombeau resplendissant*]

Henri Petit: 'S.M.I.', *Le Courrier musical*, 1 March 1933, p.116 [review of *Fantaisie burlesque*]

Paul Dambly: 'M. Olivier Messiaen', *Le Petit Journal*, 27 March 1933 [review of *Hymne au Saint-Sacrement*]

Paul Le Flem: [review of *Hymne au Saint-Sacrement*], *Comœdia*, 27 March 1933

Hector Fraggi: 'La Semaine musicale à Paris', *Le Petit Marseillais*, 29 March 1933 [review of *Hymne au Saint-Sacrement*]

Maurice Imbert: 'Concerts et récitals: Concerts Straram', *Journal des débats*, 29 March 1933 [review of *Hymne au Saint-Sacrement*]

M[arcel] B[elvianes]: 'Concerts divers: Concerts Straram', *Le Ménestrel*, 31 March 1933, p.134 [review of *Hymne au Saint-Sacrement*]

Maurice Brillant: 'Musique sacrée, musique profane', *L'Aube*, 31 March 1933 [review of *Hymne au Saint-Sacrement* and mention of José Bruyr's interview with Messiaen in *L'Écran des musiciens, seconde série*]

Henri Martelli: 'Œuvres nouvelles de Robert Casadesus, Olivier Messiaen, R. Bernard (concert de la S.M.I.)', *La Revue musicale*, no.134, March 1933, pp.213–14 [review of *Fantaisie burlesque*]

Louis Aubert: 'La Semaine musicale', *Journal*, 3 April 1933 [review of *Hymne au Saint-Sacrement*]

André George: 'La Musique au concert et au théâtre', *Les Nouvelles littéraires*, 8 April 1933 [review of *Hymne au Saint-Sacrement*]

Florent Schmitt: 'Les Concerts Straram: *Hymne au Saint-Sacrement* de M. Messiaen', *Le Temps*, 8 April 1933

Maurice Imbert: 'Les Concerts Symphoniques à Paris', *Le Courrier musical*, 15 April 1933, pp.196–8 [review of *Hymne au Saint-Sacrement* on p.196]

D[aniel-] L[esur]: 'Concerts Servais', *Le Monde musical*, 30 April 1933 [review of *Trois Mélodies*]

Henri Martelli: 'Olivier Messiaen: *Le Tombeau resplendissant*', *La Revue musicale*, no.138, July–Aug 1933, pp.128–9

André Cœuroy: 'Musicien–poète', *Beaux-Arts* [?], 10 Nov 1933 [short article]

Arthur Hoérée: 'Musique de piano', *La Revue musicale*, no.144, March 1934, pp.149–50 [review of *Fantaisie burlesque*]

Georges Dandelot: [review of *Trois Mélodies*], *Le Monde musical*, 31 Jan 1935, p.26

Denyse Bertrand: 'Concert Siohan (10 février)', *Le Ménestrel*, 15 Feb 1935, pp.53–4 [review of *L'Ascension*]

Félix Raugel: 'Récital d'orgue d'Olivier Messiaen', *Le Monde musical*, 28 Feb 1935 [review of *L'Ascension*, organ version]

Maurice Imbert: 'Les Symphoniques', *Le Courrier musical*, 1 March 1935, pp.104–6 [review of Concert Siohan, incl. *L'Ascension* on pp.104–5]

Suzanne Demarquez: 'Olivier Messiaen: *L'Ascension* (Concerts Siohan)', *La Revue musicale*, no.154, March 1935, pp.203–4

Paul Marcilly: 'Concert de musique moderne', *Le Monde musical*, March 1935 [review of a concert incl. '*Fantaisie* pour violon et piano d'Olivier Messiaen', and other works]

Jacques Ibert: 'La Vie: Concerts', *Marianne*, 3 June 1935 [review of Messiaen concert given by Line Zilgien]

[Unsigned:] 'Un nouveau groupement des compositeurs', *Comœdia*, 6 Dec 1935 [announcing the formation of La Spirale]

Jean Douël: 'La Spirale', *Le Guide musical*, Dec 1935, p.61

—: 'Paris: La Spirale', *Revue musicale belge*, 20 Jan 1936

Daniel-Lesur: 'Jeudi 30 janvier 1936', *Tablettes de la Schola Cantorum*, Feb 1936 [review of concert given by Messiaen, Delbos and Marcelle Gérar]

Henry Barraud: '*La Nativité du Seigneur* d'Olivier Messiaen – Société Nationale', *L'Art musical*, 6 March 1936

André George: 'Musique: Olivier Messiaen', *Les Nouvelles littéraires*, 14 March 1936

G[eorges] D[andelot]: 'La Nativité du Seigneur d'Olivier Messiaen', Le Monde musical, 31 March 1936

Daniel-Lesur: 'Claire Delbos, violiniste, Marcelle Gérar, cantatrice', Le Monde musical, 31 March 1936 [repr. of Feb 1936 review in Tablettes de la Schola Cantorum]

Bérenger de Miramon Fitz-James: 'L'Œuvre de Messiaen', L'Art sacré, March 1936, p.94

Paul Le Flem: 'Le Tombeau de Paul Dukas', Comœdia, 27 April 1936 [review incl. remarks on Messiaen's contribution]

Henri Martelli: 'Olivier Messiaen: La Nativité du Seigneur', La Revue musicale, no.165, April 1936, pp.291–2

Roger Vinteuil: 'Société Nationale de la Musique (25 avril)', Le Ménestrel, 1 May 1936, p.145 [review of Tombeau de Paul Dukas]

André Cœuroy: 'La Musique: Jeune France', Gringoire, 29 May 1936

—: 'Manifeste et concert des "Jeune France"', Beaux-Arts, 5 June 1936

Roger Vinteuil: 'Concert de la "Jeune France" (3 juin)', Le Ménestrel, 12 June 1936, p.192

[Unsigned:] 'Le Triptyque', L'Art musical, 13 June 1936 [review incl. Préludes and Vocalise]

Henry Barraud: 'La Jeune France – Triton (Festival Enesco) – Festival Buxtehude', L'Art musical, 26 June 1936

'Piccolo': Some Recent French Organ Music', Musical Times, June 1936, pp.528 and 537–9 [review incl. L'Ascension, La Nativité and Le Banquet céleste]

Suzanne Demarquez: 'Premier concert de Jeune France', La Revue musicale, no.167, July–Aug 1936, pp.49–50

H.H.: 'Concert d'orgue: Olivier Messiaen', Journal de Rouen, 19 Nov 1936 [review of La Nativité at Rouen Cathedral]

A.E.: 'Concerts: Olivier Messiaen', Dépêche de Rouen, 22 Nov 1936 [review of La Nativité at Rouen Cathedral]

Gilbert Chase: 'Some Young French Composers', Musical Times, Nov 1936, pp.977–9

Eugène Berteaux: 'Ciment armé. . . Derrière la porte!', La Page musicale, 19 Feb 1937 [response to Messiaen's article of 5 Feb 1937; Messiaen responded on 26 Feb 1937 with a 'Lettre ouverte à M. Eugène Berteaux' (see section I above)]

Hélène Jourdan-Morhange: 'La Grande Pitié des auditeurs', La République, 9 March 1937 [brief comments on Delbos and Messiaen]

Suzanne Demarquez: 'Société Nationale', L'Art musical, 19 March 1937 [review of two songs from Poèmes pour Mi]

Claude Arrieu: 'Société Nationale', Le Monde musical, 31 March 1937 [review of two songs from Poèmes pour Mi]

Georges Auric: 'Les Concerts', Marianne, 14 April 1937 [review of La Nativité]

Roger Vinteuil: 'La Spirale (28 avril)', Le Ménestrel, 7 May 1937, pp.147–8 [review of Poèmes pour Mi]

Marius Guerin: 'Un ménage de compositeurs: Les Messiaen', Courrier royal, 15 May 1937 [interview]

Pierre Capdevielle: 'La Spirale: Claire Delbos et Olivier Messiaen', Le Monde musical, 31 May 1937, p.140 [review of Poèmes pour Mi]

[Unsigned:] 'Les Auditions du mardi de la Revue Musicale', La Revue musicale, no.174, May 1937, pp.289–96, esp.291–2 [review of Jeune France concert]

Michel-Léon Hirsch: 'La Jeune France (4 juin)', Le Ménestrel, 11 June 1937, pp.180–1 [review of the 1937 Jeune France concert, incl. the first performance of the orchestral version of 'Action de grâces']

E[len] C. Foster: 'Young Composers in France', New York Times, 20 June 1937 [review of Jeune France concert]

Marcelle Soulage: 'Jeune France', Le Guide musical, Oct 1937

W.L. Landowski: 'Panorama radiophonique', L'Art musical, 12 Nov 1937 [report of a broadcast organ recital by Messiaen]

E.E.: 'A Mystic Composer', The Times, 11 Dec 1937 [review of André Fleury's recital, incl. four movements from La Nativité]

Pierre Auclert: 'Marcelle Bunlet et O. Messiaen aux Heures Alpines', Le Petit Dauphinois, 20 Jan 1938 [review of a concert in Grenoble incl. Poèmes pour Mi]

[Unsigned:] [untitled review of Poèmes pour Mi at the Société Nationale], New York Herald, 25 Jan 1938

R.F.: 'Société Nationale de Musique', Le Ménestrel, 28 Jan 1938, p.21 [review of Poèmes pour Mi]

Pierre Capdevielle: [untitled review of *Poèmes pour Mi* at the Société Nationale], *Le Monde musical*, 31 Jan 1938

Suzanne Demarquez: 'Triton – Société Nationale', *L'Art musical*, 4 Feb 1938, p.457 [review of *Poèmes pour Mi*]

Carol-Bernard: 'Premières auditions de la Nationale et quelques récitals', *L'Époque*, 11 Feb 1938 [review of *Poèmes pour Mi*]

[Unsigned:] 'L'Accueil aux jeunes... musical', *Paris–Midi*, 7 May 1938 [report on a concert of music by Jeune France]

F.X.N. [Felix Aprahamian]: 'French Organist and Composer', *Radio Times*, 27 May 1938, p.13 [discussion of *La Nativité*]

Suzanne Demarquez: 'Jeune France 1938 – Daniel-Lesur: *Pastorale* – André Jolivet: *Poèmes pour l'enfant* – Yves Baudrier: *Eleonora* – Olivier Messiaen: *Poèmes pour Mi*', *La Revue musicale*, no.184, June 1938, pp.382–3

[Unsigned:] 'Les Auditions du mardi de la Revue Musicale', *La Revue musicale*, no.186, Sept–Nov 1938, pp.139–45, esp. pp.141–2 [review of Jeune France concert]

A[rchibald] F[armer]: 'Organ Recital Notes', *Musical Times*, Dec 1938, pp.925–6 [scathing review of *La Nativité*]

La Nativité du Seigneur [...] *Extraits de Presse* [Paris, c.1938], 4pp. [incl. extracts from reviews, 1936–8, by Henri Sauguet, André George, Georges Auric, B. de Miramon Fitz-James, Georges Bernard, Georges Dandelot, Henry Barraud, Bernard Gavoty, Henri Martelli, André Cœuroy, Pierre Capdevielle, Daniel-Lesur, Jacques Ibert, Serge Moreaux, Gustave Samazeuilh, Maurice Brillant, A. de Montrichard, A. Engammare, Henri Hie, Otto Wend and some unsigned]

Michel-Léon Hirsch: 'Le Triton (23 janvier)', *Le Ménestrel*, 3 Feb 1939, p.28 [review of 'Prismes', i.e. *Chants de terre et de ciel*]

M. Henrion: 'La Musique religieuse', *La Page musicale*, 19 Feb 1939 [account of Messiaen recital at the Trinité]

Carol-Bernard: 'Du Palais de Chaillot à la Trinité', *L'Époque*, 16 March 1939 [review of La Sérénade concert at the Trinité with Messiaen as organist]

Suzanne Demarquez: 'La Sérénade – Quatuor Kolisch', *L'Art musical*, 24 March 1939 [review of La Sérénade concert at the Trinité]

Stan Golestan: 'Concerts et récitals', *Le Figaro*, 24 March 1939 [review of La Sérénade concert at the Trinité]

Michel-Léon Hirsch: 'La Sérénade (14 mars)', *Le Ménestrel*, 24 March 1939, p.84

Pierre Leroi: 'Concerts et récitals', *Excelsior*, 27 March 1939 [review of La Sérénade concert at the Trinité]

Paul Dambly: 'Concerts: Auditions spirituelles', *Le Petit Journal*, 10 April 1939 [review of La Sérénade concert at the Trinité]

M. Henrion: 'La Musique religieuse', *La Page musicale*, 21 April 1939 [review of La Sérénade concert at the Trinité]

Elsa Barraine: 'Tribune des musiciens d'après-guerre [...] Olivier Messiaen', *L'Art musical populaire* (Bulletin de la Fédération Musicale Populaire), no.16, April 1939, pp.1–2

A[ndré] M[angeot]: 'Mme Renée Dyonis – Mlle A. Veluard', *Le Monde musical*, 31 July 1939

V.M.: 'Première au camp', *Lumignon: Bi-mensuelle du Stalag VIIIA*, no.1, 1 April 1941, pp.3–4 [review of the first performance of *Quatuor pour la fin du Temps*]

Arthur Honegger: 'Le Quatuor Bouillon; Olivier Messiaen', *Comœdia*, 12 July 1941 [review of *Quatuor pour la fin du Temps*]

Marcel Delannoy: 'Depuis le mysticisme jusqu'au sport', *Les Nouveaux Temps*, 13 July 1941 [review of *Quatuor pour la fin du Temps*]

—: [untitled notice about free concert of music composed by Prisoners of War: Messiaen, Maurice Thiriet, Jean Martinon, conducted by Charles Münch], *Les Nouveaux Temps*, 12 Jan 1942

Arthur Honegger: 'Le Rossignol de Saint-Malo, Débuts de Mme Géori-Boué', *Comœdia*, undated cutting from May 1942 [review of Jeune France concert on 8 May 1942, incl. *Thème et variations* and three *Préludes*]

Armand Machabey: 'Olivier Messiaen', *L'Information musicale*, 22 May 1942, p.945

Pierre Capdevielle: 'Concert Jeune France (A.M.C. 8 mai)', *L'Information musicale*, 12 June 1942, p.974

Armand Machabey: 'Audition d'œuvres nouvelles (Salon de Mme Schildge-Bianchini, 3 et 16 mai)', *L'Information musicale*, 12 June 1942, p.976 [review of songs from *Chants de terre et de ciel* and *Poèmes pour Mi*]

Marcel Delannoy: 'Renée Dyonis', *Les Nouveaux Temps*, 14–15 June 1942 [review of recital with Messiaen as accompanist]

[Unsigned:] 'Le Rideau', *Paris-Soir*, 18 June 1942 [report on a forthcoming concert of music by Prisoner of War composers at the Club de France on 24 June 1942]

Arthur Honegger: 'Un nouveau langage musical', *Comœdia*, 5 Dec 1942 [introducing, and printed immediately above, Messiaen's own article 'Sur mon traité de composition']

José Bruyr: 'Les Concerts de la semaine', *Aujourd'hui*, 9 Dec 1942 [review of *Quatuor pour la fin du Temps*]

Arthur Honegger: 'Olivier Messiaen à la Pléiade', *Comœdia*, 15 May 1943 [review of *Visions de l'Amen*]

Marcel Delannoy: 'Du plastique au mystique', *Les Nouveaux Temps*, 16 May 1943 [review of *Visions de l'Amen*]

Gaston Dufy: 'La Musique: Le nouvel apport d'Olivier Messiaen', *La Semaine à Paris*, 1–15 July 1943, p.36 [review of *Visions de l'Amen*]

Serge Moreux: 'La Musique', *La Gerbe*, 29 July 1943 [review of *Visions de l'Amen*]

—: 'Olivier Messiaen', *La Gerbe*, 9 Dec 1943 [review of three organ recitals by Messiaen at the Trinité]

Roland-Manuel: 'Olivier Messiaen et la Jeune France, *Deux Apologues* de Pierre Capdevielle', *Combat*, 23 Dec 1944 [review of two *Regards* at the Concerts Triptyque]

Maurice Brillant: 'La Jeune France', *L'Aube*, 5 Jan 1945

José Bruyr: 'Un jeune grand musicien: Olivier Messiaen', *Paris mondial*, 3 April 1945 [review of *Vingt Regards*]

Bernard Gavoty ('Clarendon'): 'Les Concerts: Regard sur Olivier Messiaen', *Le Figaro*, 3 April 1945 [review of *Vingt Regards*]

Roland-Manuel: 'Olivier Messiaen et ses *Vingt Regards sur l'Enfant-Jésus*', *Combat*, 3 April 1945

L. Algazi: 'Paroles et musique', *La Marseillaise*, 4 April 1945 [review of *Vingt Regards*]

Jean Wiéner: 'Olivier Messiaen', *Ce Soir*, 4 April 1945 [brief review of *Vingt Regards*]

Claude Chamfray: 'La Musique: D'un concert. . . à l'autre', *Arts*, 6 April 1945 [review of *Vingt Regards*]

Fred Goldbeck: 'Perils de l'ingeniosité', *Le Temps présent*, 6 April 1945 [review of *Vingt Regards*]

Georges Auric: '*Vingt Regards sur l'Enfant-Jésus*', *Les Lettres françaises*, 7 April 1945

Yves Baudrier: 'Olivier Messiaen', *Volontés*, 11 April 1945 [review of *Vingt Regards*]

Marc Pincherle: 'La Musique', *Les Nouvelles littéraires*, 12 April 1945 [review of *Vingt Regards*]

Claude Rostand: 'Olivier Messiaen', *Carrefour*, 21 April 1945 [comments on Messiaen's music following an organ recital at the Palais de Chaillot]

Guy Bernard[-Delapierre]: 'Une date dans l'histoire de la musique: Les *Liturgies* d'Olivier Messiaen', *Le Pays*, 25 April 1945, pp.1–2

Roland-Manuel: 'Georges Auric, Olivier Messiaen', *Les Lettres françaises*, 28 April 1945 [review of *Trois petites Liturgies*]

Jean Wiéner: 'Événement musical', *Ce Soir*, 28 April 1945 [brief review of *Trois petites Liturgies*]

[Unsigned:] 'London Concerts [. . .] Roger Désormière', *Musical Times*, April 1945, pp.123–4 [review of *Les Offrandes oubliées*]

Hélène Tuzet: 'Les Semaines musicales françaises (mai–juin 1945): *La Nativité du Seigneur* d'Olivier Messiaen', *France*, late June or early July 1945, p.7

Guy Bernard-Delapierre: 'Olivier Messiaen', *Confluences*, June–July 1945, pp.551–6

Yves Baudrier: 'Deux œuvres nouvelles', *Quadrige*, Sept 1945, pp.27 and 30 [review of *Trois petites Liturgies*]

Bernard Gavoty: 'Musique et mystique: Le "Cas" Messiaen', *Les Études*, Oct 1945, pp.21–37

Gilbert Alphonse-Leduc: 'Réponse à Monsieur Bernard Gavoty', no publisher, 4pp., ?late 1945 [open letter responding to Gavoty's article in *Les Études*]

Jean Wiéner: 'In Memoriam', unidentified newspaper, after 2 Nov 1945 [review of *Chant des déportés*]

Hélène Tuzet: 'Musique actuelle et inactuelle', *France*, 14 Dec 1945 [review of *L'Ascension*]

Henry Barraud: 'Olivier Messiaen: Compositeur mystique?', *Contrepoints*, no.1, Dec 1945, pp.101–2

Guy Bernard-Legentil [?Guy Bernard-Delapierre]: 'Olivier Messiaen est accueilli à Londres par des tempêtes d'applaudissements', *Lumières de la ville*, 29 Jan 1946, p.21 [article, incl. short interview, about Messiaen's trip to London in Dec 1945 to perform *La Nativité* and *Visions de l'Amen*]

[Unsigned:] 'Messiaen', *New Statesman and Nation*, 9 Feb 1946, p.100 [review of *Visions de l'Amen* and two *Regards*]

Elsa Barraine: 'Olivier Messiaen', *Ce Soir*, 10 Feb 1946 [review of *Trois petites Liturgies*, and general reflections]

Gabriel Bender: 'Un entretien avec Olivier Messiaen', *Guide du concert*, 22 Feb 1946, pp.190–1

René Dumesnil: 'Le Cas Messiaen', *Journal des arts*, Feb 1946, pp.24–5

André Gauthier: 'Les Trois Liturgies intimes d'Olivier Messiaen', *Paris: Les Arts et les lettres*, 1 March 1946

Pierre Meylan: 'Un débat autour de Stravinsky', *Gazette de Lausanne*, 2 March 1946 [examines the views of Messiaen and others on Stravinsky]

Daniel-Lesur: 'Revue de la presse musicale: *Trois petites Liturgies de la Présence Divine* d'Olivier Messiaen', *Revue musicale de France*, 1 April 1946

'Y a-t-il un "Cas Messiaen"', *Le Littéraire*, 13 and 20 April 1946 [responses to the paper's 'enquête' by Arthur Honegger, Fred Goldbeck, Francis Poulenc, Claude Delvincourt and Guy Bernard-Delapierre (13 April), and Roland-Manuel, Louis Beydts, Max-Pol Fouchet, Henry Barraud and François Florand, O.P. (20 April)]

Herman Closson: 'Bruxelles: La vie artistique', *Message: Revue internationale belge*, no.55, June 1946, pp.357–61 [incl. comments on Messiaen's visit to Brussels in April 1946 and caricatures of Messiaen and Loriod on p.361]

Desmond Shawe-Taylor: 'Messiaen and Berkeley', *New Statesman and Nation*, 27 July 1946, p.63 [review of *Quatuor pour la fin du Temps*]

W.H. Haddon Squire: 'Olivier Messiaen's Quartet, Webern's Cantata Notable', *Christian Science Monitor*, 10 Aug 1946

Roland de Candé: 'Concert de fin d'année', *Plaisir de France*, January 1947 [brief review of *Vingt Regards*]

Jean-Marie Grénier: 'Revue des disques', *Images musicales*, 21 Feb 1947 [review of Loriod's Pathé recording of *Le Baiser de l'Enfant-Jésus*]

René Guillot: 'Paysages de la musique: À propos d'un récital d'orgue', *Paris–Dakar*, 7 Feb 1948 [organ music by Messiaen and others]

Bernard Gavoty ('Clarendon'): 'Les *Trois Tâla* d'Olivier Messiaen', *Le Figaro*, 18 Feb 1948

Fred Goldbeck: 'La Symphonie, elle aussi, va au cinéma... Henri Sauguet choisit le tragique et Olivier Messiaen organise la magie', *Le Figaro littéraire*, 21 Feb 1948 [review of *Trois Tâla*]

Y.H.: [untitled brief report on *Trois Tâla*], *Guide du concert*, 12, 19, 26 March 1948, p.254

Robert de Saint-Jean: 'C'est le merle noir et non le rossignol qui inspire Olivier Messiaen. A quarante ans, le musicien se prépare à écrire l'opéra dont il rêve depuis son enfance', *France-Soir*, 28–29 March 1948 [interview in which Messiaen declares that after completing the *Turangalîla-Symphonie*, his next work will be an opera]

Gaston Dufy: 'Les Grandes Œuvres de la musique contemporaine française: Olivier Messiaen', *Images musicales*, 16–23 April 1948, p.5

Suzanne Demarquez: 'Youth and Spirit Take Over in French Music', *Musical Courier*, 1 Oct 1948, p.7 [incl. discussion of Messiaen]

Léon Vallas: 'Olivier Messiaen', *Le Progrès*, 25 Jan 1949 [review of *Trois petites Liturgies*]

Robert de Fragny: 'Olivier Messiaen', *Écho sud*, 26 Jan 1949 [review of *Trois petites Liturgies*]

André Lemoine: 'Radio: Archéologie', *Le Journal musical*, ? Feb 1949 [review of a broadcast performance of *Poèmes pour Mi* on 20 Jan 1949]

M.P.P.: 'Les Concerts: Association Philharmonique', *Tout Lyon*, 9 Feb 1949 [review of *Trois petites Liturgies* in Lyon]

Ghyslaine Juramie: 'En marge de l'enregistrement des "Trois petites Liturgies": Olivier Messiaen, reflet du temps nouveau', *Images musicales*, 25 Feb 1949, pp.1 and 6

J.L.: 'Concerts: Messiaen et Villa-Lobos', *Journal musical français*, 15 March 1949 [review of *Vingt Regards*]

Henri Dufresse: '*Vingt Regards sur l'Enfant-Jésus* – Yvonne Loriod', *Images musicales*, 25 March 1949

Antoine Goléa: 'Les *Vingt Regards sur l'Enfant-Jésus*', *Images musicales*, 25 March 1949

—: 'Les Petites Liturgies d'Olivier Messiaen', *Disques*, March 1949, p.320

[Unsigned:] 'Le Jury des Concours de Rome est désormais très éclectique', *Le Monde*, 1 April 1949 [lists the members of the music jury, incl. Messiaen]

L. Courret: 'Le Disque du jour: *Trois petites Liturgies de la Présence Divine* (Olivier Messiaen)', *Combat*, 8 April 1949

A.G. [Goléa?]: 'Le Disque', *Aux Écoutes*, 20 April 1949 [brief note on the recording of *Trois petites Liturgies*]

Armand Pierhal: 'Chronique du disque', *Climats*, 29 April 1949 [review of *Trois petites Liturgies*]

Serge Moreux: 'Olivier Messiaen', *La Revue française*, April 1949, pp.101–2

[Unsigned:] 'French Composer Messiaen Joins Tanglewood Staff', *Berkshire County Eagle*, 13 July 1949 [incl. interview]

'Music [. . .] Messiaen to Tanglewood', *Newsweek*, 18 July 1949, p.67 [incl. interview]

Jay C. Rosenfeld: 'Chamber Hall Overflows for Messiaen First', *Berkshire Evening Eagle*, 25 July 1949 [review of *Quatuor*]

Olin Downes: 'Composer on Visit: Messiaen Guest Teacher at Berkshire Center', *New York Times*, 31 July 1949 [general article incl. mention of *Turangalîla* and Messiaen's class at Tanglewood]

Cyrus Durgin: '*Turangalîla*, or Love in the East Indies, or a Messiaen Afternoon', *Boston Globe*, 3 Dec 1949

Rudolph Elie: 'Symphony Concert [. . .] Turangalila Symphony of Olivier Messiaen', *Boston Herald*, 3 Dec 1949

Harold Rogers: 'Bernstein Leads 10–Movement *Turangalîla*', *Christian Science Monitor*, 3 Dec 1949

Warren Storey Smith: 'Symphony Concert', *Boston Post*, 3 Dec 1949 [review of *Turangalîla*]

Olin Downes: 'Bernstein Leads Messiaen's Work', *New York Times*, 11 Dec 1949 [review of *Turangalîla*]

Irving Kolodin: 'The Music Makers: Messiaen, Thebom, Flagstad and Puccini Make News', *New York Sun*, 12 Dec 1949 [review of *Turangalîla*]

Jean Hoyaux: 'Olivier Messiaen nous parle de sa *Turangalîla-Symphonie* qui vient d'être jouée au Carnegie Hall et à Boston', *Le Figaro littéraire*, 18 Feb 1950, p.7 [interview]

Maurice Brillant: 'Un chef-d'œuvre de Messiaen sous un titre sanscrit', ?*L'Écho*, ? July 1950 [review of *Turangalîla* at Aix]

Claude Rostand: 'Première de *Turangalîla-Symphonie*: Olivier Messiaen a produit un splendide amusement de l'oreille', unidentified cutting, summer 1950

M[artin] C[ooper]: 'The Festival at Aix-en-Provence', *Musical Times*, Sept 1950, pp.355–6 [review of *Turangalîla*]

Jean de Gibon: 'Olivier Messiaen: Un des génies les plus célèbres et les plus personnels de toute la planète', *Écho du Pays de Redon*, 27 Jan 1951 [quotes letter from Messiaen]

Bernard Gavoty ('Clarendon'): 'Messiaen peint par lui-même', *Le Figaro*, 2 Feb 1951

Jean de Gibon: 'Olivier Messiaen: Ses ascendants', *Écho du Pays de Redon*, 3 Feb 1951

—: 'Olivier Messiaen', *Écho du Pays de Redon*, 3 March 1951 [short article]

—: 'Olivier Messiaen', *Écho du Pays de Redon*, 28 April 1951 [report on performances outside France]

G.S. [?G. Simon]: 'Le Plus Grand Génie musical moderne Olivier Messiaen a passé deux jours à Redon', *Écho du Pays de Redon*, 28 July 1951 [interview]

Jean de Gibon: 'Olivier Messiaen à la Trinité de Paris', *Écho du Pays de Redon*, 27 Oct 1951 [description of Messiaen's organ playing at Mass]

—: 'Corps glorieux d'Olivier Messiaen', *Écho du Pays de Redon*, 8 Dec 1951 [review of broadcast performance]

Olivier Alain: 'Du *Banquet céleste* à la *Messe de la Pentecôte*: Olivier Messiaen parle de son œuvre d'orgue', *Journal musical français*, 13 March 1952 [interview]

Bernard Gavoty ('Clarendon'): 'Musique de chambre', *Le Figaro*, 13 May 1952 [review of *Visions de l'Amen*]

Paul Guth: 'Nébuleuses spirales, stalactites et stalagmites suggèrent des rythmes à Olivier Messiaen', *Le Figaro littéraire*, 14 Feb 1953 [interview]

Ernest Bradbury: 'Messiaen and *Turangalîla*', *Radio Times*, 19 June 1953, p.27 [article introducing the symphony's first English broadcast]

W.R. Anderson: 'Round about Radio', *Musical Times*, Aug 1953, pp.359–60 [review of *Turangalîla*]

[Unsigned:] 'Société des Concerts: Olivier Messiaen', *Le Monde*, 22 Dec 1953 [review of *Réveil des oiseaux*]

Nicole Hirsch: 'Le Chef d'orchestre Maurice Le Roux dirige le *Réveil des oiseaux*, un ouvrage descriptif d'Olivier Messiaen', *France-Soir*, 27–28 Dec 1953

Donald Mitchell: 'Some First Performances', *Musical Times*, Dec 1953, pp.576–7 [first London performance of *Chants de terre et de ciel*]

Jacques Périsson: 'Le *Réveil des Oiseaux* d'Olivier Messiaen', *Le Conservatoire*, no.29, Jan 1954, pp.17–18 [review of first Paris performance]

Claude Rostand: 'Les Grands Soirs du Petit Théâtre Marigny', *Carrefour*, 3 March 1954 [review of *Cantéyodjayâ* and *Quatre Études de rythme*]

—: 'La *Turangalila-Symphonie* d'Olivier Messiaen', *Carrefour*, 10 March 1954 [review of Paris première]

Colin Mason: 'On the Left Wing', *Musical Times*, March 1954, pp.135–6 [detailed review of the newly published *Cantéyodjayâ*]

Ernest Newman: '*Turangalila*', *The Sunday Times*, 25 April 1954

Norman Demuth: 'Messiaen and his Organ Music', *Musical Times*, April 1955, pp.203–6

Rollo Myers: 'France', *Musical Times*, May 1955, p.270 [review of *Livre d'orgue*]

Suzanne Demarquez: 'Premières auditions: Domaine musical (Petit Théâtre Marigny (10.3)', *Guide du concert*, no.107, 23 March 1956, p.867 [review of *Oiseaux exotiques*]

Maurice Roy: 'Les Disques: *Vingt Regards sur l'Enfant-Jésus*', *Revue des deux mondes*, 15 Jan 1957, pp.369–71

Suzanne Demarquez: 'Premières auditions [. . .] Domaine musical (Gaveau 30.3)', *Guide du concert*, no.151, 12 April 1957, p.893 [review of partial première of *Catalogue d'oiseaux*]

—: 'Premières auditions [. . .] *La Rousserolle effarvatte* d'Olivier Messiaen', *Guide du concert*, no.183, 7 Feb 1958, pp.727–8.

Denise Bourdet: 'Olivier Messiaen a traduit pour piano vingt-sept heures de la vie des oiseaux en Sologne', *Le Figaro littéraire*, 15 Feb 1958 [interview about *Catalogue d'oiseaux*]

Antoine Goléa: 'Olivier Messiaen a cinquante ans', *Témoignage chrétien*, 5 Dec 1958, pp.12–13

—: 'La *Turangalila* de Messiaen', *Témoignage chrétien*, 6 Feb 1959

'Olivier Messiaen a 50 ans', *Guide du concert*, no.229, 3 April 1959, pp.1090–2 [birthday tributes by Marcel Dupré, Pierette Mari, Jean-Claude Henry, Jean Barraqué and Christian de Lisle]

Suzanne Demarquez: 'Le *Catalogue d'oiseaux* d'Olivier Messiaen', *Guide du concert*, no.233, 1 May 1959, p.42

Claude Rostand: 'Quelques enregistrements sensationnels', *Carrefour*, 20 July 1960 [review of Loriod's Véga recording of *Catalogue d'oiseaux*]

—: 'Création de *Chronochromie* d'Olivier Messiaen', unidentified newspaper, Oct 1960

Martine Cadieu: 'Duo avec Messiaen', *Les Nouvelles littéraires*, 29 Dec 1960, pp.1 and 9 [interview]

Robert Siohan: 'Les Recherches d'Olivier Messiaen: Musique et ornithologie', *Le Monde*, 3 Feb 1961 [general article on Messiaen and birdsong]

Bernard Gavoty: 'Mon carnet de notes', *Journal musical français*, 6 March 1961 [incl. description of Messiaen's home]

—: Qui êtes-vous, Olivier Messiaen', *Journal musical français*, 6 April 1961 [interview]

Robert Siohan: 'Olivier Messiaen et "le charme des impossibilités"', *Les Lettres françaises*, 13–19 July 1961, pp.1 and 7 [interview]

—: '*Chronochromie* d'Olivier Messiaen', *L'Express*, 21 Sept 1961, p.43

Claude Rostand: 'Bataille pour *Chronochromie*', *Le Figaro littéraire*, Sept 1961

Suzanne Demarquez: '1er audition française: Chronochromie – O. Messiaen (Théâtre Municipal, 13 septembre), *Guide du concert*, no.323, 29 Sept 1961, p.100

[Unsigned:] 'Olivier Messiaen à l'auditorium de la RTF, Place de Bordeaux', *Les Dernières Nouvelles d'Alsace*, 6 Oct 1961 [article about *Chronochromie* in Strasbourg]

Bernard Gavoty ('Clarendon'): '*Turangalila* d'Olivier Messiaen', *Le Figaro*, 13 Oct 1961

Claude Samuel: 'Olivier Messiaen n'est plus obscur pour le grand publique', *L'Intransigeant*, 13 Oct 1961 [article on *Turangalila*]

Jacques Bourgeois: 'Écoutez, comprenez Olivier Messiaen, le compositeur de votre temps', *Elle*, end Oct 1961

Bernard Gavoty: 'Mon carnet de notes', *Journal musical français*, 6 Nov 1961 [review of *Chronochromie*]

Jacques Bourgeois: 'Au Théâtre des Champs-Élysées un chahut monstre accueille *Chronochromie* de Messiaen', *Arts*, 21–27 Feb 1962 [on the same page, another article, signed 'J.B.', entitled 'Olivier Messiaen: Une musique en vitrail']

J.H.: 'À l'École de Musique devant un auditoire choisi Mme Edith Briand et Mlle Marie-Madeleine Petit ont présenté une remarquable réalisation de *Harawî*', *Courrier de l'Ouest*, 7 March 1962

J.-Y.H. [Abbé Hameline]: '*Harawi*, chant d'amour et de mort, bouleversant chef-d'œuvre d'Olivier Messiaen', *Ouest-France*, 12 March 1962

Claude Bandieri: 'Le Plus Célèbre des musiciens français vivants, Olivier Messiaen aime bien revenir souvent en Dauphiné', *Le Dauphiné libéré*, 28 April 1963

Martine Cadieu: 'Entretiens sur l'art actuel: Martine Cadieu avec Olivier Messiaen', *Les Lettres françaises*, 7–13 Jan 1965, pp.1 and 8

[Unsigned:] 'Hommage à Olivier Messiaen', *La Libre Belgique*, 20 Feb 1965

Jacqueline Renée: 'Cécile Sauvage: Jean Tenant nous éclaire sur la grande poétesse, mère du compositeur Olivier Messiaen', *La Dépêche*, 23 Nov 1967

Claude Rostand: '*La Transfiguration de Notre-Seigneur* d'Olivier Messiaen au Festival Gulbenkian de Lisbonne, *Le Figaro littéraire*, 16 June 1969

Gerald Larner: 'Messiaen's *La Transfiguration*', *The Guardian*, undated cutting, June 1969

Stanley Sadie: 'Messiaen's Biggest Work', *The Times*, undated cutting, June 1969 [review of *La Transfiguration*]

Maurice Poté: 'Olivier Messiaen écoutera dimanche à Graslin ses *Oiseaux exotiques* au cours du concert donné', *Presse-Océan* [Nantes], 6 Jan 1970 [incl. recollections of Messiaen's studies in Nantes in 1918–19]

Brian Dennis: 'Messiaen's *La Transfiguration*', *Tempo*, no.94, autumn 1970, pp.29–30

Oliver Knussen: 'Messiaen's *Des Canyons aux étoiles. . .*', *Tempo*, no.116, March 1976, pp.39–41

Harriet Watts: 'Canyons, Colours and Birds: An Interview with Oliv[i]er Messiaen', *Tempo*, no.128, March 1978, pp.2–8

Jacques Doucelin: 'Le Martyre de saint Messiaen: Son *François d'Assise* créé à l'Opéra', *Le Figaro*, 9 Nov 1983

—: 'Ozawa: "Saint François c'est totalement crazy"', *Le Figaro*, 16 Nov 1983

Mathilde la Bardonnie: 'L'Opéra accueille Olivier Messiaen. . . Le chant de saint François. . . Christiane Eda-Pierre au ciel aux et anges. . . Catalogue en guise de biographie', *Le Monde*, 17 Nov 1983 [double-page feature on *Saint François*]

Gérard Mannoni: 'Le Rendez-vous céleste de Saint-François et de Messiaen', *Le Quotidien de Paris*, 24 Nov 1983

Jean-Louis Martinoty: 'Le Saint et le musicien: Olivier Messiaen et le temps d'oiseau', *L'Humanité*, 24 Nov 1983

Brigitte Massin: 'Messiaen: L'Opéra des oiseaux', *Le Matin*, 26 Nov 1983

Roger Tellart: 'L'Opéra de Messiaen [. . .] Voir naître un chef-d'œuvre', *La Croix*, 26 Nov 1983, pp.2–3

J[acques] D[oucelin]: 'Messiaen en majesté', *Le Figaro*, 28 Nov 1983

Jacques Doucelin: 'Sandro Sequi "l'interprète visuel"', *Le Figaro*, 28 Nov 1983

Philippe Olivier: 'Olivier Messiaen: "Je ne composerai plus jamais"', *Libération*, 28 Nov 1983

Jacques Doucelin: 'Saint François à l'Opéra: La "provocation" de Messiaen', *Le Figaro*, 29 Nov 1983

Jacques Lonchampt: 'Messiaen prêche aux oiseaux', *Le Monde*, 29 Nov 1983

Pierre Petit: '*Saint François d'Assise* d'Olivier Messiaen: L'Art naïf de la mosaïque', *Le Figaro*, 29 Nov 1983

Claude Lully: '*Saint François d'Assise*: Le Palais Garnier transformé en volière', *Le Parisien*, 30 Nov 1983

Philippe Olivier: 'François prêchi-prêcha', *Libération*, 30 Nov 1983

John Rockwell: 'Paris Opéra: The Debut of Messiaen *François*', *New York Times*, 30 Nov 1983

Claude Samuel: 'Un opéra messianique', *Le Matin*, 30 Nov 1983

Peter Stadlen: 'Messiaen's St Francis of Assisi', *Daily Telegraph*, 30 Nov 1983

Tom Sutcliffe: 'A Bird in the Hand', *The Guardian*, 30 Nov 1983 [review of *Saint François*]

Edith Walter et al.: 'Entretien-Dossier: Olivier Messiaen', *Harmonie*, Nov 1983, pp.14–25

Paul Griffiths: 'Holy Mystery, Pastel Panto', *The Times*, 1 Dec 1983 [review of *Saint François*; the 'pastel panto' is a review of Massenet's *Esclarmonde* under the same headline]

Max Loppert: 'Vital Breath of Theatre Lacking at Messiaen Première', *Financial Times*, 1 Dec 1983

J.-M. de Montrémy: 'Messiaen, le merveilleux', *La Croix*, 1 Dec 1983

Jean-Pierre le Pavec: 'Messiaen à l'Opéra: Noms d'oiseaux. *Saint François d'Assise*: Les canons du chromo liturgique', *L'Humanité*, 1 Dec 1983

Klaus Schweitzer: 'Eine unmögliche grossartige Oper', *Basler Zeitung*, 1 Dec 1983

H.H. Stuckenschmidt: 'Die Pracht des Heiligen', *Frankfurter allgemeine Zeitung*, 1 Dec 1983

Caroline Alexander: 'Frère Messiaen à l'Opéra', *Les Échos*, 2 Dec 1983

Jacques Drillon: '"Messiaen, faîtes-moi un opéra. . .": Le compositeur le plus éloigné du théâtre lyrique a choisi un anti-sujet: Saint François. Huit ans de travail pour une partition qu'on transporte dans une valise', *Nouvel Observateur*, 2 Dec 1983

Michel Parouty: 'Le Vieil Homme et Saint François', *La Tribune de Genève*, 3 Dec 1983

David Cairns: 'A Fresco for St Francis', *Sunday Times*, 4 Dec 1983

Catherine Gilbert: 'Olivier Messiaen, les oiseaux et la foi', *L'Humanité dimanche*, 4 Dec 1983

Peter Heyworth: 'Messiaen's St Francis', *The Observer*, 4 Dec 1983

Robert Serrou: 'Saint-François Super-Star: L'opéra-fleuve de Messiaen fait triomphe à Paris', *Paris-Match*, 9 Dec 1983, pp.114–21

Jacques Doucelin: 'Cinq heures d'opéra: un pari difficile: *Saint François d'Assise*', *L'Aurore*, 12 Dec 1983

Alan Rich: 'Messiaen's Saintly Vision', *Newsweek*, 12 Dec 1983

Harry Halbreich: 'Point de vue à Olivier Messiaen', *La Croix*, 14 Dec 1983

Irène Meltzheim and Père Pascal Ide: 'Le Musicien de la joie: Entretien avec Olivier Messiaen 60 années à la Trinité', *Du côté de la Trinité* [parish newspaper], March 1991, pp.1–2

Julian Anderson: 'Olivier Messiaen (1908–1992): An Appreciation', *Musical Times*, Sept 1992, pp.449–51

Paul Griffiths: '*Éclairs sur l'Au-delà*', *Tempo*, no.183, Dec 1992, pp.40–1

Charles Jourdanet: 'Il y a soixante ans Messiaen créait *Quatuor pour la fin du Temps* au stalag [. . .] Témoignage', *Nice-Matin*, 15 Jan 2001 [reminiscences of a PoW who attended the first performance of the *Quatuor*]

Index

Subentries are ordered according to life and works. In some entries Messiaen's full name is replaced by the abbreviation 'OM'.

Oiseau-cloche | Bellbird | (Anthor...